EDITION
08

Essentials of
Business Communication

NELSON EDUCATION

Essentials of Business Communication, Eighth Canadian Edition
by Mary Ellen Guffey, Dana Loewy, and Richard Almonte

Vice President, Editorial Higher Education:
Anne Williams

Publisher:
Anne-Marie Taylor

Marketing Manager:
David Stratton

Developmental Editor:
Theresa Fitzgerald

Photo Researcher:
Jessica Freedman

Permissions Coordinator:
Jessica Freedman

Production Project Manager:
Jaime Smith

Production Service:
MPS Limited

Copy Editor:
Elizabeth Phinney

Proofreader:
MPS Limited

Indexer:
Edwin Durbin

Design Director:
Ken Phipps

Managing Designer:
Franca Amore

Interior Design:
Sharon Lucas Creative

Cover Design:
Sharon Lucas Creative

Cover Image:
Stone/Getty

Compositor:
MPS Limited

Library and Archives Canada Cataloguing in Publication

Guffey, Mary Ellen, author
Essentials of business communication / Mary Ellen Guffey, Richard Almonte. – Eighth Canadian edition.

Includes index.ISBN 978-0-17-653140-9 (pbk.)

1. Business writing–Textbooks. 2. English language–Business English–Textbooks. 3. Business communication–Textbooks. I. Almonte, Richard, author II. Title.

HF5718.3.G84 2015 808'.06665 C2014-903626-4

ISBN-13: 978-0-17-653140-9
ISBN-10: 0-17-653140-8

EDITION 08

Essentials of Business Communication

Mary Ellen Guffey

Professor Emerita of Business

Los Angeles Pierce College

Dana Loewy

Business Communication Program

California State University, Fullerton

Richard Almonte

Professor, Centre for Business

George Brown College

NELSON
EDUCATION

Learning with Guffey . . .

Essentials offers a three-in-one learning package that gets results:

- Authoritative textbook
- Practical workbook
- Self-teaching grammar/mechanics handbook

From the emphasis on professionalism to *Workplace in Focus* photo essays, Guffey, Loewy, and Almonte have updated tools and created new ways to keep you interested

EMPHASIS ON GRAMMAR

Throughout the text, you are encouraged to build on your basic grammar skills. Grammar/Mechanics Checkups, Grammar/Mechanics Challenges, and Web-based grammar activities help you practise and sharpen your skills.

EMPHASIS ON PROFESSIONALISM

The Eighth Canadian Edition increases its emphasis on professional workplace behaviours and illustrates the importance of professionalism. Businesses have a keen interest in a professional workforce that effectively works together to deliver positive results that ultimately boost profits and bolster a company's image. In this edition, you'll discover the professional characteristics most valued in today's competitive workplace.

CAREER RELEVANCE

Because employers often rank communication skills among the most requested competencies, the Eighth Canadian Edition emphasizes the link between excellent communication skills and career success—helping you see for yourself the critical role business communication will play in your life.

It's Just That Easy!

and engaged. The following six pages describe features that will help students succeed in today's technologically enhanced workplace.

5.13 Instruction Message: What to Do in an Emergency

Your boss, Sue Curry, informs you one day that she is concerned about fires and safe evacuation in your office building. She asks that you, as director of Human Resources, prepare a set of procedures for employees to follow in case of fires. She thinks that the two of you can work out the procedures in a conversation, and she begins by noting that if an employee sees a fire, that person should pull the alarm and call the fire department. The number of that department is 9-911. If the fire is small, the employee can attempt to extinguish it with a fire extinguisher.

At this point, you ask your boss if the person who discovered the fire should also notify a supervisor, and your boss agrees. The supervisor is probably the one who should assess the situation and decide whether the building should be evacuated. You then begin to think about the evacuation process: what to do? Ms. Curry says that all doors should be closed and employees should secure their workstations. You ask what exactly that means, and she says employees should turn off their computers and put away important documents, but perhaps that information is unnecessary. Just stick to the main points, she says.

If employees are evacuating, they should go to the nearest exit in an orderly manner. In addition, it's very important that everyone remain calm. You ask about people with disabilities. "Sure," she says, "we should assist all visitors and persons with disabilities." Then Ms. Curry remembers that employees have been told about predetermined gathering places, and they should go there and wait for more instructions from floor monitors. It's also important that employees not re-enter the building until given the all-clear. When they are outside, they should stay out of the way of fire department personnel and equipment.

"Do you have all the information?" she asks. "Great! Now prepare a draft memo to employees for my signature."

Your Task. Draft an e-mail or memo to employees from Sue Curry, CEO. Provide brief background data and explain the main idea. List clear fire instructions. Provide your name, title, and office phone number for receivers who want more information.

Abundant Activities and Cases

Chapter concepts are translated into action as you try out your skills in activities designed to mirror real-world experiences.

Learning with Guffey . . .

Office Insider

To accentuate how excellent communication skills translate into career success, the *Office Insider* demonstrates the importance of communication skills in real-world practice.

More Before-and-After Model Documents

Before-and-after sample documents and descriptive callouts create a road map to the writing process, demonstrating the effective use of the skills being taught, as well as the significance of the revision process.

OFFICE INSIDER

Presentation skills are a primary differentiator among you and your peers. Master your presentation skills, and become the master of your career options.

Getting Ready for an Oral Presentation

In getting ready for an oral presentation, you may feel a lot of anxiety. For many people fear of speaking before a group is almost as great as the fear of pain. We get butterflies in our stomachs just thinking about it. When you feel those butterflies, though, speech coach Dianne Booher advises getting them in formation and visualizing the swarm as a powerful push propelling you to a peak performance.[3] For any presentation, you can reduce your fears and lay the foundation for a professional performance by focusing on five areas: preparation, organization, audience rapport, visual aids, and delivery.

FIGURE 6.1 Persuasive Favour Request

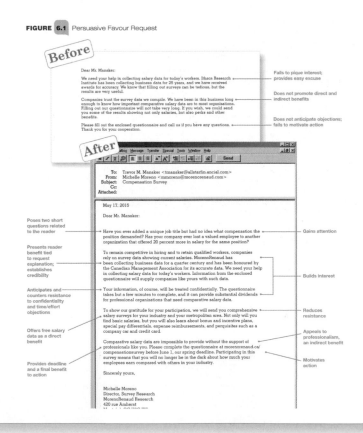

It's Just That Easy!

COMMUNICATION WORKSHOP

WEB EVALUATION: HOAX? SCHOLARLY RESEARCH? ADVOCACY?

Most of us tend to think that any information turned up via a Web search engine has somehow been evaluated as part of a valid selection process.[2] Not true. The truth is that the Internet is rampant with unreliable sites that reside side by side with reputable sites. Anyone with a computer and an Internet connection can publish anything on the Web.

Unlike library-based research materials, information at many sites has not undergone the editing or scrutiny of scholarly publication procedures. The information we read in journals and most reputable magazines is reviewed, authenticated, and evaluated. That's why we have learned to trust these sources as valid and authoritative. But information on the Web is much less reliable. Some sites are obvious hoaxes. Others exist to distribute propaganda. Still others want to sell you something. To use the Web meaningfully, you must scrutinize what you find. Here are specific questions to ask as you examine a site:

- **Currency.** What is the date of the Web page? When was it last updated? Is some of the information obviously out of date? If the information is time sensitive and the site has not been updated recently, the site is probably not reliable.
- **Authority.** Who publishes or sponsors this Web page? What makes the presenter an authority? Is a contact address available for the presenter? Learn to be skeptical about data and assertions from individuals whose credentials are not verifiable.
- **Content.** Is the purpose of the page to entertain, inform, convince, or sell? Who is the intended audience, judging from content, tone, and style? Can you assess the overall value of the content compared with that of the other resources on this topic? Web presenters with a skewed point of view cannot be counted on for objective data.
- **Accuracy.** Do the facts that are presented seem reliable to you? Do you find errors in spelling, grammar, or usage? Do you see any evidence of bias? Are footnotes provided? If you find numerous errors and if facts are not referenced, you should be alerted that the data may be questionable.

For more information on evaluating Web sites, check out the University of California at Berkeley's excellent Web site at **www.lib.berkeley.edu/TeachingLib/Guides/Internet/ Evaluate.html**.

Career Application

As interns at a news-gathering service, you have been asked to assess the quality of the following Web sites. Which of these could you recommend as sources of valid information?

- Beef Nutrition (**www.beefnutrition.org**)
- Edmunds—Where Smart Car Buyers Start (**www.edmunds.com**)
- Criticism of Apple Inc. (**http://criticismofappleinc.blog.com/**)
- EarthSave International (**www.earthsave.org**)
- The Vegetarian Resource Group (**www.vrg.org/nutshell/nutshell.htm**)
- The White House (**www.whitehouse.gov**)

Communication Workshops

Communication Workshops develop critical thinking skills and provide insight into special business communication topics such as ethics, technology, career skills, and collaboration.

Learning with Guffey . . .

Writing Plans

Ample, step-by-step writing plans help you get started quickly on organizing and formatting messages.

WRITING PLAN FOR INSTRUCTION MESSAGES

- **Subject line:** Summarize the content of the message.
- **Opening:** Expand the subject line by stating the main idea concisely in a full sentence.
- **Body:** Divide the instructions into steps. List the steps in the order in which they are to be carried out. Arrange the items vertically with bullets or numbers. Begin each step with an action verb using the imperative mood (command language such as *do this, don't do that*).
- **Closing:** Request a specific action, summarize the message, or present a closing thought. If appropriate, include a deadline and a reason.

Workplace in Focus Photo Essays

Vivid photos with intriguing stories demonstrate real-world applicability of business communication concepts. Each photo essay concludes with a critical thinking question.

WORKPLACE IN FOCUS

Trying to sell a micro car to Canadians has been a gamble for Daimler AG, manufacturer of the luxurious Mercedes-Benz brand but also maker of the diminutive Smart Fortwo. Prompted by skyrocketing gasoline prices, European and Asian drivers have long embraced small automobiles. But SUV-, truck- and van-loving Canadians? Although the Smart is well engineered and sells briskly in over 30 countries, its promoters have had to work harder to win over Canadians, especially those not living in large urban centres. *What might rural or suburban Canadian car buyers worry about most when they see an automobile such as the Smart? What strategies might reduce their resistance?*

COURTESY OF DANA LOEWY

It's Just That Easy!

WRITING IMPROVEMENT EXERCISES

Wordiness
Revise the following sentences to eliminate wordy phrases, outdated expressions, and long lead-ins.

Example: This is to notify you that at a later date we may be able to submit the report.

Revision: We may be able to submit the report later.

1. In the event that the response is at all favourable, we will in all probability start our Web site in the month of January.
2. This is to advise you that beginning with the date of April 1 all charges made after that date will be charged to your new credit card number.
3. Pursuant to your request, enclosed please find a copy of your August statement.
4. In view of the fact that our sales are increasing in a gradual manner, we must secure a loan in the amount of $50,000.
5. This is to let you know that you should feel free to use your credit card for the purpose of purchasing household items for a period of 60 days.

Needless Adverbs, Fillers, Repetitious Words
Revise the following sentences to eliminate needless adverbs, fillers (such as *there is* and *it is*), and unintentional repetition.

6. It is Web-based technology that is really streamlining administrative processes and reducing business costs for businesses.
7. It is certainly clear that there are many younger managers who are very eager but who are actually unprepared to assume management or leadership roles.
8. There are four employees who definitely spend more time in Internet recreational uses on the Internet than they spend on business-related Internet work.
9. There are definitely five advantages that computers have over a human decision maker.

Redundancies, Jargon, Slang, Clichés
Revise the following sentences to eliminate redundancies, jargon, slang, clichés, and any other wordiness.

Writing Improvement Exercises

These exercises will develop your writing skills and allow you to practise the concepts explained in the chapter.

Dear Ms. Telchinsky:

Roberta Fuyuni was in touch with me recently to request I write a reference letter for her, and I'm very pleased to do so confidentially. I understand Roberta has recently applied for the position of Manager, Food Operations, at the University Health Network. Roberta worked for me for over five years as Manager, Airline Operations.

In this position, Roberta managed a staff of between 60 and 80 cooks, packagers, logistics, and marketing and sales employees. Essentially, Roberta was second in command after me in taking care of our large business providing meals for Air Canada, WestJet, and other North American and international carriers. Roberta began as a cook, and after finishing her logistics diploma, she was promoted to Logistics Coordinator. Within two years she had earned her MBA and we promoted her again to Manager, Airline Operations, during which time she increased sales in her division by over 15%.

Besides understanding the business (ingredient purchasing and budgeting, food preparation, health and safety, logistics, marketing and sales), Roberta is well liked by both executives and employees because of her excellent soft skills. These skills came in handy as we transitioned from being owned by Cara to Gategroup. She regularly provides positive feedback to her employees, and shows initiative. For example, we were using an outdated performance review system, and Roberta developed and piloted a much more successful 360-degree system that became popular with both employees and managers.

I'm eager to aid Roberta in her transition from the airline food preparation industry to the institutional food services sector, and hope that I have explained effectively in my comments above Roberta's strong work ethic, innovative character, and ability to manage. In other words, I highly recommend Roberta without reservation. If you'd like to discuss my recommendation please contact me at the coordinates listed above.

Sincerely,

Steve Bassos
VP, Airline

Tips for Writing Letters of Recommendation
- Identify the purpose and confidentiality of the message.
- Establish your relationship with the applicant.
- Describe the length of employment and job duties, if relevant.
- Provide specific examples of the applicant's professional and personal skills.
- Compare the applicant with others in his or her field.
- Offer an overall rating of the applicant.
- Summarize the significant attributes of the applicant.
- Draw a conclusion regarding the recommendation.

Tips for Preparing Business Messages

Tips boxes summarize practical suggestions for creating effective business messages. Study them before completing your writing assignments.

Brief Contents

Preface xvii
Acknowledgments xxii

Unit 1: Communicating Today 1

1. Career Success Begins With Communication Skills 3

Unit 2: The Business Writing Process 31

2. Before You Write 34
3. Writing and Revising 56

Unit 3: Forms of Daily Business Writing 86

4. E-Mails, Messages, Texts, Social Media, Memos, Letters, and Other Daily Writing 88
5. Routine Writing Situations 127
6. Persuasive Writing Situations 160
7. Negative Writing Situations 188

Unit 4: Reporting Data 220

8. Informal Reports 223
9. Proposals and Formal Reports 257

Unit 5: Developing Speaking Skills 303

10. Communicating in Person 306
11. Business Presentations 339

Unit 6: Communicating for Employment 373

12. The Job Search, Résumés, Social Media, and Cover Letters 376
13. Interviews and Follow-Up 411

Appendixes 443

A. A Guide to Document Formats 443
B. Correction Abbreviations and Proofreading Marks 453
C. Documentation Formats 455
D. Style in Writing 465

Grammar/Mechanics Handbook 474

Key to Grammar/Mechanics Checkups 538
Notes 540
Index 547

Contents

Preface xvii
Acknowledgments xxii

Unit 1: Communicating Today 1

Chapter 1: Career Success Begins With Communication Skills 3
Becoming an Effective Business Communicator 3
Succeeding in the Changing World of Work 4
How Technology Improves Business Writing 5
Examining the Communication Process 10
Developing Better Listening Skills 12

Barriers to Effective Listening 12
Tips for Becoming an Active Listener 13
Improving Your Nonverbal Communication Skills 13

How the Eyes, Face, and Body Send Silent Messages 14
  Eye Contact 14
  Facial Expression 14
  Posture and Gestures 14
How Time, Space, and Territory Send Silent Messages 14
  Time 15
  Space 15
  Territory 15
How Appearance Sends Silent Messages 15
  Appearance of Business Documents 15
  Appearance of People 16

Tips for Improving Your Nonverbal Skills 16
What Employers Want: Professionalism 17
Understanding How Culture Affects Communication 18

Comparing Key Cultural Values 18
  Context 19
  Individualism Versus Collectivism 20
  Formality 20
  Communication Style 20
  Time Orientation 20
Learning Intercultural Workplace Skills 21

Controlling Ethnocentrism and Stereotyping 21
  Ethnocentrism 21
  Stereotypes 21
  Tolerance 21
Tips for Minimizing Oral Miscommunication Among Cross-Cultural Audiences 22
Tips for Minimizing Written Miscommunication Among Cross-Cultural Audiences 22
Globalization and Workforce Diversity 23

Tips for Effective Communication With Diverse Workplace Audiences 24
Communication Workshop 30

Unit 2: The Business Writing Process 31

Chapter 2: Before You Write 34
Basics of Business Writing 34
Writing Process for Business Messages and Oral Presentations 35

Prewriting 35
Writing 36
Revising 36
Scheduling the Writing Process 36
Analyzing the Purpose for Writing 36

Identifying Your Purpose 37
Selecting the Best Channel 37
Switching to Faster Channels 37
Anticipating the Audience 39

Profiling the Audience 39
Responding to the Profile 41
Adapting to the Task and Audience 41

Audience Benefits 41

Polite "You" View 42
Conversational but Professional 43
Positive Language 44
Courteous Language 45
Bias-Free Language 45
Plain Language and Familiar Words 47
Precise, Vigorous Words 47
Communication Workshop 54

Chapter 3: Writing and Revising 56
Writing: Researching 56

Formal Research Methods 57
Informal Research and Idea Generation 57
Writing: Organizing Data 58

Outlining 58
The Direct Pattern 59
The Indirect Pattern 60
Constructing Effective Sentences 61

Using Four Sentence Types to Achieve Variety 61
Controlling Sentence Length 62
Avoiding Three Common Sentence Faults 62
  Fragments 62
  Run-On (Fused) Sentences 63
  Comma-Splice Sentences 63
Writing: The First Draft 63
Revising: Understanding the Process of Revision 64
Concise Wording 64

Long Lead-Ins 65
Outdated Expressions 65
Needless Adverbs 66
Fillers 66
Repetitious Words 66
Redundant Words 67
Parallelism 68
Appropriate Wording 68

Jargon 68
Slang 69
Clichés 69
Instant-Messaging and Texting Speak 70
Precise Verbs 70
Active Versus Passive Voice 71
Concrete Nouns 72
Vivid Adjectives 72
Designing Documents for Readability 72

Employing White Space 73
Numbering and Bulleting Lists for Quick Comprehension 73
Adding Headings for Visual Impact 73
Revising: The Proofreading Process 75
What to Watch for in Proofreading 75
How to Proofread Documents 75
How to Proofread and Revise PDF Files 77
Communication Workshop 84

Unit 3: Forms of Daily Business Writing 86

Chapter 4: E-Mails, Messages, Texts, Social Media, Memos, Letters, and Other Daily Writing 88
Written Communication in Business 88
Communicating With Electronic Messages 89
Communicating With Paper-Based Messages 90
E-Mails and Their Proper Use 90

Knowing When to Send an E-Mail 90
Components of E-Mails 90
  Subject Line 91
  Salutation 91
  Opening 92
  Body 92
  Closing 93
Putting It All Together 93
Best Practices for Professional E-Mails 93
  Getting Started 96
  Content, Tone, and Correctness 96
  Netiquette 97
  Reading and Replying to E-Mail 97
  Personal Use 97
  Other Smart E-Mail Practices 97
Instant Messaging and Texting and Their Proper Use 98

How Instant Messaging and Texting Work 98
Pros and Cons of Instant Messaging and Texting 100
Best Practices for Instant Messaging and Texting 100
Social Media as a Business Writing Channel 101

How Businesses Use Social Networks 101
Potential Risks of Social Networks for Businesses 101
Tips for Using Social Networking Sites and Keeping Your Job 102
Sharing Information Through RSS Feeds and Social Bookmarking 103
  Really Simple Syndication 103
  Social Bookmarking 103
Podcasts, Blogs, and Wikis for Business Writing 104

Business Podcasts 104
  How Organizations Use Podcasts 104
  Delivering and Accessing Podcasts 104
  Creating a Podcast 105
Professional Blogs and Twitter 105
How Companies Use Blogs 107
  Public Relations, Customer Relations, and Crisis Communication 107
  Market Research 108
  Online Communities 108
  Internal Communication and Recruiting 108
Tips for Creating a Professional Blog 108
How Businesses Use Wikis 109
  How to Be a Valuable Wiki Contributor 110
Writing Hard-Copy Memos 110

Memo Templates 110
Preparing Memos as E-Mail Attachments 112
Writing Hard-Copy Letters 112

Permanent Record 112
Confidentiality 113
Formality and Sensitivity 113
Persuasiveness 113
Formatting Business Letters 113
  Letter Templates 113
Communication Workshop 125

Chapter 5: Routine Writing Situations 127
Routine Situation: Sharing Information 128
Routine Situation: Requesting Information or Action 129
Opening Directly 129
Details in the Body 129
Routine Situation: Replying to Shared Information or Requests 130

Subject Line Efficiency 131
Opening Directly 132
Arranging Information Logically in the Body 132

Closing Politely 132
Routine Situation: Giving Instructions 132

Dividing Instructions Into Steps 132
Revising a Message Delivering Instructions 133
Routine Situation: Making a Complaint or Claim 133

Opening With Action 135
Explaining in the Body 135
Closing Pleasantly 135
Putting It All Together 136
Routine Situation: Replying to Complaints
and Claims 136

Revealing Good News in the Opening 138
Explaining Compliance in the Body 140
Deciding Whether to Apologize 140
Showing Confidence in the Closing 140
Routine Situation: Recommending Someone 141

Identifying the Purpose in the Opening 141
Describing Performance in the Body 142
Evaluating in the Conclusion 142
Routine Situation: Expressing Goodwill 144

Thanks 144
   To Express Thanks for a Gift 145
   To Send Thanks for a Favour 146
   To Extend Thanks for Hospitality 146
Replies to Goodwill Messages 146
   To Answer a Congratulatory Note 146
   To Respond to a Pat on the Back 147
Sympathy 147
   To Express Condolences 147
Are Electronic Channels Appropriate for Goodwill
Messages? 147
Communication Workshop 159

Chapter 6: Persuasive Writing Situations 160
Using the Indirect Strategy in Persuasive Writing
Situations 160

The Components of an Indirect Persuasive Request 161
   Gain Attention 161
   Build Interest 161
   Reduce Resistance 161
   Motivate Action 162
Persuasive Situation: Asking for a Favour
or Other Action 162
Persuasive Situation: Making Complex Claims
and Complaints 164
Persuasive Situation: Getting Co-workers and
Managers Onside 165
   Persuading Other Employees 165
   Persuading Your Manager 165
Persuasive Situation: Sales and Promotional
Messages 168
   Attention 169
   Interest 170
   Desire 171
   Action 171
Putting It All Together 172
Persuasive Situation: Online Sales and Promotional
Messages 172

Selling by E-Mail 173
Using Facebook, Blogs, and Other New Media to Connect
With Customers 174
   Facebook 174
   Blogs 176
   Wikis 176
   RSS (Really Simple Syndication) 176
   Podcasting 176
   Other Social Media 176
Communication Workshop 186

Chapter 7: Negative Writing Situations 188
Dealing with Negative Situations Effectively 188

Establishing Goals in Communicating Negative News 189
The Importance of a Timely Response in Negative Situations 189
When to Use the Direct Writing Strategy
in Negative Situations 189
Negative Situation: Collection Letters 190
When to Use the Indirect Writing Strategy
in Negative Situations 191

Analyzing the Parts of an Indirect-Strategy Negative
Message 193
Buffer the Opening 193
Apologizing in the Buffer 194
Conveying Empathy in the Buffer 195
Present Your Reasons 195
Cushion the Bad News 197
Close Pleasantly 198
Negative Situation: Refusing Requests
and Claims 198
Refusing Favour Requests 199
Refusing Claims 201
Tips for Dealing with Disappointed Customers 203
Negative Situation: Sharing Negative News
with Employees 204
Delivering Bad News Personally 205
Refusing Workplace Requests 206
Announcing Negative News to Employees 207
Keeping the Indirect Strategy Ethical 209
Communication Workshop 219

Unit 4: Reporting Data 220

Chapter 8: Informal Reports 223
Understanding Report Basics 223
Functions of Reports 224

Information Reports 224
Analytical Reports 224
Report Organization 224
   Direct Strategy 224
   Indirect Strategy 225

Report Formats 225
    Electronic Format 225
    Letter Format 225
    Memo Format 226
    PowerPoint Format 227
    Template Format 228
    Manuscript Format 228
Report Delivery 228
    By E-Mail 228
    Online 228
    In Person 228
    By Mail 228

Guidelines for Writing Informal Reports 228

Define the Project 228
Gather Data 229
    Company Records 229
    Observation 229
    Surveys, Questionnaires, and Inventories 229
    Interviews 229
    Secondary Research 230
Use an Appropriate Writing Style 230
Be Objective 231
Use Headings Effectively 232

Six Kinds of Informal Reports 233

Information Reports 233
    Introduction 234
    Findings 234
    Summary 234
Progress Reports 234
Justification/Recommendation Reports 237
    Indirect Strategy 237
Feasibility Reports 238
Summary Reports 240
Minutes of Meetings 245
Communication Workshop 255

Chapter 9: Proposals and Formal Reports 257
Informal Proposals 258

Introduction 258
Background 258
Plan 258
Staffing 259
Budget 260
Authorization 261
Formal Proposals 261

Writing Formal Business Reports 262
Researching Secondary Data 264

Print Resources 264
    Books 264
    Periodicals 264
Research Databases 265
The Internet 265
    Browsers and URLs 266
    Search Tools 266
    Internet Search Tips and Techniques 266
Blogs and Social Networks 267

Generating Primary Data 268

Surveys 268
Interviews 268
Observation and Experimentation 269

Documenting Data and Plagiarism 269
    Recognizing the Purpose of Documentation 270
    What Has to Be Documented? 270
    How to Paraphrase 270
    How to Document 271
    Citing Electronic Sources 271

Organizing and Outlining Data 272

Organizational Strategies 272
    Where to Place the Conclusions and Recommendations 272
    How to Organize the Findings 272
Outlines and Headings 273

Creating Effective Graphics Using Your Data 274

Matching Graphics and Objectives 274
    Tables 275
    Bar Charts 276
    Line Charts 277
    Pie Charts 278
    Flow Charts 279
    Organization Charts 279
    Using Software to Produce Charts 279
    Photographs, Maps, and Illustrations 280

Presenting the Final Report 280

Prefatory Parts 280
Body of Report 281
    Introduction 281
    Findings 282
    Conclusions and Recommendations 282
Supplementary Parts of a Report 282
Other Ways of Presenting Formal Reports 285
Communication Workshop 301

Unit 5: Developing Speaking Skills 303

Chapter 10: Communicating in Person 306
The Importance of Professionalism, Business Etiquette, and Ethical Behaviour 306

Defining Professional Behaviour 306
    Civility 307
    Polish 307
    Business and Dining Etiquette 307
    Social Intelligence 307
    Soft Skills 307
The Relationship Between Ethics and Professional Behaviour 307
Knowing What Employers Want 308

Successful Face-to-Face Workplace Communication 310

Using Your Voice as a Communication Tool 310
   Pronunciation 311
   Tone 311
   Pitch 311
   Volume and Rate 311
   Emphasis 312
Promoting Positive Workplace Relations Through Conversation 312
   Use Correct Names and Titles 312
   Choose Appropriate Topics 312
   Avoid Negative Remarks 313
   Listen to Learn 313
   Give Sincere and Specific Praise 313
Offering Constructive Criticism at Work 313
Responding Professionally to Workplace Criticism 314
Resolving Workplace Conflicts 315
   Common Conflict Response Patterns 315
   Six-Step Procedure for Dealing with Conflict 316

Telephone, Smartphone, and Voice Mail Etiquette 316

Making Productive Phone Calls 316
Receiving Phone Calls Professionally 317
Using Smartphones for Business 318
   Location 318
   Time 319
   Volume 319
Making the Best Use of Voice Mail 319
   Receiving Voice Mail Messages 320
   Leaving Voice Mail Messages 320

Becoming a Team Player in Professional Teams 321

The Importance of Conventional and Virtual Teams in the Workplace 321
Positive and Negative Team Behaviour 322
Characteristics of Successful Professional Teams 323
   Small Size, Diverse Makeup 323
   Agreement on Purpose 323
   Agreement on Procedures 323
   Ability to Confront Conflict 323
   Use of Good Communication Techniques 323
   Ability to Collaborate Rather Than Compete 324
   Shared Leadership 324
   Acceptance of Ethical Responsibilities 324

Conducting Productive and Professional Business Meetings 325

Deciding Whether a Meeting Is Necessary 325
Selecting Participants 325
Distributing an Agenda 325

Getting the Meeting Started 326
Moving the Meeting Along 327
Dealing With Conflict 327
Handling Dysfunctional Group Members 327
Ending With a Plan 328
Following Up Actively 328
Communication Workshop 337

Chapter 11: Business Presentations 339
Getting Ready for an Oral Presentation 340

Know Your Purpose 340
Understand Your Audience 340
Organizing Content for a Powerful Impact 341
Capture Attention in the Introduction 341
Organize the Body 344
Summarize in the Conclusion 345

Building Audience Rapport Like a Pro 345

Effective Imagery 346
Verbal Signposts 346
Nonverbal Messages 347

Planning Visual Aids 347

Types of Visual Aids 348
   Slides 348
   Flipchart/Whiteboard/Blackboard 348
   Handouts 349

Designing an Impressive Slide Presentation 349

Preparing a Visually Appealing Slide Presentation 350
   Analyze the Situation and Purpose 350
   Anticipate Your Audience 351
   Adapt Text and Colour Selections 351
   Organize Your Slides 351
   Compose Your Slide Show 351
   Revise, Proofread, and Evaluate Your Slide Show 355
Using Slides Effectively in Front of an Audience 357
Practising and Preparing 357
Keeping Your Audience Engaged 358
Giving Powerful Slide Presentations in Eight Steps 358

Polishing Your Delivery and Following Up 360

Delivery Method 360
Delivery Techniques 361
   Before Your Presentation 361
   During Your Presentation 362
   After Your Presentation 363
Communication Workshop 371

Unit 6: Communicating for Employment 373

Chapter 12: The Job Search: Résumés, Social Media, and Cover Letters 376
Preparing for Employment 376

Identify Your Interests 377
Evaluate Your Qualifications 377
Recognize the Changing Nature of Jobs 378

Choose a Career Path 378
Searching for a Job Online 380
   Using the Big Employment Sites 380
   Beyond the Big Employment Sites 382
Using Traditional Job Search Techniques 382

Creating a Persuasive Résumé 383

Choose a Résumé Style 383
  Chronological 383
  Functional 384
  Combination 384
Decide on Length 384
Arrange the Parts 384
  Main Heading 385
  Career Objective 385
  Summary of Qualifications 385
  Education 386
  Work Experience or Employment History 386
  Capabilities and Skills 388
  Awards, Honours, and Activities 388
  Personal Data 388
  References 389
Using LinkedIn and Video to Bolster the Traditional
Résumé 390

LinkedIn: The "Professional" Social Media Site 390
Video Résumés 394
Applying the Final Touches to Your Résumé 395

Be Honest and Ethical 395
Polishing Your Résumé 396
Proofreading Your Résumé 397
Submitting Your Résumé 397
The Persuasive Cover Letter 398

Gaining Attention in the Opening 398
  Openings for Solicited Jobs 398
  Openings for Unsolicited Jobs 399
Building Interest in the Body 399
Action in the Closing 402
Avoiding "I" Dominance 402
Sending Your Cover Letter by E-Mail 402
Communication Workshop 409

Chapter 13: Interviews and Follow-Up 411
Employment Interviews 411
Purposes of Employment Interviews 412
Kinds of Employment Interviews 412
  Screening Interviews 412
  Hiring/Placement Interviews 412
  One-on-One Interviews 413
  Panel Interviews 413
  Group Interviews 413

Sequential Interviews 413
Stress interviews 413
Online Interviews 413
Before the Interview 414

Use Professional Phone Techniques 414
Make the First Conversation Impressive 414
Research the Target Company 415
Prepare and Practise 416
  Prepare and Rehearse Success Stories 416
  Practise Answers to Possible Questions 416
  Clean Up Any Digital Dirt 416
  Expect to Explain Problem Areas on Your Résumé 418
  Decide How to Dress 418
  Gather Items to Bring 418
Travelling to and Arriving at Your Interview 418
Fighting Fear 419
During the Interview 419

Sending Positive Nonverbal Messages and Acting
Professionally 419
  Answering Typical Questions Confidently 421
  Questions to Get Acquainted 422
  Questions to Gauge Your Interest 423
  Questions About Your Experience and Accomplishments 423
  Questions About the Future 423
  Challenging Questions 424
  Situational Questions 424
  Behavioural Questions 425
Illegal and Inappropriate Questions 426
Asking Your Own Questions 427
Ending Positively 427
After the Interview 428

Thank Your Interviewer 428
Contact Your References 428
Follow Up 430
Other Employment Documents and Follow-Up
Messages 430

Application Form 430
Application or Résumé Follow-Up Message 431
Rejection Follow-Up Message 431
Job Acceptance and Rejection Messages 432
Resignation Letter 433
Communication Workshop 441

Appendixes 443

Appendix A: A Guide to Document Formats 443
Appendix B: Correction Abbreviations and
Proofreading Marks 453
Appendix C: Documentation Formats 455
Appendix D: Style in Writing 465
Grammar/Mechanics Handbook 474

Key to Grammar/Mechanics Checkups 538
Notes 540
Index 547

Today's graduates enter working environments with ever-increasing demands. As a result of growing emphasis on team management and employee empowerment, they will be expected to gather data, solve problems, and make decisions independently. They will be working with global trading partners and collaborating with work teams in an increasingly diverse workplace. And they will be using sophisticated technologies to communicate.

Surprisingly, writing skills are becoming more and more important. In the past, businesspeople may have written a couple of business letters a month, but now they receive and send hundreds of e-mails and texts weekly. Their writing skills are showcased in every message they send. To help students develop the skills they need to succeed in today's technologically enhanced workplace, we have responded with a thoroughly revised Eighth Canadian Editionof Essentials of Business Communications.

Effective Features That Remain Unchanged

The Eighth Canadian Edition maintains the streamlined, efficient approach to communication that has equipped past learners with the skills needed to be successful in their work. It is most helpful to postsecondary and adult learners preparing themselves for new careers, planning a change in their current careers, or wishing to upgrade their writing and speaking skills. The aim of this edition is to incorporate more of the comments, suggestions, and insights provided by adopters and reviewers over the last few years. For those new to the book, some of the most popular features include the following:

- **Text/Workbook Format.** The convenient text/workbook format presents an all-in-one teaching–learning package that includes concepts, workbook application exercises, writing, speaking, and interpersonal problems, and a combination handbook/reference manual. Students work with and purchase only one volume for efficient, economical instruction.
- **Comprehensive but Concise Coverage.** An important reason for the enormous success of *Essentials of Business Communication* is that it practises what it preaches. The Eighth Canadian Edition follows the same strategy, concentrating on essential concepts presented without wasted words.
- **Writing Plans and Writing Improvement Exercises.** Step-by-step writing plans structure the writing experience so that novice writers get started quickly—without struggling to provide unknown details to unfamiliar, hypothetical cases. Many revision exercises build confidence and skills.
- **Wide Coverage of Communication Technology.** All relevant chapters build technology skills by including discussions and applications involving e-mail, instant messaging, texting, cellphones, Web research, contemporary software, online employment searches, and electronic presentations. The Eighth Canadian Edition stays on top of the use of mediated communication within organizations, including the use of social media sites like Twitter and blogs for both business and marketing communication.
- **Grammar/Mechanics Emphasis.** Each chapter features a systematic review of the Grammar/Mechanics Handbook. Readers take a short quiz to review specific concepts, and they also proofread business documents that provide a cumulative review of all concepts previously presented.

- **Challenging Cases.** The reality of the work world is that communication situations will not always easily fit the models provided in a business communication textbook. As a result, we have threaded ambiguity and complexity into the tasks so that students have a chance to use their critical thinking skills as well as their business communication skills regularly.
- **Workplace-in-Focus Feature.** Chapters contain a *Workplace in Focus* feature that connects the content being discussed in the chapter to a real-world example. These features make ideal starting points for in-class discussion.
- **Communication-Technology-in-the-News Feature.** Units open with articles from Canadian media outlets that bring home the relevance of business communication to today's technology-driven workplace. Topics covered range from texting lingo in the workplace to mastering anger when sending e-mail.
- **Plagiarism.** An unfortunate reality of the Internet age is the difficulty today's students have in understanding the need for proper citation and documentation, as well as the difficulty in understanding the seriousness of plagiarism and its difficult repercussions. We address the issue of plagiarism by offering concrete examples of the real-world ramifications of this behaviour.

 ## Revision Highlights

The following new features update the Eighth Canadian Edition:

- **Situational Focus.** The reality of business communication is that people need to be able to respond effectively in a variety of situations. This is different from memorizing a number of genres or formats. For this reason, while the Eighth Canadian Edition does include a rich introductory chapter on various daily forms of communication (e.g., text, e-mail, letter), it expands on this generic way of thinking over the next three chapters by considering important, realistic, and recurring business situations divided into three categories: routine, persuasive, and negative.
- **New and Revised End-of-Chapter Exercises and Activities.** This edition features a significant revision of the end-of-chapter exercises and activities, prepared by Marco Campagna of Algonquin College. More than half of the *Writing Improvement Exercises* are new and almost all of the *Grammar/ Mechanics Reviews* have been replaced. The *Activities and Cases* also feature more than 15 percent new content. As with the last edition, these new cases recognize the pedagogical usefulness of scripting, role-play, and performance as effective means of practising business communication skills.
- **Updated Communication Workshops.** Chapters conclude with a number of new and revised Communication Workshop features in which an enrichment activity is offered to students. These workshops cover topics that are related to but not covered in depth in the preceding chapter. They can be used as group activity assignments, in-class discussion prompts, or homework assignments.
- **Increased Analysis of New Communication Technologies.** Technology manufacturers' ability to innovate can seem to outstrip teachers' ability to contextualize the changes happening to communication. This edition stays ahead of the curve by contextualizing podcasts, Twitter, LinkedIn, Facebook, wikis, blogs, and other of-the-moment technologies in more detail than any other business communication textbook.

Other Features That Enhance Teaching and Learning

Although the Eighth Canadian Edition of *Essentials of Business Communication* packs considerable information into a small space, it covers all of the critical topics necessary in a comprehensive business communication course; it also features many teaching–learning devices to facilitate instruction, application, and retention.

- **Focus on Writing Skills.** Most students need a great deal of instruction and practice in developing basic and advanced writing techniques, particularly in view of today's increased emphasis on communication by e-mail. Writing skills have returned to the forefront since so much of today's business is transacted through written messages.
- **Realistic Emphasis.** *Essentials* devotes a chapter to the writing of e-mail, texts, and instant messages, plus other daily forms of communication, recognizing that the business world no longer operates via letter or memo, except in certain specialized situations (e.g., direct-mail sales letter, collection letters, cover letter for job application, etc.).
- **Listening, Speaking, and Nonverbal Skills.** Employers are increasingly seeking well-rounded individuals who can interact with fellow employees as well as represent the organization effectively. *Essentials* provides professional tips for managing nonverbal cues, overcoming listening barriers, developing speaking skills, planning and participating in meetings, and making productive telephone calls.
- **Coverage of Formal and Informal Reports.** Two chapters develop functional report-writing skills. Chapter 8 provides detailed instruction in the preparation of six types of informal reports, while Chapter 9 covers proposals and formal reports. For quick comprehension all reports contain marginal notes that pinpoint writing strategies.
- **Employment Communication Skills.** Successful résumés, cover letters, and other employment documents are among the most important topics in a good business communication course. *Essentials* provides the most realistic and up-to-date résumés in the field. The models show chronological, functional, combination, and computer-friendly résumés.
- **Focus on Oral Communication Skills.** Chapter 10 looks at oral interpersonal skills: person-to-person conversations, telephone communication (including cell-phone etiquette), and business meeting skills, while Chapter 11 specifically discusses business presentation skills.
- **Employment Interviewing.** *Essentials* devotes a chapter to effective interviewing techniques, including a discussion of screening interviews and hiring interviews. Chapter 13 also teaches techniques for fighting fear, answering questions, and following up.
- **Models Comparing Effective and Ineffective Documents.** To facilitate speedy recognition of good and bad writing techniques and strategies, *Essentials* presents many before-and-after documents. Marginal notes spotlight targeted strategies and effective writing. We hope that instructors turn this before-and-after technique into effective pedagogy whereby all their students' written assignments undergo the scrutiny of an editing and revising process before being handed in as final products.
- **Variety in End-of-Chapter Activities.** An amazing array of review questions, critical-thinking questions, writing improvement exercises, revision exercises, activities, and realistic case problems holds student attention and helps them apply chapter concepts meaningfully.
- **Diagnostic Test.** An optional grammar/mechanics diagnostic test helps students and instructors systematically determine specific student writing weaknesses. Students may be directed to the Grammar/Mechanics Handbook for remediation.
- **Grammar/Mechanics Handbook.** A comprehensive Grammar/Mechanics Handbook supplies a thorough review of English grammar, punctuation, capitalization style, and number usage. Its self-teaching exercises may be used for classroom instruction or for supplementary assignments. The handbook also serves as a convenient reference throughout the course and afterwards.

MindTap

MindTap for Essentials of Business Communication is a personalized teaching experience with relevant assignments that guide students to analyze, apply, and elevate thinking, allowing instructors to measure skills and promote better outcomes with ease. A fully online learning solution, MindTap combines all student learning tools—readings, multimedia, activities, and assessments—into a single Learning Path that guides the student through the curriculum. Instructors personalize the experience by customizing the presentation of these learning tools to their students, even seamlessly introducing their own content into the Learning Path. Chapter-based learning paths utilize the MindTap Reader eBook, Aplia assignments that highlight key concepts in each chapter, and oral communication activities through YouSeeU. Other MindApps Web applications let you create an engaging course with options to read the text aloud, insert video and audio, and create shared social media information. You'll also find measurable learning objectives for each unit. Instructors can access MindTap at http://www.nelson.com and http://login.cengage.com

Unparalleled Instructor Support

The Eighth Canadian Edition of *Essentials* continues to set the standard for business communication support. Classroom success is easy to achieve with the many practical ancillary items that supplement Guffey, Loewy, and Almonte's textbook.

About the Nelson Education Teaching Advantage (NETA)

The Nelson Education Teaching Advantage (NETA) program delivers research-based instructor resources that promote student engagement and higher order thinking to enable the success of Canadian students and educators. To ensure the high quality of these materials, all Nelson ancillaries have been professionally copy-edited.

Be sure to visit Nelson Education's **Inspired Instruction** website at http://www.nelson.com/inspired/ to find out more about NETA. Don't miss the testimonials of instructors who have used NETA supplements and seen student engagement increase!

Instructor Resources

All NETA and other key instructor ancillaries can be accessed through http://www.nelson.com/login and http://login.cengage.com, giving instructors the ultimate tools for customizing lectures and presentations.

- **Guffey Resource Centre** (www.nelson.com/login): Find all of your teaching and learning resources in one place! This resource centre houses all of the resources listed below as well as additional instructional support, including: teaching modules, grammar and mechanics worksheets, cases and solutions, online teaching suggestions, tips for teaching with technology, resource integration guides, and active learning activities. Please contact your local Nelson Representative to gain access to all of your instructional support.
- **NETA Test Bank:** This resource includes over 250 multiple-choice questions written according to NETA guidelines for effective construction and development of higher order questions. The Test Bank was copy-edited by a NETA-trained editor. Also included are 260 true/false questions and 130 completion questions.

    The NETA Test Bank is available in a new, cloud-based platform. **Testing Powered by Cognero®** is a secure online testing system that allows you to author, edit, and manage test bank content from any place you have Internet access. No special installations or downloads are needed, and the desktop-inspired interface, with its drop-down menus and familiar, intuitive tools, allows you to create and manage tests with ease. You can create multiple test versions in an instant, and

import or export content into other systems. Tests can be delivered from your learning management system, your classroom, or wherever you want. Testing Powered by Cognero for Essentials of Business Communication can be accessed through www.nelson.com/login and http://login.cengage.com.

- **NETA PowerPoint:** Microsoft® PowerPoint® lecture slides for every chapter have been created with an average of 25 slides per chapter, many featuring key figures, tables, and photographs from *Essentials of Business Communication*. NETA principles of clear design and engaging content have been incorporated throughout, making it simple for instructors to customize the deck for their courses.
- **Image Library:** This resource consists of digital copies of figures, short tables, and photographs used in the book. Instructors may use these jpegs to customize the NETA PowerPoint or create their own PowerPoint presentations.
- **NETA Instructor's Manual:** This resource is organized according to the textbook chapters and addresses key educational concerns, such as typical stumbling blocks student face and how to address them. Other features include answers to problems and suggested answers to exercises and cases.
- **Day One:** Day One—Prof InClass is a PowerPoint presentation that instructors can customize to orient students to the class and their text at the beginning of the course.

Innovative Resources for Students

Stay organized and efficient with **MindTap**—a single destination with all the course material and study aids you need to succeed. Built-in apps leverage social media and the latest learning technology. For example:

- ReadSpeaker will read the text to you.
- Flashcards are pre-populated to provide you with a jump start for review—or you can create your own.
- You can highlight text and make notes in your MindTap Reader. Your notes will flow into Evernote, the electronic notebook app that you can access anywhere when it's time to study for the exam.
- Self-quizzing allows you to assess your understanding.

Visit NELSONbrain.com to start using MindTap. Enter the Online Access Code from the card included with your text. If a code card is not provided, you can purchase instant access at NELSONbrain.com.

Acknowledgments

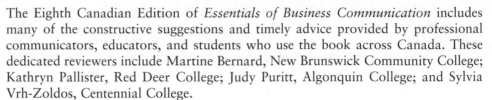

The Eighth Canadian Edition of *Essentials of Business Communication* includes many of the constructive suggestions and timely advice provided by professional communicators, educators, and students who use the book across Canada. These dedicated reviewers include Martine Bernard, New Brunswick Community College; Kathryn Pallister, Red Deer College; Judy Puritt, Algonquin College; and Sylvia Vrh-Zoldos, Centennial College.

A new edition like this would not be possible without the development team at Nelson Education. Special thanks go to Anne-Marie Taylor, Dave Stratton, Theresa Fitzgerald, Claire Horsnell, and Jaime Smith. Many thanks to Marco Campagna of Algonquin College who revised the end-of-chapter exercises and activities. We would also like to thank Naman Mahisauria and his team at MPS. Thanks also go to the copy editor, Elizabeth Phinney.

Mary Ellen Guffey
Dana Loewy
Richard Almonte

Communicating Today

CHAPTER 1
Career Success
Begins With
Communication
Skills

JPM/GETTY

COMMUNICATION TECHNOLOGY IN THE NEWS

Texting Lingo Shows Up at Office; Set Limits but Don't Discourage Young Employees

Source: Derek Sankey, "Texting lingo shows up at office." National Post *April 14, 2010, p. FP 12. Material reprinted with the express permission of POSTMEDIA NEWS, a division of Postmedia Network Inc.*

CALGARY – While Maria Bakardjieva was conducting research about how people across the world integrate the Internet and technologies into their lives, she was astounded by stories she heard from teachers.

In one group of 11- and 12-year-olds in Britain, the teacher asked her students to recount how they spent their summers. One girl wrote a paper entirely in the lingo of texting.

"It was hilarious. It was impossible. Not simply abbreviated words in the way they are spelled, but also abbreviated thoughts," recalls Ms. Bakardjieva, a professor of communication at the University of Calgary.

Now, texting shortcuts are creeping into everyday communication, even in the workplace.

"There are these discreet, almost distinct speech genres appropriate for different situations, at the same time they always overlap and influence one another and there is overflow from one into the other," Ms. Bakardjieva says.

Some academic researchers examine different speech genres and how we recognize how to communicate in different situations specific to that culture or situation. It can be a fine line for some people when deciding what's appropriate—even decipherable—in the workplace.

Technology gadgets also appear to be hampering workplace etiquette.

About 42 percent of more than 270 chief information officers across Canada with 100 or more employees stated the number of breaches in workplace etiquette have increased as a result of mobile electronic gadgets, a study by Robert Half Technology found.

"Electronic gadgets have facilitated increased productivity amongst employees, but they may also cause interruptions," says Megan Slabinski, president of Robert Half's Canadian operations.

The report identifies several examples, such as the "misguided multi-tasker," referring to somebody who thinks e-mailing or texting during a meeting demonstrates efficiency; the "broadcaster," who has no shame about when and where these mobile devices are used, such as the washroom; and the "distractor," who has good intentions by setting the device to vibrate, but a constant flow of buzzing on a desk can be a huge distraction.

It's not that proper grammar has been erased or obliterated either, but there clearly is a new genre of communication resulting from technology. Deciding on appropriate language in the workplace is common sense for many, but there is still a need for employers to be clear about it by setting guidelines, Ms. Bakardjieva says.

"People who are socialized in this culture, educated in this culture, they know how to switch from one to the other."

"[Employers] have to set clear limits. They have to engage with this problem head on and show clearly to their employees where the boundaries are drawn," she says.

At the same time, they cannot ignore the fact these technologies are ubiquitous and workers—in particular, younger generations—rely on them to carry out their tasks.

"I don't think they should be completely fascist and limiting about these things," she says. "This is the way this generation breathes. You want to have an engaged, happy employee."

Summarize the article you've just read in a two- to three-sentence paragraph. Answer the following questions, either on your own or in a small group. Be prepared to give your answers in a short presentation or in an e-mail to your instructor.

QUESTIONS:

1. How does what you've learned in this article change your perception of business communication?

2. How might what you've learned in this article change your own communication style?

3. Come up with pro and con arguments for the following debate/discussion topic: Employers need to accommodate their young employees' communication styles, instead of expecting new employees to communicate in old-fashioned ways.

Career Success Begins With Communication Skills

© YURI ARCURS/SHUTTERSTOCK

LEARNING
OBJECTIVES

1. Understand the importance of becoming an effective business communicator in today's changing workplace.

2. Identify ways in which technology helps improve business writing.

3. Discuss how to become an effective listener.

4. Analyze nonverbal communication and explain techniques for improving nonverbal communication skills.

5. Explain professionalism in the workplace.

6. Explain how culture affects communication and describe methods for improving cross-cultural communication.

7. Identify specific techniques that improve effective communication among diverse workplace audiences.

Becoming an Effective Business Communicator

People with different backgrounds bring varied views to decision making. Businesses must rely on their employees' ability to work with a diverse group of people who are located across international borders. The more effectively employees work together, the more successful their company is. In this age of information, career success is directly related to good communication, a skill that is made more challenging by tremendous changes in technology, the workforce, work environments, and the globalization of business.

Through e-mail, messaging, texting, and other technology-based communication channels, business communicators today are doing more writing than ever before. Their writing is also having a more immediate impact. This book focuses on developing business writing skills. But you will also learn to improve your listening, nonverbal, and speaking skills.

While you are born with the ability to acquire language and to listen, effective business communication skills are learned. Good communicators are not born; they are made. Your ability to thrive in the dynamic and demanding contemporary world of work will depend on many factors, some of which you cannot control. One factor that you do control, however, is how well you communicate.

The goals of this book are to teach you basic business communication skills, such as how to write an effective e-mail, memo, or letter and how to give a presentation. Anyone can learn these skills with the help of effective instructional materials and good model documents, all of which you'll find in this book. You also need practice—with meaningful feedback. You need someone such as your instructor to tell you how to modify your responses so that you can improve.

> The information revolution has made communication skills extremely important.

> Because communication skills are learned, you control how well you communicate.

We've designed this book to provide you with everything necessary to make you a successful business communicator in today's dynamic workplace. Given the increasing emphasis on communication, Canadian corporations are paying millions of dollars to communication coaches and trainers to teach employees the very skills that you are learning in this course. For example, Ottawa-based Backdraft Corporation, a leading provider of corporate writing training, and the first writing services company in the world to be granted ISO 9000 registration, lists among its clients the Royal Bank of Canada, Siemens Canada, the National Gallery of Canada, and the Government of Alberta.[1] Your coach is your instructor. Get your money's worth! Pick his or her brains.

> This book and this course might well be the most important in your postsecondary education.

Once you've had a couple of years of business experience, you may look back on this course and this textbook as the most important in your entire postsecondary education. To get started, this first chapter presents an overview. You'll take a look at (1) the changing workplace, (2) the communication process, (3) listening, (4) nonverbal communication, (5) professionalism, (6) culture and communication, and (7) workplace diversity. The remainder of the book is devoted to developing specific writing and speaking skills.

Succeeding in the Changing World of Work

The entire world of work is changing dramatically. The kind of work you'll do, the tools you'll use, the form of management you'll work under, the environment in which you'll work, the people with whom you'll interact—all are undergoing a pronounced transformation. Many of the changes revolve around processing and communicating information, as you can see in Figure 1.2 on pages 8–9. As a result, the most successful players in this new world of work will be those with highly developed communication skills. The following business trends illustrate the importance of excellent communication skills.

> Trends in the new world of work emphasize the importance of communication skills.

- **Innovative communication technologies.** E-mail, messaging, texting, social media, the Web, mobile technologies, audio- and videoconferencing—all of these technologies mean that you will be communicating more often and more rapidly than ever before. Your writing and speaking skills will be showcased and tested as never before.

- **Flattened management hierarchies.** To better compete and to reduce expenses, businesses have for years been trimming layers of management. This means that as a frontline employee, you will have fewer managers. You will be making decisions and communicating them to customers, to fellow employees, and to executives.
- **More participatory management.** Gone are the days of command-and-control management. Now, even new employees will be expected to understand and contribute to the success of the organization. Improving productivity and profitability will be everyone's job, not just management's.
- **Increased emphasis on self-directed work and project teams.** Businesses today are often run by cross-functional teams of peers. You can expect to work with a team in gathering information, finding and sharing solutions, implementing decisions, and managing conflict. Good communication skills are extremely important in working together successfully in a team environment.
- **Heightened global competition.** Because Canadian companies are required to move beyond local markets, you may be interacting with people from many different cultures. At the same time, because of increased immigration, you may be expected to interact with people from many cultures in your local market as well as in your organization.[2] As a successful business communicator, you will want to learn about other cultures. You'll also need to develop interpersonal skills including sensitivity, flexibility, patience, and tolerance.
- **New work environments.** Mobile technologies and the desire for better work/family balance have resulted in flexible working arrangements. You may be hired by one of the 23 percent of Canadian companies that offer a telecommuting option to employees.[3] Working away from the office requires exchanging even more messages in order to stay connected.
- **The move to a knowledge economy.** As Statistics Canada researchers Desmond Beckstead and Tara Vinodrai show in their paper "Dimensions of Occupational Changes in Canada's Knowledge Economy, 1971–1996," the decrease in the importance of sectors such as manufacturing and agriculture has taken place at the same time as "the importance of knowledge occupations has continuously increased over the last three decades."[4] By definition, such "knowledge occupations," many of which are in business, require excellent communication skills.

How Technology Improves Business Writing

Another basic for beginning business communicators is learning to use technology to enhance their writing efforts. Although computers and software programs cannot actually do the writing for you, they provide powerful tools that make the entire process easier and the results more professional. Technology can help you improve written documents, oral presentations, and Web pages.

1. **Designing and producing professional-looking documents, presentations, and Web pages.** Most popular word processing programs include a large selection of scalable fonts (for different character sizes and styles), italics, boldface, symbols, and styling techniques to help you produce consistent formatting and professional-looking results. Moreover, today's presentation software, such as Microsoft's PowerPoint, enables you to incorporate animated slide effects, colour, sound, pictures, and even movies into your talks for management or customers. Web document builders also help you design and construct Web pages. Another widely used software is Adobe's Portable Document Format, or PDF for short. A PDF is a file format that creates a document that is more permanent, transferable, and difficult to make changes to. Businesses use PDFs

FIGURE 1.1 Microsoft templates

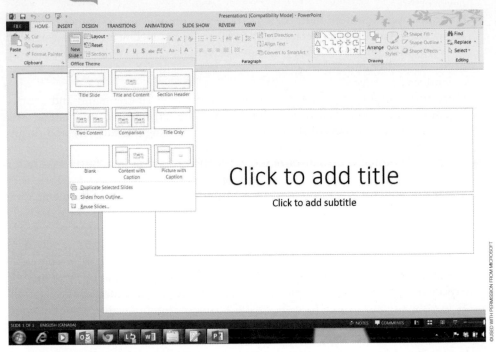

regularly for important forms that shouldn't be changed by the receiver. These tools can be used effectively to help you reinforce your message and help your audience understand and remember your message.

2. **Using templates.** One of the most useful and time-saving features of today's word processing software for the business writer is templates. As Figure 1.1 illustrates, templates are pre-formatted documents; business writers simply add the content. Any time you open up a new document in Microsoft Word, for example, on the right-hand side of your document you will see the option to choose a template. Typical templates include memos, letters, résumés, and reports. For the purposes of your business communication course, you should always choose a "professional" template, such as Word's Professional Letter template. Templates save time for business writers because, instead of memorizing the various parts of a letter (e.g., how many spaces from the top the date and address should be placed), they can now concentrate on the more important things, such as making sure grammar and style are perfected. This is not to say that knowing the parts of a letter is unimportant (see Appendix A), only that most of us don't have time to think about these features every time we sit down to write. In large companies, templates are branded using the company's logo and other design elements, and workers never write a letter or memo from "scratch" anymore. Similarly, doing an Internet search on "templates" will bring up thousands of other non-corporate and non-proprietary templates that you might use in your daily business writing.

3. **Collecting information electronically.** Information is now easily accessible through the Internet, which means workplace communication, such as presentations, are easily made more persuasive. Want to know what Apple's recent marketing campaign looked and sounded like? Google it. By using Google or other search engines, you have a wealth of information at your fingertips: newspaper articles, statistics, corporate information, peer-reviewed material, blog postings. However, you must document your borrowing of this readily available data each time you do so. Otherwise you are committing plagiarism, which has serious real-world consequences, such as firing.

Powerful writing tools can help you fight writer's block, collect information, outline and organize ideas, improve correctness and precision, add graphics, and design professional-looking documents.

4. **Adding graphics for emphasis.** Your letters, memos, and reports may be improved by the addition of graphs and artwork to clarify and illustrate data. You can import charts, diagrams, and illustrations created in database, spreadsheet, and graphics programs, or from Internet sites such as Google Images. Moreover, ready-made pictures, called clip art, can be used to symbolize or illustrate ideas.

5. **Improving correctness and precision.** Word processing programs today provide features that catch and correct spelling and typographical errors; they also provide grammar checkers that are markedly improved over earlier versions. The programs now detect many errors in capitalization, word use (such as *it's/its*), double negatives, verb use, sentence structure, number agreement, number style, and other writing faults. However, grammar programs don't actually correct the errors they detect. You must know how to do that. Similarly, these programs don't catch all misspelled words or all grammar errors (often subject–verb agreement, for example). This is especially important in Canada because most spell checkers use American spelling. For example, if you have written the word *traveling* in your memo and your spell checker hasn't caught the mistake, this is because *traveling* is the correct American spelling, whereas *travelling* is the correct Canadian spelling. You must still know how to correct your own spelling and grammar mistakes.

DILBERT   By Scott Adams

6. **Using software for team writing.** As part of today's team-based work environment, you can expect to work with others on projects. Word processing programs usually have an editing feature with commenting and strikeout that allows you to revise easily, to identify each team member's editing, and to track multiple edits. E-mail and instant messaging programs allow group members to share documents and information freely and work on the same document from several remote locations at the same time. Other computer-based communication systems such as wikis allow members of a team or community group or online group to collectively add information to an evolving site. Some wikis are free to access and create (if you Google "wiki" you'll see the variety of free sites) while others are proprietary software, such as Microsoft's SharePoint. While collaboration between team and group members is a positive aspect of computer-based writing, such collaboration also entails an extra responsibility. When a number of people are working on an assignment and using computers to piece together the various parts they've worked on, there is often a temptation not to revise the document sufficiently.

Remember to build in enough time to edit and proofread the document that has been created by pasting together the work of numerous people, so that it reads as if it was written by one person. Another danger in collaborative writing is plagiarism. Plagiarism is the stealing of another writer's words or ideas by putting them in one's own assignment without crediting the original author. Plagiarism is the most serious of academic offences, usually leading to a failing

FIGURE 1.2 Communication and Collaborative Technologies

Communication Technologies: Reshaping the World of Work

Today's workplace is changing dramatically as a result of innovative software, superfast wireless networks, and numerous technologies that allow workers to share information, work from remote locations, and be more productive in or away from the office. We are seeing a gradual progression from basic capabilities, such as e-mail, instant messaging, and calendaring, to deeper functionality, such as remote database access, multi-functional devices, and Web-based collaborative applications. Becoming familiar with modern office and collaboration technologies can help you be successful in today's digital workplace.

Telephony: VoIP

Savvy businesses are switching from traditional phone service to Voice over Internet Protocol (VoIP). This technology allows callers to communicate using a broadband Internet connection, thus eliminating long distance and local telephone charges. Higher-end VoIP systems now support unified voice mail, e-mail, click-to-call capabilities, and softphones (phones using computer networking). Free or low-cost Internet telephony sites, such as the popular Skype, are also increasingly used by businesses.

Multifunctional Printers

Stand-alone copiers, fax machines, scanners, and printers have been replaced with multifunctional devices. Offices are transitioning from a "print and distribute" environment to a "distribute and print" environment. Security measures include pass codes and even biometric thumbprint scanning to make sure data streams are not captured, interrupted, or edited.

Open Offices

Widespread use of laptop computers, wireless technology, and VoIP have led to more fluid, flexible, and open workspaces. Smaller computers and flat-screen monitors enable designers to save space with boomerang-shaped workstations and cockpit-style work surfaces rather than space-hogging corner work areas. Smaller breakout areas for impromptu meetings are taking over some cubicle space, and digital databases are replacing file cabinets.

Handheld Wireless Devices

A new generation of lightweight, handheld smartphones provide phone, e-mail, Web browsing, and calendar options anywhere there is a wireless network. Devices such as the BlackBerry and the iPhone now allow you to tap into corporate databases and intranets from remote locations. You can check customers' files, complete orders, and send out receipts without returning to the office.

Company Intranets

To share insider information, many companies provide their own protected Web sites called intranets. An intranet may handle company e-mail, announcements, an employee directory, a policy handbook, frequently asked questions, personnel forms and data, employee discussion forums, shared documents, and other employee information.

Voice Recognition

Computers equipped with voice recognition software enable users to dictate up to 160 words a minute with accurate transcription. Voice recognition is particularly helpful to disabled workers and to professionals with heavy dictation loads, such as physicians and attorneys. Users can create documents, enter data, compose and send e-mails, browse the Web, and control the desktop—all by voice.

Electronic Presentations

Business presentations in PowerPoint or Prezi can be projected from a laptop or PDA or posted online. Sophisticated presentations may include animations, sound effects, digital photos, video clips, or hyperlinks to Internet sites. In some industries, PowerPoint slides ("decks") are replacing or supplementing traditional hard-copy reports.

Collaboration Technologies: Rethinking the Way We Work Together

Global competition, expanding markets, and the ever-increasing pace of business accelerate the development of exciting collaboration tools. New tools make it possible to work together without being together. Your colleagues may be down the hall, across the country, or around the world. With today's tools, you can exchange ideas, solve problems, develop products, forecast future performance, and complete team projects any time of the day or night and anywhere in the world. Blogs and wikis, part of the so-called Web 2.0 era, are social tools that create multidirectional conversations among customers and employees. Web 2.0 moves Web applications from "read only" to "read-write," thus enabling greater participation and collaboration.

Blogs, Podcasts, and Wikis

A *blog* is a Web site with journal entries usually written by one person and comments by others. Businesses use blogs to keep customers and employees informed and to receive feedback. Company developments can be posted, updated, and categorized for easy cross-referencing. *Podcasts* are usually short audio or video clips that users can either watch on a company Web site or download and view or listen to on their computers or MP3 players on the go. A *wiki* is a Web site that allows multiple users to collaboratively create and edit pages. Information gets lost in e-mails, but blogs and wikis provide an easy way to communicate and keep track of what is said. *RSS* (really simple syndication) *feeds* allow businesspeople and customers to receive updates automatically whenever podcasts, news stories, or blog entries become available on their favourite Web sites.

Videoconferencing

Videoconferencing allows participants to meet in special conference rooms equipped with cameras and television screens. Groups see each other and interact in real time although they may be continents apart. Faster computers, rapid Internet connections, and better cameras now enable from 2 to 200 participants to sit at their own PCs and share applications, spreadsheets, presentations, and photos.

Voice Conferencing

Telephone "bridges" allow two or more callers from any location to share the same call. *Voice conferencing* (also called *audioconferencing*, *teleconferencing*, or just plain *conference calling*) enables people to collaborate by telephone. Communicators at both ends use enhanced speakerphones to talk and be heard simultaneously.

Web Conferencing

With services such as GoToMeeting, WebEx, Microsoft LiveMeeting, or the free Skype, all you need are a PC and an Internet connection to hold a meeting (*webinar*) with customers or colleagues in real time. Although the functions are constantly evolving, Web conferencing currently incorporates screen sharing, chats, slide presentations, text messaging, and application sharing.

Presence Technology

Presence technology makes it possible to locate and identify a computing device as soon as users connect to the network. This technology is an integral part of communication devices including cellphones, laptop computers, PDAs, pagers, and GPS devices. Collaboration is possible wherever and whenever users are online.

Video Phones

Using advanced video compression technology, video phones transmit real-time audio and video so that communicators can see each other as they collaborate. With a video phone, people can videoconference anywhere in the world over a broadband IP (Internet Protocol) connection without a computer or a television screen.

grade on the assignment, if not the course. When proven in the work world, plagiarism may lead to the firing of the guilty person.[5] Plagiarism is discussed in greater detail in Chapter 9.

Examining the Communication Process

As you can see, in today's workplace you can expect to be communicating more rapidly, more often, and with greater numbers of people than ever before. Since good communication skills are essential to your success, we need to take a closer look at the communication process.

Just what is communication? For our purposes communication is the transmission of information and meaning from one individual or group (the sender) to another (the receiver). The crucial element in this definition is meaning. Communication has as its central objective the transmission of meaning. The process of communication is successful only when the receiver understands an idea as the sender intended it. This classic theory of communication was first articulated by theorist Harold Lasswell (1947) and later expanded upon by Claude E. Shannon and Warren Weaver (1949). This theoretical process generally involves five steps, discussed here and shown in Figure 1.3.

1. **Sender forms an idea.** The idea may be influenced by the sender's mood, frame of reference, background, and culture, as well as the context of the situation. (For example, an accountant realizes income tax season is about to begin.)
2. **Sender encodes the idea in a message.** *Encoding* means converting the idea into words or gestures that will convey meaning. A major problem in com-

> Communication is the transmission of information and meaning from one individual or group to another.

> The communication process has five steps: idea formation, message encoding, message transmission, message decoding, and feedback.

FIGURE 1.3 Communication Process

Communication barriers may cause the communication process to break down.

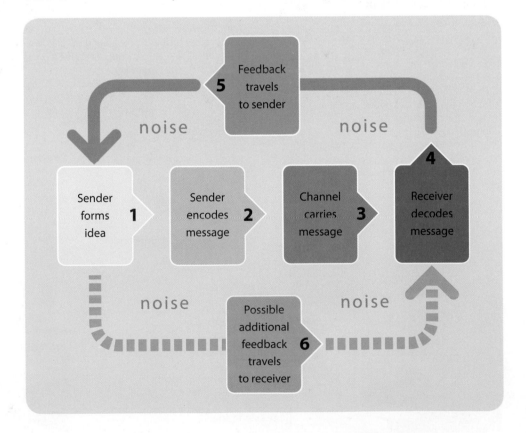

municating any message is that words have different meanings for different people. That's why skilled communicators try to choose familiar words with concrete meanings on which both senders and receivers agree. (For example, the accountant writes an e-mail asking all her clients to begin scheduling income tax appointments.)

3. **Message travels over a channel.** The medium over which the message is transmitted is the channel. Messages may be sent by computer, telephone, smartphone, traditional mail, Web site, or blog. Because both verbal and nonverbal messages are carried, senders must choose channels carefully. Any barrier that disrupts the transmission of a message in the communication process is called noise. Channel noise ranges from static that disrupts a telephone conversation to spelling and grammar errors in an e-mail message, to e-mails that are not sent because of firewalls. Such errors can damage the credibility of the sender. (For example, the accountant sends her e-mail to 125 clients in late December.)

4. **Receiver decodes message.** The person for whom a message is intended is the receiver. Translating the message into meaning involves decoding. Successful communication takes place only when a receiver understands the meaning intended by the sender. Such success is often hard to achieve because barriers and noise may disrupt the process. (For example, client reads accountant's e-mail, but decides to do his taxes himself this year.)

5. **Feedback travels to sender.** The response of the receiver creates feedback, a vital part of the entire communication process. Feedback helps the sender know that the message was received and understood. Senders can encourage feedback by including statements such as *Please let me know what you think as soon as possible*. Senders can further improve feedback by delivering the message at a time when receivers can respond. Senders should also provide only as much information as a receiver can handle. Receivers can improve the process by paraphrasing the sender's message. They might say, *Thanks for your e-mail explaining the new safe procedure*. (For example, client calls accountant, leaves voice mail thanking her for e-mail but letting her know he's going to do his taxes himself this year.)

A good critique of the work of the transmission theorists (Lasswell, Shannon, and Weaver) can be found on the Web site *Cultsock: Communication, Culture, Media* (**www.cultsock.org**) by clicking "Tm" under the Subject Index, and scrolling down to "transmission models: criticism of." For example, well-known Canadian communication theorist Marshall McLuhan (1911–1980) believed that communication couldn't be theorized in the straightforward, linear way that Lasswell, Shannon, and Weaver articulated. "McLuhan," it has been argued, "worked to disprove that communication moved in a singular line from transmitter to audience. Rather, he insisted communication was more like a field, creating an environment from which meanings were derived."[6] A good example of McLuhan's "field" is synchronous communication, such as instant messaging. In instant messaging, there's hardly enough time for the traditional communication cycle, as described by Lasswell, to take place. Receivers decode messages and send feedback almost instantaneously on a screen in real time.

As another example, McLuhan might argue that the widespread use of e-mail and texting in today's society, both at home and at work, has changed the environment in which we live. He'd be less interested in theorizing a neat pattern about how an e-mail or a text message is sent, received, and understood than in claiming that, because we now routinely use e-mail and texting, we talk on the phone and in person much less, we work much more after hours and on weekends, and so on. Where the transmission theorists saw communication as a hermetically sealed process, McLuhan would argue that the process has repercussions beyond itself.

Marshall McLuhan

Developing Better Listening Skills

Due to the synchronous, interruption-prone nature of modern technology (e.g., you may have received three text messages while reading these words, whereas if you had been reading them 30 years ago you would be much less likely to be interrupted), an incredibly important part of the communication process is effective listening and attention-paying. By many accounts, however, most of us are not very good listeners. Do you ever pretend to be listening when you're not? Do you know how to look attentive in class when your mind wanders far away? How about losing interest in people's messages when their ideas are boring or complex? Do you find it hard to focus on ideas when a speaker's clothing or mannerisms are unusual?

You probably answered yes to one or more of these questions because many of us have developed poor listening habits. In fact, some researchers suggest that we listen at only 25 percent efficiency. Such poor listening habits are costly in business. Letters must be rewritten, shipments re-shipped, appointments rescheduled, contracts renegotiated, and directions restated.

To improve listening skills, we must first recognize barriers that prevent effective listening. Then we need to focus on specific techniques that are effective in improving listening skills.

Barriers to Effective Listening

As you learned earlier, barriers and noise can interfere with the communication process. Have any of the following barriers and distractions prevented you from hearing what's said?

- **Physical barriers.** You cannot listen if you cannot hear what is being said. Physical impediments include hearing impairments, poor acoustics, and noisy surroundings. It's also difficult to listen if you're ill, tired, uncomfortable, or worried.
- **Personal barriers.** Everyone brings to the communication process a different set of cultural, ethical, and personal values. Each of us has an idea of what is right and what is important. If another person's ideas run counter to our preconceived thoughts, we tend to lose interest in his or her message and thus fail to hear.
- **Language problems.** Unfamiliar words can destroy the communication process because they lack meaning for the receiver. In addition, if a speaker's oral communication skills are compromised by a thick accent or pronunciation mistakes, listeners may be unable to understand what follows.

- **Nonverbal distractions.** Some of us find it hard to listen if a speaker is different from what we are expecting. Unusual clothing, speech mannerisms, body twitches, or a radical hairstyle or hair colour sometimes cause enough distraction to prevent us from hearing what the speaker has to say.
- **Thought speed.** Because we can process thoughts over three times faster than speakers can say them, we can become bored and allow our minds to wander.
- **Faking attention.** Most of us have learned to look as if we are listening even when we're not. Faked attention seriously threatens effective listening because it encourages the mind to engage in flights of unchecked fancy. Those who practise faked attention often find it hard to concentrate even when they want to.
- **Grandstanding.** Would you rather talk or listen? Naturally, many of us would rather talk. Since our own experiences and thoughts are most important to us, we want the attention in conversations. We sometimes fail to listen carefully because we're just waiting politely for the next pause so that we can have our turn to speak.
- **Technological barriers.** Sometimes your ability to listen attentively is undermined by your habitual need to check various devices such as your smartphone or cellphone. Different workplaces will accommodate this lack of attention in different ways, from accepting it to banning it.

Tips for Becoming an Active Listener

You can reverse the harmful effects of poor listening habits by making a conscious effort to become an active listener. This means becoming involved and taking responsibility for understanding. The following techniques will help you become an active and effective listener.

- **Stop talking.** The first step to becoming a good listener is to stop talking. Let others explain their views. Learn to concentrate on what the speaker is saying, not on what your next comment will be.
- **Control your surroundings.** Whenever possible, remove competing sounds. Close windows or doors, turn off handheld devices such as cellphones and smartphones, turn off radios and noisy appliances, and move away from loud people or engines. Choose a quiet time and place for listening.
- **Establish a receptive mindset.** Expect to learn something by listening. Strive for a positive and receptive frame of mind. If the message is complex, think of it as a mental challenge. It's hard work but good exercise to stretch and expand the limits of your mind.
- **Keep an open mind.** We all sift and filter information through our own biases and values. For improved listening, discipline yourself to listen objectively. Be fair to the speaker. Hear what is really being said, not what you want to hear.
- **Listen for main points.** Concentration is enhanced and satisfaction is heightened when you look for and recognize the speaker's central themes.
- **Capitalize on lag time.** Make use of the quickness of your mind by reviewing the speaker's points. Anticipate what's coming next. Evaluate evidence the speaker has presented. Don't allow yourself to daydream.
- **Listen between the lines.** Focus both on what is spoken and what is unspoken. Listen for feelings as well as for facts.
- **Judge ideas, not appearances.** Concentrate on the content of the message, not on its delivery. Avoid being distracted by the speaker's looks, voice, or mannerisms.
- **Be patient.** Force yourself to listen to the speaker's entire argument or message before reacting. Such restraint may enable you to understand the speaker's reasons and logic before you jump to false conclusions.
- **Take selective notes.** For some situations, thoughtful note taking may be necessary to record important facts that must be recalled later. Select only the most important points so that the note-taking process does not interfere with your concentration on the speaker's total message.
- **Provide feedback.** Let the speaker know that you are listening. Nod your head and maintain eye contact. Ask relevant questions at appropriate times. Getting involved improves the communication process for both the speaker and the listener.

> To become an active listener, stop talking, control your surroundings, develop a positive mindset, listen for main points, and capitalize on lag time.

> Listening actively may mean taking notes and providing feedback.

Improving Your Nonverbal Communication Skills

Understanding messages often involves more than listening to spoken words. Nonverbal clues, in fact, can speak louder than words. These clues include eye contact, facial expression, body movements, space, time, distance, and appearance. All these nonverbal clues affect how a message is interpreted, or decoded, by the receiver.

Just what is nonverbal communication? It includes all unwritten and unspoken messages, whether intended or not. These silent signals have a strong effect on receivers. But understanding them is not simple. Does a downward glance indicate modesty? Fatigue? Does a constant stare reflect hostility? Dullness? Do crossed arms mean defensiveness? Withdrawal? Or do crossed arms just mean that a person is cold?

> Nonverbal communication includes all unwritten and unspoken messages, intended or not.

Messages are even harder to decipher when the verbal and nonverbal codes do not agree. What would you think if Scott says he's not angry, but he slams the door when he leaves? Or what if Fatimah assures her server that the meal is excellent, but she eats very little? The nonverbal messages in these situations speak more loudly than the words.

When verbal and nonverbal messages conflict, research shows that receivers put more faith in nonverbal cues. In one study, speakers sent a positive message but averted their eyes as they spoke. Listeners perceived the total message to be negative. Moreover, they thought that averted eyes suggested lack of affection, superficiality, lack of trust, and nonreceptivity.[7]

Successful communicators recognize the power of nonverbal messages. Although it's unwise to attach specific meanings to gestures or actions, some cues broadcast by body language are helpful in understanding the feelings and attitudes of senders.

> When verbal and non-verbal messages clash, listeners tend to believe the nonverbal message.

How the Eyes, Face, and Body Send Silent Messages

Words seldom tell the whole story. Indeed, some messages are sent with no words at all. The eyes, face, and body can convey a world of meaning without a single syllable being spoken.

> The eyes are thought to be the best indicator of a speaker's true feelings.

EYE CONTACT. The eyes have been called the "windows of the soul." Even if they don't reveal the soul, the eyes are often the best indicator of a speaker's true feelings. Most of us cannot look another person straight in the eyes and lie. As a result, in Canada we tend to believe people who look directly at us. Sustained eye contact suggests trust and admiration; brief eye contact signals fear or stress. Good eye contact enables the message sender to see if a receiver is paying attention, showing respect, responding favourably, or feeling distress. From the receiver's viewpoint, good eye contact reveals the speaker's sincerity, confidence, and truthfulness.

FACIAL EXPRESSION. The expression on a person's face can be almost as revealing of emotion as the eyes. Experts estimate that the human face can display over 250,000 expressions.[8] To hide their feelings, some people can control these expressions and maintain "poker faces." Most of us, however, display our emotions openly. Raising or lowering the eyebrows, squinting the eyes, swallowing nervously, clenching the jaw, smiling broadly—these voluntary and involuntary facial expressions can add to or entirely replace verbal messages.

> Nonverbal messages often have different meanings in different cultures.

POSTURE AND GESTURES. A person's posture can convey anything from high status and self-confidence to shyness and submissiveness. Leaning toward a speaker suggests attraction and interest; pulling away or shrinking back denotes fear, distrust, anxiety, or disgust. Similarly, gestures can communicate entire thoughts via simple movements. However, the meanings of these movements differ in other cultures. Unless you know local customs, they can get you into trouble. In Canada, for example, forming the thumb and forefinger in a circle means everything's okay. But in Germany and parts of South America, the gesture is obscene.

Understanding body language, gestural literacy, and other nonverbal messages requires that you be aware that they exist and that you value their importance. To take stock of the kinds of messages being sent by your body, ask a classmate to critique your use of eye contact, facial expression, and body movements. Another way to analyze your nonverbal style is to videotape yourself making a presentation and study your performance. This way you can make sure your nonverbal cues send the same message as your words.

How Time, Space, and Territory Send Silent Messages

In addition to nonverbal messages transmitted by your body, three external elements convey information in the communication process: time, space, and distance.

TIME. How we structure and use time tells observers about our personality and attitudes. For example, if a financial planner sets aside one-hour blocks of time for client meetings, he is signalling respect for, interest in, and approval of the visitor or the topic to be discussed. If, however, he schedules only a 15-minute meeting, the client may feel less important.

People convey meaning in how they structure and organize time and how they order the space around themselves.

SPACE. How we order the space around us tells something about ourselves and our objectives. Whether the space is a bedroom, a classroom, an office, or a department, people reveal themselves in the design and grouping of their furniture. Generally, the more formal the arrangement, the more formal the communication. The way office furniture is arranged sends cues on how communication is to take place. An instructor who arranges chairs informally in a circle rather than in straight rows conveys her desire for a more open exchange of ideas. A manager who creates an open office space with few partitions separating workers' desks seeks to encourage an unrestricted flow of communication and work among areas.

TERRITORY. Each of us has certain areas that we feel are our own territory, whether it's a specific spot or just the space around us. Family members may have a favourite living-room chair, students who sit in a chair during their first class may return to that chair throughout the term, a cook might not tolerate intruders in his or her kitchen, and veteran employees may feel that certain work areas and tools belong to them.

The distance required for comfortable social interaction is controlled by culture.

We all maintain zones of privacy in which we feel comfortable. Figure 1.4 categorizes the four classic zones of social interaction among North Americans, as formulated by anthropologist Edward T. Hall.[9] Notice that North Americans are a bit standoffish; only intimate friends and family may stand closer than about 45 cm (1.5 feet). If someone violates that territory, North Americans feel uncomfortable and defensive and may step back to re-establish their space.

How Appearance Sends Silent Messages

The physical appearance of a business document, as well as the personal appearance of an individual, transmits immediate and important nonverbal messages.

APPEARANCE OF BUSINESS DOCUMENTS. The way an e-mail, letter, memo, or report looks can have either a positive or a negative effect on the receiver. Sloppy e-mails send a nonverbal message that says you are in a terrific hurry or that the reader or message is not important enough for you to care. Envelopes— through their postage, stationery, and printing—can suggest routine, important, or junk mail. Letters and reports can look neat, professional, well organized, and attractive—or just the opposite. In succeeding chapters you'll learn how to create

FIGURE 1.4 Four Space Zones for Social Interaction

ZONE	DISTANCE	USES
Intimate	0 to 45 cm (1.5 feet)	Reserved for members of the family and other loved ones.
Personal	45 cm to 123 cm (1.5 to 4 feet)	For talking with friends privately. The outer limit enables you to keep someone at arm's length.
Social	123 cm to 360 cm (4 to 12 feet)	For acquaintances, fellow workers, and strangers. Close enough for eye contact yet far enough for comfort.
Public	360 cm and over (12 feet and over)	For use in the classroom and for speeches before groups. Nonverbal cues become important as aids to communication.

"Here come the suits."

documents that send positive nonverbal messages through their appearance, format, organization, readability, and correctness.

APPEARANCE OF PEOPLE. The way you look—your clothing, grooming, and posture—sends an instant nonverbal message about you. On the basis of what they see, viewers make quick judgments about your status, credibility, personality, and potential. Because appearance is such a powerful force in business, some aspiring professionals are turning for help to image consultants. For example, Kingston, Ontario-based image consultant Catherine Bell's company Prime Impressions offers corporate training in the areas of professional attire, dining protocol, and interview coaching among many others. Bell even offers a "telecoaching" service that provides training over the phone.[10]

Tips for Improving Your Nonverbal Skills

Nonverbal communication can outweigh words in the way it influences how others perceive us. You can harness the power of silent messages by reviewing the following tips for improving nonverbal communication skills.

> Because nonverbal clues can mean more than spoken words, learn to use nonverbal communication positively.

- **Establish and maintain eye contact.** Remember that in Canada appropriate eye contact signals interest, attentiveness, strength, and credibility.
- **Use posture to show interest.** Encourage communication interaction by leaning forward, sitting or standing erect, and looking alert.
- **Improve your decoding skills.** Watch facial expressions and body language to understand the complete verbal and nonverbal message being communicated.
- **Probe for more information.** When you perceive nonverbal cues that contradict verbal meanings, politely seek additional clues (*I'm not sure I understand*, *Please tell me more about . . .*, or *Do you mean that . . .*).
- **Avoid assigning nonverbal meanings out of context.** Make nonverbal assessments only when you understand a situation or a culture.
- **Associate with people from diverse cultures.** Learn about other cultures to widen your knowledge and tolerance of intercultural nonverbal messages.
- **Appreciate the power of appearance.** Keep in mind that your personal appearance and that of your business documents and your business space send immediate positive or negative messages to receivers.

- **Observe yourself.** Ensure that your verbal and nonverbal messages agree by filming and evaluating yourself making a presentation.
- **Enlist friends and family.** Ask them to monitor your conscious and unconscious body movements and gestures to help you become a more effective communicator.

What Employers Want: Professionalism

In addition to technical knowledge in business, your future employer will expect you to show professionalism and possess what are often referred to as "soft skills." Soft skills are essential career attributes that include the ability to communicate, work well with others, solve problems, make ethical decisions, and appreciate diversity.[11] Sometimes also called *employability skills* or *key competencies*, these soft skills are desirable in all business sectors and job positions.[12]

Employers expect their employees to act in a businesslike and professional manner, yet many entry-level workers are not ready to do so or have the wrong attitudes. One employer was surprised that many of her new hires had no idea that excessive absenteeism or tardiness was grounds for termination. The new employees also seemed unaware that they were expected to devote their full energy to duties when on the job, instead of texting friends or looking at Web sites. Some recent graduates also tend to have unrealistic expectations about their salaries and working hours.

Projecting and maintaining a professional image can make a real difference in helping you to obtain the job of your dreams. Once you get that job, you are more likely to be taken seriously and promoted if you look and sound professional. New hires can sabotage their careers when they carry poor college habits into the business world. Banish the flip-flops, sloppy clothes, and instant messaging (IM) abbreviations. Think twice about sprinkling your conversation with *like*, *you know*, and uptalk (making declarative sentences sound like questions). Avoid sending the wrong message with unwitting and unprofessional behaviour. Figure 1.5 reviews conduct you will want to check to be sure you are projecting professionalism. You will learn more about soft skills and professionalism in Chapter 11.

FIGURE 1.5 Projecting Professionalism When You Communicate

	UNPROFESSIONAL	PROFESSIONAL
Speech habits	Speaking in *uptalk*, a singsong speech pattern that has a rising inflection making sentences sound like questions; using *like* to fill in mindless chatter; substituting *go* for *said*; relying on slang; or letting profanity slip into your conversation.	Recognizing that your credibility can be seriously damaged by sounding uneducated, crude, or adolescent.
E-mail	Writing e-mails with incomplete sentences, misspelled words, exclamation points, IM slang, and senseless chatting. Sloppy, careless messages send a nonverbal message that you don't care, don't know, or aren't smart enough to know what is correct.	Employers like to see subjects, verbs, and punctuation marks. They don't recognize IM abbreviations. Call it crazy, but they value conciseness and correct spelling, even in brief e-mails.
Internet	Using an e-mail address such as *hotbabe@hotmail.com, supasnugglykitty@yahoo.com,* or *buffedguy@aol.com.*	An e-mail address should include your name or a relevant, positive, businesslike expression. It should not sound cute or like a chat room nickname.
Voice mail	An outgoing message with strident background music, weird sounds, or a joke message.	An outgoing message that states your name or phone number and provides instructions for leaving a message.
Telephone	Soap operas, thunderous music, or a TV football game playing noisily in the background when you answer the phone.	A quiet background when you answer the telephone, especially if you are expecting a prospective employer's call.
Cellphones and smartphones	Taking or placing calls during business meetings or during conversations with fellow employees; raising your voice (cell yell) or engaging in cell calls that others must reluctantly overhear; using a PDA during meetings.	Turning off phone and message notification, both audible and vibrate, during meetings; using your cell only when conversations can be private.

■ Understanding How Culture Affects Communication

Comprehending the verbal and nonverbal meanings of a message is difficult even when communicators are from the same culture. But when they are from different cultures, special sensitivity and skills are necessary.

Negotiators for a Canadian company learned this lesson when they were in Japan looking for a trading partner. The Canadians were pleased after their first meeting with representatives of a major Japanese firm. The Japanese had nodded assent throughout the meeting and had not objected to a single proposal. The next day, however, the Canadians were stunned to learn that the Japanese had rejected the entire plan. In interpreting the nonverbal behavioural messages, the Canadians made a typical mistake. They assumed the Japanese were nodding in agreement as fellow Canadians would. In this case, however, the nods of assent indicated comprehension—not approval.

Every country has a common heritage, joint experience, and shared learning that produce its culture. These elements give members of that culture a complex system of shared values and customs. The system teaches them how to behave; it conditions their reactions. Comparing Canadian values with those in other cultures will broaden your world view. This comparison should also help you recognize some of the values that shape your actions and judgments of others.

Comparing Key Cultural Values

While it may be difficult to define a typical Canadian, one poll found that Canadians are convinced that a unique national identity exists—even if they are unable to agree on what it is. When asked what makes Canadian individuals distinct, respondents highlighted the tendency toward nonviolence and tolerance of others. When asked what makes Canada as a country distinct, respondents cited social programs and a nonviolent tradition as the two leading factors that make Canada different from the United States and other countries.[13]

Research shows that Canadians tend to be more collective, conforming, and conservative than their U.S. neighbours. Canadians are more supportive of civil and political institutions and collective decision making. Americans, on the other hand, tend to be much more supportive of individual decision making and questioning of collective decisions.[14]

WORKPLACE IN FOCUS

With more than 1.2 billion people and a growing reputation as the second-largest English-speaking country, India has become a hot market for outsourced call centre jobs. To accommodate the high demand for international customer support professionals in India, the city of Delhi offers hundreds of thousands of English and communication skills classes—and that is in addition to call centre training offered locally through multinational corporations such as IBM and Wipro. *What challenges do India's call centre professionals face when communicating with customers from across the globe?*

Despite the differences outlined above, most Canadians have habits and beliefs similar to those of other members of Western, technologically advanced societies. It's impossible to fully cover the many habits and beliefs of Western culture here, but we can look at four of the crucial ones that characterize the Canadian context.

CONTEXT. In a model developed by cultural anthropologist Edward T. Hall, context refers to the stimuli, environment, or ambience surrounding an event. Hall arranged cultures on a continuum, shown in Figure 1.6, from low to high in relation to context. The figure also summarizes key comparisons for today's business communicators.

Communicators in low-context cultures (such as those in North America, Scandinavia, and Germany) depend relatively little on the context of a situation—what's going on besides communication—to convey their meaning. They assume that listeners need to be briefed exactly and specifically to avoid misunderstandings. Low-context cultures tend to be logical, analytical, and action-oriented. Business communicators stress clearly articulated messages that they consider to be objective, professional, and efficient. Words are taken literally, unless sarcasm or irony is involved—and as neither is considered professional, they are left out of business communication.

Communicators in high-context cultures (such as those in China and Japan, and in Arab countries) assume that the listener is already "contexted" and does not need much background information.[15] Communicators in these cultures are more likely to be intuitive and contemplative. They may not take words literally. Instead, the meaning of a message may be implied from the social or physical setting, the relationship of the communicators, or nonverbal cues. For example, a Japanese communicator might say *yes* when he really means *no*. From the context of the situation, the Japanese speaker would indicate whether *yes* really meant *yes* or whether it meant *no*. The context, tone, time taken to answer, facial expression, and body

> Context means it's not just what's said or written that's important, but *how* it's said or written, as well as the posture, voice, and facial expression of the communicators.

FIGURE 1.6 Comparing High- and Low-Context Communicators

Culture has a powerful effect on business communicators. The following observations point out selected differences. Remember, however, that these are simplifications and that practices within a given culture vary considerably. Moreover, as globalization expands, low- and high-context cultures are experiencing change and differences may be less pronounced.

BUSINESS COMMUNICATORS IN LOW-CONTEXT CULTURES	BUSINESS COMMUNICATORS IN HIGH-CONTEXT CULTURES
Assume listeners know little and must be told everything directly.	Assume listeners are highly "contexted" and require little background.
Value independence, initiative, self-assertion.	Value consensus and group decisions.
Rely on facts, data, and logic.	Rely on relationships rather than objective data.
Value getting down to business and achieving results.	Value relationships, harmony, status, and saving face.
Keep business and social relationships separate.	Intermix business and social relationships.
Expect negotiated decisions to be final and ironclad.	Expect to reopen discussions of decisions previously negotiated.
Hold relaxed view toward wealth and power.	Defer to others based on wealth, position, seniority, and age.
Value competence regardless of position or status.	May value position and status over competence.
Have little problem confronting, showing anger, or making demands.	Avoid confrontation, anger, and emotion in business transactions.
Analyze meanings and attach face value to words.	May not take words literally; may infer meanings.

cues would convey the meaning of *yes*.[16] Communication cues are transmitted by posture, voice inflection, gestures, and facial expression.

INDIVIDUALISM VERSUS COLLECTIVISM. One of the most identifiable characteristics of Western culture is its built-in tension between individualism, an attitude of independence and freedom from control, and collectivism, the idea that the group or nation is more important than its individual citizens. Political scientist Seymour Martin Lipset has persuasively argued that Canadians are more collectivist than Americans (e.g., they support universal health care).[17] Today, however, regional tensions over oil revenues, for example, between some parts of Western Canada and Central Canada, demonstrate that Canadians' collectivist past may not be as assured in the future. Some non-Western cultures are even more collectivist than Canada. They encourage membership in organizations, groups, and teams and acceptance of group values, duties, and decisions. Members of these cultures sometimes resist independence because it fosters competition and confrontation instead of consensus.

FORMALITY. A third significant dimension of Canadian culture is its attitude toward formality. Canadians place less emphasis on tradition, ceremony, and social rules than do people in some other cultures. We dress casually and are soon on a first-name basis with others. Our lack of formality is often characterized by directness in our business dealings. Indirectness, we feel, wastes time, a valuable commodity.

This informality and directness may be confusing abroad. In Mexico, for instance, a business meeting may begin with handshakes, coffee, and an expansive conversation about the weather, sports, and other light topics. An invitation to "get down to business" might offend a Mexican executive.[18] In Japan, signing documents and exchanging business cards are important rituals. In Europe, first names are used only after long acquaintance and by invitation. In Arab, South American, and Asian cultures, a feeling of friendship and kinship must be established before business can proceed.

In Western cultures people are more relaxed about social status and the appearance of power.[19] Deference is not generally paid to individuals merely because of their wealth, position, seniority, or age. In many Asian cultures, however, these characteristics are important and must be respected. Deference and respect are paid to authority and power. Recognizing this cultural pattern, Marriott Hotel managers learned to avoid placing a lower-level Japanese employee on a floor above a higher-level executive from the same company.

COMMUNICATION STYLE. Another important dimension of our culture relates to communication style. We value straightforwardness, are suspicious of evasiveness, and distrust people who might have a "hidden agenda" or who "play their cards too close to the chest." Canadians also tend to be uncomfortable with silence and impatient with delays. Moreover, we tend to use and understand words literally. Another feature of our collective communication style is our well-known politeness. Academics, journalists, and bloggers continue to debate whether this extra-politeness is real or not: you can Google "politeness Canada" for a taste of the debate. Still, some recent informal research has proved that Canadians tend to communicate and act in a more polite and reserved way than people from other countries.[20]

TIME ORIENTATION. A fifth dimension of our culture relates to time orientation. Canadians consider time a precious commodity to be conserved. We equate time with productivity, efficiency, and money. Keeping people waiting for business appointments is considered a "waste" of time as well as rude.

However, the perception of time and how it is used are culturally learned. In some cultures time is perceived analytically. People account for every minute of the

While Canadians value both individualism and collectivism, as well as personal responsibility, other cultures emphasize group- and team-oriented values.

Canadians tend to be direct and to understand words literally.

day. In other cultures, time is holistic and viewed in larger chunks. Western cultures tend to be more analytical, scheduling appointments at 15- to 30-minute intervals. Eastern and Southern cultures tend to be more holistic, planning fewer but longer meetings. People in one culture may look at time as formal and task-oriented. In another culture, time may be seen as an opportunity to develop an interpersonal relationship. In the announcements of some international meetings, a qualifier may be inserted after the meeting time. For example, "The meeting starts at 10 a.m. Malaysian time." This tells participants whether to expect fixed or fluid scheduling.

> Canadians equate time with productivity, efficiency, and money.

Learning Intercultural Workplace Skills

The global economy needs workers with strong technical skills who also can thrive on diverse teams and interact effectively with customers and clients at home and abroad. Even if you never seek an overseas work assignment, you will need to be able to collaborate with diverse co-workers right here at home. Below we discuss how to overcome barriers to productive intercultural communication, develop strong intercultural skills, and capitalize on workplace diversity.

Controlling Ethnocentrism and Stereotyping

The process of understanding and accepting people from other cultures is often hampered by two barriers: ethnocentrism and stereotyping. These two barriers, however, can be overcome by developing tolerance, a powerful and effective aid to communication.

ETHNOCENTRISM. The belief in the superiority of one's own culture is known as ethnocentrism. This attitude is found in all cultures. If you were raised in Canada, the values just described probably seem "right" to you, and you may wonder why the rest of the world doesn't function in the same sensible fashion. A Canadian businessperson in a foreign country might be upset at time spent over coffee or other social rituals before any "real" business is transacted. In many cultures, however, personal relationships must be established and nurtured before earnest talks may proceed.

Ethnocentrism causes us to judge others by our own values. We expect others to react as we would, and they expect us to behave as they would. Misunderstandings naturally result. A Canadian who wants to set a deadline for completion of a deal may be considered pushy overseas. Similarly, a foreign businessperson who prefers a handshake to a written contract is seen as naive and possibly untrustworthy by a Canadian. These ethnocentric reactions can be reduced through knowledge of other cultures and development of flexible, tolerant attitudes.

> Ethnocentrism is the belief in the superiority of one's own culture and group.

STEREOTYPES. Our perceptions of other cultures sometimes cause us to form stereotypes about groups of people. A stereotype is an oversimplified behavioural pattern applied to entire groups. For example, the Swiss are hard-working, efficient, and neat; Germans are formal, reserved, and blunt; Americans are loud, friendly, and impatient; Canadians are polite, trusting, and tolerant; Asians are gracious, humble, and inscrutable. These attitudes may or may not accurately describe cultural norms. But when applied to individual business communicators, such stereotypes may create misconceptions and misunderstandings. Look beneath surface stereotypes and labels to discover individual personal qualities.

> A stereotype is an oversimplified behavioural pattern applied to entire groups.

TOLERANCE. Working among people from other cultures demands tolerance and flexible attitudes. As global markets expand and as our multicultural society continues to develop, tolerance becomes critical. Tolerance does not mean "putting up with" or "enduring," which is one part of its definition. Instead, tolerance is used in a broader sense. It means having sympathy for and appreciating beliefs and practices that differ from our own.

One of the best ways to develop tolerance is by practising empathy. This means trying to see the world through another's eyes. It means being non-judgmental, recognizing things as they are rather than as they "should be." It includes the ability to accept others' contributions in solving problems in a culturally appropriate manner. When a few Canadian companies began selling machinery in China, an advisor suggested that the companies rely less on legal transaction and more on creating friendships. Why? In China, the notion of friendship implies a longer-term relationship of trust and loyalty where business obligations are transacted. Instead of insisting on what "should be" (contracts and binding agreements), these companies adopted successful approaches by looking at the challenge from another cultural point of view.[21]

Making the effort to communicate with sensitivity across cultures can be very rewarding in both your work life and your personal life. The suggestions below provide specific tips for preventing miscommunication in oral and written transactions across cultures.

Tips for Minimizing Oral Miscommunication Among Cross-Cultural Audiences

When you have a conversation with someone from another culture, you can reduce misunderstandings by following these tips:

- **Use simple English.** Speak in short sentences (under 15 words) with familiar, short words. Eliminate puns, specific cultural references, slang, and jargon (special business terms). Be especially alert to idiomatic expressions that can't be translated, such as "burn the midnight oil" and "under the weather."
- **Speak slowly and enunciate clearly.** Avoid fast speech, but don't raise your voice. Over-punctuate with pauses. Always write numbers for all to see.
- **Encourage accurate feedback.** Ask probing questions, and encourage the listener to paraphrase what you say. Don't assume that a yes, a nod, or a smile indicates comprehension or assent.
- **Check frequently for comprehension.** Avoid waiting until you finish a long explanation to request feedback. Instead, make one point at a time, pausing to check for comprehension. Don't proceed to B until A has been grasped.
- **Observe eye messages.** Be alert to a glazed expression or wandering eyes. These tell you the listener is lost.
- **Accept blame.** If a misunderstanding results, graciously accept the blame for not making your meaning clear.
- **Listen without interrupting.** Curb your desire to finish sentences or to fill out ideas for the speaker. Keep in mind that Canadian listening and speaking habits may not be familiar to other cultures.
- **Remember to smile.** Roger Axtell, international behaviour expert, calls the smile the single most understood and most useful form of communication in either personal or business transactions.[22]
- **Follow up in writing.** After conversations or oral negotiations, confirm the results and agreements with follow-up e-mails. For proposals and contracts, engage a translator to prepare copies in the local language.

Tips for Minimizing Written Miscommunication Among Cross-Cultural Audiences

When you write to someone from a different culture, you can improve your chances of being understood by following these tips:

- **Adopt local styles.** Learn how documents are formatted and how letters are addressed and developed in the intended reader's country. Use local formats and styles.

- **Consider hiring a translator.** Engage a translator if (1) your document is important, (2) your document will be distributed to many readers, or (3) you must be persuasive.
- **Use short sentences and short paragraphs.** Sentences with fewer than 15 words and paragraphs with fewer than 5 lines are most readable.
- **Avoid ambiguous wording.** Avoid idioms (*once in a blue moon*), slang (*my presentation really bombed*), acronyms (*ASAP* for *as soon as possible*), abbreviations (*DBA* for *doing business as*), and jargon (*input, output, bottom line*). Use action-specific verbs (*purchase a printer* rather than *get a printer*).
- **Cite numbers carefully.** Always convert dollar figures into local currency. Avoid using figures to express the month of the year. For clarity, always spell out the month so it doesn't get confused with the day (e.g., 03/05/14 can be read as March 5, 2014 or May 3, 2014).

Globalization and Workforce Diversity

As global competition opens world markets, Canadian businesspeople will increasingly interact with customers and colleagues from around the world. At the same time, the Canadian workforce is also becoming more diverse—in race, ethnicity, age, gender, national origin, physical ability, and countless other characteristics. For example, recent Statistics Canada data shows that the Canadian labour force is made up of 8.4 million men and 7.5 million women, with the gap between the two genders closing quickly.[23]

No longer, say the experts, will the workplace be predominantly male or oriented toward Western cultural values alone. The majority of new entrants to the workforce are women, First Nations, new Canadians, and other visible-minority groups. The Canadian workforce is growing older as the baby-boom generation ages and mandatory retirement laws are abolished or changed in various parts of the country. By the year 2016, half of the Canadian population will be over 40, and 16 percent, over 65. At the same time, the proportion of people under 15 will shrink to 19 percent from the current 25 percent.[24]

While the workforce is becoming more diverse, the structure of many businesses across Canada is also changing. As you learned earlier, workers are now organized by teams. Organizations are flatter, and employees are increasingly making decisions among themselves and being asked to manage relationships with customers, suppliers, and others along the supply chain. What does all this mean for you as a future business communicator? Simply put, your job may require you to interact with colleagues and customers from around the world. Your work environment will probably demand that you cooperate effectively with small groups of co-workers. And these co-workers may differ from you in race, ethnicity, gender, age, and other ways.

A diverse work environment has many benefits. Customers want to deal with companies that reflect their values and create products and services tailored to their needs. Organizations that hire employees with different experiences and backgrounds are better able to create the customized products these customers desire. In addition, businesses with diverse workforces suffer fewer human rights complaints, fewer union clashes, and less interpersonal conflict. That's why diversity is viewed by a growing number of companies as a critical bottom-line business strategy to improve employee relationships and to increase productivity. For some businesses, diversity also makes economic sense. As Virginia Galt reports in *The Globe and Mail*, "There is one token Canadian on Western Union's national marketing team in Canada. The rest come from China, India, Colombia, Poland, the Philippines." According to Galt, while "Western Union may be further along than most employers in diversifying its work force . . . others are planning to follow suit, driven by a competitive need to expand into international markets and serve the increasingly diverse population at home."[25]

> You can expect to be interacting with customers and colleagues who may differ from you in race, ethnicity, age, gender, national origin, physical ability, and many other characteristics.

Tips for Effective Communication With Diverse Workplace Audiences

Capitalizing on workplace diversity is a challenge for most organizations and individuals. Harmony and acceptance do not happen automatically when people who are dissimilar work together. The following suggestions can help you become a more effective communicator as you enter a rapidly evolving workplace with diverse colleagues and clients.

- **Understand the value of differences.** Diversity makes an organization innovative and creative. Sameness fosters "groupthink," an absence of critical thinking sometimes found in homogeneous groups. Diversity in problem-solving groups encourages independent and creative thinking.
- **Don't expect conformity.** Gone are the days when businesses could demand that new employees or customers simply conform to the existing organization's culture. Today, the value of people who bring new perspectives and ideas is recognized. But with those new ideas comes the responsibility to listen and to allow those new ideas to grow.
- **Create zero tolerance for bias and stereotypes.** Cultural patterns exist in every identity group, but applying these patterns to individuals results in stereotyping. Assuming that Canadians of African descent are good athletes or that women are poor at math fails to admit the immense differences in people in each group. Check your own use of stereotypes and labels. Don't tell sexist or ethnic jokes. Avoid slang, abbreviations, and jargon that imply stereotypes. Challenge others' stereotypes politely but firmly.
- **Practise focused, thoughtful, and open-minded listening.** Much misunderstanding can be avoided by attentive listening. Listen for main points; take notes if necessary to remember important details. The most important part of listening, especially among diverse communicators, is judging ideas, not appearances or accents.
- **Invite, use, and give feedback.** As you learned earlier, a critical element in successful communication is feedback. You can encourage it by asking questions such as *Is there anything you don't understand?* When a listener or receiver responds, use that feedback to adjust your delivery of information. Does the receiver need more details? A different example? Slower delivery? As a good listener, you should also be prepared to give feedback. For example, summarize your understanding of what was said or agreed on.
- **Make fewer assumptions.** Be careful of seemingly insignificant, innocent workplace assumptions. For example, don't assume that everyone wants to observe the holidays with a Christmas party and a decorated tree. Celebrating only Christian holidays in December and January excludes those who honour Hanukkah, Chinese New Year, and Ramadan. Moreover, in workplace discussions, don't assume that everyone is married or wants to be, and don't assume people's sexual orientation. For invitations, avoid phrases such as "managers and their *wives*." *Spouses* or *partners* is more inclusive.
- **Learn about your cultural self.** Knowing your own cultural biases helps you become more objective and adaptable. Begin to recognize the reactions and thought patterns that are automatic to you as a result of your upbringing. Become more aware of your own values and beliefs. That way you can see them at work when you are confronted by differing values.
- **Seek common ground.** Look for areas where you and others not like you can agree or share opinions. Be prepared to consider issues from many perspectives, all of which may be valid. Accept that there is room for different points of view to coexist peacefully. Although you can always find differences, it's much harder to find similarities. Look for common ground in shared experiences, mutual goals, and similar values. Professor Nancy Adler of McGill University offers three useful methods to help people find their way through conflicts made more difficult by cultural differences: (1) Look at the problem from all participants' points of view, (2) uncover the interpretations each side is making on the basis

---

> Diversity programs have become an important business strategy because of the benefits to consumers, work teams, and organizations.

> Successful communicators invite, use, and give feedback; make few assumptions; learn about their own cultures and those of others; and seek common ground.

of their cultural values, and (3) create cultural synergy by working together on a solution that works for both sides.[26] Looking for common ground and mutual goals can help each of you reach your objectives even though you may disagree on the approach you should take.

◼ SUMMING UP AND LOOKING FORWARD

This chapter described the importance of becoming an effective business communicator. Flattened management hierarchies, participatory management, increased emphasis on work teams, heightened global competition, and innovative communication technologies are all realities that increase the need for good communication skills. Workplace software provides wonderful assistance for business communicators: you can locate information, pour content into templates, improve correctness and precision, add graphics, design professional-looking documents and presentations, and collaborate on team writing projects. But behind the "automatic professionalism" afforded by communication technology, you need to understand the communication process. Communication doesn't take place unless senders encode meaningful messages that can be decoded by receivers.

One important part of the communication process is listening. You can become a more active listener by keeping an open mind, listening for main points, capitalizing on lag time, judging ideas and not appearances, taking selective notes, and providing feedback.

The chapter also described ways to help you improve your nonverbal communication skills and professionalism.

You also learned the powerful effect that culture has on communication, and you became more aware of key cultural values. Finally, the chapter discussed ways that businesses and individuals can capitalize on workforce diversity.

The following chapters present the writing process. You will learn specific techniques to help you improve your written expression. Remember, communication skills are not inherited. They are learned.

◼ CRITICAL THINKING

1. Why should students and business professionals worry about communication when customer service, sales, and profit-making are what is important in business?

2. If you were giving a presentation and you noticed that two of your colleagues weren't listening to you but were speaking to each other, and another colleague was typing on his smartphone under the table, what would you do about it?

3. Why do we need to learn how to listen to each other when so much of communication today is done through e-mails, messaging, and texting?

4. If our behaviour is valued as a means of personal expression, do employers have the right to expect professionalism from their employees?

5. Since English is becoming the preferred language in business globally, why should Canadians take the time to learn about other cultures?

◼ CHAPTER REVIEW

1. List seven trends in the workplace that affect business communicators. How might these trends affect you in your future career?

2. Name six ways technology can help you to improve written documents.

3. Give a brief definition of the following words:

    a. Encode

    b. Channel

    c. Decode

4. List and explain 11 techniques for improving your listening skills.

5. What is nonverbal communication? Give several examples.

6. Why do employers expect professionalism in the workplace?

7. Why is good eye contact important for communicators?

8. What is the difference between individualism and collectivism? Can you think of evidence to support the argument that Canadians are more collectivist than Americans?

9. What is ethnocentrism, and how can it be reduced?

10. List and explain nine suggestions for enhancing comprehension when you are talking with people for whom English is a second language.

11. List and explain eight suggestions for becoming a more effective communicator in a diverse workplace.

ACTIVITIES AND CASES

TEAM

1.1 Getting to Know You

Your instructor wants to know more about you, your motivation for taking this course, your career goals, and your writing skills.

Your Task. Send an e-mail or write a memo of introduction to your instructor. See Chapter 4 for formats and tips on preparing e-mail messages. In your message include the following:

a. Your reasons for taking this class

b. Your career goals (both temporary and long-term)

c. A brief description of your employment, if any, and your favourite activities

d. An assessment and discussion of your current communication skills, including your strengths and weaknesses

For online classes, write a letter of introduction about yourself with the preceding information. Post your letter to your discussion board. Read and comment on the letters of other students. Think about how people in virtual teams must learn about each other through online messages.

EMAIL

1.2 Class Listening

Observe the listening habits of the students in one of your classes for a week. What barriers to effective listening did you observe? How many of the suggestions described in this chapter are being implemented by listeners in the class? Write a memo or an e-mail to your instructor describing your observations. (See Chapter 4 to learn more about memos and e-mails.)

1.3 Role Play: What Was That You Said?

Think of a recent situation in your life that matches one of these situations: someone wouldn't stop talking, so you stopped listening; there was so much noise around you that you stopped listening; you didn't agree with someone's opinions or didn't like the way he or she looked, so you stopped listening; or someone was talking and you didn't provide feedback. With a partner, write a three-minute skit that dramatizes one of the above "before" situations. Then, write another three-minute skit that dramatizes an "after" situation where the poor listening situation was improved so that you could listen actively. Perform the two skits for your class.

1.4 Video Research: Body Language in Business

YouTube is an amazing resource when searching for visual elements to add to a presentation. Imagine your boss has asked you, a manager, to improve the body language of your employees during presentations. Go to YouTube (**www.youtube.com**) and, using the search term "body language business," find three high-quality videos that you can use in a 15-minute presentation to your employees to teach them three separate body language skills or types. Either e-mail the presentation to your instructor (including YouTube links) or give the presentation in front of your class.

1.5 Role Play: You're in My Space

Working in groups of three or four, test the findings of anthropologist Edward T. Hall (see Figure 1.4 on p. 15) by writing a couple of short skits in which you turn his findings upside down. Begin by choosing a zone of social interaction (e.g., intimate), then write a one-minute skit where instead of standing at the correct distance (45 centimetres), a person communicating something intimate stands at an inappropriate distance (e.g., 4 metres) from his or her audience. Perform your skits for your class, and after each skit, ask the class what was wrong with the situation as you presented it. Can you or your classmates dramatize any situations where Hall's findings don't hold up?

1.6 Body Language

What attitudes do the following body movements suggest to you? Do these movements always mean the same thing? What part does context play in your interpretations?

a. Whistling, wringing hands

b. Bowed posture, twiddling thumbs

c. Steepled hands, sprawling sitting position

d. Rubbing hand through hair

e. Pacing back and forth, twisting fingers through hair

f. Wringing hands, tugging ears

1.7 The True Meaning of Diversity

WEB

You are the new human resources manager of a fast-growing sports apparel company, Proforme Ltée, headquartered in Laval, Quebec. The company manufactures T-shirts and baseball caps as well as more specialized clothing for soccer, tennis, and hockey players. Due to increased immigration to the Montréal area (see endnote 2), Proforme's CEO has asked you to propose a plan for diversifying the workforce. He says to you that this "should be easy as it's just a matter of hiring a few immigrants, right?" You want to please your new boss, but you quickly realize that his understanding of diversity issues needs to be updated. A good friend of yours works for the National Bank, a company that has an advanced diversity policy. You can learn some information from the company's Web site. Also research some other companies with strong diversity policies. Write your boss an e-mail that clears up his misconception about diversity (without offending him) and that proposes some positive steps Proforme can take.

Related Web site: **www.nbc.ca.** On the home page, enter "diversity" into the Search box.

1.8 Analyzing Diversity at Reebok

Reebok grew from a $12-million-a-year sport shoe company into a $3 billion footwear and apparel powerhouse without giving much thought to the hiring of employees. "When we were growing very, very fast, all we did was bring another friend into work the next day," recalled Sharon Cohen, Reebok vice president. "Everybody hired nine of their friends. Well, it happened that nine white people hired nine of their friends, so guess what? They were white, all about the same age. And then we looked up and said, 'Wait a minute. We don't like the way it looks here.' That's the kind of thing that can happen when you are growing very fast and thoughtlessly."[27]

Your Task. In what ways would Reebok benefit by diversifying its staff? What competitive advantages might diversity offer Reebok? Outline your reasoning in an e-mail message to your instructor.

1.9 Translating Idioms

Explain in simple English what the following idiomatic expressions mean. Assume that you are explaining them to people for whom English is a second language.

a. let the cat out of the bag

b. take the bull by the horns

c. he is a tightwad

d. putting the cart before the horse

e. to be on the road

f. lend someone a hand

g. with flying colours

h. turn over a new leaf

1.10 Role Play: Walking a Fine Line With a New Client

You are an account manager at an up-and-coming advertising agency in Calgary named Crane & Kim. You've recently landed a new client, IPCO Petroleum, one of Canada's best-known oil and gas producers. IPCO has hired you to perk up its image, which hasn't changed much in the last 20 years. As part of your mandate, you are to design and produce a televi-

sion commercial and a series of newspaper advertisements promoting IPCO as a progressive company. Your design and production staff has come up with an energetic new campaign that features people of various ethnicities and racial backgrounds. When Frank Pekar, director of marketing at IPCO, sees the campaign materials for the first time, he is anxious. He tells you that the blatant diversity in the materials is not really what he's looking for. Keeping in mind that you need to balance your personal belief in diversity and your belief in the strengths of diversity as a marketing tactic alongside Pekar's reservations and his importance as a client, script a five-minute skit between yourself and Pekar where you try to settle the issue. Perform your skit with a partner for your class.

1.11 Interview: The Changing World of Communication

A lot of workplaces are using new methods of communication, such as blogs, intranets, VoIP (Voice over Internet Protocol), and videoconferencing.

Your task. Interview a friend or family member who is working full-time. Ask him or her to explain the main changes in workplace communication over the past ten years. Next, ask him or her to tell you what a "day in the life" at the office is like, specifically concerning communication (for example, how many phone calls, e-mails, meetings, Web sites, blogs, instant messages, and so on he or she encounters). Then, ask him or her to offer a list of pros and cons about new communication technologies used in the workplace. Finally, ask one more communication technology-related question that you come up with by yourself. Once your interview is finished, analyze what your interviewee told you in order to summarize the information for your instructor and your class. Create a five-slide PowerPoint presentation in which you summarize your interview.

GRAMMAR/MECHANICS REVIEW 1—NOUNS

In the following sentences, underscore any inappropriate noun form, and write a correction. If a sentence is correct, write *C*.

Example: Although one exciting trip ended, several new journies awaited the travellers.

_____ 1. Setting healthy workplace boundarys is an important task for new supervisors.

_____ 2. Be sure to read the frequently asked questions before using that Web site.

_____ 3. Because world markets are expanding, many companys are going global.

_____ 4. Surprisingly, business is better on Sunday's than on week-days.

_____ 5. She said that attornies are the primary benefactors of class action suits.

_____ 6. Only the Welches and the Sanchez's brought their entire families.

_____ 7. During the late 2000's, home values dropped precipitously.

_____ 8. Both editor in chiefs followed strict copy-editing policies.

_____ 9. That financial organization employs two secretaries for four CPA's.

_____ 10. Voters in three citys refused to approve any new taxes.

_____ 11. Prizes were awarded to both runner ups in the essay contest.

_____ 12. Both cities are located in valleys that lie between mountains.

_____ 13. Our accountants insist that we list all income, expenses, and liabilitys.

_____ 14. Some typeface fonts make it difficult to distinguish between *t*'s and *i*'s.

_____ 15. Both of the homes of her brother-in-laws had many chimneys.

Document for Revision

The following document contains some writing accuracy issues, including grammar, spelling, punctuation, and style. Read the document and edit it as you go, identifying inaccuracies and fixing them. Your instructor will take up the correct answers with you.

MEMO

To: Jessica Wu-Santana
From: Martin Fitzgerald, Manager
CC:
Date: November 4, 2014
Re: Suggestion for Telecommuting Successfully

To help you become an effective telecommuter Jessica, we have a few suggestion to share with you. I understand you will be working at home for the next nine months. The following guidelines should help you stay in touch with us and complete your work satisfactory.

- Be sure to check your message bored daily, and respond immediate to those who are trying to reach you.
- Check your email at least 3 times a day, answer all message promply. Make sure that you sent copys of relevant message to the appropriate office staff.
- Transmit all spread sheet work to Scott Florio in our computer services department. He will analyze each week's activitys, and update all inventorys.
- Provide me with end of week reports' indicating the major accounts you serviced.

In preparing your work area you should make sure you have adequate space for your computer printer fax and storage. For security reasons you're working area should be off limits to your family and friends.

We will continue to hold once a week staff meetings on Friday's at 10 a.m. in the morning. Do you think it would be possible for you to attend 1 or 2 of these meeting. The next one is Friday November 17th.

I know you will enjoy working at home Jesica. Following these basic guidelines should help you accomplish your work, and provide the office with adequate contact with you.

WEB

WHAT EMPLOYERS ARE LOOKING FOR

In this workshop, you will investigate the importance, prevalence, and relevance of communication skills in today's workplace.

YOUR TASK

Choose two of the following job sites: **www.workopolis.ca, www.monster.ca, www.charityvillage.com, www.jobbank.gc.ca, www.eluta.ca.** Then, pick three different job categories that interest you (for example, accounting, marketing, administration).

- At both sites, and for each of the three job categories, find five jobs you might apply for at the end of your college/university program (2 sites × 3 categories × 5 jobs = 30 jobs).
- For each of the 30 jobs you locate, read the qualifications for the position. Make a note each time that communication skills are mentioned.
- Create three Excel spreadsheets, one for each job category. In each spreadsheet, list the hiring company, position, and communication-related skills and qualifications required.
- Once you've populated your three spreadsheets with the 30 jobs and their communication qualifications, analyze the results of your research in order to answer the following question: How important are communication skills to today's employers?

The Business Writing Process

CHAPTER 2
Before You Write

CHAPTER 3
Writing and Revising

COMMUNICATION TECHNOLOGY IN THE NEWS

Employers Slow to Embrace Web 2.0's Potential at Work

Source: Sarah Dobson, Canadian HR Reporter, May 17, 2010, Vol. 23, issue 10, p. 2. Reprinted with permission.

In June 2008, Canam Group decided to start a Facebook page in anticipation of its tri-annual managers' conference. About 200 employees at the Quebec construction company created profiles and were presented with different activities before the three-day event.

The first was a quiz assessing personality colours, which Canam used to sort people into "parties" for the opening night, as with an election (those who didn't respond to the survey were labeled "independent"). The managers were also encouraged to post pictures as part of a contest.

"Our goal was to present social media to this top management and, after that, develop our intranet the (Web) 2.0 way, using Facebook . . . to show them how easy it is to use, to publish pictures, publish videos, use a forum," said Nathalie Pilon, Canam's electronic communications manager. "We showed them what social media is and it was a real success."

Canam is now encouraging employees to use social media for business purposes. It resurrected a shelved intranet project and went on to launch other initiatives, including "CanamTube," for internal purposes such as training or CEO speeches, and a Flickr account to publish pictures of construction projects.

In May, the company hopes to publish a "Canampedia," similar to Wikipedia, providing a company lexicon that can be modified by employees. The content will be available in French and English and people can add more languages.

"Employees are asking for tools like that in the company," said Pilon. "People are asking to be able to publish content, they want to see the same thing that they see outside in the company."

Canam's attitude is a rarity, according to a recent survey from Aon Consulting Canada. Despite the proliferation of social networks, rich media outputs and online collaboration tools, organizations have been slow to adopt the power of Web 2.0. Only 12 per cent use Facebook, Twitter or similar social networks to communicate with employees or recruit potential employees while 71 per cent restrict Internet usage at work.

"A lot of employers are not really maximizing the power of this kind of communication, mostly because of fear and the fact that, on their side, they may perceive it as a high risk because it's unpredictable," said Diane McElroy, senior vice president and communications practice lead at Aon.

It's clear there's a giant gap between the workplace and people's personal lives, said Ron Shewchuk, a corporate communications consultant in Vancouver.

"These new ways of communicating have woven themselves into the very fabric of our social existence and yet they have been very slow to be adopted in the workplace," he said. "This is not something for geeks and teenagers. It really is time for the corporate world to start embracing these tools."

Many employees are not fully engaged and Web 2.0 provides access to powerful tools of engagement, said Shewchuk.

"All these social media tools are built from the ground up, to engage people, to improve collaboration, to create a sense of community, and all of these things are what drive employee engagement and drive retention."

If an employer limits or bans the use of these tools, most people will find another way.

"Why not actually sanction it and be able to control it, rather than just turning a blind eye to it?" he said.

That sentiment is backed up by a soon-to-be-released survey by Aon of 8,000 employees that found workers are already using Web 2.0 tools to get their jobs done, even if it's not directly approved by the employer. This can involve setting up networks to seek co-worker feedback around problems or informal chat pages used by global workers. They find that more efficient than what their employer has, said McElroy.

"Employers are still using the very traditional means of communication and missing a huge potential of using social media in the workplace. And it

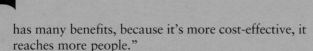

has many benefits, because it's more cost-effective, it reaches more people."

Those companies that are using these tools are largely using them for recruitment purposes, found Aon. Canam has learned, for recruitment purposes, 2.0 media are not only a good idea but necessary, said Pilon.

"New people coming in the company ask for that, they go directly to the intranet," she said.

But executive buy-in is the number-one barrier to social media implementation and rollout, according to a 2009 survey by Prescient Digital Media, which also found about one-half of organizations in the Western world have some form of Web 2.0 on the intranet, said Toby Ward, Toronto-based president and CEO of Prescient.

"Many executives don't have time to be messing around with social media and many don't understand it," he said.

Corporate reluctance can also be explained by perceived risks around giving workers the ability to comment on and rate a company or do potential damage to its reputation or trade secrets.

"That goes against traditional style of management, which is top-down: 'Why would we expose ourselves to public criticism inside the company?'" said Shewchuk.

But the risks are "far outweighed by the ability that it gives people to get information, to collaborate online, to have access to that world," he said.

There's also concern about employee productivity, but if someone is wasting time on these tools, it's a management or supervision problem, just as it is when someone goes for too many smoke breaks, said Pilon. If there is abuse of the media, Canam will treat it on a case-by-case basis, she said.

When it comes to rules and governance, fewer than one third (31 per cent) of employers have a social media policy, found Aon's survey. Canam recently published a policy to help workers understand the company's mindset and to encourage them to use the tools, she said.

Prescient's 2009 survey found about 58 per cent of companies have a governance policy and that appears to remain the same for 2010.

"It's a little disappointing that more organizations aren't doing their homework and their due diligence around this stuff," said Ward, because if people are using these tools externally, organizations are left quite vulnerable.

Summarize the article you've just read in a paragraph of two to three sentences. Answer the following questions, either on your own or in a small group. Be prepared to present your answers in a short presentation or in an e-mail to your instructor.

QUESTIONS:

1. How does what you've learned in this article change your perception of business communication?

2. How might what you've learned in this article change your own communication style?

3. Come up with pro and con arguments for the following debate/discussion topic: Social media is more of a personal communication trend than a workplace communication trend. Attempt to generate primary data for your discussion by canvassing everyone in your life who works and asking them one question: "Do you use social media at work?"

Before You Write

LEARNING OBJECTIVES

1. Understand that business writing should be audience-oriented, purposeful, and economical.

2. Identify and implement the three phases of the writing process.

3. Appreciate the importance of analyzing the task and profiling the audience for business messages.

4. Create messages that spotlight audience benefits and cultivate a "you" view.

5. Develop a conversational tone and use positive and courteous language.

6. Explain the need for inclusive language, plain but precise expression, and familiar words.

Excellent communicators concentrate on the receivers of their messages.

Basics of Business Writing

A recent Canadian Management Centre/Ipsos Reid study conducted among Canadian employees indicates that "only 42 per cent of Canadian employees . . . agree that change is communicated well in their workplace." The study concludes by stating that managers must recognize "building an engaged workforce relies heavily on leadership behaviour and communication."[1] Behind the study's findings lies a sometimes-unacknowledged reality about communication: it's not just *what* you want to say that's important; it's also *how* your audience will react upon seeing/reading/hearing your communication. In other words, all workplace communicators need to think about their audience.

Audience awareness is one of the basics of business communication. This chapter focuses on writing for business audiences. Business writing is different from other writing you have done. High-school or college projects and essays may have required you to describe your feelings, display your knowledge, or prove a thesis or argument. Business writing, however, has different goals. In preparing business messages, you'll find that your writing needs to be

- **Audience-oriented.** You will concentrate on looking at a problem from the receiver's perspective instead of seeing it from your own. An ad campaign a few years ago for Microsoft's Windows 7 phone with the tagline "Be here now" was a subtle hint that, instead of getting sidetracked by our gadgets and social media, we should remember our real-time audiences. If you Google "Windows Phone 7 ads Be Here Now" you can find the less subtle and very funny TV ads from this campaign that drive the point home.

- **Purposeful.** You will be writing to solve problems and convey information. You will have a definite purpose to fulfill in each message.
- **Professional.** You should fight the temptation to write e-mails and other messages at work that look and sound like the kind of informal messages you would send to friends.
- **Economical.** You should always try to present ideas clearly and concisely. Length, especially in these days of messaging, is not necessarily rewarded.

The ability to prepare concise, audience-centred, professional, and purposeful messages does not come naturally. Very few people, especially beginners, can sit down and compose an effective letter or report without training. But following a systematic process, studying model messages, and practising the craft can make nearly anyone a successful business writer or speaker.

Writing Process for Business Messages and Oral Presentations

Whether you are preparing an e-mail, memo, letter, or oral presentation, the process will be easier if you follow a systematic plan. Our plan breaks the entire business writing process into three phases: prewriting, writing, and revising, as shown in Figure 2.1.

As an example, let's say that you own a popular local fast-food restaurant franchise. At rush times, you've got a big problem. Customers complain about the chaotic multiple queues to approach the service counter. You once saw two customers nearly get into a fight over who was first in line. And customers are often so intent on looking for ways to improve their positions in line that they fail to look at the menu. Then they don't know what to order when their turn arrives. You want to convince other franchise owners that a single-line (serpentine) system would work better. You could telephone the owners, but you want to present a serious argument with good points that they will remember and be willing to act on when they gather for their next district meeting. You decide to write a letter that you hope will win their support.

Prewriting

The first phase of the writing process involves analyzing your purpose for writing. The audience for your letter will be other franchise owners who represent a diverse group of individuals with varying educational backgrounds. Your purpose in writing is to persuade fellow franchisees that a change in policy would improve customer service. You are convinced that a single-line system, such as that used in banks, would reduce wait times and make customers happier because they would not have to worry about where they are in line.

> Business writing is audience-oriented, purposeful, and economical.

> Following a systematic process helps beginning writers create effective messages and presentations.

> The writing process has three parts: prewriting, writing, and revising.

> The first phase of the writing process involves analyzing and anticipating the audience and then adapting to that audience.

FIGURE 2.1 The Writing Process

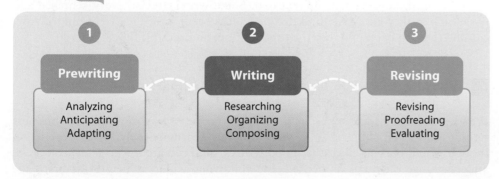

1 **Prewriting**	2 **Writing**	3 **Revising**
Analyzing Anticipating Adapting	Researching Organizing Composing	Revising Proofreading Evaluating

Prewriting also involves anticipating how your audience will react to your message. You're sure that some of the other owners will agree with you, but others might fear that customers seeing a long single line might go elsewhere. In adapting your message to the audience, you try to think of the right words and the right tone that will win approval.

Writing

The second phase of the writing process includes researching, organizing the message, and actually writing it.

The second phase of the process involves researching, organizing, and then drafting the message. In researching information for this letter, you would probably investigate other kinds of businesses that use single lines for customers. You might check out your competitors. What are other fast-food outlets doing? You might do some phoning around to see if other franchise owners are concerned about customer lines. Before writing to the entire group, you might generate ideas with a few owners to increase the number of potential solutions to the problem.

Once you have collected enough information, you would focus on organizing your letter. Should you start out by offering your solution? Or should you work up to it slowly, describing the problem, presenting your evidence, and then ending with the solution? The final step is actually drafting the letter. You'll most likely do it on your laptop or tablet so that you can make revisions easily.

Revising

The third phase of the writing process includes revising for clarity and readability, proofreading for errors, and evaluating for effectiveness.

The third phase of the process involves revising, proofreading, and evaluating your letter. After writing the first draft, you'll spend time revising the message for accuracy, clarity, conciseness, and tone. Could parts of it be rearranged to make your point more effectively? This is the time when you look for ways to improve the organization and tone of your message. Next, you'll spend time proofreading carefully to ensure correct spelling, grammar, punctuation, and format. The final step involves evaluating your entire message to decide whether it accomplishes your goal.

Scheduling the Writing Process

Although the business writing process described above shows the three phases equally, the time you spend on each varies depending on the complexity of the task, the purpose, the audience, and your schedule. Here are some rough estimates for scheduling a writing project:

- Prewriting—25 percent
- Writing—25 percent
- Revising—50 percent

These are rough guides, yet you can see that good writers spend most of their time on the final phase of revising and proofreading. What's critical to remember, perhaps surprisingly, is that revising is a major component of the writing process. It may appear that you complete one phase of the business writing process and progress to the next, always following the same order. Most business writing, however, is not that rigid. Although writers perform the tasks described, the steps may be rearranged, abbreviated, or repeated. Some writers revise every sentence and paragraph as they go. Many find that new ideas occur after they've begun to write, causing them to back up, alter the organization, and rethink their plan.

Analyzing the Purpose for Writing

We've just taken a look at the total writing process. As you develop your business writing skills, you should expect to follow this process closely. With experience, though, you'll become like other good writers and presenters who alter, compress, and rearrange the steps as needed. But following a plan is helpful at first. The remainder of this chapter covers the first phase of the writing process. You'll learn to analyze the purpose for writing, anticipate how your audience will react, and adapt your message to the audience.

Identifying Your Purpose

As you begin to write a message, ask yourself two important questions: (1) Why am I sending this message? and (2) What do I hope to achieve? Your responses will determine how you organize and present your information.

Your message may have primary and secondary purposes. For college or university work, your primary purpose may be simply to complete the assignment; secondary purposes might be to make yourself look good and to get a good grade. The primary purposes for sending business messages are typically to inform and to persuade. Secondary purposes include promoting credibility and goodwill: you and your organization want to look good in the eyes of your audience.

The primary purpose of most business messages is to inform or to persuade; the secondary purpose is to promote goodwill.

Selecting the Best Channel

After identifying the purpose of your message, you need to select the most appropriate communication channel. Some information is most efficiently and effectively delivered orally. Other messages should be written and sent out electronically. Whether to set up a meeting, send a message by e-mail, drop by someone's office, or write a report and attach it to an email depends on some of the following factors:

Choosing an appropriate channel depends on the importance of the message, the feedback required, the need for a permanent record, the cost, the formality needed, and best practices of your company.

- Importance of the message
- Amount and speed of feedback required
- Necessity of a permanent record
- Cost of the channel
- Degree of formality desired
- Best practices in your company

An interesting theory, called media richness, describes the extent to which a channel or medium recreates or represents all the information available in the original message. A richer medium, such as face-to-face conversation, permits more interactivity and feedback. A leaner medium, such as a report or proposal, presents a flat, one-dimensional message. Richer media enable the sender to provide more verbal and visual cues, as well as allowing the sender to tailor the message to the audience.

The six factors listed above will help you decide which of the channels shown in Figure 2.2 is most appropriate for delivering a message.

Switching to Faster Channels

Technology and competition continue to accelerate the pace of business today. As a result, communicators are switching to ever-faster means of exchanging information. In the past, business messages within organizations were delivered largely by hard-copy memos. Responses would typically take a couple of days. But that's too slow for today's communicators. Texting, e-mailing, and instant messaging can deliver the same information much faster than traditional channels of communication.

In fact, according to business writer Don Tapscott, within some organizations and between colleagues at different organizations, instant messaging is being added to e-mail as a popular channel choice. Tapscott even names some large companies, like IBM, that have abandoned e-mail in favour of instant messaging.[2] Instant messaging software alerts colleagues in distant locations that a co-worker is prepared to participate in an online exchange. Once signed in, individuals or entire groups can carry on and manage two-way discussions. Instant messaging resembles a conversation in which a sender types a one- or two-sentence note, followed by the receiver who types his or her response to the note. Responses appear next to the original message for both sender and receiver to see. For an example of what instant messaging can look like, see Figure 4.3 in Chapter 4. Through instant messaging, an

Chapter 02: Before You Write

FIGURE 2.2 Choosing Communication Channels

CHANNEL	BEST USE
Blog	When one person needs to present digital information easily so that it is available to others.
E-mail	When you need feedback but not immediately. Lack of security makes it problematic for personal, emotional, or private messages.
Face-to-face conversation	When you need a rich, interactive medium. Useful for persuasive, bad-news, and personal messages.
Face-to-face group meeting	When group decisions and consensus are important. Inefficient for merely distributing information.
Fax	When your message must cross time zones or international boundaries, when a written record is significant, or when speed is important.
Instant message	When you are online and need a quick response. Useful for learning whether someone is available for a phone conversation.
Letter	When a written record or formality is required, especially with customers, the government, suppliers, or others outside an organization.
Memo	When you want a written record to clearly explain policies, discuss procedures, or collect information within an organization.
Phone call	When you need to deliver or gather information quickly, when nonverbal cues are unimportant, and when you cannot meet in person.
Report or proposal	When you are delivering considerable data internally or externally.
Voice mail message	When you wish to leave important or routine information that the receiver can respond to when convenient.
Video- or teleconference	When group consensus and interaction are important but members are geographically dispersed.
Wiki	When digital information must be made available to others. Useful for collaboration because participants can easily add, remove, and edit content.

entire conversation can be completed online without the time delay that can occur when sending and responding to e-mail.

A number of years ago, *The Globe and Mail* reported that instant messaging would soon surpass e-mail as the primary way in which people interact electronically. While this prediction has not yet come true, experts like Tapscott signal that instant messaging is certainly a force to be reckoned with, especially because it is already so much a part of many young people's personal lives.[3]

Within many organizations, hard-copy memos are still written, especially for messages that require persuasion, permanence, or formality. But the channel of choice for corporate communicators today is clearly e-mail. It's fast, cheap, and easy. Thus, fewer hard-copy memos are being written. Fewer letters are also being written. That's because many customer service functions are now being served through Web-based customer relationship management tools or by e-mail.

For example, many businesses today communicate with customers through live chat, shown in Figure 2.3. Customers visit the company Web site (in the figure, Royal Bank of Canada's "RBC Chat Live" service) and chat with representatives by typing their questions and answers. Customer service representatives must have not only good typing skills but also an ability to write conversational and correct responses. One company found that it could not easily convert its telephone customer service people to chat representatives because many lacked the language skills necessary to write clear and correct messages. They were good at talking but not at writing, emphasizing that the Internet has increased the need for good writing skills.

Employee retention is a big issue these days: how do employers ensure their workers like where they're working and want to continue working there? To address this issue, a new job category, Employee Communications, has been created. Employee Communications coordinators and managers are sometimes part of the Human Resources team, and sometimes part of the Marketing team. Their job is to create employee engagement within their organization. Sara Presutto of Starbucks Canada creates employee engagement through various types of specialized meetings, as she describes in a YouTube interview at www.hrreporter.com/videodisplay/249-employee -communications-at-starbucks. Another aspect of employee communications—engagement through partnerships and events—is described by Kevin Chiu of Procter & Gamble Canada at http://canada .experiencepg.com/home/our_people/kevin_chiu _human_resources.html. *Why might organizations use multiple communication channels to transmit messages to employees? As an employee, how do you like to be engaged by your employer?*

The fact that fewer "traditional" documents (i.e., memos and letters) are being written does not make knowing how to write well less important. In fact, it makes it more important. This is because novice business communicators often assume business e-mails, instant messages, and texts can be as informal as their personal communication, for example, texting with a friend. The reality is that business writing, even if it is in quick and short formats such as with instant messages and texts and e-mails, should aim to be as structured as traditional memos and letters, especially when directed to those who are higher in your company's hierarchy, or to someone outside your organization, such as a supplier or customer.

Whether your channel choice is e-mail, messaging, hard-copy memo, or report, you'll be a more effective writer if you spend sufficient time in the prewriting phase.

Anticipating the Audience

A good writer anticipates the audience for each message: What is the reader like? How will the reader react to the message? Although you can't always know exactly who the reader is, you can imagine some characteristics of the reader. Picturing a typical reader is important in guiding what you write. By profiling your audience and shaping a message to respond to that profile, you are more likely to achieve your communication goals.

Profiling the Audience

Visualizing your audience is a pivotal step in the writing process. The questions in Figure 2.4 will help you profile your audience. How much time you devote to

> By profiling your audience before you write, you can identify the appropriate tone, language, and channel.

FIGURE 2.3 Live Chat Connects Service Reps and Customers

Customer service reps in chat sessions require solid writing skills to answer questions concisely, clearly, and conversationally. It takes a special talent to be able to think and key immediate responses that are spelled correctly and are error-free.

answering these questions depends on your message and its context. An analytical report that you compose for management or an oral presentation before a big group would, of course, demand considerable audience anticipation. On the other hand, an e-mail to a co-worker or a letter to a familiar supplier might require only a few moments of planning. No matter how short your message, spend some time

FIGURE 2.4 Asking the Right Questions to Profile Your Audience

PRIMARY AUDIENCE	SECONDARY AUDIENCE
Who is my primary reader or listener?	Who might see or hear this message in addition to the primary audience?
What are my personal and professional primary relationships with that person?	How do these people differ from the audience?
What position does the person hold in the organization?	Do I need to include more background information?
How much does that person know about the subject?	How must I reshape my message to make it understandable and acceptable to others to whom it might be forwarded?
What do I know about that person's education, beliefs, culture, and attitudes?	Should I expect a neutral, positive, or negative response to my message?

thinking about the audience so that you can adjust your words appropriately for your readers or listeners. "The most often unasked question in business and professional communication," claims a writing expert, "is as simple as it is important: *Have I thought enough about my audience?*"[4]

Responding to the Profile

Profiling your audience helps you make decisions about shaping the message. You'll discover what kind of language is appropriate, whether you're free to use specialized technical terms, whether you should explain everything, and so on. You'll decide whether your tone should be formal or informal, and you'll select the most desirable channel. Imagining whether the receiver is likely to be neutral, positive, or negative will help you determine how to organize your message.

Another advantage of profiling your audience is considering the possibility of a secondary audience. For example, let's say you start to write an e-mail to your supervisor, Sheila, describing a problem you are having. Halfway through the message you realize that Sheila could forward this message to her boss, the vice president. Sheila will not want to summarize what you said; instead she will take the easy route and merely forward your e-mail. When you realize that the vice president might see this message, you decide to back up and use a more formal tone. You remove your inquiry about Sheila's family, you reduce your complaints, and you tone down your language about why things went wrong. Instead, you provide more background information, and you are more specific in identifying items the vice president might not recognize. Analyzing the task and anticipating the audience help you adapt your message so that you can create an efficient and effective message.

◼ Adapting to the Task and Audience

After analyzing your purpose and anticipating your audience, you must convey your purpose to that audience. Adaptation is the process of creating a message that suits your audience.

One important aspect of adaptation is tone. Tone, conveyed largely by the words chosen for the message, determines how a receiver feels upon reading or hearing it. Skilled communicators create a positive tone in their messages by using a number of adaptive techniques, some of which are unconscious. These include spotlighting audience benefits, cultivating a polite "you" attitude, sounding conversational, and using inclusive language. Additional adaptive techniques include using positive expressions and preferring plain language with familiar words.

Audience Benefits

Smart communicators know that the chance of success of any message is greatly improved by emphasizing reader benefits. This means making readers see how the message affects and benefits them personally.

It is human nature for individuals to be most concerned with matters that relate directly to themselves. This is a necessary condition of existence. If we weren't interested in attending to our own needs, we could not survive.

Adapting your message to the receiver's needs means temporarily putting yourself in that person's shoes. This skill is known as *empathy*. Empathic senders think about how a receiver will decode a message. They try to give something to the receiver, solve the receiver's problems, save the receiver money, or just understand the feelings and position of that person. Which of the following messages is more appealing to the audience?

The most successful messages focus on the audience.

Sender Focus	Audience Focus
To enable us to update our shareholder records, we ask that the enclosed card be returned.	So that you can continue to promptly receive dividend cheques and information related to your shares, please return the enclosed card.
Our warranty becomes effective only when we receive an owner's registration.	Your warranty begins working for you as soon as you return your owner's registration.
The Human Resources Department requires that the online survey be completed immediately so that we can allocate our training resource funds.	By filling out the online survey, you can be one of the first employees to sign up for the new career development program.

Polite "You" View

Because receivers are most interested in themselves, emphasize *you* whenever possible.

Notice how many of the previous audience-focused messages included the word *you*. In concentrating on receiver benefits, skilled communicators naturally develop the "you" view. They emphasize second-person pronouns (*you, your*) instead of first-person pronouns (*I/we, us, our*). Whether your goal is to inform, persuade, or promote goodwill, the most attention-getting words you can use are *you* and *your*. Compare the following examples.

"I/We" View	"You" View
I have scheduled your vacation to begin May 1.	You may begin your vacation May 1.
We have shipped your order by courier, and we are sure it will arrive in time for the sales promotion on January 15.	Your order will be delivered by courier in time for your sales promotion January 15.
As a financial planner, I care about my clients' well-being.	Your well-being is the most important consideration for financial planners like me.

To see if you're really concentrating on the reader, try using the "empathy index." In one of your messages, count all the second-person references; then count all the first-person references. Your empathy index is low if the *I*'s and *we*'s outnumber the *you*'s and *your*'s.

The use of *you* is more than merely a numbers game. Second-person pronouns can be overused and misused. Readers appreciate genuine interest; on the other hand, they resent obvious attempts at manipulation. Some sales messages, for example, become untrustworthy when they include *you* dozens of times in a direct mail promotion. Furthermore, the word can sometimes create the wrong impression. Consider this statement: *You cannot return merchandise until you receive written approval.* The word *you* appears twice, but the reader feels singled out for criticism. In the following version the message is less personal and more positive: *Customers may return merchandise with written approval.* In short, avoid using *you* for general statements that suggest blame and could cause ill will.

Emphasize *you* but don't eliminate all *I* and *we* statements

In recognizing the value of the "you" attitude, however, writers do not have to sterilize their writing and totally avoid any first-person pronouns or words that show their feelings. Skilled communicators are able to convey sincerity, warmth, and enthusiasm by the words they choose. Don't be afraid to use phrases such as *I'm happy* or *We're delighted*, if you truly are. When speaking face to face, communicators show sincerity and warmth with nonverbal cues such as a smile and pleasant voice tone. In letters, memos, and e-mail messages, however, only expressive words and phrases can show these feelings. These phrases suggest hidden messages that say to readers and customers, "You are important, I am listening, and I'm honestly trying to please you."

Conversational but Professional

Most business e-mails, letters, memos, and reports are about topics that would otherwise be part of a conversation. Thus, they are most effective when they convey an informal, conversational tone instead of a formal, pretentious tone. But messages should not become so conversational that they sound overly casual and unprofessional. With the increasing use of e-mail, a major problem has developed. Sloppy, unprofessional expression appears in many e-mail messages. You'll learn more about e-mail in Chapter 4. At this point, though, we urge you to strive for a warm, conversational tone that does not include slang or overly casual wording such as texting/messaging abbreviations like LOL. The following examples should help you distinguish between three levels of diction.

> Strive for conversational expression, but also remember to be professional.

Unprofessional (low-level diction)	Conversational (mid-level diction)	Formal (high-level diction)
badmouth	criticize	denigrate
guts	nerve	courage
pecking order	line of command	dominance hierarchy
ticked off	upset	provoked
rat on	inform	betray
rip off	steal	embezzle/appropriate
TTYL	talk to you later	I'll be in touch soon about this

Unprofessional	Professional
Hey, boss, Gr8 news! Firewall now installed!! BTW, check with me b4 popping the news.	Mr. Smith, our new firewall software is now installed. Please check with me before announcing it.
Look, dude, this report is totally bogus. And the figures don't look kosher. Show me some real stats. Got sources?	Because the figures in this report seem inaccurate, please submit the source statistics.

Your goal is a warm, friendly tone that sounds professional. Talk to the reader with words that are comfortable to you. Avoid long and complex sentences. Use familiar pronouns such *I*, *we*, and *you* and an occasional contraction, such as *we're* or *I'll*. Stay away from third-person constructions such as *the undersigned*, *the writer*, and *the affected party*. Also avoid legal terminology and technical words.

Your writing will be easier to read and understand if it sounds like the following conversational examples:

Formal	Conversational
All employees are instructed to return the appropriately designated contracts to the undersigned.	Please return your contracts to me.
Pertaining to your order, we must verify the sizes that your organization requires prior to consignment of your order to our shipper.	We'll send your order as soon as we confirm the sizes you need.
The writer wishes to inform the above-referenced individual that subsequent payments may in future be sent to the address cited below.	Your payments should now be sent to us in Sudbury.
To facilitate ratification of this agreement, your negotiators urge that the membership respond in the affirmative.	We urge you to approve the agreement by voting yes.

Positive Language

> Positive language creates goodwill and gives more options to receivers.

The clarity and tone of a message are considerably improved if you use positive rather than negative language. Positive language generally conveys more information than negative language. Moreover, positive messages are uplifting and pleasant to read. Positive wording tells what *is* and what *can be done* rather than what *isn't* and what *can't be done*. For example, *Your order cannot be shipped by January 10* is not nearly as informative as *Your order will be shipped January 20*. Notice in the following examples how you can revise the negative tone to reflect a more positive impression.

Negative	Positive
We are unable to send your shipment until we receive proof of your payment.	We look forward to sending your shipment as soon as we receive your payment.
You will never regret opening an account with us.	Your new account enables you to purchase high-quality clothing at reasonable prices.
If you fail to pass the exam, you will not qualify.	You'll qualify if you pass the exam.
Although I've never had a paid position before, I have completed a work placement in a law office as an administrative assistant while completing my diploma.	My work placement experience in a lawyer's office and my recent training in legal procedures and computer applications can be assets to your organization.

Courteous Language

Maintaining a courteous tone involves not just guarding against rudeness but also avoiding words that sound demanding or preachy. Expressions such as *you should*, *you must*, and *you have to* cause people to instinctively react with *Oh, yeah?* One remedy is to turn these demands into rhetorical questions that begin with *Will you please* . . . . Giving reasons for a request also softens the tone.

Even when you feel justified in displaying anger, remember that losing your temper or being sarcastic will seldom help you accomplish your goals as a business communicator: to inform, to persuade, and to create goodwill. When you are irritated, frustrated, or infuriated, keep cool and try to defuse the situation. In dealing with customers in telephone conversations, use polite phrases such as *It was a pleasure speaking with you, I would be happy to assist you with that*, and *Thank you for being so patient.*

Less Courteous	More Courteous and Helpful
You must complete the report before Friday.	Will you please complete the report by Friday.
You should organize a car pool in this department.	Organizing a car pool will reduce your transportation costs and help preserve the environment.
This is the second time I've written. Can't you get anything right?	Please credit my account for $450. My latest statement shows that the error noted in my April 2 e-mail has not been corrected.
Am I the only one who can read the operating manual?	Let's review the operating manual together so that you can get your documents to print correctly next time.

Bias-Free Language

In adapting a message to its audience, be sure your language is sensitive and bias-free. Few writers set out to be offensive. Sometimes, though, we say things that we never thought might be hurtful. The real problem is that we don't think about the words that stereotype groups of people, such as *the boys in the mail room* or *the girls in the front office*. Be cautious about expressions that might be biased in terms of gender, race, ethnicity, age, and disability. Generally, you can avoid gender-biased language by leaving out the words *man* or *woman*, by using plural nouns and pronouns, or

Sensitive communicators avoid language that excludes people.

by changing to a gender-free word (*person* or *representative*). Avoid the *his or her* option whenever possible. It's wordy and conspicuous. With a little effort, you can usually find a construction that is graceful, grammatical, and unselfconscious.

Specify age only if it is relevant, and avoid expressions that are demeaning or subjective (such as *old guy*). To avoid disability bias, do not refer to an individual's disability unless it is relevant. When necessary, use terms that do not stigmatize disabled individuals. The following examples give you a quick look at a few problem expressions and possible replacements. The real key to bias-free communication, though, lies in your awareness and commitment. Be on the lookout to be sure that your messages do not exclude, stereotype, or offend people.

Gender-Biased	Bias-Free
female doctor, woman lawyer, cleaning woman	doctor, lawyer, cleaner
waiter/waitress, authoress, stewardess	server, author, flight attendant
mankind, man-hour, man-made	humanity, working hours, artificial
office girls	office workers
the doctor . . . he	doctors . . . they
the teacher . . . she	teachers . . . they
executives and their wives	executives and their spouses
foreman, flagman, workman	lead worker, flagger, worker
businessman, salesman	business person, sales representative
Each employee had his picture taken.	Each employee had a picture taken. All employees had their pictures taken. Each employee had his or her picture taken.

Racially or Ethnically Biased	Bias-Free
An Indian accountant was hired.	An accountant was hired.
Jim Nolan, an African Canadian, applied.	Jim Nolan applied.

Age-Biased	Bias-Free
The law applies to older people.	The law applies to people over sixty-five.
Sally Kay, 55, was transferred.	Sally Kay was transferred.
a spry old gentleman	a man
a little old lady	a woman

Disability-Biased	Bias-Free
afflicted with arthritis, suffering from . . ., crippled by . . .	has arthritis
confined to a wheelchair	uses a wheelchair

Plain Language and Familiar Words

In adapting your message to your audience, use plain language and familiar words that you think audience members will recognize. Don't, however, avoid a big word that conveys your idea efficiently and is appropriate for the audience. Your goal is to shun pompous and pretentious language. Instead, use "obvious" words. If you mean *begin*, don't say *commence* or *initiate*. If you mean *pay*, don't write *compensate*. By substituting everyday familiar words for unfamiliar ones, as shown here, you help your audience comprehend your ideas quickly.

Unfamiliar	Familiar
commensurate	equal
interrogate	question
materialize	appear
obfuscate	confuse
remuneration	pay, salary
terminate	end

DILBERT   By Scott Adams

At the same time, be selective in your use of jargon. *Jargon* describes technical or specialized terms within a field. These terms enable insiders to communicate complex ideas briefly, but to outsiders they mean nothing. Human resources professionals, for example, know precisely what's meant by *cafeteria plan* (a benefits option program), but most of us would be thinking about lunch. Geologists refer to *plate tectonics*, and physicians discuss *metastatic carcinomas*. These terms mean little to most of us. Use specialized language only when the audience will understand it.

In addition, don't be impressed by high-sounding language and legalese, such as *herein*, *herewith*, *thereafter*, and *hereinafter*. Your writing will be better if you use plain language.

Precise, Vigorous Words

Strong verbs and concrete nouns give receivers more information and keep them interested. Don't overlook the thesaurus (or the thesaurus program on your computer) for expanding your word choices and vocabulary. However, don't accept words whose meanings you don't fully understand. Whenever possible, use specific words as shown on page 49.

> How can you improve your vocabulary so that you can use precise, vigorous words?

OFFICE INSIDER

"Simple changes can have profound results . . . . Plain talk isn't only rewriting. It's rethinking your approach and really personalizing your message to the audience and to the reader."

FIGURE 2.5 Improving the Tone in an E-Mail

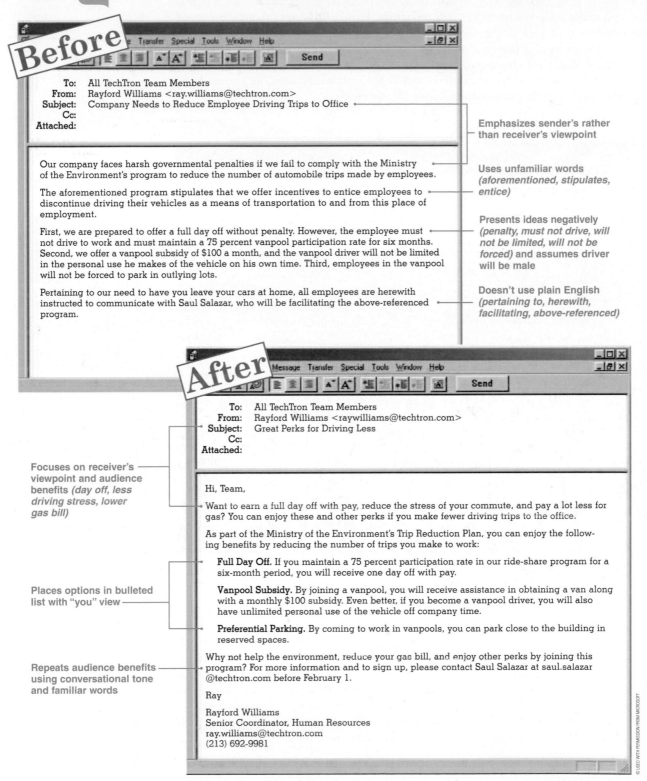

Before

To: All TechTron Team Members
From: Rayford Williams <ray.williams@techtron.com>
Subject: Company Needs to Reduce Employee Driving Trips to Office
Cc:
Attached:

Our company faces harsh governmental penalties if we fail to comply with the Ministry of the Environment's program to reduce the number of automobile trips made by employees.

The aforementioned program stipulates that we offer incentives to entice employees to discontinue driving their vehicles as a means of transportation to and from this place of employment.

First, we are prepared to offer a full day off without penalty. However, the employee must not drive to work and must maintain a 75 percent vanpool participation rate for six months. Second, we offer a vanpool subsidy of $100 a month, and the vanpool driver will not be limited in the personal use he makes of the vehicle on his own time. Third, employees in the vanpool will not be forced to park in outlying lots.

Pertaining to our need to have you leave your cars at home, all employees are herewith instructed to communicate with Saul Salazar, who will be facilitating the above-referenced program.

Emphasizes sender's rather than receiver's viewpoint

Uses unfamiliar words *(aforementioned, stipulates, entice)*

Presents ideas negatively *(penalty, must not drive, will not be limited, will not be forced)* and assumes driver will be male

Doesn't use plain English *(pertaining to, herewith, facilitating, above-referenced)*

After

To: All TechTron Team Members
From: Rayford Williams <raywilliams@techtron.com>
Subject: Great Perks for Driving Less
Cc:
Attached:

Focuses on receiver's viewpoint and audience benefits *(day off, less driving stress, lower gas bill)*

Hi, Team,

Want to earn a full day off with pay, reduce the stress of your commute, and pay a lot less for gas? You can enjoy these and other perks if you make fewer driving trips to the office.

As part of the Ministry of the Environment's Trip Reduction Plan, you can enjoy the following benefits by reducing the number of trips you make to work:

Places options in bulleted list with "you" view

Full Day Off. If you maintain a 75 percent participation rate in our ride-share program for a six-month period, you will receive one day off with pay.

Vanpool Subsidy. By joining a vanpool, you will receive assistance in obtaining a van along with a monthly $100 subsidy. Even better, if you become a vanpool driver, you will also have unlimited personal use of the vehicle off company time.

Preferential Parking. By coming to work in vanpools, you can park close to the building in reserved spaces.

Repeats audience benefits using conversational tone and familiar words

Why not help the environment, reduce your gas bill, and enjoy other perks by joining this program? For more information and to sign up, please contact Saul Salazar at saul.salazar @techtron.com before February 1.

Ray

Rayford Williams
Senior Coordinator, Human Resources
ray.williams@techtron.com
(213) 692-9981

mprecise, Dull	More Precise
a change in profits	a 25 percent hike in profits a 10 percent plunge in profits
to say	to promise, confess, understand to allege, assert, assume, judge
to think about	to identify, diagnose, analyze to probe, examine, inspect

As you revise a message, you will have a chance to correct any writing problems. Notice in Figure 2.5 what a difference revision makes. Before revision, the message failed to use familiar language. Many negative ideas could have been expressed positively. After revision, the message is shorter, is more conversational, and emphasizes audience benefits.

SUMMING UP AND LOOKING FORWARD

In this chapter you learned that good business writing is audience centred, purposeful, and economical. To achieve these results, business communicators typically follow a systematic writing process. This process includes three phases: prewriting, writing, and revising. In the prewriting phase, communicators analyze the task and the audience. They select an appropriate channel to deliver the message, and they consider ways to adapt their message to the task and the audience. Effective techniques include spotlighting audience benefits, cultivating the "you" view,

using conversational language, and expressing ideas positively and courteously. Good communicators also use inclusive language, plain and familiar words, and precise expressions.

The next chapter continues to examine the writing process. It presents additional techniques to help you become a better writer. You'll learn how to eliminate repetitious and redundant wording, as well as how to avoid wordy prepositional phrases, long lead-ins, needless adverbs, and misplaced modifiers. You'll also take a closer look at spell checkers and grammar checkers.

CRITICAL THINKING

1. As a business communicator, you are encouraged to profile or "visualize" the audience for your messages. How is this possible if you don't really know the people who will receive a sales letter or who will hear your business presentation?

2. If adapting your tone to your audience and developing reader benefits are so important, why do we see so much writing that fails to reflect these suggestions?

3. Discuss the following statement: "The English language can be dangerous—it is filled with terms that are easily

misinterpreted as derogatory and others that are blatantly insulting."

4. Why is writing in a natural, conversational tone difficult for many people?

5. Is it ethical to always write in a positive tone, as this chapter has advised? What if the message you're conveying is a bad one, such as a firing, demotion, or loss of sales?

6. Why should you be courteous at work even if someone hasn't been courteous to you?

CHAPTER REVIEW

1. Name four ways in which business writing differs from other writing.

2. List the three phases of the business writing process and summarize what happens in each phase. Which phase requires the most time?

3. What factors are important in selecting an appropriate channel to deliver a message?

4. How does profiling the audience help a business communicator prepare a message?

5. What is meant by *audience benefit*? Give an original example.

6. List three specific techniques for developing a warm, friendly, and conversational tone in business messages.

7. Why does positive language usually tell more than negative language? Give an original example.

8. What can make language biased? Offer some original examples.

9. What are the advantages of using plain English when communicating?

WRITING IMPROVEMENT EXERCISES

Audience Benefits and the "You" View

Revise the following sentences to emphasize the perspective of the audience and the "you" view.

1. To help us process your order with our new database software, we need you to go to our Web site and fill out the customer information required.

2. Under a new policy, reimbursement of travel expenses will be restricted to those related to work only.

3. To avoid suffering the kinds of monetary losses experienced in the past, our credit union now prohibits the cashing of double-endorsed checks presented by our customers.

4. We are pleased to announce an arrangement with HP that allows us to offer discounted computers in the student bookstore.

5. We are pleased to announce that you have been approved to enroll in our management trainee program.

6. Our warranty goes into effect only when we have received the product's registration card from the purchaser.

7. Unfortunately, the computer and telephone systems will be down Thursday afternoon for upgrades to improve both systems.

8. As part of our company effort to be friendly to the environment, we are asking all employees to reduce paper consumption by communicating by e-mail and avoiding printing.

Conversational, Professional Tone

Revise the following sentences to make the tone conversational yet professional.

Example: As per your recent request, the undersigned is happy to inform you that we are sending you forthwith the brochures you requested.

Revision: I'm happy to send you the brochures you requested.

9. Pertaining to your request, the above-referenced items (printer toner and supplies) are being sent to your Oakdale office, as per your telephone conversation of April 1.

10. Kindly inform the undersigned whether or not your representative will be making a visitation in the near future.

11. It's totally awesome that we still got the contract, like, after the customer amped up his demands, but our manager pushed back.

12. BTW, dude, we've had some slippage in the schedule but don't have to dump everything and start from ground zero.

13. To facilitate ratification of this agreement, your negotiators urge that the membership respond in the affirmative.

14. R head honcho wz like totally raggety bkuz I wz sick n stuff n mist the team meet. Geez!

Positive Expression

Revise the following statements to make them more positive.

15. Customers are ineligible for the 10 percent discount unless they show their membership cards.

16. Titan Insurance Company will not process any claim not accompanied by documented proof from a physician showing that the injuries were treated.

17. If you fail to comply with each requirement, you will not receive your $50 rebate.

18. We must withhold remuneration until you complete the job satisfactorily.

19. Although you apparently failed to consult the mounting instructions for your Miracle Wheatgrass Extractor, we are enclosing a set of clamps to fasten the device to a table. A new set of instructions is enclosed.

20. Your application cannot be processed because you neglected to insert your telephone number.

Unbiased Language

Revise the following sentences to eliminate terms that are considered sexist or that suggest stereotypes.

21. Any applicant for the position of fireman must submit a medical report signed by his physician.

22. Every employee is entitled to see his personnel file.

23. All waiters and waitresses are covered under our new benefits package.

24. A salesman would have to use all his skills to sell those condos.

25. Executives and their wives are invited to the banquet.

Plain Language and Familiar Words

Revise the following sentences to use plain expression and familiar words.

26. We are offering a pay package that is commensurate with other managers' remuneration.

27. The seller tried to obfuscate the issue by mentioning closing and other costs.

28. Even after officers interrogated the suspect, solid evidence failed to materialize.

29. In dialoguing with the owner, I learned that you plan to terminate our contract.

Precise, Vigorous Language

Revise the following sentences to use precise, vigorous language.

30. The document was bad.

31. The employee asked for a raise.

32. A director presented a report.

ACTIVITIES AND CASES

2.1 Selecting Communication Channels

Your Task. Using Figure 2.2, suggest the best communication channels for the following messages. Assume that all channels shown are available. Be prepared to explain your choices.

1. As department manager, you wish to inform four members of a training session scheduled for three weeks from now.

2. As assistant to the vice president, you are to investigate the possibility of developing work placement programs with several nearby colleges and universities.

3. You wish to send price quotes for a number of your products in response to a request from a potential customer in Taiwan.

4. You must respond to a notice from the Canada Revenue Agency insisting that you did not pay the correct amount for last quarter's employee remittance.

5. As a manager, you must inform an employee that continued tardiness is jeopardizing her job.

6. Members of your task force must meet to discuss ways to improve communication among 500 employees at 12 branches of your company. Task force members are from Toronto, Winnipeg, Calgary, Regina, and Halifax.

7. You need to know whether Davinder in Printing can produce a special pamphlet for you within two days.

2.2 Weighing the Pros and Cons of Instant Messaging

The company you work for is finding that e-mail response time is beginning to lag. Anecdotally, managers are hearing that employees are taking up to 72 hours to respond to routine e-mail requests for information, updates, and so forth. Because the company is embarking on its annual "ReThink" exercise, you figure it's time to introduce instant messaging as a way of ensuring rapid response. ReThink, by the way, is the company's way of taking stock of the good and bad things that have happened in the last year, and of brainstorming ideas for future improvements.

Your Task. Form teams of 3 to 5. Go to Google Talk's Web site (**www.google.ca/talk**) and download the instant messaging software. Add your team members as contacts. Start chatting about this year's ReThink. Offer suggestions and make criticisms for five to ten minutes. Now, pick a team leader. Have that team leader send a traditional e-mail to all teammates asking them to offer suggestions and constructive criticism for this year's ReThink. Now that you've talked about ReThink using both instant messaging and traditional e-mail, which communication channel is more effective? Why? If possible, demonstrate the "thread" of conversation in the instant messaging channel and the e-mail channel to your instructor or class.

2.3 Turning Negatives Into Positives

There has been a lot of bad business news in the past couple of years. Between the lingering recession and the catastrophic train derailment and explosion in Lac-Mégantic, Quebec, the world has witnessed large corporations going bankrupt or having to be bailed out by taxpayers, CEOs losing their jobs due to mismanagement of corporate disasters, and national governments negotiating bailouts (e.g., Ireland, Greece). From the point of view of one of the bailed-out companies or governments or corporations suffering from bad media publicity, how do you move the focus away from the negative news and toward a more positive perspective?

Your Task. In your school's library databases or on the Internet, using a search term such as "bad publicity," see if you can find a source that gives good advice on how companies or governments can turn negatives into positives. Then, imagine that your college or university has just experienced a horrible health or environmental disaster, or some large-scale scandal that has been reported in the media. Create some business communications for various stakeholders (e.g., students, parents, media, government, corporate partners) that turn negatives into positives. Present your communications to your instructor or to the class.

2.4 When the Audience Is Your Superior

Imagine that you are a new employee working for a large corporation. You've been on the job six months and your best friend suddenly announces she's getting married—next weekend, on a whim. You've known her for 15 years, and you really want to be at her wedding. Unfortunately, the day and time that the wedding is taking place are unconventional: next Friday at 11:00 a.m. As a result, you'll need to ask for the whole day off.

Your task. Write two e-mails to your boss. In the first one, break the three fundamental rules of good business writing: make the e-mail not audience-oriented, unpurposeful, and uneconomical. In the second e-mail, correct the three broken rules. Once you're finished, put the first e-mail on a handout and see how many of your classmates notice where you've broken the rules. Then, show your classmates your second version and see whether or not they agree about how you decided to improve the e-mail.

GRAMMAR/MECHANICS REVIEW 2—PRONOUNS

Study each of the following statements. Choose the pronoun that completes the statement correctly.

_____its_____ **Example:** Our Safety Committee just submitted (its, their) report.

_____ 1. We expected Mr. Thomas to call. Was it (he, him) who left the message?

_____ 2. Every member of the men's bowling team must have (his, his or her, their) picture taken.

_____ 3. Just between you and (me, I), a new salary schedule will soon be announced.

_____ 4. (Who, Whom) did you say was having trouble with the virus protection software?

_____ 5. Most applications arrived on time, but (yours, your's) was late.

_____ 6. Because of outstanding sales, the company gave bonuses to Mark and (me, I).

_____ 7. My friend and (I, me, myself) could not decide on an apartment to share.

_____ 8. The offices are similar, but (ours, our's) is cheaper to rent.

_____ 9. Please distribute the supplies to (whoever, whomever) ordered them.

_____ 10. Everyone except the manager and (I, me, myself) was eligible for a bonus.

_____ 11. No one is better able to lead the team than (he, him, himself).

_____ 12. It became clear that (we, us) employees would have to speak up for ourselves.

_____ 13. Someone on the women's team left (their, her) shoes in the van.

_____ 14. Next year I hope to earn as much as (she, her, herself).

_____ 15. Every homeowner should check (their, his or her, his) fire insurance.

💬 GRAMMAR/MECHANICS CHALLENGE—2

The document in Figure 2.6 contains some writing accuracy issues, including grammar, spelling, punctuation, and style. In addition, it doesn't take into consideration the advice on tone covered in this chapter. Read the document and edit it as you go, identifying inaccuracies and needed changes and fixing them. Your instructor will take up the correct answers with you.

FIGURE 2.6 E-Mail Sample

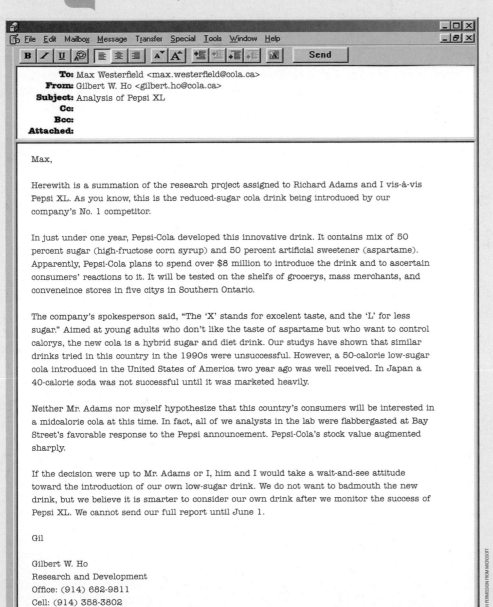

SHARPENING YOUR SKILLS FOR CRITICAL THINKING, PROBLEM SOLVING, AND DECISION MAKING

Gone are the days when management expected workers to follow the leader blindly and do only what they were told. Today, you'll be expected to think critically. You'll be solving problems and making decisions. Much of this book is devoted to helping you solve problems and communicate those decisions to management, fellow workers, clients, governments, and the public. Faced with a problem or an issue, most of us do a lot of worrying before making a decision. All that worrying can become directed thinking by channelling it into the following procedure.

1. **Identify and clarify the problem.** Your first task is to recognize that a problem exists. Some problems are big and unmistakable, such as failure of a courier service to get packages to customers on time. Other problems may be continuing annoyances, such as regularly running out of toner for an office copy machine. The first step in reaching a solution is pinpointing the problem area.

2. **Gather information.** Learn more about the problem situation. Look for possible causes and solutions. This step may mean checking files, calling suppliers, or brainstorming with fellow workers. For example, the courier service would investigate the tracking systems of the airlines carrying its packages to determine what is going wrong.

3. **Evaluate the evidence.** Where did the information come from? Does it represent various points of view? What biases could be expected from each source? How accurate is the information gathered? Is it fact or opinion? For example, it is a fact that packages are missing; it is an opinion that they are merely lost and will turn up eventually.

4. **Consider alternatives and implications.** Draw conclusions from the gathered evidence and pose solutions. Then weigh the advantages and disadvantages of each alternative. What are the costs, benefits, and consequences? What are the obstacles, and how can they be handled? Most important, what solution best serves your goals and those of your organization? Here's where your creativity is especially important.

5. **Choose and implement the best alternative.** Select an alternative and put it into action. Then, follow through on your decision by monitoring the results of implementing your plan. The courier company decided to give its unhappy customers free delivery service to make up for the lost packages and downtime. Be sure to continue monitoring and adjusting the solution to ensure its effectiveness over time.

Career Application

Let's return to the fast-food franchise problem discussed earlier in this chapter, in which some franchise owners are unhappy with the multiple lines for service. Customers don't seem to know where to stand to be next in line. Tempers flare when aggressive customers cut in line, and other customers spend so much time protecting their places in line that they fail to study the menu. Then they don't know what to order when they approach the counter. As a franchise owner, you would like to find a solution to this problem. Any changes in procedures, however, must be approved by all the franchise owners in a district. That means you'll have to get a majority to agree. You know that management feels that the multi-line system accommodates higher volumes of customers more quickly than a single-line system. Moreover, the problem of perception is important. What happens when customers open the door to a restaurant and see a long, single line? Do they stick around to learn how fast the line is moving?

- Individually or with a team, use the critical thinking steps outlined here. Begin by clarifying the problem.
- Where could you gather information to help you solve this problem? Would it be wise to see what your competitors are doing? How do banks handle customer lines? Airlines? Sports events?
- Evaluate your findings and consider alternatives. What are the pros and cons of each alternative?
- Choose the best alternative. Present your recommendation to your class and give your reasons for choosing it.

Related Web site: **www.cfa.ca/About_Us/Code_of_Ethics**

CHAPTER
03

Writing and Revising

1. Contrast different methods of researching data and generating ideas for messages.
2. Explain how to organize information into outlines.
3. Compare direct and indirect patterns for organizing messages.
4. Identify components of effective sentences.
5. Revise messages to achieve conciseness, clarity, and impact.
6. Revise messages to achieve visual persuasiveness.
7. Describe effective techniques for proofreading documents.

Writing naturally may seem easy, but it's not. It takes instruction and practice and patience (i.e., you need to fight the temptation to check Facebook, listen to your MP3 player, etc.). You've already learned some techniques for writing naturally (using a conversational tone, positive language, plain and familiar words). This chapter presents additional writing tips that make your communication not only natural but also professional.

Figure 3.1 reviews the entire writing process. In Chapter 2 we focused on the prewriting stage. This chapter addresses the second and third stages, which include researching, organizing, composing, revising, and proofreading.

Writing: Researching

The second stage of the writing process involves research, which means collecting the necessary information to prepare a message.

No experienced businessperson would begin writing a message to a customer or client or manager before collecting the needed information. We call this collection process *research*. Research is necessary before beginning to write because the information you collect helps shape the message. Discovering significant information after a message is completed often means starting over and reorganizing. To avoid frustration and inaccurate messages, collect information that answers this primary question:

• What does the receiver need to know about this topic?

When the message involves action, search for answers to secondary questions:

• What is the receiver to do?
• How is the receiver to do it?
• When must the receiver do it?
• What will happen if the receiver doesn't do it?

FIGURE 3.1 The Writing Process

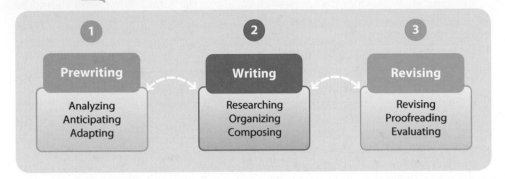

Whenever your communication problem requires more information than you have in your head or at your fingertips, you must conduct research. This research may be formal or informal.

Formal Research Methods

Long reports and complex business problems generally require some use of formal research methods. Let's say you are a product manager for a major soft drink manufacturer, and your boss asks you to evaluate the impact on traditional soft drink sales of energy drinks. Or as a sales manager for a major hotel chain let's assume you've been asked to investigate methods for increasing profitability. Both tasks require more data than you have in your head or at your fingertips. To conduct formal research, you could:

- **Search secondary sources.** Most people at work begin research by going to search engines like Google. On Google, you can find articles, corporate information, government information, as well as information on solutions providers like consultants. You can also find sources through an online public library catalogue. The catalogue will let you search for books as well as specialized articles in research databases. More rarely, secondary sources are also available in hard copy, such as books and newspapers and magazines in a library, or old non-digitized company files.
- **Go directly to the source.** For first-hand information, you can create your own sources by doing primary research. For the soft drink report, for example, you could find out what consumers really think about energy drinks versus soft drinks by conducting interviews or surveys, by putting together questionnaires, or by organizing focus groups. For the profitability report, you could interview experts such as business and hospitality professors to find out whether your company has been overlooking a tactic to boost its profitability. Formal research includes structured sampling and controls that allow investigators to make accurate judgments and valid predictions.
- **Conduct experiments.** Instead of asking for the target audience's opinion, experimental researchers present choices with controlled variables. Let's say, for example, that the soft drink manufacturer wants to determine at what price and under what circumstances consumers would switch from a soft drink to an energy drink. The results of such experimentation would provide valuable data for managerial decision making.

Because formal research techniques are particularly necessary for reports, you'll study them more extensively in Chapters 8 and 9.

Informal Research and Idea Generation

Most routine tasks—such as composing e-mails, messages, letters, informational reports, and oral presentations—require data that you can collect informally. Here are some techniques for collecting informal data and for generating ideas:

- **Search your company.** If you are responding to an inquiry, you can often find the answer by investigating your company's files or by consulting colleagues.

> Formal research may include searching libraries and electronic databases or investigating primary sources.

> Good sources of primary information are interviews, surveys, questionnaires, and focus groups.

OFFICE
INSIDER

*"Writing today is not a frill
for the few, but an essential
skill for the many."*

- **Talk with your manager.** Get information from the individual who gave you the assignment. What does that person know about the topic? What slant should be taken? What other sources would he or she suggest?
- **Interview the target audience.** Consider talking with individuals at whom the message is aimed. They can provide clarifying information that tells you what they want to know and how you should shape your remarks.
- **Conduct an informal survey.** Gather unscientific but helpful information via questionnaires or telephone surveys. In preparing a report predicting the success of a proposed fitness centre, for example, circulate a questionnaire asking for employee reactions.
- **Brainstorm for ideas.** Alone or with others, come up with ideas for the writing task at hand, and record at least a dozen ideas without judging them. Small groups are especially fruitful in brainstorming because people spin ideas off one another.

Writing: Organizing Data

Once you've collected data, you need to find a way to organize it. Organizing includes two processes: grouping and patterning. Well-organized messages group similar items together; ideas follow a sequence that helps the reader understand relationships and accept the writer's views. Unorganized messages proceed without structure or pattern, jumping from one thought to another. Such messages fail to emphasize important points. Puzzled readers can't see how the pieces fit together, and they become frustrated and irritated. Many communication experts regard poor organization as the greatest failing of business writers. A simple technique can help you organize data: the outline.

Outlining

In developing simple messages, some writers make a quick ideas list of the topics they wish to cover. They then compose a message at their computers directly from the list.

A simple way to organize data is the outline.

Most writers, though, need to organize their ideas—especially if the project is complex—into a hierarchy, such as an outline. The beauty of preparing an outline is that it gives you a chance to organize your thoughts before you start to choose specific words and sentences. Figure 3.2 shows a format for an outline.

FIGURE 3.2 Sample Outline

Awards Ceremony Costs

I. Venue
    A. Rentals
        1. Microphone
        2. Screen projector
        3. Tablecloths
    B. Extra staff
        1. Security guard
        2. Set-up, clean-up staff
        3. Speaker honorarium
II. Food
    A. Pre-awards
        1. Nonalcoholic beverages
        2. Appetizers
    B. Post-awards
        1. Alcohol
        2. Dinner
        3. Dessert
III. Awards
    A. Certificates
    B. Cash prizes

FIGURE 3.3 Audience Response Determines Patterns of Organization

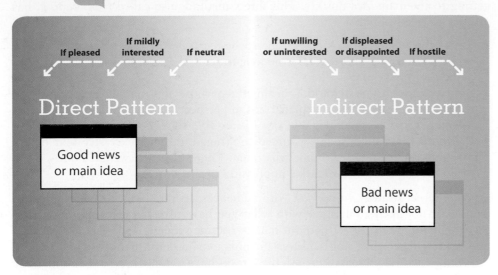

The Direct Pattern

After preparing an outline, you will need to decide where in the message you will place the main idea. Placing the main idea at the beginning of the message is called the *direct pattern*. In the direct pattern the main idea comes first, followed by details, explanation, or evidence. Placing the main idea later in the message (after the details, explanation, or evidence) is called the *indirect pattern*. The pattern you select is determined by how you expect the audience to react to the message, as shown in Figure 3.3.

In preparing to write any message, you need to anticipate the audience's reaction to your ideas and frame your message accordingly. When you expect the reader to be pleased, mildly interested, or, at worst, neutral—use the direct pattern. That is, put your main point—the purpose of your message—in the first or second sentence. Compare the direct and indirect patterns in the following memo openings. Notice how long it takes to get to the main idea in the indirect opening.

> Business messages typically follow either (1) the direct pattern, with the main idea first, or (2) the indirect pattern, with the main idea following explanation and evidence.

Indirect Opening	Direct Opening
Bombardier is seeking to improve the process undertaken in producing its annual company awards ceremony. To this end, the Marketing Department, which is in charge of the event, has been refining last year's plan, especially as regards the issue of rental costs and food and beverage costs.	The Marketing Department at Bombardier suggests cutting costs for the annual awards ceremony by adjusting the way we order food and the way we handle rentals.

Tips for Writing Outlines

- Define the main topic in the title.
- Divide the topic into major components, preferably three to five.
- Break the components into subpoints.
- Use details, illustrations, and evidence to support subpoints.
- Don't put a single item under a major component if you have only one subpoint; integrate it with the main item above it or reorganize.
- Strive to make each component exclusive (no overlapping).

Explanations and details should follow the direct opening. What's important is getting to the main idea quickly. This direct method, also called *frontloading*, has at least three advantages:

- **Saves the reader time.** Many businesspeople can devote only a few moments to each message. Messages that take too long to get to the point may lose their readers along the way.
- **Sets a proper frame of mind.** Learning the purpose up front helps the reader put the subsequent details and explanations in perspective. Without a clear opening, the reader may be thinking, *Why am I being told this?*
- **Prevents frustration.** Readers forced to struggle through excessive text before reaching the main idea become frustrated. They resent the writer. Poorly organized messages create a negative impression of the writer.

The direct strategy works best with audiences that are likely to be receptive to or at least not likely to disagree with what you have to say. Typical business messages that follow the direct pattern include routine requests and responses, orders and acknowledgments, non-sensitive memos, e-mails, informational reports, and informational oral presentations. All these tasks have one element in common: none has a sensitive subject that will upset the reader.

The Indirect Pattern

When you expect the audience to be uninterested, unwilling, displeased, or perhaps even hostile, the indirect pattern is more appropriate. In this pattern you don't reveal the main idea until after you have offered an explanation and the evidence.

WORKPLACE IN FOCUS

When the Deepwater Horizon rig exploded in the Gulf of Mexico in 2010, millions of barrels of oil spread to coastlines, harming wildlife and displacing thousands of citizens. Later the same year a similar disaster took place when a pipeline owned by Canadian energy company Enbridge ruptured in Michigan, sending unrefined oil into the nearby Kalamazoo River. Although BP established a multi-billion dollar emergency fund to compensate businesses and citizens for their economic losses, victims became distressed when the independent agency in charge of financial disbursements sent form letters denying payment to more than 300,000 claimants, mostly for insufficient documentation on applications. *Ideally, how should claims administrators organize messages when denying claims to disaster victims?*

This approach works well with three kinds of messages: (1) bad news, (2) ideas that require persuasion, and (3) sensitive news, especially when being transmitted to superiors. The indirect pattern has these benefits:

- **Respects the feelings of the audience.** Bad news is always painful, but the pain can be lessened when the receiver is prepared for it.
- **Encourages a fair hearing.** Messages that may upset the reader are more likely to be read when the main idea is delayed. Beginning immediately with a piece of bad news or a persuasive request, for example, may cause the receiver to stop reading or listening.
- **Minimizes a negative reaction.** A reader's overall reaction to a negative message is generally improved if the news is delivered gently.

Typical business messages that could be developed indirectly include letters and memos that decline requests, deny claims, and refuse credit. Persuasive requests, sales letters, sensitive messages, and some reports and oral presentations also benefit from the indirect strategy. You'll learn more about how to use the indirect pattern in Chapters 6 and 7.

In summary, business messages may be organized directly, with the main idea first, or indirectly, with the main idea delayed. Although these two patterns cover many communication problems, they should not be considered universal. Every business transaction is distinct. Some messages are mixed: part good news, part bad; part goodwill, part persuasion. In upcoming chapters you'll practise applying the direct and indirect patterns in typical situations. Then, you'll have the skills and confidence to evaluate communication problems and vary these patterns depending on the goals you wish to achieve.

Constructing Effective Sentences

After deciding how to organize your message, you're ready to begin drafting it. The most compelling and effective messages contain a variety of sentence patterns rather than repeating the same pattern.

> Use a variety of sentence types to avoid boring, monotonous writing.

Using Four Sentence Types to Achieve Variety

Messages that repeat the same sentence pattern soon become boring. The way you construct your sentences can make your messages interesting and readable. To avoid monotony and to add spark to your writing, use a variety of sentence types. You have four sentence types from which to choose: simple, compound, complex, and compound-complex.

A **simple sentence**, shown in the following example, contains one complete thought (an independent clause) with a subject (underlined once) and predicate verb (underlined twice):

SNC Lavalin saw an opportunity.

A **compound sentence** contains two complete but related thoughts. The two thoughts (independent clauses) may be joined (a) by a conjunction such as *and, but,* or *or;* (b) by a semicolon; or (c) by a conjunctive adverb such as *however, consequently,* or *therefore.* Notice the punctuation in these examples:

Our team project was difficult.

Our team project was difficult; we were happy with the results.

Our team project was difficult; however, we were happy with the results.

A **complex sentence** contains an independent clause (a complete thought) and a dependent clause (a thought that cannot stand by itself). Dependent clauses are often introduced by words such as *although, since, because, when,* and *if.* When dependent clauses precede independent clauses, they always are followed by a comma.

> When <u>we finished</u> our team project, <u>we held</u> a team party.

A **compound-complex sentence** contains at least two independent clauses and one dependent clause. Because these sentences are usually long, use them sparingly.

> Although this team project <u>is</u> completed, soon <u>we'll begin</u> work on another; however, <u>it will be</u> less challenging.

Controlling Sentence Length

Sentences of 20 or fewer words have the most impact.

Regardless of the type of sentence, remember that sentence length can influence readability. Because your goal is to communicate clearly, try to limit your sentences to 20 or fewer words. The American Press Institute reports that reader comprehension drops off markedly as sentences become longer:

SENTENCE LENGTH	COMPREHENSION RATE
8 words	100%
15 words	90%
19 words	80%
28 words	50%

Avoiding Three Common Sentence Faults

As you craft your sentences, beware of three common traps: fragments, run-on (fused) sentences, and comma-splice sentences. If any of these faults appears in a business message, the writer immediately loses credibility.

Fragments are broken-off parts of sentences and should not be punctuated as sentences.

FRAGMENTS. One of the most serious errors a writer can make is punctuating a fragment as if it were a complete sentence. A fragment is usually a broken-off part of a complex sentence.

Fragment	Revision
Because most transactions require a permanent record. Good writing skills are critical.	Because most transactions require a permanent record, good writing skills are critical.
The recruiter requested a writing sample. Even though the candidate seemed to communicate well.	The recruiter requested a writing sample even though the candidate seemed to communicate well.

Fragments often can be identified by the words that introduce them—words such as *although, as, because, even, except, for example, if, instead of, since, such as, that, which,* and *when*. These words introduce dependent clauses. Make sure such clauses always connect to independent clauses.

RUN-ON (FUSED) SENTENCES. A sentence with two independent clauses must be joined by a coordinating conjunction (*and, or, nor, but*) or by a semicolon (;). Without a conjunction or a semicolon, a run-on sentence results.

When two independent clauses are run together without punctuation or a conjunction, a run-on (fused) sentence results.

Run-on	Revision
Most job seekers present a printed résumé some are also using Web sites as electronic portfolios.	Most job seekers present a printed résumé. Some are also using Web sites as electronic portfolios.
One candidate sent an e-mail résumé another sent a traditional résumé.	One candidate sent an e-mail résumé; another sent a traditional résumé.

COMMA-SPLICE SENTENCES. A comma splice results when a writer joins (splices together) two independent clauses with a comma. Independent clauses may be joined with a coordinating conjunction (*and, or, nor, but*) or a conjunctive adverb (*however, consequently, therefore,* and others). Notice that clauses joined by coordinating conjunctions require only a comma. Clauses joined by a coordinating adverb require a semicolon. The three following examples illustrate three ways to revise comma splices. Notice that the first one uses a conjunction (*and*), the second uses a conjunctive adverb (*however*), and the third uses only a semicolon.

Comma Splice	Possible Revisions
Some employees responded by e-mail, others picked up the telephone.	Some employees responded by e-mail, and others picked up the telephone.
	Some employees responded by e-mail; however, others picked up the telephone.
	Some employees responded by e-mail; others picked up the telephone.

💬 Writing: The First Draft

Writers who haven't completed the preparatory work of researching and organizing often suffer from "writer's block" and sit staring at the computer screen. It's easier to get started if you have organized your ideas and established a plan. Preparing a first draft is also easier if you have a quiet environment in which to concentrate. In a time when many routine messages are tapped out on tablets or smartphones in meetings, on the bus, or at lunch, businesspeople with important messages to compose need to consciously set aside time and not allow calls, visitors, or other interruptions. This is a good technique for students as well.

Find a quiet place in which to write.

As you begin drafting your document, keep in mind that you are writing the first draft, not the final copy. Experts suggest that you draft quickly, sometimes known as *sprint writing*. According to one university writing centre, "The purpose of the initial draft is to produce raw material, not to dazzle the critics with your finely shaped prose."[1] As you write out each idea, imagine that you are talking to the reader. Don't let yourself get bogged down. If you can't think of the right word, insert a substitute or type "find perfect word later."[2]

Another technique that helps you draft your message is reading it back to yourself, aloud. Sometimes a sentence or group of sentences don't seem complete or persuasive on the screen. However, reading them aloud can cause you to see in which direction you might continue, or if a change in direction is required.

Finally, don't forget to save as you go. There's nothing worse than writing for 5 or 15 or 30 minutes only to have your device lose everything you've written.

Revising: Understanding the Process of Revision

Once you've written a complete draft of a business document, it's time to begin revising your work so it can be sent to its intended audience. Revising means improving the content and sentence structure of your message. It may include adding to, cutting, and changing what you've written. Proofreading involves correcting the grammar, spelling, punctuation, format, and mechanics of your message.

Both revising and proofreading require a little practice to develop your skills. Take a look at Figure 3.6 on page 76. Notice how the revised version of this paragraph is clearer, more concise, and more vigorous because we removed a lot of extra words that were not adding to the message. Major ideas stand out when they are not covered up by unnecessary words.

Many professional writers compose the first draft quickly without worrying about language, precision, or correctness. Then they revise and polish extensively. Other writers prefer to revise as they go—particularly for shorter business documents. Whether you revise as you go or do it when you finish a document, you'll want to focus on concise wording.

> The third phase of the writing process includes revision, proofreading, and evaluating.

> Some communicators write the first draft quickly; others revise and polish as they go.

> Main points are easier to understand in concise messages.

> A wordy phrase can often be reduced to a single word.

Concise Wording

In business, time is money. Translated into writing, this saying means that concise messages save reading time and, thus, money. In addition, messages that are written directly and efficiently are easier to read and comprehend. In the revision process, look for shorter ways to say what you mean. Examine every sentence you write. Could the thought be conveyed in fewer words? Notice how the following wordy expressions could be put more concisely.

Wordy	Concise
at a later date	later
at this point in time	now
afford an opportunity	allow
are of the opinion that	believe, think that
at the present time	now, currently

Wordy	Concise
despite the fact that	though
due to the fact that	because, since
during the time	while
feel free to	please
for the period of	for
fully cognizant of	aware of
in addition to the above	also
in spite of the fact that	even though
in the event that	if
in the amount of	for
in the near future	soon
in view of the fact that	because
in as much as	since
more or less	about
until such time as	until

Long Lead-Ins

Delete unnecessary introductory words and phrases. The main idea of the sentence often follows the words *that* or *because*.

> Avoid long lead-ins that delay the reader from reaching the meaning of the sentence.

Wordy	Concise
I am sending you this announcement to let you all know that the office will be closed Monday.	The office will be closed Monday.
You will be interested to learn that you can now be served at our Web site.	You can now be served at our Web site.
I am writing this letter because Dr. Rahib Peshwar suggested that your organization was hiring trainees.	Dr. Rahib Peshwar suggested that your organization was hiring trainees.

Outdated Expressions

The world of business has changed greatly in the past century. Yet some business writers continue to use antiquated phrases and expressions borrowed from a period when the language of business was exceedingly formal. Replace outdated expressions such as those shown here with more modern phrasing:

> Replace outdated expressions with modern, concise phrasing.

Outdated Expressions	Modern Phrasing
are in receipt of	have received
as per your request	at your request
attached hereto	attached
enclosed please find	enclosed is/are
pursuant to your request	at your request
thanking you in advance	thank you
I trust that	I think, I believe
under separate cover	separately

Needless Adverbs

Eliminating intensifying adverbs such as *very*, *definitely*, *quite*, *completely*, *extremely*, *really*, *actually*, *somewhat*, and *rather* streamlines your writing. Omitting these intensifiers generally makes you sound more credible and businesslike.

Wordy	Concise
We *actually* did not *really* give his plan a *very* fair trial.	We did not give his plan a fair trial.
Professor Anna Pictou offers an *extremely* fine course that students *definitely* appreciate.	Professor Anna Pictou offers a fine course that students appreciate.

Fillers

Good writers avoid crowding sentences with excess words. Beginning an idea with *there is* usually indicates that writers are having a hard time deciding what the main idea of the sentence should be. Used correctly, *there* indicates a specific place (*I placed the box there*). Used as fillers, *there* and occasionally *it* merely take up space.

Wordy	Concise
There are three vice presidents who report directly to the president.	Three vice presidents report directly to the president.
It is the client who should make application for licensing.	The client should apply for licensing.

Repetitious Words

Avoid the monotony of unintentionally repeated words.

Communicators who want to create vibrant sentences vary their words to avoid unintentional repetition. Notice how monotonous the following announcement sounds:

Employees will be able to elect an additional six employees to serve with the four previously elected employees who currently comprise the employees' board of directors. To ensure representation, shift employees will be electing one shift employee as their sole representative.

In this example the word *employee* is used six times. In addition, the last sentence begins with the word *representation* and ends with the similar word *representative*. An easier-to-read version follows:

Employees will be able to elect an additional six representatives to serve with the four previously elected members of the employees' board of directors. To ensure representation, shift workers will elect their own board member.

In the second version, synonyms (*representatives, members, workers*) replaced *employee*. The last sentence was reworked by using a pronoun (*their*) and by substituting *board member* for the repetitious *representative*. Variety of expression can be achieved by searching for appropriate synonyms and by substituting pronouns.

Good writers are also alert to the overuse of the articles *a*, *an*, and particularly *the*. Often the word *the* can simply be omitted, particularly with plural nouns.

Wordy	Improved
The committee members agreed on many rule changes.	Committee members agreed on many rule changes.

Redundant Words

Repetition of words to achieve emphasis or effective transition is an important writing technique discussed in the previous chapter. The needless repetition, however, of words whose meanings are clearly implied by other words is a writing fault called *redundancy*. For example, in the expression *final outcome*, the word *final* is redundant and should be omitted, since *outcome* implies finality. Learn to avoid redundant expressions such as the following:

Redundant	Concise
absolutely essential	essential
adequate enough	adequate
basic fundamentals	fundamentals *or* basics
big in size	big
combined together	combined
exactly identical	identical
each and every	each *or* every
necessary prerequisite	prerequisite
new beginning	beginning
refer back	refer
repeat again	repeat
true facts	facts

Chapter 03: Writing and Revising

Parallelism

Parallelism adds conciseness because sentences written so that their parts are balanced or parallel are easy to read and understand. To achieve parallel construction, use similar structures to express similar ideas. For example, the words *computing, coding, recording,* and *storing* are parallel because the words all end in *-ing.* To express the list as *computing, coding, recording,* and *storage* is disturbing because the last item is not what the reader expects. Try to match nouns with nouns, verbs with verbs, and clauses with clauses. Your goal is to keep the wording balanced in expressing similar ideas.

Lacks Parallelism	Illustrates Parallelism
The policy affected all vendors, suppliers, and *those involved with consulting.*	The policy affected all vendors, suppliers, and *consultants.* (Matches nouns)
Our primary goals are to increase productivity, reduce costs, and *the improvement of product quality.*	Our primary goals are to increase productivity, reduce costs, and *improve product quality.* (Matches verbs)
We are scheduled to meet in Atlanta on January 5, *we are meeting in Montréal on the 15th of March,* and in Chicago on June 3.	We are scheduled to meet in Atlanta on January 5, *in Montréal on March 15,* and in Chicago on June 3. (Matches phrases)
Shelby audits all accounts lettered A through L; accounts lettered M through Z are audited by Andrew.	Shelby audits all accounts lettered A through L; Andrew audits accounts lettered M through Z. (Matches clauses)
Our Grey Cup ads have three objectives: 1. We want to increase product use. 2. Introduce complementary products. 3. Our corporate image will be enhanced.	Our Grey Cup ads have three objectives: 1. Increase product use 2. Introduce complementary products. 3. Enhance our corporate image (Matches verbs in listed items)

Appropriate Wording

In the world of business, it's important that you choose the most economical or concise words to get your point across (after all, time is money), but it's just as important that these words be appropriate. "Appropriate" in the world of business is easy to explain—it means professional as opposed to friendly, formal or semiformal as opposed to informal, and precise as opposed to long-winded.

Jargon

Except in certain specialized contexts, you should avoid jargon and unnecessary technical terms. Jargon is special terminology that is peculiar to a particular activity or profession. For example, geologists speak knowingly of *exfoliation, calcareous ooze,* and *siliceous particles.* Engineers are familiar with phrases such as *infrared processing flags, output latches,* and *movable symbology.* Telecommunication experts use such words and phrases as *protocol, mode,* and *asynchronous transmission.* Business professionals are especially prone to using jargon, with words and phrases such as *leverage, ramp up, in the pipeline, cascade, pushback,* and *bullish or bearish* being just a few of the many you may find in the business section of the newspaper or in your local office.

Ask high-tech shoppers if they want a tablet with a microprocessor containing two or more cores that process multiple data streams into rich multimedia content fast, and you will encounter only blank stares. But ask if they want a tablet with multiple brains that can download songs, play videos, and allow the user to instant message with friends at the same time, and you have made a sale. *In what situations should communicators avoid using complex or technical language?*

Every field has its own special vocabulary. Using that vocabulary within the field is acceptable and even necessary for accurate, efficient communication. Don't use specialized terms, however, if you have reason to believe that your reader or listener may misunderstand them.

Slang

Slang is composed of informal words with arbitrary and extravagantly changed meanings. Slang words quickly go out of fashion because they are no longer appealing when everyone begins to understand them. Consider the following excerpt from an e-mail sent by a ski resort company president to his executive team: "Well guys, the results of our customer survey are in and I'm massively stoked by what I'm hearing. Most of our customers are totally happy with the goods, and I just want to congratulate all my peeps on a job well done!"

The meaning here is considerably obscured by the use of slang. Good communicators, of course, aim at clarity and avoid unintelligible slang.

DILBERT   **By Scott Adams**

Clichés

Clichés are expressions that have become exhausted by overuse. These expressions lack not only freshness but also clarity. Most are meaningless to people from other cultures. The following partial list contains representative clichés you should avoid in business writing.

Clichés are dull and sometimes ambiguous.

below the belt	last but not least
better than new	make a bundle
beyond the shadow of a doubt	pass with flying colours
easier said than done	quick as a flash
exception to the rule	shoot from the hip
fill the bill	stand your ground
first and foremost	true to form
hard facts	one in a million
keep your nose to the grindstone	

Instant-Messaging and Texting Speak

Although there has been widespread adoption of communication technology in the workplace (e-mails, instant messages, etc.), the technology came in far faster than new rules could be put in place about how it should be used. The boundary between personal use of communication technology (between friends and family) and professional use of communication technology (between co-workers) has been blurred. Not everyone is happy about this blurring, and you can Google "instant-message speak" to get a taste of the debate raging among bloggers, journalists, and others.

What ends up happening is that the shorthand we sometimes use in personal texts, e-mails, and instant messages—expressions like CUL8R (instead of "see you later")—creeps into our professional workplace messages. You can visit **www.webopedia.com/quick_ref/textmessageabbreviations.asp** for hundreds more such abbreviations. It would be unrealistic to insist that such shorthand should never be used, but a rule you definitely should follow as a new business communicator is never to use such shorthand when your message is going to a customer, to another audience outside your company (e.g., government), to a manager or other employee higher up than you in the company's hierarchy, or to a fellow employee with whom you've never communicated before. In such cases, continue to use standard, more formal diction.

Precise Verbs

> Precise verbs make your writing forceful, clear, and lively.

Effective writing creates meaningful images in the mind of the reader. Such writing is marked by concrete and descriptive words. Ineffective writing is often dulled by abstract and generalized words. The most direct way to improve lifeless writing is through using precise verbs. Precise verbs describe action in a way that is understandable for the reader. These verbs deliver the force of the sentence. Select verbs that will help the reader see precisely what is happening.

General	Precise
Our salesperson will *contact* you next week.	Our salesperson will (*telephone, e-mail, visit*) you next week.
The CEO *said* that we should contribute.	The CEO (*urged, pleaded, demanded*) that we contribute.
We must *consider* this problem.	We must (*clarify, remedy, rectify*) this problem.
The newspaper was *affected* by the strike.	The newspaper was (*crippled, silenced, demoralized*) by the strike.

The power of a verb is diminished when it is needlessly converted to a noun. This happens when verbs such as *acquire*, *establish*, and *develop* are made into nouns (*acquisition*, *establishment*, and *development*). These nouns then receive the central emphasis in the sentence. In the following pairs of sentences, observe how forceful the original verbs are compared with their noun forms.

Weak (Noun-Centred)	Strong (Verb-Centred)
Acquisition of park lands was made recently by the provincial government.	The provincial government *acquired* park lands recently.
The webmaster and the designer had a *discussion* concerning graphics.	The webmaster and the designer *discussed* graphics.
Both companies must grant *approval* of the merger.	Both companies must *approve* the merger.

Active Versus Passive Voice

Colleagues and clients prefer active-voice sentences because they are direct, clear, and concise; however, the passive voice has distinct uses. In composing messages, you may use the active or passive voice to express your meaning. In the active voice, the subject is the doer of the action (*The manager hired Jake*). In the passive voice, the subject is acted upon (*Jake was hired by the manager*). Notice that in the passive voice, the attention shifts from the doer to the receiver of the action. You don't even have to reveal the doer if you choose not to. The active voice is more direct, clear, and concise. Nevertheless, the passive voice is useful in certain instances such as the following:

- **To emphasize an action or the recipient of the action.** *An investigation was launched.*
- **To de-emphasize negative news.** *Cash refunds cannot be made.*
- **To conceal the doer of an action.** *An error was made in our sales figures.*

How can you tell whether a verb is active or passive? Identify the subject of the sentence and decide whether the subject is doing the acting or is being acted upon. For example, in the sentence *An appointment was made for January 1*, the subject is *appointment*. The subject is being acted upon; therefore, the verb (*was made*) is passive. Another clue in identifying passive-voice verbs is that they generally include a *to be* helping verb, such as *is, are, was, were, be, being*, or *been*. Figure 3.4 summarizes effective uses for active and passive voice.

FIGURE 3.4 Using Active and Passive Voice Effectively

Use the active voice for directness, vigour, and clarity.

DIRECT AND CLEAR IN ACTIVE VOICE	INDIRECT AND LESS CLEAR IN PASSIVE VOICE
The manager completed performance reviews for all employees.	Performance reviews were completed for all employees by the manager.
Evelyn initiated a customer service blog last year.	A customer service blog was initiated last year.
Coca-Cola created a Sprite page in Facebook to advertise its beverage.	A Sprite page was created in Facebook by Coca-Cola to advertise its beverage.

Use the passive voice to be tactful or to emphasize the action rather than the doer.

LESS TACTFUL OR EFFECTIVE IN ACTIVE VOICE	MORE TACTFUL OR EFFECTIVE IN PASSIVE VOICE
We cannot grant you credit.	Credit cannot be granted.
The CEO made a huge error in projecting profits.	A huge error was made in projecting profits.
I launched a successful fitness program for our company last year.	A successful fitness program was launched for our company last year.

Chapter 03: Writing and Revising

Concrete Nouns

Concrete nouns help readers visualize the meanings of words.

Nouns name persons, places, and things. Abstract nouns name concepts that are difficult to visualize, such as *automation, function, justice, institution, integrity, form, judgment,* and *environment.* Concrete nouns name objects that are more easily imagined, such as *desk, car,* and *light bulb.* Nouns describing a given object can range from the very abstract to the very concrete—for example, *object, motor vehicle, car, convertible, Mustang.* All of these words or phrases can be used to describe a Mustang convertible. However, a reader would have difficulty envisioning a Mustang convertible when given just the word *object* or even *motor vehicle* or *car.*

In business writing, help your reader "see" what you mean by using concrete language.

General	Concrete
a change in our budget	*a 10 percent reduction* in our budget
that company's product	*Motorola's Minitor V* pager
a person called	*Mrs. Tomei, the administrative assistant,* called
we *improved* the assembly line	*we installed 26 ARC Mate 120iC Series robots* on the assembly line

Vivid Adjectives

A thesaurus (on your computer or in book form) helps you select precise words and increase your vocabulary.

Including highly descriptive, dynamic adjectives makes writing more vivid and concrete. Be careful, though, not to overuse them or to lose objectivity in selecting them.

General	Vivid
The report was on time.	The *detailed 12-page report* was submitted on time.
Clayton needs a better truck.	Clayton needs a *rugged, four-wheel-drive Dodge* truck.
We enjoyed the movie.	We enjoyed the *entertaining* and *absorbing* movie.
	Overkill: We enjoyed the *gutsy, exciting, captivating,* and *thoroughly marvellous* movie.

🗨 Designing Documents for Readability

Well-designed documents improve your messages in two important ways. First, they enhance readability and comprehension. Second, they make readers think you are a well-organized and intelligent person. In the revision process, you have a chance to adjust formatting and make other changes so that readers grasp your main points quickly. Significant design techniques to improve readability include appropriate use of white space, margins, typefaces, numbered and bulleted lists, and headings for visual impact.

Employing White Space

Empty space on a page is called *white space*. A page crammed full of text or graphics appears busy, cluttered, and unreadable. To increase white space, use headings, bulleted or numbered lists, short paragraphs, and effective margins. As discussed earlier, short sentences (20 or fewer words) improve readability and comprehension, as do short paragraphs (eight or fewer printed lines). As you revise, think about shortening long sentences. Also consider breaking up long paragraphs into shorter chunks. Be sure, however, that each part of the divided paragraph has a topic sentence.

Numbering and Bulleting Lists for Quick Comprehension

One of the best ways to ensure rapid comprehension of ideas is through the use of numbered or bulleted lists. Lists provide high "skim value." This means that readers can browse quickly and grasp main ideas. By breaking up complex information into smaller chunks, lists improve readability, understanding, and retention. They also force the writer to organize ideas and write efficiently.

In the revision process, look for items that could be converted to lists and follow these techniques to make your lists look professional:

- **Numbered lists:** Use for items that represent a sequence or reflect a numbering system.
- **Bulleted lists:** Use to highlight items that don't necessarily show a chronology.
- **Capitalization:** Capitalize the initial word of each line.
- **Punctuation:** Add end punctuation only if the listed items are complete sentences.
- **Parallelism:** Make all the lines consistent; for example, start each with a verb.

In the following examples, notice that the list on the left presents a sequence of steps with numbers. The bulleted list does not show a sequence of ideas; therefore, bullets are appropriate. Also notice the parallelism in each example. In the numbered list, each item begins with a verb. In the bulleted list, each item follows an adjective/noun sequence. Business readers appreciate lists because they focus attention. Be careful, however, not to use so many that your messages look like grocery lists.

> Numbered lists represent sequences; bulleted lists highlight items that may not show a sequence.

Numbered List	Bulleted List
Our recruiters follow these steps when hiring applicants:	To attract upscale customers, we feature the following:
1. Examine the application. 2. Interview the applicant. 3. Check the applicant's references.	• Quality fashions • Personalized service • A generous return policy

Adding Headings for Visual Impact

Headings are an effective tool for highlighting information and improving readability. They encourage the writer to group similar material together. Headings help the reader separate major ideas from details. They enable a busy reader to skim familiar or less important information. They also provide a quick preview or review. Headings appear most often in reports, which you will study in greater detail in Chapters 8 and 9. However, main headings, subheadings, and category headings can also improve readability in e-mail messages, memos, and letters. In the following example they are used with bullets to summarize categories.

Our company focuses on the following areas in the employment process:

- **Attracting applicants.** We advertise for qualified applicants, and we also encourage current employees to recommend good people.

- **Interviewing applicants.** Our specialized interviews include simulated customer encounters as well as scrutiny by supervisors.
- **Checking references.** We investigate every applicant thoroughly; we contact former employers and all listed references.

In Figure 3.5 the writer was able to convert a dense, unappealing e-mail message into an easier-to-read version by applying document design. Notice that

FIGURE 3.5 Using Document Design to Improve Readability

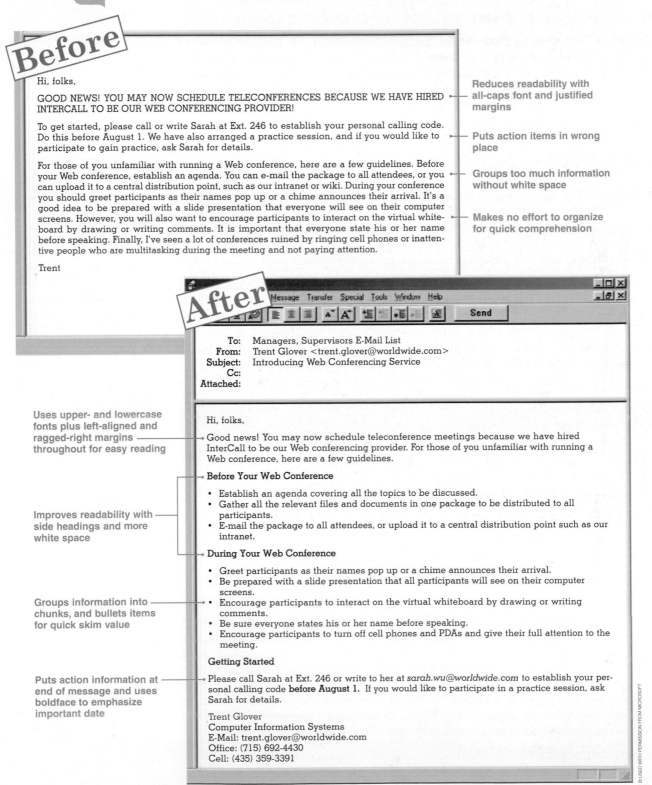

Chapter 03: Writing and Revising NEL

the all-caps font in the first paragraph makes its meaning difficult to decipher. Justified margins and lack of white space further reduce readability. In the revised version, the writer changed the all-caps font to upper- and lowercase and also used ragged-right margins to enhance visual appeal. One of the best document design techniques in this message is the use of headings and bullets to help the reader see chunks of information in similar groups. All of these improvements are made in the revision process. You can make any message more readable by applying the document design techniques presented here.

Revising: The Proofreading Process

Once you have the message in its final form, it's time to proofread. Don't proofread earlier because you may waste time checking items that are eventually changed or omitted.

What to Watch for in Proofreading

Careful proofreaders check for problems in these areas:

- **Spelling.** Now's the time to consult the dictionary. Is *recommend* spelled with one or two *c*'s? Do you mean *affect* or *effect*? Use your computer spell checker, but don't rely on it. See the Communication Workshop section on pages 84–85 to learn more about the benefits and hazards of computer spell checkers.
- **Grammar.** Locate sentence subjects. Do their verbs agree with them? Do pronouns agree with their antecedents? Review the principles in the Grammar/ Mechanics Handbook if necessary. The Communication Workshop discusses grammar checkers more extensively, but we recommend not using them until you've mastered grammar, mechanics, and punctuation on your own.
- **Punctuation.** Make sure that introductory clauses are followed by commas. In compound sentences put commas before coordinating conjunctions (*and*, *or*, *but*, *nor*). Double-check your use of semicolons and colons.
- **Names and numbers.** Compare all names and numbers with their sources, because inaccuracies are not immediately visible. Especially verify the spelling of the names of individuals receiving the message. Most of us immediately dislike someone who misspells our name.
- **Format.** Be sure that letters, printed memos, and reports are balanced on the page. Compare their parts and format with those of standard documents shown in Appendix A. If you indent paragraphs, be certain that all are indented.
- **Consistency.** Make sure all words are spelled and formatted the same way throughout your document. For example, spelling *cheque* the Canadian way three times and then twice the American way (*check*) reduces your credibility as a business writer and confuses readers.

> Good proofreaders check spelling, grammar, punctuation, names, numbers, format, and consistency.

How to Proofread Documents

When revising printed documents, you will manually apply standard proofreading marks, such as those shown in Figure 3.6. Some people refer to this as "hard" proofing because you are marking hard copies. Today, however, you will often be proofreading and marking digital documents. This is especially true when you are collaborating with someone who is not nearby.

Revising digital documents with digital proofing tools is known as "soft" proofing. Soft proofing has many advantages. Corrections and edits can be transferred electronically among authors, editors, proofreaders, and typesetters—and then on to the printer without pen ever touching paper. Revising digitally can save mailing costs and days of production time by avoiding sending hard-copy proofs back and forth. The disadvantages of soft proofing include tired eyes, especially when you are working on long documents. An even greater disadvantage is the fear of losing your work because of a computer crash.

FIGURE **3.6** Hard Proofreading Marks With Sample Proofread

ℐ	Delete	∧	Insert
≡	Capitalize	⌗∧	Insert space
/lc	Lowercase (don't capitalize)	⋀	Insert punctuation
∩	Transpose	⊙	Insert period
⌣	Close up	¶	Start paragraph

Marked Copy

~~This is to inform you that~~ beginning september 1, the doors
lc leading to the West side of the building will have alarms.
Because ~~of the fact that~~ these ~~exits~~ doors also function as fire exits,
they can not ~~actually~~ be locked, consequently, we are instaling
alrams. Please ~~utilize~~ use the east side exists to avoid setting off
the ear splitting alarms.

Regardless of its hazards, digital proofing is definitely a skill you should learn. You have a number of tool options. You might use simple word processing tools such as strikethrough and colour. In the example shown in Figure 3.7, strikethroughs in red identify passages to be deleted. The Strikethrough function is located on the **Font** tab in MS Word. We used blue to show inserted words, but you may choose any colour you prefer.

Another way to revise digitally is to use the MS Word Insert **Comment** and **Track Changes** features, which are discussed below and illustrated in more detail in the Communication Workshop feature starting on page 84.

It's good practice for new business writers to first get used to editing on paper before trying to edit on-screen. The reality is, though, that in most workplaces today documents are edited using the straightforward Track Changes function in Word.

Track Changes applies different colours to indicate any changes you make to the wording of your document. The feature also creates a comment bubble on the right side of the screen that explains exactly what has been changed (see Figure 3.8 on page 78). The advantage of Track Changes is that it shows you the new, improved wording while retaining the older wording, and let's you decide whether or not you'd like to accept your proposed change.

If you are going to proofread on paper (e.g., during a peer editing session in your business communication course), the process is described below.

- Print a copy, preferably double-spaced.
- Allow adequate time to proofread carefully. A common excuse for sloppy proofreading is lack of time.
- Be prepared to find errors. One student confessed, "I can find other people's errors, but I can't seem to locate my own." Psychologically, we don't expect to find errors, and we don't want to find them. You can overcome this obstacle by anticipating errors and congratulating, not criticizing, yourself each time you find one.

FIGURE 3.7 Revisions Done Manually (Hard) vs. Digitally (Soft)

Revising Printed Documents Manually

~~This is a short note to let you know that,~~ as you requested, I ~~made an~~
~~investigation of~~ investigated several of our competitors' Web sites. Attached ~~hereto~~ is a
summary of my findings. ~~of my investigation.~~ I was ~~really~~ most interested in
~~making a comparison of the employment of strategies for~~ comparing marketing strategies as well
as ~~the use of~~ navigational graphics ~~used~~ to guide visitors through the sites.
~~In view of the fact that~~ Because we will be revising our own Web site ~~in the near~~
~~future,~~ soon, I was ~~extremely~~ intrigued by the organization, ~~kind of~~ marketing
tactics, and navigation at ~~each and~~ every site I visited.

Revising Printed Documents Digitally

~~This is a short note to let you know that, as~~ As you requested, I ~~made an~~
~~investigation of~~ investigated several of our competitors' Web sites.
Attached ~~hereto~~ is a summary of my findings. ~~of my investigation.~~ I was
~~really~~ most interested in ~~making a comparison of the employment of~~
~~strategies for~~ comparing marketing strategies as well as ~~the use of~~
navigational graphics ~~used~~ to guide visitors through the sites. ~~In view of~~
~~the fact that~~ Because we will be revising our own Web site ~~in the near~~
~~future~~ soon, I was ~~extremely~~ intrigued by the organization, ~~kind of~~
marketing tactics, and navigation at ~~each and~~ every site I visited.

- Read the message at least twice—once for meaning and the second time to identify grammar, mechanics, and style errors. For very long documents (book chapters and long articles or reports), read a third time to verify consistency in formatting.
- For documents that must be perfect, read complex passages of the message aloud. Spell names and difficult words, note capitalization, and read punctuation.
- Use standard proofreading marks, shown in Figure 3.6, to indicate changes. A more complete list of proofreading marks appears in Appendix B.

Proofreaders use these standard marks to indicate revisions.

How to Proofread and Revise PDF Files

As business writers depend more and more on PDF (portable document format) documents, you will want to learn how to edit them. A rich array of PDF tools from Adobe Acrobat can make markup and work flow fairly intuitive. That is, you can usually see how to perform a function without reading instructions. You can insert, replace, highlight, delete, or underline material as well as add notes, all with an insertion point that looks similar to that used in traditional proofreading, as shown in Figure 3.8. The next time you have a PDF document open on your screen, go to the Tools menu, choose Annotate, and then add a note. Adobe Acrobat enables you to add comments easily, but these markup tools require your computer to be running Adobe.

FIGURE 3.8 Proofreading and Marking PDF Files

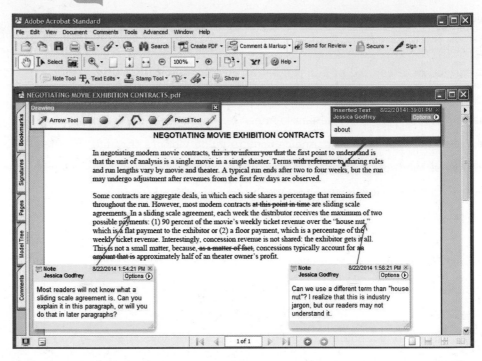

SUMMING UP AND LOOKING FORWARD

This chapter explained the second phase of the writing process including researching, organizing, composing, revising, and proofreading. Before beginning a message requiring research, business writers collect data, either formally or informally. Information for a message can then be organized into a list or an outline. Depending on the expected reaction of the receiver, the message can be organized directly (for positive reactions) or indirectly (for negative reactions or when persuasion is necessary).

Once a message has been composed, it should be revised before it's sent. To revise for conciseness, look for wordy phrases that can be shortened and eliminate outdated expressions and empty fillers. Also watch for repetitive words and redundancies among other errors. To revise for appropriateness, look for non-simple, declarative language. For example, eliminate jargon unless it is clear to receivers, and avoid slang and clichés altogether. The best writing includes precise verbs, concrete nouns, and vivid adjectives. After revising, you're ready for the last step in the writing process: proofreading. Watch for irregularities in spelling, grammar, punctuation, names and numbers, and format. Although documents are often proofread on-screen, you should know how to proofread from a printed copy. Longer documents (e.g., reports) should be proofread several times. Also, complex documents should be revised with readability and visual persuasiveness in mind (e.g., white space and graphic highlighting). Proofreading is now aided by tools such as Word's Track Changes and Adobe's annotating tool for PDFs.

In Chapters 2 and 3 you've studied the writing and revision process. Now it's time for you to put these techniques to work. Chapter 4 introduces you to the main business writing formats, while Chapters 5 to 7 discuss common writing situations in which you'll need to employ these formats.

CRITICAL THINKING

1. What research methods other than Google can you choose from when you're asked to research something at work?

2. Why is the organization of a message so important?

3. Does writing sentences effectively have any real-world effects?

4. If your boss writes in a flowery, formal tone and relies on outdated expressions, should you follow that style also?

5. If you notice a co-worker using uncredited sources while drafting a presentation or report, what should you do about it?

6. Why is audience analysis so important in choosing the pattern of organization for a business message?

7. Why are short sentences and short paragraphs appropriate for business communication?

8. Why might it be unethical to use the indirect method of organizing a message?

▌ CHAPTER REVIEW

1. What is the difference between formal and informal research?
2. What is the difference between a list and an outline?
3. What is frontloading, and what are its advantages?
4. When is the indirect method appropriate, and what are the benefits of using it?
5. What are the main types of sentences?
6. Which writing errors cause a lack of conciseness?
7. What types of wording cause a lack of appropriateness?
8. List and explain four strategies for improving document readability.
9. What six areas should you especially pay attention to when you proofread?
10. Should you proofread when you are writing or after you finish? Why?
11. How can technology aid proofreading and revising?
12. How is revising different from proofreading?

▌ WRITING IMPROVEMENT EXERCISES

Wordiness
Revise the following sentences to eliminate wordy phrases, outdated expressions, and long lead-ins.

Example: This is to notify you that at a later date we may be able to submit the report.

Revision: We may be able to submit the report later.

1. In the event that the response is at all favourable, we will in all probability start our Web site in the month of January.
2. This is to advise you that beginning with the date of April 1 all charges made after that date will be charged to your new credit card number.
3. Pursuant to your request, enclosed please find a copy of your August statement.
4. In view of the fact that our sales are increasing in a gradual manner, we must secure a loan in the amount of $50,000.
5. This is to let you know that you should feel free to use your credit card for the purpose of purchasing household items for a period of 60 days.

Needless Adverbs, Fillers, Repetitious Words
Revise the following sentences to eliminate needless adverbs, fillers (such as *there is* and *it is*), and unintentional repetition.

6. It is Web-based technology that is really streamlining administrative processes and reducing business costs for businesses.
7. It is certainly clear that there are many younger managers who are very eager but who are actually unprepared to assume management or leadership roles.
8. There are four employees who definitely spend more time in Internet recreational uses on the Internet than they spend on business-related Internet work.
9. There are definitely five advantages that computers have over a human decision maker.

Redundancies, Jargon, Slang, Clichés
Revise the following sentences to eliminate redundancies, jargon, slang, clichés, and any other wordiness.

Example: Last but not least, Tobias collected together as much support material as possible to avoid getting burned in cash losses or bottom-line profits.

Revision: Finally, Tobias collected as much support material as possible to avoid losing cash or profits.

10. First and foremost, we plan to emphasize an instructional training program.
11. It was the consensus of opinion of members of the committee that the committee should meet at 11 a.m. in the morning.
12. If you will refer back to the contract, you will definitely find that there are specific specifications to prevent anyone from blowing the budget.

13. This memorandum serves as an advance warning that all books and magazines borrowed from the library must be taken back to the library by June 1.

14. In view of the fact that our last presentation failed, we are at this point in time convinced that we must include only the most absolutely essential selling points this time.

15. In the normal course of events, we would wait until such time as we had adequate enough credit reports.

Precise Verbs

Revise these sentences, centring the action in the verbs.

Example: Ms. Tulita gave an appraisal of the Web site.

Revision: Ms. Tulita appraised the Web site.

16. The webmaster made a description of the project.

17. Can you bring about a change in our company travel policy?

18. Web-based customer service will produce the effect of reduction in overall costs.

19. In writing this proposal, we must make application of new government regulations.

20. The board of directors made a recommendation affirming abandonment of the pilot project.

21. An investigator made a determination of the fire damages.

22. We hope to have production of our new line of products by January.

23. The duty of the comptroller is verification of departmental budgets.

24. Please make a correction in my account to reflect my late payment.

Vivid Words

Revise the following sentences to include vivid and concrete language. Add appropriate words.

Example: They said it was a long way off.

Revision: Management officials announced that the merger would not take place for two years.

25. Our new copier is fast.

26. An employee from that company notified us about the change in date.

27. Please contact them soon.

28. They said that the movie they saw was good.

29. Workers improved when they saw the big picture.

30. The report was weak.

Revising Sentences

Revise the following sentences. Identify whether the mistake is a sentence fragment, run-on sentence, or comma splice.

31. Although they began as a side business for Disney. Destination weddings now represent a major income source.

32. About 2,000 weddings are held yearly. Which is twice the number just ten years ago.

33. Weddings may take place in less than one hour, however the cost may be as much as $5,000.

34. Limousines line up outside Disney's wedding pavilion, ceremonies are scheduled in two-hour intervals.

35. Many couples prefer a traditional wedding others request a fantasy experience.

Sentence Types

For each of the numbered sentences, select the letter that identifies its type:

 a. Simple sentence   c. Complex sentence

 b. Compound sentence d. Compound-complex sentence

36. Canadians pride themselves on their informality.

37. When Canadians travel abroad on business, their informality may be viewed negatively.

38. Informality in Asia often equals disrespect; it is not seen as a virtue.

39. The order of first and last names in Asia may be reversed, and this causes confusion to Canadians and Europeans.

40. When you are addressing someone, ask which name a person would prefer to use; however, be sure you can pronounce it correctly.

Organizing Paragraph Sentences

Study the list of seven sentences below from an interoffice memo to hospital staff. Then answer the following questions:

41. Which sentence should be the topic sentence?

42. Which sentence(s) should be developed in a separate paragraph?

43. Which sentences should become support sentences?

1. *The old incident report form caused numerous problems and confusion.*

2. *One problem was that employees often omitted important information.*

3. *The Hospital Safety Committee has revised the form used for incident reports.*

4. *Another problem was that inappropriate information was often included that might expose the hospital to liability.*

5. *The Hospital Safety Committee has scheduled a lunchtime speaker to discuss prevention of medication mistakes.*

6. *Factual details about the time and place of the incident are important, but speculation on causes is inappropriate.*

7. *The new form will be available on April 1.*

 ACTIVITIES AND CASES

3.1 Editing Done Three Ways

Return to Activity 2.4 from the last chapter. If you completed this activity, you should have two different documents: the first e-mail and the second e-mail.

Your Task. Using traditional editing as described in this chapter (with proofreading marks made in pen or pencil on the page itself), edit your two e-mails. Alternatively, edit two e-mails by one of your classmates. Next, try editing the same two e-mails on-screen. Use Microsoft Word's Track Changes feature. How long did it take you to edit the e-mails this way? Did you prefer this way to the traditional way? Why or why not? Finally, try editing the same two e-mails on-screen using Word's Insert Comment feature. How long did it take you to edit the e-mails this way compared to the other two ways? What are the pros and cons of using only the Insert Comment feature? Explain to your fellow students in a short presentation the editing process you've just completed.

3.2 Editing Other Peoples' Writing

As the employee with the best communication skills, you are frequently asked to edit messages. The following e-mail has problems with flabby expressions, long lead-ins, *there is/are* fillers, redundancies, trite business phrases, and other writing techniques you have studied. You may (a) use standard proofreading marks (see Appendix B) to correct the errors here, or (b) download the document from **www.nelson.com/guffeyessentials8ce** and revise it at your computer.

Your instructor may ask you to use the Track Changes feature in Word to show your editing comments. Turn on Track Changes on the Review tab. Click Show Markup. Place your cursor at an error, click New Comment, and key your edit in the bubble box provided. Study the guidelines in the Grammar/Mechanics Handbook as well as the lists of Confusing Words and Frequently Misspelled Words to sharpen your skills.

FIGURE 3.9 Editing With Track Changes

To: Roger M. Karjala <r.m.karjala@cwbank.com>
From: Keiko Kurtz <k.kurtz@cwbank.com>
Subject: Suggestion for Improvement of Customer Relations
Cc:

Roger,

Because of the fact that you asked for suggestions on how to improve customer relations I am submitting my idea. I am writing you this message to let you know that I think we can improve customer satisfaction easy by making a change in our counters.

Last December glass barriers were installed at our branch. There are tellers on one side and customers on the other. The barriers have air vents to be able to allow we tellers to carry on communication with our customers. Management thought that these bullet proof barriers would prevent and stop thiefs from jumping over the counter.

However there were customers who were surprised by these large glass partitions. Communication through them is really extremely difficult and hard. Both the customer and the teller have to raise there voices to be heard. Its even more of a inconvenience when you are dealing with an elderly person or someone who happens to be from another country. Beyond a shadow of a doubt, these new barriers make customers feel that they are being treated impersonal.

I did research into the matter of these barriers and made the discovery that we are the only bank in town with them. There are many other banks that are trying casual kiosks and open counters to make customers feel more at home.

Although it may be easier said than done, I suggest that we actually give serious consideration to the removal of these barriers as a beginning and initial step toward improving customer relations.

Keiko Kurtz
E-mail: k.kurtz@cwbank.com
Support Services
(780) 549-2201

GRAMMAR/MECHANICS REVIEW 3—VERBS

Study each of the following statements. Underline any verbs that are used incorrectly. In the space provided, write the correct form (or *C* if correct).

_____is_____   **Example** Are you certain that the database of our customers' names and addresses <u>are</u> secure?

_____   1. In the company's next annual report is a summary of our environmental audit and a list of charitable donations.

_____   2. Only one of the top-ranking executives have been insured.

_____   3. Toronto-Dominion Bank, along with the other four large banks, offer a variety of savings plans.

_____   4. Neither the plans that this bank offers nor the service just rendered by the teller are impressive.

_____ 5. Finding a good bank and selecting a savings/chequing plan often require considerable research and study.

_____ 6. The budget analyst wants to know whether the Equipment Committee are ready to recommend a printer.

_____ 7. Either of the printers that the committee selects is acceptable to the budget analyst.

_____ 8. If Ms. Davis had chose the Maximizer Plus savings plan, her money would have earned maximum interest.

_____ 9. Although the applications have laid there for two weeks, they may still be submitted.

_____ 10. Jessica acts as if she was the manager.

_____ 11. One of the reasons that our Alaskan sales branches have been so costly are the high cost of living.

● GRAMMAR/MECHANICS CHALLENGE—3

Document for Revision

The e-mail in Figure 3.10 has faults in grammar, punctuation, conversational language, outdated expressions, sexist language, concise wording, long lead-ins, and many other problems. Use standard proofreading marks (see Appendix B) to correct the errors. Study the guidelines in the Grammar/Mechanics Handbook to sharpen your skills. When you finish, your instructor may show you the revised version of this e-mail.

FIGURE 3.10 Agent's Packages

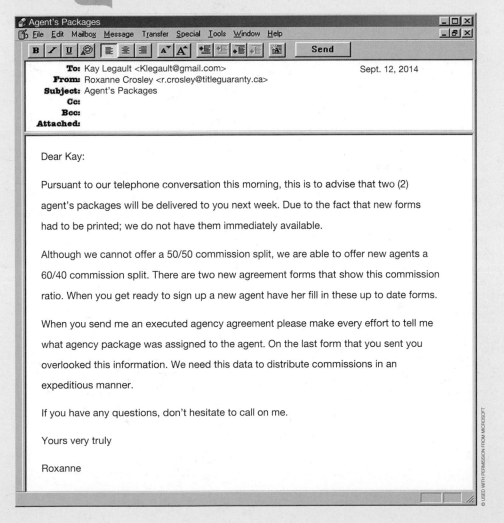

To: Kay Legault <Klegault@gmail.com>
From: Roxanne Crosley <r.crosley@titleguaranty.ca>
Subject: Agent's Packages
Cc:
Bcc:
Attached:

Sept. 12, 2014

Dear Kay:

Pursuant to our telephone conversation this morning, this is to advise that two (2) agent's packages will be delivered to you next week. Due to the fact that new forms had to be printed; we do not have them immediately available.

Although we cannot offer a 50/50 commission split, we are able to offer new agents a 60/40 commission split. There are two new agreement forms that show this commission ratio. When you get ready to sign up a new agent have her fill in these up to date forms.

When you send me an executed agency agreement please make every effort to tell me what agency package was assigned to the agent. On the last form that you sent you overlooked this information. We need this data to distribute commissions in an expeditious manner.

If you have any questions, don't hesitate to call on me.

Yours very truly

Roxanne

REVISING AND EDITING DOCUMENTS IN MS WORD

Collaborative writing and editing projects are challenging. Fortunately, Microsoft Word offers many useful tools to help team members edit and share documents electronically. Three simple but useful editing tools are Text Highlight Colour, Font Colour, and Strikethrough, which you learned about on page 76. These tools, included on the Office Home tab, enable reviewers to point out editing changes. For example, notice how you can use Strikethrough to delete a wordy lead-in or use yellow highlighting to call attention to a misspelled word:

~~This is just a note to let you know that~~ I would appreciate you're help in preparing the announcement about tornado safety tips.

Complex projects, however, may require more advanced editing tools such as Track Changes and Insert Comment.

Track Changes

To suggest specific editing changes to other team members, Track Changes is useful. When this tool is in effect, all changes to a document are recorded in a different colour, with one colour for each reviewer. New text is underlined, and a vertical line appears in the margin to show where changes were made. Text that has been deleted is crossed out. Suggested revisions offered by different team members are identified and dated. The original writer may accept or reject these changes. In Word 2007, you will find Track Changes in the Review menu.

Insert Comment

By using the Insert Comment feature, you can point out problematic passages or errors, ask or answer questions, and share ideas without changing or adding text. When more than one person adds a comment, each comment appears in a different colour and is identified by the individual writer's name and a date/time stamp.

To use this tool in Word 2007, fill in the User Information section. To facilitate adding, reviewing, editing, or deleting comments, click the New Comment button on the Review tab. Then type your comment. In the Draft and Outline views, the reviewing pane opens on the left side or bottom of the screen so that you can enter a comment. In the Print Layout and Web Layout views, a new balloon appears on the right side of the screen.

Career Application

On the job, you will likely be working with others on projects that require the production of written documents. During employment interviews, employers may ask whether you have participated in team projects using collaborative software. To be able to answer that question favourably, take advantage of this opportunity to work on a collaborative document using the features described above.

YOUR TASK

1. Divide into two-person teams. Download the file for Figure 3.9: Editing With Track Changes at **www.nelson.com/guffeyessentials8ce** or type it into a Word document.

2. Team member 1: Edit the message using Track Changes, making all necessary corrections. Save the letter with a file name such as *TrackChangesEdit*.

3. Team Member 2: Edit the message using only the Insert Comment function. Save the letter with a file name such as *InsertCommentsEdit*.

4. Both team members: Compare the edit done with Track Changes and the edit done with Insert Comment. Which is faster and more efficient for an editor? Which is easier for a writer to understand? Which will be most effective at work? Why? Explain your answers to these questions in a brief presentation with two to three PowerPoint slides.

UNIT
03

Forms of Daily Business Writing

CHAPTER 4
E-Mails, Messages, Texts, Social Media, Memos, Letters, and Other Daily Writing

COMMUNICATION TECHNOLOGY IN THE NEWS

Watch Your (Digital) Mouth

Amber MacArthur, "Watch your (digital) mouth, Globe and Mail," July 21, 2010, globeandmail.com, http://www.theglobeandmail.com/news/technology/digital-culture/trending-tech/watch-your-digital-mouth/article1647223. © The Globe and Mail Inc. All Rights Reserved.

According to blogger Cindy Alvarez, there are six kinds of angry emails, ranging from name-calling emails to "frustration-laden tirade emails."

Most of us try to resist sending these types of messages, but sometimes the temptation is overwhelming. It's easy to think that anger management can be just a click away.

But if you want to keep your friends, your job, and your sanity, but are prone to writing angry-sounding messages, take ToneCheck for a spin.

This temper-tracking tool professes to "stop email confusion before it happens." The software, developed by Moncton-based company Lymbix, flags emotional words and phrases, and gives users a chance to make changes before hitting send.

Through a number of positive ratings, such as affection and amusement, to a number of negative ratings, such as fear and anger, the tool analyzes messages for "Tone Tolerance." For example, their online demo identifies this example sentence as one that would prompt review.

"It is time to solidify matters or move on."

ToneCheck describes these words as angry and offers the sender a chance to modify the tone within a preview window.

The email add-on is currently only available for Microsoft Outlook. During the beta release, ToneCheck is free. As for other compatibility beyond Windows, ToneCheck is working on supporting web-based clients.

I interviewed Matt Eldridge, founder and CEO of ToneCheck's parent company, Lymbix.

Amber: How did you come up with the idea for ToneCheck?

Matt: I was a partner and Director of Franchising for a dotcom private sale real estate company, and I found I was good at closing deals face to face and over the phone, but when it came to emails I was losing deals. I found that the tone in my emails was being interpreted as aggressive or harsh and because of that, potential franchise buyers were walking away. I thought there must be a solution, some kind of tone checker that I could download into my email to help with this problem, but after a lot of research discovered there was no such solution. I then started to think about spellcheck and grammar check and really believed that a tone check could be the next step in the natural evolution of those tools.

And voila, ToneCheck was born.

Amber: How big of an issue are negative emails?

Matt: Emails that are seen as negative because tone has been misinterpreted are a very big problem. You have a 50/50 chance of somebody ascertaining the correct tone of your email message and seeing as billions of emails are sent each day, we are solving a very big problem. English as second language is a very lucrative market that I am also excited about, as connotation is lost in translation.

Amber: Where do you plan on developing your product next?

Matt: We will expand beyond Outlook as market demand increases. We chose Outlook strategically because of the client's 500 million users. With that kind of market dominance it made the most sense to tackle that beast first. I have always wanted to build a company with mass market appeal and with our suite of solutions, I believe we will do just that.

Amber: What has been the response so far?

Matt: The response has been overwhelming, with amusement, contentment, excitement and gratitude topping the list. We are solving a problem that almost everyone can identify with and because of that we are starting to gain a lot of traction. We want to help the world communicate more clearly and for people to be truly understood!

Summarize the blog posting you've just read in a paragraph of two to three sentences. Answer the following questions, either on your own or in a small group. Be prepared to present your answers in a short presentation or in an e-mail to your instructor.

QUESTIONS:

1. How does what you've learned in this article change your perception of business communication?

2. How might what you've learned in this article change your own communication style?

3. Come up with pro and con arguments for one of the following debate/discussion topics:

   a) Worrying about the tone of your e-mails at work is a waste of time.

   b) Tools like ToneCheck make us less responsible writers.

CHAPTER
04

E-Mails, Messages, Texts, Social Media, Memos, Letters, and Other Daily Writing

Written Communication in Business

Today's workplaces are still far from paperless, but increasingly, written information is exchanged electronically and on the go. Written communication has become a dynamic, interactive activity. This is quite different than traditional written communication before the Internet, which was a somewhat static exchange between sender and receiver, as per the model of communication we looked at in Chapter 1. Writers today are empowered by their devices (desktops, laptops, tablets, smartphones) to be active participants who correspond with colleagues and outsiders, but who also create content, review products, and edit and share all kinds of information, among other activities.

Today, data are stored on and accessed from remote networks, not just on individual computers. This storing and accessing of data along with software applications in remote network clusters, or "clouds," is called *cloud computing*. Also, virtual private networks (VPN) offer secure access to company information from any location in the world that provides an Internet connection. In addition, in many businesses, desktop computers are fast becoming obsolete with the adoption of ever-smaller laptops, netbooks, smartphones, tablets, and other compact mobile devices. As a result, mobile and cloud computing are the two most important technological trends impacting business communication today.

Businesspeople today are connected—and writing—at all times. Many of them are expected to remain tethered to their jobs (i.e., respond to messages on their smartphones) wherever they are, even on weekends or while on vacation. Some argue that the communications technology revolution of the last 20 years has resulted in amazing productivity gains. However, others point out that technological advances have perhaps created more work (i.e., the 50-hour workweek without overtime for those "i-workers" lucky enough to snag and keep a promising position in a tough economy).

You are probably already sharing photos and music and other files digitally with your friends and family. Even though this technology has entered the workplace, this does not mean your workplace written messages should look and sound the same as your personal written messages. The main difference is the level of structure and formality, which needs to be higher at work than at home. The importance of maintaining this difference is perhaps the most important lesson in business communication today.

This chapter explores how to "do" electronic communication professionally, specifically e-mail, instant messaging, and text messaging in the workplace. You'll also learn about business writing in podcasts, wikis, and social networking sites. Finally, you'll look back at traditional business correspondence: the writing of memos and letters. Knowledge of these traditional forms is still required, despite the ascendancy of electronic communication. Knowing how to write an effective message (whatever the form) saves you time, reduces stress, and builds your image as a professional.

Communicating With Electronic Messages

A number of electronic communication channels enable businesspeople to exchange information rapidly and efficiently. All of these new electronic channels display your writing skills.

- **E-mail.** E-mail involves the transmission of messages through computers and networks. Users can send messages to a single or multiple recipients. When messages arrive in a simulated mailbox, recipients may read, print, forward, store, or delete them. E-mail is most appropriate for short messages that deliver routine requests and responses. It is inappropriate for sensitive, confidential, or lengthy documents. Used professionally, e-mail is a powerful business tool. You will learn more about safe and smart e-mail practices below.

- **Instant messaging.** More interactive than e-mail, instant messaging (IM) involves the exchange of text messages in real time between two or more people logged into an IM service. IM creates a form of private chat room so that individuals can carry on conversations similar to telephone calls. IM is especially useful for back-and-forth online conversations, such as a customer communicating with a technical support person to solve a problem. Like e-mail, instant messaging creates a permanent text record and must be used carefully.

- **Texting.** Sending short messages (160 or fewer characters) from mobile phones and other wireless devices is called *text messaging*, or *texting* for short. This method is available on smartphones and cellphones. Mobile phones can be connected with instant message services, the Web, desktop computers, and even landline telephones. Busy communicators use text messaging for short person-to-person inquiries and responses that keep them in touch while away from the office. Clearly this channel is not appropriate for longer messages that require thought and revision.

- **Social media.** The best-known form of quickly evolving social media is Facebook, but LinkedIn and Twitter are almost as popular. Sites such as Instagram and Pinterest are also gaining popularity due to their highly visual appearance. As its name suggests, social media is about bringing people together, and businesses use social media sites to promote their products, share annual reports, report on sustainability efforts, encourage community partnerships, and so forth. As such, social media is less of a one-to-one communication channel like instant messaging or texting than a one-to-many channel used mostly for marketing and promotion purposes.

- **Podcasts.** A podcast is a digital media file that is distributed over the Internet and downloaded on portable media players and personal computers. Podcasts

Downsized organizations, work teams, increased employee empowerment, and global competition mean more emphasis on internal communication.

are distinguished by their ability to be syndicated, subscribed to, or downloaded automatically when new content is added. In business, podcasts are useful for improving customer relations, marketing, training, product launches, and "viral" marketing (creating online "buzz" about new products).

- **Blogs.** A blog is a Web site with journal entries usually written by one person with comments added by others. It may combine text, images, and links to other blogs or Web pages. Businesses use blogs to keep customers and employees informed and to receive feedback. Company news can be posted, updated, and categorized for easy cross-referencing. Blogs may be a useful tool for marketing and promotion as well as for showing a company's personal side.
- **Wikis.** A wiki is a Web site that enables multiple users to collaboratively create and edit pages. A wiki serves as a central location where shared documents can be viewed and revised by a large or dispersed team. Because a wiki can be used to manage and organize meeting notes, team agendas, and company calendars, it is a valuable project management tool.

Communicating With Paper-Based Messages

Although the business world is quickly switching to electronic and digital communication channels, paper-based documents still serve important functions.

- **Business letters.** Writers draft business letters on company stationery when a permanent record is necessary, when confidentiality is important, when sensitivity and formality are essential, and when a persuasive, well-considered presentation is required. Business letters in English have been around since the early 1500s,[1] and they are still used today as you'll see in some of the situations described in Chapters 5, 6, and 7.
- **Interoffice memos.** Paper-based interoffice memos were invented in the 1870s when large businesses became complex and needed a quick way for information to be transmitted.[2] Today, e-mail has diminished the use of memos, but employees do sometimes use memos to convey confidential internal information. Memos are also still useful for explaining organizational procedures or policies (e.g., dress code; bullying) that become permanent guidelines. Later in this chapter you will learn the various components of interoffice memos, and in Chapters 5, 6, and 7, you'll encounter situations in which a memo may need to be written.

💬 E-Mails and Their Proper Use

E-mail messages are a standard form of communication within organizations. As such, they will probably become your most common business communication channel. These electronic messages perform critical tasks such as informing employees, contacting clients, requesting data, supplying responses, confirming decisions, and giving directions. They generally have a similar format and structure.

Knowing When to Send an E-Mail

E-mail is an appropriate channel for short, informal messages that request information and respond to inquiries. It is especially effective for messages to multiple receivers and messages that must be archived (saved). An e-mail is also appropriate as a cover document when sending longer attachments. E-mail, however, is not always a substitute for face-to-face conversations, telephone calls, business letters, or memos, as we'll see when we discuss these more traditional channels below.

Components of E-Mails

E-mails should contain five parts: (a) an informative subject line that summarizes the message, (b) a salutation, (c) an opening that quickly reveals the main idea (e.g., information, instruction, request, concern, question), (d) a body that explains and/or justifies the main idea, and (e) a professional/friendly closing. E-mails are good at delivering direct messages such as good news (e.g., office closing at noon on Friday), standard information (e.g., meeting times), or routine requests (e.g., please help Sheila get up to speed on the Macquarrie file). They may not the best channel to deliver difficult, complex messages, unless there is an attachment involved.

WRITING PLAN FOR E-MAILS

- **Subject line:** Summarize the main idea in condensed form.
- **Salutation:** Say hello politely.
- **Opening:** Reveal the main idea immediately in expanded form.
- **Body:** Explain and justify the main idea using headings, bulleted lists, and other "high-skim" features when appropriate.
- **Closing:** Include action information, dates, or deadlines; or if appropriate, a summary of the message or a closing thought.

SUBJECT LINE. In e-mails, an informative subject line is extremely important. If your subject line summarizes your central idea, thus providing quick identification for reading and for filing, there is a greater chance it will be paid attention to (or found when someone is searching for it at a later date). Remember that businesspeople receive dozens if not hundreds of e-mails per day. To ensure your e-mail is noticed, your subject line must be specific. Messages without subject lines or with general subject lines may be automatically deleted.

A sure way to have your message deleted or ignored is to use a one-word heading such as *Issue, Problem, Important,* or *Help.* Including a word such as *Free* is dangerous because it may trigger spam filters. Try to make your subject line "talk" by including a verb (e.g., *Reviewing MTO proposal draft*). Or, explain the purpose of the message and how it relates to the reader (e.g., *Answer to question about bonuses*). Remember that a subject line is usually written in an abbreviated style, often without articles (*a, an, the*). It need not be a complete sentence, and it does not end with a period.

> A subject line must be concise but meaningful.

Poor Subject Line	Improved Subject Line
Trade Show	Need You to Showcase Two Items at Our Next Trade Show
Staff Meeting	Rescheduling Staff Meeting for 1 P.M. on May 12
Important!	Please Respond to Job Satisfaction Survey
Parking Permits	Obtain New Employee Parking Permits From HR

SALUTATION. A holdover from letter-writing, e-mails (at least the first one in a chain between you and your correspondent) should include a salutation. The most common salutation is *Hi* as in *Hi, Rachna.* Depending on the receiver (e.g., client, boss) or the situation (e.g., bad news, complaint, asking for a favour), you may sometimes choose to use *Dear* as in *Dear Rachna.* After the initial e-mails have been exchanged, you may find you switch to a one-word salutation such as *Rachna,* or you may stop using any salutation and begin with the opening of the e-mail itself.

OPENING. Most e-mails cover non-sensitive information that can be handled in a straightforward manner. Open e-mails by frontloading; that is, reveal the main idea (information, instruction, request, concern, question) immediately. Even though the purpose of the e-mail is summarized in the subject line, that purpose should be restated—and amplified—in the first sentence. Busy readers want to know immediately why they are reading a message. As you learned in Chapter 3, most messages should begin directly. Notice how the following indirect opener can be improved by frontloading.

Indirect Opening	Direct Opening
For the past six months, the Human Resources Development Department has been considering changes in our employee benefit plan.	Please review the following proposal regarding employee benefits and let me know by May 20 if you approve these changes.

BODY. The body provides more information about the reason for writing. It explains and discusses the subject logically. Effective e-mails should discuss only one topic. Limiting the topic helps the receiver act on the subject and file it appropriately. A writer who, for example, describes a computer printer problem and also requests permission to attend a conference runs a 50 percent failure risk. The receiver may respond to the printer problem but delay or forget about the conference request.

The body of e-mails should have high "skim value." This means that information should be easy to read and comprehend. As covered in the section on document design in Chapter 3, many techniques improve readability. You should use bulleted lists, numbered lists, appropriate typefaces and fonts, and headings, as in the examples below.

Instead of This	Try This
Here are the instructions for operating the copy machine. First, you insert your copy card in the slot. Then you load paper in the upper tray. Last, copies are fed through the feed tray.	Follow these steps to use the copy machine: 1. *Insert* your copy card in the slot. 2. *Load* paper in the upper tray. 3. *Feed* copies through the feed tray.

Instead of This	Try This		
On May 16 we will be in Regina, and Dr. Susan Dillon is the speaker. On June 20, we will be in Saskatoon, and Dr. Diane Minger is the speaker.	**Date** May 16 June 20	**City** Regina Saskatoon	**Speaker** Dr. Susan Dillon Dr. Diane Minger

Instead of This	Try This
To keep exercising, you should make a written commitment to yourself, set realistic goals for each day's workout, and enlist the support of a friend.	To keep exercising, you should (a) make a written commitment to yourself, (b) set realistic goals for each day's workout, and (c) enlist the support of a friend.

CLOSING. Generally, you will close an e-mail with action information or questions, dates, or deadlines. For certain e-mails it may be appropriate to close with a summary of the message, or a closing thought. Here again the value of thinking through the message before actually writing it becomes apparent. The closing is where readers look for deadlines and action language. An effective memo or e-mail closing might be *Please send me the PowerPoint deck by June 15 so that we can have your data before our July planning session.*

In more complex messages, a summary of the main points may be an appropriate closing. If no action request is made and a closing summary is unnecessary, you might end with a simple concluding thought *(I'm glad to answer your questions* or *This sounds like a useful project).* You don't need to close messages to co-workers with goodwill statements such as those found in letters to customers or clients. However, some closing thought is often necessary to prevent a feeling of abruptness.

Closings can show gratitude or encourage feedback with remarks such as *I sincerely appreciate your help* or *What are your ideas on this proposal?* Other closings look forward to what's next, such as *How would you like to proceed?* Avoid closing with overused expressions such as *Please let me know if I may be of further assistance.* This ending sounds mechanical and insincere. In addition, it's good practice to include a closing salutation such as *Cheers, Bye,* or *Thanks,* followed by your first name. If the context is right, a more formal closing salutation such as *Sincerely* or *Warm regards* can be used in e-mails. Sometimes, business writers don't type their name after the *Cheers.* Instead, they simply type a comma after *Cheers* and let their signature block act as their name, as the writer does in Figure 4.2.

Putting It All Together

To see the development of a complete e-mail, look at Figure 4.1. It shows the first draft and revision of an e-mail that Madeleine Espinoza, senior marketing manager, wrote to her boss, Keith Milton. Although it contained solid information, the first draft was so wordy and dense that the main points were lost.

In the revision stage, Madeleine realized that she needed to reorganize her message into an opening, a body, and a closing. She desperately needed to improve its readability. In reviewing what she had written, she recognized that she was talking about two main problems. She discovered that she could present a three-part solution. These ideas didn't occur to her until she had written the first draft. Only in the revision stage was she able to see that she was talking about two separate problems as well as a three-part solution. The revision process can help you think through a problem and clarify a solution.

As she revised, Madeleine was more aware of the subject line, salutation, opening, body, and closing of her message. She used an informative subject line and opened directly by explaining why she was writing. Her opening outlined the two main problems so that her reader understood the background of the recommendations that followed. In the body of the message, Madeleine identified three corrective actions, and she highlighted them for improved readability. Notice that she listed her three recommendations using numbers with boldface headings. Bullets don't always transmit well in e-mail messages. Madeleine closed her message with a deadline and a reference to the next action to be taken.

To see what a well-formatted e-mail looks like, take a look at Figure 4.2. The figure shows a request/question e-mail that has an effective subject line, salutation, opening, body, and closing. The writer uses graphic highlighting techniques to make the e-mail easier to read.

Best Practices for Professional E-Mails

In 2000, the Internet handled about 10 billion e-mails a day. According to Radicati Group Inc., in 2012 that number had gone up to 145 billion per day, of which 90 billion are workplace e-mails and 55 billion, personal e-mails.[3] The number will clearly be much higher soon, given the increased use of BlackBerrys, iPhones, and other

> E-mail has become an essential means of communication within organizations as well as with customers and suppliers.

FIGURE **4.1** Revising an E-Mail

Before

To:　Keith Milton <keith.milton@apex.com>
From:　Madeleine Espinoza <madeleine.espinoza@apex.com>
Subject:　Problems ●———————————————————————————— **Uses one-word, meaningless subject line**
Cc:
Attached:

———————————————————————————— **No salutation included**

Pursuant to your request, I am responding. Your inquiry of April 29 suggested that you ●——— **Fails to reveal purpose quickly**
wanted to know how to deal with the database problems.

In my opinion the biggest problem is that it contains a lot of outdated information, including
customers who haven't purchased anything in five or more years. Another problem is that the ●——— **Buries two problems and three-part solution in difficult-to-read paragraph**
old database is not compatible with the new software that is being used by our mailing
service, and this makes it difficult to merge files. After much thought, I think I can solve both
problems by starting a new database. This would be the place where we put the names of all
new customers. And we would have it keyed using Access software. The problem with
outdated information could be solved by finding out if the customers in our old database wish
to continue receiving our newsletter and product announcements. Finally we would rekey the ●——— **Forgets to conclude with next action and end date**
names of all active customers in the new database. Does this make sense?

Maddy ●————— **Does not provide full contact information**

After

To:　Keith Milton <keith.milton@apex.com>
From:　Madeleine Espinoza <madeleine.espinoza@apex.com>
Provides informative ———— Subject:　How to Improve Our Customer Database
subject line summarizing Cc:
purpose Attached:

Salutation added ———————— ●Hi, Keith,

Opens with concise ———————— ●As you requested, I am submitting my recommendations for improving our customer data-
purpose and highlights base. The database has two major problems. First, it contains many names of individuals who
two problems have not made purchases in five or more years. Second, the format is not compatible with the
new Access software used by our mailing service.

The following three steps, however, should solve both problems:

1. **Build a new database.** Effective immediately, enter the names of all new customers in a new
database using Access software.

Organizes body in num- 2. **Determine the status of customers in our old database.** Send out a mailing asking whether
bered list for readability recipients wish to continue receiving our newsletter and product announcements.

3. **Rekey the names of active customers.** Enter the names of all responding customers in our
new database so that we have only one active database.

Closes with key benefit, ———— ●These changes will enable you, as team leader, to send mailings only to active customers.
deadline, and next action Please let me know by May 10 whether you think these recommendations are workable. If so, I
will investigate costs.

Maddy

Provides name and full ———— ●Madeleine M. Espinoza
contact information Senior Marketing Manager
E-Mail: madeleine.espinoza@apex.com
●Office: (658) 348-8835
●Cell: (632) 348-9820

smartphones. Statistics Canada reports that 81 percent of Canadian private-sector
enterprises use e-mail, while 100 percent of Canadian public-sector workplaces do
so.[4] Companies acknowledge that e-mail has become an indispensable means of
internal communication as well as an essential link to customers and suppliers.

At the same time, as a recent high-profile case demonstrates, companies are
also finding the widespread use of e-mail problematic. A major Canadian bank
recently sued ten of its former employees for what it claimed was illegal use of

FIGURE 4.2 Formatting an E-Mail

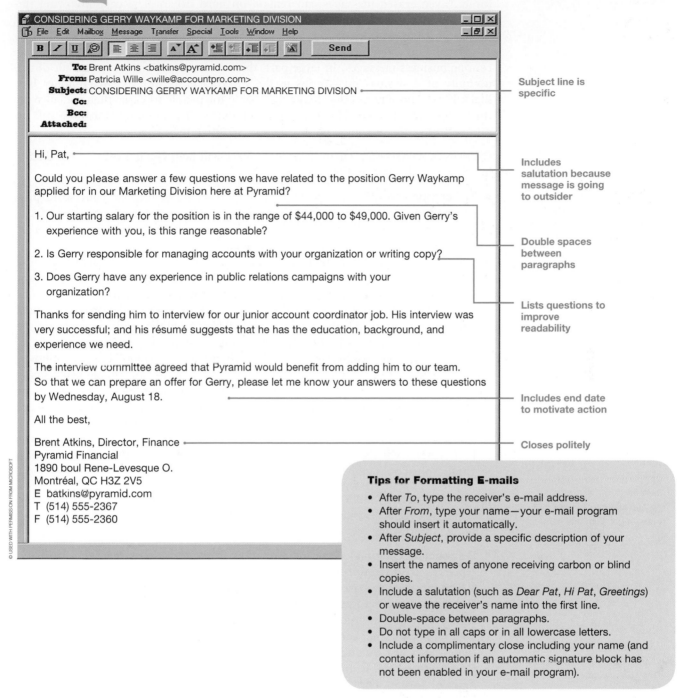

CONSIDERING GERRY WAYKAMP FOR MARKETING DIVISION	_ □ X
File Edit Mailbox Message Transfer Special Tools Window Help	_ ᵭ X

B *I* U   A A **Send**

To: Brent Atkins <batkins@pyramid.com>
From: Patricia Wille <wille@accountpro.com>
Subject: CONSIDERING GERRY WAYKAMP FOR MARKETING DIVISION ──── Subject line is specific
Cc:
Bcc:
Attached:

Hi, Pat, ──── Includes salutation because message is going to outsider

Could you please answer a few questions we have related to the position Gerry Waykamp applied for in our Marketing Division here at Pyramid?

1. Our starting salary for the position is in the range of $44,000 to $49,000. Given Gerry's experience with you, is this range reasonable? ──── Double spaces between paragraphs

2. Is Gerry responsible for managing accounts with your organization or writing copy?

3. Does Gerry have any experience in public relations campaigns with your organization? ──── Lists questions to improve readability

Thanks for sending him to interview for our junior account coordinator job. His interview was very successful; and his résumé suggests that he has the education, background, and experience we need.

The interview committee agreed that Pyramid would benefit from adding him to our team. So that we can prepare an offer for Gerry, please let me know your answers to these questions by Wednesday, August 18. ──── Includes end date to motivate action

All the best,

Brent Atkins, Director, Finance ──── Closes politely
Pyramid Financial
1890 boul Rene-Levesque O.
Montréal, QC H3Z 2V5
E batkins@pyramid.com
T (514) 555-2367
F (514) 555-2360

Tips for Formatting E-mails

- After *To*, type the receiver's e-mail address.
- After *From*, type your name—your e-mail program should insert it automatically.
- After *Subject*, provide a specific description of your message.
- Insert the names of anyone receiving carbon or blind copies.
- Include a salutation (such as *Dear Pat*, *Hi Pat*, *Greetings*) or weave the receiver's name into the first line.
- Double-space between paragraphs.
- Do not type in all caps or in all lowercase letters.
- Include a complimentary close including your name (and contact information if an automatic signature block has not been enabled in your e-mail program).

company-issued smartphones.[5] The employees used the communication devices to send e-mails to each other discussing the setting up of a new and rival company to the bank. The employees obviously didn't realize that the e-mails sent using the smartphones were not private, and that the bank was fully within its rights to store these e-mails.

Today, the average e-mail may remain in the company's computer system for several years. And, in an increasing number of cases, the only impression a person has of the e-mail writer is from a transmitted message; they never actually meet. That's why it's important to take the time to organize your thoughts, compose carefully, and ensure correct grammar and punctuation.

Savvy e-mail communicators are also learning its dangers. They know that their messages can travel (intentionally or unintentionally) to unexpected destinations. A quickly drafted note may end up in the boss's mailbox or forwarded to an unintended receiver. Making matters worse, computers—like elephants—never forget. Even erased messages can remain on hard drives. The case involving the bank discussed above is a cautionary tale for any company-employed business writer naive enough to assume e-mail is a simple, private, two-way communication system.

Despite its dangers and limitations, e-mail is the channel of choice for sending routine business messages. In large part, this increased popularity is a result of the ubiquity of desktops and laptops in the workplace, as well as smartphones like BlackBerrys and iPhones that make it possible for people to carry their e-mail with them wherever they go. However, other channels of communication may still be more effective for sending complex data or sensitive messages.

GETTING STARTED. The following pointers will help you get off to a good start in using e-mail safely and effectively.

- **Try composing offline.** Especially for important messages, use your word processing program to write offline. Then cut and paste your message to your e-mail. This prevents "self-destructing" (losing all your writing through some glitch or pressing the wrong key) when working online.
- **Get the address right.** E-mail addresses can be long and complex, often including letters, numbers, dashes, and underscores. Omit one character or misread the letter *l* for the number *1*, and your message will be returned. Solution: use your electronic address book frequently and use the Reply feature in your e-mail program—most e-mail programs include the correct e-mail address from the original message in the reply message. And double-check every address that you key in manually.
- **Avoid misleading subject lines.** With an abundance of "spam" clogging inboxes and the fear of computer viruses that are spread by e-mail attachments, many e-mail users ignore or delete messages with unclear subject lines. Make sure your subject line is specific and helpful. Generic tags such as "Hello" and "How are you?" may cause your message to be deleted before it is opened.
- **Apply the top-of-screen test.** When readers open your message and look at the first screen, will they see what is most significant? Your subject line and first paragraph should convey your purpose.

CONTENT, TONE, AND CORRECTNESS. Although e-mail seems as casual as a telephone call, it definitely is not. Because it produces a permanent record, think carefully about what you say and how you say it.

- **Be concise.** Omit unnecessary information. Remember that screens are small and typefaces are often difficult to read. Organize your ideas tightly. If you must send a long message, prepare an attachment and use the e-mail as a cover message.
- **Don't send anything you wouldn't want published.** E-mail creates a permanent record that does not go away even when deleted. Every message is a corporate communication that can be used against you or your employer. Don't write anything that you wouldn't want your boss, your family, or a judge to read.
- **Don't use e-mail to avoid contact.** E-mail is inappropriate for breaking bad news or for resolving arguments. For example, it is improper to fire a person by e-mail. It is also a poor channel for clashing with supervisors, subordinates, or others. Before risking hurt feelings, call or pay the person a visit.
- **Care about correctness.** People are still judged by their writing, whether electronic or paper-based. Sloppy e-mail messages (with missing apostrophes, haphazard spelling, and jumbled writing) make readers work too hard. They resent not only the information but also the writer.
- **Care about tone.** Your words and writing style affect the reader. Avoid sounding curt, negative, or domineering. A good way to ensure your tone is appropriate is never to respond in anger—responding angrily almost always leads to more headaches.

> Because e-mail is now the most popular communication channel, messages should be well organized, carefully composed, and grammatically correct.

> Avoid sending e-mails that are longer than one screen.

> Avoid humorous or sarcastic expressions that may be misunderstood.

"Be careful what you write. My wonderful, charming, brilliant boss reads everyone's email."

- **Resist humour and sarcasm.** Without the nonverbal cues conveyed by your facial expression, your voice, and your gestures, humour can easily be misunderstood.

NETIQUETTE. Although e-mail is an evolving communication channel, a number of rules of polite online interaction apply.

- **Don't copy everyone.** Send copies only to people who really need to see the message. It is unnecessary to document every business decision and action with an electronic paper trail.
- **Don't reply to an entire cc list.** Think carefully about whether your reply needs to be seen by everyone on the message or just the person who sent you the message.
- **Don't send or forward spam.** It has recently become illegal in Canada to send spam. For more information, see the Government of Canada's Web site on the new law: **fightspam.gc.ca/eic/site/030.nsf/eng/h_00039.html.**
- **Use capital letters only for emphasis or for titles.** Avoid writing entire messages or phrases in all caps, which is equivalent to shouting.
- **Announce attachments.** If you're sending an attachment, tell your receiver in the body of your e-mail. Consider summarizing or highlighting important aspects of the attachment briefly in the e-mail.
- **Consider asking for permission before forwarding.** For messages containing private or project-specific information, obtain approval before forwarding to others.

READING AND REPLYING TO E-MAIL. The following tips can save you time and frustration when reading and answering e-mails.

- **Scan all messages in your inbox before replying to each individually.** Because subsequent messages often affect the way you respond, read them all first, especially those from the same sender.
- **Print only when necessary.** Generally, read and answer most messages online without printing. Use folders to archive messages that should be saved. Print only those messages that are complex, controversial, or involve significant decisions and follow-up.
- **Acknowledge receipt.** If you can't reply immediately, say when you can (*Will respond Friday*).
- **Don't automatically return the sender's message.** When replying, avoid irritating your recipients by returning the entire "thread" or sequence of messages on a topic, unless the thread needs to be included to provide context for your remarks.
- **Revise the subject line if the topic changes.** When replying or continuing an e-mail exchange, revise the subject line as the topic changes.
- **Respond to messages quickly and efficiently.** Set yourself a goal of replying to all messages on the day they are received. After answering e-mails, file them in a project-specific folder if necessary.
- **Never respond when you are angry.** Calm down before replying to an upsetting message. You will come up with different and better options after thinking about what was said. If possible, iron out differences in person.

PERSONAL USE. Remember that office computers are meant for work-related communication.

- **Limit use of company computers for personal matters.** Unless your company specifically allows it, don't use your employer's computers for personal messages, personal shopping, or entertainment.
- **Assume that all e-mail is monitored.** Employers legally have the right to monitor e-mail, and about 60 percent of them do so.

OTHER SMART E-MAIL PRACTICES. Depending on your messages and audience, the following tips promote effective electronic communication.

- **Design messages effectively.** When a message is long, help the reader with headings, bulleted lists, and perhaps an introductory summary that describes what will follow. Although these techniques lengthen a message, they shorten reading time.

Cathy

- **Consider cultural differences.** Be clear and precise in your language. Remember that figurative clichés (*pull up stakes*, *playing second fiddle*), sports references (*hit a home run*, *play by the rules*), and slang (*cool*, *stoked*) can cause confusion abroad.
- **Double-check before hitting the Send button.** Have you included everything? Avoid the necessity of sending a second message, which makes you look careless. Edit for grammar and style and tone (remember, no anger or sarcasm!) and ensure your answer makes sense before sending.

Instant Messaging and Texting and Their Proper Use

Making their way from teen bedrooms to office boardrooms, instant messaging and text messaging have become permanent and powerful communication tools. IM enables you to use the Internet to communicate in real time in private chat rooms with one or more individuals. It is like live e-mail or a text telephone call. More and more workers are using it as a speedy communication channel to exchange short messages.

Text messaging, or texting, is another popular means for exchanging brief messages in real time. Usually delivered by smartphone, texting requires a short message service (SMS) supplied by a cellphone service provider. When multimedia files are being shared on a phone, MMS (or multimedia messaging service) is required.

How Instant Messaging and Texting Work

To send an instant message, you might use Microsoft's Windows Live Messenger, Yahoo! Messenger, or AOL's Instant Messenger, or newer services such as Google Talk, Digsby, and Trillian Astra that integrate social network updates.[6] Once service is installed, you enter your name and password to log on. The software checks to see if any of the users in your contact list are currently logged in. If the server finds any of your contacts, it sends a message back to your computer. If the person you wish to contact is online, you can click that person's name and a window opens that you can enter text into. You enter a message, such as that shown in Figure 4.3, and click Send. Unlike e-mail, IM and texting provide no elaborate page layout options. The text box is small, and pressing the Enter key sends the message. Obviously, it is designed for brief but fast text interaction.

New applications allow people to use IM not only on their computers but also on their handheld devices such as the popular iPhone, shown in Figure 4.4. Many smartphones work on a 3G or 4G cellphone network where they consume minutes, but they may also allow generally free Wi-Fi access where available.

Texting, on the other hand, usually requires a smartphone or PDA, and users are charged for the service, often by choosing a flat rate for a certain number of text or media messages per month. Voice over Internet Protocol (VoIP) providers,

FIGURE 4.3 Sample Workplace Instant Message Conversation

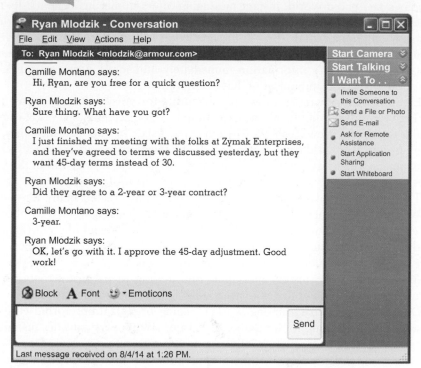

Ryan Mlodzik - Conversation

File   Edit   View   Actions   Help

To: Ryan Mlodzik <mlodzik@armour.com>

Camille Montano says:
  Hi, Ryan, are you free for a quick question?

Ryan Mlodzik says:
  Sure thing. What have you got?

Camille Montano says:
  I just finished my meeting with the folks at Zymak Enterprises,
  and they've agreed to terms we discussed yesterday, but they
  want 45-day terms instead of 30.

Ryan Mlodzik says:
  Did they agree to a 2-year or 3-year contract?

Camille Montano says:
  3-year.

Ryan Mlodzik says:
  OK, let's go with it. I approve the 45-day adjustment. Good
  work!

Start Camera
Start Talking
I Want To . .
  Invite Someone to this Conversation
  Send a File or Photo
  Send E-mail
  Ask for Remote Assistance
  Start Application Sharing
  Start Whiteboard

Block   A Font   Emoticons

Send

Last message received on 8/4/14 at 1:26 PM.

such as Skype, now offer texting. For a small fee, Skype subscribers can send text messages to SMS-enabled cellphones in Canada and IM messages both domestically and internationally. Skype and other formerly computer-based applications are simultaneously available on mobile devices and are making communication on the go more convenient than ever before.

FIGURE 4.4 Texting With a Smartphone

Apple's iPhone (and its competitors, such as Samsung's Galaxy) allows you to text, i.e., have brief written conversations in real-time with other texters, in a highly visual, user-friendly medium.

Pros and Cons of Instant Messaging and Texting

In today's fast-paced world, instant messaging offers numerous benefits. Its major attraction is real-time communication with colleagues anywhere in the world—so long as a cellphone signal or a Wi-Fi connection is available. IM is a convenient alternative to the telephone and may eventually even replace e-mail. Because IM allows people to share information immediately and make decisions quickly, its impact on business communication has been dramatic.

Like IM, texting can be a low-cost substitute for voice calls, delivering a message between private mobile phone users quietly and discreetly. SMS is particularly popular in Europe, New Zealand, Australia, and Asia.[7] In bulk text messages, companies around the world provide news alerts, financial information, and advertising to customers. Texts have been used in game shows for TV voting, and in the United States most notably to select contestants on *American Idol*.

The immediacy of instant and text messaging has created many fans. A user knows right away whether a message was delivered. Messaging avoids phone tag and eliminates the downtime associated with personal telephone conversations. Another benefit includes "presence functionality." Co-workers can locate each other online, thus avoiding having to hunt down someone who is out of the office. Many people consider instant messaging and texting to be productivity boosters because they enable them to get answers quickly and allow multitasking.

Despite its popularity among workers, some organizations forbid employees to use instant messaging for a number of reasons. Employers consider instant messaging yet another distraction in addition to the interruptions caused by the telephone, e-mail, and the Web. Organizations also fear that privileged information and company records will be revealed through public instant messaging systems, which hackers can easily penetrate. Organizations worry about *phishing* (fraudulent) schemes, viruses, malware, and *spim* (IM spam).

Like e-mail, instant and text messages can become evidence in lawsuits. Moreover, companies may fear instant messaging and texting because businesses are required to track and store messaging conversations to comply with legal requirements. This task adds significant expense to an operating budget. Finally, IM and texting have been implicated in inappropriate workplace uses such as *sexting*.

> Organizations may ban instant messaging because of productivity, security, litigation, and compliance fears.

Best Practices for Instant Messaging and Texting

Instant messaging can definitely save time and simplify communications with co-workers and customers. Before using IM or text messaging on the job, however, be sure you have permission. Do not use public systems without checking with your supervisor. If your organization does allow IM and texting, you can use it efficiently and professionally by following these best practices:

- Learn about your organization's IM and texting policies. Are you allowed to use instant messaging? With whom may you text?
- Don't text or IM while driving a car. Pull over if you must read or send a message.
- Make yourself unavailable when you need to complete a project or meet a deadline.
- Organize your contact lists to separate business contacts from family and friends.
- Keep your messages simple and to the point. Avoid unnecessary chitchat, and know when to say goodbye.
- Don't use IM or texts to send confidential or sensitive information.
- Be aware that instant messages and texts can be retrieved. As with e-mail, don't say anything that would damage your reputation or that of your organization.
- If personal messaging is allowed, keep it to a minimum. Your organization may prefer that personal chats be done during breaks or the lunch hour.
- Show patience by not blasting multiple messages to co-workers if a response is not immediate.
- Keep your presence status current so that people trying to reach you don't waste their time.

- Beware of jargon, slang, and abbreviations, which, although they may reduce keystrokes, may be confusing and appear unprofessional.
- Respect your receivers by employing proper grammar, spelling, and proofreading.

Social Media as a Business Writing Channel

Far from being only entertaining leisure sites, social networking sites such as Facebook and Twitter are used by businesses to communicate with customers and other stakeholders. Social networking sites enable businesses to connect with customers and employees, persuade customers to buy products and services, share company news, and exchange ideas.

How Businesses Use Social Networks

Some firms use social online communities for brainstorming and teamwork. They provide the collaboration tools and watch what happens. BT Group (formerly British Telecom) has about 11,000 employees on Facebook in addition to offering its own internal social network. A BT Group IT executive says that his company can observe online relationships to see how information travels and decision making occurs. The company is able to identify teams that form spontaneously and naturally and then assigns targeted projects to them. Idea generators are easy to spot. The BT executive considers these contributors invaluable, suggesting that "a new class of supercommunicators has emerged."[8]

Other companies harness the power of online communities to boost their brand image or to provide a forum for collaboration, as in the Netflix example in Figure 4.5. McDonald's has a strong presence on Facebook boasting nearly 1.5 million "fans." The fast-food chain also maintains a private networking site, StationM, for its 650,000 hourly employees in 15,000 locations across the United States and Canada.[9]

U.S.-based insurer MetLife has launched connect.MetLife, an online social network collaboration tool. Resembling Facebook, this internal networking tool sits safely behind the corporate firewall.[10] Consumer electronics chain Best Buy has created its own social network, Blue Shirt Nation, with currently more than 20,000 participants, most of them sales associates. IBM's in-house social network, Beehive, has 30,000 employees on it. Managers notice avid networkers who create buzz and promote the brand. The drawback is that quieter employees may be overlooked.[11]

Potential Risks of Social Networks for Businesses

Online social networks hold great promise for businesses while also presenting some risk. Most managers want plugged-in employees with strong tech skills. They like to imagine their workers as brand ambassadors. They fantasize about their products becoming overnight sensations thanks to viral marketing. However, they also fret about incurring productivity losses, compromising trade secrets, attracting the wrath of huge Internet audiences, and facing embarrassment over inappropriate and damaging employee posts.[12]

Businesses take different approaches to the "dark side" of social networking. Some, such as Zappos.com, take a hands-off approach to employee online activity. Others, such as IBM, have drafted detailed policies to cover all forms of self-expression online. Some of IBM's guidelines include being honest about one's identity, accepting personal responsibility for published posts, and hitting Send only after careful thought. The technology giant asks its workers to avoid any controversies outside their professional role. The company wants workers to "add value" as they are building their social reputations, not dwell on trivia.[13] Finally, Enterprise Rent-A-Car and other organizations block some or all social media sites.

Younger workers in particular are often stunned when their employers block access to Facebook, Gmail, and other popular Web destinations. One 27-year-old

> Social networking sites allow businesses to connect with customers and employees, sell products and services, share company news, and exchange ideas.

FIGURE 4.5 How Companies Use Facebook: Netflix

Large corporations thrive on Facebook. *Slate* magazine recently ranked Coca-Cola, with over 5 million fans, as "first among companies with the best Facebook presences." Newer companies such as Netflix involve customers in rating their products and services on Facebook to establish a social media presence.

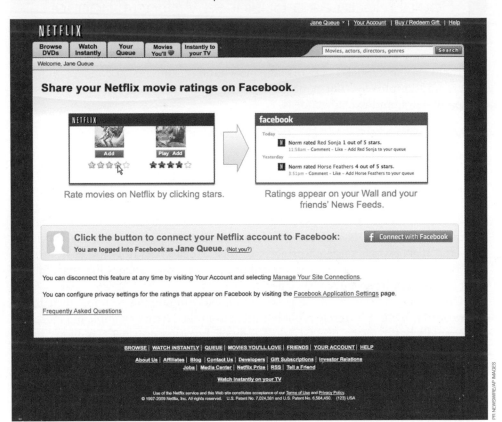

complained in the media about his former employer: "It was a constant battle between the people that saw technology as an advantage, and those that saw it as a hindrance."[14] The key is to strike a balance between allowing employees access to the Web and protecting security and ensuring productivity.

Tips for Using Social Networking Sites and Keeping Your Job

Experts agree that, as with any public online activity, users of social networking sites would do well to exercise caution. Privacy is a myth, and sensitive information should not be shared lightly, least of all risqué photographs. Furthermore, refusing "friend" requests or "unfriending" individuals could jeopardize professional relationships. Consider the following tip by career counsellor Julie Powell[15] if you like to visit social networking sites and want to keep your job: Establish boundaries. Don't share information online that you would not be comfortable sharing openly in the office.

The advice to think twice before posting online applies to most communication channels used on the job. Facebook expert and blogger Nick O'Neill cautions account holders never to assume that the content they post on a social networking site is protected unless they have activated the privacy option. Many users leave their pages open and risk trouble with their employers by assuming that online comments are hidden from view.[16] Even privacy settings, however, do not guarantee complete protection from prying eyes.

Among the many risks in the cyber world are inappropriate photographs and making "friends" online. Tags make pictures searchable so that an embarrassing college

WORKPLACE IN FOCUS

While most social networking sites connect people in cyberspace, Foursquare's geosocial networking service connects people in real spaces. Launched in 2009, the location-sharing app encourages mobile device users to "check in" at local stores, restaurants, and offices. The GPS feature sends meet-up alerts whenever contacts from one's social network are in the vicinity. Professionals tout Foursquare's face-to-face networking potential; Starbucks uses the service to deliver mobile customer rewards programs. How is mobile computing changing the way we do business?

incident may resurface years later. Another potential minefield, says consultant Rachel Weingarten, is rejecting friend requests from some colleagues while accepting such offers from others.[17] The snubbed co-worker may harbour ill feelings as a result. Blocking a user for no apparent reason could also be interpreted as a rude rejection.

Sharing Information Through RSS Feeds and Social Bookmarking

You may wonder how businesspeople navigate the vast resources available on the Internet. Seeking information on the Web that is relevant to you and your business can be time-consuming. Really simple syndication (RSS for short) is a time saver, allowing users to monitor many news sources in one convenient spot. Likewise, social bookmarking helps busy professionals stay informed about topics of interest and negotiate the vast information jungle of the Web.

> RSS feeds allow users to monitor many news sources at once.

REALLY SIMPLE SYNDICATION. RSS, a fast and easy way to search and manage information, is a data file format capable of transmitting changing Web content. News organizations, bloggers, and other online information providers syndicate (i.e., publish and distribute) their content to subscribers. RSS documents are called feeds or channels, and they can be read most efficiently with a Web-based feed reader (also known as an aggregator), an easy-to-use software application. Feeds help alert subscribers to up-to-the-minute blog entries, news items, videos, and podcasts from various sources.

How does RSS work? Each time a syndicated Web site is updated, a summary of the new information travels by RSS feed to the site's subscribers. Users can read RSS feeds within their Internet browsers and in e-mail programs such as MS Outlook, or use popular news aggregators such as Google Reader, Bloglines, SharpReader, NetNewsWire, and Straw. Web-based feed readers also work well with mobile devices, helping busy executives keep up with customized news feeds on the go.

Forward-looking companies such as retailer Target, online travel sites such as Travelocity, and many airlines have been using RSS feeds to alert customers to weekly sales and special offers.

SOCIAL BOOKMARKING. In the battle for "eyeballs" on the Internet, social bookmarking is another critical component. Business Web sites, blogs, and other online content gain an edge if readers link to them and, thus, share content with other online users. Digg, delicious, reddit, StumbleUpon, and squidoo are just a few of the many fast-growing social bookmarking and content aggregator (collector)

> In what ways is social bookmarking helpful to business users?

Web sites. Social bookmarking helps users search, organize, manage, and store bookmarks on the Web with the help of metadata—that is, information tags or keywords.

Many Web sites, blogs, and other content providers on the Internet offer various widgets or icons of social bookmarking sites to enable content sharing. Web publishers hope readers will link their information to social bookmarking sites and alert others to the information.

Perhaps you can see now how RSS feeds and social bookmarking sites could help you stay abreast of breaking news from many sources and save you valuable time. Whether you wish to grab a broadcast from your favourite news source or check the most recent sports scores, look for the square orange RSS feed icon, or, on most high-traffic Web sites, you will also see Share links, or widgets, that will take you to social bookmarking sites.

Podcasts, Blogs, and Wikis for Business Writing

Podcasts, blogs, and wikis are part of the new user-centred virtual environment called Web 2.0. Far from being passive consumers, today's Internet users have the power to create Web content; interact with businesses and each other; review products, self-publish, or blog; contribute to wikis; or tag and share images and other files. Individuals wield enormous power because they can potentially reach huge audiences. For this reason, businesses often rightly fear the wrath of disgruntled employees and customers. On the other hand, this connectedness also allows businesses to curry favour with influential plugged-in opinion leaders.

The widespread use of the Web means that, in the online world, Internet users can bypass gatekeepers who filter content in the traditional print and visual media. Hence, even extreme views often reach audiences of thousands or even millions. The dangers are obvious. Fact checking often falls by the wayside, buzz may become more important than truth, and a single keystroke can make or destroy a reputation. This section addresses prudent business uses of podcasts, blogs, and wikis because you are likely to encounter these and other electronic communication tools on the job.

Business Podcasts

The words *broadcast* and *iPod* combined to create the word *podcast*; however, audio and video files can be played on any number of devices, not just Apple's iPod. Podcasts can extend from short clips of a few minutes to 30-minute or longer digital files. Naturally, large video files gobble up a lot of memory, so they tend to be streamed on a Web site rather than downloaded.

HOW ORGANIZATIONS USE PODCASTS. Like blogging, podcasting has experienced large growth and has spread among various user groups online. Major news and media organizations podcast radio and television shows. Podcasts are also used in education. Students can access instructors' lectures, listen to interviews, watch sporting events, and access other content. Apple's iTunes U distributes free educational podcasts from Berkeley, Stanford, and other universities. Canadian universities such as McGill and Alberta have strong podcast sites. Check out McGill University's series of podcasts on contemporary issues in business at **http://podcasts.mcgill.ca/business -leadership.** Corporations, such as Canadian accounting giant PwC, use podcasting to enrich their client service offerings. Check out PwC's series of podcasts on contemporary issues in business at **www.pwc.com/ca/en/strategy-talks/index.jhtml.** Unlike streaming video that users can view only with an active Internet connection, podcasts encoded as MP3 files can be downloaded to a computer, a smartphone, or an MP3 player to be enjoyed on the go, often without subsequent Web access.

DELIVERING AND ACCESSING PODCASTS. Businesses have embraced podcasting for sending audio and video messages that do not require a live presence yet offer a friendly human face. Because they can broadcast repetitive information that does not require interaction, podcasts can replace costlier live teleconferences. Many

Used by the news media, in education, and in corporate training, podcasts are digital audio or video files that can be downloaded to a computer or watched on a smartphone.

organizations now train their sales force with podcasts that are available any time. Real estate agents create podcasts to enable buyers to take virtual walking tours of available properties at their leisure. Human resources policies can also be presented in the form of podcasts for unlimited viewing on demand or when convenient. Marketing pitches also lend themselves to podcasting.

Podcasts are featured on media Web sites and company portals or shared on social networking sites and blogs. They can usually be streamed or downloaded as media files. Really simple syndication (RSS) allows the distribution of current information published in podcasts, blogs, video files, and news items. Users can select RSS feeds from various sources and personalize the information they wish to receive.

CREATING A PODCAST. Producing a simple podcast does not require sophisticated equipment. With inexpensive recording, editing, and publishing software such as the popular Propaganda, ePodcast Creator, Audacity, or Gabcast, users can inform customers, mix their own music, or host interviews. In fact, any digital recorder can be used to create a high-quality simple podcast, especially if the material is scripted and well rehearsed. If you are considering creating your own podcast, here are a few tips:

> Creating a simple, yet professional podcast is easy and relatively inexpensive.

- **Decide whether to record one podcast or a series.** You can create a one-time podcast for a specific purpose or a series of podcasts on a related subject. Make sure you have enough material to sustain a steady flow of information.
- **Download software.** The program Audacity is available for free; other popular recording and editing software programs are relatively inexpensive.
- **Obtain hardware.** Depending on the sound quality you desire, you may need a sophisticated microphone and other audio equipment. The recording room must be properly shielded against noise, echo, and other interference. Many universities and some libraries provide language labs that feature recording booths.
- **Organize the message.** Make sure your broadcast has a beginning, middle, and end. Build in some redundancy. Tell the listeners what you will tell them, then tell them, and finally, tell them what you have told them. This principle, known to effective PowerPoint users, also applies to podcasting. Previews, summaries, and transitions are important to help your audience follow the message.
- **Choose an extemporaneous or scripted delivery.** Think about how you will deliver the information, whether speaking freely or using a manuscript. Extemporaneous delivery means that you prepare, but you use only brief notes. It usually sounds more spontaneous and natural than reading from a script, but it can also lead to redundancy, repetition, and flubbed lines. Reading from a script, if done skillfully, can sound natural and warm. However, in the wrong hands, reading can come across as mechanical and amateurish.
- **Prepare and practise.** Before recording, do a few practise runs. Editing audio or video is difficult and time-consuming. Try to get your recording right, so that you won't have to edit much.
- **Publish and distribute your message.** If you post the podcast to a blog, you can introduce it and solicit your audience's feedback. Consider distributing your podcast through an RSS feed.

Professional Blogs and Twitter

A blog is a Web site with journal entries on any imaginable topic. It is usually written by one person, although some blogs feature multiple commentators. Typically, readers leave feedback. Businesses use blogs to keep customers and employees informed and to interact with them. The biggest advantage of business blogs is that they potentially reach a far-flung, vast audience.

> Blogs are online journals used by companies to communicate internally with employees and externally with customers.

Marketing and advertising firms and their clients are looking closely at blogs because blogs can produce unbiased consumer feedback faster and more cheaply than such staples of consumer research as focus groups and surveys. Employees and executives at companies such as Boeing, Target, and Whole Foods maintain blogs. They use blogs to communicate internally with employees and externally with clients. Currently,

28 percent of Fortune 500 companies are blogging.[18] As an online diary or journal, a blog allows visitors to leave public comments. At this time, writers have posted 163 million blogs, and this number is growing by about 76,000 blogs per day.[19]

Twitter falls between the blog and social media categories. It is often referred to as a microblogging service, but it also invites social networking. It allows users to share brief status updates called tweets about their lives and their whereabouts online. Twitter users can access the service by computer or with their smartphones.

In some industries, companies are using Twitter and other social media to monitor what is being said about them, to engage with customers, and to market to other businesses. There are good and bad ways of doing this, as you'll see by reading Buzz Bishop's recent blog post on the topic "How to Use a Company Twitter Account" at **www.cyberbuzz.com/2009/03/13/how-to-use-a-company-twitter-account.**

In tweets of 140 characters or fewer, Starbucks replies to customer questions, while social media veteran Southwest Airlines has a particularly impressive online presence, boasting 12 million monthly visits to its Web site, 1.3 million Facebook fans, and 1 million Twitter followers.[20] An early adopter of Facebook and Twitter, the quirky airline appointed "tweet watchers" who troubleshoot air travellers' problems. Other airlines also tweet actively, as you can see in Figure 4.6.[21]

FIGURE 4.6 Corporate Twitter Feed

True North Airlines
Welcome to the Twitter page of True North Airlines. Our Twitter feed is active between 8:00 am and 4:00 pm EST seven days a week!
Vancouver, BC Joined 2009

Tweets	Photos/Videos	Following	Followers		
65K	817	9.5K	257K		Follow

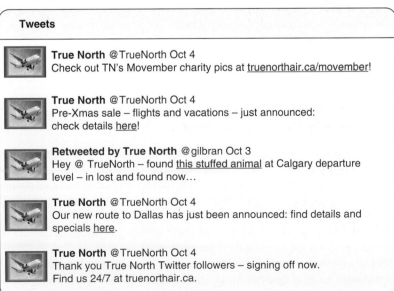

Tweets

True North @TrueNorth Oct 4
Check out TN's Movember charity pics at truenorthair.ca/movember!

True North @TrueNorth Oct 4
Pre-Xmas sale – flights and vacations – just announced: check details here!

Retweeted by True North @gilbran Oct 3
Hey @ TrueNorth – found this stuffed animal at Calgary departure level – in lost and found now…

True North @TrueNorth Oct 4
Our new route to Dallas has just been announced: find details and specials here.

True North @TrueNorth Oct 4
Thank you True North Twitter followers – signing off now.
Find us 24/7 at truenorthair.ca.

How Companies Use Blogs

The potential applications of blogs in business are vast. Like other Web 2.0 phenomena, corporate blogs usually invite feedback and help build communities. Specifically, companies use blogs for public relations, customer relations, crisis communication, market research, viral marketing, internal communication, and recruiting.

PUBLIC RELATIONS, CUSTOMER RELATIONS, AND CRISIS COMMUNICATION. One of the prominent uses of blogs is to provide up-to-date company information to the press and the public. Blogs can be written by the marketing department, executives, or by rank-and-file employees. Canadian food company McCain's blog—"the all good blog" shown in Figure 4.7—promotes itself as a place to share what inspires the company. Iconic Canadian clothing manufacturer Roots takes a different approach, with a visual Blog on Tumblr called "The Lodge." General Electric's Global Research blog addresses industry insiders and the interested public. Similarly, after experimenting with in-house blogs and proprietary social networks, Best Buy introduced BBY, Best Buy Community, a blog and social networking site for employees and managers. The company's chief marketing officer, Barry Judge, runs a corporate blog on a Web site bearing his name.

A company blog is a natural forum for late-breaking news, especially when disaster strikes. Business bloggers can address rumours and combat misinformation. Although a blog cannot replace other communication channels in an emergency, it should be part of the overall effort to soothe the public's emotional reaction with a human voice of reason.

FIGURE 4.7 A Corporate Blog

McCain Foods' blog, *The All Good Blog*, includes user-friendly features such as a search function, a list of contributors, a list of popular topics, and an simple navigation menu bar.

MARKET RESEARCH. Because most blogs invite feedback, they can be invaluable sources of opinion from customers and industry experts. In addition to monitoring visitor comments on their corporate blogs, many companies now have appointed employees who scrutinize the blogosphere for buzz, and positive and negative postings about their organization and products.

ONLINE COMMUNITIES. Like Twitter, which has a loyal core following, company blogs can attract a devoted community of participants who want to keep informed about company events, product updates, and other news. In turn, those enthusiasts can contribute new ideas. Similar to Dell's *IdeaStorm*, Starbucks' blog *Ideas In Action* solicits product and service ideas from customers.

INTERNAL COMMUNICATION AND RECRUITING. Blogs can be used to keep virtual teams on track and to share updates on the road. Members in remote locations can stay in touch by smartphone and other devices, exchanging text, images, sound, and video clips. In many companies, blogs have replaced hard-copy publications in offering late-breaking news or tidbits of interest to employees. They feature profiles of high-performing workers, information about benefits, and so forth. Blogs mirror the company culture and present an invaluable opportunity for job candidates to size up a potential employer and the people working there.

Tips for Creating a Professional Blog

Blogging has grown up as a commercial activity and now offers sound business opportunities. Some bloggers make a living, although most remain unknowns in the boundless thickets of information on the Internet. To even have a shot at competing with established blog sites, consider the following guidelines for starting a successful business blog:

> Like all business messages, blog entries must be well targeted, carefully crafted, and professional.

- **Identify your audience.** As with any type of communication, you must know your audience to decide what to write to get people to read your blog. Does your blog stand out? What makes you interesting and unique?
- **Find a home for your blog.** You can use software that will let you attach a blog function to your Web site. Alternatively, you can join a blog hosting site that will provide a link on your Web site to attract visitors. You can usually find templates and other options to help build traffic to your site, especially if you use trackers that identify recent posts and popular message threads. According to Blogtap, currently the top three blog hosting sites are WordPress, Google Blogger, and TypePad.[22]
- **Craft your message.** Blog about topics that showcase your expertise and insights. Offer a fresh, unique perspective on subjects your audience cares about. Your writing should be intriguing and sincere. Experts suggest that authors get to know the blogosphere in their industry and comment on what other bloggers are writing about. Stick with what you know.
- **Make "blogrolling" work for you.** Your goal is to attract repeat visitors to your blog. One way to achieve this objective is to increase traffic between blogs. "Blogrolling" means that you provide links to other sites or blogs on the Web that you find valuable and that are related to your business or industry. Respond to other bloggers' postings and link to them.
- **Attract search engines by choosing the right keywords.** In headlines and text, emphasize potential search terms that may draw traffic to your site. Focus on one topic and use a variety of synonyms to propel your blog to the top of search engine listings. An import company doing business with China would want to stress the keywords *import* and *China* as well as *trade, Asia,* and so forth, in addition to more industry-specific terms, such as *toys.*
- **Blog often.** Provide fresh content regularly. Stay current. Stale information puts off visitors. Post short, concise messages, but do so often.
- **Monitor the traffic to your site.** If necessary, vary your subject to attract interest. If traffic slows down, experiment with new themes while staying within your

core business and expertise. Also, evaluate the effectiveness of your publishing platform. Some blog publishing sites are more valuable than others in increasing your blog's visibility to search engines.

- **Seek permission.** If you are employed, explore your company's blogging policy. Even if neither a policy nor a prohibition against blogging exists, avoid writing about your employer, co-workers, customers, and events at the office, however veiled your references may be. The Internet is abuzz with stories about bloggers who got fired for online indiscretions.
- **Stay away from inappropriate topics.** Whether you are a rank-and-file employee or a freelance blogger, remember not to write anything you wouldn't want your family, friends, and the public at large to read. Blogs are not private journal entries; therefore, don't entrust to them any risqué, politically extreme, or private information.

How Businesses Use Wikis

At least as important to business as blogs are wikis. A wiki is a Web site that employs easy-to-use collaborative software to allow users to create documents that can be edited by tapping into the same technology that runs the well-known online encyclopedia Wikipedia. Large companies, such as BT Group (previously British Telecom), use wikis to connect company representatives with developers and create a community that will contribute to the knowledge base of a product or service.[23] With its Forum Nokia, the Finnish cellphone maker is one of many companies—for example, IBM, Microsoft, and Disney—that maintain wikis. Most corporate projects are facilitated with the help of wikis, a tool that is especially valuable across vast geographic distances and multiple time zones.

> Teams use wikis to create and edit documents, whether across geographic distances and multiple time zones or in-house.

Far from being just a tool for geeks, wikis are used beyond information technology departments. The five main uses range from providing a shared internal knowledge base to storing templates for business documents.

- **The global wiki.** For companies with a global reach, a wiki is an ideal tool for information sharing between headquarters and satellite offices. Team members can easily edit their work and provide input to the home office and each other.

FIGURE 4.8 A Corporate Wiki

SAS, a leading provider of business analytics software, maintains a corporate wiki. The wiki is used as a knowledge base where employees can go to look up topics, such as data mining, or post information.

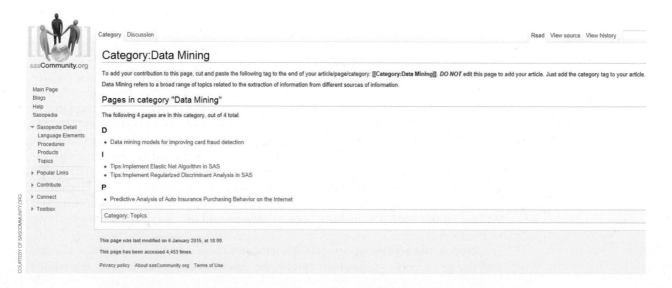

- **The wiki knowledge base.** Teams or departments use wikis to collect and disseminate information to large audiences, thereby creating a database for knowledge management. For example, an IT department may compile frequently asked questions that help users resolve the most common problems themselves. Human resources managers may update employee policies, make announcements, and convey information about benefits. A sample knowledge-base wiki can be found in Figure 4.8.
- **Wikis for meetings.** Wikis can facilitate feedback before and after meetings or serve as repositories of meeting minutes. In fact, wikis may replace some meetings, yet still keep a project on track. An often-cited example of a huge global wiki meeting is IBM's famous massive online discussion and brainstorming session that involved more than 100,000 participants from more than 160 countries.
- **Project management with wikis.** Wikis offer a highly interactive environment ideal for projects by enabling information to be centralized for easy access and user input. All participants have the same information available and can share ideas more freely than in traditional face-to-face meetings. Instead of a top-down information flow, wikis empower employees and foster a team environment in which ideas can thrive.
- **Documentation and wikis.** Wikis can help to document projects large and small as well as technical and non-technical. Wikis may also provide templates for reports.

HOW TO BE A VALUABLE WIKI CONTRIBUTOR. Whether you wish to contribute to a wiki on the Web or at work, try to be an effective participant. As with most electronic communication, abide by the conventions of polite society, and follow commonsense rules. Show respect and watch out for improper or ambiguous language. Don't attack or otherwise severely criticize another contributor.

> To be productive when working on a wiki project, be polite, follow the guidelines established by the editors, and respect other contributors.

Pay attention to correct grammar and spelling, and verify your facts. Every comment you contribute is essentially published on the Web and available to any reader. If the content appears on the company intranet, it is there for the whole company to see. Wikipedia, a wiki that is trying to marry credibility with its desire for openness, has had to introduce many safeguards in its 11-year history to deal with vandals (i.e., people who "deface" a posting).

Follow the guidelines for contributors, and give credit where credit is due. Contributors to a wiki are part of a team, not individual authors who can reasonably expect recognition or maintain control over their writing. When borrowing, be sure to cite your sources to avoid plagiarism.

Writing Hard-Copy Memos

Before e-mail, interoffice memos (along with phone calls and face-to-face discussions) were the primary communication channel for delivering information within organizations. Memos are still useful for important internal messages that require a permanent record or formality. For example, organizations use memos to explain and enforce changes in procedures and for new official instructions.

> Hard-copy memos are useful for internal messages that require a permanent record or formality.

MEMO TEMPLATES. Some organizations have their own memo templates. In addition to the name of the organization, these templates include the basic elements of *Date*, *To*, *From*, and *Subject*. Large organizations may include other identifying headings, such as *File Number*, *Floor*, *Extension*, *Location*, and *Distribution*.

If your company or organization doesn't have its own template for memos, simply open a new Word document, go to Templates (usually in the File menu), and search for memos. Word offers a number of memo templates you can use. Start writing in the template, making sure to save as you go. A typical memo is shown in Figure 4.9.

Notice the following important elements: there are spaces between the title and the guidewords, and spaces among the guidewords—this increases readability.

FIGURE 4.9 Typical Business Memo

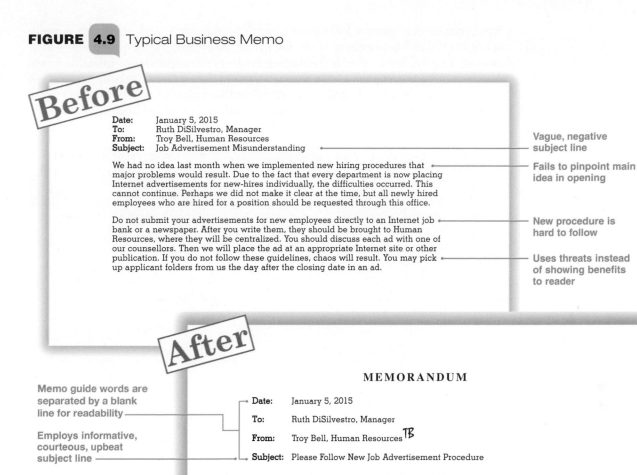

Before

Date: January 5, 2015
To: Ruth DiSilvestro, Manager
From: Troy Bell, Human Resources
Subject: Job Advertisement Misunderstanding ● — — — — — — — Vague, negative
                                                                 subject line

We had no idea last month when we implemented new hiring procedures that ● — — Fails to pinpoint main
major problems would result. Due to the fact that every department is now placing   idea in opening
Internet advertisements for new-hires individually, the difficulties occurred. This
cannot continue. Perhaps we did not make it clear at the time, but all newly hired
employees who are hired for a position should be requested through this office.

Do not submit your advertisements for new employees directly to an Internet job ● — New procedure is
bank or a newspaper. After you write them, they should be brought to Human   hard to follow
Resources, where they will be centralized. You should discuss each ad with one of
our counsellors. Then we will place the ad at an appropriate Internet site or other
publication. If you do not follow these guidelines, chaos will result. You may pick ● — Uses threats instead
up applicant folders from us the day after the closing date in an ad.   of showing benefits
                                                                                       to reader

After

MEMORANDUM

Memo guide words are
separated by a blank
line for readability — — — — — ● Date: January 5, 2015

                                 To: Ruth DiSilvestro, Manager

                                 From: Troy Bell, Human Resources ᵀᴮ

Employs informative,
courteous, upbeat
subject line — — — — — — — — — ● Subject: Please Follow New Job Advertisement Procedure

Combines "you" view with — — ● To find the right candidates for your open positions as fast as possible, we are
main idea in opening   implementing a new routine. Effective today, all advertisements for departmental
                                job openings should be routed throuqh the Human Resources Department.

Explains why change in — — — — A major problem resulted from the change in hiring procedures implemented last
procedures is necessary   month. Each department is placing job advertisements for new-hires individually,
                                when all such requests should be centralized in this office. To process applications
                                more efficiently, please follow this procedure:

Lists easy-to-follow   1. Write an advertisement for a position in your department.
steps and starts each — — — —
step with a verb   2. Bring the ad to Human Resources and discuss it with one of our counsellors.

                                3. Let Human Resources place the ad at an appropriate Internet job bank or
                                    submit it to a newspaper.

                                4. Pick up applicant folders from Human Resources the day following the closing
                                    date provided in the ad.

Closes by reinforcing — — — — ● Following these guidelines will save you work and will also enable Human
benefits to reader   Resources to help you fill your openings more quickly. Call Ann Edmonds at
                                Ext. 2505 if you have questions about this procedure.

Omits a closing and — — — — —
signature

Tips for Formatting Interoffice Memos

Use MS Word's templates to select a memo format and begin filling
in the template. If a template is not available, follow these steps:
• Set one tab to align entries evenly after *Subject*.
• Leave 1 or 2 blank lines after the subject line.
• Single-space all but the shortest memos.
  Double-space between paragraphs.
• For a two-page memo, use a second-page heading
  with the addressee's name, page number, and date.
• Handwrite your initials after your typed name.

Next, notice that memos follow the writing pattern discussed earlier for e-mails: specific subject line, opening with main idea, body that explains the main idea, closing. Finally, notice that alone among business correspondence forms, a memo does not include an opening or a closing salutation (i.e., *Hi* or *Dear* or *Sincerely* or *Cheers*). This is because memos were developed to save time and to be impersonal. See Appendix A for more details on memo (and fax, a form of memo) formatting.

WRITING PLAN FOR MEMOS

- **Subject line:** Summarizes the content of the memo.
- **Opening:** Expands the subject line by stating the main idea concisely in a full sentence.
- **Body:** Provides background data and explains the main idea. Consider using lists, bullets, or headings to improve readability. In describing a procedure or giving instructions, use command language (*do this*, *don't do that*).
- **Closing:** Requests a specific action, summarizes the message, or presents a closing thought. If appropriate, includes a deadline and a reason.

> To deliver a long or formal document, send a cover e-mail with an attachment.

PREPARING MEMOS AS E-MAIL ATTACHMENTS. Because e-mail is inappropriate for writing overly long documents or for items that require formality or permanence, with such messages, writers may prepare the information in standard memo format and send the memo as an attachment with a cover e-mail.

When attaching a document to an e-mail, be sure to include identifying information in the attachment. This is because the cover e-mail message may become separated from the attachment, and the receiver won't know who sent the attachment. If your e-mail attachment is a memo, there shouldn't be any problems, as memos identify the date, sender, receiver, and subject.

◼ Writing Hard-Copy Letters

Before memos and e-mail, business was carried on for centuries using letters. Despite the widespread use of e-mail and other electronic communication channels, in certain situations letters are still the preferred channel for communicating *outside* an organization. Such letters may be sent to suppliers, government agencies, other businesses, and, most important, customers. Letters to customers receive a high priority because they are seen as important by receivers (not surprisingly, given how rarely we get actual letters in the mail anymore), encourage product feedback, project a favourable image of the organization, and promote future business.

> Business letters are important for messages requiring a permanent record, confidentiality, formality, sensitivity, and a well-considered presentation.

A letter remains a powerful and effective channel for businesspeople to get their message across. Business letters are particularly necessary when (a) a permanent record is required; (b) confidentiality is paramount; (c) formality and sensitivity are essential; and (d) a persuasive, well-considered presentation is important.

PERMANENT RECORD. Many business transactions require a permanent record. For example, when a company enters into an agreement with another company, business letters introduce the agreement and record decisions and points of understanding. Although telephone conversations and e-mails may be exchanged, important details are generally recorded in business letters that are kept in company files. Business letters deliver contracts, explain terms, exchange ideas, negotiate agreements, answer vendor questions, and maintain customer relations.

CONFIDENTIALITY. By convention, mail is opened by the person to whom it is addressed. This means that letters are confidential (unless someone decides not to obey the convention just described).

FORMALITY AND SENSITIVITY. Business letters presented on company stationery carry a sense of formality and importance not possible with e-mail. They look important. They send the following nonverbal message: the writer considered the message to be so significant and the receiver so important that the writer cared enough to write a real message. Business letters deliver more information than e-mail because they are written on stationery that usually is printed with company information such as logos, addresses, titles, and contact details.

PERSUASIVENESS. When a business communicator must be persuasive and can't do it in person, a business letter is more effective than other communication channels. Letters can persuade people to change their actions, adopt new beliefs, make donations, contribute their time, and try new products. Hard-copy letters are a powerful tool to promote services and products, boost online and retail traffic, and solicit contributions. This is because they represent deliberate communication; in other words, someone had to think carefully about what went into the letter, and how it was organized.

Formatting Business Letters

A business letter conveys silent messages beyond its printed words. The letter's appearance and format reflect the writer's carefulness and experience, much like your appearance during a job interview may convey messages about you. A short letter bunched at the top of a sheet of paper, for example, looks as though it were prepared in a hurry or by an amateur.

> Letters are deliberate (not impulsive) forms of written communication.

LETTER TEMPLATES. Many organizations will have their own letter templates, including their logo and company name and address. Unless instructed not to, always use your company's letter template when drafting a letter.

If your company or organization doesn't have its own template for letters, simply open a new Word document, go to Templates (usually in the File menu), and search for letters. Word offers a number of letter templates you can use. Choose one that looks professional and formal, not informal or too busy. Start writing in the template, making sure to save as you go. A typical letter is shown in Figure 4.10.

Notice the following important elements: the letter begins with your company's letterhead—the company name and any logo associated with the company, plus your address. A few spaces underneath the letterhead is the date of the letter. A few spaces further down is the name and address of the person to whom you're writing. Then, there is an opening salutation (like in an e-mail), which usually begins with *Dear*. The letter opens after the salutation. It has a body that explains the main point of the letter. The letter closes politely, and ends with a closing salutation (usually *Sincerely*) plus a signature and title. See Appendix A for more details about letter formatting.

WRITING PLAN FOR LETTERS

- **Letterhead:** Your company name, logo, and address.
- **Date and address:** The date of the letter followed by the name and address to which it is being sent.
- **Body:** Three sections: an opening, the body that explains your main reason for writing, and a polite closing.
- **Closing salutation and signature:** A polite "goodbye" with your signature and title.

FIGURE 4.10 Typical Business Letter

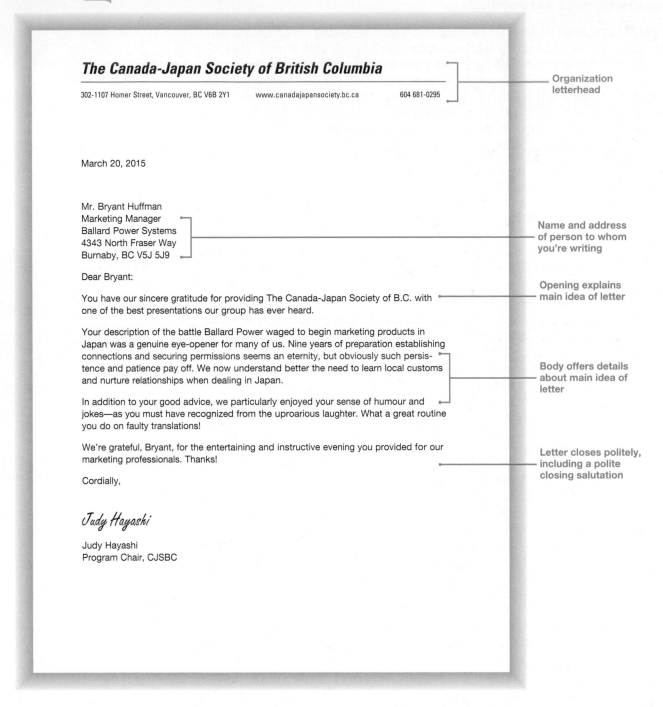

The Canada-Japan Society of British Columbia

302-1107 Homer Street, Vancouver, BC V6B 2Y1   www.canadajapansociety.bc.ca   604 681-0295

Organization
letterhead

March 20, 2015

Mr. Bryant Huffman
Marketing Manager
Ballard Power Systems
4343 North Fraser Way
Burnaby, BC V5J 5J9

Name and address
of person to whom
you're writing

Dear Bryant:

You have our sincere gratitude for providing The Canada-Japan Society of B.C. with
one of the best presentations our group has ever heard.

Opening explains
main idea of letter

Your description of the battle Ballard Power waged to begin marketing products in
Japan was a genuine eye-opener for many of us. Nine years of preparation establishing
connections and securing permissions seems an eternity, but obviously such persistence and patience pay off. We now understand better the need to learn local customs
and nurture relationships when dealing in Japan.

Body offers details
about main idea of
letter

In addition to your good advice, we particularly enjoyed your sense of humour and
jokes—as you must have recognized from the uproarious laughter. What a great routine
you do on faulty translations!

We're grateful, Bryant, for the entertaining and instructive evening you provided for our
marketing professionals. Thanks!

Letter closes politely,
including a polite
closing salutation

Cordially,

Judy Hayashi

Judy Hayashi
Program Chair, CJSBC

SUMMING UP AND LOOKING FORWARD

People working in business exchange messages externally and internally. They do so using forms of business writing. The first main form is electronic messages, including e-mails, instant messages, text messages, social media posts, podcasts, blogs, and wikis. The second main form is paper-based messages, including business letters and interoffice memos.

Because messages are increasingly being exchanged electronically, this chapter presented many techniques for sending and receiving safe and effective e-mails and instant messages and texts. Writing posts on social media, and writing podcast, blog, and wiki material, also requires you to follow basic rules. Businesspeople are still using hard-copy memos to convey confidential information or important company-wide messages, while hard-copy letters are also used in situations when formality, a permanent record, confidentiality, or persuasiveness are required.

 CRITICAL THINKING

1. "E-mail is no longer a cutting-edge tool," says a recent newspaper article. "But it is clear that some people still do not know how to use it effectively."[24] What are the major complaints about the use of business e-mail?

2. Consider this statement: *Instant messaging and texting are too informal for business use*. Do you agree or disagree? Why?

3. Why are lawyers and technology experts warning companies to store, organize, and manage computer data, including e-mails and instant and text messages, with greater diligence?

4. Compare your personal use of social media with corporate use of social media. What are the similarities and differences?

5. Are podcasts and blogs really as revolutionary as they seem? To what degree are podcasts a new version of a radio broadcast? And to what degree is a blog just a technical version of a diary or journal?

6. When was the last time you (or someone you know who works full time) came across a memo? What about the last time you (or he or she) received a letter? Could the memo or letter have been replaced by an e-mail or other electronic communication, or did it need to be hard copy? Why?

7. *Ethical Issue*: Should managers have the right to monitor the e-mails, messages, and texts of employees? Why or why not? What if employees are warned that electronic messages could be monitored? If a company wanted to create its own electronic communication policy, what guidelines should be included?

CHAPTER REVIEW

1. Explain why have companies adopted the use of electronic communication.

2. For what reasons is hard-copy correspondence (i.e., memos and letters) still useful?

3. What structural elements contribute to an effective e-mail?

4. What e-mail etiquette suggestions show respect for others?

5. What are the most important practices when sending instant and text messages at work?

6. How is social media a form of business writing?

7. How are podcasting, blogging, and wikis forms of business writing?

8. What structural elements make up an effective memo?

9. What are the main structural differences between a letter and a memo (and an e-mail)?

WRITING IMPROVEMENT EXERCISES

Message Openers

Your Task. Compare the following sets of message openers. Circle the letter of the opener that illustrates a direct opening. Be prepared to discuss the weaknesses and strengths of each.

1. An e-mail requesting information about creating a Facebook presence:

   a. We want to start our business fan page on Facebook, but we are not sure how to ensure visibility and participation, and we worry about the privacy risks and data safety. We have many questions and would like information about Facebook and social media in general.

   b. Please answer the following questions about creating a business fan page on Facebook and protecting our network from intrusions and malicious attacks.

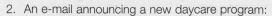

2. An e-mail announcing a new daycare program:

   a. Employees interested in enrolling their children in our new low-cost daycare program are invited to an HR orientation on September 15.

   b. For several years we have studied the possibility of offering a daycare option for those employees who are parents. Until recently, our management team was unable to agree on the exact parameters of this benefit, but now some of you will be able to take advantage of this option.

3. An e-mail message announcing an employee satisfaction survey:

   a. We have noticed recently an increased turnover among our sales staff. We are concerned about this troubling development and would like to study its causes. We have hired an outside consulting firm to gauge the attitudes of our salespeople in confidential qualitative interviews.

   b. The consulting firm Strelitz & Kaus Research Associates will soon conduct in-depth qualitative interviews to explore the satisfaction among our sales staff and recommend strategies to stem the tide of recent departures.

4. A memo announcing a new procedure:

   a. It has come to our attention that some staff members write blogs, sometimes publicly addressing sensitive company information. We respect the desire of employees to express themselves and would like to continue allowing the practice, but we decided to provide binding rules to ensure the company's and the bloggers' safety.

   b. The following new policy for blog authors will help staff members to create posts that will maintain the integrity of the company's sensitive information and keep the writers safe.

Opening Paragraphs and Subject Lines

Your Task. The following opening paragraphs to memos are wordy and indirect. After reading each paragraph, identify the main idea. Then, write an opening sentence that illustrates a more direct opening and include a subject line.

5. Several staff members came to me and announced their interest in learning more about telecommuting and government telework policies. As most of you know, these areas of concern are increasingly important for most government workers here in Washington, D.C. A seminar titled "Telecommuting and Telework Policies" is being conducted March 22. I am allowing the following employees to attend the seminar: Darrell Walters, Akil Jackson, and Amy Woods.

6. Your MegaCorp Employees Association has secured for you discounts on auto repair, carpet purchases, travel arrangements, and many other services. These services are available to you if you have a Buying Power Card. All MegaCorp employees are eligible for their own private Buying Power Cards.

Bulleted and Numbered Lists

7. E-mails and memos frequently contain bulleted or numbered lists, which you learned about in this chapter.

Your Task. Revise the following wordy paragraph into an introductory statement and a short list with category headings. Should the list be numbered or bulleted?

   Our office could implement better environmental practices such as improving energy efficiency and reducing our carbon footprint. Here are three simple things we can do to make our daily work practices greener. For one thing, we can power down. At night we should turn off monitors, not just log off our computers. In addition, we could "Light Right." This means installing energy-efficient lighting throughout the office. A final suggestion has to do with recycling. We could be recycling instantly if we placed small recycling bins at all workstations and common-use areas.

8. **Your Task.** Revise the following wordy paragraph into an introductory statement with a concise list that has three bullet points. Could you use category headings for your bullet points?

   If you are a job candidate interviewing for a job, you should follow a few guidelines that most people consider basic. You will be more successful if you do these things. One of the first things to do is get ready. Before the interview, successful candidates research the target

company. That is, they find out about it. If you really want to be successful, you will prepare success stories. Wise candidates also clean up any digital dirt that may be floating around the Internet. Those are a few of the things to do before the interview. During the interview, the best candidates try to sound enthusiastic. They answer questions clearly but with short, concise responses. They also are prepared to ask their own questions. After the interview, when you can relax a bit, you should remember to send a thank-you note to the interviewer. Another thing to do after the interview is contact references. One last thing to do, if you don't hear from the interviewer within five days, is follow up with an inquiry.

 ## ACTIVITIES AND CASES

4.1 Document Critique: Dealing with Excessive E-mail

The following e-mail from Stella Soto requests feedback from her managerial staff; however, her first draft contains many writing faults.

Your Task. Analyze the message. List its weaknesses and then outline an appropriate writing plan. If your instructor directs, revise the message.

Date: December 18, 2014

To: Amsoft Manager List

From: Stella Soto <stella.soto@amsoft.com>

Subject: E-Mail Problems

Cc:

Bcc:

Dear Managers,

As Amsoft vice president, I am troubled by a big problem. I am writing this note to ask for your help and advice to address an urgent problem—the problem of excessive e-mail. If you will do me the favour of answering the questions below, I'm sure your ideas will assist us in the development of a plan that should benefit your staff, yourself, and our organization will be improved. Your responses in writing to these questions (preferably by December 22) will help me prepare for our supervisory committee meeting on January 4. Everyone had the expectation that e-mail would be a great big productivity tool. I'm afraid that its use is becoming extremely excessive. For our organization it is actually cutting into work time. Did you know that one study found that the average office worker is spending 2 hours a day on e-mail? In our organization we may be spending even more then this. Its exceedingly difficult to get any work done because of writing and answering an extra ordinary number of e-mails coming in each and every day. Excessive e-mail is sapping the organization's strength and productivity. I would like to have your answers to some questions before the above referenced dates to help us focus on the problem.

Can you give a ballpark figure for how many e-mail messages you receive and answer on a personal basis each day? Think about how many hours the staff members in your department spend on e-mail each day. Approximately how many hours would you estimate? Do you have any ideas about how we can make a reduction in the volume of e-mail messages being sent and received within our own organization? Do you think that e-mail is being used by our employees in an excessive manner?

I'm wondering what you think about an e-mail-free day once a week. How about Fridays? I appreciate your suggestions and advice in developing a solution to the problem of controlling e-mail and making an improvement in productivity.

Stella

1. List at least five weaknesses of this message.

2. Outline a writing plan for this message.

4.2 Document Critique: Facts About Corporate Instant Messaging

The following interoffice memo reports information from a conference, but it is poorly written.

Your Task. Analyze the memo. List its weaknesses and then outline an appropriate writing plan. If your instructor directs, revise the memo.

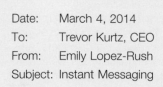

Date: March 4, 2014

To: Trevor Kurtz, CEO

From: Emily Lopez-Rush

Subject: Instant Messaging

Thanks for asking me to attend the Instant Messaging Conference. It was sponsored by Pixel Link and took place March 2. Do you think you will want me to expand on what I learned at the next management council meeting? I believe that meeting is March 25.

Anyway, here's my report. Jason Howard, the conference leader, told us that over 80 million workers are already using instant messaging and that it was definitely here to stay. But do the risks outweigh the advantages? He talked about benefits, providers, costs involved, and risks. The top advantages of IM are speed, documentation, and it saves costs. The major problems are spam, security, control, and disruptive. He said that the principal IM providers for consumers were Windows Live Messenger and Yahoo Messenger. Misuse of IM can result in reductions in productivity. However, positive results can be achieved with appropriate use. Although some employees are using consumer IM services, for maximum security many organizations are investing in enterprise-level IM systems, and they are adopting guidelines for employees. These enterprise-level IM systems range in cost from $30 to $100 per user licence. The cost depends on the amount of functionality.

This is just a summary of what I learned. If you want to hear more, please do not hesitate to call.

1. List at least five weaknesses of this interoffice memo.

2. Outline a writing plan for this memo.

4.3 Document Critique: Planning a Charity Golf Event

The following e-mail from Seth Jackson requests information about planning a charity golf tournament. His first draft must be revised.

Your Task. Analyze the message. List its weaknesses and then outline an appropriate writing plan. If your instructor directs, revise the message. Could this message benefit from category headings?

Date: February 1, 2014

To: Kaitlin Merek <kmerek@monarch.ca>

From: Seth Jackson <seth.jackson@cox.ca>

Subject: Need Help!

The Children's Resource Centre badly needs funds. We have tried other things, but now we want to try a charity golf event. In view of the fact that you have expertise in this area and since you volunteered to offer your assistance, I am writing this e-mail to pick your brain, so to speak, in regard to questions that have to do with five basic fundamentals in the process of preparation. I'm going to need your answers in these areas before February 15. Is that possible? Maybe you would rather talk to me. Should I contact you?

In regard to the budget, I have no idea how to estimate costs. For example, what about administrative costs? How about marketing? And there are salaries, cellphone rentals, copiers, and a lot of other things.

I also need help in choosing a golf course. Should it be a public course? Or a private course? Resort? One big area that I worry about is sponsors. Should I go after one big sponsor? But let's say I get Pepsi to be a sponsor. Then do I have to ban Coke totally from the scene?

Another big headache is scoring. I will bet you can make some suggestions for tabulating the golf results. And posting them. By the way, did you see that Tiger Woods is back in the winner's circle?

I have noticed that other golf tournaments have extra events, such as a pairing party to introduce partners. Many also have an awards dinner to award prizes. Should I be planning extra events?

Seth Jackson
Philanthropy and Gifts Coordinator
Children's Resource Centre

1. List at least five weaknesses of this request e-mail.

2. Outline a writing plan for this message.

4.4 Document Critique: New Process for Reporting Equipment Repairs

The following is a manager's first draft of an e-mail describing a new process for reporting equipment repairs. The message is addressed to one employee, but it will also be sent to others.

Your Task. Analyze the message. List its weaknesses and then outline an appropriate writing plan. If your instructor directs, revise the message.

Date: April 25, 2014

To: Faith Benoit <Faith.Benoit@stcc.ca>

From: Mia Murillo <Mia.Murillo@stcc.ca>

Subject: Repairs

Cc:

Bcc:

We have recently instituted a new procedure for all equipment repairs. Effective immediately, we are no longer using the "Equipment Repair Form" that we formerly used. We want to move everyone to an online database system. These new procedures will help us repair your equipment faster and keep track of it better. You will find the new procedure at http://www.BigWebDesk.ca. That's where you log in. You should indicate the kind of repair you need. It may be for AudioVisual, Mac, PC, or Printer. Then you should begin the process of data entry for your specific problem by selecting Create New Ticket. The new ticket should be printed and attached securely to the equipment. Should you have questions or trouble, just call Sylvia at Extension 255. You can also write to her at *Sylvia.Freeman@stcc.ca.* The warehouse truck driver will pick up and deliver your equipment as we have always done in the past.

1. List at least five weaknesses of this e-mail message.
2. Outline a writing plan for this message.

4.5 Memo That Informs: Change in Insurance Premiums

You are the benefits manager for a national furniture retail chain, The Home Centre, headquartered in Richmond, British Columbia. Most of the full-time employees who work for the chain pay into an employee benefits plan. This plan includes dental and vision care, prescription drug coverage, and other benefits. One of the most expensive benefits employees pay for is long-term disability (LTD) insurance. Recently, your insurance provider, Cansafe, has informed you that due to the high number of recent long-term disability claims, premiums for long-term disability insurance will have to rise substantially, on the order of 15 percent. For the average employee, this means an increase of more than $20 per month.

Your Task. Your job requires you to write a well-organized memo informing The Home Centre employees about the impending increase. From past experience, you know that employees who are closer to retirement are big supporters of long-term disability insurance, whereas younger employees tend to be frustrated by the high premiums.

Related Web site: Sun Life's site has a useful description of LTD insurance at **www.sunlife.ca/Plan/Health/Disability+insurance?vgnLocale=en_CA**.

4.6 E-Mail That Informs and Requests: Dress Code Controversy

`WEB`

`TEAM`

As the Montréal-based director of Human Resources at Sensational, you have not had a good week. The national media recently reported the fact that Sensational—a leading women's fashion chain—has been taken before the Nova Scotia Human Rights Commission to defend against a claim by a young woman. The young woman recently applied for a job at a Halifax Sensational location and was told in a pre-interview with a manager that "she'd never be hired if she wore her headdress to work." Citing the Commission's Web site claim that "It's against the law to fire an employee because he wears clothing that is required by his religion," the young woman lodged a complaint.[25] Head office in Vancouver has been in damage-control mode ever since.

Your Task. Quickly realizing the effects the negative media reporting will have, you draft an e-mail to all employees. The purpose of the e-mail is to reaffirm that Sensational abides by and supports all Canadian human rights legislation, and, at the same time, that employees should not talk to any media that may ask them for comments. You realize that these two messages are somewhat contradictory (one positive, one negative), but you feel time is of the essence.

Related Web site: Nova Scotia Human Rights Commission (**www.gov.ns.ca/humanrights**).

MEMO

WEB

4.7 Response E-Mail or Memo: Office Romance Off Limits?

Where can you find the hottest singles scene today? Some would say in your workplace. Because people are working long hours and have little time for outside contacts, relationships often develop at work. Estimates suggest that one third to one half of all romances begin at the office. Your boss is concerned about possible problems resulting from workplace relationships. What happens if a relationship between a superior and subordinate results in perceived favouritism? What happens if a relationship ends in a nasty breakup? Your boss would like to simply ban all relationships between employees. However, that's not likely to work. He asks you, his assistant, to learn what guidelines could be established regarding office romances.

Your Task. Using research databases or the Internet, look for articles about workplace romance. From various articles, select four or five suggestions that you could make to your boss in regard to protecting an employer. Why is it necessary for a company to protect itself? Discuss your findings and reactions with your team. Individually or as a group, submit your findings and reactions in a well-organized, easy-to-read e-mail or memo to your boss (your instructor). You may list main points from the articles you research, but use your own words to write the message.

4.8 Request E-Mail or Memo: Old Habits Die Hard

Over ten years ago, the province of Manitoba introduced The Non-Smokers Health Protection Act to make "smoking . . . prohibited in all enclosed public places and indoor workplaces." The legislation was mostly popular, but some companies in the province have been finding that their employees are not necessarily obeying the law at all times.

Your Task. As Lindsay Harapa, director of Human Resources, write an e-mail attaching a memo to all department managers of Imperial Foods, a large food products company in Winnipeg. Remind employees of the provincial law, and tell the managers that you want them to set up departmental committees to mediate any smoking conflicts before complaints surface. Explain why this is a good policy.

Related Web site: Highlights of Manitoba's legislation can be found at **www.gov.mb.ca/ healthyliving/smokingban.html**.

WEB

4.9 Instant Messaging at Local Auto Dealer

Read the following log of a live IM chat between a customer service representative and a visitor to a Glendora car dealership's Web site.

Your Task. Discuss in class how Alex could have made this interaction with a customer more effective. Is his IM chat with Mr. Rhee professional, polite, and respectful? If your instructor directs, rewrite Alex's responses to Mr. Rhee's queries.

Service rep:	Hey, I'm Alex. How's it goin? Welcome to Harkin BMW of Glendora!
Customer:	??
Service rep:	Im supposed to provid live assistance. What can I do you for?
Customer:	I want buy car.
Service rep:	May I have your name fist?
Customer:	Jin Bae Rhee
Service rep:	Whoa! Is that a dude's name? Okay. What kind? New inventory or preowned?
Customer:	BMW. 2014 model. for family, for business.
Service rep:	New, then, huh? Where are you from?
Customer:	What car you have?
Service rep:	We got some that will knock your socks off.
Customer:	I want green car, low mileage, less gasoline burn.

Service rep:	My man, if you can't afford the gas on these puppies, you shouldn't buy a Beemer, you know what I mean? Or ya want green color?
Customer:	?
Service rep:	Okeydoke, we got a full lineup. Which series, 3, 5, 6, or 7? Or an X3 or X5? A Z4 convertible?
Customer:	760 sedan?
Service rep:	Nope. We got just two 550i, one for $68,695 and one for 71,020
Customer:	Eureopean delivery?
Service rep:	Oh, I know zip about that. Let me find someone who does. Can I have your phone number and e-mail?
Customer:	i prefer not get a phone call yet … but 299-484-9807 is phone numer and jrhee@techtrade.com email
Service rep:	Awsome. Well give you a jingle back or shoot you an email pronto! Bye.

4.10 Response E-Mail: Rescheduling Interviews to Accommodate a Travelling Boss

MEMO

Your boss, Michael Kaufman, has scheduled three appointments to interview applicants for the position of project manager. All of these appointments are for Thursday, May 5. However, he now must travel to Toronto that week. He asks you to reschedule all the appointments for one week later. He also wants a brief background summary for each candidate.

Although frustrated, you call each person and are lucky to arrange these times. Saul Salazar, who has been a project manager for nine years with Summit Enterprises, agrees to come at 10:30 a.m. Kaitlyn Grindell, who is a systems analyst and a consultant to many companies, will come at 11:30. Mary Montgomery, who has an MA and six years of experience as senior project coordinator at High Point Industries, will come at 9:30 a.m. You are wondering whether Mr. Kaufman forgot to include Grace Ho, operations personnel officer, in these interviews. Ms. Ho is usually part of the selection process.

Your Task. Write an e-mail to Mr. Kaufman including all the information he needs.

4.11 Procedure Memo: Standardizing Purchase Requests

The purchasing department handles purchases for a growing family company. Some purchase orders arrive on the proper forms, but others are memos or handwritten notes that are barely legible. The owner wants to establish a standard procedure for submitting purchase requests. The purchase requests must now be downloaded from the company intranet. To provide the fastest service, employees should fill out the purchase request. Employees must include the relevant information: date, quantities, catalogue numbers, complete descriptions, complete vendor mailing address and contact information, delivery requirements, and shipping methods. The purchasing department should receive the original, and the sender should keep a copy. An important step in the new procedure is approval by the budget manager on the request form.

Your Task. As assistant manager in the purchasing department, write an interoffice memo or e-mail to all employees informing them of the new procedure.

4.12 Information E-Mail: Choosing a Holiday Plan

EMAIL

In the past your company offered all employees 11 holidays, starting with New Year's Day in January and proceeding through Christmas Day the following December. Other companies offer similar holiday schedules. In addition, your company has given all employees one floating holiday. That day was determined by a company-wide vote. As a result, all employees had the same day off. Now, management is considering a new plan that involves a floating holiday that each employee may choose. Selections, however, would be subject to staffing needs within individual departments. If two people wanted the same day, the employee with the most seniority would have the day off.

Your Task. As a member of the human resources staff, write an e-mail to employees. This message should provide information as well as ask employees to choose between continuing the current company-wide uniform floating holiday and instituting a new plan for an individual floating holiday. Be sure to establish an end date.

4.13 Social Networking: Building an Online Community on Facebook

Chances are you already have a Facebook profile and communicate with friends and family. You may be a fan of a celebrity or a business. Now you can also become a fan of your business communication class if your instructor decides to create a course page on Facebook. The main purpose of such a social networking site for a class is to exchange links and interesting stories relevant to the material being learned. Intriguing tidbits and business news might also be posted on the "wall" to be shared by all signed-up fans. Everybody, even students who are quiet in class, could contribute. However, before you can become a fan of your business communication class, it needs to be created online.

Your Task. If you posted a profile on Facebook, all you need to do is search for the title of the newly created business communication Facebook page and become a fan. If you don't have an account yet, begin by signing up at **www.facebook.com**. On-screen prompts make it easy for you to build a profile.

4.14 Request IM: Don't Abuse the Casual Friday Policy

You work in a government ministry as manager of 25 customer service representatives. You've been with the ministry for ten years, and two years ago your fellow managers adopted a policy allowing casual dress (e.g., short skirts, shorts, T-shirts, jeans) on Fridays. Any employee wishing to "dress down" could do so by bringing along a donation for the local food bank. Also two years ago, the ministry installed instant messaging software so that employees could be in touch with each other more quickly and more informally. Over the past few months, you've noticed employees abusing the casual Friday policy by wearing casual clothing on other days of the week.

Your Task. Send an instant message early on a Monday morning to your 25 customer service reps informing them that the casual Friday policy needs to be followed. Assume that a trouble-making customer service rep named Ed responds to your message, as does Yanique, a very young recently hired rep. Create an IM conversation, imagining what Ed's and Yanique's responses will be to your message and how you will reply. How will you stay on top of this situation and ensure that your directions are being followed?

GRAMMAR/MECHANICS REVIEW 4—PREPOSITIONS AND CONJUNCTIONS

Study each of the following statements. Write *a* or *b* to indicate the sentence in which the idea is expressed more effectively. For more practice, you will find a set of Bonus Grammar/Mechanics Checkups with immediate feedback at your premium Web site, **www.nelson.com/guffeyessentials8ce**.

Example

<u> b </u>   a.   Gentry graduated high school last year.

        b.   Gentry graduated from high school last year.

___ 1. a.   What type of printer do you prefer?

          b.   What type printer do you prefer?

___ 2. a.   I hate when my cell rings during meetings.

          b.   I hate it when my cell rings during meetings.

___ 3. a.   Bullets make this message easier to read then that one.

          b.   Bullets make this message easier to read than that one.

___ 4. a.   Blogrolling is when you provide links to other blogs.

          b.   Blogrolling involves the provision of links to other blogs.

___ 5. a.   It seems as if we have been working on this project forever.

          b.   It seems like we have been working on this project forever.

___ 6. a.   Does anyone know where the meeting is?

          b.   Does anyone know where the meeting is at?

___ 7. a.   A wiki is better then a blog for workplace updates.

          b.   A wiki is better than a blog for workplace updates.

___ 8. a.   Were you transferred to the home office in Montréal or to the office of the branch in Ottawa?

          b.   Were you transferred to the Montréal home office or the Ottawa branch office?

___ 9. a.   Cloud computing is where your files and programs are stored in huge Internet data centres.

          b.   Cloud computing involves storing files and programs at huge Internet data centres.

___ 10. a.   Where shall we move the computer to?

          b.   Where shall we move the computer?

___ 11. a.   Job seekers should keep their online profiles free of risqué photos, profanity, and negative comments.

          b.   Job seekers should keep their online profiles free of risqué photos, profanity, and they should avoid negative comments.

___ 12. a.   His blog comments were informative like we hoped they would be.

          b.   His blog comments were informative as we hoped they would be.

___ 13. a.   Jeremy had an interest in and an aptitude for computer researching.

          b.   Jeremy had an interest and aptitude for computer researching.

___ 14. a.   She joined both of the social networking sites.

          b.   She joined both social networking sites.

___ 15. a.   As soon as she graduated college, she was eligible for the job.

          b.   As soon as she graduated from college, she was eligible for the job.

◾ GRAMMAR/MECHANICS CHALLENGE—4

Document for Revision

The following memo has faults in grammar, punctuation, spelling, capitalization, number form, repetition, wordiness, and other areas. Use standard proofreading marks (see Appendix B) to correct the errors. When you finish, your instructor can show you the revised version of this memo.

Lux Hotels and Spas Inc.

Memo

DATE: March 2, 2014

TO: Department Heads, Managers, and Supervisors

FROM: James Robbins, Director, Human Resources

SUBJECT: Submitting Appraisals of Performance by April 15th

Please be informed that performance appraisals for all you're employees' are due, before April 15th. These appraisal are esspecially important and essential this year. Because of job changes, new technologys and because of office re-organization.

To complete your performance appraisals in the most effective way, you should follow the procedures described in our employee handbook, let me briefly make a review of those procedures;

1. Be sure each and every employee has a performance plan with 3 or 4 main objective.

2. For each objective make an assessment of the employee on a scale of 5 (consistently excedes requirements) to 0 (does not meet requirements at all.

3. You should identify 3 strengths that he brings to the job.

4. Name 3 skills that he can improve. These should pertain to skills such as Time Management rather then to behaviours such as habitual lateness.

5. The employee should be met with to discuss his appraisal.

6. Finish the appraisal and send the completed appraisal to this office.

We look upon appraisals like a tool for helping each worker assess his performance. And enhance his output. If you would like to discuss this farther, please do not hessitate to call me.

WHOSE COMPUTER OR SMARTPHONE IS IT, ANYWAY?

Many companies today provide their employees with computers, and some provide smartphones with Internet access. Should employees be able to use those devices for online shopping, personal messages, personal work, and listening to music or playing games?

But It's Harmless

According to a recent poll, one third of Canadian workers has Internet access at work and four out of five of these say they log on for personal reasons, such as sending personal e-mails, checking out news or sports headlines, comparison shopping, checking investments, and making online purchases. While the poll did not determine whether this activity occurred during work or in the employee's spare time, the potential for abuse and evidence of abuse have led a growing number of employers in Canada to consider developing policies governing Internet use and also to monitor the online activities of employees.[26] To justify much of this personal activity, workers claim that pursuing personal online activities is performance enhancing, as it keeps them at their desks rather than in the shopping malls or at the water cooler.

Companies Cracking Down—What's Reasonable?

Employers are less happy about increasing use of bandwidth for personal online activities. In a recent survey, 60 percent of employers say they are or plan to be monitoring their workers' online activity by 2015.[27]

Some companies try to enforce a "zero tolerance" policy, prohibiting any personal use of company equipment, while others allow some personal activity. In Canada, under the Privacy Act and Charter of Rights and Freedoms, employees have a "reasonable expectation" of privacy in the workplace, but that expectation can be met simply by notifying employees that they are being monitored.[28] Currently many employers provide no guidelines on reasonable Internet use. As well, what some employers regard as a firing offence, others view as acceptable personal use. As Paul Kent-Snowsell, a Vancouver lawyer specializing in Internet cases, warns, "It has always been cause for dismissal if you're not using company time to do company work."[29] At the same time, Robert Lendvai, marketing director for Ottawa's Kyberpass Corporation, a maker of network security software, indicates that while Canadian corporations use the security features of his company's software, only about one in five activates the monitoring capabilities.[30]

Career Application

As an administrative assistant at Big C Technologies in Vancouver, you have just received an e-mail from your boss asking for your opinion. It seems that many employees have been shopping online; one person actually received four personal packages couriered to him in one morning. Although reluctant to do so, management is considering installing monitoring software that not only tracks Internet use but also allows extensive blocking of Web sites, such as porn, hate, and game sites.

YOUR TASK

- In teams or as a class, research and discuss the problem of workplace abuse of e-mail and the Internet.
- Should full personal use be allowed?
- In terms of equipment, are computers and their links to the Internet similar to office telephones?
- Should employees be allowed to access the Internet for personal use if they log on to their own private e-mail accounts?

- Should management be allowed to monitor all Internet use?
- Should employees be warned if e-mail is to be monitored?
- What specific reasons can you give to support an Internet crackdown by management?
- What specific reasons can you give to oppose a crackdown?

Decide whether you support or oppose a crackdown. Explain your views in an e-mail or a memo to your boss, Roberta Everson (reverson@bigc.com), or in a traditional in-class debate.

Related Web sites: Visit the Webspy site (**www.webspy.com**) for a detailed look at a leading Internet surveillance software product available for purchase by corporations and organizations. For information on Canada's privacy laws and regulations, visit the Web site of the Office of the Privacy Commissioner of Canada (www.privcom.gc.ca).

CHAPTER 05

Routine Writing Situations

LEARNING OBJECTIVES

1. Identify routine business writing situations.
2. Explain the relationship between routine writing situations and the direct plan for business writing.
3. Write messages that share information.
4. Write messages that request information and/or action.
5. Write reply messages to clients, customers, or co-workers.
6. Write instruction messages.
7. Write claim/complaint and adjustment messages.
8. Write recommendation messages.
9. Write goodwill messages.

In Chapter 4 you learned that recent estimates indicate that about 145 billion e-mails are sent every day, with many of them being workplace e-mails. The same source that produced this statistic also claims that "new research [shows] that only one in four emails is essential for work. And only 14% of work emails were considered critically important."[1] This should not come as a surprise.

Once you think about it, you'll realize that most often when you write to someone at work, it's a routine need that leads you to write, not a highly important need. For example, you might need to relay information, answer an e-mail, ask a question, request something, explain how to do something, lodge a simple complaint, or give someone a pat on the back. These largely positive messages are routine and straightforward; they help workers in organizations conduct everyday business. Before e-mail became ubiquitous at work, these messages were dealt with through face-to-face conversations, phone calls, or, in the case of instructions, recommendations, or complaints, perhaps in a memo or letter.

In today's world of work, routine situations requiring you to write could include needing to tell or explain something to a co-worker (e.g., why Prezi is more effective than PowerPoint for a certain occasion). Or, you might find yourself in the situation of needing to ask a question or ask for help (e.g., can a colleague proofread a PowerPoint deck for you). Another routine situation in business that requires writing is replying to a colleague or client or manager who's been in touch with you (e.g., an account experiencing a problem with the solution you sell). Sometimes, you need to give instructions on how to do something, and this will lead you to write him or her (e.g., how to fill out benefit forms on a new online system). In situations when something in business goes wrong (but in a routine sort

> Only about 14 percent of work e-mails are considered critically important; most others are routine.

of way), you may decide to write a claim or complaint message (e.g., an order is short or missing certain products). On the other hand, in situations when someone asks for your recommendation, or has provided help or hospitality and needs to be thanked, you will want to write a recommendation or goodwill message (e.g., a manager introduced you to her boss in a complimentary way and you want to say thanks).

Recall from Chapter 3 that whenever you write a business message, you have two choices for how to do so. Choosing the direct method means you will place your main idea up front in the message. Choosing the indirect method means that before you announce your main idea you'll explain why the main idea is coming, buffer the main idea, or otherwise delay getting to the main point. Clearly, as the word "routine" suggests, the type of situations we'll be discussing in the rest of this chapter take place frequently—probably every day. Therefore, it only makes sense to write routine messages using the direct method. Otherwise, you're taking up too much of your correspondent's time and too much of their screen.

> Written messages responding to routine situations should use the direct method of getting right to the main point.

💬 Routine Situation: Sharing Information

As mentioned above, one of the two most common routine situations at work is wanting or needing to share information with someone (the other person is asking for something). For example, imagine that you work in a marketing research company. You routinely give presentations to clients using presentation technology. You've always used Microsoft's PowerPoint software, but you've heard and read about Prezi, a competing software, which does things a bit differently. A colleague down the hall writes to you one day to share some information. In Figure 5.1, Scott MacIntyre texts his colleague Myna St. Jean about Prezi, a PowerPoint alternative.

> ### WRITING PLAN FOR SHARING INFORMATION
> - **Opening:** Say hi; set the context for sharing.
> - **Body:** Share your information.
> - **Closing:** Sign off with your name and perhaps a closing salutation.

FIGURE 5.1 Routine Message Sharing Information

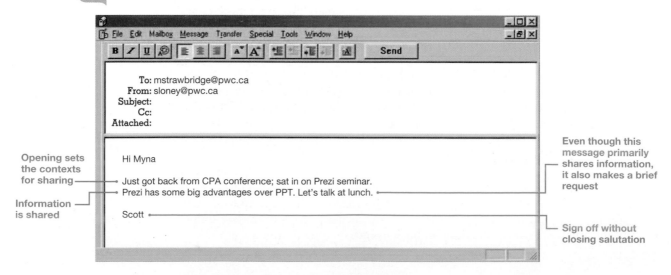

Opening sets the contexts for sharing

Information is shared

Even though this message primarily shares information, it also makes a brief request

Sign off without closing salutation

◼ Routine Situation: Requesting Information or Action

Many business messages are written to request information or action. Although the specific subject of each inquiry may differ, the similarity of purpose in routine requests enables writers to use the following writing plan.

> ### WRITING PLAN FOR AN INFORMATION OR ACTION REQUEST
>
> - **Opening:** Ask the most important question first or express a polite command.
> - **Body:** Explain the request logically and courteously. Ask other questions if necessary.
> - **Closing:** Request a specific action with an end date, if appropriate, and show appreciation.

Opening Directly

The most emphatic positions in a letter are the openings and closings. Readers tend to look at them first. The writer should capitalize on this tendency by putting the most significant statement first. The first sentence of an information request is usually a question or a polite command. It should not be an explanation or justification, unless resistance to the request is expected. When the information requested is likely to be forthcoming, immediately tell the reader what you want. This saves the reader's time and may ensure that the message is read. A busy executive who skims the mail, quickly reading subject lines and first sentences only, may grasp your request rapidly and act on it. A request that follows a lengthy explanation, on the other hand, may never be found.

> *Readers find the openings and closings of letters most valuable.*

An e-mail inquiring about hotel accommodations, shown in Figure 5.2, begins immediately with the most important idea. Can the hotel provide meeting rooms and accommodations for 250 people? Instead of opening with an explanation of who the writer is or how the writer happens to be writing this letter, the letter begins directly.

If several questions must be asked, you have two choices. You can ask the most important question first, as shown in Figure 5.2. An alternative opening begins with a summary statement, such as *Will you please answer the following questions about providing meeting rooms and accommodations for 250 people from May 25 through May 29, 2015*. Notice that the summarizing statement sounds like a question but has no question mark. That's because it's really a command disguised as a question. Rather than bluntly demanding information (*Answer the following questions*), we often soften commands by posing them as questions. Such statements, called rhetorical questions, should not be punctuated as questions because they do not require answers.

Details in the Body

The body of a message that requests information should provide necessary details and should be easy to read. Remember that the quality of the information obtained from a request letter depends on the clarity of the inquiry. If you analyze your needs, organize your ideas, and frame your request logically, you are likely to

> *The body of a request message may contain an explanation or a list of questions.*

FIGURE 5.2 E-mail Requesting Information

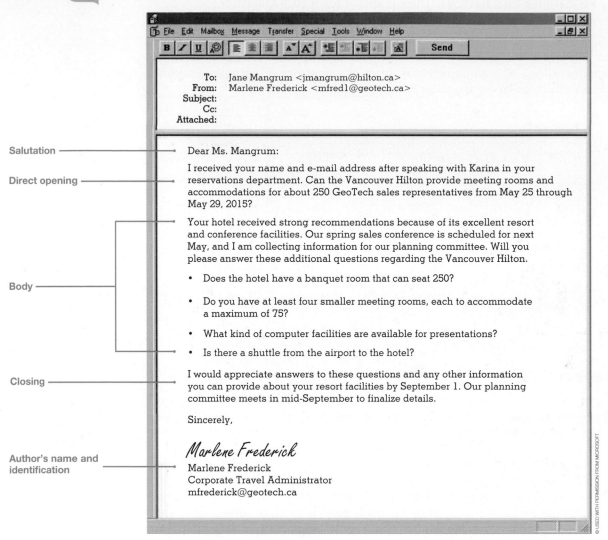

Salutation ——————— Dear Ms. Mangrum:

Direct opening ——————— I received your name and e-mail address after speaking with Karina in your reservations department. Can the Vancouver Hilton provide meeting rooms and accommodations for about 250 GeoTech sales representatives from May 25 through May 29, 2015?

Body ——————— Your hotel received strong recommendations because of its excellent resort and conference facilities. Our spring sales conference is scheduled for next May, and I am collecting information for our planning committee. Will you please answer these additional questions regarding the Vancouver Hilton.

- Does the hotel have a banquet room that can seat 250?

- Do you have at least four smaller meeting rooms, each to accommodate a maximum of 75?

- What kind of computer facilities are available for presentations?

- Is there a shuttle from the airport to the hotel?

Closing ——————— I would appreciate answers to these questions and any other information you can provide about your resort facilities by September 1. Our planning committee meets in mid-September to finalize details.

Sincerely,

Author's name and identification ——————— Marlene Frederick
Marlene Frederick
Corporate Travel Administrator
mfrederick@geotech.ca

To: Jane Mangrum <jmangrum@hilton.ca>
From: Marlene Frederick <mfred1@geotech.ca>
Subject:
Cc:
Attached:

receive a meaningful answer that doesn't require a follow-up message. Whenever possible, itemize the information to improve readability. Notice that the questions in Figure 5.2 are bulleted, and they are parallel. They demonstrate an excellent use of graphic highlighting.

Use the final paragraph to ask for specific action, to set an end date if appropriate, and to express appreciation, as shown in Figure 5.2.

> The ending of a request message should tell the reader what you want done and when.

It's always appropriate to end a request message with appreciation for the action that will be taken. Your appreciation will sound most sincere if you avoid mechanical, tired expressions, and just say what you mean such as *Thanks in advance* or *Sincerely*.

Routine Situation: Replying to Shared Information or Requests

> Before responding to requests, gather facts, check figures, and seek approval if necessary.

Often, the business situation calls for you to respond favourably to requests for information or action. A customer wants information about a product. A supplier asks to arrange a meeting. Another business inquires about one of your procedures. But before responding to any inquiry, be sure to check your facts and figures carefully.

Any message sent from one business to another is considered a legally binding contract. If a policy or procedure needs authorization, seek approval from a supervisor or executive before writing the message. In complying with requests, you'll want to apply the same direct pattern you used in making requests.

WRITING PLAN FOR A REPLY MESSAGE

- **Subject line:** Identify previous correspondence.
- **Opening:** Deliver the most important information first.
- **Body:** Explain and clarify information, provide additional information if appropriate, and build goodwill.
- **Closing:** End politely.

Subject Line Efficiency

An information response message should contain a subject line that helps the reader recognize the topic immediately. Efficient business communicators use a subject line to refer to earlier correspondence so that in the first sentence, the most important spot in a letter, they are free to emphasize the main idea. Notice in Figure 5.3 that the subject line identifies the subject completely.

> Use the subject line to refer to previous correspondence.

FIGURE 5.3 E-mail Response to Customer

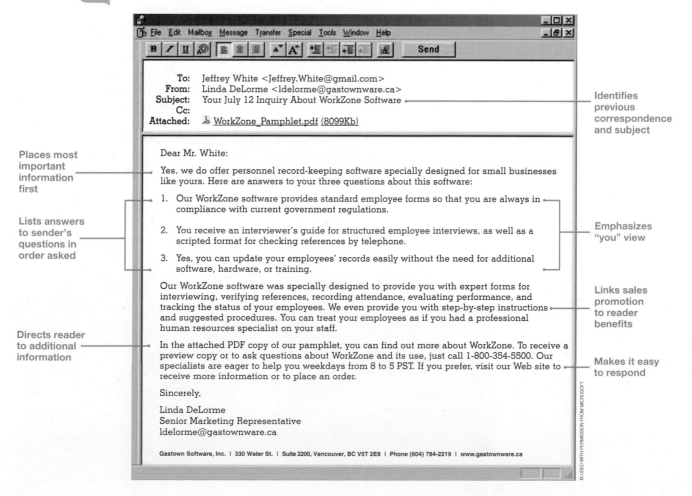

Identifies previous correspondence and subject

Places most important information first

Lists answers to sender's questions in order asked

Directs reader to additional information

Emphasizes "you" view

Links sales promotion to reader benefits

Makes it easy to respond

To: Jeffrey White <Jeffrey.White@gmail.com>
From: Linda DeLorme <ldelorme@gastownware.ca>
Subject: Your July 12 Inquiry About WorkZone Software
Cc:
Attached: WorkZone_Pamphlet.pdf (8099Kb)

Dear Mr. White:

Yes, we do offer personnel record-keeping software specially designed for small businesses like yours. Here are answers to your three questions about this software:

1. Our WorkZone software provides standard employee forms so that you are always in compliance with current government regulations.

2. You receive an interviewer's guide for structured employee interviews, as well as a scripted format for checking references by telephone.

3. Yes, you can update your employees' records easily without the need for additional software, hardware, or training.

Our WorkZone software was specially designed to provide you with expert forms for interviewing, verifying references, recording attendance, evaluating performance, and tracking the status of your employees. We even provide you with step-by-step instructions and suggested procedures. You can treat your employees as if you had a professional human resources specialist on your staff.

In the attached PDF copy of our pamphlet, you can find out more about WorkZone. To receive a preview copy or to ask questions about WorkZone and its use, just call 1-800-354-5500. Our specialists are eager to help you weekdays from 8 to 5 PST. If you prefer, visit our Web site to receive more information or to place an order.

Sincerely,

Linda DeLorme
Senior Marketing Representative
ldelorme@gastownware.ca

Gastown Software, Inc. | 330 Water St. | Suite 2200, Vancouver, BC V5T 2E8 | Phone (604) 784-2219 | www.gastownware.ca

© USED WITH PERMISSION FROM MICROSOFT

Opening Directly

In the first sentence of an information response, deliver the information the reader wants. Avoid wordy, drawn-out openings (*I have before me your letter of February 6, in which you request information about . . .*). More forceful and more efficient is an opener that answers the inquiry (*Here is the information you wanted about . . .*). When agreeing to a request for action, announce the good news promptly (*I will be happy to speak to your business communication class on the topic of . . .*).

Arranging Information Logically in the Body

When answering a group of questions or providing considerable data, arrange the information logically and make it readable by using lists, tables, headings, bold-face, italics, or other graphic devices. When customers or prospective customers inquire about products or services, your response should do more than merely supply answers. You'll also want to promote your organization and products. Be sure to present the promotional material with attention to the "you" view and to reader benefits (*You can use our standardized tests to free you from time-consuming employment screening*). You'll learn more about special techniques for developing sales and persuasive messages in Chapter 6.

> A good way to answer questions is to number or bullet each response.

Closing Politely

To avoid abruptness, include a pleasant closing remark that shows your willingness to help the reader. Provide extra information if appropriate. Tailor your remarks to fit this letter and this reader. Since everyone appreciates being recognized as an individual, avoid form-letter closings (e.g., *If we may be of further assistance, . . .*).

🗨 Routine Situation: Giving Instructions

Instruction messages must clearly explain how to complete a task. You may be asked to write instructions about how to repair a paper jam in the photocopier, order supplies, file a grievance, or hire new employees. Like requests and responses, instruction messages follow a straightforward, direct approach. They must use plain English and be especially clear. Instructions clearly explain how to complete a task, but they may also cover policies and official procedures, which establish rules of conduct to be followed within an organization.

Dividing Instructions Into Steps

Before writing instructions for a process, be sure you understand the process completely. Create logical steps in the correct order. Practice completing the procedure yourself first. Here is a writing plan that will help you get started:

> **WRITING PLAN FOR INSTRUCTION MESSAGES**
> - **Subject line:** Summarize the content of the message.
> - **Opening:** Expand the subject line by stating the main idea concisely in a full sentence.
> - **Body:** Divide the instructions into steps. List the steps in the order in which they are to be carried out. Arrange the items vertically with bullets or numbers. Begin each step with an action verb using the imperative mood (command language such as *do this, don't do that*).
> - **Closing:** Request a specific action, summarize the message, or present a closing thought. If appropriate, include a deadline and a reason.

The most effective way to list directions is to use command language called the imperative mood. Think recipes, owner manuals, and assembly instructions. The imperative mood differs from the indicative mood in that it requests an action, whereas the indicative mood describes a statement as shown here:

Indicative Mood	Imperative (Command) Mood
The contract should be sent immediately.	Send the contract immediately.
The first step involves loading the software.	Load the software first.
A survey of employees is necessary to learn what options they prefer.	Survey employees to learn the options they prefer.

If you are asked to prepare a list of instructions that is not part of a message, include a title such as "How to Clear Paper Jams." Include an opening paragraph explaining why the instructions are needed.

Revising a Message Delivering Instructions

Figure 5.4 shows the first draft of an interoffice memo written by Troy Bell. His memo was meant to announce a new method for employees to follow in advertising open positions. However, the tone was negative, the explanation of the problem rambled, and the new method was unclear. Notice, too, that Troy's first draft told readers what they *shouldn't* do (*Do not submit advertisements for new employees directly to an Internet job bank or a newspaper*). It is more helpful to tell readers what they *should* do. Finally, Troy's first memo closed with a threat instead of showing readers how this new practice will help them.

In the revision Troy improved the tone considerably. The subject line contains a *please*, which is always pleasant to see even if one is giving an order. The subject line also includes a verb and specifies the purpose of the memo. Instead of expressing his ideas with negative words and threats, Troy revised his message to explain objectively and concisely what went wrong.

Troy realized that his original explanation of the new procedure was vague and unclear. To clarify the instructions, he itemized and numbered the steps. Each step begins with an action verb in the imperative (command) mood (*Write, Bring, Let,* and *Pick up*). It is sometimes difficult to force all the steps in a list into this kind of command language. Troy struggled, but by trying different wording, he finally found verbs that worked.

> Numbered steps and action verbs improve the clarity of instructions.

Why should you go to so much trouble to make lists and achieve parallelism? Because readers can comprehend what you have said much more quickly. Parallel language also makes you look professional and efficient.

In writing messages that deliver instructions, be careful of tone. Today's managers and team leaders seek employee participation and cooperation. These goals can't be achieved, though, if the writer sounds like a dictator or an autocrat. Avoid making accusations and blaming people. Rather, explain changes, give reasons, and suggest benefits to the reader. Assume that employees want to contribute to the success of the organization and to their own achievement. Notice in the Figure 5.4 revision that Troy tells readers that they will save time and have their open positions filled more quickly if they follow the new method.

◼ Routine Situation: Making a Complaint or Claim

In business many things can go wrong—promised shipments are late, warranted goods fail, contracts are breached, or service is disappointing. When you as a customer must write to identify or correct a wrong, the message is called a *complaint*

FIGURE 5.4 Memo Delivering Instructions

Before

Date:	January 5, 2015
To:	Ruth DiSilvestro, Manager
From:	Troy Bell, Human Resources
Subject:	Job Advertisement Misunderstanding

Uses vague, negative subject line

We had no idea last month when we implemented a new hiring process that major problems would result. Due to the fact that every department is now placing Internet advertisements for new-hires individually, the difficulties occurred. This cannot continue. Perhaps we did not make it clear at the time, but all newly hired employees who are hired for a position should be requested through this office.

Fails to pinpoint main idea in opening

Do not submit your advertisements for new employees directly to an Internet job bank or a newspaper. After you write them, they should be brought to Human Resources, where they will be centralized. You should discuss each ad with one of our specialists. Then we will place the ad at an appropriate Internet site or other publication. If you do not follow these guidelines, chaos will result. You may pick up applicant folders from us the day after the closing date in an ad.

Makes new process hard to follow

Uses threats instead of showing benefits to reader

After

MEMORANDUM

Date:	January 5, 2015
To:	Ruth DiSilvestro, Manager
From:	Troy Bell, Human Resources TB
Subject:	Please Follow New Job Advertisement Process

Employs informative, courteous, upbeat subject line

To find the right candidates for your open positions as fast as possible, we are implementing a new routine. Effective today, all advertisements for departmental job openings should be routed through the Human Resources Department.

Combines "you" view with main idea in opening

A major problem resulted from the change in hiring procedures implemented last month. Each department is placing job advertisements for new-hires individually, when all such requests should be centralized in this office. To process applications more efficiently, please follow these steps:

Explains why change in procedures is necessary

1. Write an advertisement for a position in your department.

2. Bring the ad to Human Resources and discuss it with one of our specialists.

3. Let Human Resources place the ad at an appropriate Internet job bank or submit it to a newspaper.

4. Pick up applicant folders from Human Resources the day following the closing date provided in the ad.

Lists easy-to-follow steps and starts each step with a verb

Following these guidelines will save you work and will also enable Human Resources to help you fill your openings more quickly. Call Ann Edmonds at Ext. 2505 if you have questions about this process.

Closes by reinforcing benefits to reader

Tips for Writing Instructions
- Arrange each step in the order it should be completed.
- Start each instruction with an action verb in the imperative (command) mood.
- Be careful of tone when writing messages that give orders.
- Show reader benefits if you are encouraging use of the process.

or a *claim*. Straightforward complaints and claims are those to which you expect the receiver to agree readily. While your first impulse may be to make a phone call, send an e-mail, or use the company's "Contact Us" form online, you may not get the results you seek. You may need to use the letter channel to ensure your complaint or claim is taken more seriously. Below is the writing plan for a complaint or claim that uses a direct approach.

> **WRITING PLAN FOR A COMPLAINT OR CLAIM**
> - **Opening:** Describe clearly the desired action.
> - **Body:** Explain the nature of the complaint or claim, explain how the complaint or claim is justified, and provide details regarding the action requested.
> - **Closing:** End pleasantly with a goodwill statement and include an end date if appropriate.

Opening With Action

If you have a legitimate claim, you can expect a positive response from a company. Smart businesses today want to hear from their customers. That's why you should open a claim letter with a clear statement of the problem or with the action you want the receiver to take. You might expect a replacement, a refund, a new order, credit to your account, correction of a billing error, free repairs, free inspection, or cancellation of an order.

When the remedy is obvious, state it immediately (*Please send us 24 Royal hot-air popcorn poppers to replace the 24 hot-oil poppers sent in error with our order shipped January 4*). When the remedy is less obvious, you might ask for a change in policy or procedure or simply for an explanation (*Because three of our employees with confirmed reservations were refused rooms at your hotel on September 16, would you please clarify your policy regarding reservations and late arrivals*).

Explaining in the Body

In the body of a claim letter, explain the problem and justify your request. Provide the necessary details so that the difficulty can be corrected without further correspondence. Avoid becoming angry or trying to lay blame. Bear in mind that the person reading your letter is seldom responsible for the problem. Instead, state the facts logically, objectively, and unemotionally; let the reader decide on the causes.

Include copies of all pertinent documents such as invoices, sales receipts, catalogue descriptions, and repair records. (By the way, be sure to send copies and not your originals, which could be lost.) When service is involved, cite names of individuals spoken to and dates of calls. Assume that a company honestly wants to satisfy its customers—because most do. When an alternative remedy exists, describe it (*If you are unable to send 24 Royal hot-air popcorn poppers immediately, please credit our account now and notify us when they become available*).

Closing Pleasantly

Conclude a claim letter with a courteous statement that promotes goodwill and expresses a desire for continued relations. If appropriate, include an end date (*We realize that mistakes in ordering and shipping sometimes occur. Because we've enjoyed your prompt service in the past, we hope that you will be able to send us the hot-air poppers by January 15*).

Finally, in making complaints and claims, act promptly. Delaying makes them appear less important. Delayed complaints or claims are also more difficult to verify.

By taking the time to put your claim in writing, you indicate your seriousness. A hard-copy complaint or claim (i.e., a letter) also gestures toward the seriousness with which you take the message, and may net you a fuller response. Either way, be sure to keep a copy of your complaint or claim message.

Putting It All Together

Figure 5.5 shows a hostile claim e-mail that vents the writer's anger but accomplishes little else. Its tone is belligerent, and it assumes that the company intentionally overcharged the customer. Furthermore, it fails to tell the reader how to remedy the problem. The revision chooses a more "permanent" and formal channel—a letter. It tempers the tone, describes the problem objectively, and provides facts and figures. Most importantly, it specifies exactly what the customer wants done.

Notice that the letter in Figure 5.5 is shown with the return address typed above the date. This personal business style may be used when typing on paper without a printed letterhead.

Routine Situation: Replying to Complaints and Claims

Even the best-run and best-loved businesses occasionally receive claims or complaints from consumers. When a company receives a claim and decides to respond favourably, the message is called an *adjustment*. Most businesses make adjustments promptly: they replace merchandise, refund money, extend discounts, send coupons, and repair goods. Businesses make favourable adjustments to legitimate claims for two reasons.

First, consumers are often protected by law for recovery of damages. If, for example, you find an insect in a package of frozen peas, the food processor of that package is bound by contractual law to replace it. If you suffer injury, the processor may be liable for damages. Second, and more obviously, most organizations genuinely want to satisfy their customers and retain their business. This is especially true since the advent of social media. The last thing companies want are complaints going viral on Facebook or Twitter, which can lead to a damaged reputation, poorer sales, and the need for a time-consuming and expensive crisis communications process.

FIGURE 5.5 Claim Letter

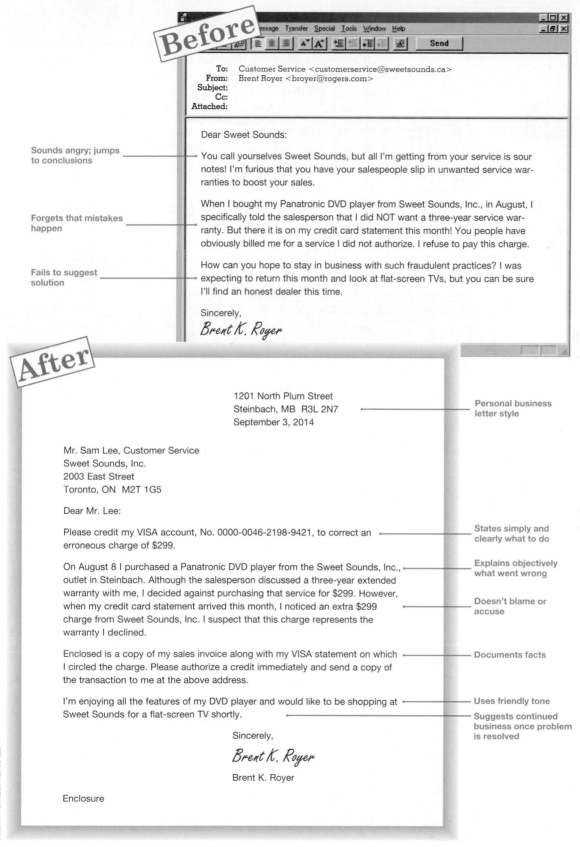

Before

To:	Customer Service <customerservice@sweetsounds.ca>
From:	Brent Royer <broyer@rogers.com>
Subject:	
Cc:	
Attached:	

Dear Sweet Sounds:

Sounds angry; jumps to conclusions — You call yourselves Sweet Sounds, but all I'm getting from your service is sour notes! I'm furious that you have your salespeople slip in unwanted service warranties to boost your sales.

Forgets that mistakes happen — When I bought my Panatronic DVD player from Sweet Sounds, Inc., in August, I specifically told the salesperson that I did NOT want a three-year service warranty. But there it is on my credit card statement this month! You people have obviously billed me for a service I did not authorize. I refuse to pay this charge.

Fails to suggest solution — How can you hope to stay in business with such fraudulent practices? I was expecting to return this month and look at flat-screen TVs, but you can be sure I'll find an honest dealer this time.

Sincerely,

Brent K. Royer

After

1201 North Plum Street
Steinbach, MB R3L 2N7
September 3, 2014

Personal business letter style

Mr. Sam Lee, Customer Service
Sweet Sounds, Inc.
2003 East Street
Toronto, ON M2T 1G5

Dear Mr. Lee:

Please credit my VISA account, No. 0000-0046-2198-9421, to correct an erroneous charge of $299. — **States simply and clearly what to do**

On August 8 I purchased a Panatronic DVD player from the Sweet Sounds, Inc., outlet in Steinbach. Although the salesperson discussed a three-year extended warranty with me, I decided against purchasing that service for $299. However, when my credit card statement arrived this month, I noticed an extra $299 charge from Sweet Sounds, Inc. I suspect that this charge represents the warranty I declined. — **Explains objectively what went wrong** / **Doesn't blame or accuse**

Enclosed is a copy of my sales invoice along with my VISA statement on which I circled the charge. Please authorize a credit immediately and send a copy of the transaction to me at the above address. — **Documents facts**

I'm enjoying all the features of my DVD player and would like to be shopping at Sweet Sounds for a flat-screen TV shortly. — **Uses friendly tone** / **Suggests continued business once problem is resolved**

Sincerely,

Brent K. Royer

Brent K. Royer

Enclosure

HOW TO WIN AN ARGUMENT WITH A CUSTOMER:

YOU'RE RIGHT.

GOFF

© TED GOFF, WWW.TEDGOFF.COM

In responding to customer claims, you must first decide whether to grant the claim. Unless the claim is obviously fraudulent or excessive, you will probably grant it. When you say yes, your adjustment message will be good news to the reader. Deliver that good news by using the direct pattern as shown in the writing plan below. When your response is no, the indirect pattern might be more appropriate. Chapter 7 discusses the indirect pattern for conveying negative news.

You have three goals in adjustment messages:

- Rectifying the wrong, if one exists
- Regaining the confidence of the customer
- Promoting further business

WRITING PLAN FOR REPLYING TO A COMPLAINT OR CLAIM

- **Subject line (optional):** Identify the previous correspondence.
- **Opening:** Grant request or announce the adjustment immediately. Include resale or sales promotion if appropriate.
- **Body:** Provide details about how you are complying with the request. Try to regain the customer's confidence, and include resale or sales promotion if appropriate.
- **Closing:** End positively with a forward-looking thought, express confidence in future business relations, and avoid referring to unpleasantness.

Revealing Good News in the Opening

Instead of beginning with a review of what went wrong, present the good news immediately. When Amy Hopkins responded to Sound, Inc.'s claim about a missing shipment, her first draft, shown at the top of Figure 5.6, was angry. No wonder. Sound, Inc., had apparently provided the wrong shipping address, and the goods were returned. But once Amy and her company decided to send a second shipment and comply with the customer's claim, she had to give up the anger and strive to retain the goodwill and the business of this customer. The improved version of her letter announces that a new shipment will arrive shortly.

If you decide to comply with a customer's claim, let the receiver know immediately. Don't begin your letter with a negative statement (*We are very sorry to hear that you are having trouble with your Sno-Flake ice crusher*). This approach reminds the reader of the problem and may rekindle the heated emotions or unhappy feelings experienced when the claim was written. Instead, focus on the good news. The following openings for various letters illustrate how to begin a message with good news.

You may take your Sno-Flake ice crusher to Ben's Appliances at 310 First Street, Moose Jaw, where it will be repaired at no cost to you.

Thanks for your letter about your new Winter-Buster tires. You are certainly justified in expecting them to last more than 12,000 km.

We agree with you that the warranty on your iPod Nano should be extended for six months.

The enclosed cheque for $325 demonstrates our desire to satisfy our customers and earn their confidence.

In announcing that you will grant a claim, be sure to do so without a grudging tone—even if you have reservations about whether the claim is legitimate. Once you decide to comply with the customer's request, do so happily. Avoid half-hearted or

FIGURE 5.6 Adjustment Letter

Before

Sir:

Fails to reveal good news immediately; blames customer

In response to your recent complaint about a missing shipment, it's very difficult to deliver merchandise when we have been given the wrong address.

Creates ugly tone with negative words and sarcasm

Our investigators looked into your problem shipment and determined that it was sent immediately after we received the order. According to the shipper's records, it was delivered to the warehouse address given on your stationery: 3590 University Avenue, Saint John, New Brunswick E2M 1G7. Unfortunately, no one at that address would accept delivery, so the shipment was returned to us. I see from your current stationery that your company has a new address. With the proper address, we probably could have delivered this shipment.

Sounds grudging and reluctant in granting claim

Although we feel that it is entirely appropriate to charge you shipping and restocking fees, as is our standard practice on returned goods, in this instance we will waive those fees. We hope this second shipment finally catches up with you.

Sincerely,

Amy Hopkins

After

Ew ELECTRONIC WAREHOUSE
930 Abbott Park Place
Saint John, New Brunswick E3L 0T7

February 21, 2015

Mr. Jeremy Garber
Sound, Inc.
2293 Second Avenue
Saint John, NB E3M 2R5

Dear Mr. Garber:

Uses customer's name in salutation

SUBJECT: YOUR FEBRUARY 20 LETTER ABOUT YOUR PURCHASE ORDER

You should receive by February 28 a second shipment of the speakers, headphones, and other electronic equipment that you ordered January 20.

Announces good news immediately

The first shipment of this order was delivered January 28 to 3590 University Avenue, Saint John, NB. When no one at that address would accept the shipment, it was returned to us. Now that I have your letter, I see that the order should have been sent to 2293 Second Avenue, Saint John, New Brunswick E3M 2R5. When an order is undeliverable, we usually try to verify the shipping address by telephoning the customer. Somehow the return of this shipment was not caught by our normally painstaking shipping clerks. You can be sure that I will investigate shipping and return procedures with our clerks immediately to see if we can improve existing methods.

Regains confidence of customer by explaining what happened and by suggesting plans for improvement

As you know, Mr. Garber, our volume business allows us to sell wholesale electronics equipment at the lowest possible prices. However, we do not want to be so large that we lose touch with valued customers like you. Over the years our customers' respect has made us successful, and we hope that the prompt delivery of this shipment will earn yours.

Closes confidently with genuine appeal for customer's respect

Sincerely,

Amy Hopkins

Amy Hopkins
Distribution Manager

c David Cole
Shipping Department

reluctant responses (*Although the Sno-Flake ice crusher works well when it is used properly, we have decided to allow you to take yours to Ben's Appliances for repair at our expense*).

Explaining Compliance in the Body

In responding to claims, most organizations sincerely want to correct a wrong. They want to do more than just make the customer happy. They want to stand behind their products and services; they want to do what's right.

In the body of the message, explain how you are complying with the claim. In all but the most routine claims, you should also seek to regain the confidence of the customer. You might reasonably expect that a customer who has experienced difficulty with a product, with delivery, with billing, or with service has lost faith in your organization. Rebuilding that faith is important for future business.

How to rebuild lost confidence depends on the situation and the claim. If procedures need to be revised, explain what changes will be made. If a product has defective parts, explain how the product is being improved. If service is faulty, describe genuine efforts to improve it. Notice in Figure 5.6 that the writer promises to investigate shipping procedures to see if improvements might prevent future mishaps.

Sometimes the problem is not with the product but with the way it's being used. In other instances customers misunderstand warranties or inadvertently cause delivery and billing mix-ups by supplying incorrect information. Remember that rational and sincere explanations will do much to regain the confidence of unhappy customers.

In your explanation avoid emphasizing negative words such as *trouble*, *regret*, *misunderstanding*, *fault*, *defective*, *error*, *inconvenience*, and *unfortunately*. Keep your message positive and upbeat.

Deciding Whether to Apologize

Whether to apologize is a debatable issue. Some experts argue that apologies remind customers of their complaints and are therefore negative, and that overuse of apologizing leads to a meaningless "apology culture."[2] These writers avoid apologies; instead they concentrate on how they are satisfying the customer. Real messages that respond to customers' claims, however, often include apologies. If you feel that your company is at fault and that an apology is an appropriate goodwill gesture, by all means include it. Be careful, though, not to admit negligence. You'll learn more about responding to negative messages in Chapter 7.

Showing Confidence in the Closing

End positively by expressing confidence that the problem has been resolved and that continued business relations will result. You might mention the product in a favourable light, suggest a new product, express your appreciation for the customer's business, or anticipate future business. It's often appropriate to refer to the desire to be of service and to satisfy customers. Notice how the following closings illustrate a positive, confident tone.

> Your Sno-Flake ice crusher will help you remain cool and refreshed this summer. For your additional summer enjoyment, consider our Smoky Joe tabletop gas grill, shown in the enclosed summer catalogue. We genuinely value your business and look forward to your future orders.

> We hope that this refund cheque convinces you of our sincere desire to satisfy our customers. Our goal is to earn your confidence and continue to justify that confidence with quality products and matchless service.

> You were most helpful in telling us about this situation and giving us an opportunity to correct it. We sincerely appreciate your cooperation.

Most businesses comply with claims because they want to promote customer goodwill.

Because negative words suggest blame and fault, avoid them in letters that attempt to build customer goodwill.

End your letter by looking ahead positively.

In all your future dealings with us, you will find us striving our hardest to earn your confidence by serving you with efficiency and sincere concern.

Routine Situation: Recommending Someone

Recommendation messages may be written to nominate people for awards and for membership in organizations. They may also be used to let someone within the organization know about the good work or skills being displayed by an employee. Most frequently, though, they are written to evaluate present or former employees as part of the job application process.

The central concern in these messages is honesty. When writing a recommendation, you should avoid exaggerating or distorting a candidate's qualifications to cover up weaknesses or to destroy the person's chances. Ethically and legally, you have a duty to the candidate as well as to other employers to describe that person truthfully and objectively. You don't, however, have to endorse everyone who asks. Since recommendations are generally voluntary, you can—and should—resist writing recommendations for individuals you can't truthfully support. Ask these people to find other recommenders who know them or their performance better.

Some businesspeople today refuse to write recommendations for former employees because they fear lawsuits. Others argue that recommendations are useless because they're always positive. Despite the general avoidance of negatives, well-written recommendations do help match candidates with jobs. Hiring companies learn more about a candidate's skills and potential. As a result, they are able to place a candidate properly. Therefore, you should learn to write such messages because you will surely be expected to do so in your future career.

For recommendation messages, use the direct strategy as described in the following writing plan.

> You may write messages recommending people to someone else within your organization or outside of it, for awards, for membership in organizations, or for employment.

WRITING PLAN FOR A HARD-COPY EMPLOYMENT RECOMMENDATION

- **Opening:** Identify the applicant, the position, and the reason for writing. State that the message is confidential. Establish your relationship with the applicant. Describe the length of employment or relationship.
- **Body:** Describe job duties. Provide specific examples of the applicant's professional and personal skills and attributes. Compare the applicant with others in his or her field.
- **Closing:** Summarize the significant attributes of the applicant. Offer an overall rating. Draw a conclusion regarding the recommendation.

> The opening of a letter of recommendation should establish the reason for writing and the relationship of the writer.

Identifying the Purpose in the Opening

Begin an employment recommendation by identifying the candidate and the position sought, if it is known. State that your remarks are confidential, and suggest that you are writing at the request of the applicant. Describe your relationship with the candidate, as shown here:

> Ms. Cindy Rosales, whom your organization is considering for the position of media trainer, requested that I submit confidential information

on her behalf. Ms. Rosales worked under my supervision for the past two years in our Video Training Centre.

Letters that recommend individuals for awards may open with more supportive statements, such as the following:

> I'm very pleased to nominate Robert Walsh for the Employee-of-the-Month award. For the past 16 months, Mr. Walsh served as staff accountant in my division. During that time he distinguished himself by . . . .

Describing Performance in the Body

> **A good recommendation describes general qualities ("organizational and interpersonal skills") backed up by specific evidence that illustrates those qualities.**

The body of an employment recommendation should describe the applicant's job performance and potential. Employers are particularly interested in such traits as communication skills, organizational skills, people skills, the ability to work with a team, the ability to work independently, honesty, dependability, ambition, loyalty, and initiative. In describing these traits, be sure to back them up with evidence. One of the biggest weaknesses in letters of recommendation is that writers tend to make global, non-specific statements (*He was careful and accurate* versus *He completed eight financial statements monthly with about 99 percent accuracy*). Employers prefer definite, task-related descriptions:

> As a training development specialist, Ms. Rosales demonstrated superior organizational and interpersonal skills. She started as a Specialist I, writing scripts for interactive video modules. After six months she was promoted to team leader. In that role she supervised five employees who wrote, produced, evaluated, revised, and installed 14 computer/videodisc training courses over a period of 18 months.

Be especially careful to support any negative comments with verification (not *He was slower than other customer service reps* but *He answered 25 calls an hour, while most service reps average 40 calls an hour*). In reporting deficiencies, be sure to describe behaviour (*Her last two reports were late and had to be rewritten by her supervisor*) rather than evaluate it (*She is unreliable and her reports are careless*).

Evaluating in the Conclusion

> **The closing of a recommendation presents an overall ranking and may provide an offer to supply more information by telephone.**

In the final paragraph of a recommendation, you should offer an overall evaluation. Indicate how you would rank this person in relation to others in similar positions. Many managers add a statement indicating whether they would re-hire the applicant, given the chance. If you are strongly supportive, summarize the candidate's best qualities. In the closing you might also offer to answer questions by telephone. Such a statement, though, could suggest that the candidate has weak skills and that you will make damaging statements orally but not in print. Here's how our sample letter might close:

> Ms. Rosales is one of the most productive employees I have supervised. I would rank her in the top 10 percent of all the media specialists with whom I have worked. Were she to return to Waterloo, we would be pleased to re-hire her. If you need additional information, call me at (519) 555-3019.

General letters of recommendation, written when the candidate has no specific position in mind, can begin with a salutation like *To Prospective Employers*. More specific recommendations, to support applications to known positions, address an individual. This type of specific recommendation letter is shown in Figure 5.7.

FIGURE 5.7 Recommendation Letter

Gate Gourmet

2498 Brittania Rd. E., Mississauga, ON L4W 2P7   E-Mail: sbassos@gategourmet.com   Phone: 905-405-4100
Web: www.gategourmet.com

March 2, 2015

Bonnie Telchinsky, HR Specialist
University Health Network
288 University Ave., Suite 1216
Toronto, ONM5A 2C8

Dear Ms. Telchinsky:

Roberta Fuyuni was in touch with me recently to request I write a reference letter for her, and I'm very pleased to do so confidentially. I understand Roberta has recently applied for the position of Manager, Food Operations, at the University Health Network. Roberta worked for me for over five years as Manager, Airline Operations.

In this position, Roberta managed a staff of between 60 and 80 cooks, packagers, logistics, and marketing and sales employees. Essentially, Roberta was second in command after me in taking care of our large business providing meals for Air Canada, WestJet, and other North American and international carriers. Roberta began as a cook, and after finishing her logistics diploma, she was promoted to Logistics Coordinator. Within two years she had earned her MBA and we promoted her again to Manager, Airline Operations, during which time she increased sales in her division by over 15%.

Besides understanding the business (ingredient purchasing and budgeting, food preparation, health and safety, logistics, marketing and sales), Roberta is well liked by both executives and employees because of her excellent soft skills. These skills came in handy as we transitioned from being owned by Cara to Gategroup. She regularly provides positive feedback to her employees, and shows initiative. For example, we were using an outdated performance review system, and Roberta developed and piloted a much more successful 360-degree system that became popular with both employees and managers.

I'm eager to aid Roberta in her transition from the airline food preparation industry to the institutional food services sector, and hope that I have explained effectively in my comments above Roberta's strong work ethic, innovative character, and ability to manage. In other words, I highly recommend Roberta without reservation. If you'd like to discuss my recommendation please contact me at the coordinates listed above.

Sincerely,

Steve Bassos
VP, Airline

Tips for Writing Letters of Recommendation
- Identify the purpose and confidentiality of the message.
- Establish your relationship with the applicant.
- Describe the length of employment and job duties, if relevant.
- Provide specific examples of the applicant's professional and personal skills.
- Compare the applicant with others in his or her field.
- Offer an overall rating of the applicant.
- Summarize the significant attributes of the applicant.
- Draw a conclusion regarding the recommendation.

Figure 5.7 illustrates a complete job application letter of recommendation and provides a summary of writing tips. After naming the applicant and the position sought, the letter describes the applicant's present duties. Instead of merely naming positive qualities (*He is personable, possesses superior people skills, works well with a team, is creative, and shows initiative*), these attributes are demonstrated with specific examples and details.

🗨 Routine Situation: Expressing Goodwill

Goodwill messages, which include thanks, recognition, and sympathy, sometimes intimidate communicators. Finding the right words to express feelings is sometimes more difficult than writing ordinary business documents. Also, as humans we find it easier to criticize than we do to praise.

Writers tend to procrastinate when it comes to goodwill messages, or else they send a ready-made card or pick up the telephone. Remember, though, that the personal sentiments of the sender are always more expressive and more meaningful to readers than are printed cards or oral messages. Taking the time to write gives more importance to our well-wishing. Personal notes also provide a record that can be reread, and treasured.

In expressing thanks, recognition, or sympathy, you should always do so promptly. These messages are easier to write when the situation is fresh in your mind. They also mean more to the recipient. And don't forget that a prompt thank-you message carries the hidden message that you care and that you consider the event to be important. You will learn to write four kinds of goodwill messages—thanks, congratulations, praise, and sympathy. Instead of writing plans for each of them, we recommend that you concentrate on the five Ss. Goodwill messages should be

- **Selfless.** Be sure to focus the message solely on the receiver, not the sender. Don't talk about yourself; avoid such comments as *I remember when I . . . .*
- **Specific.** Personalize the message by mentioning specific incidents or characteristics of the receiver. Telling a colleague *Great speech* is much less effective than *Great story about Potash Corp. marketing in Washington.* Take care to verify names and other facts.
- **Sincere.** Let your words show genuine feelings. Rehearse in your mind how you would express the message to the receiver orally. Then transform that conversational language to your written message. Avoid pretentious, formal, or flowery language (*It gives me great pleasure to extend felicitations on the occasion of your firm's 20th anniversary*).
- **Spontaneous.** Keep the message fresh and enthusiastic. Avoid canned phrases (*Congratulations on your promotion*; *Good luck in the future*). Strive for directness and naturalness, not creative brilliance.
- **Short.** Although goodwill messages can be as long as needed, try to accomplish your purpose in only a few sentences. What is most important is remembering an individual. Such caring does not require documentation or wordiness. Individuals and business organizations often use special note cards or stationery for brief messages.

Thanks

When someone has done you a favour or when an action merits praise, you need to extend thanks or show appreciation. Letters (or tweets) of appreciation may be written to customers for their orders, to hosts and hostesses for their hospitality, to individuals for kindnesses performed, and especially to customers who complain. After all, complainers are actually providing you with "free consulting reports from the field." One recent study found that "83% of the complainants that received a [Twitter] reply liked or loved the fact that the company responded."[3] Complainers who feel that they were listened to may become the greatest promoters of an organization.

Because the receiver will be pleased to hear from you, you can open directly with the purpose of your message. The e-mail in Figure 5.8 thanks a speaker who addressed a local professional association. Although such thank-you messages can be quite short, this one is a little longer because the writer wants to

---

Messages that express thanks, recognition, and sympathy should be written promptly.

Goodwill messages are most effective when they are selfless, specific, sincere, spontaneous, and short.

Send letters of thanks to customers, hosts, and individuals who have performed kind acts.

OFFICE INSIDER

"Saying 'Thank You' is an important concept in our business. When people are sincerely appreciated for their efforts, they tend to be more effective and do a better job."

FIGURE 5.8 E-Mail Thank-You for a Favour

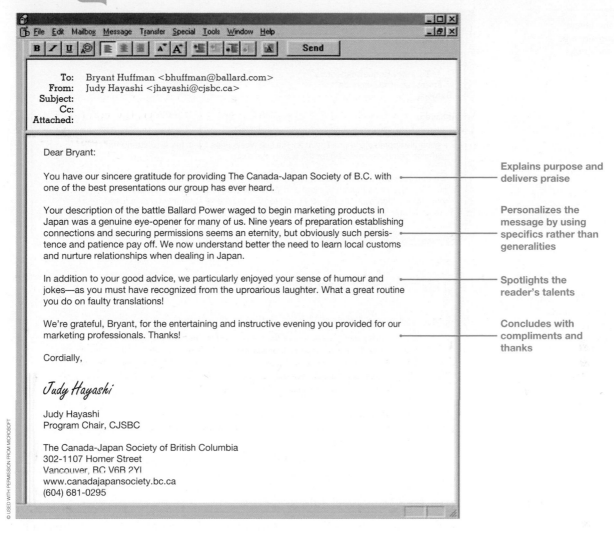

Dear Bryant:	
You have our sincere gratitude for providing The Canada-Japan Society of B.C. with one of the best presentations our group has ever heard.	**Explains purpose and delivers praise**
Your description of the battle Ballard Power waged to begin marketing products in Japan was a genuine eye-opener for many of us. Nine years of preparation establishing connections and securing permissions seems an eternity, but obviously such persistence and patience pay off. We now understand better the need to learn local customs and nurture relationships when dealing in Japan.	**Personalizes the message by using specifics rather than generalities**
In addition to your good advice, we particularly enjoyed your sense of humour and jokes—as you must have recognized from the uproarious laughter. What a great routine you do on faulty translations!	**Spotlights the reader's talents**
We're grateful, Bryant, for the entertaining and instructive evening you provided for our marketing professionals. Thanks!	**Concludes with compliments and thanks**

Figure content:

To: Bryant Huffman <bhuffman@ballard.com>
From: Judy Hayashi <jhayashi@cjsbc.ca>
Subject:
Cc:
Attached:

Cordially,

Judy Hayashi

Judy Hayashi
Program Chair, CJSBC

The Canada-Japan Society of British Columbia
302-1107 Homer Street
Vancouver, BC V6B 2Y1
www.canadajapansociety.bc.ca
(604) 681-0295

lend importance to the receiver's efforts. Notice that every sentence relates to the receiver and offers enthusiastic praise. And, by using the receiver's name along with contractions and positive words, the writer makes the letter sound warm and conversational.

Written notes that show appreciation and express thanks are significant to their receivers. In expressing thanks, you can send a text or an e-mail, or when appropriate and meaningful, write a short hard-copy note in a special card and deliver it by hand. The following messages provide models for expressing thanks for a gift, for a favour, and for hospitality.

TO EXPRESS THANKS FOR A GIFT

Thanks, Laura, to you and the other members of the department for honouring me with the elegant Waterford crystal vase at the party celebrating my twentieth anniversary with the company.

The height and shape of the vase are perfect to hold roses and other bouquets from my garden. Each time I fill it, I'll remember your thoughtfulness in choosing this lovely gift for me.

> Identify the gift, tell why you appreciate it, and explain how you will use it.

TO SEND THANKS FOR A FAVOUR

> Say what the favour means using sincere, simple statements.

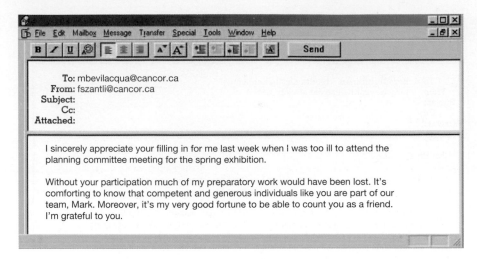

To: mbevilacqua@cancor.ca
From: fszantli@cancor.ca
Subject:
Cc:
Attached:

I sincerely appreciate your filling in for me last week when I was too ill to attend the planning committee meeting for the spring exhibition.

Without your participation much of my preparatory work would have been lost. It's comforting to know that competent and generous individuals like you are part of our team, Mark. Moreover, it's my very good fortune to be able to count you as a friend. I'm grateful to you.

TO EXTEND THANKS FOR HOSPITALITY

> Compliment the fine food, charming surroundings, warm hospitality, excellent host and hostess, and good company.

Jeffrey and I want you to know how much we enjoyed the dinner party for our department that you hosted Saturday evening. Your charming home and warm hospitality, along with the lovely dinner and sinfully delicious chocolate dessert, combined to create a truly memorable evening.

Most of all, though, we appreciate your kindness in cultivating togetherness in our department. Thanks, Jennifer, for being such a special person.

Replies to Goodwill Messages

By all means, respond to goodwill messages. They are attempts to connect personally, to reach out and form professional and/or personal bonds. Failing to respond to notes of congratulations and most other goodwill messages is like failing to say "You're welcome" when someone says "Thank you." Responding to such messages is simply the right thing to do. Avoid minimizing your achievements with comments that suggest you don't really deserve the praise or that the sender is exaggerating your good qualities.

TO ANSWER A CONGRATULATORY NOTE

Thanks for your kind words regarding my award, and thanks, too, for sending me the newspaper clipping. I truly appreciate your thoughtfulness and warm wishes.

TO RESPOND TO A PAT ON THE BACK

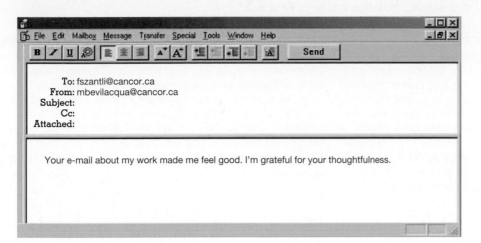

> Take the time to respond to any goodwill message you receive.

Sympathy

Most of us can bear misfortune and grief more easily when we know that others care. Messages expressing sympathy are probably more difficult to write than any other kind of message. "Sympathy" cards from the store make the task easier—but they are far less meaningful. Grieving friends want to know what you think—not what card writers think. In writing a personalized sympathy note, (1) refer to the death or misfortune sensitively, using words that show you understand what a crushing blow it is; (2) in the case of a death, praise the deceased in a personal way; (3) offer assistance without going into excessive detail; and (4) end on a reassuring, forward-looking note. Sympathy messages may be electronic, but handwriting is more personal.

> Sympathy messages should refer to the misfortune sensitively and offer assistance.

TO EXPRESS CONDOLENCES

> We are deeply saddened, Gayle, to learn of the death of your husband. Warren's kind nature and friendly spirit endeared him to all who knew him. He will be missed.
>
> Although words seem empty in expressing our grief, we want you to know that if we can help you or lighten your load in any way, you just have to let us know.

> In condolence notes, mention the loss tactfully and recognize the good qualities of the deceased. Assure the receiver of your concern, offer assistance, and conclude on a positive, reassuring note.

Are Electronic Channels Appropriate for Goodwill Messages?

In expressing thanks or responding to goodwill messages, handwritten notes are most impressive. However, if you frequently communicate with the receiver by e-mail or text and if you are sure your note will not get lost, then sending an electronic goodwill message is acceptable according to the Emily Post Institute.[4]

To express sympathy immediately after learning of a death or accident, you might precede a phone call or a written condolence message with an e-mail. E-mail is a fast and non-intrusive way to show your feelings. However, advises the Emily Post Institute, immediately follow with a handwritten note. Remember that e-mails are quickly gone and forgotten. Handwritten messages remain and can be returned to. Your thoughtfulness is more lasting if you take the time to write a handwritten message on stationery or in a card.

⬛ SUMMING UP AND LOOKING FORWARD

In this chapter you learned to that there are numerous routine situations in the workplace that require a written message. These routine messages may share information, request information and action, or make complaints and claims. You also saw how you should respond positively to information requests and customer complaints and claims. Finally, you learned how to write recommendation and goodwill messages. Virtually all of these routine messages use the direct strategy. They open immediately with the main idea followed by details and explanations. A question you'll need to settle for yourself is which communication format or channel suits your direct, routine message best: an e-mail, a text, a letter, a memo, or a card? Often, this decision is easy: you reply using the same method as the person who wrote to you. But when you're the first to start the communication chain, you'll need to decide thoughtfully.

While most routine messages are positive, occasionally, you will have to deny routine requests and deliver bad news. In Chapter 7 you will learn to use the indirect strategy in conveying negative news. But first, in Chapter 6, you'll learn how to use written messages to persuade customers, clients, and co-workers.

⬛ CRITICAL THINKING

1. When you're sharing information using a brief text or instant message, why does it make sense to have a plan in mind for your message?

2. Since brevity is valued in business writing, is it ever wise to respond with more information than requested? Why or why not?

3. Should resale or sales promotion information be included in a letter that responds to a claim letter from a customer? Why or why not?

4. Which is more effective in claim messages—anger or objectivity? Why?

5. Why is it important to regain the confidence of a customer when you respond to a claim?

6. Is it ethical to send a recommendation letter that's positive when you have reservations about the candidate's past performance?

7. Goodwill messages may not seem routine in today's fast-paced world of business. Do you agree or disagree with this statement. Why?

CHAPTER REVIEW

1. List five routine situations in business that may require a message.

2. What determines whether you write a letter directly or indirectly?

3. How do you organize a message that shares information?

4. List two ways that you could begin an inquiry message that asks many questions.

5. What three elements are appropriate in the closing of a request for information?

6. What is a complaint or claim message? Provide an original example based on your own recent business experience.

7. What are the three goals when responding to a customer claim letter?

8. Why do some companies comply with nearly all claims?

9. What information should the opening in a letter of recommendation include?

10. The best goodwill messages include what five characteristics?

WRITING IMPROVEMENT EXERCISES

Improving Opening Paragraphs

Revise the following openings so that they are more direct. Add information if necessary.

1. Despite the economy, Western Bank has been investigating the possibility of initiating an internship program within our Financial Services Department. I have been appointed as the point person to conduct research regarding our proposed program. We are fully aware of the benefits of a strong internship program, and our management team is eager to take advantage of some of these benefits. We would be deeply appreciative if you would be kind enough to help us out with answers to a number of specific questions.

2. My name is Kimberly Sanchez, and I am assistant to the manager of Information Services & Technology at Onyz, Inc. We are interested in your voice recognition software that we understand allows you to dictate and copy text without touching a keyboard. We are interested in answers to a number of questions, such as the cost for a single-user license and perhaps the availability of a free trial version. Will you please answer the following questions.

3. Your letter of March 4 has been referred to me. Pursuant to your inquiry, I have researched your question in regard to whether or not we offer our European-style patio umbrella in colours. This unique umbrella is one of our most popular items. Its 10-foot canopy protects you when the sun is directly overhead, but it also swivels and tilts to virtually any angle for continuous sun protection all day long. It comes in two colours: cream and forest green.

4. I am pleased to receive your inquiry regarding the possibility of my acting as a speaker at the final semester meeting of your business management club on May 2. The topic of online résumés interests me and is one on which I think I could impart helpful information to your members. Therefore, I am responding in the affirmative to your kind invitation.

5. So far I have been happy with my Timex Ironman watch, but lately it's been rather erratic. The display has been fading, and the numerals are hard to read. I suspected that a new battery was needed, but the problem remained even after a new one was inserted. I wore the watch while surfing and I suspect that water may have penetrated the watch. Can you recommend a convenient service location to have the watch looked at?

Writing Instructions

Revise the following wordy, dense paragraphs into a set of concise instructions. Include an introductory statement.

6. Orders may be placed at our Web site by following certain steps. Here they are. As a visitor to our site, you should first look over everything and find the items you want from our catalogue. Then your shopping cart is important. You will add items to your shopping cart. When you are finished adding things to your shopping cart, the next step is to proceed to checkout. But wait! Have you created a new account? After creating a new account, we next need to know what shipping address to ship your items to. We will also need to have you choose a shipping method. Then you will be expected to provide payment information. Finally, you are nearly done! Payment information must be provided, and then you are ready to review your order and submit it.

7. If you want to make a YouTube video, here are some important tips for those who have not done it before. First, you will need to obtain a video recording device such as a cellphone, webcam, or camcorder. Another thing you will have to do is make a decision on whether or not to make a video blog, comedy skit, how-to video, or a video that is about travel. Remember that your video must be no more than 15 minutes long for traditional YouTube membership accounts. You will want to create a video with good light quality, and that usually means daytime recording. Finally, be sure to use editing software to change or delete anything.

8. A number of employees have asked about how to make two-sided copies. Here's what to do. The copy for side 1 of the original goes face down on the Document Glass. Then the Document Cover should be closed. Next you should select the quantity that you require. To copy side 1, you should then press Start. Now you remove the first original and place the second original face down on the Document Glass. The Document Cover should be closed. Now you remove side 1 copy from the Output Tray. It should be inserted face down into the Paper Bypass Tray. Then select the Alternate Paper Tray and press Start.

ACTIVITIES AND CASES

5.1 Information Request: Can I Do a Co-op Placement at Your Firm?

You are a second-semester interior design student at Algonquin College in Ottawa. As part of your four-year applied degree program, you are required to complete a 20-week co-op term. Rather than using the services of the college's co-op office, which normally helps students find co-op positions, you've decided to strike out on your own. Being fluently bilingual, you decide you'd like to move to Montréal for your co-op term. You've narrowed your search down to one well-known design firm, Leroux + Smythe, and you have a lot of questions. For example, has the firm used co-op students before? If so, what typical tasks did the students perform? Another question you'd like answered is whether the firm can pay a salary or at least an honorarium for your 20-week placement. Also, you'd like to know what kinds of clients the firm has for its design services. Finally, you're interested in finding out the amount of French you'll have to write and speak during your placement. You decide to write the company a letter requesting information.

1. What should you include in the opening of this information request?
2. What should the body of your letter contain?
3. How can your phrase your questions most effectively?
4. How should you close this letter?

Your Task. Using your own return address, write a personal business letter requesting information about a co-op placement to Claudette Garneau, Manager Human Resources, Leroux + Smythe, 1450 rue Maclennan, Montréal, QC H3X 2Y4.

Related Web site: Information on Algonquin College's program in interior design is available at **www2.algonquincollege.com/mediaanddesign/program/bachelor-of-applied-arts-interior-design**. Information on co-op placements is available at **www.algonquincollege.com/coop**.

5.2 Claim Request: Free Samples Are Surprisingly Costly

As marketing manager of Caribou Mountain Ranch, you are very annoyed with Quantum Enterprises. Quantum provides imprinted promotional products for companies. Your resort was looking for something special to offer in promoting its vacation packages. Quantum offered free samples of its promotional merchandise, under its "No Surprise" policy.

You figured, what could you lose? So on January 11 you placed a telephone order for a number of samples. These included three kinds of jumbo tote bags and a square-ended barrel bag with fanny pack, as well as a deluxe canvas attaché case and two colours of garment-dyed sweatshirts. All items were supposed to be free. You did think it odd that you were asked for your company's MasterCard number, but Quantum promised to bill you only if you kept the samples.

When the items arrived, you weren't pleased, and you returned them all on January 21 (you have a postal receipt showing the return). But your February credit card statement showed a charge of $239.58 for the sample items. You called Quantum in February and spoke to Lane, who assured you that a credit would be made on your next statement. However, your March statement showed no credit. You called again and received a similar promise. It's now April and no credit has been made. You decide to write and demand action. Circle the correct choice in the following items.

1. To open this claim letter, you should
   a. provide a complete chronology of what happened with all the dates and facts.
   b. tell Quantum how sick and tired you are of this game it is playing.
   c. explain carefully how much of your valuable time you have spent on trying to resolve this matter.
   d. describe the action you want taken.

2. In writing this claim letter, you should assume that Quantum
   a. regularly uses this trick to increase its sales.
   b. made an honest mistake and will rectify the problem.
   c. has no intention of crediting your account.
   d. reacts only when threatened seriously.

3. In the body of this claim letter, you should
   a. describe briefly what has taken place.
   b. refer to specific dates and names of people contacted.
   c. enclose copies of any relevant documents.
   d. do all of the above.

4. The closing of this claim letter should
   a. refer to your lawyer, whom Quantum will hear from if this matter is not settled.
   b. explain what action you want taken and by when.
   c. make sure that Quantum knows that you will never use their products again.
   d. threaten to spread the word among the travel industry that Quantum can't be trusted.

Your Task. After circling your choices, write a claim letter that documents the problem and states the action you want taken. Add any information you feel is necessary. Address your letter to Ms. Kayla Tutshi, Customer Service, Quantum Enterprises, 1505 Victory Drive, Kamloops, BC V2C 4X3.

5.3 Information Request: Helping Raise Puppies to Become Dog Guides

WEB

As an assistant in the Corporate Social Responsibility Office of your corporation, you have been given an unusual task. Your manager wants to expand the company's philanthropic and community relations mission and especially employee volunteerism. She heard about the Lions Foundation of Canada Dog Guides, a program in which trainers breed and raise puppies for dog guide training. She thinks this would be an excellent outreach program for the company's employees. They could give back to the community in their role as foster parents to a future dog guide, groomers/bathers of dog guides in training, kennel workers, or special events workers. To pursue the idea, she asks you to request information about the program and ask questions about whether a company could sponsor a program encouraging employees to act as volunteers. She hasn't thought it through very carefully and relies on you to raise logical questions, especially about costs for volunteers.

Your Task. Write an information request to Sandy Turney, Executive Director, Lions Foundation of Canada Dog Guides, P.O. Box 907, Oakville, ON L6J 5E8. Include an end date and a reason.

For more information on the dog guide program, go to **www.dogguides.com/index.html**.

5.4 Information Request: Searching for a Social Media Specialist

EMAIL

As the director of corporate communication for HomeCentre, a large home supply store, you are charged with looking into the possible hiring of a social media specialist who can monitor cyberspace and be ready to respond to both negative and positive messages. Such specialists can help build a company's brand and promote its online reputation. They can also develop company guidelines for employee use and encourage staffers to spread the good word about the organization.

Petco, supplier of pet supplies and services, recently hired Natalie Malaszenko as its director of social media and commerce. Her assignment at Petco was to envision and articulate the company's social media strategy for the future. To that end, she created fan pages on Facebook, opened several Twitter accounts, and wrote a company blog. In addition to Petco, other organizations have hired social media officers, including Scotiabank, Canon Canada, L'Oréal, Steam Whistle Brewing, and Bell Media.

To learn more about social media, you decide to go to Rick Trumka, who was recommended as a social media consultant by your CEO, David Seldenberg. You understand that Mr. Trumka has agreed to provide information and will be paid by HomeCentre. You decide that this is not a matter that can be handled quickly by a phone call. You want to get answers in writing.

Many issues concern you. For one thing, you are worried about the hiring process. You have no idea about a reasonable salary for a social media specialist. You don't know where to place that person within your structure: in corporate communications, marketing, customer service, or exactly where? Another thing that disturbs you is how to judge a candidate. What background would you require? Do colleges actually award degrees in social networking? How will you know the best candidate? And what about salary? Should you be promising a full-time salary for doing what most people consider to be fun?

Your Task. Compose an e-mail inquiry to *rick.trumka@mediaresources.com*. Explain your situation and list specific questions. Mr. Trumka is not an employment source; he is a consultant who charges for his information and advice. Make your questions clear and concise. You realize that Mr. Trumka would probably like to talk on the phone or visit you, but make clear that you want a written response so that you can have a record of his information to share when you report to the CEO.

5.5 Information Request: Culture Vultures Seeking Adventure

WEB

You just watched a great television show about cheap travel in Europe, and you think you'd like to try it next summer. The program described how some people want to get away from it all; others want to see a little of the world. Some want to learn a different language; some want to soak up a bit of culture. The "get-away" group, the program advised, should book a package trip to a Contiki resort where they relax and soak up the sun. But "culture vultures" and FITs (free independent travellers) should select the countries they want to visit and plan their own trips. You decide to visit France, Spain, and Portugal.

Begin planning your trip by gathering information from the country's tourist office or Web site. Many details need to be worked out. What about visas? How about inoculations? Since your budget will be limited, you need to stay in hostels whenever possible. Where are they? Are they private? Some hostels accept only people who belong to their organization. You really need to get your hands on a list of hostels for every country before departure. You are also interested in any special transport passes for students, such as a Eurail Pass. And while you are at it, find out if they have any special guides for student travellers. All this information can be secured from a tourist office.

Your Task. Using the Internet, you found an address for information: Tourist Office of Spain in Canada, 3402–2 Bloor Street West, Toronto, ON M4W 3E2 (**www.spain.info/ca/TourSpain**). Write a letter requesting information. If you prefer another country, find its tourist office address. Because this is a personal business letter, include your return address above the date.

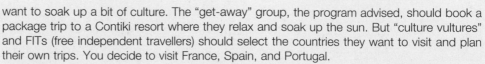

5.6 Information Request: Meeting in Haines Junction at the Dalton Trail Lodge

Your company, Software Solutions, has just had an enormously successful two-year sales period. The CEO has asked you, as marketing manager, to arrange a fabulous conference/retreat as a thank-you gift for all 20 engineers, product managers, and salespeople. She wants the company to host a four-day combination sales conference/vacation/retreat at some spectacular location. She suggests that you start by inquiring at the Dalton Trail Lodge in Haines Junction, Yukon. You check its Web site and get some good information. However, you decide to write a letter so that you can have a permanent, formal record of all the resorts you investigate. You estimate that your company will require about 20 rooms. You'll also need about three conference rooms for one and a half days. You want to know room rates, conference facilities, and outdoor activity possibilities for families. You have two time periods that would be possible: September 18–22 or October 4–8. You know that these are off-peak times, and you wonder if you can get a good room rate. What is the most economical way to get to Haines Junction from Software Solutions' headquarters in Prince George, B.C.? One evening you will want to host a banquet for about 140 people. The CEO wants a report from you by April 1.

Your Task. Write a well-organized information request to Dalton Trail Lodge, c/o Grayling Camp Enterprises, Box 5331, Haines Junction, YT Y0B 1L0.

Related Web site: **www.daltontrail.com**.

5.7 Information Request: Computer Code of Conduct

As an assistant in your college's or university's campus computer centre, you have been asked by your supervisor to help write an updated code of conduct for use of the centre facilities. This code will spell out which behaviour and activities are allowed in your centre and which are not. The first thing you are to do is conduct a search on the Internet to see what other college or university computing centres have written as conduct codes.

Your Task. Search the Internet employing variations of the keywords "computer code of conduct." Print two or three codes that seem appropriate. Write an e-mail to the director of an educational computer centre asking for further information about its code and its effectiveness. Include at least five significant questions. Attach your printouts to your letter.

5.8 Information Request: Backpacking Cuisine

Assume that you are Marc Vannault, manager of a health spa and also an ardent backpacker. You are organizing a group of hikers for a wilderness trip to Yukon. One item that must be provided is freeze-dried food for the three-week trip. You are unhappy with the taste and quality of backpacking food products currently available. You expect to have a group of hikers who are older, affluent, and natural-food enthusiasts. Some are concerned about products containing preservatives, sugar, and additives. Others are on diets restricting cholesterol, fat, and salt.

You heard that Outfitters, Inc., offers a new line of freeze-dried products. You want to know what they offer and whether they have sufficient variety to serve all the needs of your group. You need to know where their products can be purchased and what the cost range is. You'd also like to try a few of their items before placing a large order. You are interested in how they produce the food products and what kinds of ingredients they use. If you have any items left over, you wonder how long they can be kept and still be usable.

Your Task. Write an information request letter to Karie Osborne, Outfitters, Inc., 1169 Willamette Street, Canmore, AB T0L 2P2.

5.9 Direct Claim: New Iron Gate Needs Work

You work for JPM, Johnson Property Management, in Calgary, Alberta. Your employer specializes in commercial real estate. Just yesterday one of your business tenants in the trendy NW 23rd Avenue neighbourhood complained about problems with an iron gate you had installed by Chung Iron Works just six months earlier, on August 20. Apparently, the two doors of the gate have settled and don't match in height. The gate gets stuck. It takes much force to open, close, and lock the gate. The iron gate was painted, and in some spots rust is bleeding onto the previously pristine white paint. The shop owner at 921 NW 23rd Ave., Calgary, AB T2P 4K1, is petite and has complained to you about struggling with the gate at least twice a day when opening and closing her store.

You realize that you will have to contact the installer, Chung Iron Works, and request that the company inspect the gate and remedy the problem. Only six months have passed, and you recall that the warranty for the gate was for one year. To have a formal record of the claim and because Chung Iron Works does not use e-mail, you decide to write a claim letter.

Your Task. Address your letter to Jin Ree at Chung Iron Works, 2255 NW Yeon Avenue in Calgary, AB T3R 7N6. To jog his memory, you will enclose a copy of the company's proposal/invoice. Your business address is 1960 NE Irving Street, Calgary, AB T2L 8N1, phone (403) 335-5443 and fax (403) 335-5001.

5.10 Claim Letter: Undersized French Doors

As Julie Chen, owner of Smart Interiors, you recently completed a kitchen remodel that required double-glazed, made-to-order oak French doors. You ordered them by telephone on July 2 from Custom Wood, Inc. When they arrived on July 25, your carpenter gave you the bad news: the doors were cut too small. Instead of measuring a total of 3.23 square metres, the doors measured 3.13 square metres. In your carpenter's words, "No way can I stretch those doors to fit these openings!" You waited three weeks for these doors, and your clients wanted them installed immediately. Your carpenter said, "I can rebuild this opening for you, but I'm going to have to charge you for my time." His extra charge came to $455.50.

You feel that the people at Custom Wood should reimburse you for this amount, since it was their error. In fact, you actually saved them money by not returning the doors. You decide to write to Custom Wood and enclose a copy of your carpenter's bill. You wonder whether you should also include a copy of Custom Wood's invoice, even though it does not show the exact door measurements. You are a good customer of Custom Wood, having used their quality doors and windows on many other jobs. You're confident that it will grant this claim.

Your Task. Write a claim letter to Jay Brandt, Marketing Manager, Custom Wood, Inc., 401 Main Street, Vancouver, BC V1L 2E6.

5.11 Direct Claim: Can't Attend Management Seminar

Assiniboine Executive Training Institute offered a seminar titled "Enterprise Project Management Protocol" that sounded terrific. It promised to teach project managers how to estimate scope of work, report status, write work packages, and cope with project conflicts. Because your company often is engaged in large cross-functional projects, it decided to send four key managers to the seminar to be held June 1–2 at the Assiniboine headquarters in Winnipeg. The fee was $2,200 each, and it was paid in advance. About six weeks before the seminar, you learned that three of the managers would be tied up in projects that would not be completed in time for them to attend.

Your Task. On your company letterhead, write a claim letter to Addison Firchuk, Registrar, Assiniboine Executive Training Institute, Suite 901–100 Lombard Avenue, Winnipeg, MB R3B 0X2. Ask that the seminar fees for three employees be returned because they cannot attend. Give yourself a title and supply any details necessary.

5.12 Claim Letter: Deep Desk Disappointment

Assume that you are Monica Keil, President, Keil Consulting Services, 423 Lawrence Avenue, Montréal, QC H5L 2E3. Since your consulting firm is doing very well, you decide to splurge and purchase a fine executive desk for your own office. You order an expensive desk described as "North American white oak embellished with hand-inlaid walnut cross-banding." Although you do not ordinarily purchase large, expensive items by mail, you are impressed by the description of this desk and by the money-back guarantee promised in the catalogue.

When the desk arrives, you know that you have made a mistake—it is not the high-quality product that you had anticipated. The wood finish is rough, the grain looks splotchy, and many of the drawers do not pull out easily. The advertisement has promised "full suspension, silent ball-bearing drawer slides." You are disappointed with the desk and decide to send it back, taking advantage of the money-back guarantee.

Your Task. Write a letter to Rodney Harding, Marketing Manager, Big Spruce Wood Products, P.O. Box 488, Sandpoint, BC V5N 7L8. You want your money refunded. You're not sure whether the freight charges can be refunded, but it's worth a try. Supply any details needed.

EMAIL

5.13 Instruction Message: What to Do in an Emergency

Your boss, Sue Curry, informs you one day that she is concerned about fires and safe evacuation in your office building. She asks that you, as director of Human Resources, prepare a set of procedures for employees to follow in case of fires. She thinks that the two of you can work out the procedures in a conversation, and she begins by noting that if an employee sees a fire, that person should pull the alarm and call the fire department. The number of that department is 9-911. If the fire is small, the employee can attempt to extinguish it with a fire extinguisher.

At this point, you ask your boss if the person who discovered the fire should also notify a supervisor, and your boss agrees. The supervisor is probably the one who should assess the situation and decide whether the building should be evacuated. You then begin to think about the evacuation process: what to do? Ms. Curry says that all doors should be closed and employees should secure their workstations. You ask what exactly that means, and she says employees should turn off their computers and put away important documents, but perhaps that information is unnecessary. Just stick to the main points, she says.

If employees are evacuating, they should go to the nearest exit in an orderly manner. In addition, it's very important that everyone remain calm. You ask about people with disabilities. "Sure," she says, "we should assist all visitors and persons with disabilities." Then Ms. Curry remembers that employees have been told about predetermined gathering places, and they should go there and wait for more instructions from floor monitors. It's also important that employees not re-enter the building until given the all-clear. When they are outside, they should stay out of the way of fire department personnel and equipment.

"Do you have all the information?" she asks. "Great! Now prepare a draft memo to employees for my signature."

Your Task. Draft an e-mail or memo to employees from Sue Curry, CEO. Provide brief background data and explain the main idea. List clear fire instructions. Provide your name, title, and office phone number for receivers who want more information.

TEAM

CRITICAL THINKING

5.14 Information Response: Avoiding Employee Gifts That Are Re-gifted

A friend of yours, Megan Stowe, is an executive with a large insurance company. One day in late October, you see her at an industry conference in St. John's, Newfoundland. Afterward, you decide to head down to Water Street for a coffee at a nearby café. After the usual small talk, she says, "You know, I'm beginning to hate the holidays. Every year it gets harder to choose presents for our staff. Once we gave fruitcakes, which I thought were tasty and elegant, but it turns out a lot of our people re-gifted them to other people before Christmas." As an executive training coach, you say, "Well, what's your gift goal? Do you want to encourage your employees? Are you just saying thanks? Or do you want your gifts to act as a retention tool to keep good people on your team?" Megan responds, "I never thought of it that way. Our company doesn't really have a strategy for holiday gifts. It's just something we do every year. Do you have any ideas?"

As it turns out, you have a lot of ideas. You've developed a gift list based on the reasons talented people stay in organizations. Megan asks you to get in touch next week explaining some of the gift ideas. She thinks she will be able to retain your services for this advice.

Your Task. Using your library databases and the Internet, research articles and information on corporate gift giving. As a consultant, prepare a letter with a sampling of gift-giving ideas addressed to Megan Stowe, Vice President, Human Resources, London Life Insurance Company, 255 Dufferin Ave., London, ON N6A 4K1.

5.15 Information Response: Backpacking Cuisine

As Karie Osborne, owner of Outfitters, Inc., producer of freeze-dried backpacking foods, answer the inquiry of Marc Vannault (see Activity 5.7). You are eager to have Mr. Vannault sample your new all-natural line of products containing no preservatives, sugar, or additives. You want him to know that you started this company two years ago after you found yourself making custom meals for discerning backpackers who rejected typical camping fare. Some of your menu items are excellent for individuals on restricted diets. Some dinners are cholesterol-, fat-, and salt-free, but he'll have to look at your list to see for himself.

You will send him your complete list of dinner items and the suggested retail prices. You will also send him a sample "Saturday Night on the Trail," a four-course meal that comes with fruit candies and elegant appetizers. All your food products are made from choice ingredients in sanitary kitchens that you supervise personally. They are flash-frozen in a new vacuum process that you have patented. Although your dried foods are meant to last for years, you don't recommend that they be kept beyond 18 months because they may deteriorate. This could happen if a package were punctured or if the products became overheated.

Your Task. Respond to Marc Vannault, 322 East Drive, Penticton, BC V2A 1T2. By the way, your products are currently available at High-Country Sports Centre, 19605 Rocky Mountain Highway, Calgary, AB T8L 1Z8. Large orders may be placed directly with you, and you offer a 5 percent discount on direct orders.

5.16 Information Response: Massage Necessary

As a general practitioner, you've noticed that many of your patients have begun to ask for a letter stating that you've recommended they have massage therapy. The reason your patients need the letter is that some insurance plans will not reimburse for massage expenses unless a medical doctor has stated—in writing—that the treatment is necessary. Rather than writing a new letter each time a patient makes this request, you decide to develop a template that can be stored on your computer. The only thing you will have to change is the date and the name of the patient.

Your Task. Write a short information response letter that can be sent to any insurance plan/company. In the letter, make clear that your patient needs massage for an underlying condition, and not for a workplace or accident-related injury (some insurance companies will not pay if the condition requiring treatment is a result of an accident or workplace incident).

5.17 Order Response: Unfortunately, We're Fully Booked . . .

CRITICAL THINKING

As the sales manager of the Dalton Trail Lodge in Haines Junction, Yukon, you sometimes wish you had an infinite number of rooms to offer prospective guests. It seems to often happen that people all want to stay at the lodge at the same times. You recently received a letter from Software Solutions in Prince George, B.C. (Activity 5.5). Unfortunately, you have to tell Software Solutions that both dates it requested are already fully booked at the lodge. That's the bad news. The good news as you see it is that the periods immediately after the ones requested by Software Solutions are free (i.e., September 25–29 and October 11–15). You are very eager to get the booking, even though you are aware that the dates of the lodge's availability don't exactly match up with Software Solutions' request.

Your Task. Because you consider time to be of the essence, you decide to reply via e-mail to this letter. In your e-mail, you encourage Software Solutions to get in touch via telephone or by reply e-mail so that a solution to the situation can be reached more quickly.

5.18 Claim Response: Undersized French Doors

As Jay Brandt, manager of Custom Wood, Inc., you have a problem. Your firm manufactures quality pre-cut and custom-built doors and frames. You have received a letter dated August 3 from Julie Chen (Activity 5.9). Ms. Chen is an interior designer, and she complains that the oak French doors she recently ordered for a client were made to the wrong dimensions.

Although they were the wrong size, she kept the doors and had them installed because her clients were without outside doors. However, her carpenter charged an extra $455.50 to install them. She claims that you should reimburse her for this amount, since your company was responsible for the error. You check her July 2 order and find that the order was filled correctly. In a telephone order, Ms. Chen requested doors that measured 3.13 square metres and that's what you sent. Now she says that the doors should have been 3.23 square metres.

Your policy forbids refunds or returns on custom orders. Yet, you remember that around July 2 you had two new people working the telephones taking orders. It's possible that they did not hear or record the measurements correctly. You don't know whether to grant this claim or refuse it. But you do know that you must look into the training of telephone order takers and be sure that they verify all custom-order measurements. It might also be a good idea to have your carpenters call a second time to confirm custom measurements.

Ms. Chen is a successful interior designer and has provided Custom Wood with a number of orders. You value her business but aren't sure how to respond. You'd like to remind her that Custom Wood has earned a reputation as a premier manufacturer of wood doors and frames. Your doors feature prime woods, meticulous craftsmanship, and award-winning designs. And the engineering is ingenious.

Your Task. Decide how to treat this claim and whether to respond by letter or e-mail. The addresses are Julie Chen, Smart Interiors, 3282 Richmond Road, Vancouver, BC V5Y 2A8 and jchen@smartinteriors.ca. You might mention that you have a new line of greenhouse windows that are available in three sizes. Include a brochure describing these windows.

5.19 Claim Response: Deep Desk Disappointment

As Rodney Harding, Marketing Manager of Big Spruce Wood Products, it is your job to reply to customer claims, and today you must respond to Monica Keil, President of Keil Consulting Services (Activity 5.11). You are disturbed that she is returning the executive desk (Invoice No. 3499), but your policy is to comply with customer wishes. If she doesn't want to keep the desk, you will certainly return the purchase price plus shipping charges. Desks are occasionally damaged in shipping, and this may explain the marred finish and the sticking drawers.

You want Ms. Keil to give Big Spruce Wood Products another chance. After all, your office furniture and other wood products are made from the finest hand-selected woods by master artisans. Since she is apparently furnishing her office, send her another catalogue and invite her to look at the traditional conference desk on page 10-E. This is available with a matching credenza, file cabinets, and accessories. She might be interested in your furniture-leasing plan, which can produce substantial savings.

Your Task. Write to Monica Keil, President, Keil Consulting Services, 423 Lawrence Avenue, Montréal, QC H5L 2E3 or mkeil@keilconsulting.ca. In granting her claim, promise that you will personally examine any furniture she may order in the future.

5.20 Recommendation Letter: Telling It Like It Is

You are a business communication professor at a community college. Your students do a co-op semester from May to August as part of their program. In March, some of your students start asking for recommendation letters. This spring in particular has been heavy with requests, and one sticks in your mind. Jeff Brown, a second-year student, who has been in two of your classes, asks for a recommendation letter. He is applying for entry-level customer service jobs in the banking industry. You are Jeff's business communication professor, and you've got little to complain about. Jeff has been averaging an A in your two courses, his writing and speaking skills are superior, he thinks critically, solves problems in original ways, and is a good team player. Unfortunately, he's managed to demonstrate all of these strong skills and maintain his high average while continually skipping classes and arriving late for the classes he does show up to. You want to give Jeff a good recommendation, but you realize that in the work world, absenteeism and showing up late aren't treated as lightly as at college.

Your Task. Write a general letter of recommendation for Jeff Brown.

5.21 Thanks for the Favour: I Got a Job!

You are Jeff Brown from Activity 5.19. It took you only three weeks of co-op job hunting and you landed a great job with Scotiabank. You'd like to thank your business communication professor for the recommendation letter s/he wrote for you in early March. You're busy with end of term and final exams, though, so you put writing the thank-you letter off till late April, more than six weeks since the recommendation letter was written.

Your Task. Write a letter thanking your professor.

5.22 Response to Thanks: Congratulations on Your New Job
As the professor from Activity 5.19, you've just received Jeff Brown's handwritten letter of thanks. You're off for your vacation at this point, and only checking in at the office once a week. You don't have Jeff's mailing address, but you do have his e-mail address.

Your Task. Send Jeff an e-mail responding to his letter of thanks.

5.23 Sympathy Message: To a Spouse

Your Task. Imagine that a co-worker was killed in an automobile accident. Write a letter of sympathy to his or her spouse.

5.24 Information Request
You are in the second year of the Hairstylist program at Algonquin College and will be graduating shortly. You and your sister have inherited a small amount of money from an aunt who recently passed away, and you are looking for ways to put your inheritance to good use. Your sister is graduating from the Esthetician program at the same college, and together you would like to purchase a hair salon and aesthetics franchise called Hair Clippers and Best Face Forward. There are already two successful franchises in Ottawa; one is located in the west end, the other in downtown Ottawa. You and your sister would like to obtain information on opening another franchise in the east end, close to where the two of you are living. Some of the information you would like to gather includes the total investment required to start the franchise, whether a portion of the investment can be financed, and whether you can rent your own equipment. You would also like to know whether the east end would be a feasible location, whether training is available, and, since this is your first venture operating a small business, the nature of support provided to franchisees. You would appreciate any other information that Hair Clippers and Best Face Forward can offer, since you are also contemplating other investment options.

Your Task. Write an information request letter or e-mail to Martha Jones, Business Manager, Hair Clippers and Best Face Forward Franchise, 53 St. Laurent Boulevard, Ottawa, ON K2R 5R3, asking for detailed information on starting your own franchise business. Include at least five significant questions.

🔲 GRAMMAR/MECHANICS REVIEW 5—COMMAS 1

Study each of the following statements and insert necessary commas. In the space provided, write the number of commas that you add; write *0* if no commas are needed. Check your answers against the correct responses at the back of the book. If your answers are different than the correct responses, study carefully the principles shown in parentheses.

__2__   **Example**   The hiring manager is looking for candidates who are conscientious adaptable and flexible.

___ 1. We do not as a rule hire anyone who has not been interviewed.

___ 2. You may be sure Ms. Ebert that we will notify you immediately.

___ 3. Digital networking involves having your job hunt and qualifications spread virally among friends former colleagues and professional associates.

___ 4. We have scheduled two interviews for December 5 at the Hyatt Regency in Edmonton beginning at 1 p.m.

___ 5. As a matter of fact job hunters regularly flub by submitting their résumés to multiple recruiters and hiring managers at the same firm.

___ 6. In the meantime please remember that today's hiring managers regularly search the Internet before hiring anyone.

___ 7. One hiring manager even found digital dirt on a candidate that went back to March 1 2005 in Chicago.

___ 8. Anne Lublin volunteered to move from St. John's Newfoundland to St. Andrew's New Brunswick for a job.

___ 9. Eric Wong Teresa Cabrillo and Elise Rivers are the final three candidates.

___ 10. The benefits package mailed to Ms. Dawn Summers 1339 Kearsley Street Kingston ON arrived exactly five days after it was mailed.

___ 11. Many job candidates think needless to say that they will find a job by searching the big job boards.

___ 12. Experienced job counsellors feel however that the best way to find a job is through personal networking.

___ 13. Before going to his interview, Jon did three things: researched the hiring company prepared success stories and practised answering questions.

___ 14. Valuable job leads can develop from projecting yourself online and making sure everyone you know is aware that you are looking for a job.

___ 15. I'm pleased to meet you Mr. Powell.

GRAMMAR/MECHANICS CHALLENGE—5

Document for Revision

The following e-mail has faults in grammar, punctuation, spelling, number form, and wordiness. Use standard proofreading marks (see Appendix B) to correct the errors. When you finish, your instructor can show you the revised version of this e-mail.

TO: <bspring@cmail.ca>

SUBJECT: Your January 11 Letter Requesting Information About New All Natural Products

Dear Mr. Spring, We have received your letter of January 11 in which you inquire about our all-natural products. Needless to say, we are pleased to be able to answer in the affirmative. Yes, our new line of freeze dried back packing foods meet the needs of older adults and young people as well. You asked a number of questions, and here are answers to you're questions about our products.

- Our all natural foods contains no perservatives, sugars or additives. The inclosed list of dinner items tell what foods are cholesterol-, fat-, and salt-free.

- Large orders recieve a five percent discount when they're placed direct with Outfitters, Inc. You can also purchase our products at Centre Sportif Estrie, 1960 rue Fabre, Sherbrooke, QC, J1L 3C7.

- Outfitters, Inc., food products are made in our sanitary kitchens which I personally supervise. The foods are flash froze in a patented vacum process that retain freshness, texture and taste.

- Outfitters, Inc. food products are made from choice ingredients that combines good taste and healful quality.

- Our foods stay fresh and tasty for up to 18 months.

Mr. Spring I started Outfitters, Inc., two years ago after making custom meals for discerning back packers who rejected typical camping fare. What a pleasure it is now to share my meals with back packers like you.

I hope you'll enjoy sample meal we recently mailed you. "Saturday Night on the Trail" is a four-coarse meal complete with fruit candys and elegant appetizers. Please call me personally at (604) 459-3342 to place an order, or to ask other questions about my backpacking food products.

Sincerely,

OIL REFINERY CLEANS UP ITS ACT

For years companies have been aware of the corporate social responsibility (CSR) movement. Corporate social responsibility is defined as "a company's environmental, social and economic performance and the impacts of the company on its internal and external stakeholders."[5]

In a recent high-profile case in Saint John, well-known corporation Irving Oil experienced "three malfunctions at [its] refinery [that] caused a grey, gritty dust to layer parts of Saint John."[6] An investigation was undertaken by the federal Department of Environment, but surprisingly to some residents of Saint John, no charges were laid against Irving Oil.

Department of Environment spokesperson Jennifer Graham told the media that charges were not laid because "the incident that occurred would be considered sort of an upset that the company couldn't control." A local environmental activist saw things differently, however. Gordon Dalzell claims that "the case illustrates problems with the Department of Environment's ability to enforce air quality rules," and that "the department needs better tools to hold industrial polluters accountable."

As part of its social responsibility initiatives, Irving Oil decided to distribute vouchers to affected residents of Saint John entitling them to free car and house washing.

Career Application

In a class discussion, consider these questions:

- Why are companies increasingly interested in social responsibility?
- Who is directly accountable when a company's social responsibility initiatives still leave the public unhappy?
- What are the advantages and disadvantages of detailed codes of social responsibility for companies?

YOUR TASK

You are an assistant corporate communications manager at Irving Oil. Your boss, the Director of Corporate Communications, asks you to research best practices in crisis communications, especially relating to environmental cases (e.g., pipeline spills, etc.). The Director asks you to draft a memo summary for her by next week. She also implies that if she likes what she sees, she may use your research at an upcoming high-level meeting. Using library databases and the Web, research crisis communications relating to businesses and the environment, and write an e-mail attaching a draft memo to your boss, Sherry Cardinal, as instructed.

Related Web sites: Visit Irving Oil's corporate social responsibility site at **www.irvingoil.com/corporate_social _responsibility** and read an article about environmental crisis communications at **www.rosehillcommunications .com/Crisis_Communication_Messaging.pdf**.

CHAPTER

06

Persuasive Writing Situations

LEARNING OBJECTIVES

1. Understand why the indirect strategy is used to persuade and how the strategy works.

2. Request favours and other actions persuasively.

3. Write persuasive claim request messages.

4. Present persuasive new ideas within organizations.

5. Analyze techniques used in persuasive sales and promotional messages.

6. Compose various persuasive electronic sales and promotional messages.

The ability to persuade is a primary factor in personal and business success.

Persuasion is the ability to make people think or do what you would like them to think or do. Clearly, developing the ability to persuade is a key factor in the success you achieve in your business messages, in your career, and in your interpersonal relations. Persuasive individuals are highly valued in today's successful organizations; they tend to become decision makers, managers, executives, and entrepreneurs because their ideas generally prevail. Or, through their persuasive messaging, they make or surpass their sales targets or add value to the organization in some other way.

This chapter will examine techniques for writing persuasively in response to a number of common workplace situations. These include times when you must request a favour or other action, persuade either colleagues or managers or both, or make a claim. In addition to request situations, persuasion plays a big part when you need to write one of the many types of sales and promotional messages (e.g., a direct sales letter). Perhaps the most persuasive writing situation of all—that of the cover letter—is dealt with separately in Chapter 12.

Using the Indirect Strategy in Persuasive Writing Situations

An indirect persuasion strategy is necessary in your day-to-day relations with busy co-workers, managers, people in outside organizations, and the general public because you will meet resistance when trying to persuade. This resistance is natural because most people who are trying to persuade others are asking for something that is valuable: money (e.g., in a sales presentation; in a streetcorner charity solicitation situation), time (e.g., in a negotiation over increased vacation time), or goods (e.g., in a situation when a donation is requested).

Knowing that you will encounter resistance, it only makes sense that you should reduce or counter the resistance of the person with whom you've been in touch before actually asking for what you want. For example, if after eight years of working for a furniture manufacturing company as a territory sales manager, with six straight years of growth in your sales but no growth to speak of in your vacation time, you may decide to ask your manager for more time off. Knowing that your company overall has had a slow sales period (not in your territory, however), you know you can't simply make a direct request to your boss: "Ken, I've been thinking it's time I received an increase in my vacation time." Instead, you'll need an indirect strategy that begins with countering resistance: "Ken, I've got some ideas the other territory managers can use to emulate my reps' success in growing business in these tough times. Can we talk about the ideas over lunch this week? When we meet, I'd also like to make a formal request for two extra days of vacation time going forward. After eight years with the company and a lot of success in my job, I feel this is an appropriate time for me to see a small bump in my vacation time. Let me know a time that works for you."

As the example above shows, the indirect strategy is akin to the classic sports move (e.g., in hockey, basketball, or football) known as a "deke"; that is, evading your opponent by making him or her think you're going to skate, dribble, or run one way, only to quickly move the other way before reverting to your original direction. In persuasive writing (and speaking) situations, you similarly seek to draw attention away from the reality of your attempt to persuade a skeptical person by talking about something else, only to come back to your difficult but necessary request.

The indirect strategy requires more practice and experience than the direct strategy you used in the previous chapter to deal with routine writing situations. For this reason, pay close attention to the writing plans in this chapter as they show you how to perform the "persuasive moves" necessary to make things happen in the world of work. Also try the end-of-chapter Activities and Cases to build your persuasive writing skills.

The Components of an Indirect Persuasive Request

The indirect strategy contains separate strategies, but in a successful persuasive message, all four appear together as a unified whole. The order of the four strategies is not, though, set in stone; for example, not every persuasive situation will require you to build interest before you reduce resistance. However, most persuasive messages begin by gaining attention and end by motivating action.

GAIN ATTENTION. In the brief opening of the message, gain the reader's attention by describing a problem, making an unexpected statement, mentioning a reader benefit, paying the reader a compliment, or posing a stimulating question. For example, in a persuasive voice mail message left by a local theatre company to its current subscribers, the speaker might begin by mentioning a listener benefit: *All of our returning subscribers will be able to take advantage of special access to our subscribers' lounge, as well as to after-show talks by members of the cast and creative team!*

BUILD INTEREST. The message's body is intended to keep the reader's attention and persuade him or her that the request is reasonable. This section is often the longest part of the message, as it includes the use of facts and statistics, expert opinion, direct benefits to the receiver, examples, and specific details, as well as indirect benefits to the receiver. In the theatre subscription example, the person leaving the voice mail may build interest by stating, *We rely on our subscribers to join us year after year because your subscription helps generate the largest part of our revenue. Government grants and donations currently make up 30 percent of our revenue. This is why we need subscribers to keep coming back . . . .*

REDUCE RESISTANCE. A crucial step in preparing the body of a persuasive message, yet one that is often left out by novice writers, is that of putting oneself in the receiver's shoes and asking: What kinds of problems might the receiver have with my request? For example, the person selling theatre subscriptions may be instructed to reduce the argument that people have many other important uses for their time and money. She may do this by arguing that, while people are busy and have many priorities, supporting the arts is important for the cultural life of the city and the quality of life of those enjoying the theatre. To counter this perceived resistance, the speaker anticipates and names this resistance in her voice mail, and then counters it with a benefit: *Even though we understand you have competing priorities for your hard-earned money, we also know that supporting the arts is good for our city and good for our health. An evening at the theatre is a surefire way to leave the pressures and worries of everyday life behind for a few hours.*

MOTIVATE ACTION. Finally, no persuasive message is complete without the sender closing by telling the receiver exactly what he or she wants, and when he or she wants it. The goal is to sound confident but not pushy, and to motivate the reader to say yes. In essence, a persuasive message should end with a specific request that is confident but not demanding. In the theatre subscription example, the voice mail might end: *I'm sorry I missed you tonight, but I'll try you again tomorrow after dinner time. In the meantime, feel free to give me a call at (416) 922-0018 and ask for Helen if you'd like to re-subscribe immediately. I can offer you the special access to the subscribers' lounge and after-show talks until March 15.*

◼ Persuasive Situation: Asking for a Favour or Other Action

Requests for large favours generally require persuasive strategies.

Asking for a favour implies that you want someone to do something for nothing—or for very little. Common examples are requests for the donation of time, money, energy, a name, resources, talent, skills, or expertise. On occasion, everyone needs to ask a favour. Small favours, such as asking a co-worker to lock up the office for you on Friday, can be straightforward and direct. Little resistance is expected. Larger favours, though, require careful planning and an indirect strategy. A busy executive is asked to serve on a committee to help disadvantaged children; a florist is asked to donate table arrangements for a charity fundraiser; a well-known author is asked to speak before a local library group—why should they agree to do so? In each instance, persuasion is necessary to overcome the recipient's natural resistance.

People are more likely to grant requests if they see direct or indirect benefits to themselves.

Fortunately, many individuals and companies are willing to grant requests for time, money, information, cooperation, and special privileges. They grant these favours for a variety of reasons. They may be interested in your project, or they may see goodwill potential for themselves. Often, though, they comply because they see that others will benefit from the request. Professionals sometimes feel obligated to contribute their time or expertise to "give back to the community."

Figure 6.1 shows a persuasive favour request from Michelle Moreno. Her research firm seeks to persuade other companies to complete a questionnaire regarding salary data. For most organizations, salary information is strictly confidential. What can she do to convince strangers to part with such private information?

The hurriedly written first version of the request suffers from many faults. It fails to pique the interest of the reader in the opening. It also provides an easy excuse for Mr. Mansker to refuse (*filling out surveys can be tedious*). In the body, Mr. Mansker doesn't receive any incentive to accept the request. The writing is self-serving and offers few specifics. In addition, the draft does not anticipate objections and fails to suggest counterarguments. Lastly, the closing does not motivate action by providing a deadline or a final benefit.

In the revised version, Michelle begins her persuasive favour request by posing two short questions that spotlight the need for salary information. To build interest and establish trust, she mentions that MorenoRenaud has been collecting business data for a quarter century and has received awards from the Canadian Marketing

FIGURE **6.1** Persuasive Favour Request

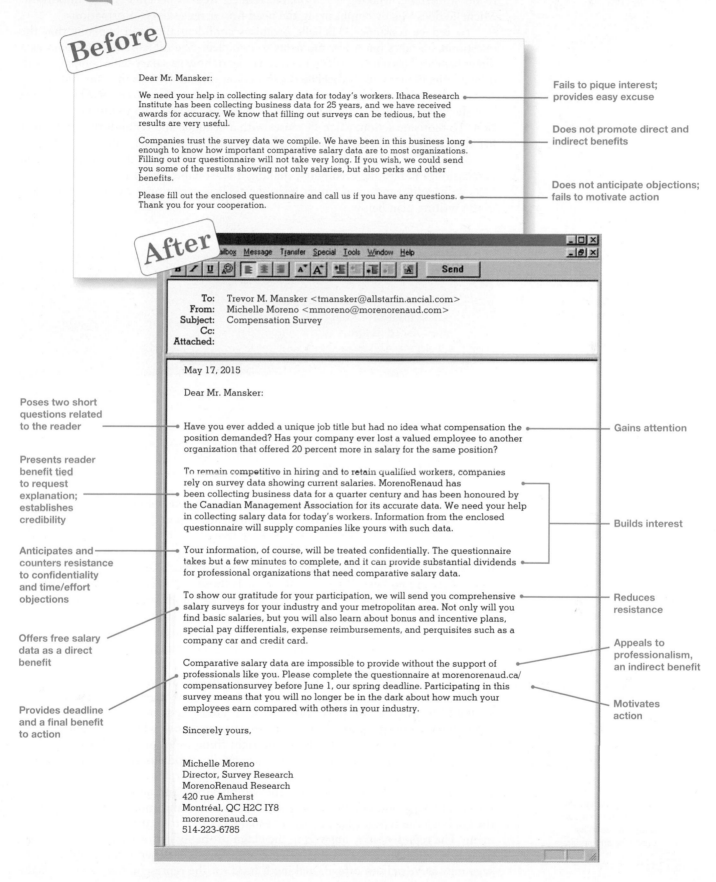

Before

Dear Mr. Mansker:

We need your help in collecting salary data for today's workers. Ithaca Research Institute has been collecting business data for 25 years, and we have received awards for accuracy. We know that filling out surveys can be tedious, but the results are very useful.

Companies trust the survey data we compile. We have been in this business long enough to know how important comparative salary data are to most organizations. Filling out our questionnaire will not take very long. If you wish, we could send you some of the results showing not only salaries, but also perks and other benefits.

Please fill out the enclosed questionnaire and call us if you have any questions. Thank you for your cooperation.

Fails to pique interest; provides easy excuse

Does not promote direct and indirect benefits

Does not anticipate objections; fails to motivate action

After

To:	Trevor M. Mansker <tmansker@allstarfin.ancial.com>
From:	Michelle Moreno <mmoreno@morenorenaud.com>
Subject:	Compensation Survey
Cc:	
Attached:	

Send

May 17, 2015

Dear Mr. Mansker:

Have you ever added a unique job title but had no idea what compensation the position demanded? Has your company ever lost a valued employee to another organization that offered 20 percent more in salary for the same position?

To remain competitive in hiring and to retain qualified workers, companies rely on survey data showing current salaries. MorenoRenaud has been collecting business data for a quarter century and has been honoured by the Canadian Management Association for its accurate data. We need your help in collecting salary data for today's workers. Information from the enclosed questionnaire will supply companies like yours with such data.

Your information, of course, will be treated confidentially. The questionnaire takes but a few minutes to complete, and it can provide substantial dividends for professional organizations that need comparative salary data.

To show our gratitude for your participation, we will send you comprehensive salary surveys for your industry and your metropolitan area. Not only will you find basic salaries, but you will also learn about bonus and incentive plans, special pay differentials, expense reimbursements, and perquisites such as a company car and credit card.

Comparative salary data are impossible to provide without the support of professionals like you. Please complete the questionnaire at morenorenaud.ca/compensationsurvey before June 1, our spring deadline. Participating in this survey means that you will no longer be in the dark about how much your employees earn compared with others in your industry.

Sincerely yours,

Michelle Moreno
Director, Survey Research
MorenoRenaud Research
420 rue Amherst
Montréal, QC H2C IY8
morenorenaud.ca
514-223-6785

Poses two short questions related to the reader

Presents reader benefit tied to request explanation; establishes credibility

Anticipates and counters resistance to confidentiality and time/effort objections

Offers free salary data as a direct benefit

Provides deadline and a final benefit to action

Gains attention

Builds interest

Reduces resistance

Appeals to professionalism, an indirect benefit

Motivates action

Association. Developing credibility is especially important when persuading strangers to do something. Making a reasonable request tied to benefits is also important. Michelle does this by emphasizing the need for current salary information.

To reduce resistance, Michelle promises confidentiality and explains that the questionnaire takes but a few moments to complete. She offers free salary data as a direct benefit. This data may help the receiver learn how its salary scale compares with others in its industry. But Michelle doesn't count on this offer as the only motivator. As an indirect benefit, she appeals to the professionalism of the receiver. She's hoping that the receiver will recognize the value of providing salary data to the entire profession. To motivate action, Michelle closes with a deadline and reminds the reader that her company need not be in the dark about comparative salaries within its industry.

This favour request incorporates many of the techniques that are effective in persuasion: establishing credibility, making a reasonable and precise request, tying facts to benefits, and overcoming resistance. These techniques can be summarized in the writing plan below.

> Persuasive claim and complaint messages make reasonable requests backed by solid evidence.

WRITING PLAN FOR A PERSUASIVE REQUEST

- **Gain attention** in the opening.
- **Build interest** in the body.
- **Reduce resistance** in the body.
- **Motivate action** in the closing.

Persuasive Situation: Making Complex Claims and Complaints

Let's say you buy a new car and the transmission repeatedly requires servicing. When you finally get tired of taking it in for repair, you decide to send an e-mail to the car manufacturer's district office, asking that the company install a new transmission in your car. You know that your request will be resisted. You must convince the manufacturer that replacement, not repair, is needed. Routine claim situations, when there are no "gray" areas at all, such as those you encountered in Chapter 5, should be straightforward and direct. Persuasive claims and complaints, on the other hand, are generally more effective when they are indirect.

> Use persuasion when you must change attitudes or produce action.

The organization of an effective persuasive claim or complaint message centres on the closing and the persuasion. First, decide what action you want taken to satisfy the claim. Then, decide how you can prove the worth of your claim. Plan carefully the reasoning you will follow in convincing the reader to take the action you request. If the claim is addressed to a business, the most effective appeals are generally to the organization's pride in its products and its services. Refer to its reputation for integrity and your confidence in it. Show why your claim is valid and why the company will be doing the right thing in granting it. Most organizations are sincere in their efforts to showcase quality products and services that gain consumer respect.

> The most successful appeals are to a company's pride in its products and services.

Although claim messages often contain an aspect of complaint, try not to be angry. Hostility and emotional threats toward an organization do little to achieve the goal of a claim message. Claims are usually referred to a customer service department. The representative answering the claim probably had nothing to do with the design, production, delivery, or servicing of the product or service. An abusive message may serve only to offend, making it hard for the representative to evaluate the claim rationally.

A writing plan for an indirect persuasive claim or complaint follows the steps below.

WRITING PLAN FOR A COMPLEX CLAIM OR COMPLAINT

- **Gain attention** in the opening by paying the receiver a compliment.
- **Build interest** in the body by explaining and justifying the claim or complaint with convincing reasons and without anger.
- **Reduce resistance** in the body by subtly suggesting the responsibility of the receiver. Appeal to the receiver's sense of fairness or desire for customer satisfaction.
- **Motivate action** in the closing by explaining exactly what action you want taken and when.

Observe how the claim e-mail shown in Figure 6.2 illustrates the suggestions above. When Arte International Furnishings in Concord, Ontario, purchased two VoIP systems, it discovered that they would not work without producing an annoying static sound. The company's attempt, via the Internet, to return the VoIP systems has been ignored by the retailer. Despite these difficulties, notice the writer's positive opening, her well-documented claims, and her specific request for action.

Persuasive Situation: Getting Co-workers and Managers Onside

When it comes to persuasion, the hierarchy at work determines how you write—whether you choose a direct or indirect approach, for example. You may consider what type and amount of evidence to include, depending on whether you wish to persuade your co-workers or your own manager or other managers. The authority of your audience may also help you decide whether to adopt a formal or informal tone.

PERSUADING OTHER EMPLOYEES. Instructions or directives moving downward from employees to other employees whom they manage (i.e., direct reports) usually require little persuasion. Employees expect to be directed in how to perform their jobs. These messages (such as information about procedures, equipment, or customer service) follow the direct pattern, with the purpose immediately stated. However, employees are sometimes asked to perform in a capacity outside their work roles or to accept changes that are not in their best interests (such as pay cuts, job transfers, or reduced benefits). Occasionally, superiors need to address sensitive workplace issues such as bullying eradication or diversity programs. Similarly, supervisors may want to create buy-in when introducing a healthier cafeteria menu or mandatory volunteering effort. In these instances, a persuasive message using the indirect pattern may be most effective.

The goal is not to manipulate employees or to deceive them with trickery. Rather, the goal is to present a strong but honest argument, emphasizing points that are important to the receiver or the organization. In business, honesty is not just the best policy—it is the only policy. People see right through puffery and misrepresentation. For this reason, the indirect pattern is effective only when supported by accurate, honest evidence.

PERSUADING YOUR MANAGER. Another form of persuasion within organizations centres on suggestions made by employees to their managers. Convincing management to adopt a procedure or invest in a product or new equipment generally requires skillful communication. Managers are just as resistant to change as others are. Knowing

FIGURE **6.2** Complex Indirect Claim

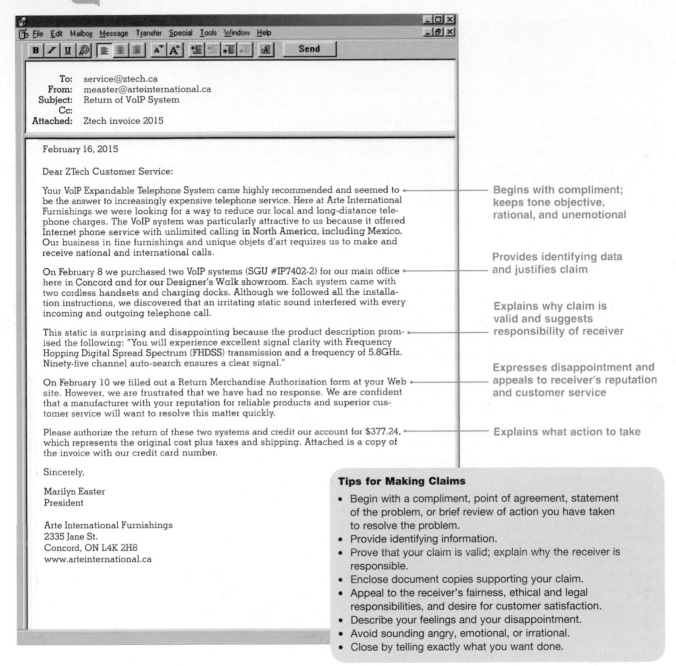

To: service@ztech.ca	
From: measter@arteinternational.ca	
Subject: Return of VoIP System	
Cc:	
Attached: Ztech invoice 2015	

February 16, 2015

Dear ZTech Customer Service:

Your VoIP Expandable Telephone System came highly recommended and seemed to be the answer to increasingly expensive telephone service. Here at Arte International Furnishings we were looking for a way to reduce our local and long-distance telephone charges. The VoIP system was particularly attractive to us because it offered Internet phone service with unlimited calling in North America, including Mexico. Our business in fine furnishings and unique objets d'art requires us to make and receive national and international calls.

— Begins with compliment; keeps tone objective, rational, and unemotional

On February 8 we purchased two VoIP systems (SGU #IP7402-2) for our main office here in Concord and for our Designer's Walk showroom. Each system came with two cordless handsets and charging docks. Although we followed all the installation instructions, we discovered that an irritating static sound interfered with every incoming and outgoing telephone call.

— Provides identifying data and justifies claim

This static is surprising and disappointing because the product description promised the following: "You will experience excellent signal clarity with Frequency Hopping Digital Spread Spectrum (FHDSS) transmission and a frequency of 5.8GHz. Ninety-five channel auto-search ensures a clear signal."

— Explains why claim is valid and suggests responsibility of receiver

On February 10 we filled out a Return Merchandise Authorization form at your Web site. However, we are frustrated that we have had no response. We are confident that a manufacturer with your reputation for reliable products and superior customer service will want to resolve this matter quickly.

— Expresses disappointment and appeals to receiver's reputation and customer service

Please authorize the return of these two systems and credit our account for $377.24, which represents the original cost plus taxes and shipping. Attached is a copy of the invoice with our credit card number.

— Explains what action to take

Sincerely,

Marilyn Easter
President

Arte International Furnishings
2335 Jane St.
Concord, ON L4K 2H8
www.arteinternational.ca

Tips for Making Claims

- Begin with a compliment, point of agreement, statement of the problem, or brief review of action you have taken to resolve the problem.
- Provide identifying information.
- Prove that your claim is valid; explain why the receiver is responsible.
- Enclose document copies supporting your claim.
- Appeal to the receiver's fairness, ethical and legal responsibilities, and desire for customer satisfaction.
- Describe your feelings and your disappointment.
- Avoid sounding angry, emotional, or irrational.
- Close by telling exactly what you want done.

precisely what you're asking for and providing evidence of why the request is necessary is critical when employees submit recommendations to their manager. It's also important to be realistic in your requests, recognizing that your manager has other employees he or she manages whose needs may be different from your own. Equally important when asking something of your manager is to focus on his or her needs. How can you make your suggestion sound like something your manager also wants or needs?

Obviously, when you set out to persuade someone at work who is above you in the company hierarchy, do so carefully. Use words like *suggest* and *recommend*, and craft sentences using conditional verb tenses such as: *It might be a good idea if . . .*; *We might think about doing . . .* The conditional tense lets you offer suggestions without threatening the person's authority.

In Figure 6.3 you can see a persuasive memo (attached to an e-mail) written by Marketing Assistant Monica Cho, who wants her manager to authorize the purchase

OFFICE INSIDER

When you create the impression that you are a person of honesty and integrity, you will have a considerable advantage over someone who is perceived otherwise.

FIGURE **6.3** E-mail Cover Note With Attached Interoffice Persuasive Memo

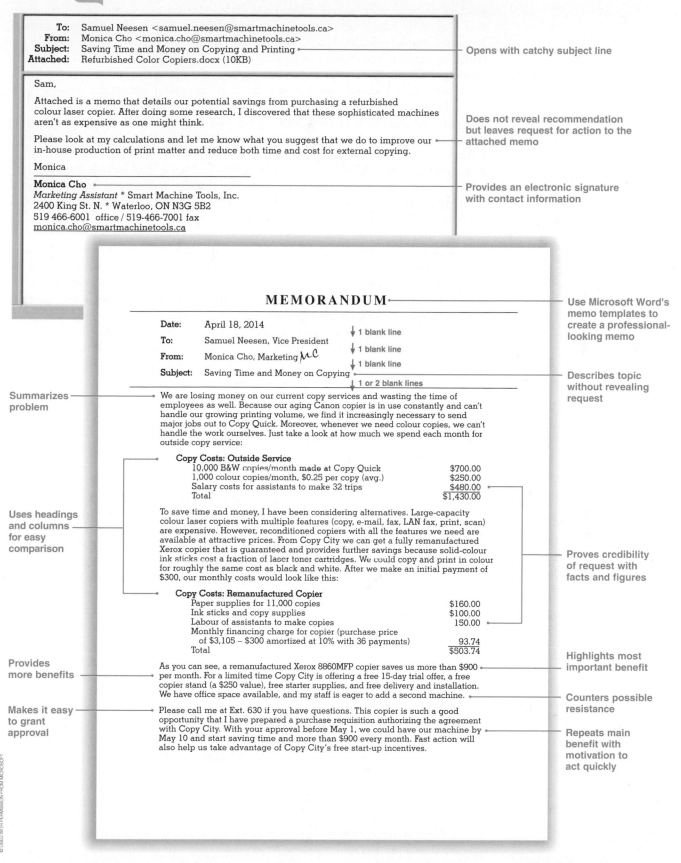

To: Samuel Neesen <samuel.neesen@smartmachinetools.ca>
From: Monica Cho <monica.cho@smartmachinetools.ca>
Subject: Saving Time and Money on Copying and Printing ●——— Opens with catchy subject line
Attached: Refurbished Color Copiers.docx (10KB)

Sam,

Attached is a memo that details our potential savings from purchasing a refurbished
colour laser copier. After doing some research, I discovered that these sophisticated machines ——— Does not reveal recommendation
aren't as expensive as one might think. but leaves request for action to the
attached memo

Please look at my calculations and let me know what you suggest that we do to improve our ●———
in-house production of print matter and reduce both time and cost for external copying.

Monica

Monica Cho ●——— Provides an electronic signature
Marketing Assistant * Smart Machine Tools, Inc. with contact information
2400 King St. N. * Waterloo, ON N3G 5B2
519 466-6001 office / 519-466-7001 fax
monica.cho@smartmachinetools.ca

MEMORANDUM ●——— Use Microsoft Word's
memo templates to
create a professional-
looking memo

Date: April 18, 2014 ↓ 1 blank line
To: Samuel Neesen, Vice President ↓ 1 blank line
From: Monica Cho, Marketing M.C ↓ 1 blank line
Subject: Saving Time and Money on Copying ●——— Describes topic
↓ 1 or 2 blank lines without revealing
request

Summarizes ——— We are losing money on our current copy services and wasting the time of
problem employees as well. Because our aging Canon copier is in use constantly and can't
handle our growing printing volume, we find it increasingly necessary to send
major jobs out to Copy Quick. Moreover, whenever we need colour copies, we can't
handle the work ourselves. Just take a look at how much we spend each month for
outside copy service:

Copy Costs: Outside Service
10,000 B&W copies/month made at Copy Quick $700.00
1,000 colour copies/month, $0.25 per copy (avg.) $250.00
Salary costs for assistants to make 32 trips $480.00
Total $1,430.00

Uses headings To save time and money, I have been considering alternatives. Large-capacity
and columns colour laser copiers with multiple features (copy, e-mail, fax, LAN fax, print, scan)
for easy are expensive. However, reconditioned copiers with all the features we need are
comparison available at attractive prices. From Copy City we can get a fully remanufactured Proves credibility
Xerox copier that is guaranteed and provides further savings because solid-colour of request with
ink sticks cost a fraction of laser toner cartridges. We could copy and print in colour facts and figures
for roughly the same cost as black and white. After we make an initial payment of
$300, our monthly costs would look like this:

Copy Costs: Remanufactured Copier
Paper supplies for 11,000 copies $160.00
Ink sticks and copy supplies $100.00
Labour of assistants to make copies 150.00
Monthly financing charge for copier (purchase price
of $3,105 – $300 amortized at 10% with 36 payments) 93.74
Total $503.74

Highlights most
important benefit

Provides As you can see, a remanufactured Xerox 8860MFP copier saves us more than $900 ●———
more benefits per month. For a limited time Copy City is offering a free 15-day trial offer, a free
copier stand (a $250 value), free starter supplies, and free delivery and installation.
We have office space available, and my staff is eager to add a second machine. ●——— Counters possible
resistance

Makes it easy Please call me at Ext. 630 if you have questions. This copier is such a good
to grant opportunity that I have prepared a purchase requisition authorizing the agreement
approval with Copy City. With your approval before May 1, we could have our machine by ●——— Repeats main
May 10 and start saving time and more than $900 every month. Fast action will benefit with
also help us take advantage of Copy City's free start-up incentives. motivation to
act quickly

© USED WITH PERMISSION FROM MICROSOFT

of a multi-function colour laser copier. She has researched the prices, features, and maintenance costs of the machines. They often serve as copiers, faxes, scanners, and printers and can cost several thousand dollars. Monica has found an outstanding deal offered by a local office supplier. Because Monica knows that her boss, Samuel Neesen, favours "cold, hard facts," she lists current monthly costs for copying at Copy Quick to increase her chances of gaining approval. Finally, she calculates the amortization of the purchase price and monthly costs of running the new colour copier.

Notice that Monica's memo isn't short. A successful persuasive message will typically take more space than a direct message because proving a case requires evidence. In the end, Monica chose to send her memo as an e-mail attachment accompanied by a polite, short e-mail message because she wanted to keep the document format in Microsoft Word intact. She also felt that the message was too long to paste into an e-mail. Monica's persuasive memo and her e-mail include a subject line that announces the purpose of the message without disclosing the actual request. By delaying the request until she has had a chance to describe the problem and discuss a solution, Monica prevents the reader's premature rejection.

The strength of this persuasive document, though, is in the clear presentation of comparison figures showing how much money the company can save by purchasing a remanufactured copier. Buying a copier that uses low-cost solid ink instead of expensive laser cartridges is another argument in this machine's favour. Although the organization pattern is not obvious, the memo does follow most of the Writing Plan for a Persuasive Request from the beginning of this chapter, by beginning with an attention-getter (a frank description of the problem), building interest (with easy-to-read facts and figures), providing benefits, and reducing resistance. Notice that the conclusion suggests what action is to be taken, makes it easy to respond, and repeats the main benefit to motivate action.

> When selling an idea to management, writers often are successful if they make a strong case for saving or earning money.

Persuasive Situation: Sales and Promotional Messages

Sales messages use persuasion to promote specific products and services. The focus in this part of the chapter is on direct-mail sales letters, but the communication strategy you will learn here can be applied to all forms of sales and promotions, including print, online, social and digital media, as well as traditional copywriting for radio and TV advertisements. Smart companies strive to develop a balanced approach to their overall marketing strategy, including both traditional direct mail as well as social/digital marketing when appropriate.

Sales letters are generally part of a package that may contain a brochure, price list, illustrations, testimonials, and other persuasive appeals. Professionals who specialize in traditional direct-mail services have made a science of analyzing a market, developing an effective mailing list, studying the product, preparing a sophisticated campaign aimed at a target audience, and motivating the reader to act. You have probably received many direct-mail packages, often called "junk mail."

> Traditional direct-mail marketing uses snail mail or flyering; new media marketing uses e-mail, social media, and digital media.

Because sales letters are usually written by marketing communications specialists, you may never write one on the job. Why, then, learn how to write a sales letter? In many ways, every message we draft is a form of sales letter. We sell our ideas, our organizations, and ourselves. When you apply for a job, you are both the seller and the product. Learning the techniques of sales writing will help you be more successful in any communication that requires persuasion and promotion. Furthermore, you will recognize sales strategies, thus enabling you to become a more perceptive consumer of ideas, products, and services.

> Learning to write sales letters helps you sell yourself and your ideas as well as become a smarter consumer.

Your primary goal in writing a sales message is to get someone to devote a few moments of attention to it.[1] You may be promoting a product, a service, an idea, or yourself. In each case the most effective messages will follow a writing plan. This is the same recipe we studied earlier, but the ingredients are different.

WRITING PLAN FOR A SALES MESSAGE: AIDA

Professional marketers and salespeople follow the AIDA pattern (attention, interest, desire, and action) when persuading consumers. In addition to telemarketing and personal selling, this pattern works very well for written messages.

- **Opening:** Gain *attention*. Offer something valuable; promise a benefit to the reader; ask a question; or provide a quotation, fact, product feature, testimonial, startling statement, or personalized action setting.
- **Body:** Build *interest*. Describe central selling points and make rational and emotional appeals. Elicit *desire* in the reader and reduce resistance. Use testimonials, money-back guarantees, free samples, performance tests, or other techniques.
- **Closing:** Motivate *action*. Offer a gift, promise an incentive, limit the offer, set a deadline, or guarantee satisfaction.

> The AIDA pattern (attention, interest, desire, and action) is used in selling because it is highly effective.

ATTENTION. One of the most critical elements of a sales letter is its opening paragraph, the attention-getter. This opener should be short (one to five lines), honest, relevant, and stimulating. Marketing pros have found that eye-catching typographical arrangements or provocative messages, such as the following, can hook a reader's attention:

- **Offer:** A free trip to Hawaii is just the beginning!
- **Benefit:** Now you can raise your sales income by 50 percent or even more with the proven techniques found in . . . .
- **Open-ended suggestive question:** Do you want your family to be safe?
- **Quotation or proverb:** Necessity is the mother of invention.

WORKPLACE IN FOCUS

Trying to sell a micro car to Canadians has been a gamble for Daimler AG, manufacturer of the luxurious Mercedes-Benz brand but also maker of the diminutive Smart Fortwo. Prompted by skyrocketing gasoline prices, European and Asian drivers have long embraced small automobiles. But SUV-, truck- and van-loving Canadians? Although the Smart is well engineered and sells briskly in over 30 countries, its promoters have had to work harder to win over Canadians, especially those not living in large urban centres. *What might rural or suburban Canadian car buyers worry about most when they see an automobile such as the Smart? What strategies might reduce their resistance?*

- **Compliment:** Life is full of milestones. You have reached one. You deserve . . . .
- **Fact:** A recent *Maclean's* poll says that three quarters of Canadians are not happy with the quality of financial advice they're receiving.
- **Product feature:** Electronic stability control, ABS, and other active and passive safety features explain why the ultra-compact new Smart Fortwo has achieved a four-star crash rating in Quebec.
- **Testimonial:** The most recent J.D. Power survey of "initial quality" shows that BMW ranks at the top of brands with the fewest defects and malfunctions, ahead of Chrysler, Hyundai, Lexus, Porsche, and Toyota.
- **Startling statement:** Let the poor and hungry feed themselves! For just $100 they can.
- **Personalized action setting:** It's 6:30 p.m. and you are working overtime to meet a pressing deadline. Suddenly your copier breaks down. The production of your colour-laser brochures screeches to a halt. How you wish you had purchased the Worry-Free-Anytime service contract from Canon.

Other openings calculated to capture attention might include a solution to a problem, an anecdote, a personalized statement using the receiver's name, or a relevant current event.

INTEREST. In this phase of your sales message, you should describe clearly the product or service. Think of this part as a promise that the product or service will satisfy the audience's needs. In simple language, emphasize the central selling points that you identified during your prewriting analysis. Those selling points can be developed using rational or emotional appeals.

Rational appeals are associated with reason and intellect. They translate selling points into references to making or saving money, increasing efficiency, or making the best use of resources. In general, rational appeals are appropriate when a product is expensive, long lasting, or important to health, security, and financial success. Emotional appeals relate to status, ego, and sensual feelings. Appealing to the emotions is sometimes effective when a product is inexpensive, short-lived, or nonessential. Many clever sales messages, however, combine emotional and rational strategies for a dual appeal. Consider these examples:

Rational Appeal

Cheery Maids is a one-stop solution: for one low monthly charge, you will receive biweekly visits by a team of our professional, fully-bonded cleaning staff who will clean your house from top to bottom. Enjoy both peace of mind and your time away from work without having to do your own cleaning.

Emotional Appeal

Tired of 9 to 5? Tired of commutes that seem to stretch longer and longer each day? Tired of getting home only to find you need to cook and clean the house because it's such a mess? Let Cheery Maids take part of the "tired" out of your life by providing you with cheerful, competitively priced home cleaning services.

Dual Appeal

By signing up today with Cheery Maids, you'll receive two free cleans in the next calendar year. Not only will you be able to leave the "dirty work" to our trained professionals, you'll have money left over to enjoy a couple of relaxing nights out at dinner and a movie with the family—on us!

A physical description of your product is not enough, however. Experienced salespeople know that no matter how well you know your product, no one is persuaded by cold, hard facts alone. In the end, "people buy because of the product benefits."[2] Your job is to translate those cold facts into warm feelings and reader

Build interest by describing the benefits a product or service offers and by making rational or emotional appeals.

Rational appeals focus on making or saving money, increasing efficiency, or making good use of resources.

Emotional appeals focus on status, ego, and sensual feelings.

benefits. Let's say a sales letter promotes a hand cream made with Vitamin A and aloe and cocoa butter extracts. Those facts become *Nature's hand helpers—including soothing aloe and cocoa extracts, and firming Vitamin A—form invisible gloves that protect your sensitive skin against the hardships of work, harsh detergents, and constant environmental assaults.*

DESIRE. The goal at this stage in the sales message is to elicit desire in the reader and to overcome resistance. You also try to make the audience want the product or service, and to anticipate objections, focus strongly on reader benefits. Here the promises of the attention and interest sections are covered in great detail. Marketing pros use a number of techniques to elicit desire in their audience and to overcome resistance.

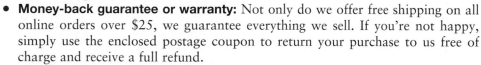

- **Testimonials:** *I always receive friendly and on-time service when I take my car to a Canadian Tire mechanic for servicing. I just wouldn't go anywhere else!*—Vince McRae, Edmundston, NB.
- **Names of satisfied users (with permission, of course):** See the bottom of this message to learn about some of the IT professionals who are already taking advantage of our conference webinar subscription service and are 100% satisfied with the experience.
- **Money-back guarantee or warranty:** Not only do we offer free shipping on all online orders over $25, we guarantee everything we sell. If you're not happy, simply use the enclosed postage coupon to return your purchase to us free of charge and receive a full refund.
- **Free trial or sample:** "Welcome to the wine store. Would you care for a sample of a wonderful new white wine? Go ahead and enjoy a piece of cheddar and a cracker—they pair nicely with the minerally quality of this Riesling . . . I have a coupon for $1 off per bottle if you'd like to take some home . . . . "
- **Performance tests, polls, or awards:** At Luce this week, Chef Ferretti, who's just back from Washington, D.C., where he won the prestigious North American Chef Competition for best innovative dish, is offering a three-course tasting menu including one-course wine pairing for $89.

In addition, you need to anticipate objections and questions the receiver may have. When possible, translate these objections into selling points (*Tax season can be a stressful time and you want to make sure you can trust the person who prepares your income tax returns. For this reason we offer a free 30-minute consultation with one of our tax preparation specialists who will walk you through your return and explain how we arrived at our calculations.*). Be sure, of course, that your claims are accurate and do not stretch the truth.

When price is an obstacle, consider these suggestions:

- Delay mentioning price until after you have created a desire for the product.
- Show the price in small units, such as the price per month or per ten downloads of a magazine subscription service.
- Demonstrate how the reader saves money by, for instance, subscribing for two or three years.
- Compare your prices with those of a competitor.
- If applicable, offer advantageous financing terms.

> Techniques for motivating action include offering a gift or incentive, limiting an offer, and guaranteeing satisfaction.

ACTION. All the effort put into a sales message is wasted if the reader fails to respond. To make it easy for readers to act, you can provide a reply card, a stamped and pre-addressed envelope, a toll-free telephone number, a convenient Web address, or a promise of a follow-up call. Because readers often need an extra push, consider including additional motivators, such as the following:

- **Offer a gift:** You will receive a free iPod nano with the purchase of any new car.
- **Promise an incentive:** With every new, paid subscription, we will plant a tree in one of Canada's pollution-busting boreal forests.
- **Limit the offer:** Only the first 100 customers receive free cheques.
- **Set a deadline:** You must act before June 1 to get these low prices.
- **Guarantee satisfaction:** We will return your full payment if you are not entirely satisfied—no questions asked.

The final paragraph of the sales letter carries the call to action. This is where you tell readers what you want done and give them reasons for doing it. Most sales letters also include postscripts because they make irresistible reading. Even readers who might skim over or bypass paragraphs are drawn to a P.S. Therefore, use a postscript to reveal your strongest motivator, to add a special inducement for a quick response, or to re-emphasize a central selling point.

Putting It All Together

Sales letters are a preferred marketing medium because they can be personalized, directed to target audiences, and filled with a more complete message than other advertising media. However, direct mail is expensive. That is why the total sales message is crafted so painstakingly.

Figure 6.4 shows a sales letter addressed to a target group of existing bank customers. To sell the new Groceries Plus Mastercard, the letter incorporates all four AIDA components of an effective persuasive message. Notice that the personalized action-setting opener places the reader in a familiar situation (walking into a supermarket) and draws an analogy between the choosing which aisle to go down first and choosing between many credit cards.

The writer develops a rational central selling point (a credit card that earns you free groceries is one you'll use happily) and repeats this selling point in all the components of the letter. Notice, too, how a testimonial from a satisfied customer lends support to the sales message, and how the closing pushes for action. Also, see how call-outs (bolded, indented attention-grabbing messages) appear within the body of the letter.

Because the price of the credit card (a $100 yearly fee) is not a selling feature, it is mentioned only on the reply card. This sales letter repeats its strongest motivator—$25 in free groceries for signing up—in the high-impact P.S. line.

 ## Persuasive Situation: Online Sales and Promotional Messages

To make the best use of limited advertising dollars while reaching a great number of potential customers, many businesses are turning to the Internet and to digital marketing campaigns in particular. Much like traditional direct mail, digital marketing can attract new customers, keep existing ones, encourage future sales, cross-sell, and cut costs. As consumers become more comfortable and secure with online purchases, they will receive more e-mail sales messages.

In fact, by growing a healthy 16 percent, online advertising will continue to outpace overall ad spending, predicts the Interactive Advertising Bureau, an industry association.[3] Consultants forecast that the fastest-growing segment of interactive advertising continues to be "socially enabled" advertising: ads that link to some form of social media.[4]

In the future, customers will be more likely to receive ads for products and services they actually use and like, and they can always opt out of receiving such marketing e-mails. An eConsultancy study of 1,400 U.S. consumers found that

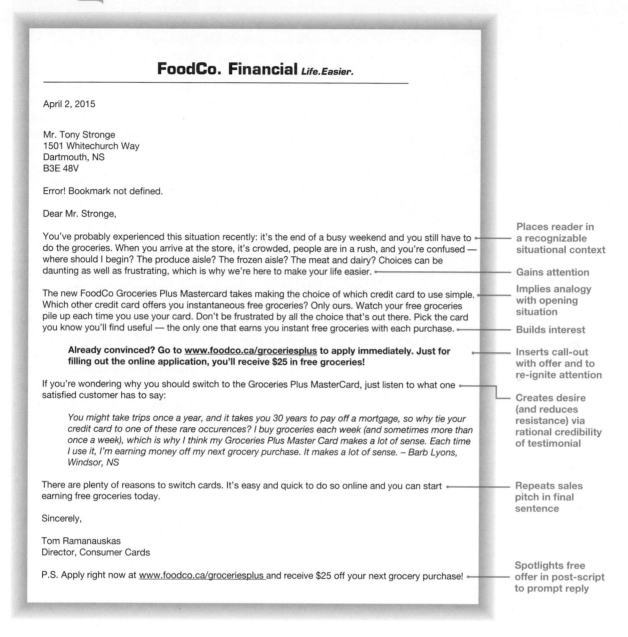

FoodCo. Financial *Life.Easier.*

April 2, 2015

Mr. Tony Stronge
1501 Whitechurch Way
Dartmouth, NS
B3E 48V

Error! Bookmark not defined.

Dear Mr. Stronge,

You've probably experienced this situation recently: it's the end of a busy weekend and you still have to do the groceries. When you arrive at the store, it's crowded, people are in a rush, and you're confused — where should I begin? The produce aisle? The frozen aisle? The meat and dairy? Choices can be daunting as well as frustrating, which is why we're here to make your life easier.

Places reader in a recognizable situational context
Gains attention

The new FoodCo Groceries Plus Mastercard takes making the choice of which credit card to use simple. Which other credit card offers you instantaneous free groceries? Only ours. Watch your free groceries pile up each time you use your card. Don't be frustrated by all the choice that's out there. Pick the card you know you'll find useful — the only one that earns you instant free groceries with each purchase.

Implies analogy with opening situation
Builds interest

Already convinced? Go to www.foodco.ca/groceriesplus to apply immediately. Just for filling out the online application, you'll receive $25 in free groceries!

Inserts call-out with offer and to re-ignite attention

If you're wondering why you should switch to the Groceries Plus MasterCard, just listen to what one satisfied customer has to say:

Creates desire (and reduces resistance) via rational credibility of testimonial

> *You might take trips once a year, and it takes you 30 years to pay off a mortgage, so why tie your credit card to one of these rare occurences? I buy groceries each week (and sometimes more than once a week), which is why I think my Groceries Plus Master Card makes a lot of sense. Each time I use it, I'm earning money off my next grocery purchase. It makes a lot of sense. – Barb Lyons, Windsor, NS*

There are plenty of reasons to switch cards. It's easy and quick to do so online and you can start earning free groceries today.

Repeats sales pitch in final sentence

Sincerely,

Tom Ramanauskas
Director, Consumer Cards

P.S. Apply right now at www.foodco.ca/groceriesplus and receive $25 off your next grocery purchase!

Spotlights free offer in post-script to prompt reply

42 percent prefer to receive ads by e-mail compared to 3 percent who favoured social networking sites and only 1 percent who preferred Twitter.[5]

Selling by E-Mail

If your organization requires an online sales message, try using the following techniques gleaned from the best-performing e-mails.

Communicate only with those who have given permission! By sending messages only to "opt-in" folks, you greatly increase your "open rate"—those e-mail messages that will be opened. E-mail users detest spam. However, receivers are surprisingly receptive to offers tailored specifically for them. Remember that today's customer is somebody—not anybody.

> Send only targeted, not "blanket," mailings. Include something special for a select group.

Today's promotional e-mail often comes with colourful and eye-catching graphics and a minimum of text. To allow for embedded images, sound, and even video, the e-mail is coded in HTML and can be viewed in an e-mail program or an

Internet browser. Software programs make it easy to create e-newsletters for e-mail distribution. Figure 6.5 shows one such promotional message in HTML format by live music search engine Live Nation. It was sent by e-mail to customers who had bought tickets from Live Nation. They had to create an account and sign up to receive e-newsletters and periodic promotions like this one.

The principles you have learned to apply to traditional sales messages also work with electronic promotional tools. However, some fundamental differences are obvious when you study Figure 6.5. Online sales messages are much shorter than direct mail, feature colourful graphics, and occasionally even have sound or video clips. They offer a richer experience to readers who can click hyperlinks to access content that interests them. When such messages are sent out as ads or periodic e-newsletters, they may not have salutations or closings. Rather, they may resemble Web pages.

Here are a few guidelines that will help you create effective online sales messages:

- **Craft a catchy subject line.** Offer discounts or premiums: *Spring Sale: Buy now and save 20 percent!* Promise solutions to everyday work-related problems. Highlight hot new industry topics. Invite readers to scan a top-ten list of items such as issues, trends, or people.
- **Keep the main information "above the fold."** E-mail messages should be top heavy. Primary points should appear early in the message so that they capture the reader's attention.
- **Make the message short, conversational, and focused.** Because on-screen text is taxing to read, be brief. Focus on one or two central selling points only.
- **Convey urgency.** Top-performing sales e-mails state an offer deadline or demonstrate why the state of the industry demands action on the reader's part. Good messages also tie the product to relevant current events.
- **Sprinkle testimonials throughout the copy.** Consumers' own words are the best sales copy. These comments can serve as call-outs or be integrated into the copy.
- **Provide a means for opting out.** It is polite and a good business tactic to include a statement that tells receivers how to be removed from the sender's mailing database.

Using Facebook, Blogs, and Other New Media to Connect With Customers

Besides the static one-directional e-mail sales and promotions channel, businesses are increasingly looking to social media and blogs to send out their persuasive and promotional messages to partner firms and customers. These new tools can also be useful internally when communicating with employees.

FACEBOOK. Facebook is the Web's dominant social network. Founder and CEO Mark Zuckerberg is confidently predicting a billion Facebook members in the near future. The current number of over 600 million users already represents a huge resource for businesses eager to connect with their customers in unprecedented ways. Nike's three-minute commercial "Write the Future" was first launched on the company's Facebook site. The video went viral, and over one weekend, the number of Nike's Facebook fans doubled from 1.6 million to 3.1 million. Soft-drink giant Coca-Cola maintains by far the largest presence on Facebook with more than 12 million fans. The company's vice president of global interactive marketing, Carol Kruse, said that Coca-Cola has made Facebook a central focus of its marketing plans.[6]

A recent study by public relations giant Burson-Marsteller suggests that social media, with Facebook foremost among them, offer huge research and brand-building opportunities. Media-savvy businesses face a public that wants to be heard. If they listen to and engage with users, companies can positively affect their customers'

FIGURE 6.5 E-Mail Sales Message to Opt-In Recipients

LIVE NATION® SPECIAL OFFER

Christina Perri: The 'Burning Gold' Meet & Greet Package
Upgrade for Meet & Greet, Photo and more!

Already have a ticket to the Demi Lovato World Tour with special guest Christina Perri? Upgrade to The 'Burning Gold' Meet & Greet Package to meet Christina! Don't miss this chance to meet and take a photo with one of your favorite singer/songwriters.

Meet & Greet VIP Packages include:*

- Individual Photo Op with Christina Perri
- VIP commemorative laminate
- Limited edition Christina Perri VIP gift item
- Early entrance into the venue
- On-site VIP host

Upgrade your ticket to a VIP package today!

BUY NOW

Find Christina Perri Meet & Greet Packages in Your City!

Date	Venue	City	
09/06/14	Baltimore Arena	Baltimore, MD	Buy Now
09/07/14	The Union Center	Albany, NY	Buy Now
09/09/14	Peterson Events Center	Pittsburgh, PA	Buy Now
09/14/14	American Airlines Arena	Miami, FL	Buy Now
09/15/14	Amway Center	Orlando, FL	Buy Now
09/23/14	Sprint Center	Kansas City, MO	Buy Now
09/25/14	Pepsi Center	Denver, CO	Buy Now
09/27/14	Staples Center	Los Angeles, CA	Buy Now
09/28/14	Viejas Arena	San Diego, CA	Buy Now
10/02/14	Comcast Arena at Everett	Everett, WA	Buy Now
10/04/14	Rexall Place	Edmonton, AB	Buy Now
10/05/14	Scotiabank Saddledome	Calgary, AB	Buy Now
10/07/14	Credit Union Centre	Saskatoon, SK	Buy Now
10/10/14	Denny Sanford Premier Center	Sioux Falls, SD	Buy Now
10/11/14	I Wireless Center	Moline, IL	Buy Now
10/14/14	United Center	Chicago, IL	Buy Now
10/15/14	KFC Yum Center	Louisville, KY	Buy Now
10/17/14	Mohegan Sun	Uncasville, CT	Buy Now
10/19/14	Bell Centre	Montreal, QC	Buy Now
10/20/14	FirstOntario Centre	Hamilton, ON	Buy Now
10/22/14	Verizon Wireless Arena	Manchester, NH	Buy Now
10/24/14	Giant Center	Hershey,PA	Buy Now
10/25/14	Prudential Center	Newark, NJ	Buy Now
10/27/14	Barclays Center	Brooklyn, NY	Buy Now

*Please note : Your merchandise items that are included in the package will be available for pickup at the venue the day of the show. All VIP tickets will be issued at the designated VIP check in location (or other designated location at the venue) prior to the show on the date of the event only. Check in location information will be emailed out 3-5 days prior to the day of the show. All packages are will-call only except for in the state of NY. All packages are NON-REFUNDABLE and NON-TRANSFERABLE outside the first 24 hrs. of purchase. All sales are final. You must bring a valid PHOTO ID matching the MAIN ATTENDEE name on this order. Those who cannot present a photo ID matching the ATTENDEE name on the order will be turned away. Please note: This offer is not valid if tickets are purchased through TM+. Christina Perri The 'Burning Gold' Meet & Greet Packages cannot be resold. Please check with the venue directly for any age restriction.

beliefs as well as counter potentially negative perceptions.[7] Almost 80 percent of major global companies market their brands and communicate with the public on social media sites.[8] Despite concerns after repeated privacy breaches, to proponents of social media, sites such as Facebook promise advertising that is less obtrusive and more tailored to users' needs than traditional, widely distributed ads.

BLOGS. In the right hands, blogs can be powerful marketing tools. Information technology giant Hewlett-Packard (HP) invites guest bloggers to contribute to its site as advisors to small businesses, for example. Executives, HP employees, and outside experts discuss a wide range of technology- and company-related topics. Although not overtly pushing a marketing message, ultimately HP wants to generate goodwill; hence, the blogs serve as a public relations tool.[9] Nearly half of the CEOs questioned in one survey said they believe blogs are useful for external public relations, and 59 percent said they find blogs valuable for internal communication.[10] Many companies now use blogs to subtly market their products and develop a brand image.

WIKIS. Wikis generally facilitate collaboration inside organizations, but they also do so between companies, thus generating goodwill. A wiki contains digital information available on a Web portal or on a company's protected intranet where visitors can add or edit content. One big advantage of wikis is the ease of information and file sharing. Perhaps the best-known wiki is the online encyclopedia Wikipedia.

In business, wiki users can quickly document and publish a complex process to a group of recipients. GigaSpaces, a U.S.-based software and cloud computing leader, uses a wiki program called Confluence to host its public online help system, as well as for internal organizational purposes. As one corporate user of this wiki software says, it "dramatically improves the user experience for our customers."[11] GigaSpaces is just one company using a wiki platform to satisfy its customers and in turn sell them further solutions for their business problems.

RSS (REALLY SIMPLE SYNDICATION). RSS is yet another tool for keeping customers and business partners up to date. Many companies now offer RSS feeds, a format for distributing news or information about recent changes on their Web sites, in wikis, or in blogs. Recipients subscribe to content they want using RSS reader software. Alternatively, they receive news items or articles in their e-mail.[12] The RSS feeds help users keep up with their favourite Web magazines, Web sites, and blogs. As a promotional tool, this medium can create interest in a company and its products.

PODCASTING. Podcasting is emerging as an important Internet marketing tool. Business podcasts are content-rich audio or video files featuring company representatives, business experts, or products and services. They can be distributed by RSS or downloaded from company Web sites and played back on a computer or an MP3 player.

OTHER SOCIAL MEDIA. Social media such as Twitter are a very important part of marketing today. As Tamar Weinberg, author of *The New Community Rules: Marketing on the Social Web*, has shown, Twitter, for example, has been used successfully by both large and small companies to increase sales and to perform other functions such as crisis management.[13] Clearly, business communicators today—especially those who work in publicity, advertising, marketing, and sales—have to become experts at the relatively new communication genres such as social media, whose interfaces are radically different than that of the traditional letter: more flexible, colourful, touchable, changeable, and so on.

SUMMING UP AND LOOKING FORWARD

The ability to persuade is a powerful and versatile communication tool. In this chapter you learned to apply the indirect strategy in writing claim letters, making favour requests, writing persuasive suggestions within organizations, and writing sales letters. You also learned basic techniques for developing successful online sales messages. The techniques suggested here will be useful in many other contexts beyond the writing of these business documents. You will find that logical organization of arguments is also extremely effective in expressing ideas orally or any time you must overcome resistance to change.

Not all business messages are strictly persuasive. Occasionally, you must deny requests and deliver bad news. In the next chapter you will learn to use the indirect strategy in conveying negative news.

CRITICAL THINKING

1. Why is the ability to persuade a significant trait in both business and personal relations?

2. The organization of a successful persuasive claim centres on the reasons and the closing. Why?

3. Why not just write all favour requests directly? Discuss.

4. In a world of depleted forests and overflowing landfills, why does junk mail still thrive? Is it ethical? Should something be done to curb it?

5. Some individuals will never write a sales letter. Why is it nevertheless important for them to learn the techniques for doing so?

CHAPTER REVIEW

1. What is the difference between direct and indirect benefits to individuals we may want to persuade?

2. Explain how you would decide whether to use the direct pattern or the indirect pattern.

3. List eight tips for making claims and complaints.

4. What are the most important considerations when trying to persuade people within your organization?

5. List at least ten ways to gain a reader's attention in the opening of a sales letter.

6. Name five writing techniques that reduce resistance in a sales message.

7. Name six techniques for motivating action in the closing of a sales message.

8. Describe the main advantages of using business podcasts, blogs, wikis, and social media.

9. What techniques do writers of successful online sales messages use?

WRITING IMPROVEMENT EXERCISES

Strategies

Your Task. For each of the following situations, check the appropriate writing strategy.

Direct Strategy	Indirect Strategy	
_____	_____	1. A request from one company to another to verify the previous employment record of a job applicant
_____	_____	2. An announcement that must convince employees to stop smoking, start exercising, and opt for a healthy diet to lower health care expenses and reduce absenteeism
_____	_____	3. An e-mail message to employees telling them that the company parking lot will be closed for one week while it is being resurfaced
_____	_____	4. A letter to a cleaning service demanding a refund for sealing a dirty tiled floor and damaging a fresh paint job

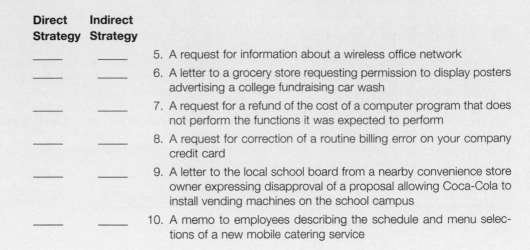

	Direct Strategy	Indirect Strategy	
	_____	_____	5. A request for information about a wireless office network
	_____	_____	6. A letter to a grocery store requesting permission to display posters advertising a college fundraising car wash
	_____	_____	7. A request for a refund of the cost of a computer program that does not perform the functions it was expected to perform
	_____	_____	8. A request for correction of a routine billing error on your company credit card
	_____	_____	9. A letter to the local school board from a nearby convenience store owner expressing disapproval of a proposal allowing Coca-Cola to install vending machines on the school campus
	_____	_____	10. A memo to employees describing the schedule and menu selections of a new mobile catering service

---

● ACTIVITIES AND CASES

6.1 Action Request: Protesting Plastic-Wrapped Bananas

Your Task. Analyze the following message and list its weaknesses. If your instructor directs, revise the message. A copy of this e-mail is provided at **www.nelson.com/guffeyessentials8ce** for revision online.

To: Members of the 7-Eleven Franchise Owners Association of Ontario
From: Nicholas Barajas <nicholas.barajas@hotmail.com>
Subject: Can You Believe Plastic-Wrapped Bananas?

Hey, have you heard about this new thing coming at us? As a 7-Eleven franchise owner and member of the 7-Eleven Franchise Owners Association of Ontario, I am seriously put off about this move to wrap our bananas in plastic. Sure, it would extend their shelf life to five days. And I know that our customers want yellow—not brown—bananas. But wrapping them in plastic?? I mentioned this at home, and my teenage daughter immediately turned up her nose and said, "A banana wrapped in plastic? Eeeyooo! Do we really need more plastic clogging up the environment?" She's been studying sustainability and said that more plastic packaging is not a sustainable solution to our problem.

I realize that we 7-Eleven franchisees are increasingly dependent on fresh food sales as cigarette sales tank. But plastic-wrapped bananas is going too far, even if the wrapping slows ripening. As members of the 7-Eleven Franchise Owners Association, we have to do something. I think we could insist that our supplier Fresh Del Monte come up with a wrapper that's biodegradable. On the other hand, extending the shelf life of bananas cuts the carbon footprint by cutting down all those deliveries to our stores.

We have a meeting of franchisees coming up on January 20. Let's resist this banana thing!

Nick

1. List at least five faults.
2. Outline a writing plan for a persuasive request.
   Opening:
   Body:
   Closing:

6.2 Favour Request: Inviting a Speaker
Your Task. Analyze the following poorly written invitation. List its weaknesses and outline a writing strategy. If your instructor directs, revise it.

Dear Dr. Schulz:

Because you're a local Nanaimo author, we thought it might not be too much trouble for you to speak at our Canadian Association of Independent Management banquet May 5. Some of us business students here at Glenbow Valley College admired your book *Beyond Race and Gender,* which appeared last spring and became such a hit across the country. One of our instructors said you were now the country's management guru. What exactly did you mean when you said that Canada is the "Mulligan stew" of the Americas?

Because we have no funds for honoraria, we have to rely on local speakers. Dr. Lester Pierfont and Deputy Mayor Shirley Slye were speakers in the past. Our banquets usually begin at 6:30 with a social hour, followed by dinner at 7:30 and the speaker from 8:30 until 9:00 or 9:15. We can arrange transportation for you and your wife if you need it.

We realize that you must be very busy, but we hope you'll agree. Please let our advisor, Duncan Rankin, have the favour of an early response.

1. List at least five weaknesses.
2. Outline a writing plan for a favour request.

    Opening:

    Body:

    Closing:

6.3 Persuasive Suggestion: Asking for Tuition Reimbursement

Your Task. Analyze the poorly written e-mail in Figure 6.6. List its weaknesses. If your instructor directs, revise it.

1. List at least five weaknesses in this e-mail.
2. Outline a writing plan for this e-mail.

    Opening:

    Body:

    Closing:

FIGURE 6.6 Tuition Help

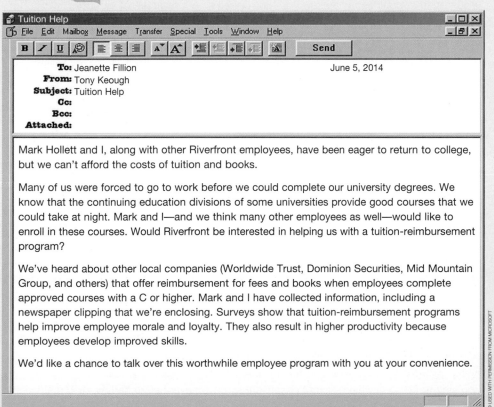

6.4 Sales Letter: Analyzing the Pitch

Read the following sales letter and analyze its effectiveness by answering the questions listed after the letter.

Dear Friend of University of Prince Edward Island,

You are part of a special group of alumni—doctors, lawyers, bankers, managers, professors—who have a wide variety of credit cards available to them. For this reason I am inviting you to choose the superior benefits of the UPEI *Platinum Preferred* Visa credit card.

The UPEI Alumni Association has planned, in association with Atlantic Bank, a superior credit card with excellent benefits, personalized customer care, and best of all, no annual fee.

Each purchase made with your UPEI *Platinum Preferred* Visa card leads directly to a contribution to the UPEI Alumni Association. This extra benefit costs nothing, but allows the Association to continue its vital work on campus and in the community.

Yours sincerely,

Margaret Simpson
Director of Alumni Relations
UPEI Alumni Association

a. What technique captures the reader's attention in the opening? Is it effective?

b. What are the central selling points?

c. Does the letter use rational, emotional, or a combination of appeals? Explain.

d. What technique builds interest in the product? Are benefits obvious?

e. How is price handled?

f. Does the letter anticipate reader resistance and offer counterarguments?

g. What action is the reader to take? How is the action made easy?

Your Task. Revise the above letter, adding any improvements you think necessary based on your answers to the above questions.

TEAM

6.5 Persuasive Claim: Excessive Legal Fees

You are the business manager for McConnell's, a producer of gourmet ice cream. McConnell's has 12 ice-cream shops in the Toronto area and a reputation for excellent ice cream. Your firm was approached by an independent ice-cream vendor who wanted to use McConnell's name and recipes for ice cream to be distributed through grocery stores and drugstores. As business manager you worked with a law firm, Peretine, Valcon, and Associates, to draw up contracts regarding the use of McConnell's name and quality standards for the product.

When you received the bill from Louis Peretine, you couldn't believe it. The bill itemized 38 hours of attorney preparation, at $300 per hour, and 55 hours of paralegal assistance, at $75 per hour. The bill also showed $415 for telephone calls, which might be accurate because Mr. Peretine had to converse with McConnell's owners, who were living in Ireland at the time. However, you doubt that an experienced attorney would require 38 hours to draw up the contracts in question.

Perhaps some error was made in calculating the total hours. Moreover, you have checked with other businesses and found that excellent legal advice can be obtained for $200 per hour. McConnell's would like to continue using the services of Peretine, Valcon, and Associates for future legal business. Such future business is unlikely if an adjustment is not made on this bill.

Your Task. Write a persuasive request to Louis Peretine, Legal Counsel, Peretine, Valcon, and Associates, 2690 Whyte Avenue, Toronto, ON M2N 2E6.

6.6 Persuasive E-Mail: Scheduling Meetings More Strategically

The following message, with names changed, was actually sent.

Your Task. Based on what you have learned in this chapter, improve this e-mail. Expect the staff to be somewhat resistant because they have never before had meeting restrictions.

From: Dina Waterman <dwaterman@promosell.ca>
To: All Managers
Cc:
Subject: Scheduling Meetings

Please be reminded that travel in the greater Vancouver area is time-consuming. In the future we are asking that you set up meetings that

1. Are of critical importance
2. Consider travel time for the participants
3. Consider phone conferences (or video or e-mail) in lieu of face-to-face meetings
4. Meetings should be at the location where most of the participants work and at the most opportune travel times
5. Travelling together is another way to save time and resources.

We all have our traffic horror stories. A recent one is that a certain manager was asked to attend a one-hour meeting in Ladner. This required one hour of travel in advance of the meeting, one hour for the meeting, and two and a half hours of travel through Vancouver afterward. This meeting was scheduled for 4 p.m. Total time consumed by the manager for the one-hour meeting was four and a half hours.

Thank you for your consideration.

6.7 Persuasive Internal E-Mail Request: Convincing Your Boss to Blog

You have just read Steve Rubel's *Micro Persuasion* blog, in which he cites an interesting study of chief executives and blogging.[14] It turns out that a majority of CEOs believe blogs to be useful for internal (59 percent) and external communication (47 percent). However, only 7 percent of the CEOs interviewed actually blog, although 18 percent expect to host a company blog within two years.

Your boss, Simon Dawkins, is a technophobe who is slow in adopting the latest information technology. You know that it will be a difficult sell, but you believe that corporate blogging is an opportunity not to be missed.

Your Task. Decide what industry your company is part of, then write a persuasive e-mail message to Simon Dawkins attempting to convince him that blogging is a useful public-relations and internal communication tool and that he or someone he officially designates should start a company blog. Anticipate Dawkins' fears. Naturally, a blogger has to be prepared even for unflattering comments. If your instructor directs, visit the blogs of companies such as Google (**http://googleblog.blogspot.com**), Microsoft (**http://blogs.msdn.com**), or Rogers (**http://redboard.rogers.com**). You can search for company blogs in Google. Select the More tab on top of the screen and click Blogs.

6.8 Persuasive Favour Request: Helping Out a Worthy Charity

You have been a supporter of the World Partnership Walk since you were 17 years old. Now, five years later, you have graduated from college and are working as the office manager for a small Ottawa-based law firm, Fraser, Ahmet, and Grandpre. Last year, you were able to persuade the three partners in the firm to become local corporate sponsors for the Ottawa World Partnership Walk. This year, you'd like to be more ambitious and recruit other local law firms to make a corporate donation. This year's walk happens at a busy time: soon after the annual Terry Fox Run and just before the annual AIDS Walk Ottawa. Still, you believe the World Partnership Walk is worthy of support by area law firms.

Your Task. Write a letter that you will personalize and send to 15 small and medium-sized Ottawa-area law firms requesting that they become corporate sponsors for this year's World Partnership Walk.

Related Web site: For more information on the World Partnership Walk, go to **www .worldpartnershipwalk.com**.

6.9 Persuasive E-Mail: Overusing Overnight Shipments

WEB

As office manager of Cambridge Software, write a memo persuading technicians, engineers, programmers, and other employees to reduce the number of overnight or second-day mail shipments. Your Federal Express, Canada Post, and other shipping bills have been higher than expected, and you feel that staff members are overusing these services.

Encourage employees to send messages by e-mail. Sending an e-mail costs almost nothing, whether it's sent locally or halfway around the world. Storing larger documents on secure FTP sites is another easy way to share documents. Attaching smaller documents—whether as Word files or as PDF documents—is replacing faxing and couriering in today's business world. Obviously, there's a huge difference between the "almost nothing" cost of an e-mail and potentially hundreds of dollars for overnight courier service. If employees have to send a package, they should, whenever possible, obtain the courier service account number of the recipient and use it for charging the shipment.

Your Task. Ask employees to decide whether receivers are really going to mind receiving an e-mail document they have to read on screen or print out. You'd like to reduce overnight delivery services voluntarily by 50 percent over the next two months. Unless a sizable reduction occurs, there may be significant consequences (e.g., suspension of courier privileges). Address your e-mail to all employees.

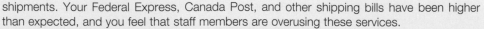

6.10 Persuasive Letter or E-Mail: Inviting an Alumna to Speak

As public relations director for the Business and Accounting Association on your campus, you have been asked to find a keynote speaker for the first meeting of the school year. The owner of a successful local firm, TempHelp4You, is an alumna of your university. You think not only that many students would enjoy learning about how she started her business, but also that some might like to sign up with her temporary help agency. She would need to prepare a 30-minute speech and take questions after the talk. The event will be held from noon until 1:30 p.m. on a date of your choosing in Branford Hall. You can offer her lunch at the event and provide her with a parking permit that she can pick up at the information kiosk at the main entrance to your campus. You need to have her response by a deadline you set.

Your Task. Write a direct approach e-mail to Marion Minter in which you ask her to speak at your club's meeting. Send it to *mminter@temphelp4you.com*.

6.11 Sales Letter: Fitness at the Local Brewery

Health research shows that 33 percent of Canadians between the ages of 20 and 64 are overweight.[15] Long-term health risks could be reduced if overweight employees shed their excess weight.

As a sales representative for Fitness Associates, you think your fitness equipment and programs could be instrumental in helping people lose weight. With regular exercise at an on-site fitness centre, employees lose weight and improve overall health. As employee health improves, absenteeism is reduced and overall productivity increases. And employees love working out before or after work. They make the routine part of their work day, and they often have work buddies who share their fitness regimen.

Though many companies resist spending money to save money, fitness centres need not be large or expensive to be effective. Studies show that moderately sized centres coupled with motivational and training programs yield the greatest success. For just $30,000, Fitness Associates will provide exercise equipment including stationary bikes, weight machines, and treadmills. Their fitness experts will design a fitness room, set up the fitness equipment, and design appropriate programs. Best of all, the one-time cost is usually offset by cost savings within one year of centre installation. For additional fees, FA can also provide fitness consultants for employee fitness assessments. FA specialists will also train employees on proper use of the equipment, and they will clean and manage the facility—for an extra charge, of course.

Your Task. Write a sales letter to Ms. Kathleen Stewart, Human Resources VP, Good Times Brewing Company, 3939 Brewery Row, Moose Jaw, SK S6H 0V9. Assume you are writing on company letterhead. Ask for an appointment to meet with her. Send her a brochure detailing the products and services that Fitness Associates provides. As an incentive, offer a free fitness assessment for all employees if Good Times Brewing installs a fitness facility by December 1.

6.12 Sales Letter: Persuading an Old Friend to Switch to ACCuracy Plus

You are the owner of Software Solutions, a Prince George, B.C.–based software consultancy. Recently, at a major industry trade show in Chicago, you were introduced to a new accounting software package, ACCuracy Plus. Quickly realizing its merits, you signed a deal with the American manufacturer to become the exclusive sales agent for the software in Canada, west of Ontario. Now that you own the right to sell the software, you have to make some sales. One day, while brainstorming possible clients, you remember your old friend from college, Tim Thom. While reading the newspaper last year you found out that Tim Thom has been promoted to VP Operations for Health & Co., a Victoria-based national retail chain selling vitamins, supplements, and natural foods. Even though you haven't seen or spoken to Tim in over eight years, you used to be good friends, and you believe a persuasive sales letter about your new software will not go unanswered. The question is, should you make a strong pitch for a sale, or should you just pitch for a get-together over lunch?

Your Task. Write a persuasive sales letter to Tim Thom, where you try to interest him in switching from his current accounting software to ACCuracy Plus.

Related Web sites: To build interest in ACCuracy Plus, browse the Internet for the features of its competitors such as AccPac (**www.accpac.com**) and Dynamics GP (**www.microsoft .com/dynamics/gp/default.mspx**). Be careful not to plagiarize when you write your letter.

6.13 New Media Alumni Campaign

WEB

Your college or university has traditionally been very conservative in contacting its alumni about donations. For example, there is a paper-based alumni magazine that is mailed out three times a year to all alumni. Also, there is a paper-based letter mailer that goes out once a year to alumni asking them to donate to the scholarship and building funds. Recognizing that social media, blogs, and other new media are revolutionizing the way people get their information, entertain themselves, and plan their lives, the new alumni director at your institution decides that something has to change.

Your Task. As the new alumni coordinator, examine the alumni Web sites of various postsecondary institutions, but not your own, looking for evidence of new media presence/use. Then, create a persuasive online sales campaign (which may include a traditional Web page, or a social media page, or a combination of the two) whose goal is to persuade recent alumni (who've graduated in the past five years) to stay connected with your institution and to make a regular donation. What can you offer these people in return for their time and money?

Related Web Site: Visit **www.alumnifutures.com/2011/03/chiclets.html** for a critique of the omnipresent links to social media on alumni Web sites.

6.14 Claim Request: Not-So-Automatic Refund

CRITICAL THINKING

You work for Signet Hotels, a large chain of hotels and resort properties. A recent business trip took you to Argentina, where you had two days off and a chance to do a lot of shopping. The Argentine peso is currently trading at one third the value of the Canadian dollar, so everything you purchased was a third of the cost of buying it in Canada. You bought some souvenirs for your family, some clothing for yourself (including a leather jacket), and an anniversary gift for your partner: an expensive silver bowl. In total, your purchases came to about 1,000 Argentine pesos, or $300 Canadian. At three of the stores in which you shopped, you were offered the opportunity for rebate of your sales tax, through a company called Global Blue Tax Free. In essence, if you fill out some paperwork and save your receipts, once you get to the airport, Global is supposed to give you your tax back. You figure you'll get back about 200 pesos or $70 Canadian. When you get to the airport in Buenos Aires, everything goes smoothly. Global asks if you'd like your refund issued via cheque or directly onto your credit card. You choose the credit card option. Back in Canada, you wait for two months without receiving the refund on your credit card statement.

Your Task. Write a short claim request e-mail to the Manager of Refunds at Global Blue Tax Free.

Related Web site: **www.global-blue.com**.

6.15 Persuasive Claim: Overcharged and Unhappy

As regional manager for an electronics parts manufacturer, you and two other employees attended a conference in Halifax on May 4 and 5. You stayed at the Country Inn because your company recommends that employees use this hotel chain. Generally, your employees have liked their accommodations, and the rates have been within your company's budget. Now, however, you are unhappy with the charges you see on your company's credit statement from Country Inn. When your department's administrative assistant made the reservations, she was assured that you would receive the weekend rates and that a hot breakfast—in the hotel restaurant, the Atrium—would be included in the rate. You hate those "continental" breakfasts of cold sweet rolls and instant coffee, especially when you have to leave early and won't get another meal until afternoon. So you and the other two employees went to the restaurant and ordered a hot meal from the menu. When you receive the credit statement, though, you see a charge for $114 for three champagne buffet breakfasts in the Atrium on May 5. You hit the ceiling! For one thing, you didn't have a buffet breakfast and certainly had no champagne. The three of you got there so early that no buffet had been set up. You ordered pancakes and sausage, and for this you were billed $35 each. You are outraged! What's worse, your company may charge you personally for exceeding the expected rates.

In looking back at this event, you remembered that other guests on your floor were having a "continental" breakfast in a lounge on your floor. Perhaps that's where the hotel expected all guests on the weekend rate to eat. However, your administrative assistant had specifically asked about this matter when she made the reservations, and she was told that you could order breakfast from the menu at the hotel's restaurant.

Your Task. You want to straighten out this matter, and you can't do it by telephone because you suspect that you will need a written record of this entire mess. Write a claim request to Customer Service, Country Inn, Inc., 428 Church Street, Halifax, NS B2Y 3Y2. Should you include a copy of the credit statement showing the charge?

GRAMMAR/MECHANICS REVIEW 6—COMMAS 2

Study each of the following statements and insert necessary commas. In the space provided, write the number of commas that you add; write *0* if no commas are needed.

_1_ **Example**   When preparing for a job interview you should conduct considerable research into the target company.

____ 1. If candidates appear overly eager or desperate they may blow the opportunity.

____ 2. Some job seekers are becoming more aggressive and they often end up hurting their chances.

____ 3. You can be best prepared if you look up information about the hiring company and if you know more than just the basics about the company's leadership and core businesses.

____ 4. Deborah Wang who is the founder of an executive search firm says that the most successful candidates offer examples of past accomplishments.

____ 5. Most firms are looking for reliable hardworking candidates who can explain how they will contribute to the organization.

____ 6. During the last 16 months the number of qualified candidates has doubled.

____ 7. The position of marketing manager which has been open for the past six months is difficult to fill.

____ 8. Recruiters look for candidates who are a strong fit for a particular position and who have exactly the skills required.

____ 9. When interviewing a recent candidate the recruiter said that the applicant clearly and effectively explained how he could cut costs and increase sales.

____ 10. The candidates who had the best qualifications were screened by means of telephone interviews before being offered in-person interviews.

Review of Commas 1 and 2

____ 11. To learn about your target company read recent company press releases annual reports media coverage and industry blogs.

____ 12. After he was hired Joseph was told to report for work on Monday May 15 in Toronto.

<u>___</u> 13. Regarding the subject of pay which may come up early in an interview it's better to hold off the discussion until you have been extended a job offer.

<u>___</u> 14. As a matter of fact the salary you request may impact the organization's decision to hire you.

<u>___</u> 15. Although she wasn't excited about the opportunity Julie scheduled an interview for Tuesday February 3 at 2 p.m.

 # GRAMMAR/MECHANICS CHALLENGE—6

Document for Revision

The following persuasive internal memo has faults in grammar, punctuation, spelling, number form, wordiness, and negative words. Use standard proofreading marks (see Appendix B) to correct the errors. When you finish, your instructor can show you the revised version of this memo.

Beverage Inc.

MEMO

To: Sara W. Morrisseau, Vice President
From: Jackson Pardell, Market Research
CC:
Date: August 5, 2015
Re: ANALYSIS OF GULPIT XL

Here is a summery of the research of Clemence Willis' and myself. Regarding the reduced sugar sports drink being introduced by our No. 1 compititor, GulpIT.

In just under a years time GulpIT developed this new drink, it combines together a mixture of 50 percent sugar and 50 percent artificial sweetener. Apparently GulpIT plans to spend over $8 million to introduce the drink, and to assess consumers reactions to it. It will be tested on the shelfs of convience stores grocerys and other mass merchants in five citys in the Atlantic provinces.

The companys spokesperson said, "The 'X' stands for excelent taste, and the 'L' stands for less sugar." Aimed at young adult's who don't like the taste of sweetener but who want to control calories. The new sports drink is a hybrid sugar and diet drink. Our studys show that simular drinks tryed in this country in the 1980's were unsucessful. On the other hand a 50 calorie low sugar sports drink introduced in Europe two year ago was well received, similarly in Japan a 40 calorie soda is now marketed sucessfully by a cola manufactuerer.

However our research in regard to trends and our analysis of GulpIT XL fails to indicate that this countrys consumers will be interested in a midcalorie sports drink. Yet the Toronto Stock Exchanges response to GulpITs announcement of it's new drink was not unfavourable.

In view of the foregoing the writer and his colleague are of the opinion that we should take a wait and see attitude. Toward the introduction of our own low sugar sports drink.

KEEPING SALES LETTERS LEGAL AND ETHICAL

In promoting products and writing sales letters, be careful about the words you choose and the claims you make. How far can you go in praising and selling your product?

- **Puffery.** In a sales letter, you can write, *Hey, we've got something fantastic! It's the very best product on the market!* Called "puffery," such promotional claims are not taken literally by reasonable consumers.

- **Proving your claims.** If a juice maker touts its product as something close to a magic elixir ("health in a bottle," "antioxidant superpower") that can keep even prostate cancer at bay, it had better have competent and reliable scientific evidence to support the claim. Such a claim goes beyond puffery and requires proof. Two recent cases in the U.S. show how puffery quickly becomes problematic. The Federal Trade Commission (FTC) has accused the makers of Pom Wonderful of hyping the health benefits of the pomegranate juice that sells for five to six times as much as ordinary cranberry juice. The FTC and the Better Business Bureau also considered deceptive a logo used by United Egg Producers ("Animal Care Certified"), which misled consumers by suggesting a higher standard of animal care than was the case. The logo can no longer be used. In a litigious society, marketers who exaggerate are often taken to court.

- **Celebrity endorsements.** The unauthorized use of a celebrity's name, likeness, or nickname is not permitted in sales messages. For example, in the U.S., animal rights organization PETA used an image of First Lady Michelle Obama alongside Oprah Winfrey, Tyra Banks, and Carrie Underwood in ads bearing the tagline "Fur-Free and Fabulous!" but failed to secure permission, thus garnering a measured response from the White House that Ms. Obama did not condone the ad. Hip-hop artist 50 Cent settled a lawsuit with Taco Bell under undisclosed terms after suing the chain for allegedly using his persona and trademark to promote new menu items.

- **Misleading statements.** You cannot tell people that they are winners or finalists in a sweepstake unless they actually are. Similarly, you can't make critical comments about the competition unless you can prove the criticism. Rogers, a leading Canadian telecommunications company, is currently involved in litigation with the federal Competition Bureau. In a series of ads for its Chatr cellphone service, Rogers implied that competitors had more "dropped calls" than Chatr. The Competition Bureau did not agree there was evidence of such a difference, and took Rogers to court.[16] Similarly, it is deceptive to invite unsuspecting consumers to cash a cheque that will then hook them into entering a legal contract or a subscription. Finally, companies may not misrepresent the nature, characteristics, qualities, or geographic origin of goods or services they are promoting. Companies have been warned against making misleading "green" marketing claims and confusing consumers about so-called eco-friendly products.

- **Unwanted merchandise.** If you enclose unsolicited merchandise with a letter, you may not require the receiver to pay for it or return it. Express Publishing, for example, sent a copy of its *Food & Wine Magazine's Cookbook* with a letter inviting recipients to preview the book. "If you don't want to preview the book, simply return the advance notice card within 14 days." Courts, however, have ruled that recipients are allowed to retain, use, or discard any unsolicited merchandise without paying for it or returning it. Some companies that advertise free trial periods have been found to routinely ignore cancellation requests, send unwanted merchandise, and charge customers' credit cards for it.

Career Application

Assume you work for a consumer goods company like Procter and Gamble or Unilever that brings new consumer products (e.g., medicine, household cleaners, personal grooming products, food, etc.) to market every quarter. Due to the exploding cost of litigation, your VP is worried that the company does not know enough about how Canada's Competition Bureau deals with complaints about false advertising. She asks you to research the Competiton Bureau's recent rulings to find if there are any patterns in its rulings.

YOUR TASK

To complete this task, go to **www.competitionbureau.gc.ca/eic/site/cb-bc.nsf/eng/home** and click on Legal Opinions and Actions, then click on Court Decisions. Review at least 10 cases and see if you can find a common thread. Report on your findings in an e-mail or memo to your boss.

Negative Writing Situations

LEARNING OBJECTIVES

1. Explain the importance of dealing with negative situations quickly and appropriately.

2. List the goals of communicating in negative situations.

3. Identify situations in which a direct-strategy negative message is appropriate.

4. Apply the direct pattern in routine negative messages, such as collection letters.

5. Identify situations in which an indirect-strategy negative message is appropriate.

6. Apply the indirect pattern in refusing requests, refusing claims, and announcing bad news to customers and employees.

7. Explain when the indirect strategy may be unethical.

OFFICE INSIDER

"Despite the fact that we sometimes have to send negative messages at work, it is imperative to turn the situation around and focus on lessons learned and experience gained."

Dealing with Negative Situations Effectively

Even the best-run businesses will sometimes make mistakes. Goods arrive late or are not delivered at all, products fail, service disappoints, billing is mishandled, or customers are misunderstood. You may have to write messages ending business relationships, declining proposals, announcing price increases, refusing requests for donations, terminating employees, turning down invitations, or responding to unhappy customers. You might have to apologize for mistakes in orders, the rudeness of employees, overlooked appointments, pricing errors, faulty accounting, defective products, or jumbled instructions. As a company representative, you may even have to respond to complaints voiced to the world on Twitter, Facebook, or consumer comment Web sites.

Every businessperson must occasionally deliver negative news. Because bad news disappoints, irritates, and sometimes angers the receiver, such messages must be written thoughtfully. The bad feelings associated with disappointing news can generally be reduced if the receiver knows the reasons for the rejection, feels that the news was revealed sensitively, and believes that the matter was treated seriously and fairly.

In this chapter you will learn when to use the direct strategy and when to use the indirect strategy to deliver negative news. You will learn the goals of business communicators when writing negative messages and learn techniques for achieving those goals.

Establishing Goals in Communicating Negative News

Delivering bad news is not the easiest writing task you may have, but it can be gratifying if you do it effectively. As a business communicator dealing with a negative situation, the following are your goals:

- **Explain clearly and completely.** Your message should be so clear that the receiver understands and, we hope, accepts the bad news. The receiver should not have to call or write to clarify the message.
- **Project a professional image.** You will strive to project a professional and positive image of you and your organization. Even when irate customers use a threatening tone or overstate their claims, you must use polite language, control your emotions, and respond with clear explanations of why a negative message was necessary.
- **Convey empathy and sensitivity.** Negative news is better accepted if it is delivered sensitively. Use language that respects the receiver and attempts to reduce bad feelings. Accepting blame, when appropriate, and apologizing goes far in smoothing over negative messages. But avoid creating legal liability or responsibility for you or your organization.
- **Be fair.** Show that the situation or decision was fair, impartial, and rational. Receivers are far more likely to accept negative news if they feel they were treated fairly.
- **Maintain friendly relations.** Make an effort to include statements that show your desire to continue pleasant relations with the receiver. As you learned in Chapter 5, in writing routine adjustment messages, one of your goals is to regain the confidence of customers.

These goals are ambitious, and we are not always successful in achieving them all. With experience, however, you will be able to vary these strategies and adapt them to your organization's specific communication needs.

The Importance of a Timely Response in Negative Situations

Because of the speed and ubiquity of communication in the workplace today (i.e., many if not most employees have smartphones, are on social media, etc.), bad news—which has always "travelled fast"—now travels even faster and sometimes gets broadcast outside the company to people and organizations that shouldn't really be seeing it. For this reason, timeliness is extremely important when communicating in negative situations.

Whenever possible, negative situations such as firings, restructurings, and company-related crises should be dealt with immediately and personally. As one crisis communications expert argues, "the timeliness of communication is paramount in a crisis,"[1] and existing communication approval systems may need to be stepped around to deliver the message quickly. That said, timeliness is not so vital that you should switch to informal and inappropriate communication channels. For example, texting termination notices (as some managers and owners have begun to do) is a poor communication choice because it indicates that the terminated employee is so unimportant that an informal text was deemed the appropriate way to fire him or her.[2]

When to Use the Direct Writing Strategy in Negative Situations

In any negative situation, you have a choice between two basic strategies for delivering negative news: direct and indirect. Which approach is best suited for your particular message? To answer this question, you will analyze how your

> The sting of bad news can be reduced by giving reasons, communicating sensitively, and treating the receiver fairly.

> The goals in communicating negative news are explaining clearly, acting professionally, conveying empathy, being fair, maintaining friendly relations, and dealing with the situation in a timely fashion.

receiver will react to this news as well as the degree of negativity included in the message.

Not all negative situations at work are crises or involve personal misfortune. In these cases, as a business communicator, you should feel free to use a direct-strategy negative message. The direct strategy, with the bad news appearing first followed by the reasons and a pleasant closing, is effective in situations such as the following:

The direct pattern is appropriate when the bad news is not damaging, when the receiver might overlook the bad news, when the organization expects directness, when the receiver prefers directness, or when firmness is necessary.

- **When the bad news is not damaging.** If the bad news is insignificant (such as a small increase in cost) and doesn't personally affect the receiver, then the direct strategy certainly makes sense.
- **When the receiver may overlook the bad news.** With the crush of e-mails and other communications today, many readers skim messages, looking only at the opening. If they don't find substantive material, they may discard the message. Rate increases, changes in service, new policy requirements—these critical messages may require boldness to ensure attention.
- **When organizations prefer directness.** Some companies expect all internal messages and announcements—even bad news—to be straightforward and presented without frills.
- **When the receiver prefers directness.** Busy managers may prefer directness. Such shorter messages enable the reader to get in the proper frame of mind immediately. If you suspect that the reader prefers that the facts be presented immediately, use the direct pattern.
- **When firmness is necessary.** Messages that must demonstrate determination and strength should not use delaying techniques. For example, the last in a series of collection letters that seek payment of overdue accounts may require a direct opener.

WRITING PLAN FOR A DIRECT-STRATEGY NEGATIVE MESSAGE

- **Bad news** in the opening
- **Reason(s)** for bad news in the body
- **Pleasant closing**

Figure 7.1 shows an example of a typical direct-strategy negative message that follows the writing plan above. In this case, a routine notice arrives in your mailbox (or inbox) announcing a price increase in your phone service. Notice that the bad news is communicated in the opening sentence of the message. The reason comes after. Also notice how much shorter this message is than the indirect-style negative messages we will examine later in the chapter.

Negative Situation: Collection Letters

One of the most important processes in business is the collection process. Collection is the steps a company takes to ensure that its unpaid invoices get paid. The first phase in the collection process is usually the sending of a short reminder letter or e-mail that lets the client or customer know that his or her invoice is outstanding. Best practices stipulate that a copy of the outstanding invoice should be attached to this short reminder message, in case the client has misplaced the original.

An understanding of how to write a direct negative message becomes useful in the second step of the collection process. If the client or customer with the outstanding

FIGURE 7.1 Direct-Strategy Negative Message

SASKATOON HYDRO

January 2015

To valued Saskatoon Hydro customers,

As of January 1, 2015, rates for electricity in the city of Saskatoon are rising. — Bad news in opening of message

Provincial generator SaskPower has brought in these changes to more accurately reflect the cost of generation and distribution of energy. — Reasons for bad news in body of message

We appreciate your continued business. Comments and questions may be directed to the website below. — Pleasant closing

Sincerely,

Luke Roberts
Director, Customer Satisfaction
www.saskhydro.ca/ratechange

---

invoice does not reply in a timely manner to the short reminder message, it is time to write a direct bad-news message demanding payment. Figure 7.2 shows a typical example of such a message.

The main objective of a bad-news collection letter is to receive payment, but also to make sure that the goodwill of the client or customer is retained. According to the Web site of Credit Guru Inc. (**www.creditguru.com/collectionletters.htm**), a company that offers advice on the collection process, the main features of a well-written collection letter are a reminder of the dates of the invoice, a reminder of the total amount outstanding, a request for immediate payment or payment by a specified date, a request for the payment to be sent by the quickest means (e.g., courier), and finally, a sense of urgency coupled with an unapologetic and non-threatening tone.[3]

 ## When to Use the Indirect Writing Strategy in Negative Situations

When dealing with a negative situation that will upset or irritate the receiver, business communicators use the indirect pattern. The direct method clearly saves time and is preferred by some who consider it to be more professional and even more ethical than the indirect method. Others think that revealing bad news slowly and indirectly shows sensitivity to the receiver. By preparing the receiver, you tend to soften the impact. The indirect strategy enables you to keep the reader's attention

> The indirect pattern softens the impact of bad news.

FIGURE **7.2** Direct-Strategy Collection Letter

FRASER, AHMET, AND GRANDPRE

3017–66 Avenue Northwest, Suite 222
Edmonton, AB T6H 1Y2

August 14, 2014

Tom Przybylski
Unity Ltd.
9 Givins Dr., Unit 5
Edmonton, AB T2A 4X3

Dear Mr. Przybylski:

Re: Invoice No. 443-2010

Outstanding Amount Due: $19,567.87

You are indebted to the firm of Fraser, Ahmet, and Grandpre in the amount of $19,567.87, for services rendered and for which you were invoiced on March 30, 2014. A copy of the outstanding invoice is enclosed for your reference, as is a copy of a reminder letter sent to you on July 2, 2014.

Unless we receive a certified cheque or money order, payable to Fraser, Ahmet, and Grandpre, in the amount of $19,567.87, or unless satisfactory payment arrangements are made within seven (7) business days, we are left no choice but to pursue collection of the amount owing. We are not prepared to continue carrying your accounts receivable and we will take all necessary steps for the recovery of this amount from you.

We do not wish to proceed in this fashion and would appreciate your cooperation instead. We look forward to hearing from you on or before August 21, 2014.

Yours sincerely,

Pat McAfee

Pat McAfee
Office Manager/Collections Clerk

until you have been able to explain the reasons for the bad news, whereas a direct and blunt announcement of disappointing news might cause the receiver to stop reading and toss the message aside or delete it.

The most important part of an indirect-strategy negative message is the explanation, which you'll learn about shortly. The indirect strategy consists of four main parts, shown in Figure 7.3:

- **Buffer.** Introduce the message with a neutral statement that makes the reader continue reading.
- **Reasons.** Explain why the bad news was necessary and that the matter was taken seriously.

FIGURE **7.3** Four Parts of an Indirect-Strategy Negative Message

Buffer	Reasons	Bad News	Closing
Open with a neutral but meaningful statement that does not mention the bad news.	Explain the causes of the bad news before disclosing it.	Reveal the bad news without emphasizing it. Provide an alternative or compromise, if possible.	End with a personalized, forward-looking, pleasant statement. Avoid referring to the bad news.

- **Bad news.** Provide a clear but understated announcement of the bad news that might include an alternative or a compromise.
- **Closing.** End with a warm, forward-looking statement that might mention good wishes, gifts, or a sales promotion.

Analyzing the Parts of an Indirect-Strategy Negative Message

Even though it may be impossible to make the receiver happy when delivering negative news, you can reduce bad feelings and resentment by structuring your message sensitively. As you have just learned, most negative messages contain some or all of these parts: buffer, reasons, bad news, and closing. Figure 7.4 presents these four parts of the indirect strategy in greater detail, with suggested elements you can include in each part. This section also discusses apologies and how to convey empathy in delivering bad news.

> To reduce negative feelings, use a buffer to open sensitive bad-news messages.

Buffer the Opening

A buffer is a device that reduces shock or pain. To buffer the pain of bad news, begin your message with a neutral but meaningful statement that makes the reader continue reading. The buffer should be relevant and concise. Although it should avoid revealing the bad news immediately, it should not convey a false impression that good news follows. It should provide a natural transition to the explanation that follows. The individual situation, of course, will help determine what you should put in the buffer. Here are some possibilities for opening indirect negative messages.

> A buffer opens an indirect negative message with a neutral, concise, relevant, and upbeat statement.

> A good buffer may include the best news, a compliment, appreciation, facts regarding the problem, a statement indicating understanding, or an apology.

FIGURE **7.4** Elements of an Indirect-Strategy Negative Message

Buffer	Reasons	Bad News	Closing
• Best news • Compliment • Appreciation • Agreement • Facts • Understanding • Apology	• Cautious explanation • Reader or other benefits • Company policy explanation • Positive words • Evidence that matter was considered fairly and seriously	• Embedded placement • Passive voice • Implied refusal • Compromise • Alternative	• Forward look • Information about alternative • Good wishes • Freebies • Resale • Sales promotion

- **Best news.** Start with the part of the message that represents the best news. For example, in a Web site announcement plus in-branch signage that discloses reduced operating hours but increased staffing, you might say *Beginning July 1, we're adding extra staff in our branch locations and we'll be open to serve you between 9:30 a.m. and 4:30 p.m.*
- **Compliment.** Praise the receiver's accomplishments, organization, or efforts, but do so with honesty and sincerity. For instance, in a letter declining an invitation to speak, you could write *I admire the United Way for its fundraising projects in our community. I am honoured that you asked me to speak Friday, November 5.*
- **Appreciation.** Convey thanks to the reader for doing business, for sending something, for a service or job well done, for showing confidence in your organization, for expressing feelings, or simply for providing feedback. In a letter terminating an employee's contract, you might say *Thank you for your work on the past two seasons of* Riley's Cove. *Your efforts contributed to a wonderful television program enjoyed across Canada.* Avoid thanking the reader, however, for something you are about to refuse.
- **Agreement.** Make a relevant statement with which both sender and receiver can agree. A letter that rejects an application for a credit card might be phrased *Having access to a credit card is an important part of your financial well-being. While we thank you for your recent application for a GoldPlus Visa Card, your application did not meet our criteria for approval. However, we're happy to offer you a Classic Visa Card . . . .*
- **Facts.** Provide objective information that introduces the bad news. For example, in a memo announcing cutbacks in the hours of the employees' cafeteria, you might say *During the past five years the number of employees eating breakfast in our cafeteria has dropped from 32 percent to 12 percent.*
- **Understanding.** Show that you care about the reader. In announcing a product defect, the writer can still manage to express concern for the customer: *We know you expect superior performance from all the products you purchase from OfficeCity. That's why we're writing personally about the Excell printer cartridges you recently ordered.*

Apologizing in the Buffer

You learned about apologies in adjustment situations in Chapter 5. We expand that discussion here because apologies are often part of negative situations. The truth is that sincere apologies work. A study of letters responding to customer complaints revealed that 67 percent carried an apology of some sort.[4] An apology is defined as an "admission of blameworthiness and regret for an undesirable event."[5] Apologies to customers are especially important if you or your company erred. They cost nothing, and they go a long way in soothing hard feelings. Here are some tips on how to apologize effectively in business messages:

- **Apologize sincerely.** People dislike apologies that sound hollow (*We regret that you were inconvenienced* or *We regret that you are disturbed*). Focusing on your regret does not convey sincerity. Explaining what you will do to prevent recurrence of the problem projects sincerity.
- **Accept responsibility.** One CEO was criticized for the following weak apology: *I want our customers to know how much I personally regret any difficulties you may experience as a result of the unauthorized intrusion into our computer systems.* Communication experts faulted this apology because it did not acknowledge responsibility.[6]
- **Use good judgment.** Don't admit blame if it might prompt a lawsuit.

Consider these poor and improved apologies:

Poor Apology	Improved Apology
We regret that you are unhappy with the price of frozen yogurt purchased at one of our self-serve scoop shops.	We are genuinely sorry that you were disappointed in the price of frozen yogurt recently purchased at one of our self-serve scoop shops. Your opinion is important to us, and we appreciate your giving us the opportunity to look into the problem you describe.
We apologize if anyone was affected.	I apologize for the frustration our delay caused you. As soon as I received your message, I began looking into the cause of the delay and realized that our delivery tracking system must be improved.

Conveying Empathy in the Buffer

One of the hardest things to do in apologies is to convey sympathy and empathy. As discussed in Chapter 2, *empathy* is the ability to understand and enter into the feelings of another. When ice storms trapped JetBlue Airways passengers on hot planes for hours, CEO Neeleman wrote a letter of apology that sounded as if it came from his heart. He said, "Dear JetBlue Customers: We are sorry and embarrassed. But most of all, we are deeply sorry." Later in his letter he said, "Words cannot express how truly sorry we are for the anxiety, frustration, and inconvenience that you, your family, friends, and colleagues experienced."[7] Neeleman put himself into the shoes of his customers and tried to experience their pain.

> Empathy involves understanding and entering into the feelings of someone else.

Here are other examples of ways to express empathy in written messages:

- **In writing to an unhappy customer:** *We did not intentionally delay the shipment, and we sincerely regret the disappointment and frustration you must have suffered.*
- **In terminating employees:** *It is with great regret that we must take this step. Rest assured that I will be more than happy to write letters of recommendation for anyone who asks.*
- **In responding to a complaint:** *I am deeply saddened that our service failure disrupted your sale, and we will do everything in our power to . . . .*
- **In showing genuine feelings:** *You have every right to be disappointed. I am truly sorry that . . . .*

"Dear Valued Customer: We're sorry, but company policy forbids apologies. Sincerely yours."

Present Your Reasons

The most important part of an indirect negative message is the section that explains why a negative decision is necessary. Without sound reasons for denying a request or refusing a claim, a message will fail, no matter how cleverly it is organized or written. As part of your planning before writing, you analyzed the problem and decided to refuse a request for specific reasons. Before disclosing the bad news, try to explain those reasons. Providing an explanation reduces feelings of ill will and improves the chances that the reader will accept the bad news.

> Bad-news messages should explain reasons before stating the negative news.

- **Explain clearly and cautiously.** If the reasons are not confidential or legally questionable, you can be specific: *Growers supplied us with a limited number of patio*

roses, and our demand this year was twice that of last year. In responding to a billing error, explain what happened: *After you informed us of an error on your January bill, we investigated the matter and admit the mistake was ours. Until our new automated system is fully online, we are still subject to human error. Rest assured that your account has been credited as you will see on your next bill.* In refusing a favour request, explain why the request can't be fulfilled: *On January 17 we have a board of directors meeting that I must attend.* However, in an effort to be the "good guy," don't make dangerous or unrealistic promises: *Although we can't contribute now, we expect increased revenues next year and promise a generous gift then.*

> Readers accept bad news more readily if they see that someone benefits.

- **Cite plausible reader benefits.** Readers are more open to bad news if in some way, even indirectly, it may help them. In refusing a customer's request for free hemming of skirts and slacks, a clothing company wrote: "We tested our ability to hem skirts a few years ago. This process proved to be very time-consuming. We have decided not to offer this service because the additional cost would have increased the selling price of our skirts substantially, and we did not want to impose that cost on all our customers."[8] Readers also accept bad news more readily if they recognize that someone or something else benefits, such as other workers or the environment: *Although we would like to consider your application, we prefer to fill managerial positions from within.* Avoid trying to show reader benefits, though, if they appear insincere: *To improve our service to you, we're increasing our brokerage fees.*

- **Explain company policy.** Readers don't like blanket policy statements prohibiting something: *Company policy prevents us from making cash refunds* or *Proposals may be accepted from local companies only* or *Company policy requires us to promote from within.* Instead of hiding behind company policy, gently explain why the policy makes sense: *We prefer to promote from within because it rewards the loyalty of our employees. In addition, we've found that people familiar with our organization make the quickest contribution to our team effort.* By offering explanations, you demonstrate that you care about your readers and are treating them as important individuals.

- **Choose positive words.** Because the words you use can affect a reader's response, choose carefully. Remember that the objective of the indirect pattern is to hold the reader's attention until you've had a chance to explain the reasons justifying the bad news. To keep the reader in a receptive mood, avoid expressions that might cause the reader to tune out. Be sensitive to negative words such as *claim, error, failure, fault, impossible, mistaken, misunderstand, never, regret, unwilling, unfortunately,* and *violate.*

- **Demonstrate fairness.** In explaining reasons, demonstrate to the reader that you take the matter seriously, have investigated carefully, and are making an unbiased decision. Customers are more accepting of disappointing news when they feel that their requests have been heard and that they have been treated fairly. Avoid deflecting responsibility, known as "passing the buck," or blaming others within your organization. Such unprofessional behaviour makes the reader lose faith in you and your company.

Cushion the Bad News

Although you can't prevent the disappointment that bad news brings, you can reduce the pain somewhat by breaking the news sensitively. Be especially considerate when the reader will suffer personally from the bad news. A number of thoughtful techniques can lessen the impact.

> Techniques for cushioning bad news include positioning it strategically, using the passive voice, emphasizing the positive, implying the refusal, and suggesting alternatives or compromises.

- **Position the bad news strategically.** Instead of spotlighting it, enclose the bad news between other sentences, perhaps among your reasons. Try not to let the refusal begin or end a paragraph—the reader's eye will linger on these high-visibility spots. Another technique that reduces shock is putting a painful idea in a subordinate clause: *Although the board did not award you a bonus this year, we are thankful for your enthusiasm and loyalty and highly encourage you to apply once again next year.* Subordinate clauses often begin with words such as *although, as, because, if,* and *since.*

- **Use the passive voice.** Passive-voice verbs enable you to describe an action without connecting the action to a specific person. Whereas the active voice focuses attention on a person (*We don't accept unsolicited proposals*), the passive voice highlights the action (*Unsolicited proposals are not accepted because . . .*). Use the passive voice for the bad news. In some instances you can combine passive-voice verbs and a subordinate clause: *Although unsolicited proposals are not currently being accepted, we encourage you to try again beginning March 30, after which time our policy may have changed.*

- **Accentuate the positive.** As you learned earlier, messages are far more effective when you describe what you can do instead of what you can't do. Rather than *We will no longer accept requests for product changes after June 1*, try a more positive appeal: *We are accepting requests for product changes until June 1.*

- **Imply the refusal.** It's sometimes possible to avoid a direct statement of refusal. Often, your reasons and explanations leave no doubt that a request has been denied. Explicit refusals may be unnecessary and at times cruel. In this refusal to contribute to a charity, for example, the writer never actually says no: *Because we will soon be moving into new offices, all our funds are earmarked for moving and furnishings. We hope that next year we'll be able to support your worthwhile charity.* This implied refusal is effective even though the bad news is not stated. The danger of an implied refusal, of course, is that it can be so subtle that the reader misses it. Be certain that you make the bad news clear, thus preventing the need for further correspondence.

- **Suggest a compromise or an alternative.** A refusal is not so harsh—for the sender or the receiver—if a suitable compromise, substitute, or alternative is available. In denying permission to a class to visit a research facility, for instance, this writer softens the bad news by proposing an alternative: *Although class tours of the entire research facility are not given due to safety and security reasons, we do offer tours of parts of the facility during our open house in the fall.* You can further reduce the impact of the bad news by refusing to dwell on it. Present it briefly (or imply it), and move on to your closing.

Close Pleasantly

Closings to bad-news messages might include a forward look, an alternative, good wishes, special offers, and resale or sales promotional information.

After explaining the bad news sensitively, close the message with a pleasant statement that promotes goodwill. The closing should be personalized and may include a forward look, an alternative, good wishes, special offers, resale information, or an off-the-subject remark.

- **Forward look.** Anticipate future relations or business. A letter that refuses a contract proposal might read: *Thank you for your bid. We look forward to working with your talented staff when future projects demand your special expertise.*

- **Alternative follow-up.** If an alternative exists, end your letter with follow-through advice. For example, in a letter rejecting a customer's demand for replacement of landscaping plants, you might say *We will be happy to give you a free inspection and consultation. Please call 746-8112 to arrange a date for a visit.* In a message to a prospective home buyer: *Although the lot you saw last week is now sold, we do have two excellent view lots available at a slightly higher price.* In reacting to an Internet misprint: *Please note that our Web site contained an unfortunate misprint offering $850-per-night Banff luxury chalets at $85. Although we cannot honour that rate, we are offering a special half-price rate of $425 to those who responded.*

- **Good wishes.** A conversation in which someone is fired or downsized might read: *We want you to know your contribution here has been highly valued, and we wish you all the best as you look for rewarding work in a different setting. Please be in touch with your manager about securing a reference.*

- **Special offers.** When customers complain—primarily about food products or small consumer items—companies often send coupons, samples, or gifts to restore confidence and to promote future business. In response to a customer's complaint about a frozen dinner, you could write *Thank you for your loyalty and for sharing in our efforts to make Green Valley frozen entrées the best they can be. We appreciate your input so much that we'd like to buy you dinner. We've enclosed a coupon to cover the cost of your next entrée.*

- **Resale or sales promotion.** When the bad news is not devastating or personal, references to resale information or promotion may be appropriate: *The laptops you ordered are unusually popular because they have more plug-ins for peripheral devices than any other laptop in their price range. To help you locate additional accessories for these computers, we invite you to visit our Web site at . . ., where our online catalogue provides a huge selection of peripheral devices such as stereo speakers, printers, personal digital assistants, and digital pagers.*

Avoid endings that sound superficial, insincere, inappropriate, or self-serving. Don't invite further correspondence (*If you have any questions, do not hesitate . . .*), and don't refer again to the bad news. Take another look at the elements in Figure 7.4 whenever you need to review writing sensitive negative messages.

● Negative Situation: Refusing Requests and Claims

The indirect strategy is appropriate when refusing requests for time, money, information, or action.

As you move forward in your career and become a professional or a representative of an organization, you may receive requests for favours or contributions. When you must refuse these requests, you will first think about how well you know the receiver and how he or she will react to your refusal and decide whether to use the direct or the indirect strategy. You may also have to say *no* to customer claims, deny credit, and deal with disappointment and even anger. At the same time, your goal is to resolve the situation in a prompt, fair, and tactful manner. If you have any doubt, use the indirect strategy and the following writing plan:

WRITING PLAN FOR REFUSING REQUESTS OR CLAIMS

- **Buffer:** Start with a neutral statement on which both reader and writer can agree, such as a compliment, an appreciative comment, a quick review of the facts, or an apology. Add a key idea or word that acts as a transition to the reasons.
- **Reasons:** Present valid reasons for the refusal, avoiding words that create a negative tone. Include resale or sales promotion material if appropriate.
- **Bad news:** Soften the blow by de-emphasizing the bad news, using the passive voice, accentuating the positive, or implying a refusal. Suggest a compromise, alternative, or substitute if possible. The alternative can be part of the bad news or part of the closing.
- **Closing:** Renew good feelings with a positive statement. Avoid referring to the bad news. Include resale or promotion information, if appropriate. Look forward to continued business.

Refusing Favour Requests

Requests for favours, money, information, and action may come from charities, friends, or business partners. Many are from people representing commendable causes, and you may wish you could comply. However, resources are usually limited.

Two versions of a request refusal are shown in Figure 7.5 on the next page. A magazine writer requested salary information for an article, but this information could not be released. The ineffective version begins with needless information that could be implied. The second paragraph creates a harsh tone with such negative words as *sorry, must refuse, violate,* and *liable.* Since the refusal precedes the explanation, the reader probably will not be in a receptive frame of mind to accept the reasons for refusing. Notice, too, that the bad news is emphasized by its placement in a short sentence at the beginning of a paragraph. It stands out and adds more weight to the rejection already felt by the reader.

Moreover, the refusal explanation is overly graphic, containing references to possible litigation. The tone at this point is threatening and unduly harsh. Then, suddenly, the author throws in a self-serving comment about the high salary and commissions of his salespeople. Instead of offering constructive alternatives, the ineffective version reveals only tiny bits of the desired data. Finally, the closing sounds too insincere and doesn't build goodwill.

In the more effective version of this refusal, the opening reflects the writer's genuine interest in the request. But it does not indicate compliance. The second sentence acts as a transition by introducing the words *salespeople* and *salaries,* repeated in the following paragraph. Reasons for refusing this request are objectively presented in an explanation that precedes the refusal. Notice that the refusal (*Although specific salaries and commission rates cannot be released*) is a subordinate clause in a long sentence in the middle of a paragraph. To further soften the blow, the letter offers an alternative. The cordial closing refers to the alternative, avoids mention of the refusal, and looks to the future.

It's always easier to write refusals when alternatives can be offered to soften the bad news. But often no alternatives are possible. The refusal shown in Figure 7.6 involves a delicate situation in which a manager has been asked by his superiors to violate a contract. Several of the engineers for whom he works have privately asked

> In refusing requests, avoid a harsh tone or being too explicit; offer constructive alternatives whenever possible.

FIGURE 7.5 Refusing an External Favour Request

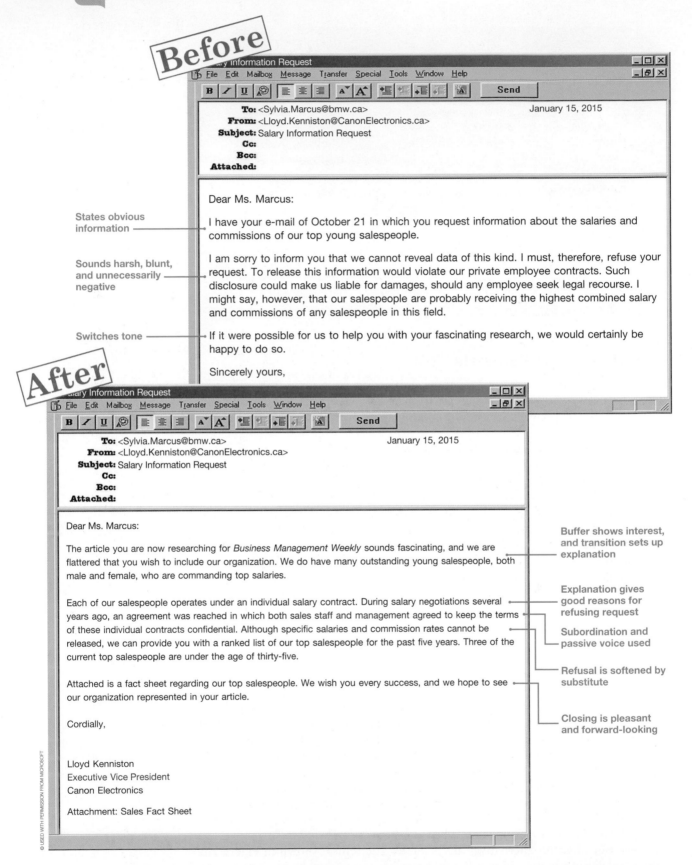

FIGURE 7.6 Refusing an Internal Favour Request

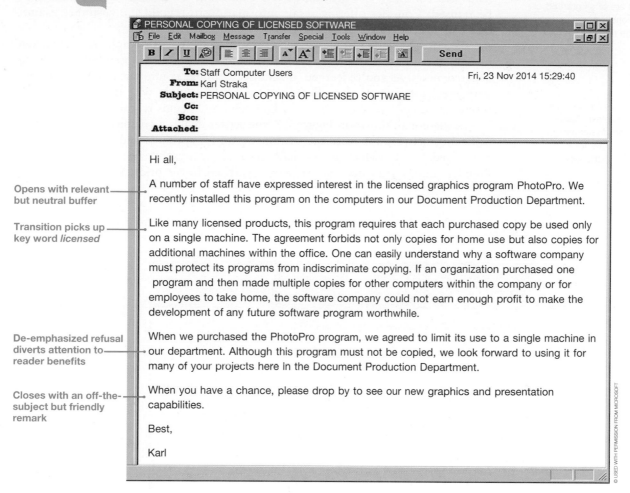

Opens with relevant but neutral buffer

Transition picks up key word *licensed*

De-emphasized refusal diverts attention to reader benefits

Closes with an off-the-subject but friendly remark

---

him to make copies of a licensed software program for them. They apparently want this program for their personal computers. Making copies is forbidden by the terms of the software licensing agreement, and the manager refuses to do this. Rather than saying no to each engineer who asks him, he sends all affected staff the e-mail shown in Figure 7.6.

The opening tactfully avoids suggesting that any engineer has actually asked to copy the software program. These professionals may prefer not to have their private requests made known. A transition takes the reader to the logical reasons against copying. Notice that the tone is objective, neither preaching nor condemning. The refusal is softened by being linked with a positive statement (*Although this program must not be copied, we look forward to using it for many of your projects here . . .*). To divert attention from the refusal, the memo ends with a friendly, off-the-subject remark.

Refusing Claims

Customers occasionally want something they are not entitled to or something you can't grant. They may misunderstand warranties or make unreasonable demands. Because these customers are often unhappy with a product or service, they are emotionally involved. Writing or saying *no* to emotionally involved receivers will probably be your most challenging communication task. As publisher Malcolm Forbes observed, "To be agreeable while disagreeing—that's an art."[9]

Fortunately, the reasons-before-refusal plan helps you be empathic and artful in breaking bad news. Obviously, in denial letters you will need to adopt the proper tone. Don't blame customers, even if they are at fault. Avoid "you" statements that

> In denying claims, writers use the reasons-before-refusal strategy to set an empathic tone and buffer the bad news.

Although customer claims are often granted, occasionally some must be refused.

sound preachy *(You would have known that cash refunds are impossible if you had read your contract)*. Use neutral, objective language to explain why the claim must be refused. Consider offering resale information to rebuild the customer's confidence in your products or organization.

Claims that cannot be approved because the customer or employee is mistaken, misinformed, unreasonable, or possibly even dishonest, are essentially delivering negative news. As you've learned, the indirect strategy communicates negative news with the least pain. It also allows the sender to explain why the claim must be refused before the reader realizes the bad news and begins resisting.

When refusing customer claims, explain objectively and do not assume that the customer is foolish or dishonest.

In the e-mail shown in Figure 7.7, the writer denies a customer's claim for the difference between the price the customer paid for speakers and the price she saw advertised locally (which would have resulted in a cash refund of $151). While Premier Sound Sales does match any advertised lower price, the price-matching

FIGURE 7.7 Refusing a Claim

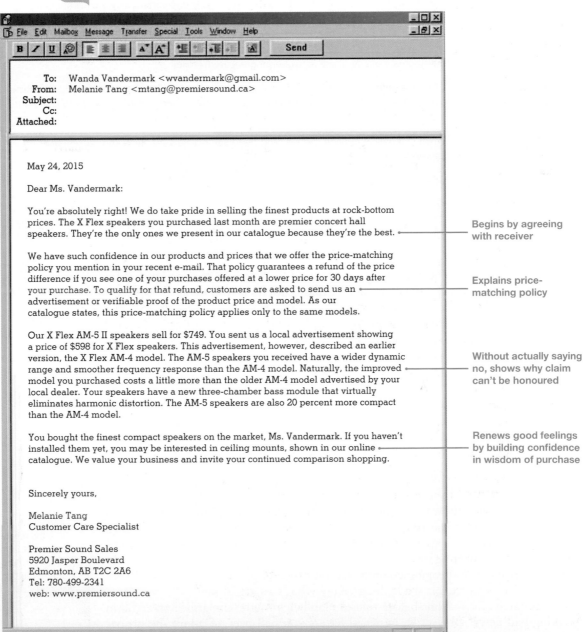

To: Wanda Vandermark <wvandermark@gmail.com>
From: Melanie Tang <mtang@premiersound.ca>
Subject:
Cc:
Attached:

May 24, 2015

Dear Ms. Vandermark:

You're absolutely right! We do take pride in selling the finest products at rock-bottom prices. The X Flex speakers you purchased last month are premier concert hall speakers. They're the only ones we present in our catalogue because they're the best. ● — Begins by agreeing with receiver

We have such confidence in our products and prices that we offer the price-matching policy you mention in your recent e-mail. That policy guarantees a refund of the price difference if you see one of your purchases offered at a lower price for 30 days after your purchase. To qualify for that refund, customers are asked to send us an ● — Explains price-matching policy advertisement or verifiable proof of the product price and model. As our catalogue states, this price-matching policy applies only to the same models.

Our X Flex AM-5 II speakers sell for $749. You sent us a local advertisement showing a price of $598 for X Flex speakers. This advertisement, however, described an earlier version, the X Flex AM-4 model. The AM-5 speakers you received have a wider dynamic range and smoother frequency response than the AM-4 model. Naturally, the improved ● — Without actually saying no, shows why claim can't be honoured model you purchased costs a little more than the older AM-4 model advertised by your local dealer. Your speakers have a new three-chamber bass module that virtually eliminates harmonic distortion. The AM-5 speakers are also 20 percent more compact than the AM-4 model.

You bought the finest compact speakers on the market, Ms. Vandermark. If you haven't installed them yet, you may be interested in ceiling mounts, shown in our online ● — Renews good feelings by building confidence in wisdom of purchase catalogue. We value your business and invite your continued comparison shopping.

Sincerely yours,

Melanie Tang
Customer Care Specialist

Premier Sound Sales
5920 Jasper Boulevard
Edmonton, AB T2C 2A6
Tel: 780-499-2341
web: www.premiersound.ca

policy applies only to exact models. This claim must be rejected because the advertisement the customer submitted shows a different, older speaker model.

The e-mail to Wanda Vandermark opens with a buffer that agrees with a statement in the customer's letter. It repeats the key idea of product confidence as a transition to the second paragraph. Next comes an explanation of the price-matching policy. The writer does not assume that the customer is trying to pull a fast one. Nor does the writer suggest that the customer is a dummy who didn't read or understand the price-matching policy.

The safest path is a neutral explanation of the policy along with precise distinctions between the customer's speakers and the older ones. The writer also gets a chance to re-sell the customer's speakers and demonstrate what a quality product they are. By the end of the third paragraph, it's evident to the reader that her claim is unjustified.

Notice how most of the components in an effective claim refusal are woven together in this letter: buffer, transition, explanation, and pleasant closing. The only missing part is an alternative, which was impossible in this situation.

Tips for Dealing with Disappointed Customers

Whenever possible, disappointed customers should be dealt with immediately and personally. Customer complaints about products and services now appear on sites such as Complaints.com and iRipoff.com, as well as on Facebook, Twitter, and MySpace. Companies are responding by joining social media and telling their own stories, putting a positive spin on potentially damaging, viral word of mouth.

Whether companies deal with unhappy customers online or up close and personal, they face the same challenges. Maintaining market share and preserving goodwill require sensitive and skillful communication. Many business professionals strive to control the damage and resolve such problems in the following manner:[10]

- Call the individual involved.
- Describe the problem and apologize.
- Explain why the problem occurred, what your company is doing to resolve it, and how it will ensure that the problem will not happen again.
- Follow up with a message that documents the phone call and promotes goodwill.

Dealing with problems immediately is very important in resolving conflict and retaining goodwill. Hard-copy correspondence has become too slow for problems that demand immediate attention. But written electronic messages are good substitutes when personal contact is impossible, to establish a record of the incident, to formally confirm follow-up procedures, and to promote good relations.

A follow-up e-mail to a client complaint is shown in Figure 7.8. Consultant Eva Ngombe found herself in the embarrassing position of explaining why she had given out the name of her client to a salesperson. The client, Accordia Resources International, had hired her firm, Cartus Consulting Associates, to help find an appropriate service for outsourcing its payroll functions. Without realizing it, Eva had mentioned to a potential vendor (Payroll Services, Inc.) that her client was considering hiring an outside service to handle its payroll. An overeager salesperson from Payroll Services immediately called on Accordia, thus angering the client. The client had hired the consultant to avoid this very kind of intrusion. Accordia did not want to be hounded by vendors selling their payroll services.

When she learned of the problem, the first thing consultant Eva Ngombe did was call her client to explain and apologize. She was careful to control her voice and rate of speaking. A low-pitched, deliberate pace gives the impression that you are thinking clearly, logically, and reasonably—not emotionally and certainly not irrationally. However, she also followed up with the e-mail shown in Figure 7.8. The e-mail not only confirms the telephone conversation but also adds some formality. It sends the nonverbal message that the writer takes the matter seriously and that it is important enough to warrant a written message.

"As soon as you realize there is a problem, let your client know by phone or, if possible, in person. It's better to let them hear bad news from you than to discover it on their own because it establishes your candour."

FIGURE 7.8 Follow-Up Message to Client Complaint

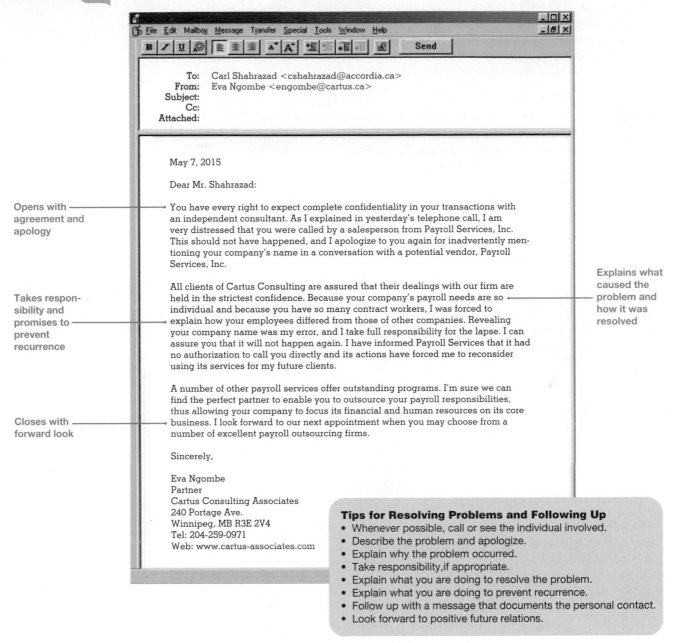

Opens with agreement and apology

Takes responsibility and promises to prevent recurrence

Closes with forward look

Explains what caused the problem and how it was resolved

May 7, 2015

Dear Mr. Shahrazad:

You have every right to expect complete confidentiality in your transactions with an independent consultant. As I explained in yesterday's telephone call, I am very distressed that you were called by a salesperson from Payroll Services, Inc. This should not have happened, and I apologize to you again for inadvertently mentioning your company's name in a conversation with a potential vendor, Payroll Services, Inc.

All clients of Cartus Consulting are assured that their dealings with our firm are held in the strictest confidence. Because your company's payroll needs are so individual and because you have so many contract workers, I was forced to explain how your employees differed from those of other companies. Revealing your company name was my error, and I take full responsibility for the lapse. I can assure you that it will not happen again. I have informed Payroll Services that it had no authorization to call you directly and its actions have forced me to reconsider using its services for my future clients.

A number of other payroll services offer outstanding programs. I'm sure we can find the perfect partner to enable you to outsource your payroll responsibilities, thus allowing your company to focus its financial and human resources on its core business. I look forward to our next appointment when you may choose from a number of excellent payroll outsourcing firms.

Sincerely,

Eva Ngombe
Partner
Cartus Consulting Associates
240 Portage Ave.
Winnipeg, MB R3E 2V4
Tel: 204-259-0971
Web: www.cartus-associates.com

Tips for Resolving Problems and Following Up
- Whenever possible, call or see the individual involved.
- Describe the problem and apologize.
- Explain why the problem occurred.
- Take responsibility, if appropriate.
- Explain what you are doing to resolve the problem.
- Explain what you are doing to prevent recurrence.
- Follow up with a message that documents the personal contact.
- Look forward to positive future relations.

Many consumer problems are handled with letters, either written by consumers as complaints or by companies in response. However, e-mail and social media sites on the Internet are increasingly emerging as channels for delivering and responding to complaints and negative messages.

Negative Situation: Sharing Negative News with Employees

Bad news, whether delivered in person or in writing, is usually better received when reasons are given first.

A tactful tone and a reasons-first approach help preserve friendly relations with customers. These same techniques are useful when delivering bad news within organizations. Interpersonal bad news might involve telling the boss that something went wrong or confronting an employee about poor performance. Organizational bad news might involve declining profits, lost contracts, harmful lawsuits, public relations controversies, and changes in policy. Whether you use a direct or an indirect strategy in delivering that news depends primarily on the anticipated reaction of the audience. Generally, bad news is better received when reasons are given first. Within organizations, you may find yourself giving bad news in person or in writing.

Delivering Bad News Personally

Whether you are an employee or a supervisor, you may have the unhappy responsibility of delivering bad news. First, decide whether the negative information is newsworthy. For example, trivial, non-criminal mistakes or one-time bad behaviours are best left alone. However, fraudulent travel claims, consistent hostile behaviour, or failing projects must be reported.[11] For example, you might have to tell the boss that the team's computer crashed losing all its important files. As a team leader or supervisor, you might be required to confront an underperforming employee. If you know that the news will upset the receiver, the reasons-first strategy is most effective. When the bad news involves one person or a small group nearby, you should generally deliver that news in person. Here are pointers on how to do so tactfully, professionally, and safely:[12]

- **Gather all the information.** Cool down and have all the facts before marching in on the boss or confronting someone. Remember that every story has two sides.
- **Prepare and rehearse.** Outline what you plan to say so that you are confident, coherent, and dispassionate.
- **Explain: past, present, future.** If you are telling the boss about a problem such as the computer crash, explain what caused the crash, the current situation, and how and when you plan to fix it.
- **Consider taking a partner.** If you fear a "shoot the messenger" reaction, especially from your boss, bring a colleague with you. Each person should have a consistent and credible part in the presentation. If possible, take advantage of your organization's internal resources. To lend credibility to your view, call on auditors, inspectors, or human resources experts.
- **Think about timing.** Don't deliver bad news when someone is already stressed or grumpy. Experts also advise against giving bad news on Friday afternoon when people have the weekend to dwell on it.
- **Be patient with the reaction.** Give the receiver time to vent, think, recover, and act wisely.

When you must deliver bad news in person, be sure to gather all the information, prepare, and rehearse.

WRITING PLAN FOR SHARING NEGATIVE NEWS WITH EMPLOYEES

- **Buffer:** Start with a neutral or positive statement that transitions to the reasons for the bad news. Consider opening with the best news, a compliment, appreciation, agreement, or solid facts. Show understanding.
- **Reasons:** Explain the logic behind the bad news. Provide a rational explanation using positive words and displaying empathy. If possible, mention reader benefits.
- **Bad News:** Position the bad news so that it does not stand out. Be positive, but don't sugarcoat the bad news. Use objective language.
- **Closing:** Provide information about an alternative, if one exists. If appropriate, describe what will happen next. Look forward positively.

Refusing Workplace Requests

Occasionally, managers must refuse requests from employees. In Figure 7.9 you see the first draft and revision of a message responding to a request from a key specialist, Melvin Arroyo. He wants permission to attend a conference. However, he can't attend the conference because the timing is bad; he must be present at budget planning meetings scheduled for the same two weeks. Normally, this matter would be discussed in person. However, Melvin has been travelling among branch offices, and he just hasn't been in the office recently.

The vice president's first inclination was to send a quickie e-mail, as shown in the Figure 7.9 draft, and "tell it like it is." However, the vice president realized that this message was going to hurt and that it had possible danger areas. Moreover, the message misses a chance to give Melvin positive feedback. An improved version of the e-mail starts with a buffer that delivers honest praise (*pleased with the exceptional leadership you have provided* and *your genuine professional commitment*). By the way, don't be stingy with compliments; they cost you nothing. The buffer

FIGURE 7.9 Refusing an Internal Request

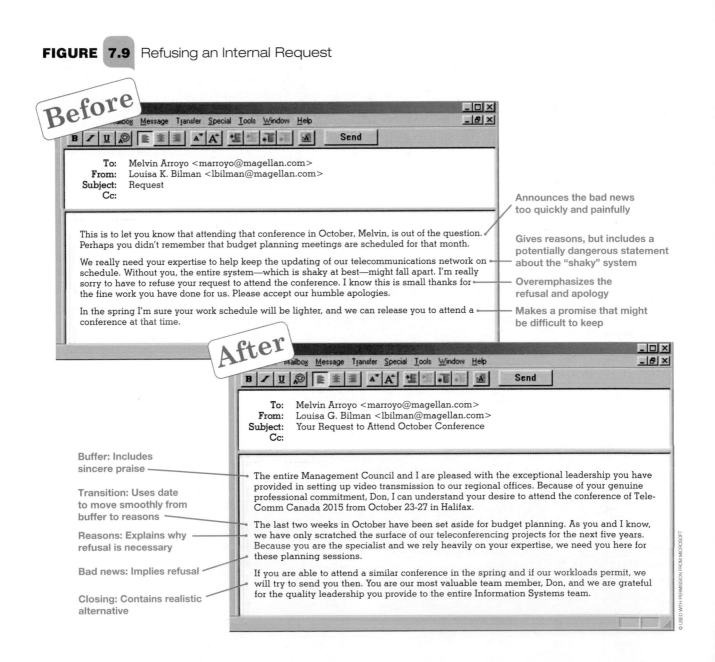

Before

To:	Melvin Arroyo <marroyo@magellan.com>
From:	Louisa K. Bilman <lbilman@magellan.com>
Subject:	Request
Cc:	

This is to let you know that attending that conference in October, Melvin, is out of the question. Perhaps you didn't remember that budget planning meetings are scheduled for that month. — Announces the bad news too quickly and painfully

We really need your expertise to help keep the updating of our telecommunications network on schedule. Without you, the entire system—which is shaky at best—might fall apart. I'm really sorry to have to refuse your request to attend the conference. I know this is small thanks for the fine work you have done for us. Please accept our humble apologies. — Gives reasons, but includes a potentially dangerous statement about the "shaky" system / Overemphasizes the refusal and apology

In the spring I'm sure your work schedule will be lighter, and we can release you to attend a conference at that time. — Makes a promise that might be difficult to keep

After

To:	Melvin Arroyo <marroyo@magellan.com>
From:	Louisa G. Bilman <lbilman@magellan.com>
Subject:	Your Request to Attend October Conference
Cc:	

Buffer: Includes sincere praise — The entire Management Council and I are pleased with the exceptional leadership you have provided in setting up video transmission to our regional offices. Because of your genuine professional commitment, Don, I can understand your desire to attend the conference of Tele-Comm Canada 2015 from October 23-27 in Halifax.

Transition: Uses date to move smoothly from buffer to reasons
Reasons: Explains why refusal is necessary — The last two weeks in October have been set aside for budget planning. As you and I know, we have only scratched the surface of our teleconferencing projects for the next five years. Because you are the specialist and we rely heavily on your expertise, we need you here for these planning sessions.

Bad news: Implies refusal
Closing: Contains realistic alternative — If you are able to attend a similar conference in the spring and if our workloads permit, we will try to send you then. You are our most valuable team member, Don, and we are grateful for the quality leadership you provide to the entire Information Systems team.

also includes the date of the meeting, used strategically to connect the reasons that follow.

The middle paragraph provides reasons for the refusal. Notice that they focus on positive elements: Melvin is the specialist; the company relies on his expertise; and everyone will benefit if he passes up the conference. In this section it becomes obvious that the request will be refused. The writer is not forced to say *No, you may not attend.* Although the refusal is implied, the reader gets the message.

The closing suggests a qualified alternative (*if our workloads permit, we will try to send you then*). It also ends positively with gratitude for Melvin's contributions to the organization and with another compliment (*you're a valuable player*). The improved version focuses on explanations and praise rather than on refusals and apologies. The success of this message depends on sincerity and attention to the entire writing process, not just on using a buffer or scattering a few compliments throughout.

Announcing Negative News to Employees

Many of the same techniques used to deliver bad news personally are useful when organizations face a crisis or must deliver bad news to their workers and other groups. Smart organizations involved in a crisis prefer to communicate the news openly to employees and stakeholders. A crisis might involve serious performance problems, a major relocation, massive layoffs, a management shakeup, or public controversy. Instead of letting rumours distort the truth, managers explain the organization's side of the story honestly and promptly. Morale can be destroyed when employees learn of major events affecting their jobs through the grapevine or from news accounts—rather than from management.

> Organizations can sustain employee morale by communicating bad news openly and honestly.

When bad news must be delivered to employees, management may want to deliver the news personally. With large groups, however, this is generally impossible. Instead, organizations deliver bad news through many channels, including traditional interoffice memos and e-mails. In addition, organizations are disseminating important information through the company intranet and other document management platforms. The intranet may feature up-to-date news, blog postings, videos, and webcasts. Still, interoffice memos seem to function most effectively because they are more formal and make a permanent record. The above writing plan outlines the content for such a message.

For example, in many businesses today, employee extended health care plans are increasing in cost. Northern Industries, Inc., had to announce a substantial increase to its employees; Figure 7.10 shows two versions (posted on the company intranet) of its negative message to employees. The first version opens directly with the bad news. No explanation is given for why employee monthly deductions are rising. Although Northern Industries has been absorbing the increasing costs in the past and has not charged employees, it takes no credit for this. Instead, the tone of the memo is defensive and unsatisfying to receivers.

The improved version of this negative memo, shown at the bottom of Figure 7.10, uses the indirect pattern. Notice that it opens with a relevant, upbeat buffer regarding extended health care benefits—but says nothing about increasing monthly costs. For a smooth transition, the second paragraph begins with a key idea from the opening (comprehensive package). The reasons section discusses rising costs with explanations and figures. The bad news (*you will be paying $119 a month*) is clearly presented but embedded within the paragraph.

> In announcing bad news to employees, consider starting with a neutral statement or something positive.

Throughout, the writer Victor Markelson strives to show the fairness of the company's position. The ending, which does not refer to the bad news, emphasizes how much the company is paying and what a wise investment it is. Notice that the entire memo demonstrates a kinder, gentler approach than that shown in the first draft. Of prime importance in breaking bad news to employees is providing clear, convincing reasons that explain the decision.

Chapter 07: Negative Writing Situations

FIGURE 7.10 Message Announcing Negative Employee News

Before

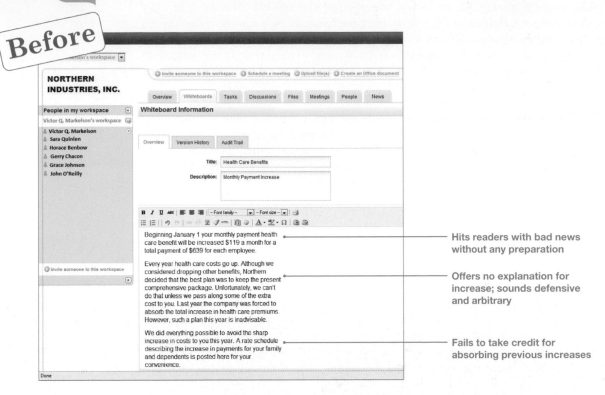

Hits readers with bad news without any preparation

Offers no explanation for increase; sounds defensive and arbitrary

Fails to take credit for absorbing previous increases

After

Begins with positive buffer

Explains why costs are rising

Reveals bad news clearly but embeds it in paragraph

Ends positively by stressing the company's major share of the costs

Keeping the Indirect Strategy Ethical

You may worry that the indirect pattern is unethical or manipulative because the writer deliberately delays the main idea. But consider the alternative. Breaking bad news bluntly can cause pain and hard feelings. By delaying bad news, you soften the blow somewhat, as well as ensure that your reasoning will be read while the receiver is still receptive. Your motives are not to deceive the reader or to hide the news. Rather, your goal is to be a compassionate, yet effective, communicator.

The key to ethical communication lies in the motives of the sender. Unethical communicators intend to deceive. For example, Victoria's Secret, the clothing and lingerie chain, once offered free $10 gift certificates. However, when customers tried to use the certificates, they found that they were required to make a minimum purchase of $50 worth of merchandise.[13] For this misleading, deceptive, and unethical offer, the chain paid a $100,000 fine. Although the indirect strategy provides a setting in which to announce bad news, it should not be used to avoid or misrepresent the truth.

> The indirect strategy is unethical only if the writer intends to deceive the reader.

SUMMING UP AND LOOKING FORWARD

When faced with delivering negative news, you must first analyze the situation and the intended receiver: Is this extremely difficult news or routine negative news? Is the receiver just going to shrug or is he or she going to be heartbroken? Depending on your analysis of the negative situation, you can write the negative news directly, or you can write it indirectly by presenting a buffer and reasons first. Many business communicators prefer the indirect strategy because it tends to preserve goodwill. In some instances, however, the direct strategy is more effective in delivering bad news.

In this chapter you learned the goals in communicating bad news, and you studied many techniques for delivering bad news sensitively. Then, you learned to apply those techniques in refusing typical requests for favours, money, information, and action. Furthermore, you studied techniques for denying claims, refusing credit, and dealing with disappointed customers. You also gained insight into how companies deliver bad news to audiences inside the organization. Finally, you were taught to recognize unethical applications of the indirect strategy. Now that you understand how to write routine, persuasive, and negative messages within your company and outside of it, you're ready to learn about writing longer, more specialized and less frequent business documents such as proposals and reports. Chapter 8 introduces informal reports, and Chapter 9 discusses proposals and formal reports.

CRITICAL THINKING

1. Communication author Dana Bristol-Smith likens delivering bad news to removing a Band-Aid—you can do it slowly or quickly. She thinks that doing so quickly is better, particularly when companies must give bad news to employees.[14] Do you agree or disagree?

2. A survey of business professionals revealed that most respondents reported that every effort should be made to resolve business problems in person.[15] Why is this logical? Why is this problematic?

3. Respected industry analyst Gartner Research issued a report naming social networking as one of the top ten "disruptive" (innovative, game-changing) influences shaping information technology today.[16] Should organizations fear Web sites where consumers post negative messages about products and services? What actions can companies take in response to this disruptive influence?

4. Does bad news travel faster and farther than good news? Why? What implications would this have for companies responding to unhappy customers?

5. Why might it be a bad idea to be blunt and terse toward people on a budget when denying them credit?

6. Why is the "reasons" section of a negative news message so important?

7. **Ethical Issue:** Radio Shack infamously fired 400 of its employees by e-mail a few years ago. More recently, the CEO of electric-car manufacturer Tesla, Elon Musk, used his blog to announce layoffs. Why do most business communicators and management experts frown upon such behaviour? Do you agree or disagree with these experts?

CHAPTER REVIEW

1. What are the business communicator's most important goals in communicating negative news?
2. In what situations is the direct negative strategy a good idea?
3. List the four main parts of the indirect strategy for revealing bad news.
4. In what situations is the indirect negative strategy a good idea?
5. List seven possibilities for opening negative news messages.
6. List at least five words that might affect readers negatively.
7. How can the passive voice be used effectively in negative news messages? Provide an original example.
8. Aside from using a buffer and the indirect strategy, what other techniques can you employ that will cushion the blow of negative news?
9. How can you ensure that you close a negative news message pleasantly and maintain the reader's goodwill?
10. What are some tips for business writers wishing to apologize effectively?
11. What does conveying empathy mean in delivering apologies?
12. The indirect organization strategy may seem unethical or manipulative because the writer deliberately delays the main idea. Explain how the indirect strategy can be ethical.

WRITING IMPROVEMENT EXERCISES

Passive-Voice Verbs

Passive-voice verbs may be preferable in breaking bad news because they enable you to emphasize actions rather than personalities. Compare these two refusals:

Active voice: I cannot authorize you to take three weeks of vacation in July.
Passive voice: Three weeks of vacation in July cannot be authorized.

Your Task. Revise the following refusals so that they use passive-voice instead of active-voice verbs.

1. We do not allow used merchandise to be returned or exchanged.
2. Managers may not advertise any job openings until those positions have first been posted internally.
3. Your car rental insurance does not cover large SUVs.
4. We cannot meet the sales income projected for the fourth quarter.
5. Titan Insurance Company will not process any claim not accompanied by documented proof showing that a physician treated the injuries.

Subordinate Clauses

You can further soften the effect of bad news by placing it in an introductory subordinate clause that begins with *although*, *since*, or *because*. The emphasis in a sentence is on the independent clause. Instead of saying *We cannot serve you on a credit basis*, try *Because serving you on a credit basis is currently not possible, please consider taking advantage of our cash discounts and sale prices*.

Your Task. Revise the following so that the bad news is de-emphasized in a dependent clause that precedes an independent clause. Use the passive voice and "you" view whenever it is appropriate and safe.

6. Unfortunately, we cannot accept personal checks or unauthorized credit. We encourage you to submit your credit application online before coming to the eBay auction.
7. We appreciate your interest in our organization, but we are unable to extend an employment offer to you at this time.

8. It is impossible for us to ship your complete order at this time. However, we are able to send the two armless task chairs immediately.

9. Air Pacific cannot possibly honour the $51 flight to Fiji that erroneously appeared on Travelocity. We are eager, however, to provide a compromise price to customers who booked at the erroneous price.

ACTIVITIES AND CASES

7.1 Follow-up Apology: Naming-Rights-for-Computer-Sales Agreement Goes Sour

As the director of partnerships for Inspire Canada, the largest retailer of computers in the country, you signed an agreement four months ago in July with Macdonald College, a community college in Picton, Ontario. The agreement stipulated that, in exchange for the naming rights to the college's new academic building (now known as the Inspire Canada Information Centre), your company would provide computer hardware, software, and printers at a deep discount to the college for a five-year period. But now you have a difficult situation on your hands.

Over the past two months, the president of the college has been calling you almost weekly to complain about the problematic rollout of the agreement between Inspire Canada and the college. "Your company's name is on our building, and the media have painted you as a great corporate responsibility success story, but you haven't kept your half of the agreement," is typical of the messages you've received from the president. She has told you that your computer equipment has been shipped late in 90 percent of orders, causing severe problems for students and professors in September. Also, printers have malfunctioned in 85 percent of the labs on campus, causing widespread late submission of assignments. In response, you recently called the president and told her that Inspire is "doing everything it can to improve shipping procedures." You also promised to look into the printer problem.

Discuss the following options in resolving this business problem.

1. Following a telephone call to this unhappy customer, what should you do next?

   a. Leave it. A telephone call is enough. You did what you could to explain the problem, and words will not solve the problem anyway.

   b. Wait to see whether this customer calls again. After all, the next move is up to her. Respond only after repeated complaints.

   c. Send a short e-mail message repeating your apology and explanation.

   d. Immediately send a letter that apologizes, explains, and shows how seriously you have taken the problem and the customer's complaint.

2. You decide to write a follow-up letter. To open this letter, you should begin with

   a. A neutral statement, such as *This letter is in response to your telephone complaint*.

   b. A defensive statement that protects you from legal liability, such as *As I mentioned on the telephone, you are the only customer who has complained about shipping problems*.

   c. An apologetic statement that shows you understand and take responsibility for the problem.

   d. An off-the-subject remark, such as *We're happy to hear that the college has increased its enrolment this fall*.

3. In the body of the follow-up letter, you should

   a. explain why the problem occurred.

   b. describe what you are doing to resolve the problem.

   c. promise that you will do everything possible to prevent the problem from happening again.

   d. do all of the above.

4. In the closing of this letter, you should

   a. avoid apologizing because it may increase your legal liability.

   b. show appreciation for the customer's patience and patronage.

  c. explain that company policy prohibits you from revealing the exact nature of the shipping and printer problems.

  d. provide an action deadline.

Your Task. After circling your choices and discussing them in your class, write a follow-up message to Dr. Marianne Porter, President, Macdonald College, 35 Regent St., Picton, ON K0K 3BC or mporter@macdonald.ca. In your message, be proactive about solutions, but consider also that Dr. Porter has implied she may leak the story to the local and national media and/or seek the advice of the college's lawyer.

7.2 Request Refusal: No New Droid for You

What follows is a letter to a customer who demanded a brand-new replacement Droid smartphone under her wireless phone protection plan.

Current date

Ms. Lynda Brownsmith
2402 Pretoria Street
Orleans, ON K2B 8N7

Dear Ms. Brownsmith:

This letter is being sent to you to inform you that warranty repairs or replacements are not available for damage caused by operator fault. The dot inside your smartphone indicates in bright red that the device suffered prolonged exposure to liquid. The phone also shows signs of heavy external abuse—quite rightly excluded from coverage under your protection plan.

  Your phone retailer, Premier Wireless, at 901 Ste. Charles Avenue, forwarded your device to us. Our service technician made an inspection. That's when he discovered that your Droid had not been treated with proper caution and care. He said he had never seen such a gunky phone interior, and that without a doubt the gadget was subjected to blunt force on top of that! You are lucky that the touch screen did not crack or break and that you didn't lose all your data irretrievably since you apparently didn't bother to arrange for a backup. Today's smartphones are sophisticated high-tech devices. They must be handled with utmost respect. You wouldn't believe how many users accidentally drop their phones into the toilet.

  Our Peace of Mind Plan gets rave reviews from users. They love the protection their expensive equipment enjoys at a low monthly cost of $5.99. However, the manufacturer's warranty on your Droid covers only this one thing: manufacturing defects. Your warranty has expired by now, but it wouldn't cover neglect and abuse anyway. Your Peace of Mind Plan is in effect but only covers you for theft, loss, and malfunction. It explicitly excludes liquid and physical damage. In any case, there is always a deductible of $89. We can't replace the Droid at no charge. But we could sell you a remanufactured model, at a cost of $49 plus tax. Your other option is to purchase a new device at full retail cost. Furthermore, since you have a two-year contract, you will be eligible for an upgrade as you are nearing month 20.

  Let us know what you want to do. We pride ourselves on our unparalleled customer service.

Sincerely,

Your Task.
1. List at least five weaknesses in this letter.
2. Outline a plan for writing a refusal to a request.

  Buffer:
  Reasons:
  Bad news:
  Closing:

TEAM

7.3 Customer Bad News: Costly SUV Upgrade

Steven Chan, a consultant from Regina, Saskatchewan, was surprised when he picked up his rental car from Budget at the Calgary airport over Easter weekend. He had reserved a full-size car, but the rental agent told him he could upgrade to a Ford Excursion for an additional $25 a day. "She told me it was easy to drive," Mr. Chan reported. "But when I saw it, I realized it was huge—like a tank. You could fit a full-size bed inside."

On his trip Mr. Chan managed to scratch the paint and damage the rear-door step. He didn't worry, though. He thought the damage would be covered because he had charged the rental on his American Express card. He knew that the company offered backup car rental insurance coverage. To his dismay, he discovered that its car rental coverage excluded large SUVs. "I just assumed they'd cover it," he confessed. He wrote to Budget to complain about not being warned that certain credit cards may not cover damage to large SUVs or luxury cars.

Budget agents always encourage renters to sign up for Budget's own "risk product." They don't feel that it is their responsibility to study the policies of customers' insurance carriers and explain what may or may not be covered. Moreover, they try to move customers into their rental cars as quickly as possible and avoid lengthy discussions of insurance coverage. Customers who do not purchase insurance are at risk. Mr. Chan does not make any claim against Budget, but he is upset about being "pitched" to upgrade to the larger SUV, which he didn't really want.[17]

Your Task. As a member of the customer care staff at Budget, respond to Mr. Chan's complaint. Budget obviously is not going to pay for the SUV repairs, but it does want to salvage his goodwill and future business. Offer him a coupon worth two days' free rental of any full-size sedan. Write to Steven Chan, 201–548 Hillsdale Street, Regina, SK S32 0A2.

7.4 Internal Refusal: Want to Telecommute? Learn to Communicate

Pamela Gershon, a young software developer from Edmonton, Alberta, is thrilled at the prospect of working from home where she would be able to take care of her two small children, three dogs, and a cat. Like many forward-looking employers, Northrop Grumman Corporation, a leading aerospace and defence technology company, is encouraging workers to consider telecommuting. The company has created a formal program with specific policies explaining eligibility and requirements. Currently, only positions in technical sales, information technology, Web and graphic design, and software development qualify for telecommuting. In addition, workers must be dependable, self-motivated, and organized. Because telecommuting is a sought-after privilege, employees with proven high performance, seniority, minimal absenteeism, and superb communication skills receive priority consideration. Telecommuters need to follow company policies determining work hours, break times, and work schedules, even off site. Moreover, they must visit the main office located on CFB Cold Lake at least once every two weeks to report to their supervisors in person.

Northrop Grumman promotes telecommuting because it benefits the company as well as its workers. In addition to flexibility, telecommuters usually experience gains in productivity and efficiency. The employer lowers overhead costs and is able to retain valuable workers who may not be able or willing to commute to remote corporate offices.[18]

Pamela has been a diligent worker, but after only a year and a half at Northrop Grumman, she doesn't have the seniority needed for a successful application. Her performance has been satisfactory but not outstanding. It seems as if she still needs time to prove herself. In addition, her major weakness is average communication skills, something her supervisor has already discussed with Pamela.

Your Task. Draft a memo addressed to Pamela Gershon for Human Resources Director Gabrielle Anicker turning down Pamela's telecommuting application. Be gentle but honest in revealing your reasons for the *no*, but don't close the door on a future application once Pamela meets certain conditions.

7.5 Request Refusal: The End of Free Credit Reports

You are part of the customer service team at Experian, the largest supplier of consumer and business credit information in the world. Experian took over TRW Information Systems & Services back in 1996. Experian currently employs more than 11,000 people in North America, the United Kingdom, Continental Europe, Africa, and Asia Pacific. As a service to consumers, Experian at one time provided complimentary credit reports. However, it now offers them only in certain locations and to certain groups of people.

Experian's Web site explains its new policy in its FAQ (frequently asked questions) section. Your supervisor says to you, "I guess not everyone is able to learn about our new policy by going to our Web site, because we still receive a lot of phone requests for free reports. I'm unhappy with a letter we've been using to respond to these requests. I want you to compose a draft of a new form letter that we can send to people who inquire. You should look at our Web site to see who gets free reports and in what locations."

Because you are fairly new to Experian, you ask your boss what prompted the change in policy. She explains, "It was a good idea, but it got out of hand. So-called 'credit repair' companies would refer their clients to us for free credit reports, and then they advised their clients to dispute every item on the report. We had to change our policy. But you can read more about it at our Web site."

Your Task. You resolve to study the Experian Web site closely. Your task is to write a letter refusing the requests of people who want free credit reports. But you must also explain the reasons for the change in policy, as well as its exceptions. Decide whether you should tell consumers how to order a copy and how to pay for it. Although your letter will be used repeatedly for such requests, address your draft to Ms. Cherise Benoit, 250 Rue Bruce, Montréal, QC H2X 1E1. Sign it with your boss's name, Elisabeth Bourke.

7.6 Bad News for Customers: These Funds Are Worth Holding On To

You are a financial planner in Hamilton, Ontario, with over 200 clients. Since you began your practice as a financial planner, you have been a strong believer in BMC's mutual funds, which are heavily invested in the financial services sector. Over the past few years, though, these funds have been underperforming dismally. For example, in 2009, when the S&P/TSX Index was 10.5 percent, BMC funds were averaging 2.2 percent; in 2014 when the index was at 11.9 percent, BMC funds averaged 2.5 percent; and in 2015 when the Index is at 10.9 percent, BMC funds are averaging –0.1 percent. BMC funds have been criticized in major newspapers of late, and for the past few months you have had at least five clients per week calling to sell their funds. You believe BMC funds are still a good value because the financial services sector will rebound soon. Also, with Canadian demographic trends pointing to a large retired population in the next decade, you believe BMC funds are a smart investment.

Your Task. Write a letter to your clients in which you discuss the recent bad news about BMC funds, but at the same time, in which you attempt to put this bad news into a broader context.

Related Web site: For general information on Canadian mutual fund performance, go to **www .morningstar.ca**.

7.7 Credit Refusal: Camcorders for Rudy's Camera Shop

As a Uniworld Electronics sales manager, you are delighted to land a sizable order for your new Canon Vixia camcorder. This hot new camcorder features a sleek, lightweight design, brilliant optical quality, vibrant images, and outstanding image capture in low-light conditions.

The purchase order comes from Rudy's Camera Shop, a retail distributor in Victoria, British Columbia. You send the order on to Pamela Kahn, your credit manager, for approval of the credit application attached. To your disappointment, Pam tells you that Rudy's Camera doesn't qualify for credit. Experian, the credit-reporting service, reports that extending credit to Rudy's would be risky for Uniworld. But Experian did offer to discuss your client's report with him.

Because you think you can be more effective in writing than on the telephone, you decide to write to Rudy's Camera with the bad news and offer an alternative. Suggest that Rudy's order a smaller number of the Canon camcorders. If it pays cash, it can receive a 2 percent discount. After Rudy's has sold these fast-moving camcorders, it can place another cash order through your toll-free order number. With your fast delivery system, its inventory will never be depleted. Rudy's can get the camcorders it wants now and can replace its inventory almost overnight. Credit Manager Kahn tells you that your company generally reveals to credit applicants the name of the credit-reporting service it used and encourages them to investigate their credit record.

Your Task. Write a credit refusal to Ron Kasbekar, Rudy's Camera Shop, 316 Lucas Drive, Victoria, BC V8N 1H6. Add any information needed.

7.8 Refusing a Claim: Evicting a Noisy Neighbour

As Robert Hsu, you must deny the request of Arman Aryai, one of the tenants in your three-storey office building. Mr. Aryai, a Chartered Accountant, demands that you immediately evict a neighbouring tenant who plays loud music throughout the day, interfering with Mr. Aryai's conversations with clients and with his concentration. The noisy tenant, Bryant Haperot, seems to operate an entertainment booking agency and spends long hours in his office.

You know you can't evict Mr. Haperot immediately because of his lease. Moreover, you hesitate to do anything drastic because paying tenants are hard to find. You called your lawyer, and he said that the first thing you should do is talk to the noisy tenant or write him a letter asking him to tone it down. If this doesn't work within 30 days, you could begin the eviction process.

Your Task. Decide on a course of action. Because Mr. Aryai doesn't seem to answer his telephone, you must write to him. You need a permanent record of this decision anyway. Write to Arman Aryai, CA, Suite 203, Pico Building, 1405 Bower Boulevard, Vancouver, BC V6L 1Y3 or aryai@aplusaccountants.ca. Deny his request, but tell him how you plan to resolve the problem.

7.9 Customer Bad News: Sorry—Smokers Must Pay

Recently, the Century Park Hotel embarked on a two-year plan to provide enhanced value and improved product quality to its guests. It always strives to exceed guest expectations. As part of this effort, Century Park has been refurbishing many rooms with updated finishes. The new carpet, paint, upholstery, and draperies, however, absorb the heavy odour of cigarette smoke. In order to protect the hotel's investment, Century Park enforces a strict non-smoking policy for selected rooms.

Century Park makes sure that guests know about its policy regarding smoking in non-smoking rooms. It posts a notice in each designated room, and it gives guests a handout from the manager detailing its policy and the consequences for smoking. The handout clearly says, "Should a guest opt to disregard our non-smoking policy, we will process a fee of $150 to the guest's account." For those guests who prefer to smoke, a smoking accommodation can be provided.

On May 10 Wilson M. Weber was a guest in the hotel. He stayed in a room clearly marked "Non-smoking." After he left, the room cleaners reported that the room smelled of smoke. According to hotel policy, a charge of $150 was processed to Mr. Weber's credit card. Mr. Weber has written to demand that the $150 charge be removed. He doesn't deny that he smoked in the room. He just thinks that he should not have to pay.

Your Task. As hotel manager, deny Mr. Weber's claim. You would certainly like to see Mr. Weber return as a Century Park guest, but you cannot budge on your non-smoking policy. Address your response to Mr. Wilson M. Weber, 634 Wetmore Avenue, Saskatoon, SA M5A 3G8.

7.10 Credit Refusal: Cash Only at GoodLife Fitness Clubs

As manager of the Moncton GoodLife Fitness Club, you must refuse the application of Monique Cooper for an Extended Membership. This is strictly a business decision. You liked Monique very much when she applied, and she seems genuinely interested in fitness and a healthful lifestyle. However, your Extended Membership plan qualifies the member for all your testing, exercise, recreation, yoga, and aerobics programs. This multi-service program is expensive for the club to maintain because of the huge staff required. Applicants must have a solid credit rating to join. To your disappointment, you learned that Monique's credit rating is decidedly negative. Her credit report indicates that she is delinquent in payments to four businesses, including Pros Athletic Club, your principal competitor.

You do have other programs, including your Drop In and Work Out plan, which offers the use of available facilities on a cash basis. This plan enables a member to reserve space on the racquetball and handball courts. The member can also sign up for yoga and exercise classes, space permitting. Because Monique is far in debt, you would feel guilty allowing her to plunge in any more deeply.

Your Task. Refuse Monique Cooper's credit application, but encourage her cash business. Suggest that she make an inquiry to the credit-reporting company Experian to learn about her credit report. She is eligible to receive a $10 credit report if she mentions this application. Write to Monique Cooper, 303 Magnetic Blvd., Moncton, NB E1A 4B8 or mcooper@mymail.ca.

7.11 Employee Bad News: Strikeout for Expanded Office Teams

Assume you are Walter Cervello, vice president of operations at Copiers Plus, 508 W. Inverary Road, Kingston, ON K2G 1V8. Recently several of your employees requested that their spouses or friends be allowed to participate in Copiers Plus's intramural sports teams. Although the teams play only once a week during the season, these employees claim that they can't afford more time away from friends and family. Over 100 employees currently participate in the eight coed volleyball and softball teams, which are open to company employees only. The teams were designed to improve employee friendships and to give employees a regular occasion to have fun together.

If non-employees were to participate, you're afraid that employee interaction would be limited. And while some team members might have fun if spouses or friends were included, you're not so sure all employees would enjoy it. You're not interested in turning intramural sports into "date night." Furthermore, the company would have to create additional teams if many non-employees joined, and you don't want the administrative or equipment costs of more teams. Adding teams would also require changes to team rosters and game schedules, which could be a problem for some employees. You do understand the need for social time with friends and families, but guests are welcome as spectators at all intramural games. Besides, the company already sponsors a family holiday party and an annual company picnic.

Your Task. Write an e-mail or hard-copy memo to the staff denying the request of several employees to include non-employees on Copiers Plus's intramural sports teams.

7.12 Employee Bad News: Refusing Holiday Season Event
In the past your office has always sponsored a holiday season party at a nice restaurant. As your company has undergone considerable downsizing and budget cuts during the past year, you know that no money is available for holiday entertaining.

Your Task. As executive vice president, send an e-mail to Dina Gillian, office manager. Dina asked permission to make restaurant reservations for this year's holiday party. Refuse Dina, but offer some alternatives. How about a potluck dinner?

CRITICAL THINKING

7.13 Customer Bad News: Image Consultant Plays Bad Guy
As the owner of Polished Pro Image Consultants, you hate the part of your job that requires you every so often to write collection letters. Your work is all about making people look good, so when they don't pay their bills, it's difficult for you to get in touch with them—it's as if nothing you taught them has sunk in. Still, as a small business owner, you cannot afford a collections clerk, and you dread the cost of hiring a third-party collection agency to take care of your outstanding accounts. Recently, you provided extensive consulting services to David M. Fryer, a local businessperson who will be running in the next election to be the local Member of Parliament. You billed Mr. Fryer for 18 hours at $100 per hour for in-person consulting, plus another 10 hours at $50 per hour for telephone consulting. In total, your invoice dated May 14, 2014, amounted to $2,300 plus HST. A reminder e-mail you sent to Mr. Fryer on June 30 went unanswered, and you've decided now that August has arrived, it's time to act. The only thing holding you back is that Mr. Fryer is prominent in your community, and while you definitely want your invoice paid, you're not sure you want to get on his bad side.

Your Task. Write a collection letter to Mr. David M. Fryer, President, Hexago Plastics, 230 Queen St., Saint John, NB E3K 4N6.

7.14 Employee Bad News: The Worst Publicity Ever
Sometimes relaying negative news using new communications technology can turn into a public relations disaster. A case in the United States demonstrates just how bad things can become.

Your Task. Do two sets of secondary research: first, type the phrase "e-mail termination radio shack" into an Internet search engine such as Google. How many articles about the infamous Radio Shack "firing by e-mail" situation can you find? Next, type the same phrase into an online research database in your college or university library. How many articles can you find now? Develop a three-slide PowerPoint presentation in which you offer (a) a short explanation of what happened, (b) a short explanation of the difference in tone between the articles you found via the Internet and those you found via the research database, and (c) a suggestion to Radio Shack and other employers about a better channel and message they can use when delivering negative messages such as the one in this case.

7.15 Announcing Bad News to Customers
You are the owner of Miss Twinkle's Treats, a small bakery in London, Ontario. The delicious cakes, squares, cookies, and breads that Miss Twinkle's is known for are made from scratch daily at your location on the outskirts of the city. Although you operate a small storefront, most of your business comes from supplying local restaurants and coffee shops with your tantalizing treats. You own a small truck that is used to deliver orders to your customers throughout the London area. Although Miss Twinkle's is financially successful, rising costs have severely

undercut your profits over the past few months. You know that you are not the only business owner dealing with rising prices—many of your suppliers have raised their prices over the last year. Specifically, the higher price of wheat and sugar has resulted in a drastic increase in your production costs. Previously, you did not charge for deliveries made to your wholesale clients. However, you now feel that you have no choice but to add a delivery charge to each order to cover your increased costs and the rising price of gas.

Your Task. As the owner of Miss Twinkle's Treats, write a letter to your clients in which you announce a $20 charge per delivery. See if you can come up with an offer or special to placate your customers. Use the indirect writing strategy and explain your reasons for introducing the charge.

7.16 Employee Bad News: Refusing the Use of Instant Messaging on the Job

As the vice president of the Green Group, an environmental firm, you've had a request from team leader Emily Tsonga. She wants to know whether her team can use instant messaging on the job. Emily is working on the plans for an environmentally friendly shopping centre, Westbury Mall. Her team project is moving ahead on schedule, and you have had excellent feedback from the shopping centre developers.

Emily's team is probably already using instant messaging through public systems, and this worries you. You are concerned about security, viruses, and wasted time. However, the company has been considering a secured "enterprise-level" instant messaging system. The principal drawbacks are that such a system is expensive, requires administration, and limits use to organizational contacts only. You are not sure your company will ever adopt such a system.

You will have to refuse Emily's request, but you want her to know how much you value her excellent work on developing sustainability and green building techniques for the Westbury Mall project. You know you cannot get by with a quick refusal. You must give her solid reasons for rejecting her request.

Your Task. Send an e-mail to Emily Tsonga at etsonga@greengroup.ca refusing her request. See Chapter 4 for more information on the pros and cons of instant messaging. Also do research on the Internet or in a library database to understand better the risks of instant messaging.

GRAMMAR/MECHANICS REVIEW—7

The following sentences contain errors in grammar, punctuation, capitalization, number style, usage, and spelling. Write a corrected version of each sentence.

1. The first province by province report describing Canada's tobacco use and tobacco control laws were recently released.

2. The report which was compiled by statistics canada showed adult smoking rates that varied from 5% of the population in alberta, to twelve percent in quebec.

3. As expected quebecs pattern of deaths related to smoking was nearly twice that of albertas.

4. Hailed by anti-tobacco groups as proof of the need for more stricter National regulations the report was dismissed by the tobacco industry as "old news".

5. Statistics canada said that the comparisons might stimulate changes in some provinces, but that the report was not part of any particular policy drive.

6. "Children are particularly vulnerable to second-hand smoke because they breathe faster than adults inhale more air proportionate to their body mass and their lungs are still growing and developing reported ugnat et al in the Canadian journal of public health.

7. Most likely to attract attention, are data related to smoking among High School students.

8. The 8 provinces with the lowest cigarette taxs has a higher than average number of smokers.

9. The provinces of newfoundland and british columbia have the highest provincial tobacco taxes at $22 a pack rank in the middle on percentage of smokers.

10. The québec-based "ACTI-Menu" health programs non smoking campaign encourages smokers who want to quit to pair up with a non smoking partner. Both partners sign a pledge with the smoker agreeing not to smoke for the period of march 1st to april 12th.

11. Walker Merryman a spokesperson for the tobacco institute said "This report is more rehash than research, it is not terribly useful for understanding why kids smoke".

12. Anti-tobacco supporters are urging government to support a proposal to severely restrict: advertising marketing and distribution of tobacco products.

13. The province of quebec however faces the biggest problem, nearly twenty-four percent of it's students who were daily smokers 15 to 19 years of age, reported smoking within the month in which they were surveyed.

14. In 2004 7% of young people aged 10 to 19 were beginning to smoke.

15. The governments tobacco education and information officer explained that its hard to restrict smoking when the provinces economy is linked so close to gaming which is linked to tobacco.

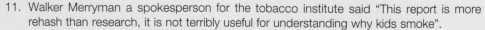 GRAMMAR/MECHANICS CHALLENGE—7

Document for Revision

The e-mail in Figure 7.11 has faults in grammar, punctuation, spelling, number form, and negative words. Use standard proofreading marks (see Appendix B) to correct the errors. When you finish, your instructor can show you the revised version of this message.

FIGURE 7.11 Order Confirmation

Order Confirmation

File Edit Mailbox Message Transfer Special Tools Window Help

B I U | | | | A A | | | | | | **Send**

To: Ragu Raghavan   May 3, 2015
From: Andy Weiss
Subject: Order Confirmation
Cc:
Bcc:
Attached:

Dear Mr. Raghavan:

You will be recieving shortly the handimaid service and utility carts you ordered along with 5 recycling stack bins. Unfortunately, the heavy duty can crusher is not available but it will be sent from the factory in St John's Newfoundland and should reach you by May 31st.

You may place any future orders, by using our toll free telephone number (1-800-577-9241), or our toll-free fax number (1-800-577-2657). If you need help with any items ask for one of the following sales represenatives, Ben Crowchild, Susan Fried, or Rick Woo. When the items you order are in our currant catalogue it will be shipped the same day you place you're order. For products to be custom imprinted please provide a typed or printed copy with your order.

Remember we are the only catalogue sales company that guarantees your full satisfaction. If you are not pleased we'll arrange for a prompt refund, credit or replacement. We'll also refund or credit all shipping costs associated with the returned items. We want your business!

COMMUNICATION WORKSHOP

● INTERCULTURAL ISSUES: PRESENTING BAD NEWS IN OTHER CULTURES

To minimize disappointment, Canadians generally prefer to present negative messages indirectly. Other cultures may treat bad news differently, as illustrated in the following:

- In Germany business communicators occasionally use buffers but tend to present bad news directly.
- British writers tend to be straightforward with bad news, seeing no reason to soften its announcement.
- In Latin countries the question is not how to organize negative messages but whether to present them at all. It is considered disrespectful and impolite to report bad news to superiors. Therefore, reluctant employees may fail to report accurately any negative situations to their bosses.
- In Thailand the negativism represented by a refusal is completely alien; the word *no* does not exist. In many cultures negative news is offered with such subtleness or in such a positive light that it may be overlooked or misunderstood by literal-minded Americans.
- In many Asian and some Latin cultures, one must look beyond an individual's actual words to understand what is really being communicated. One must consider the communication style, the culture, and especially the context. Consider the following phrases and their possible meanings:

Phrase	Possible Meaning
I agree.	I agree with 15 percent of what you say.
We might be able to.	Not a chance!
We will consider it.	*We* will consider it, but *the real decision maker* will not.
That is a little too much.	That is outrageous!
Yes.	Yes, I'm listening. *OR*: Yes, you have a good point.
	OR: Yes, I understand, but I don't necessarily agree.

Career Application

Interview fellow students or work colleagues who are from other cultures. Collect information regarding the following questions:

- How is negative news handled in their cultures?
- How would typical business communicators refuse a request for a business favour (such as a contribution to a charity)?
- How would typical business communicators refuse a customer's claim?
- How would an individual be turned down for a job?

YOUR TASK

Report the findings of your interviews in a class discussion or memo report. In addition, collect samples of foreign business letters. You might ask foreign students, your campus admissions office, or local export/import companies whether they would be willing to share business letters from other countries. You can also use the Internet and search terms such as "Business Etiquette" or "Business Letters or Writing" and "Africa" or "Asia" for example. Compare letter styles, formats, tone, and writing strategies. How do these elements differ from those in typical North American business letters?

UNIT 04

Reporting Data

CHAPTER 8
Informal Reports

CHAPTER 9
Proposals and
Formal Reports

COMMUNICATION TECHNOLOGY IN THE NEWS

BlackBerry Etiquette Has Yet to Be Defined

Do you check your BlackBerry during work meetings? Do you do it furtively under the table, while your colleagues are distracted by a presentation?

Do you leave it in front of you so you can give it the occasional peck whenever it buzzes? Or are you bold enough in the board room to hold it up while you type your replies, a practice that's provoked comedian Jerry Seinfeld to respond, "Can I just pick up a magazine and read it in front of your face while you're talking to me?"

Unless you work in a company that bans BlackBerry use in meetings, you've seen all these behaviours. Most likely, you've been that person. But is it bad etiquette? Don't the pressures of time and overflowing inboxes make this a necessary evil of the 21st century workplace?

Other journalists who have taken time out from deleting e-mail to investigate this burning issue have concluded that polite society abhors the employee whose eyes wander from the PowerPoint presentation to the new e-mail alert.

But as someone who struggles to ignore the siren buzz of the BlackBerry, I demand leave to appeal this collective ruling by the media's finest minds. After all, every new technology that transforms communications encounters resistance from the old guard. Surely the cool kids accept that it is possible to concentrate on a meeting and accept e-mail requests for other meetings at the same time?

It didn't take much Googling to find some research that confirmed my hunch: while 68 per cent of the baby-boom generation born before 1964 think that the use of smartphones during meetings is distracting, just 49 per cent of the under-30s see a problem. As this 2008 LexisNexis survey helpfully points out, that's less than half. If the person running your meeting is a Generation Y'er, there's a better than even chance that she won't mind you checking your e-mail.

Still, most of us have bosses who are too old to skateboard to work. What does Generation X think of BlackBerry peckers? I asked John Freeman, a member of that demographic and the author of *The Tyranny of E-mail*:

"You never have everyone's full attention in a meeting any longer, and I think that's why meetings are becoming so ineffective," he wrote in a non-tyrannical e-mail.

"Whether it's the lot who try to thumb under the table, or those who brazenly do it in the open, the message, from a significant group of those gathered, is—I have other things to do. Which totally defeats the purpose of meeting: you want to create a sense of group purpose. And on top of that it's rude."

But John, I can multitask. It may look like I'm updating my Facebook status under the table, but a co-worker has sent me an urgent question and I can answer that and concentrate on your presentation at the same time. Surely I can get an expert on multitasking to back me up here.

I called Clifford Nass, a professor of communication at Stanford University in California. Nass was part of a group that researched the concentration skills of students who frequently multitasked while consuming media. Did he find that those of us who listen and e-mail at the same time are an elite brigade of hyper-efficient workers? Not exactly.

"The more you multitask, the worse you become at it," he said. According to the Stanford team's research, there's a cost to memory and attention when you switch from one task to another. And that cost increases for people who multitask heavily.

So the science suggests that the appearance of not paying attention when you check your e-mail in a meeting mirrors the reality: however much you think you're paying attention to two things at once, you're not.

And yet the BlackBerry sits there in my pocket, calling to me throughout the meeting: Check me! Check me! What can I do?

"You have to become more cognisant that what you're doing is likely to be offensive to others," said

BlackBerry Etiquette Has Yet to Be Defined (*continued*)

Robert Gordon, who coaches adults with attention deficit hyperactivity disorder (ADHD).

Gordon, who is based in Toronto, says the strategy for executives struggling with ADHD is to separate them from their distractions. So in the case of a BlackBerry, that means shutting it off. I make a final plea. Rob, there are parts of many meetings that aren't relevant to me. What if I check my e-mail then?

"Then the onus falls on the person calling the meeting to be more focused on the agenda," he said.

So there's the answer. It's not my fault I'm rudely checking my BlackBerry. It's your fault for not making the meeting more interesting. And that's just plain bad etiquette.

Summarize the article you've just read in a two- to three-sentence paragraph. Answer the following questions, either on your own or in a small group. Be prepared to present your answers in a short presentation or in an e-mail to your instructor.

QUESTIONS:

1. How does what you've learned in this article change your perception of business communication?

2. How might what you've learned in this article change your own communication style?

3. Come up with pro and con arguments for the following debate/discussion topic: BlackBerrys and other electronic devices should be banned from workplace meetings and presentations.

Informal Reports

©CHRIS SCHMIDT/ISTOCKPHOTO.COM

LEARNING OBJECTIVES

1. Describe informal business reports, including functions, organization, formats, and delivery methods.
2. Develop informal reports by gathering data effectively and understanding effective style.
3. Identify and explain functions of six types of informal reports.
4. Write informal informational reports.
5. Write informal analytical reports.

💬 Understanding Report Basics

Good report writers are good at simplifying facts so that anyone can understand them. Collecting information and organizing it clearly and simply into meaningful reports are skills that all successful businesspeople today require. In this age of information, reports play a significant role in helping decision makers solve problems. You can learn to write good reports by examining basic techniques and by analyzing appropriate models.

Because of their abundance and diversity, business reports are difficult to define. They may range from informal e-mail trip reports to formal 200-page financial forecasts. Some reports may be presented orally in front of a group using PowerPoint, while other reports appear as e-mails, memos, or in template forms. Still others consist primarily of numerical data, such as tax reports or profit-and-loss statements.

Although reports vary in length, content, format, organization, and level of formality, they all have one common purpose: they are organized attempts to answer business questions and solve business problems in writing or in presentation format. In this chapter we'll concentrate on informal written reports. Reports are informal when the information included in them deals with routine or recurring events, or when decisions taken based on the report have a relatively low financial threshold. Decisions with large budgets attached usually come after a formal report has been researched and presented; you'll look at formal reports in Chapter 9.

> Informal reports are relatively short (under ten pages) and are usually written in memo or letter format. Sometimes, they are attached to e-mails or presented in the body of the e-mail itself if the context is quite informal.

Functions of Reports

Most reports can be classified into two functional categories: information reports and analytical reports.

Information Reports

Reports that present data without analysis or recommendations are primarily informational. Although writers collect and organize facts, they are not expected to analyze the facts (i.e., say what the facts mean) for readers. A trip report describing an employee's visit to a conference, for example, simply presents information. Other reports that present information without analysis could involve routine operations (e.g., an incident report in a fast-food restaurant), compliance with regulations (e.g., a status update on a new government regulation rollout in a bank), or company policies and procedures (e.g., a status update on employee reaction to enforcement of a new company policy in a manufacturing company).

Analytical Reports

Reports that provide analysis and conclusions as well as data are analytical. If requested, writers also supply recommendations. Analysis is the process of breaking down a problem into its parts in order to understand it better and solve it (e.g., each time you write an outline, as shown in Figure 3.2 on page 58, you are analyzing a problem). Analytical reports attempt to provide the insight necessary to persuade readers to act or change their opinions. For example, a recommendation report that compares several potential locations for an employee fitness club might recommend one site, but not until after it has analyzed and discussed the alternatives. This analysis should persuade readers to accept the writer's choice. Similarly, a feasibility report that analyzes the ability of a private chef school to open a satellite campus in a nearby city will either say yes this can be done or no it can't, but it will also discuss the alternative course of action.

Report Organization

Like routine, persuasive, or negative messages, reports may be organized using the direct or indirect method. The reader's expectations and the content of a report determine its pattern of development, as shown in Figure 8.1.

DIRECT STRATEGY. When the purpose for writing is presented close to the beginning, the organizational strategy is direct. Information reports, such as the memo attachment shown in Figure 8.4, are usually arranged directly. They open with an introduction, followed by the facts and a summary. In Figure 8.4 the writer explains what happened at a work conference. The memo attachment begins with an introduction. It then presents the facts, which are listed using headings for greater readability. The memo ends with a summary, appreciation, and a complimentary close.

Analytical reports may also be organized directly, especially when readers are supportive or are familiar with the topic. Many busy executives prefer this pattern because it gives them the results of the report immediately. They don't have to spend time wading through the facts, findings, discussion, and analyses to get to the two items they are most interested in—the conclusions and recommendations. You should be aware, though, that unless readers are familiar with the topic, they may find the direct pattern confusing. Some readers prefer the indirect pattern because it seems logical and mirrors the way we solve problems.

FIGURE 8.1 Audience Analysis and Report Organization

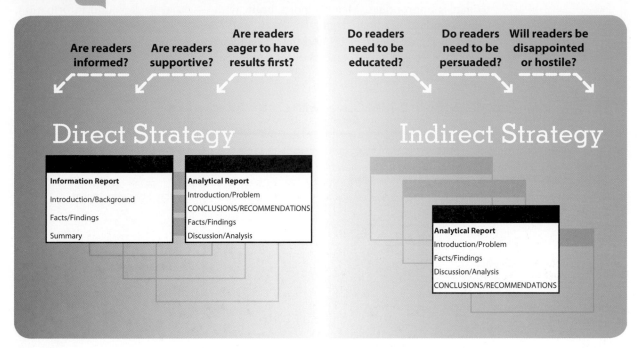

Are readers informed? **Are readers supportive?** **Are readers eager to have results first?**

Do readers need to be educated? **Do readers need to be persuaded?** **Will readers be disappointed or hostile?**

Direct Strategy

Information Report
Introduction/Background
Facts/Findings
Summary

Analytical Report
Introduction/Problem
CONCLUSIONS/RECOMMENDATIONS
Facts/Findings
Discussion/Analysis

Indirect Strategy

Analytical Report
Introduction/Problem
Facts/Findings
Discussion/Analysis
CONCLUSIONS/RECOMMENDATIONS

INDIRECT STRATEGY. When the conclusions and recommendations, if requested, appear at the end of the report, the organizational pattern is indirect. Such reports usually begin with an introduction or description of the problem, followed by facts and interpretation from the writer. They end with conclusions and recommendations. This pattern is helpful when readers are unfamiliar with the problem. It is also useful when readers must be persuaded or when they may be disappointed in or hostile toward the report's findings. The writer is more likely to retain the reader's interest by first explaining, justifying, and analyzing the facts and then making recommendations. This pattern also seems most rational to readers because it follows the normal thought process: problem, alternatives (facts), solution.

Report Formats

The format of a report is governed by its length, topic, audience, and purpose. After considering these elements, you will probably choose from among the following six formats.

> How you format a report depends on its length, topic, audience, and purpose.

ELECTRONIC FORMAT. In today's less formal workplace, informal reports are often sent as e-mails. The report is either written in the body of the e-mail, or it is attached to the e-mail as a memo, a letter, or PowerPoint slides. For example, the progress report in Figure 8.5 (p. 236) is sent from an employee to her manager. It is perhaps more formal than the average e-mail (i.e., it has an introduction, a body with headings, and a conclusion). Increasingly, businesses encourage employees to upload reports to the company intranet or FTP site, especially for team-based writing. Firms provide software that enables workers to update information about their activities, progress on a project, and other information about their on-the-job performance.

LETTER FORMAT. Use letter format for short (usually eight or fewer pages) informal reports addressed outside an organization. Prepared using a company's letterhead, a letter report, like the one in Figure 8.2, contains a date, inside address, salutation, and complimentary close. Although they may carry information similar to that found in correspondence, letter reports usually are longer and show more careful organization than most letters. They also include headings.

MEMO FORMAT. For short informal reports that stay within organizations, memo format is appropriate. Memo reports begin with essential background information, using standard headings: *Date*, *To*, *From*, and *Subject*, as shown in the information report in Figure 8.4 (p. 235) and the recommendation report in Figure 8.6 (p. 238). Like letter reports, memo reports differ from regular memos in length, use of headings,

FIGURE 8.2 Informational Report: E-Mail Cover with Letter Attachment

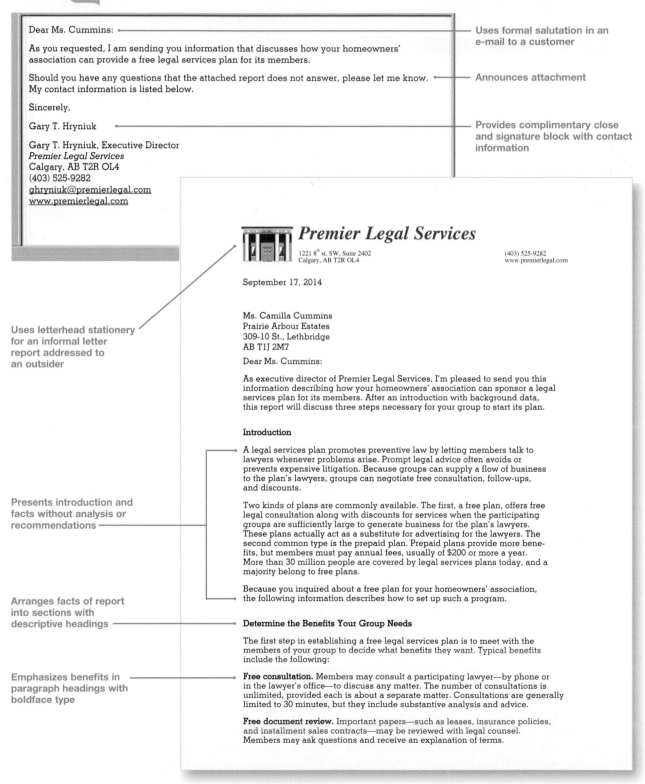

Dear Ms. Cummins:

As you requested, I am sending you information that discusses how your homeowners' association can provide a free legal services plan for its members.

Should you have any questions that the attached report does not answer, please let me know. My contact information is listed below.

Sincerely,

Gary T. Hryniuk

Gary T. Hryniuk, Executive Director
Premier Legal Services
Calgary, AB T2R OL4
(403) 525-9282
ghryniuk@premierlegal.com
www.premierlegal.com

Uses formal salutation in an e-mail to a customer

Announces attachment

Provides complimentary close and signature block with contact information

Uses letterhead stationery for an informal letter report addressed to an outsider

Premier Legal Services

1221 8th st. SW, Suite 2402
Calgary, AB T2R OL4

(403) 525-9282
www.premierlegal.com

September 17, 2014

Ms. Camilla Cummins
Prairie Arbour Estates
309-10 St., Lethbridge
AB T1J 2M7

Dear Ms. Cummins:

As executive director of Premier Legal Services, I'm pleased to send you this information describing how your homeowners' association can sponsor a legal services plan for its members. After an introduction with background data, this report will discuss three steps necessary for your group to start its plan.

Introduction

Presents introduction and facts without analysis or recommendations

A legal services plan promotes preventive law by letting members talk to lawyers whenever problems arise. Prompt legal advice often avoids or prevents expensive litigation. Because groups can supply a flow of business to the plan's lawyers, groups can negotiate free consultation, follow-ups, and discounts.

Two kinds of plans are commonly available. The first, a free plan, offers free legal consultation along with discounts for services when the participating groups are sufficiently large to generate business for the plan's lawyers. These plans actually act as a substitute for advertising for the lawyers. The second common type is the prepaid plan. Prepaid plans provide more benefits, but members must pay annual fees, usually of $200 or more a year. More than 30 million people are covered by legal services plans today, and a majority belong to free plans.

Arranges facts of report into sections with descriptive headings

Because you inquired about a free plan for your homeowners' association, the following information describes how to set up such a program.

Determine the Benefits Your Group Needs

The first step in establishing a free legal services plan is to meet with the members of your group to decide what benefits they want. Typical benefits include the following:

Emphasizes benefits in paragraph headings with boldface type

Free consultation. Members may consult a participating lawyer—by phone or in the lawyer's office—to discuss any matter. The number of consultations is unlimited, provided each is about a separate matter. Consultations are generally limited to 30 minutes, but they include substantive analysis and advice.

Free document review. Important papers—such as leases, insurance policies, and installment sales contracts—may be reviewed with legal counsel. Members may ask questions and receive an explanation of terms.

FIGURE 8.2 (Continued)

Identifies second and succeeding pages with headings

Uses parallel side headings for consistency and readability

Includes complimentary close and signature

Ms. Camilla Cummins   Page 2   September 17, 2014

Discount on additional services. For more complex matters, participating lawyers will charge members 75 percent of the lawyer's normal fee. However, some organizations choose to charge a flat fee for commonly needed services.

Select the Lawyers for Your Plan

Groups with geographically concentrated memberships have an advantage in forming legal plans. These groups can limit the number of participating lawyers and yet provide adequate service. Generally, smaller panels of lawyers are advantageous.

Assemble a list of candidates, inviting them to apply. The best way to compare prices is to have candidates submit their fees. Your group can then compare fee schedules and select the lowest bidder, if price is important. Arrange to interview lawyers in their offices.

After selecting a lawyer or a panel, sign a contract. The contract should include the reason for the plan, what the lawyer agrees to do, what the group agrees to do, how each side can end the contract, and the signature of both parties. You may also wish to include references to malpractice insurance, assurance that the group will not interfere with the lawyer–client relationship, an evaluation form, a grievance procedure, and responsibility for government filings.

Publicize the Plan to Your Members

Members won't use a plan if they don't know about it, and a plan will not be successful if it is unused. Publicity must be vocal and ongoing. Announce it in newsletters, flyers, meetings, and on bulletin boards.

Persistence is the key. All too frequently, leaders of an organization assume that a single announcement is all that's needed. They expect members to see the value of the plan and remember that it is available. Most organization members, though, are not as involved as the leadership. Therefore, it takes more publicity than the leadership usually expects in order to reach and maintain the desired level of awareness.

Summary

A successful free legal services plan involves designing a program, choosing the lawyers, and publicizing the plan. To learn more about these steps or to order a $45 how-to manual, call me at (403) 525-9282.

Sincerely,

Gary T. Hryniuk

Gary T. Hryniuk
Executive Director

GTR:pas

Tips for Letter Reports
- Use letter format for short informal reports sent to outsiders.
- Organize the facts into divisions with consistent headings.
- Single-space the body.
- Double-space between paragraphs.
- Leave two blank lines above each side heading, if space allows.
- Create side margins of 1 to 1.25 inches.
- Start the date 2 inches from the top or one blank line below the last line of the letterhead.
- Add a second-page heading, if necessary, consisting of the addressee's name, the page number, and the date.

and deliberate organization. Note that the writer in Figure 8.2 attaches the report to an e-mail message, which introduces the attachment.

POWERPOINT FORMAT. Because reports are often presented within companies to managers and other employees, it has become quite common today for informal internal reports to be created in PowerPoint. During a presentation, the PowerPoint slides are used to help the presenter discuss the report. The presenter can also choose to e-mail or otherwise distribute the PowerPoint "deck" (i.e., slide file) before the presentation or afterwards.

TEMPLATE FORMAT. Templates (either company-produced or available online, for example, from Microsoft Word) are often used for repetitive data, such as monthly sales reports, performance appraisals, merchandise inventories, expense claims, and personnel and financial reports. Standardized headings in these templates save time for the writer. Templates also make similar information easy to locate and ensure that all necessary information is provided.

MANUSCRIPT FORMAT. For longer, more formal reports, use manuscript format. These reports are usually printed on plain paper instead of letterhead stationery or memo forms. They begin with a title followed by systematically displayed headings and subheadings. You will see examples of proposals and formal reports using manuscript format in Chapter 9.

Report Delivery

<aside>
Written reports can be delivered in person, by mail, or electronically.
</aside>

Once reports are written, you must decide what channel to use to deliver them to your readers. Written business reports can be delivered in the following ways:

BY E-MAIL. Reports in any format can be attached to an e-mail (or sometimes even drafted in the body of the message). When using this channel, you will introduce the report and refer clearly to the attachment in the body of your e-mail. Figure 8.7 (p. 241) shows an e-mail that announces the enclosed feasibility report and goes to a recipient within the organization. Other figures in this chapter also show a report attached to an e-mail cover.

ONLINE. You might choose to make your report available online. Many report writers today are making their reports available to their readers on the Web. One common method for doing this involves saving the report as a Portable Document Format (PDF) file and then uploading it to the company's Web site, FTP site, intranet, or some form of "cloud" storage system. This is an inexpensive method of delivery and allows an unlimited number of readers access to the report. If the report contains sensitive or confidential information, access to the document can be password protected. Within companies, the move to cloud computing (where memory is located on a server accessible by multiple employees, not on one employee's laptop or desktop), means that reports can be stored in an employee's cloud and made visible to other employees.

IN PERSON. If you are located close to the reader, deliver your report in person. This delivery method works especially well when you would like to comment on the report or clarify its purpose. Delivering a report in person also makes the report seem more important or urgent.

BY MAIL. In a few instances, hard-copy reports may still be delivered by mail. You can send your reports by interoffice mail, Canada Post, or a commercial delivery service such as UPS or FedEx.

<aside>
OFFICE INSIDER

A nonprofit organization polled 120 businesses to find out what type of writing they required of their employees. More than half of the business leaders responded that they "frequently" or "almost always" produce technical reports (59 percent), formal reports (62 percent), and memos and correspondence (70 percent).
</aside>

Guidelines for Writing Informal Reports

Your natural tendency in preparing a report may be to sit down and begin writing immediately. If you follow this urge, however, you will very likely have to rewrite or even start again. Reports take planning, beginning with defining the project and gathering data. The following guidelines will help you plan your project.

Define the Project

Begin the process of report writing by defining your project. Do this by stating, in writing, the problem to be solved, the question to be answered, or the task to

Chapter 08: Informal Reports

be completed. Then, move on to writing a statement of purpose. Ask yourself this question: Am I writing this report to inform, to analyze, to solve a problem, or to persuade? The answer should be a clear, accurate statement identifying your purpose—why you are writing the report. In informal reports the statement of purpose may be only one sentence; that sentence usually becomes part of the introduction. Notice how the following introductory statement describes the purpose of the report:

> This report presents information regarding professional development activities coordinated and supervised by the Human Resources Department between the first of the year and the present.

After writing a statement of purpose, analyze who will read your report. If your report is intended for your immediate supervisors and they are supportive of your project, you need not include extensive details, historical development, definition of terms, or persuasion. Other readers, however, may require background information and persuasive strategies.

The expected audience for your report influences your writing style, research method, vocabulary, areas of emphasis, and communication strategy. Remember, too, that your audience may consist of more than one set of readers. Reports are often distributed to secondary readers who may need more details than the primary reader.

Begin a report by being able to state the problem to be solved, question to be answered, or task to be completed. Then, draft a statement of purpose. Be able to explain why you are writing the report.

Gather Data

A professional report is based on solid, accurate, verifiable facts. Typical sources of factual information for informal reports include (1) company records; (2) observation; (3) surveys, questionnaires, and inventories; (4) interviews; and (5) secondary research.

The facts for reports are often obtained from company records, observation, surveys, interviews, and secondary research.

COMPANY RECORDS. Many business-related reports begin with an analysis of company files. From them you can observe past performance and methods used to solve previous problems. You can collect pertinent facts that will help determine a course of action. For example, if a telecommunications company is interested in revamping the design of the bills it sends to customers, the project manager assigned to this task would want to gather examples of previous bill designs to ensure that improvements are made and old designs aren't reused.

OBSERVATION. Another logical source of data for many problems lies in personal observation and experience. For example, if you were writing a report on the need for additional computer equipment, you might observe how much the current equipment is being used and for what purpose.

SURVEYS, QUESTIONNAIRES, AND INVENTORIES. Primary data from groups of people can be collected most efficiently and economically by using surveys, questionnaires, and inventories. For example, if you were part of a committee investigating the success of a campus recycling program, you might begin by using a questionnaire to survey use of the program by students and faculty. You might also do some informal telephoning to see if departments on campus know about the program and are using it.

INTERVIEWS. Talking with individuals directly concerned with the problem produces excellent primary information. Interviews also allow for one-on-one communication, thus giving you an opportunity to explain your questions and ideas in eliciting the most accurate information. For example, a food company adding a new low-fat organic bar to its nutrition bar line would solicit interview or focus-group feedback before releasing the new product to the market. Questions posed to people

paid to taste the sample bar might include "Did you find the bar tasty? Nutritious? Healthy?" and "Did you find the packaging attractive? Easy to open?"

SECONDARY RESEARCH. You will probably be interested in finding examples from other organizations that shed light on the problem identified in your report. For example, an automobile parts manufacturer eager to drum up new business in the hybrid and electric vehicle market could do in-house research or pay for professional research into hybrid and electric vehicle manufacturing. Hundreds of articles on this topic are available electronically through online library databases and other online resources. From a home, office, or library computer, you can obtain access to vast amounts of information provided by governments, newspapers, magazines, and companies from all over the world. Also, you may decide to use the Internet to conduct secondary research on your topic. Using search engines such as Google and Google Scholar will also yield hundreds of results on any topic.

When doing secondary research on the Internet, an extra step must be taken that isn't necessary when using library databases. You need to verify the accuracy of your sources. Because the Internet is a public space where anyone can post information, you must be able to separate credible, useful information from opinion and non-credible sources. You do this by asking yourself a number of questions, which are discussed in more detail in the Communication Workshop at the end of this chapter.

Use an Appropriate Writing Style

Like other business messages, reports can range from informal to formal, depending on their purpose, audience, and setting. Research reports from consultants to their clients tend to be rather formal. Such reports must project an impression of objectivity, authority, and impartiality. But a report to your boss describing a trip to a conference (as in Figure 8.4 on p. 235) would probably have informal elements. You can see the differences between formal and informal styles in Figure 8.3.

FIGURE 8.3 Report-Writing Styles

	INFORMAL WRITING STYLE	FORMAL WRITING STYLE
Use for . . .	Reports for familiar audiences Non-controversial reports Most reports for company insiders	Theses Research studies Controversial or complex reports (especially to outsiders)
Effect is . . .	Feeling of warmth, personal involvement, closeness	Impression of objectivity, accuracy, professionalism, fairness Distance created between writer and reader
Characteristics are . . .	Use of first-person pronouns (*I, we, me, my, us, our*) Use of contractions (*can't, don't*) Emphasis on active-voice verbs (*I conducted the study*) Shorter sentences; familiar words Occasional use of humour, metaphors Occasional use of colourful speech Acceptance of author's opinions and ideas	Absence of first-person pronouns; use of third-person (*the researcher, the writer*) Absence of contractions (*cannot, do not*) Use of passive-voice verbs (*the study was conducted*) Complex sentences; long words Absence of humour and figures of speech Reduced use of colourful adjectives and adverbs Elimination of "editorializing" (author's opinions, perceptions)

In this chapter we are most concerned with an informal writing style. Your informal reports will probably be written for familiar audiences and involve non-controversial topics. You may use first-person pronouns (*I, we, me, my, us, our*) and contractions (*I'm, we'll*). You'll emphasize active-voice verbs and strive for shorter sentences using familiar words.

Whether you choose a formal or informal writing style, remember to apply the writing techniques you have learned in earlier chapters. The same techniques you have been using to compose effective memos, letters, and e-mails apply to developing outstanding reports. Business reports must be clear and concise. They should be written using topic sentences, support sentences, and transitional expressions to build coherence. Avoid wordiness, outdated expressions, slang, jargon, and clichés in your reports. Finally, proofread all business reports carefully to make sure that they contain no errors in spelling, grammar, punctuation, names and numbers, or format.

Be Objective

Reports are convincing only when the facts are believable and the writer is credible. You can build credibility in a number of ways:

- **Present both sides of an issue.** Even if you favour one possibility, discuss both sides and show through logical reasoning why your position is superior. Remain impartial, letting the facts prove your point.
- **Separate fact from opinion.** Suppose a manager wrote *We are rapidly becoming the go-to division within the organization.* This opinion is difficult to prove, and it may damage the credibility of the writer. A more convincing statement might

be *Our closing rate has increased 12 percent over the past year, and we've been cited three times in* Marketing *magazine in the past 18 months.* After you have made a claim or presented an important statement in a report, ask yourself *Is this a verifiable fact?* If the answer is no, rephrase your statement to make it sound more reasonable.

- **Be sensitive and moderate in your choice of language.** Don't exaggerate. Instead of saying *most people think . . .,* it might be more accurate to say *Some people think . . . .* Better yet, use specific figures such as *Sixty percent of employees agree . . . .* Also avoid using labels and slanted expressions. Calling someone a *loser,* a *control freak,* or an *elitist* demonstrates bias. If readers suspect that a writer is prejudiced, they may discount the entire argument.

- **Cite sources.** Tell your readers where the information came from. For example, *In a recent conference call with sector analyst Rachna Jayasingh, October 15, she mentioned . . .,* or The Wall Street Journal *(August 10, p. 40) reports that . . . .* By referring to respected sources, you lend authority and credibility to your statements. Your words become more believable and your argument more convincing. In Chapter 9 you will learn how to document your sources properly.

Use Headings Effectively

Functional headings show the outline of a report; talking headings provide more information.

Headings are helpful to both the report reader and the writer. For the reader they serve as an outline of the text, highlighting major ideas and categories. They also act as guides for locating facts and pointing the way through the text. Moreover, headings provide resting points for the mind and for the eye, breaking up large chunks of text into manageable and inviting segments. For the writer, headings force organization of the data into meaningful blocks.

You may choose functional or talking headings. Functional headings describe the function of the section (such as *Introduction, Discussion of Findings,* and *Summary*) and help the writer outline a report; they are used in the progress report shown in Figure 8.5 (p. 236). Talking headings, on the other hand, (such as *Students Perplexed by Shortage of Parking* or *Short-Term Parking Solutions*) tell a story about the section, and provide more information to the reader. Many of the examples in this chapter use functional headings for the purpose of instruction. To provide even greater clarity, you can make headings both functional and descriptive, such as *Recommendations: Shuttle and New Structures.* Whether your headings are talking or functional, keep them brief and clear. Here are general tips on displaying headings effectively:

- **Consistency.** The cardinal rule of headings is that they should be consistent. In other words, don't use informational headings in three of four cases and a talking heading in the fourth case. Or, don't use bolded headings for 80 percent of your report and underlined headings for the other 20 percent.
- **Strive for parallel construction.** Use balanced expressions such as *Direct Costs* and *Hidden Costs* rather than *Direct Costs* and *Costs Unaccounted For.*
- **Use only short first- and second-level headings.** Many short business reports contain only one or two levels of headings. For such reports use first-level headings (centred, bolded) and/or second-level headings (flush left, bolded). See Figure 9.4 in the next chapter for examples of how such headings look on the page.
- **Capitalize and underline carefully.** Most writers use all capital letters (without underlines) for main titles, such as the report, chapter, and unit titles. For first- and second-level headings, they capitalize only the first letter of main words. For additional emphasis, they use a bold font.
- **Keep headings short but clear.** Try to make your headings brief (no more than eight words) but understandable. Experiment with headings that concisely tell who, what, when, where, and why.

- **Don't enclose headings in quotation marks.** Quotation marks are appropriate only for marking quoted words or words used in a special sense, such as slang. They are unnecessary in headings.
- **Don't use headings as antecedents for pronouns such as *this, that, these, and those*.** For example, when the heading reads *Fund Highlights*, don't begin the following sentence with *These have been discussed earlier, but it's worth summarizing once again . . . .*

Six Kinds of Informal Reports

You are about to examine six types of informal reports frequently written in business. In many instances the boundaries of the types overlap; distinctions are not always clear-cut. Individual situations, goals, and needs may make one report take on some characteristics of a report in another category. Still, these general types, presented here in a brief overview, are helpful to beginning writers. The reports will be illustrated and discussed in more detail below.

> Reports that provide data are informational; reports that draw conclusions and make recommendations are analytical.

- **Information reports.** Reports that collect and organize information are informative or investigative. They may record routine activities such as daily, weekly, and monthly reports of sales or profits. They may investigate options, performance, or equipment. Although they provide information, they do not analyze that information.
- **Progress reports.** Progress reports monitor unusual or non-routine activities. For example, progress reports would keep management informed about a committee's preparations for a trade show 14 months from now. Such reports usually answer three questions: (1) Is the project on schedule? (2) Are corrective measures needed? (3) What activities are next?
- **Justification/recommendation reports.** Recommendation and justification reports are similar to information reports in that they present information. However, they offer analysis in addition to data. They attempt to solve problems by evaluating options and offering recommendations. Usually these reports revolve around a significant company decision.
- **Feasibility reports.** When a company or organization must decide whether to proceed with a plan of action based on a previously accepted recommendation, it may require a feasibility report that establishes how possible the plan is. For example, a company has decided to redesign its Web site, but how feasible is it to have the redesign accomplished in six months' time? A feasibility report would examine the practicality of implementing the recommendation or proposal.
- **Summary reports.** A summary condenses the primary ideas, conclusions, and recommendations of a longer report or publication. Employees may be asked to write summaries of technical or research reports. Students may be asked to write summaries of periodical articles or books to sharpen their writing skills.
- **Minutes of meetings.** A record of the proceedings and action points of a meeting is called "the minutes." Although informal business meetings today take place without minutes being recorded, many companies, organizations, clubs, committees, and boards still require minutes to be recorded. The person delegated to take notes at a meeting usually turns them into the minutes, distributes them to the participants after the meeting, asks for revisions, and then files the report. You'll find more information on meetings in Chapter 10.

Information Reports

Writers of information reports provide information without drawing conclusions or making recommendations. You saw this earlier in Figure 8.2. Some information reports are highly standardized, such as police reports, hospital admittance reports, monthly sales reports, or statistical reports on government program use. Many of these are fill-in reports using templates for recurring data and situations. Other information reports are more personalized, as illustrated in Figure 8.4 (p. 235). They often include these sections:

INTRODUCTION. The introduction to an information report may be called *Introduction* or *Background*. In this section do the following: (1) explain why you are writing, (2) describe what methods and sources were used to gather information and why they are credible, (3) provide any special background information that may be necessary, (4) give the purpose of the report, if known, and (5) offer a preview of your findings. You'll notice in Figure 8.4 that not all five of these criteria are met, nor is a heading included, because it is a short, informal information report. However, if you were writing an information report for a client in manuscript format, you would use the heading *Introduction* and try to fit in all five criteria.

FINDINGS. The findings section of a report may also be called *Observations, Facts, Results,* or *Discussion*. Important points to consider in this section are organization and display. Consider one of these methods of organization: (1) chronological, (2) alphabetical, (3) topical, or (4) most important to least important. You'll notice that in Figure 8.4, the writer uses a topical method of organization, with the three topics being the booth, trends, and customers/prospects.

To display the findings effectively, number paragraphs, underline or boldface key words, or use other graphic highlighting methods such as bullets. Be sure that words used as headings are parallel in structure. If the findings require elaboration, either include this discussion with each segment of the findings or place it in a separate section entitled *Discussion*.

SUMMARY. A summary section is optional. If it is included, use it to summarize your findings objectively and impartially, or to set the stage for the report that follows. The information report shown in Figure 8.4 summarizes the size and scope of the show attended, then previews the topics that will be covered in the body of the report.

Notice how easy this information report is to read. Short paragraphs, ample use of graphic highlighting (i.e. headings), white space, and concise writing all contribute to improved readability.

Progress Reports

Continuing projects often require progress reports to describe their status. These reports may be external (telling customers how their projects are advancing) or internal (informing management of the status of activities). Progress reports typically follow this development strategy:

- The purpose and nature of the project
- A complete summary of the work already completed
- A thorough description of work currently in progress, including personnel, methods, and obstacles, as well as attempts to remedy obstacles
- A forecast of future activities in relation to the scheduled completion date, including recommendations and requests

In Figure 8.5 Avrom Gil explains the market research project being done on the impact of a recent industry/consumer show. He begins with a statement summarizing the research project in relation to the expected completion date. He then updates the client with a brief summary of the project's progress. He emphasizes the present status of the project and offers some preliminary data to build interest, and concludes by describing the next steps to be taken.

FIGURE 8.4 Informational Report: E-Mail Cover With Memo Attachment

Hi, Dave!

As you requested, I am sending you the attached trip report describing my amazing experiences at the largest IT trade show in the world, the CeBIT.

Thank you for the opportunity. I networked with lots of people and, yes, I had a blast.

Cheers,
Prakash

Prakash Kohli, Developer
Future Engine, Inc.
408.532.3434 Ext. 811
pkohli@future-engine.com
www.future-engine.com

Uses informal form of address

Announces attachment

Uses informal yet professional language

Includes complimentary close and signature block

FUTURE ENGINE, INC.
MEMORANDUM

Date: March 16, 2015

To: David Wong, IT Director

From: Prakash Kohli, Developer PK

Subject: Trip Report from the CeBIT Trade Show in Hannover, Germany

Identifies the event

As you know, I attended the huge CeBIT computer show in Hannover on March 4–9. CeBIT runs for six days and attracts almost 500,000 visitors from Germany, Europe, and all over the world to the famed Hannover fairgrounds. It features 27 halls full of technology and people. If you've been to Comdex Las Vegas in the fall, think of a show that is easily five times larger. Let me describe our booth, overall trends, and the contacts I made in Hannover.

Focuses on three main points

Our Booth at the Fair

Our Future Engine booth spanned two floors. The ground floor had a theater with large screen, demonstration stations, and partners showing their products and services. Upstairs we had tables and chairs for business meetings, press interviews, food, and drinks—along with a cooking area and a dishwasher. Because no one has time to get food elsewhere, we ate in the booth.

Hot Tech Trends

Summarizes key information

The top story at this year's CeBIT was Green IT. The expo management decided to spotlight a range of topics dealing with Green IT, showcasing many approaches in the Green IT Village in Hall 9. The main focus centered on highly energy-efficient solutions and power-saving technologies and their contribution to climate protection. *Green IT* is the big buzzword now and was even dubbed the "Megatrend of this expo" by the organizer. Only the future will tell whether Green IT will be able to spawn attractive new business areas.

Customers and Prospects

CeBIT is a fantastic way to connect with customers and prospects. Sometimes it's a way of meeting people you only knew virtually. In this case, we had three fans of our Internetpakt.com podcast visit us at the booth: Jürgen Schmidt, Karin Richter, and Peter Jahn of MEGAFunk. All three came in our white FE T-Shirts, which could only be rewarded with new black Internetpakt.com T-Shirts. All in all, we made about 600 contacts and have 50 solid leads. The visit was definitely worthwhile and will pay off very soon.

Highlights the value of the trip

In closing, this was probably one of the best conference experiences I've ever had. Customers and partners like FE; they are excited about our technology, and they want more. Some know us because of our software solutions and were surprised to learn that we sell hardware, too (this is a good sign). All want us to grow and gain in influence.

Shows appreciation and mentions expenses

Check out my CeBIT photo gallery on Flickr for some more impressions of our booth at CeBIT with comments. Thank you for giving me the opportunity to network and to experience one of the biggest trade shows in the business. My itemized expenses and receipts are attached.

Tips for Trip Reports
- Use memo format for short informal reports sent within the organization.
- Identify the event (exact date, name, and location) and preview the topics to be discussed.
- Summarize in the body three to five main points that might benefit the reader.
- Itemize your expenses, if requested, on a separate sheet. Mention this in the report.
- Close by expressing appreciation, suggesting action to be taken, or synthesizing the value of the trip or event.

FIGURE 8.5 Progress Report

Hi Lina,

Please find attached the requested progress report.

If you have any questions, please give me a call.

Best,
Avrom

Short, professional e-mail introduces attached progress report.

PROGRESS OF CANDESIGN 2016 RESEARCH PROJECT

To: ltersigni@canevent.ca
From: agil@westwindresearch.ca
Subject: Progress of CanDesign 2016 Research Project

[attachment]

Dear Ms. Tersigni,

Market research on the impact of CanDesign 2015 and implications for CanDesign 2016 has entered the analysis stage (phase 3). We are on schedule, based on our original project plan, and our final report will be available to you after February 27, 2015.

Section describes completed work concisely

Accomplished so far

We have completed the first two phases of the project. Phase 1 (completed February 5, 2015) involved designing the survey questionnaire. Phase 2 (completed February 19, 2015) involved distributing the questionnaire to two groups: paid attendees of CanDesign 2015 and industry professionals, as well as collecting results. Over 700 completed questionnaires have been received to date (85% of target).

Section discusses current activities.

Current work

My team is analyzing the results of the questionnaire. Early results show high satisfaction levels (~80%) among attendees, but a small drop in satisfaction among industry professionals (~72%) compared with (~75% last year). In addition, a significant number of both attendees and professionals (~25% and ~27%) express dissatisfaction with the show Web site, especially its navigation design. We will be correlating 2015 results to both 2013 and 2014 results in hopes of showing trends.

Section lists tasks still to be completed.

Still to come

Before submitting our final report, we will need to perform the rest of our analysis and correlations. Also, we are convening two focus groups (as per project plan) to see whether one-on-one contact with attendees and industry professionals confirms the results of the questionnaires.

One unresolved issue is renumeration for focus group attendees. Before we invite attendees, I will need confirmation about what we can offer attendees at our focus groups. I will be in touch later today to speak with you about this.

We are largely on track for the completion of this market research project and look forward to sharing results with you on or after February 27.

Tips for Writing Progress Reports
- Identify the purpose and the nature of the project immediately.
- Supply background information only if the reader must be educated.
- Describe the work completed.
- Discuss the work in progress, including personnel, activities, methods, and locations.
- Identify problems and possible remedies.
- Consider future activities.
- Close by giving the expected date of completion.

Some business communicators use progress reports to do more than merely report progress. These reports can also be used to offer ideas and suggest possibilities. Let's say you are reporting on the progress of redesigning the company Web site. You might suggest a different way to handle customer responses. Instead of making an official recommendation, which might be rejected, you can lay the foundation for a change within your progress report. Progress reports can also be used to build the image of a dedicated, conscientious employee.

Justification/Recommendation Reports

Both managers and employees must occasionally write reports that justify or recommend something, such as buying equipment, changing a procedure, hiring an employee, consolidating departments, or investing funds. Large organizations sometimes prescribe how these reports should be organized; they use forms of templates with conventional headings. At other times, such reports are not standardized. For example, an employee takes it upon himself to write a report suggesting improvements in telephone customer service because he feels strongly about it. When you are free to select an organizational plan yourself, however, let your audience and topic determine your choice of direct or indirect structure.

> Justification/recommendation reports analyze a problem, discuss options, and present a recommendation, solution, or action to be taken.

For non-sensitive topics and recommendations that will be agreeable to readers, you can organize directly according to the following sequence:

- In the introduction identify the problem or need briefly.
- Announce the recommendation, solution, or action concisely and with action verbs.
- Discuss pros, cons, and costs. Explain more fully the benefits of the recommendation or steps to be taken to solve the problem.
- Conclude with a summary specifying the recommendation and action to be taken.

Lara Brown, an executive assistant at a large petroleum and mining company in Calgary, applied the preceding process in writing the recommendation report shown in Figure 8.6. Her boss, the director of Human Resources, asked her to investigate ways to persuade employees to quit smoking. Lara explained that the company had banned smoking many years ago inside the buildings but never tried very hard to get smokers to actually kick the habit. Lara's job was to gather information about the problem and learn how other companies have helped workers stop smoking. The report would go to her boss, but Lara knew he would pass it along to the management council for approval.

If the report were just for her boss, Lara would put her recommendation right up front because she was sure he would support it. But the management council is another story. The managers need to be persuaded because of the costs involved— and because some of them are smokers. Therefore, Lara put the alternative she favoured last. To gain credibility, Lara footnoted her sources. She had enough material for a ten-page report, but she kept it to two pages to conform to her company's report policy.

INDIRECT STRATEGY. When a reader may oppose a recommendation or when circumstances suggest caution, do not rush to reveal your recommendation. Consider using the following sequence for an indirect approach to your recommendations:

- Refer to the problem in general terms, not to your recommendation, in the subject line.
- Describe the problem or need your recommendation addresses. Use specific examples, supporting statistics, and authoritative quotes to lend credibility to the seriousness of the problem.

Chapter 08: Informal Reports

- Discuss alternative solutions, beginning with the least likely to succeed.
- Present the most promising alternative (your recommendation) last.
- Show how the advantages of your recommendation outweigh its disadvantages.
- Summarize your recommendation. If appropriate, specify the action it requires.
- Ask for authorization to proceed, if necessary.

Feasibility Reports

Feasibility reports examine the practicality and advisability of following a course of action. They answer this question: Will this plan or proposal work? Feasibility reports are typically internal reports written to advise on matters such as consolidating departments, offering a wellness program to employees, or hiring an outside firm to handle a company's accounting or computing operations. These

> Feasibility reports analyze whether a proposal or plan will work.

FIGURE 8.6 Justification/Recommendation Report, Direct Strategy, APA Style

Date: October 11, 2015

To: Gordon McClure, Director, Human Resources

From: Lara Brown, Executive Assistant *LB*

Subject: Smoking Cessation Programs for Employees

At your request, I have examined measures that encourage employees to quit smoking. As company records show, approximately 23 percent of our employees still smoke, despite the antismoking and clean-air policies we adopted in 2014. To collect data for this report, I studied professional and government publications; I also inquired at companies and clinics about stop-smoking programs.

This report presents data describing the significance of the problem, three alternative solutions, and a recommendation based on my investigation.

Significance of Problem: Health Care and Productivity Losses

Employees who smoke are costly to any organization. The following statistics show the effects of smoking for workers and for organizations:

- Absenteeism is 40 to 50 percent greater among smoking employees.
- Accidents are two to three times greater among smokers.
- Bronchitis, lung and heart disease, cancer, and early death are more frequent among smokers (Arhelger, 2012, p. 4).

Although our clean-air policy prohibits smoking in the building, shop, and office, we have done little to encourage employees to stop smoking. Many workers still go outside to smoke at lunch and breaks. Other companies have been far more proactive in their attempts to stop employee smoking. Many companies have found that persuading employees to stop smoking was a decisive factor in reducing their health insurance premiums. Following is a discussion of three common stop-smoking measures tried by other companies, along with a projected cost factor for each (Rindfleisch, 2012, p. 4).

Alternative 1: Literature and Events

The least expensive and easiest stop-smoking measure involves the distribution of literature, such as "The Ten-Step Plan" from Smokefree Enterprises and government pamphlets citing smoking dangers. Some companies have also sponsored events such as the Great Canadian Smoke-Out, a one-day occasion intended to develop group spirit in spurring smokers to quit. "Studies show, however," says one expert, "that literature and company-sponsored events have little permanent effect in helping smokers quit" (Mendel, 2011, p. 108).

    Cost: Negligible

Avoids revealing recommendation immediately

Uses headings that combine function and description

Introduces purpose of report, tells method of data collection, and previews organization

Documents data sources for credibility; uses APA style citing author and year in the text

FIGURE **8.6** *(Continued)*

Gordon McClure   October 11, 2015   Page 2

Alternative 2: Stop-Smoking Programs Outside the Workplace

Local clinics provide treatment programs in classes at their centers. Here in Calgary we have the Smokers' Treatment Centre, ACC Motivation Centre, and New-Choice Program for Stopping Smoking. These behaviour-modification stop-smoking programs are acknowledged to be more effective than literature distribution or incentive programs. However, studies of companies using off-workplace programs show that many employees fail to attend regularly and do not complete the programs.

> Cost: $1,200 per employee, three-month individual program ●————— **Highlights costs for**
> (Your-Choice Program)   **easy comparison**
> $900 per employee, three-month group session

Alternative 3: Stop-Smoking Programs at the Workplace

Many clinics offer workplace programs with counsellors meeting employees in ●————— **Arranges alternatives** company conference rooms. These programs have the advantage of keeping a **so that most effective** firm's employees together so that they develop a group spirit and exert pressure **is last** on each other to succeed. The most successful programs are on company premises and also on company time. Employees participating in such programs had a 72 percent greater success record than employees attending the same stop-smoking program at an outside clinic (Honda, 2011, p. 35). A disadvantage of this arrangement, of course, is lost work time—amounting to about two hours a week for three months.

> Cost: $900 per employee, two hours per week of release time for three
> months

Conclusions and Recommendation ●————— **Summarizes findings**
                                          and ends with specific
                                          recommendation

Smokers require discipline, counselling, and professional assistance to kick the nicotine habit, as explained at the Canadian Cancer Society Web site ("Guide to Quitting Smoking," 2012). Workplace stop-smoking programs on company time are more effective than literature, incentives, and off-workplace programs. If our goal is to reduce health care costs and lead our employees to healthful lives, we should invest in a workplace stop-smoking program with release time for smokers. Although the program temporarily reduces productivity, we can expect to recapture that loss in lower health care premiums and healthier employees.

Therefore, I recommend that we begin a stop-smoking treatment program on ●————— **Reveals recommendation** company premises with two hours per week of release time for participants for **only after discussing all** three months. **alternatives**

Lists all references ————● Gordon McClure   October 11, 2015   Page 3
in APA Style   **References**

Magazine ————————● Arhelger, Z. (2012, November 5). The end of smoking. *Canadian Business*,
                                    pp. 3–8.

Web site article ————————● Guide to quitting smoking. (2012, October 17). Retrieved from the Canadian
                                    Cancer Society Web site: http://www.cancer.ca

Journal article, database ————————● Honda, E. M. (2011) Managing anti-smoking campaigns: The case for company
                                    programs. *Management Quarterly 32*(2), 29–47. Retrieved from
                                    http://search.ebscohost.com/

Book ————————● Mendel, I. A. (2011) *The puff stops here*. Toronto: Science Publications.

Newspaper article ————————● Rindfleisch, T. (2012, December 4). Smoke-free workplaces can help smokers
                                    quit, expert says. *Evening Chronicle*, p. 4.

Tips for Memo Reports
- Use memo format for short (eight or fewer pages) informal reports within an organization.
- Create side margins of 1 to 1.25 inches.
- Start the date 2 inches from the top or 1 blank line below the last line of the letterhead.
- Sign your initials on the *From* line.
- Use an informal, conversational style.
- For a receptive audience, put recommendations first.
- For an unreceptive audience, put recommendations last.

reports may also be written by consultants called in to investigate a problem. The focus in these reports is on the decision: stopping or proceeding with the proposal. Since your role is not to persuade the reader to accept the decision, you'll want to present the decision immediately. In writing feasibility reports, consider this plan:

- Announce your decision immediately.
- Describe the background and problem necessitating the proposal.
- Discuss the benefits of the proposal.
- Describe any problems that may result.
- Calculate the costs associated with the proposal, if appropriate.
- Show the time frame necessary for implementation of the proposal.

Elizabeth Webb, customer service manager for a large insurance company in London, Ontario, wrote the feasibility report shown in Figure 8.7. Because her company had been losing customer service reps (CSRs) after they were trained, she talked with the vice president about the problem. He didn't want her to take time away from her job to investigate what other companies were doing to retain their CSRs. Instead, he suggested that they hire a consultant to investigate. The vice president then wanted to know whether the consultant's plan was feasible. Although Elizabeth's report is only one page long, it provides all the necessary information: background, benefits, problems, costs, and time frame.

Summary Reports

> A summary condenses the primary ideas, conclusions, and recommendations of a longer publication.

In today's knowledge economy, information is what drives organizations. Information is important because without it, business decisions cannot be made. Because there is a huge amount of information available today on any given topic (e.g., the millions of pages of Internet material), people who make decisions don't always have the time to read and review all the information on a particular problem, issue, or topic. Therefore, decision makers need the essential elements of an issue or problem presented in a short, logical, easy-to-understand format that helps them quickly grasp what's vital.

Any time you take what someone else has written or said and reduce it to a concise, accurate, and faithful version of the original—in your own words—you are summarizing. A well-written summary report does three things: (1) it provides all the important points from the original without introducing new material; (2) it has a clear structure that often reflects the structure of the original material; and (3) it is independent of the original, meaning the reader of the summary can glean all essential information in the original without having to refer to it.

The ability to summarize well is a valuable skill for a number of reasons. Businesspeople are under pressure today to make decisions based on more information than ever before. Someone who can summarize that information into its key parts is way ahead of someone who cannot. Second, summarizing is a key communication task in many businesses today. For instance, in Figure 8.8 below, a vice president of Human Resources asks one of his HR consultants to do research on the use of BlackBerrys in the workplace, as the company they work at has been experiencing some problems. Third, the ability to summarize makes you a better writer. As you learn to pick apart the structure of articles, reports, and essays written by professional writers such as journalists, you can introduce their tricks of the trade into your own writing. Finally, as part of writing the more complex reports discussed in Chapter 9, you will have to write executive summaries of your own work. Why not learn how to do this by summarizing other peoples' writing first?

FIGURE 8.7 Feasibility Report, Direct Strategy

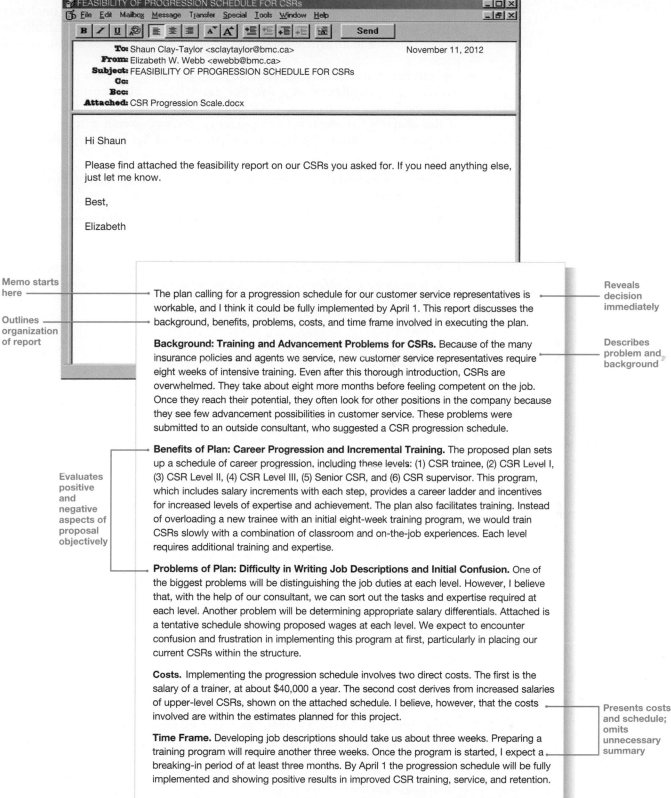

FEASIBILITY OF PROGRESSION SCHEDULE FOR CSRs

File Edit Mailbox Message Transfer Special Tools Window Help

To: Shaun Clay-Taylor <sclaytaylor@bmc.ca>   November 11, 2012
From: Elizabeth W. Webb <ewebb@bmc.ca>
Subject: FEASIBILITY OF PROGRESSION SCHEDULE FOR CSRs
Cc:
Bcc:
Attached: CSR Progression Scale.docx

Hi Shaun

Please find attached the feasibility report on our CSRs you asked for. If you need anything else, just let me know.

Best,

Elizabeth

Memo starts here

Outlines organization of report

The plan calling for a progression schedule for our customer service representatives is workable, and I think it could be fully implemented by April 1. This report discusses the background, benefits, problems, costs, and time frame involved in executing the plan.

Reveals decision immediately

Background: Training and Advancement Problems for CSRs. Because of the many insurance policies and agents we service, new customer service representatives require eight weeks of intensive training. Even after this thorough introduction, CSRs are overwhelmed. They take about eight more months before feeling competent on the job. Once they reach their potential, they often look for other positions in the company because they see few advancement possibilities in customer service. These problems were submitted to an outside consultant, who suggested a CSR progression schedule.

Describes problem and background

Benefits of Plan: Career Progression and Incremental Training. The proposed plan sets up a schedule of career progression, including these levels: (1) CSR trainee, (2) CSR Level I, (3) CSR Level II, (4) CSR Level III, (5) Senior CSR, and (6) CSR supervisor. This program, which includes salary increments with each step, provides a career ladder and incentives for increased levels of expertise and achievement. The plan also facilitates training. Instead of overloading a new trainee with an initial eight-week training program, we would train CSRs slowly with a combination of classroom and on-the-job experiences. Each level requires additional training and expertise.

Evaluates positive and negative aspects of proposal objectively

Problems of Plan: Difficulty in Writing Job Descriptions and Initial Confusion. One of the biggest problems will be distinguishing the job duties at each level. However, I believe that, with the help of our consultant, we can sort out the tasks and expertise required at each level. Another problem will be determining appropriate salary differentials. Attached is a tentative schedule showing proposed wages at each level. We expect to encounter confusion and frustration in implementing this program at first, particularly in placing our current CSRs within the structure.

Costs. Implementing the progression schedule involves two direct costs. The first is the salary of a trainer, at about $40,000 a year. The second cost derives from increased salaries of upper-level CSRs, shown on the attached schedule. I believe, however, that the costs involved are within the estimates planned for this project.

Presents costs and schedule; omits unnecessary summary

Time Frame. Developing job descriptions should take us about three weeks. Preparing a training program will require another three weeks. Once the program is started, I expect a breaking-in period of at least three months. By April 1 the progression schedule will be fully implemented and showing positive results in improved CSR training, service, and retention.

There are four steps to writing an effective summary:

- **Read the material carefully for understanding.** Ideally, you will read the original three times: the first time to understand the topic; the second time with a pen, pencil, or highlighter in hand to underline the main points (usually no more than three in an article-length piece); and the third time to see the overall pattern.
- **Lay out the structure of your summary.** Simply write the main points you've underlined or highlighted in a list. For example, the HR consultant summarizing the Regina *Leader-Post* article in Figure 8.8 (also found at the beginning of this chapter) has identified three main points, one overall pattern, and one solution or conclusion. To lay out the structure of her summary, she would write:

1. There is evidence that younger workers don't view the use of BlackBerrys during meetings as a distraction from what's going on.

2. Experts agree that using BlackBerrys during meetings is distracting.

3. Experts also agree that multitasking becomes inefficient after a certain point.

4. The solution to using BlackBerrys at work is to recognize that this behaviour is potentially offensive to others and to separate oneself from the source of one's distraction.

FIGURE 8.8 Marked-Up Article for Summary

BlackBerry etiquette has yet to be defined

Richard Baum

Reuters

Saturday, May 15, 2010

Do you check your BlackBerry during work meetings? Do you do it furtively under the table, while your colleagues are distracted by a presentation?

Do you leave it in front of you so you can give it the occasional peck whenever it buzzes? Or are you bold enough in the board room to hold it up while you type your replies, a practice that's provoked comedian Jerry Seinfeld to respond, "Can I just pick up a magazine and read it in front of your face while you're talking to me?"

Unless you work in a company that bans BlackBerry use in meetings, you've seen all these behaviours. Most likely, you've been that person. But is it bad etiquette? Don't the pressures of time and overflowing inboxes make this a necessary evil of the 21st century workplace?

Other journalists who have taken time out from deleting e-mail to investigate this burning issue have concluded that polite society abhors the employee whose eyes wander from the PowerPoint presentation to the new e-mail alert.

But as someone who struggles to ignore the siren buzz of the BlackBerry, I demand leave to appeal this collective ruling by the media's finest minds. After all, every new technology that transforms communications encounters resistance from the old guard. Surely the cool kids accept that it is possible to concentrate on a meeting and accept e-mail requests for other meetings at the same time?

Main Point # 1

Evidence = Survey

It didn't take much Googling to find some research that confirmed my hunch: while 68 per cent of the baby-boom generation born before 1964 think that the use of smartphones meetings is distracting, just 49 per cent of the under-30s-see-a-problem. As this 2008 LexisNexis survey helpfully points out, that's less than half. If the person running your meeting is a Generation Y'er, there's a better than even chance that she won't mind you checking your e-mail.

Still, most of us have bosses who are too old to skateboard to work. What does Generation X think of BlackBerry Peckers? I asked John Freeman, a member of that demographic and the author of The Tyranny of Email:

"You never have everyone's full attention in a meeting any longer, and I think that's why meetings are becoming so ineffective" he wrote in a non-tyrannical e-mail.

Main Point # 2
Evidence =
Expert opinion
(author)

"Whether it's the lot who try to thumb under the table, or those who brazenly do it in the open, the message, from a significant group of those gathered, is — I have other things to do. Which totally defeats the purpose of meeting: you want to create a sense of group purpose. And on top of that it's rude."

But John, I can multitask. It may look like I'm updating my Facebook status under the table, but a co-worker has sent me an urgent question and I can answer that and concentrate on your presentation at the same time. Surely I can get an expert on multitasking to back me up here.

I called Clifford Nass, a professor of communication at Stanford University in California. Nass was part of a group that researched the concentration skills of students who frequently multi-tasked while consuming media. Did he find that those of us who listen and e-mail at the same time are an elite brigade of hyper-efficient workers? Not exactly.

"The more you multitask, the worse you become at it," he said. According to the Stanford team's research, there's a cost to memory and attention when you switch from one task to another. And that cost increases for people who multitask heavily.

Main Point # 3
Evidence =
Expert opinion
(professor)

So the science suggests that the appearance of not paying attention when you check your e-mail in a meeting mirrors the reality: however much you think you're paying attention to two things at once, you're not.

And yet the BlackBerry sits there in my pocket, calling to me throughout the meeting: Check me! Check me! What can I do?

"You have to become more cognisant that what you're doing is likely to be offensive to others," said Robert Gordon, who coaches adults with attention deficit hyperactivity disorder (ADHD).

Gordon, who is based in Toronto, says the strategy for executives struggling with ADHD is to sepa-rate them from their distractions. So in the case of a BlackBerry, that means shutting it off. I make a final plea. Rob, there are parts of many meetings that aren't relevant to me. What if I check my e-mail then?

Solution/
Conclusion

"Then the onus falls on the person calling the meeting to be more focused on the agenda," he said.

So there's the answer. It's not my fault I'm rudely checking my BlackBerry. It's your fault for not making the meeting more interesting. And that's just plain bad etiquette.

Source: Richard Baum, "Blackberry etiquette has yet to be defined." Regina Leader Post, May 15, 2010, page G4.

- **Write a first draft.** In this step, you take your list from the step before (which may use the original author's exact language in many parts) and convert it into your own words. Our summary writer might write something like this:

    As requested, I've researched ~~the topic of~~ current opinion on the use of BlackBerrieys in the workplace.

    One useful article I found was by Richard Baum in the Regina *Leader-Post*. In his article ~~called~~ "BlackBerry etiquette has yet to be defined" (May 15, 2010), Baum makes ~~a number of main points and supports his~~ the following points ~~with~~ using two types of evidence.

    - Baum's main point is that there is a difference of opinion in the workplace. Younger workers see BlackBerry use as okay, while older workers don't. He ~~s~~cites a LexisNexis survey from 2008 to back up this point.

    - The second point Baum makes is that the use of BlackBerrys in meetings and presentations is distracting. He supports this point with quotes from experts like authors and professors.

- The next point ~~made by~~ Baum makes is that multitasking with a BlackBerry (one of the device's selling points) becomes inefficient after a certain point. Again he uses a professor of communication to support this point.

- Baum's conclusion is that BlackBerr~~ie~~ys do need to be put away at certain points in order not to create distractions that irritate~~s~~ other workers and lead~~s~~ to less efficiency at work.

I appreciated the opportunity to provide this summary. If there's anything else you need, please let me know.

Sincerely,

Bailey Bingley

- **Proofread and revise.** The final step of writing a summary, like any written document, is to proofread for grammar, spelling, punctuation, and style mistakes and to rewrite where necessary. In the example above, the summary writer found a number of mistakes in her draft (shown with strikethrough). A proofread and revised final version of this descriptive summary report appears in Figure 8.9.

FIGURE 8.9 Summary Report

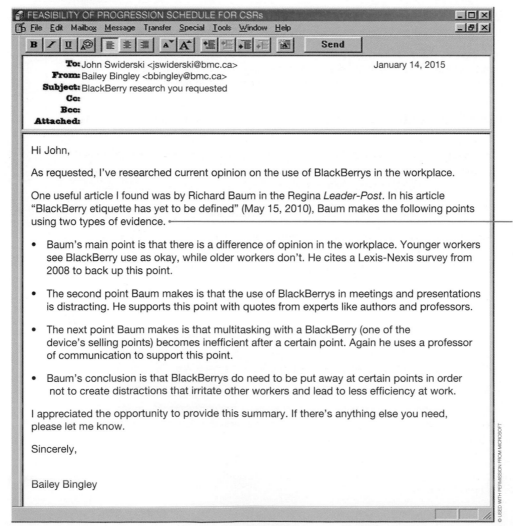

FEASIBILITY OF PROGRESSION SCHEDULE FOR CSRs

File Edit Mailbox Message Transfer Special Tools Window Help

Send

To: John Swiderski <jswiderski@bmc.ca>   January 14, 2015
From: Bailey Bingley <bbingley@bmc.ca>
Subject: BlackBerry research you requested
Cc:
Bcc:
Attached:

Hi John,

As requested, I've researched current opinion on the use of BlackBerrys in the workplace.

One useful article I found was by Richard Baum in the Regina *Leader-Post*. In his article "BlackBerry etiquette has yet to be defined" (May 15, 2010), Baum makes the following points using two types of evidence.

- Baum's main point is that there is a difference of opinion in the workplace. Younger workers see BlackBerry use as okay, while older workers don't. He cites a Lexis-Nexis survey from 2008 to back up this point.

- The second point Baum makes is that the use of BlackBerrys in meetings and presentations is distracting. He supports this point with quotes from experts like authors and professors.

- The next point Baum makes is that multitasking with a BlackBerry (one of the device's selling points) becomes inefficient after a certain point. Again he uses a professor of communication to support this point.

- Baum's conclusion is that BlackBerrys do need to be put away at certain points in order not to create distractions that irritate other workers and lead to less efficiency at work.

I appreciated the opportunity to provide this summary. If there's anything else you need, please let me know.

Sincerely,

Bailey Bingley

Although the article is about Blackberrys, the findings apply to smartphones in general.

Minutes of Meetings

Minutes provide a summary of the proceedings of meetings. Traditional minutes, illustrated in Figure 8.10, are written whenever a formal meeting has taken place. If you are the secretary or note taker of a meeting, you'll want to write minutes that do the following:

- Provide the name of the group, as well as the date, time, and place of the meeting.
- Identify the names of attendees and absentees, if appropriate.
- Describe the disposition of previous minutes (not required in informal meetings).
- Record new business, announcements, and reports.
- Include the precise wording of motions; record the vote and action taken.
- Conclude with the name and signature of the person recording the minutes.

Notice in Figure 8.10 that the writer of the minutes summarizes discussions rather than capturing every comment. However, when a decision is made, it is recorded as close to verbatim (i.e., word for word) as possible.

In more formal meetings, before a decision is taken a "motion" must be called and that motion voted on by the majority in the room. A formal minutes report would list these motions (who made it, seconded it, and the fact that it was passed), but few organizations use formal minutes any longer.

> Meeting minutes record summaries of old business, new business, announcements, and reports, as well as the precise wording of motions.

FIGURE 8.10 Minutes Report

Lor-Dan Produce Distribution
Safety Committee
Bi-annual Meeting Minutes
September 14, 2015

Present: A. Faccinelli, T. Loredan, M. Baransky, V. Singh

Absent: B. Fortier

Topics Discussed

1. Strategizing for our next Safe At Work inspection. Ministry of Labour officials will most probably be visiting the warehouse in early 2016 — we want to improve our scores. Should we hold a company-wide meeting, or rely on managers to filter down best practices within specific areas? Should we reach out to competitors who scored higher in 2013 to solicit advice?

2. Complying with Occupational Health and Safety Act provisions on Workplace Harrassment and Violence. We haven't drafted our policy yet, and are behind many of our competitors. Ministry of Labour regularly does blitz inspections looking for compliance in this area. Who should draft policy? Target dates? How do we make sure all Lor-Dan employees know and understand eventual policy?

Decisions

1. Hold company-wide meeting by November 1, 2015, to explain Safe at Work inspections and compliance. Reach out to two competitors by October 15, 2015, for advice on more successful compliance with Ministry inspections.

2. Harrassment and Violence policy should be drafted by subcommittee by October 15, 2015, for draft discussion at above meeting. Publish harassment and violence brochure and posters for distribution to employees and posting in warehouse.

Action Items

1. V. Singh and B. Fortier to organize meeting on or by November 1, 2015.
2. A. Faccinelli to contact competitors for advice by October 15, 2015.
3. T. Loredan, M. Baransky, and one employee to form subcommittee to draft harassment/violence policy by October 15, 2015.
4. Once above policy is finalized, ask C. Coletor (Director, HR) to print and distribute internally (estimated by November 15, 2015).

Next Meeting: March 15, 2016 Room and Agenda TBA

SUMMING UP AND LOOKING FORWARD

This chapter presented six types of informal business reports: information reports, progress reports, justification/recommendation reports, feasibility reports, summaries, and minutes of meetings. Information reports generally provide data only. But justification/recommendation reports as well as feasibility reports and sometimes summary reports are more analytical in that they also evaluate the information, draw conclusions, and make recommendations. This chapter also discussed a number of possible formats, delivery methods, and style choices for reports. The chapter's model documents illustrating six informal sample reports would be considered relatively informal. Longer, more formal reports are necessary for major investigations and research leading to important decisions. These reports and proposals, along with suggestions for research methods, are presented in Chapter 9.

CRITICAL THINKING

1. Why are most informal reports written using the direct strategy?
2. Is there a significant difference between a report that provides information and a regular e-mail or other message that provides information?
3. Is it a good idea to always provide analysis when asked to write reports, or are there times when it's okay to present information only?
4. Compare and contrast justification/recommendation reports and feasibility reports. How can you easily remember the difference?
5. *Providing a summary is both an exercise in information gathering and an analytical task.* Discuss this statement and provide examples to back it up.

CHAPTER REVIEW

1. List six kinds of informal reports and describe the goal of each one.
2. Explain the difference between providing information and providing an analysis of information.
3. Why are there two different patterns of organization for informal reports?
4. List the main report formats and give a realistic example of each one.
5. Match each situation below with the appropriate informal report.
   a. Your supervisor asks you to read a long technical report and write a report that condenses the important points.
   b. You want to tell management about an idea you have for improving a procedure that you think will increase productivity.
   c. You just attended a meeting at which you were the only person taking notes. The person who ran the meeting sends you an e-mail asking if you could remind him of the important decisions that were made.
   d. As Engineering Department office manager, you have been asked to describe your highly regarded computer system for another department.
   e. As a police officer, you are writing a report of an arrest.
   f. At a mail-order catalogue company, your boss asks you to investigate ways to reduce the time that customers are kept waiting for service representatives to take their telephone orders. She wants your report to examine the problem and offer solutions.
6. If you were about to write the following reports, where would you gather information? Be prepared to discuss the specifics of each choice.
   a. You are a student representative on a curriculum committee. You are asked to study the course requirements in your major and make recommendations.
   b. As department manager, you must write job descriptions for several new positions you wish to establish in your department.
   c. You are proposing to management that a copier in your department be replaced.
   d. You must document the progress of a 12-month advertising campaign to alter the image of a clothing manufacturer's jeans.

7. What three questions do progress reports typically address?

8. What is the purpose of a meeting minutes report?

9. Information reports generally contain what three parts?

10. What items should you include in an article summary that your employer asks you to write?

11. What is the main difference between a descriptive summary and an evaluative summary?

12. Why are headings so important in report writing?

 WRITING IMPROVEMENT EXERCISES

1. **Practise Summarizing.** Summarize the magazine article below in a 150-word e-mail to your business partner.

2. **Practise Summarizing.** Summarize the newspaper article on page 248 in a 150-word e-mail to your boss.

3. **Practise Summarizing/Role Play.** Choose a newspaper or magazine article related to business and summarize it. Look ahead to Figure 11.3 (p. 343) and turn your article summary into an oral presentation outline. Give your summary as a short presentation to your class, as if they were your work colleagues at a weekly staff meeting.

Patients rewarded

by Greg Fjetland, November 22, 2004

After her 13-year-old daughter Jessica was diagnosed with a rare brain tumour, Marlene Petersen of Kelowna, B.C., felt almost overwhelmed by the demands on her time. New to the province, with four other children at home and as many as six medical appointments for Jessica on just one day, "You can imagine how stressful the situation was," says Petersen. Fortunately, she was able to make use of a new health service launched in October.

NavaHealth, a for-profit, privately owned company, leads B.C. residents through the labyrinthine health-care system by providing support and patient advocacy. With NavaHealth's president Elisabeth Riley helping her to understand Jessica's treatment, Petersen found coping with her daughter's illness far less overwhelming. "There's so much information coming at you, you can't remember it all," says Petersen. "You have questions that you forget to ask. And your emotions get in the way."

NavaHealth is the brainchild of Riley, currently dean of the School of Health Sciences at the British Columbia Institute of Technology. Riley began the planning for NavaHealth after she was laid off in the summer of 2002 from her position as president and CEO of the Children's & Women's Health Centre of B.C. in Vancouver. She realized from her long experience in the health sector that a service gap was widening. "The medical system is increasingly complex," says Riley. "It's not the fault of the system; it's just that medicine is so complex. We had only a doctor and a nurse in the system 50 years ago, and now look at how many health professionals and alternatives there are."

So Riley laid the groundwork for her new enterprise, including hiring IT professionals to create a database for health information and hiring registered nurses as "health navigators." With 10 navigators now working throughout British Columbia, NavaHealth provides services in person, by phone and e-mail.

Navigators not only will accompany clients to appointments—the doctors are informed first—but can point out a wide range of appropriate services, including directing the client to community support services such as grief counselling, or private services such as contractors to adapt a home for handicap needs.

Riley is the sole owner of NavaHealth. She charges $100 an hour for the services of a navigator, which she splits with the RN. After an initial free consultation, payment is on a fee-for-service basis. Riley says she funded the launch of NavaHealth entirely out of her pocket. She watches her budget carefully: when a reporter calls her long distance on her cellphone, she calls him back on her land line to reduce the charges.

Helping patients comprehend their medical options is a large market, but where Riley might really strike gold is in targeting her services at what she calls the Sandwich Generation: those adults with both aging parents and children at home to care for. It's a market strongly supported by the demographics of the mid-life baby boomers who live in one part of the country while their parents live elsewhere. "Anyone who has had to balance the demands of caring for an aging parent along with demands from their work and their own family, knows how challenging that can be," Riley says.

While the British Columbia Medical Association doesn't have an official position on patients hiring paid consultants to accompany them to the doctor's office, BCMA president Dr. Jack Burak admits to some concerns. First, it's not a service that all patients can afford equally, and secondly, a patient with a paid advocate may expect a longer appointment with a doctor who has only limited time available. "I don't know how you meld those two concerns," Burak says.

Riley says the market will decide. Since opening her doors, she's received inquiries for her service from across the country and she estimates NavaHealth will break even within six months. Riley intends to expand her service nationwide with head offices in every province within five years. Now that's a healthy ambition.

Source: Patients Rewarded, by Greg Fjetland, Canadian Business, November 22, 2004. Reprinted with permission.

TORONTO STAR

Boom in housing for executives on move

TONY WONG

BUSINESS REPORTER, May 25, 2005

David Morton has had just about every kind of request from executives moving to Toronto on short-term assignments and looking for housing. For a Fortune 500 company executive with a substantial monthly budget of $40,000, Morton was able to find a mansion in Rosedale, considered one of Toronto's best neighbourhoods.

The client's main requests were that the backyard be big enough for his children and their dog, and that the home be recently renovated.

While living in Rosedale isn't the typical request, Morton, the owner of MAC Furnished Rentals Inc., can place you in furnished accommodation for a short-term stay in Toronto from $3,000 a month all the way up to the $40,000 range and beyond.

"They could be moving for a new posting, to fill a short-term position, to look after a maternity leave—the reasons vary," said Morton, who has more than 100 units in Ottawa, Toronto and Sudbury.

According to a Royal LePage Relocation Services study released yesterday, the corporate-housing market in Canada was a $230 million business in 2004.

The most expensive city to relocate to was Vancouver, where it cost an average of $2,950 a month for furnished accommodation, or about $98 per night. Toronto was in close second place at $2,935, followed by Fort McMurray at $2,905.

Toronto has the largest supply of units, but Calgary, with less than a quarter of the population, comes in a close second because of the highly mobile oil and gas industry.

Royal LePage places Fort McMurray, with a population of just 56,000, in third place, but calls it the "corporate-housing capital of Canada," with the lowest vacancy rate driven by the boom in oil-sands production.

In Fort McMurray, the average stay is 90 days, compared with 47 in Toronto and 58 in Vancouver.

"The amount of corporate activity out of (Fort McMurray) is staggering," said Robert Peterman, director of assignment solutions for Royal LePage. "You're talking about one of the biggest oil-production areas in the world, and most of it is coming from that area."

Peterman said the corporate-housing market has grown significantly over the past several years, thanks to an improving economy.

Morton said his company, which started five years ago, has grown about 20 per cent annually.

While the Toronto area has experienced a surge of growth over the past several years, some of that was curtailed last year. Some smaller players left the business due to competition from rising vacancy rates caused by heavy condominium development and a downturn caused by the increase in the Canadian dollar, boosting prices for foreign filmmakers and other visitors, said Royal LePage.

While the market is generally made up of small, independent operators, the returns are now attractive enough to garner the attention of bigger chains, said Peterman.

"The corporate-housing market in Canada is extremely fragmented," Royal LePage said in its report. "Local suppliers range from independent investors with a single furnished suite to large full-suite hotels. Amenities, services and quality vary enormously."

In Toronto, several developers are looking at specially built suite lodges specifically for the corporate, long-term-stay market.

"If you look a few years back, most of the big firms had their own furnished apartments they could move their executives to," said Morton.

With corporate downsizing in the 1990s, the furnished apartments were sold, leaving a vacuum in the market that was filled by operators such as Morton.

Peterman said companies generally use furnished apartments over hotels as a "lifestyle choice" rather than a cost-saving issue, although it is generally cheaper to use corporate accommodations rather than place employees in hotel rooms.

"Some people do prefer living out of hotels. But if you are moving somewhere for three months, you generally would probably prefer to live in a bigger unit with a full kitchen and more of a home-like atmosphere," said Peterman.

It's also something of a misconception to think that placing an employee on temporary assignment rather than relocating him or her entirely is always more cost effective, Peterman said: "You've got to pay for accommodations, and then there are the bi-weekly trips back home, so this can add up pretty quickly."

ACTIVITIES AND CASES

TEAM

8.1 Evaluating Headings and Titles

Identify the following report headings and titles as "talking" or "functional/descriptive." Discuss the usefulness and effectiveness of each.

1. Background
2. Oil Imports Slow in China
3. Discussion of Findings
4. Rosier Job Outlook: Emerging From the Crisis

5. Recommendation: Return to Stocks Is Paying Off Again
6. Adobe Exceeds Expectations on Creative Suite Sales
7. Best Android Apps for Business: PocketCloud, Ignition, and TouchDown
8. Budget

8.2 Information Report: The Less Glamorous Side of Being an Entrepreneur

WEB

You and three friends have decided to open a consulting business in Kitchener, Ontario. You're all recent business college grads and, rather than work for a large corporation, you'd like to strike out on your own. The area you'd like to concentrate on is branding for not-for-profit organizations and educational institutions. Your three friends have already staked out the glamorous side of things, including business development, which leaves you with the "nuts and bolts." The company has been registered, but none of its banking issues have been dealt with. Your partners ask you to send them an e-mail about which bank has "the best deal" as well as "any other stuff you can find out."

Your Task. Write an e-mail information report to your three partners investigating opening up a business account at two financial institutions. Do some more research into what it takes to start a small business and include this information in your report.

Related Web site: The government of Ontario maintains an excellent site on starting a small business in that province; see **www.ontariocanada.com/ontcan/1medt/smallbiz/en/sb_yrguide_main_en.jsp**.

8.3 Information Report: Canadian Tech Company Expands into Asia

WEB

You work in business development for Hydrogenics, a Mississauga, Ontario–based producer of clean energy products. Hydrogenics already has an office in Tokyo, but the owners feel they need to expand its Asian operations. Your boss has asked you to investigate the partnership opportunities available for investors in Korea and China. He gives you a tight deadline of one week, and asks for the report to be sent to him via e-mail with any attachments you think are important.

Your Task. Investigate the mechanics of opening an office and/or investing in Korea and China. Report your findings in an e-mail to your boss, Bob Khan.

Related Web sites: Important background information can be found at **www.hydrogenics.com**, **www.investkorea.org**, and **www.fdi.gov.cn/pub/FDI_EN/default.htm**.

8.4 Information Report: Showcasing Your Work Experience

Your instructor wants to learn about your employment. Select a position you now hold or one that you have held in the past. If you have not been employed, choose a campus, professional, or community organization to which you belong. You may also select an internship or volunteer activities.

Your Task. Write an informational report describing your employment or involvement. As an introduction describe the company and its products or services, its ownership, and its location. As the main part of the report, describe your position, including its tasks and the skills required to perform these tasks. Summarize by describing the experience you gained. Your memo report should be single-spaced and one and a half to two pages long and should be addressed to your instructor.

8.5 Progress Report: Making Headway Toward Your Educational Goal

CRITICAL THINKING

You made an agreement with your parents (or spouse, relative, or partner) that you would submit a progress report at this time describing the headway you have made toward your educational goal (employment, certificate, diploma, degree).

Your Task. In memo format write a progress report that fulfills your promise to describe your progress toward your educational goals. Address your progress report to your parents, spouse, relative, or partner. In your memo (1) describe your goal; (2) summarize the work you have completed thus far; (3) discuss thoroughly the work currently in progress, including your successes and anticipated obstacles; and (4) forecast your future activities in relation to your scheduled completion date.

8.6 Progress Report: Designing a Template for HR

You are the assistant to the Director of Human Resources at BASF's head office in Mississauga, Ontario. At a recent meeting of the management board, it was decided that the employee review process required an overhaul. Instead of once-yearly meetings with their immediate superior to "discuss any issues," the company has decided to institute a more accountable process in which all employees (including managers) must write a yearly progress report.

Your Task. Develop a template report for your boss, Sue Swinton, Director of Human Resources, that can be filled out by all BASF Canada employees at all ten locations once a year. Keep in mind that employees are generally unenthusiastic about the employee review process. In other words, your template must be easy to fill out and logical.

Related Web sites: BASF Canada's site is at **www2.basf.us/basf-canada/index_e.shtm**. You may also want to research best practices in performance management and the employee review process.

8.7 Recommendation Report: What Is It About Advertising?

You are the CEO of a mid-size Oakville, Ontario–based advertising agency named Slam! Your company is in the enviable position of having secured the advertising contract for the 2015 Pan/Parapan American Games in Toronto. The problem is, you can't seem to keep your employees around long enough to ensure continuity within projects. It seems as though the advertising business is a revolving door: new college and university grads are eager to work for you, but six months later, once you've trained them, they leave for more lucrative jobs at other agencies. You're too busy to figure out a solution or policy; in fact you're so busy you haven't got around to hiring a Human Resources manager. Instead you ask your research manager to write you a report on some possible solutions.

Your Task. As the research manager at Slam!, research and write a short e-mail recommendation report for your boss outlining some possible solutions to the "revolving door" problem. Your boss's thriftiness is well known, so you'll have to be careful about how you phrase any expensive solutions.

Related Web site: An article at the following URL provides some general solutions to employee retention: **www.bcjobs.ca/re/hr-resources/human-resource-advice/recruitment-and-retention/employee-retention-ideas**—ideas-for-retaining-top-performers; however, you should also do other research on the topic of employee retention. Be careful not to plagiarize from your sources when completing this report. Information on the Pan/Parapan American Games can be found at **www.toronto2015.org**.

8.8 Progress Report: Filling in Your Supervisor

As office manager for the Vancouver Humane Society (**www.vancouverhumanesociety.bc.ca**), an organization that rescues and finds homes for abandoned and abused animals, you have been asked to come up with ways to increase community awareness of your organization. For the past month, you have been meeting with business and community leaders, conducting Web research, and visiting with representatives from other nonprofit organizations. Your supervisor has just asked you to prepare a written report to outline what you have accomplished so far.

Your Task. In memo format, write a progress report to your supervisor. In your memo (a) state whether the project is on schedule, (b) summarize the activities you have completed thus far, (c) discuss thoroughly the work currently in progress, and (d) describe your future activities. Also let your supervisor know any obstacles you have encountered and whether the project is on schedule.

8.9 Justification/Recommendation Report: Solving a Campus Problem

In any organization, room for improvement always exists. Your college or university campus is no different. You are the member of a student task force that has been asked to identify problems and suggest solutions.

In groups of two to five, investigate a problem on your campus, such as inadequate parking, slow registration, poor class schedules, an inefficient bookstore, a weak job-placement program, unrealistic degree requirements, or a lack of internship programs. Within your group develop a solution to the problem. If possible, consult the officials involved to ask for their input in arriving at a feasible solution. Do not attack existing programs; instead, strive for constructive discussion and harmonious improvements.

Your Task. After reviewing the persuasive techniques discussed in Chapter 6, write a justification/recommendation report in memo or letter format. Address your report to the college or university president.

8.10 Justification/Recommendation Report: Developing a Company E-Mail and Web-Use Policy

As a manager in a midsize financial services firm, you are aware that members of your department frequently use e-mail and the Internet for private messages, shopping, games, and other personal activities. In addition to the strain on your company's computer network, you worry about declining productivity, security problems, and liability issues. When you walked by one worker's computer and saw what looked like pornography on the screen, you knew you had to do something. Although workplace privacy is a controversial issue for unions and employee-rights groups, employers have legitimate reasons for wanting to know what is happening on their computers. A high percentage of lawsuits involve the use and abuse of e-mail. You think that the executive council should establish some kind of e-mail and Web-use policy. The council is generally receptive to sound suggestions, especially if they are inexpensive. You decide to talk with other managers about the problem and write a justification/recommendation report.

In teams of two to five, discuss the need for an e-mail and Web-use policy. Using the Web, find sample policies used by other firms. Look for examples of companies struggling with lawsuits over e-mail abuse. Find information about employers' rights to monitor employees' e-mail and Web use. Use this research to determine what your company's e-mail and Web-use policy should cover. Each member of the team should present and support his or her ideas regarding what should be included in the policy and how to best present your ideas to the executive council.

Your Task. Write a convincing justification/recommendation report in memo or letter format to the executive council based on the conclusions you draw from your research and discussion. Decide whether you should be direct or indirect.

8.11 Justification/Recommendation Report: Diversity Training— Does It Work?

Employers recognize the importance of diversity awareness and intercultural sensitivity in the workplace because both are directly related to productivity. It is assumed that greater harmony also minimizes the threat of lawsuits. An interest in employee diversity training has spawned numerous corporate trainers and consultants, but after many years of such training, some recent studies seem to suggest that they may be ineffective or deliver mixed results at best. A 2009 article in the trade magazine *Canadian HR Reporter* concluded that diversity training does not necessarily change bias, for example, against lesbian, gay, and transgendered employees.[1]

Search the Internet and your library's databases for information about diversity training. Examine articles favourable to diversity training and those that exhibit a more pessimistic view of such efforts.

Your Task. As a group of two to five members, write a memo report to your boss (address it to your instructor) and define diversity training. Explain which measures companies take to make their managers and workers culturally aware and respectful of differences. If you have personally encountered such training, draw on your experience in addition to your research. Your report should answer the question *Does diversity training work?* If yes, recommend steps your company should take to become more sensitive to minorities. If no, suggest how current practices could be improved to be more effective.

8.12 Justification Report: Evaluating Your Curriculum

You have been serving as a student member of a curriculum advisory committee. The committee is expected to examine the course requirements for a degree, diploma, or certificate in your area.

Your Task. In teams of three to five, decide whether the requirements are realistic and practical. What improvements can your team suggest? Interview other students, faculty members, and employers for their suggestions. Prepare a justification report in e-mail or memo format to send to the president of your college or university proposing your suggestions. You anticipate that the head of your faculty or department may need to be persuaded to make any changes. Consider delaying your recommendations until after you have developed a foundation of explanation and reasons.

8.13 Justification Report: Purchasing New Equipment

In your work or your training position, identify equipment that needs to be purchased or replaced (e.g., computer, printer, modem, DVD player, copier, digital camera, etc.). Gather information about two different models or brands.

Your Task. Write a justification report comparing the two items. Establish a context by describing the need for the equipment. Discuss the present situation, emphasizing the current deficiencies. Describe the advantages of acquiring the new equipment.

8.14 Feasibility Report: Starting an International Student Organization

To fulfill a student project in your department, you have been asked to submit a letter report to the dean evaluating the feasibility of starting an organization of international students on campus.

Your Task. Find out how many international students are on your campus, what nations they represent, how one goes about starting an organization, and whether a faculty sponsor is needed. Assume that you have conducted an informal survey of international students. Of the 39 who filled out the survey, 31 said they would be interested in joining. Write a mini-report in memo or letter format to the dean outlining the advisability of starting an international student organization on your college campus.

8.15 Summary Report: Condensing an Article About E-Mail Privacy

Your boss is worried because the company has no formal e-mail policy. Should employees be allowed to use e-mail for personal messages? May management monitor the messages of employees? She asks you to research this topic (or another topic on which you and your instructor agree).

Your Task. Using library databases, find a useful newspaper, magazine, or other periodical article (around 1,000 words). In a one-page document, summarize the major points of the article. Also evaluate its strengths and weaknesses. Attach this summary document to an e-mail that you send to your boss, Justine Toller, Division Manager.

WEB

8.16 Summary Report: Putting Business Blogs and Social Media to Work

Your supervisor has just learned about using blogs or social media such as Facebook and Twitter to communicate with the public. She wants to learn more. She asks you to conduct Internet and database research to see what has been written about the business uses of blogs or social media.

Your Task. Using an electronic database or the Web, find an article that discusses the use of blogs or social media as communication vehicles. In a memo report addressed to your boss, Jina Ree, summarize the primary ideas, conclusions, and recommendations presented in the article. Be sure to identify the author, article name, periodical, and date of publication in your summary. Also include your reaction to and evaluation of the article.

8.17 Minutes: Recording the Proceedings of a Meeting

Ask your instructor to let you know when the next all-faculty or division or departmental meeting is taking place on your campus. Or, ask your student association or student council representative to let you know when the next association or council meeting is taking place. Or, next time you're at work or at your co-op job, ask your boss to let you sit in on a meeting. Volunteer to act as note taker or secretary for this meeting.

Your Task. Record the proceedings of the meeting you attend in an informal meeting minutes report. Focus on reports presented, motions/action items, votes, and decisions reached.

8.18 Role Play: Everyone's Taking Minutes

Next time you have a group or team related to one of your school assignments, videotape or audiotape one of your group or team meetings. Then, turn that meeting into a scripted skit. Perform the skit in front of your class.

Your Task. As an audience member, watch the skit discussed above. Assume you are the note taker at the meeting. Create a minutes report for the meeting you just watched. Are there any elements of a meeting the group/team missed (e.g., motions, action statements, etc.)?

8.19 Longer Report: Solving a Problem

Choose a business or organization with which you are familiar and identify a problem, such as poor quality, indifferent service, absenteeism at organization meetings, uninspired cafeteria food, outdated office equipment, unresponsive management, lack of communication, under-appreciated employees, wasteful procedures, or a similar problem.

Your Task. Describe the problem in detail. Assume you are to report to management (or to the leadership of an organization) about the nature and scope of the problem. Decide which kind of report to prepare (information, recommendation, justification), and choose the format. How would you gather data to lend authority to your conclusions and recommendations? Determine the exact topic and report length after consultation with your instructor.

 ## GRAMMAR/MECHANICS REVIEW 8—SEMICOLONS AND COLONS

Study each of the following statements. Insert any necessary punctuation. Use the delete sign to omit unnecessary punctuation. In the space provided, indicate the number of changes you made. If you make no changes, write *0*. This exercise concentrates on semicolon and colon use, but you will also be responsible for correct comma use.

_2_ **Example** Jessica Mayer's task is to ensure that her company has enough cash to meet its obligations moreover she is responsible for finding ways to reduce operating expenses.

___ 1. Short-term financing refers to a period of one year or less long-term financing on the other hand refers to a period of more than one year.

___ 2. Jessica Mayer's firm must negotiate short-term financing during the following months October November and December.

___ 3. Jessica was interested in her company's finances however she was also seeking information about improving her personal credit score.

___ 4. Having a long history of making payments on time on all types of credit accounts is important to lenders therefore you should strive to make timely payments.

___ 5. Two of the most highly respected and popular banks for short-term financing are: CIBC and TD Bank.

___ 6. People with Fico scores of 700 to 800 are good credit risks people with scores of 400 or less are poor credit risks.

___ 7. Jessica learned that three factors account for about a third of one's credit score (a) length of credit history (b) new credit and (c) type of credit.

___ 8. She attended a credit conference featuring the following speakers Jonathon Cruz certified financial consultant Credit Specialists Margaret Lee founder Credit Solutions and Judith Plutsky legal counsel Liberty Financial.

___ 9. Opening several new credit accounts in a short period of time can lower your credit score but scores are not affected by multiple inquiries from credit score agencies.

___ 10. Your credit score ignores some surprising factors for example your age salary and occupation.

___ 11. Credit Solutions which is a nonprofit counselling and debt management service says that two factors account for two-thirds of your credit score (1) your payment history and (2) the amount owed versus available credit.

___ 12. If you want specific information from Credit Solutions send your request to Margaret Lee 3520 Troy Highway Simcoe Ontario K2D-1G8.

___ 13. Margaret Lee who founded Credit Solutions employs an experienced courteous staff however she also responds to personal requests.

___ 14. Interest rates are at historic lows they may never be this low again.

___ 15. Margaret Lee said "If your goal is to increase your credit score take a look at folks with the highest credit scores. They have four to six credit card accounts no late payment and at least one installment loan with an excellent payment history."

Document for Revision

The progress report shown in Figure 8.11 has faults in grammar, punctuation, spelling, number form, wordiness, and word use. Use standard proofreading marks (see Appendix B) to correct the errors. When you finish, your instructor can show you the revised version of this report.

FIGURE 8.11 Progress Report

To: John Peters <jpeters@zedfilms.ca>   January 10, 2015
From: Kalare Jegsee <kjegsee@zedfilms.ca>
Subject: Progress Report on Sites for "Great Canadian Cook Off" Series
Cc:
Bcc:
Attached:

This email will outline the progress of my location search for our "Great Canadian Cook Off" series, which begins to shooting in April. My location search has been undertaken in the downtown Toronto area, because the gratest number of restaurants are found there.

<u>What I've done so Far:</u> As requested by you, I've searched for restaurants that have a professional kitchen, that are not crampped in size, and which are avaliable for rental during our shoting period and renting for less than $1,000 per day. This required a week's worth of telephoning around the city to narrow down the possibilities. After my phoning I had narrowed down the search to five restaurants: Lisa's; On the Avenue; Trattoria Umberto, Avignon; and also the Mackenzie House. At this point I have had meetings with the owners of the first two restaurants named above. Bot Lisa's and On the Avenue fit our criterias, but Lisas is pretty cramped in size.

<u>What I still Need To Do:</u> As you can see from what I've said above, there are three restaurants I've yet to visit. I have meetings scheduled for this Thursday and Friday at all three. I realized while visiting Lisa's and On the Avenue that we should probably be add another criteria which is; what kind of front-of-house facilities do they have. In other words, if the dining area itself is not attractive (we may be using this for extra shots, e.g. one on one interviews), there isn't much points going with this location. So I will keep this extra criteria in mind when I meet with the other 3 restaurants.

I'll send u a final report narrowing my list of five down to 2 by early next week (probably Monday!). Please let me know if you have any questions.

Cheers,

Kalare

WEB EVALUATION: HOAX? SCHOLARLY RESEARCH? ADVOCACY?

Most of us tend to think that any information turned up via a Web search engine has somehow been evaluated as part of a valid selection process.[2] Not true. The truth is that the Internet is rampant with unreliable sites that reside side by side with reputable sites. Anyone with a computer and an Internet connection can publish anything on the Web.

Unlike library-based research materials, information at many sites has not undergone the editing or scrutiny of scholarly publication procedures. The information we read in journals and most reputable magazines is reviewed, authenticated, and evaluated. That's why we have learned to trust these sources as valid and authoritative. But information on the Web is much less reliable. Some sites are obvious hoaxes. Others exist to distribute propaganda. Still others want to sell you something. To use the Web meaningfully, you must scrutinize what you find. Here are specific questions to ask as you examine a site:

- **Currency.** What is the date of the Web page? When was it last updated? Is some of the information obviously out of date? If the information is time sensitive and the site has not been updated recently, the site is probably not reliable.
- **Authority.** Who publishes or sponsors this Web page? What makes the presenter an authority? Is a contact address available for the presenter? Learn to be skeptical about data and assertions from individuals whose credentials are not verifiable.
- **Content.** Is the purpose of the page to entertain, inform, convince, or sell? Who is the intended audience, judging from content, tone, and style? Can you assess the overall value of the content compared with that of the other resources on this topic? Web presenters with a skewed point of view cannot be counted on for objective data.
- **Accuracy.** Do the facts that are presented seem reliable to you? Do you find errors in spelling, grammar, or usage? Do you see any evidence of bias? Are footnotes provided? If you find numerous errors and if facts are not referenced, you should be alerted that the data may be questionable.

For more information on evaluating Web sites, check out the University of California at Berkeley's excellent Web site at **www.lib.berkeley.edu/TeachingLib/Guides/Internet/Evaluate.html**.

Career Application

As interns at a news-gathering service, you have been asked to assess the quality of the following Web sites. Which of these could you recommend as sources of valid information?

- Beef Nutrition (**www.beefnutrition.org**)
- Edmunds—Where Smart Car Buyers Start (**www.edmunds.com**)
- Criticism of Apple Inc. (**http://criticismofappleinc.blog.com/**)
- EarthSave International (**www.earthsave.org**)
- The Vegetarian Resource Group (**www.vrg.org/nutshell/nutshell.htm**)
- The White House (**www.whitehouse.gov**)
- Prime Minister of Canada (**http://pm.gc.ca/eng/**)
- National Anti-Vivisection Society (**www.navs.org**)
- Dow Chemical Company (**www.dow.com**)
- Dow: A Chemical Company on the Global Playground (**www.dowethics.com**)
- Smithsonian Institution (**www.si.edu**)
- Drudge Report (**www.drudgereport.com**)
- Canadian Cancer Society (**www.cancer.ca**)
- Ova Prima Foundation (**www.ovaprima.org/**)

YOUR TASK

If you are working with a team, divide the preceding list among team members. If you are working individually, select four of the sites. Answer the questions in the preceding checklist as you evaluate each site. Summarize your evaluation of each site in a memo report to your instructor or in team or class discussion. Consider the following questions:

- What evidence can you find to determine whether these sites represent hoaxes, personal opinion, or reliable information?
- Are the sources for factual information clearly listed so that they can be verified?
- Can you tell who publishes or sponsors the page?
- Are the organization's biases clearly stated?
- Is advertising clearly differentiated from informational content?
- Would you use these sites for scholarly research? Why or why not?

CHAPTER

09

Proposals and Formal Reports

© LISE GAGNE/ISTOCKPHOTO.COM

LEARNING OBJECTIVES

1. Write effective informal business proposals.

2. Describe how to prepare to write a formal report.

3. Collect data effectively from secondary sources, especially electronic sources.

4. Generate primary data from surveys, interviews, observation, and experimentation.

5. Explain accurate documentation of data and the consequences of plagiarism.

6. Organize report data, create an outline, and write effective titles.

7. Illustrate data using tables, charts, and graphs.

8. Sequence the main parts of a formal report.

Proposals are persuasive offers to solve problems, provide services, or sell equipment or other products. Let's say that the City of Fredericton wants to upgrade the laptops and software in its Human Resources Department. Once it knows exactly what it wants, it prepares a request for proposal (RFP) specifying its requirements. It then publishes the RFP, and companies interested in bidding on the job submit proposals. RFPs were traditionally publicized in newspapers, but today they're published on special Internet sites, such as **www.merx.com**, which is the best-known Canadian RFP site.

Both large and small companies, organizations, and agencies are increasingly likely to use RFPs to solicit competitive bids on their projects. This enables them to compare "apples to apples." That is, they can compare the prices different companies would charge for completing the same project. RFPs also work for companies in situations where needs are not clear. An RFP can be issued stating broad expectations and goals within which bidding companies offer innovative solutions and price quotes. In most cases, a proposal also acts as a legal statement of work from which a contract for services is developed.

Many companies earn a sizable portion of their income from sales resulting from proposals. It's important to realize that not all proposals are solicited—that is, published in the newspaper or on Web sites. Unsolicited proposals are also important business documents. For example, if you are a consultant who specializes in coaching and team-building skills, you can send an unsolicited proposal to a large organization such as a bank, offering your services.

The ability to write effective proposals, whether solicited or unsolicited, is especially important today. In writing proposals, the most important thing to

> Proposals are persuasive offers to solve problems, provide services, or sell equipment.

> Both large and small companies today often use requests for proposals (RFPs) to solicit competitive bids on projects.

remember is that they are sales presentations. They must be persuasive, not merely mechanical descriptions of what you can do. You may recall from Chapter 6 that effective persuasive sales messages build interest by emphasizing benefits for the reader, reduce resistance by detailing your expertise and accomplishments, and motivate action by making it easy for the reader to understand and respond.

Informal Proposals

Informal proposals may contain an introduction, background information, the plan, staffing requirements, a budget, and an authorization request.

Proposals may be informal or formal; the distinction is primarily in length and format. Informal proposals are often presented in letter format. Sometimes called letter proposals, they contain six principal parts: introduction, background, proposal, staffing, budget, and authorization request. The informal letter proposal shown in Figure 9.1 illustrates all six parts of a letter proposal. This proposal is addressed to a Calgary dentist who wants to improve patient satisfaction.

Introduction

Effective proposal openers capture interest by promising extraordinary results or resources or by identifying key benefits, issues, or outcomes.

Most proposals begin by explaining briefly the reasons for the proposal, highlighting the writer's qualifications, and briefly previewing the price and timeline of the job to be undertaken. To make your introduction more persuasive, use persuasive techniques to gain the reader's attention. One proposal expert suggests these possibilities:

- Hint at extraordinary results with details to be revealed shortly.
- Promise low costs or speedy results.
- Mention a remarkable resource (well-known authority, new computer program, well-trained staff) available exclusively to you.
- Identify a serious problem (worry item) and promise a solution, to be explained later.
- Specify a key issue or benefit that you feel is the heart of the proposal.[1]

For example, in the introduction of the proposal shown in Figure 9.1, Alex Parsons focused on a key benefit. In this proposal to conduct a patient satisfaction survey, she thought that the client, Dr. Atala, would be most interested in specific recommendations for improving service to her patients. But Parsons didn't hit on this benefit until after the first draft had been written. Indeed, it's often a good idea to put off writing the introduction to a proposal until after you have completed other parts. For longer proposals the introduction also describes the scope and limitations of the project, as well as outlining the organization of the material to come.

Background

The background section identifies the problem and discusses the goals or purposes of the project. The background is also the place to go over some recent history. In other words, briefly summarize what circumstances led to you writing the proposal. For example, in Figure 9.1, the "history" of the situation is alluded to in the sentence *We know that you have been incorporating a total quality management system in your practice.*

In a proposal, your aim is to convince the reader that you understand the problem completely. Thus, if you are responding to an RFP, this means repeating its language. For example, if the RFP asks for the *design of a maintenance program for high-speed mail-sorting equipment*, you would use the same language in explaining the purpose of your proposal. This section might include segments entitled *Basic Requirements*, *Most Critical Tasks*, and *Most Important Secondary Problems*.

Plan

In the plan section, you should discuss your methods for solving the problem. In some proposals this is tricky, because you want to disclose enough of your plan to secure the contract without giving away so much information that your services

OFFICE INSIDER

"To conquer writer's block in proposal writing, begin with a bulleted list of what the customer is looking for. This list is like a road map; it gets you started and keeps you headed in the right direction."

aren't needed. Without specifics, though, your proposal has little chance, so you must decide how much to reveal. Explain what you propose to do and how it will benefit the reader. Remember, too, that a proposal is a sales presentation. Sell your methods, product, and "deliverables"—items that will be left with the client. In this section some writers specify how the project will be managed, how its progress will be audited, and what milestones along the way will indicate the project is progressing as planned. Most writers also include a schedule of activities or a timetable showing when events take place.

> The plan section must give enough information to secure the contract but not so much detail that the services are not needed.

Staffing

The staffing section of a proposal describes the credentials and expertise of the project leaders and the company as a whole. A well-written staffing section describes the capabilities of the whole company. Although the example in Figure 9.1 does not do so, staffing sections often list other high-profile jobs that have been undertaken

FIGURE 9.1 Informal Proposal, Letter Format

InFocus Market Research
research | PR | consulting

1 Providence Plaza | Calgary, AB T1A 4E5
Phone (403) 628-3011

June 2, 2015

Kimberly Atala, DDS
1789 Clarkson Avenue
Calgary, AB T1L 5G4

Dear Dr. Atala:

Grabs attention with "hook" that focuses on key benefit

Understanding the views of your patients is the key to meeting their needs. InFocus Market Research is pleased to propose a plan to help you become even more successful by learning what patients expect of your practice, so that you can improve your services.

Uses opening paragraph in place of introduction

Background and Goals

We know that you have been incorporating a total quality management system in your practice. Although you have every reason to believe your patients are pleased with your services, you may want to give them an opportunity to discuss what they like and possibly don't like about your office. Specifically, your purposes are to survey your patients to (a) determine the level of their satisfaction with you and your staff, (b) elicit their suggestions for improvement, (c) learn more about how they discovered you, and (d) compare your "preferred" and "standard" patients.

Identifies four purposes of survey

Announces heart of proposal

Proposed Plan

On the basis of our experience in conducting many local and national customer satisfaction surveys, InFocus proposes the following plan:

Divides total plan into logical segments for easy reading

Survey. We will develop a short but thorough questionnaire probing the data you desire. Although the survey instrument will include both open-ended and closed questions, it will concentrate on the latter. Closed questions enable respondents to answer easily; they also facilitate systematic data analysis. The questionnaire will gauge patients' views of courtesy, professionalism, accuracy of billing, friendliness, and waiting time. After you approve it, the questionnaire will be sent to a carefully selected sample of 300 patients whom you have separated into groupings of "preferred" and "standard."

Describes procedure for solving problem or achieving goals

Analysis. Survey data will be analyzed by demographic segments, such as patient type, age, and gender. Using state-of-the art statistical tools, our team of seasoned experts will study (a) satisfaction levels, (b) the reasons for satisfaction or dissatisfaction, and (c) the responses of your "preferred" compared to "standard" patients. Moreover, our team will give you specific suggestions for making patient visits more pleasant.

Report. You will receive a final report with the key findings clearly spelled out, Dr. Atala. Our expert staff will draw conclusions based on the results. The report will include tables summarizing all responses, divided into preferred and standard clients.

FIGURE 9.1 *(Continued)*

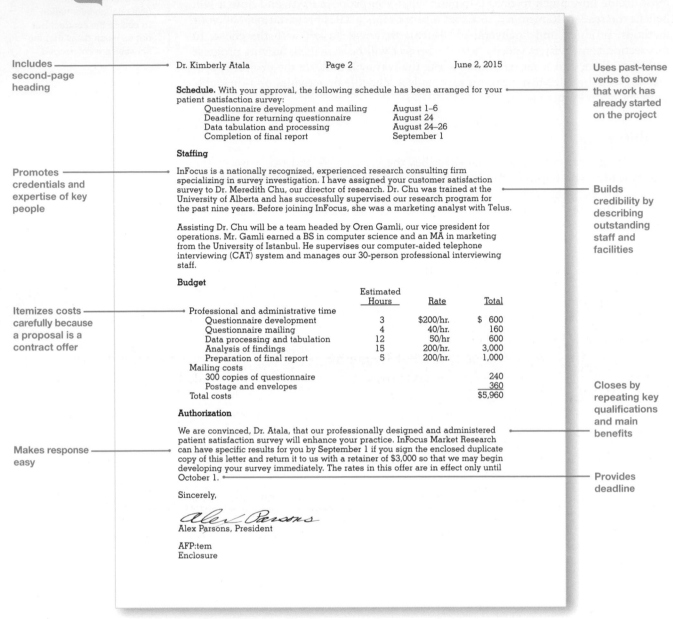

Includes second-page heading

Promotes credentials and expertise of key people

Itemizes costs carefully because a proposal is a contract offer

Makes response easy

Uses past-tense verbs to show that work has already started on the project

Builds credibility by describing outstanding staff and facilities

Closes by repeating key qualifications and main benefits

Provides deadline

Dr. Kimberly Atala   Page 2   June 2, 2015

Schedule. With your approval, the following schedule has been arranged for your patient satisfaction survey:

Questionnaire development and mailing	August 1–6
Deadline for returning questionnaire	August 24
Data tabulation and processing	August 24–26
Completion of final report	September 1

Staffing

InFocus is a nationally recognized, experienced research consulting firm specializing in survey investigation. I have assigned your customer satisfaction survey to Dr. Meredith Chu, our director of research. Dr. Chu was trained at the University of Alberta and has successfully supervised our research program for the past nine years. Before joining InFocus, she was a marketing analyst with Telus.

Assisting Dr. Chu will be a team headed by Oren Gamli, our vice president for operations. Mr. Gamli earned a BS in computer science and an MA in marketing from the University of Istanbul. He supervises our computer-aided telephone interviewing (CAT) system and manages our 30-person professional interviewing staff.

Budget

	Estimated Hours	Rate	Total
Professional and administrative time			
Questionnaire development	3	$200/hr.	$ 600
Questionnaire mailing	4	40/hr.	160
Data processing and tabulation	12	50/hr.	600
Analysis of findings	15	200/hr.	3,000
Preparation of final report	5	200/hr.	1,000
Mailing costs			
300 copies of questionnaire			240
Postage and envelopes			360
Total costs			$5,960

Authorization

We are convinced, Dr. Atala, that our professionally designed and administered patient satisfaction survey will enhance your practice. InFocus Market Research can have specific results for you by September 1 if you sign the enclosed duplicate copy of this letter and return it to us with a retainer of $3,000 so that we may begin developing your survey immediately. The rates in this offer are in effect only until October 1.

Sincerely,

Alex Parsons

Alex Parsons, President

AFP:tem
Enclosure

---

by the company as a way of building interest and reducing resistance. For example, before she mentioned Dr. Chu and Mr. Gamli, Parsons could have said, *Among our well-known clients are Husky Energy and the Calgary Board of Education.*

The staffing section may also identify the size and qualifications of the support staff, along with other resources such as computer facilities and special programs for analyzing statistics. In longer proposals, résumés of key people may be provided. The staffing section is a good place to endorse and promote your staff.

Budget

The most important item in proposals, many would argue, is the budget, a list of project costs. You need to prepare this section carefully because it represents a contract; you can't raise the price later—even if your costs increase. You can—and should—protect yourself with a deadline for acceptance. In the budget section

> Because a proposal is a legal contract, the budget must be researched carefully.

some writers itemize hours and costs; others present a total sum only. A proposal to install a complex computer system might, for example, contain a detailed line-by-line budget. In the proposal shown in Figure 9.1, Parsons felt that she needed to justify the budget for her firm's patient-satisfaction survey, so she itemized the costs. But the budget included for a proposal to conduct a one-day seminar to improve employee communication skills might be a lump sum only. Your analysis of the project and your audience will help you decide what kind of budget to prepare.

Authorization

Informal proposals need to close with a request for approval or authorization. In addition, the closing should remind the reader of key benefits and motivate action. It might also include a deadline date beyond which the offer is invalid. At some companies, such as Hewlett-Packard, authorization to proceed is not part of the proposal. Instead, it is usually discussed after the customer has received the proposal. In this way the customer and the sales account manager are able to negotiate terms before a formal agreement is drawn. Either way, learning to write an authorization section—which must find a way of saying you want the job without appearing too greedy or needy—is an important persuasive exercise.

Formal Proposals

Formal, detailed proposals became a staple in various industries in the 1950s, as a way of streamlining the bidding for government-funded projects. These formal proposals differ from informal proposals in size and format. Formal proposals respond to big projects and may range from 5 to 200 or more pages, and as you can imagine, writing a formal proposal to bid on a multi-million-dollar contract requires careful preparation, expertise, and countless staff hours. In addition, the tone used in formal proposals is often more formal than the tone used in informal proposals. For example, the about-to-be finished project to build a train link to Toronto's Pearson Airport from downtown (the Union Pearson Express) has been a huge engineering and logistical undertaking. The proposals by AirLinx Partners Inc. to build a station at the airport and three kilometres of track, and by Sumitomo Corporation of America to build the train cars,[2] would have been much longer than the two-page letter proposal in Figure 9.1.

To facilitate comprehension and reference, formal proposals are organized into many parts. In addition to the six basic parts just described, formal proposals contain some or all of the following additional parts: copy of the RFP, letter of transmittal, abstract and/or executive summary, title page, table of contents, figures, and

In a move reminiscent of suburban bomb shelters of the Cold War era, urban planners are preparing "lilypad cities" to house survivors if climate disaster fears ever materialize. Should the planet become inundated by rising sea levels, these zero-emission ships could literally bob around the globe as self-sustaining habitats, complete with energy supplied from solar panels and wind turbines. Designed by award-winning Belgian architect Vincent Callebaut, and inspired by the shape of lilypads, the giant floating metropolises are both stylish and loaded with the comforts of modern living. *What organizations might submit proposals in the development of lily-pad cities?*

appendixes containing such items as detailed budgets and staffing information. In this book we will not discuss formal proposals in detail because it is unlikely that a business communicator in an entry-level position would have to write such a detailed proposal. Formal proposal writing is usually handled either by consultants or by employees with significant experience in this area.

Proposals in the past were always paper-based and delivered by mail or special messenger. Today, however, companies increasingly prefer online proposals. Receiving companies may transmit the electronic proposal to all levels of management without ever printing a page; this appeals to many environmentally conscious organizations.

> Formal proposals respond to big projects and may contain 200 or more pages.

Well-written proposals win contracts and business for companies and individuals. In fact, many companies, especially those that are run on a consulting model, depend entirely on proposals to generate their income. Companies such as Microsoft, Hewlett-Packard, and IBM employ staffs of people that do nothing but prepare proposals to compete for new business. For more information about industry standards and resources, visit the Web site of the Association of Proposal Management Professionals (**www.apmp-canada.ca**).

Writing Formal Business Reports

Whenever a business problem requires research (as in the example in Figure 9.1 concerning InFocus Market Research and Dr. Kimberly Atala), a formal report (or presentation, or both) is often part of the main deliverable to the client. We can define a formal business report, then, as a written solution to a business issue or problem. These formal reports typically have three overall characteristics: a formal tone, a traditional structure, and considerable length. While this makes them sound similar to formal proposals, there's an important difference: proposals present an offer to do work or provide something, whereas reports represent the end product of thorough investigation and analysis.

Formal research reports in business serve a very important function. They provide management with vital data, analysis, and recommendations for decision making. In this section we will consider the entire process of writing a formal report: preparing to write; researching, generating, documenting, organizing, and illustrating data; and presenting the final report.

Like proposals and informal reports, formal reports begin with a definition of the project. Probably the most difficult part of this definition is limiting the scope of the report. Every project has limitations. Decide at the outset what constraints influence the range of your project and how you will achieve your purpose. How much time do you have for completing your report? How much space will you be allowed for reporting on your topic? How accessible are the data you need? How thorough should your research be?

If you are writing about low morale among employees who work shifts, for example, how many of your 475 employees should you interview? Should you limit your research to company-related morale factors, or should you consider external factors over which the company has no control? In investigating variable-rate mortgages, should you focus on a particular group, such as first-time homeowners in a specific area, or should you consider all mortgage holders? The first step in writing a report, then, is determining the precise boundaries of the topic.

Once you have defined the project and limited its scope, write a statement of purpose. The statement of purpose should describe the goal, scope, significance, and limitations of the report. Notice how the following statement includes all four criteria:

> The purpose of this report is to explore employment possibilities for entry-level paralegal workers in the city of St. John's. It will consider typical salaries, skills required, opportunities, and working conditions. This research is significant because of the increasing number of job openings in the electronic health records field. This report will not consider health care sector secretarial employment, which represents a different employment focus.

A formal business research report is characterized by serious tone, traditional structure, and considerable length.

The planning of every report begins with a statement of purpose explaining the goal, significance, and limitations of the report.

WORKPLACE IN FOCUS

Hailed as the largest science experiment in history, the Large Hadron Collider is a multibillion-dollar atom-smasher out to uncover the origins of the universe. Buried 100 metres below Meyrin, Switzerland, the massive particle accelerator uses barrel-shaped solenoids and supercooled magnets to recreate conditions believed to have existed during the Big Bang. Physicists at CERN built the collider to investigate the existence of extra dimensions and "dark matter"—an invisible mass that may comprise much of the universe. Despite public fears that the atomic project could unleash an Earth-swallowing black hole, scientists backing the collider have issued formal reports affirming its safety. *Why is it important for CERN to provide accurate documentation in its safety reports?*

▣ Researching Secondary Data

One of the most important steps in the process of writing a report is doing research that will help solve the business problem at hand. A report is only as good as its data, so you'll want to spend considerable time collecting data before you begin writing.

Primary data come from firsthand experience and observation; secondary data, from reading articles, books, Web sites, reports, and statistics.

Data fall into two broad categories, primary and secondary. Primary data result from firsthand experience and observation. Secondary data come from reading what others have experienced and observed. One of the best-known organizations that researches primary data is Consumers Union (**www.consumerreports.org**), a nonprofit organization headquartered in Yonkers, New York. After testing all kinds of consumer goods in its National Testing and Research Center—everything from cars to computers to fitness equipment—Consumers Union publishes its results in its best-selling magazine, *Consumer Reports*. Once published, the primary data generated in the Yonkers lab becomes secondary data. Now anyone—a student, a parent, a potential customer, or a newspaper reporter—can use the data. Secondary data are easier and less expensive to develop than primary data, which might involve interviewing large groups or sending out questionnaires.

Secondary research is where nearly every research project should begin. Often, something has already been written about your topic. Reviewing secondary sources can save time and effort and help you avoid costly primary research to develop data that already exist. Most secondary material is available in online databases conveniently located in your school or company library.

Print Resources

Although researchers are increasingly turning to electronic data, some data are available only in print.

Although we've seen a steady move away from print to electronic data, some information is still most easily accessible in print. For example, articles published in peer-reviewed academic journals, which are sometimes important when researching business problems, may not be available on the public or open Internet. If your company doesn't pay for a subscription to research databases (many companies do not), you may have to rely on your local reference library to find peer-reviewed articles in journals. Sometimes these journals are in old-fashioned hard-copy format on shelves. More often they are found in databases that your local public library system subscribes to and makes available to its patrons. Similarly, because many daily newspapers have instituted pay-firewalls (i.e., you must be a paid member to access most stories), you may find you need to get your hands on a hard-copy version of the *National Post* or *The Globe and Mail* to track down a useful article from the business section. Knowing where to find these hard-copy versions of academic journals and daily newspapers in your local library is still an important asset.

If you are an infrequent library user, begin your research by talking with a reference librarian about your project. These librarians won't do your research for you, but they will steer you in the right direction. Most libraries also help you understand their computer, cataloguing, and retrieval systems by providing brochures, handouts, and workshops.

Books provide historical, in-depth data; periodicals provide limited but current coverage.

BOOKS. Although sometimes outdated, depending on how quickly a particular body of knowledge changes, books provide excellent in-depth data and interpretation on many subjects. For example, if you are investigating best practices in Web site design, you will find numerous books with valuable information in your nearest library. Books are located through online catalogues that can be accessed in the library, on any campus computer, or from home with an Internet connection and valid password. Most library catalogues today enable you to learn not only whether a book is in the library's holdings but also whether it is currently available.

PERIODICALS. Magazines, newspapers, and journals are called periodicals because of their recurrent or periodic publication. Articles in journals and other periodicals will be extremely useful to you because they are concise, limited in scope, and current, and can supplement information in books. For example, if you want to understand the latest trends and research in the business communication field, you would browse through recent volumes of the *Journal of Business Communication*. And if you're studying the fluctuating prices of commodities like food and energy, a reputable newspaper's business section would be a good place to start to get oriented to the topic.

Research Databases

As a writer of business reports today, you will most likely do much of your secondary research using online research databases. Many researchers turn to databases first because they are fast, focused, and available online. Databases are exactly what they sound like: large collections of information in electronic format. In this case, the information is almost every article published in every newspaper, magazine, academic journal, and trade journal. A huge amount of information, by any measure. By using these online resources you can look for the secondary data you require without ever leaving your office or home.

The strength of databases lies in the fact that they are current and field-specific. For example, if you go to the George Brown College Library Web site (**library .georgebrown.ca**), you will instantly see the "Start Your Research" title and right underneath it a box that says "Articles & Databases." Clicking here, you can choose the area of you research (e.g., Business, Health, Hospitality, Technology) and click Go. Doing so will take you to a list of databases of information in your particular area of research. If you click on Business, for example, a list of over 50 different databases appears. These business databases contain articles from magazines, newspapers, and academic journals, but they also contain statistical information, encyclopedia information, company information, and various other important business information. Your own library will have similar resources. Libraries pay for these databases partly through your tuition fees. If in your workplace you do not have access to an institution's databases, your local public library (e.g., Vancouver Public Library) will have databases available for your use (assuming you have a valid library card!).

Learning how to use an online database takes some practice. We suggest you go to your local urban library site and experiment with online databases. Choose a topic like *trends in business communication* and see what you come up with. Try to find one current article from a newspaper, a magazine, and a journal. Do you get better results when you use the basic or the advanced search function? Do you get better results by separating the topic into parts, for example, *trends* and *business* and *communication*, or by typing in the whole phrase at once? If you're having trouble, you can always sign up for a free guided seminar at your library, or ask a librarian for help next time you're there.

> Most researchers today begin by looking in online databases, which are collections of almost every article published in any publication.

> Review information online through research databases that are accessible by computer and searchable.

The Internet

Growing at a dizzying pace, the Internet includes an enormous collection of pages created by people around the world. The Internet is interactive, mobile, and user-friendly with multimedia content ranging from digital sound files to vivid images and video files. With trillions of pages of information available on the Internet, chances are that if you have a question, an answer exists online. To a business researcher, the Internet offers a wide range of organizational and commercial information. You can expect to find such items as product and service facts, public relations material, mission statements, staff directories, press releases, current company news, government information, selected article reprints, collaborative scientific project reports, stock research, financial information, and employment information.

The Internet is unquestionably one of the greatest sources of information now available to anyone needing simple facts quickly and inexpensively. But finding relevant, credible information can be frustrating and time-consuming. The constantly changing contents of the Internet and its lack of organization irritate budding

> The Internet is a collection of hypertext pages that offer information and links to trillions of pages.

researchers. Moreover, content isn't always reliable. Anyone posting a site is a publisher without any quality control or guarantee. The problem of gathering information is complicated by the fact that the total number of Web sites recently surpassed 600 million, growing at a rate of about 5 percent or 30 million new sites each month.[3] Therefore, to succeed in your search for information and answers, you need to understand how to browse the Internet and use search engines. You also need to understand how to evaluate the information you find.

BROWSERS AND URLs. Searching the Internet requires a browser, such as Microsoft Internet Explorer, Safari, or Firefox. Browsers are software programs that enable you to view the graphics and text of, as well as access links to, Web pages. To locate the Web page of a specific organization, you need its Web site address, or URL (Uniform Resource Locator). URLs are case and space sensitive, so be sure to type the address exactly as it is printed. For most companies, the URL follows the pattern of **www.xyzcompany.com**. Your goal is to locate the top-level Web page (called the *home page* and, in certain cases, *portal*) of an organization's site. On this page you will generally find an overview of the site contents or a link to a site map. If you can't guess a company's URL, you can usually find it quickly using Google (**www.google.ca**).

Internet access has gone mobile in the last few years, as increasingly sophisticated smartphones, netbooks, and tablet devices such as the iPad now offer nearly the same functions as desktop and laptop computers do. Mobile browsers, also called mini browsers, are small versions of their bigger cousins, Internet Explorer or Firefox. Businesspeople can surf Web pages and write e-mail on the go with devices such as the popular BlackBerry and iPhone, which fit into their pockets. Similarly, users can listen to podcasts, digital recordings of radio programs, and other audio and video files on demand. Podcasts are distributed for downloading to a computer or an MP3 audio player such as the iPod and can be enjoyed anywhere you choose.

SEARCH TOOLS. The Internet is packed with amazing information. Instead of visiting libraries or searching reference books when you need to find something, you can now turn to the Web for all kinds of facts. However, finding what you are looking for on the Web is hopeless without powerful, specialized search tools, such as Google, Bing, and Yahoo Search. A search tool, also called a search engine, is a service that indexes, organizes, and often rates and reviews Web pages. Some search tools rely on people to maintain a catalogue of Web sites or pages. Others use software to identify key information. They all begin a search based on the keywords that you enter. The most-used search engine at this writing is Google. It has developed a huge following with its ease of use and its "uncanny ability to sort through millions of Web pages and put the sites you really want at the top of its results pages."[4]

INTERNET SEARCH TIPS AND TECHNIQUES. To conduct a thorough search for the information you need, use these tips and techniques:

- **Use two or three search tools.** Different Internet search engines turn up different results. However, at this writing, Google consistently turns up more reliable "hits" than other search engines.
- **Know your search tool.** When connecting to a search service for the first time, always read the description of its service, including its FAQs (Frequently Asked Questions), Help, and How to Search sections. In Google, for example, there are special sub-search areas (e.g., news, images, videos, books, scholar) that can refine or speed up your search process.
- **Understand case sensitivity.** Generally use lowercase for your searches, unless you are searching for a term that is typically written in upper- and lowercase, such as a person's name.

- **Use nouns as search words and as many as eight words in a query.** The right key words—and more of them—can narrow your search considerably.
- **Use quotation marks.** When searching for a phrase, such as *cost-benefit analysis,* most search engines will retrieve documents having all or some of the terms. This and/or strategy is the default of most search engines. To locate occurrences of a specific phrase, enclose it in quotation marks.
- **Omit articles and prepositions.** Known as "stop words," articles and prepositions don't add value to a search. Instead of *request for proposal,* use *proposal request.*
- **Proofread your search words.** Make sure you are searching for the right thing by proofreading your search words carefully. For example, searching for *sock market* will come up with substantially different results than searching for *stock market.*
- **Save the best.** To keep better track of your favourite Web sites, save them as bookmarks or favourites.
- **Keep trying.** If a search produces no results, check your spelling. Try synonyms and variations on words. Try to be less specific in your search term. If your search produces too many hits, try to be more specific. Think of words that uniquely identify what you are looking for, and use as many relevant keywords as possible. Use a variety of search engines, and repeat your search a few days later.

Blogs and Social Networks

The Internet continues to grow and expand, offering a great variety of virtual communities and collaboration tools. Mentioned most frequently are blogs and social networking sites. Far from being mere entertainment, these resources are affecting the way we do business today.

One of the newest ways to locate secondary information on the Web is through the use of *blogs.* Blogs are used by business researchers, students, politicians, the media, and many others to share and gather information. Marketing firms and their clients are looking closely at blogs because blogs can produce unbiased consumer feedback faster and more cheaply than such staples of consumer research as focus groups and surveys.[5] Research published by Technorati confirms that 42 percent of its respondents blog about brands they like or dislike.[6] Employees and executives at companies such as Google, Rogers, IBM, McCain, and Hewlett-Packard maintain blogs. They use blogs to communicate internally with employees and externally with clients.[7]

A blog is an online diary or journal that allows visitors to leave public comments. At this time, writers have posted 153 million blogs, according to BlogPulse statistics.[8] However, only about half of these blogs are active, meaning that posts were published within the last three months. A recent Pew Internet study suggested that 32 percent of adult Internet users read a blog once a month and only 17 percent used Twitter or other status-update services.[9] Although blogs may have been overrated in their importance, they do represent an amazing new information stream if used wisely. Be sure to evaluate all blog content using the checklist provided in the Communication Workshop at the end of Chapter 8.

At least as important to business as blogs are social media sites. Far from being only entertaining leisure sites, social networks such as Facebook and Twitter are used by businesses to enable teams to form spontaneously and naturally and then to assign targeted projects to them. Social media is also used by business to "listen and engage in customer conversations, address customer complaints and feedback more quickly, and proactively provide information to customers, as well as positively influence customer's opinions."[10] However, these exciting new online tools require sound judgment when researchers wish to use them. For example, if using social networking to promote a product as a marketer, are you ethically compromised by invading the privacy of unsuspecting members of the public?

> Blogs, wikis, and informal online networks can be used to generate primary or secondary data.

◼ Generating Primary Data

Primary data come from firsthand experience.

Although you'll begin a business report by searching for secondary data, you'll need primary data to give a complete, up-to-date, and original picture. Business reports that solve specific current problems typically rely on primary, firsthand data. If, for example, management wants to discover the cause of increased employee turnover in its Halifax office, it must investigate conditions in Halifax by collecting recent information. Providing answers to business problems often means generating primary data through surveys, interviews, observation, or experimentation.

Surveys

Surveys yield efficient and economical primary data for reports.

Surveys collect data from groups of people. When companies develop new products, for example, they often survey consumers to learn their needs. The advantages of surveys are that they gather data economically and efficiently. Traditionally mailed, e-mailed, and online surveys reach big groups nearby or at great distances. Moreover, surveys are easy to respond to because they're designed with closed-ended, quantifiable questions. It's easy to pick an answer on a professionally designed survey, thus improving the accuracy of the data.

Surveys, of course, have disadvantages. Most of us rank them as an intrusion on our increasingly important private time, so response rates may be no higher than 10 percent. Furthermore, those who do respond may not represent an accurate sample of the overall population, thus invalidating generalizations for the group. Let's say, for example, that an insurance company sends out a survey questionnaire asking about provisions in a new policy. If only older people respond, the survey data cannot be used to generalize what people in other age groups might think.

A final problem with surveys has to do with truthfulness. Some respondents exaggerate their incomes or distort other facts, thus causing the results to be unreliable. Nevertheless, surveys are still considered the best way to generate data for business and student reports.

Interviews

Interviews with experts produce useful report data, especially when little has been written about a topic.

Some of the best report information, particularly on topics about which little has been written, comes from individuals. These individuals are usually experts or veterans in their fields. Consider both in-house and outside experts for business reports. Tapping these sources will call for in-person, e-mail, or telephone interviews. To elicit the most useful data, try these techniques:

- **Locate an expert.** Ask managers and other individuals whom they consider to be most knowledgeable about a particular field or industry. Check Web sites of professional organizations and consult articles about the topic or related topics. Most people enjoy being experts or at least recommending them. You could also post an inquiry to an Internet group. Choose your groups carefully, though, to avoid being flooded with unwanted correspondence.
- **Prepare for the interview.** Learn about the individual you're interviewing as well as the background and terminology of the topic. Let's say you're interviewing a corporate communication expert about producing an in-house company blog. You ought to be familiar with terms such as *font* and software such as WordPress or Movable Type. In addition, be prepared by making a list of questions that pinpoint your areas of interest in the topic. Ask the interviewee if you may record the talk.
- **Maintain a professional attitude.** Call before the interview to confirm the arrangements, and then arrive on time. Be prepared to take notes if your recorder fails (and remember to ask permission beforehand if you want to record). Dress professionally, and use your body language to convey respect.
- **Make your questions objective and friendly.** Don't get into a debating match with the interviewee. And remember that you're there to listen, not to talk! Use open-ended, rather than yes-or-no, questions to draw experts out.

- **Watch the time.** Tell interviewees in advance how much time you expect to need for the interview. Don't overstay your appointment.
- **End graciously.** Conclude the interview with a general question, such as *Is there anything you'd like to add?* Express your appreciation, and ask permission to phone or e-mail later if you need to verify points.

Observation and Experimentation

Some kinds of primary data can be obtained only through firsthand observation and investigation. How long does a typical caller wait before a customer service representative answers the call? How is a new piece of equipment operated? Are complaints of sexual harassment being taken seriously? Observation produces rich data, but that information is especially prone to charges of subjectivity. One can interpret an observation in many ways. Thus, to make observations more objective, try to quantify them. For example, record customer telephone wait time for 60-minute periods at different times throughout a week. Or compare the number of sexual harassment complaints made with the number of investigations undertaken and resulting actions.

When you observe, plan ahead. Arrive early enough to introduce yourself and set up whatever equipment you think is necessary. Make sure you have received permissions beforehand, particularly if you are recording. In addition, take notes, not only of the events or actions but also of the settings. Changes in environment often have an effect on actions. Famous for his out-of-the box thinking, Howard Schultz, the CEO of Starbucks, is known to hate research, advertising, and customer surveys. Instead of relying on sophisticated marketing research, Schultz visits 25 Starbucks locations a week to learn about his customers.[11]

Experimentation produces data suggesting causes and effects. Informal experimentation might be as simple as a pretest and post-test in a college course. Did students expand their knowledge as a result of the course? More formal experimentation is undertaken by scientists and professional researchers who control variables to test their effects. Assume, for example, that Mordens' of Winnipeg Candy Manufacturing wants to test the hypothesis (which is a tentative assumption) that chocolate lifts people out of depression. An experiment testing the hypothesis would separate depressed individuals into two groups: those who ate chocolate (the experimental group) and those who did not (the control group). What effect did chocolate have? Such experiments are not done haphazardly, however. Valid experiments require sophisticated research designs, careful attention to matching the experimental and control groups, and ethical considerations.

> Some of the best report data come from firsthand observation and investigation.

Documenting Data and Plagiarism

One common complaint of college and university professors is that their students don't understand the importance of documentation. Documentation is the act of showing where your information came from, whether in a business report, in an academic essay, or in a workplace presentation. Young people sometimes find it hard to understand that *all* information, whether it comes from a book, a magazine, a newspaper, a pamphlet or brochure, a Web site, or a blog, is theoretically the "property" of someone else. If you use it and don't say that you've used it, you're stealing.

Put yourself in the shoes of a journalist. She makes her living by writing for a newspaper. If you take a phrase or a sentence or a paragraph from what she's written and place it in your report or presentation without acknowledging that fact, you're infringing on her rights—you're stealing from her. Not documenting sources is dishonest, ethically problematic, and illegal. The crime is called plagiarism, and all colleges and universities have strict policies against it, including penalties such as a zero grade on the plagiarized assignment and sometimes a mention on your final transcript. If your instructor has not already discussed your institution's policy, you should ask him or her to do so.

Plagiarism is the act of *not* documenting your sources, of taking another person's ideas or published words and not acknowledging that fact. Any time you quote directly, paraphrase, or summarize information from a source, you must document it.

RECOGNIZING THE PURPOSE OF DOCUMENTATION. As a careful business writer and presenter, you should document your data properly for the following reasons:

- **To strengthen your argument.** Including good data from reputable sources will convince readers of your credibility and the logic of your reasoning.
- **To protect yourself.** Acknowledging your sources keeps you honest. It's unethical and illegal to use others' ideas without proper documentation.
- **To instruct the reader/audience.** Citing references enables readers and listeners to pursue a topic further and make use of the information themselves.

WHAT HAS TO BE DOCUMENTED? When you write reports, especially in college, you are continually dealing with other people's ideas. You are expected to conduct research, synthesize ideas, and build on the work of others. But you are also expected to give proper credit for borrowed material. To avoid plagiarism, you must give credit whenever you use the following:[12]

- Another person's ideas, opinions, examples, or theory
- Any facts, statistics, graphs, and drawings that are not common knowledge
- Quotations of another person's actual spoken or written words
- Paraphrases of another person's spoken or written words

Information that is common knowledge requires no documentation. For example, the statement *Many businesspeople agree that* The Report on Business *is among Canada's top mainstream business sources* would require no citation. Statements that are not common knowledge, however, must be documented. For example, *Alberta is home to seven of Canada's top ten fastest-growing large cities* would require a citation because most people don't know this fact (in this case the information came from a story on Huffingtonpost.ca quoting Statistics Canada's 2011 census).[13] Cite sources for proprietary information such as statistics organized and reported by a newspaper or magazine. You probably use citations to document direct quotations, but you must also cite ideas that you summarize in your own words.

HOW TO PARAPHRASE. In writing reports and using the ideas of others, you will probably rely heavily on *paraphrasing*, which means restating an original passage in your own words and in your own style. To do a good job of paraphrasing, follow these steps:

1. Read the original material carefully to comprehend its full meaning.
2. Write your own version without looking at the original.
3. Avoid repeating the grammatical structure of the original and merely replacing words with synonyms.
4. Reread the original to be sure you covered the main points but did not borrow specific language.

To better understand the difference between plagiarizing and paraphrasing, study the following passages. Notice that the writer of the plagiarized version uses the same grammatical construction as the source and often merely replaces words with synonyms. Even the acceptable version, however, requires a reference to the source author.

Original Source

While the BlackBerry has become standard armor for executives, a few maverick leaders are taking action to reduce e-mail use . . . . The concern, say academics and management thinkers, is misinterpreted messages, as well as the degree to which e-mail has become a substitute for the nuanced conversations that are critical in the workplace.[14]

Plagiarized Version

Although smartphones are standard among business executives, some pioneering bosses are acting to lower e-mail usage. Business professors and management experts are concerned that messages are misinterpreted and that e-mail substitutes for nuances in conversations that are crucial on the job (Last name, year).

Acceptable Paraphrase

E-mail on the go may be the rage in business. However, some executives are rethinking its use, as communication experts warn that e-mail triggers misunderstandings. These specialists believe that e-mail should not replace the more subtle face-to-face interaction needed on the job (Last name, year).

> The plagiarized version uses the same sentence structure as the original and makes few changes other than replacing some words.

> The acceptable paraphrase presents ideas from a different perspective and uses a different sentence structure than the original.

HOW TO DOCUMENT. Documentation is achieved through citations. A citation is how you tell your reader from where the idea or phrase or sentence was borrowed (e.g., an endnote citation, an APA-style citation, an MLA-style citation, etc.). The original reason behind citations (before plagiarism became a big problem) was to allow anyone reading your work to find your sources should he or she wish to do additional research. If someone says to you, "But you didn't cite it!" he or she means you didn't include a proper citation.

For example, in a report that reads *In a recent Vancouver Province article, Blake Spence, Director of Transportation, argues that Toronto's transit system must be modernized and expanded to cope with the influx of tourists expected during the 2015 Pan American Games (A17)*, the MLA-style citation is the combination of the lead-in, *Blake Spence . . . argues*, and the page reference, *(A17)*. The basic elements of an MLA-style in-text citation are the author's name and the page number. There will be times when you don't have these two pieces of information. For more information on such cases, as well as the two main citation methods—footnote/endnote (or Chicago style) and parenthetic (or APA and MLA style)—please read Appendix C. Also study Figure 9.17 (pages 283–292) to see how sources are documented there. Besides in-text citations, you will cite each source you've used (primary and secondary) at the end of your report on a page called the "Works Cited" or "References" page. There is a specific format for how this is done, also found in Appendix C.

CITING ELECTRONIC SOURCES. Research has become an extension of our fingertips. We log on and search the Internet as if it's part of us, unlike earlier generations of students, who experienced a separation between themselves and research sources. They had to physically get to a library, wander around, find books and magazines on shelves, flip through pages to find material, copy that material into a notebook, then go back home and copy it on a typewriter or computer. It's therefore no surprise that plagiarism is on the rise. As a recent article in the *Ottawa Citizen* points out, 53 percent of undergraduate students in Canada admit to "copying a few sentences from a written source or the Internet" without citing.[15]

Precisely because it's so easy to do, Internet plagiarism is a difficult problem to root out. Some students today even believe that they're not doing anything wrong by copying information from the Internet. Unfortunately, the reality is that this act constitutes academic dishonesty, and all academic institutions penalize dishonesty with a range of penalties, from a zero on the assignment, to revoking admission from a course or a program, to displaying evidence of academic dishonesty on academic transcripts. It's your responsibility as a business communicator, both at school and at work, not to plagiarize from the Internet.

When citing electronic media, you should hold the same goals as for print sources. That is, you want to give credit to the author and to allow others to

OFFICE INSIDER

Changing the words of an original source is not sufficient to prevent plagiarism. If you have retained the essential idea of an original source, and have not cited it, then no matter how drastically you may have altered its context or presentation, you have still plagiarized.

locate the same or updated information easily. However, since electronic sources are less stable than books or magazines, citation guides recommend more information be provided when citing electronic sources than when citing print sources. Since electronic sources can be changed easily, multiple publication dates may need to be included as well as the date on which the source was used. For an electronic source, your citation should include the author's name (when available), document title, Web page or online database title, access date, and Web address. See Appendix C for more detailed information and examples of citing electronic sources.

Organizing and Outlining Data

Once you have collected the data for a report and recorded that information on notes or printouts, you are ready to organize it into a coherent plan of presentation. First, you should decide on an organizational strategy, and then, following your plan, you will want to outline the report. Poorly organized reports lead to frustration; therefore, it is important to organize your report carefully so that readers will understand, remember, or be persuaded.

Organizational Strategies

The readability and effectiveness of a report are greatly enhanced by skillful organization of the information presented. As you begin the process of organization, ask yourself two important questions: (a) Where should I place the conclusions/recommendations? and (b) How should I organize the findings?

> In the direct strategy, conclusions and recommendations come first; in the indirect strategy, they are last.

WHERE TO PLACE THE CONCLUSIONS AND RECOMMENDATIONS. As you recall from earlier instruction, the direct strategy requires that we present main ideas first. In formal reports that would mean beginning with your conclusions and recommendations. For example, if you were studying five possible locations for a proposed shopping centre, you would begin with the recommendation of the best site. Use this strategy when the reader is supportive and knowledgeable. However, if the reader isn't supportive or needs to be informed, the indirect strategy may be better. This strategy involves presenting facts and discussion first, followed by conclusions and recommendations. Since formal reports often seek to educate the reader, this order of presentation is often most effective. Following this sequence, a study of possible locations for a shopping centre would begin with data regarding all proposed sites followed by an analysis of the information and conclusions drawn from that analysis.

> Organize report findings chronologically, geographically, topically, or by one of the other methods shown in Figure 9.2.

HOW TO ORGANIZE THE FINDINGS. After collecting your facts, you need a coherent plan for presenting them. Below we describe three organizational patterns: chronological, geographical, and topical. You will find these and other patterns summarized in Figure 9.2. The pattern you choose depends on the material collected and the purpose of your report.

- **Chronological order.** Information sequenced along a time frame is arranged chronologically. This plan is effective for presenting historical data or for describing a procedure. Agendas, minutes of meetings, progress reports, and procedures are usually organized by time. A description of the development of a multinational company, for example, would be chronological. A report explaining how to obtain federal funding for a project might be organized chronologically. Often topics are arranged in a past-to-present or present-to-past sequence.
- **Geographical or spatial arrangement.** Information arranged geographically or spatially is organized by physical location. For instance, a report analyzing a

FIGURE 9.2 Organizational Patterns for Reports

PATTERN	DEVELOPMENT	USE
Chronology	Arrange information in a time sequence to show history or development of topic.	Useful in showing time relationships, such as five-year profit figures or a series of events leading to a problem
Geography/ Space	Organize information by regions or areas.	Appropriate for topics that are easily divided into locations, such as East Coast and West Coast, etc.
Topic/ Function	Arrange by topics or functions.	Works well for topics with established categories, such as a report about categories of company expenses
Compare/ Contrast	Present problem and show alternative solutions. Use consistent criteria. Show how the solutions are similar and different.	Best used for "before and after" scenarios or for problems with clear alternatives
Journalism Pattern	Arrange information in paragraphs devoted to *who, what, when, where, why*, and *how*. May conclude with recommendations.	Useful with audiences that need to be educated or persuaded
Value/Size	Start with the most valuable, biggest, or most important item. Discuss other items in descending order.	Useful for classifying information in, for example, a realtor's report on home values
Importance	Arrange from most to least important or build from least to most important.	Appropriate when persuading the audience to take a specific action or change a belief
Simple/ Complex	Begin with simple concept; proceed to more complex idea.	Useful for technical or abstract topics
Best Case/ Worst Case	Describe the best and worst possible outcomes.	Useful when dramatic effect is needed to achieve results; helpful when audience is uninterested or uninformed
Convention	Organize the report using a prescribed plan that all readers understand.	Useful for many operational and recurring reports such as weekly sales reports

company's national sales might be divided into sections representing geographical areas such as the East Coast, Quebec, Southern Ontario, Northern Ontario, the Prairies, and the West Coast.

- **Topical or criteria arrangement.** Some subjects lend themselves to arrangement by topic or criteria. A report analyzing changes that need to be made to improve a company's Web site is an example. The report could be organized by *Possible Models and Competitor Models* or by the criteria used to judge effective Web sites, such as *Usability, Navigation, Content, and Other Design Issues.*

Outlines and Headings

Most writers agree that the clearest way to show the organization of a report topic is by recording its divisions in an outline. Although the outline isn't part of the final report, it is a valuable tool for the writer. It reveals at a glance the overall organization of the report. As you learned in Chapter 3, outlining involves dividing a topic into major sections and supporting those with details. Figure 9.3 shows a short outline for a report about forms of business ownership. Rarely is a real outline so perfectly balanced; some sections are usually longer than others.

> Outlines show the organization and divisions of a report.

The main points used to outline a report often become the main headings of the written report, amplified with facts, statistics, quotations, and other data. In Chapter 8 you studied tips for writing different types of headings. Formatting those headings depends on what level they represent. Major headings, as you can see in

FIGURE 9.3 Outline for a Report

FORMS OF BUSINESS OWNERSHIP

I. Sole proprietorship (*first main topic*)
    A. Advantages of sole proprietorship (*first subdivision of Topic I*)
        1. Minimal capital requirements (*first subdivision of Topic A*)
        2. Control by owner (*second subdivision of Topic A*)
    B. Disadvantages of sole proprietorship (*second subdivision of Topic I*)
        1. Unlimited liability (*first subdivision of Topic B*)
        2. Limited management talent (*second subdivision of Topic B*)
II. Partnership (*second main topic*)
    A. Advantages of partnership (*first subdivision of Topic II*)
        1. Access to capital (*first subdivision of Topic A*)
        2. Management talent (*second subdivision of Topic A*)
        3. Ease of formation (*third subdivision of Topic A*)
    B. Disadvantages of partnership (*second subdivision of Topic II*)
        1. Unlimited liability (*first subdivision of Topic B*)
        2. Personality conflicts (*second subdivision of Topic B*)

Figure 9.4, are centred and typed in bold font. Second-level headings start at the left margin, and third-level headings are bolded, situated at the beginning of a paragraph, and followed by a period.

Creating Effective Graphics Using Your Data

> Effective graphics clarify numerical data and simplify complex ideas.

After collecting and interpreting information, you need to consider how best to present it. If your report contains complex data and numbers, you may want to consider graphics such as tables and charts. These graphics clarify data, create visual interest, and make numerical data meaningful. By simplifying complex ideas and emphasizing key data, well-constructed graphics make key information more understandable and easier to remember. In contrast, readers tend to be bored and confused by text paragraphs packed with complex data and numbers. Use the following points as a general guide to creating effective graphics in a report:

- Clearly identify the contents of the visual aid with meaningful titles and numbering (e.g., *Figure 1: Internet Use at Canadian Companies*).
- Refer the reader to the visual aid by discussing it in the text and mentioning its location and figure number (e.g., *as Figure 1 below shows . . .*).
- Locate the visual aid close to its reference in the text.
- Strive for vertical placement of visual aids. Readers are disoriented by horizontal pages in reports.
- Give credit to the source if appropriate (e.g., *Source: Statistics Canada*).

You need to understand, however, that the same data can be shown in many forms. For example, a company's quarterly sales can be displayed in a chart, table, or graph. That's why you need to know how to match the appropriate graphic with your objective and how to incorporate it into your report.

Matching Graphics and Objectives

Before creating the best graphics, you should first decide what data you want to highlight and which graphics are most appropriate to your objectives. Tables? Bar charts? Pie charts? Line charts? Surface charts? Flow charts? Organization charts?

FIGURE 9.4 Heading Levels in Reports

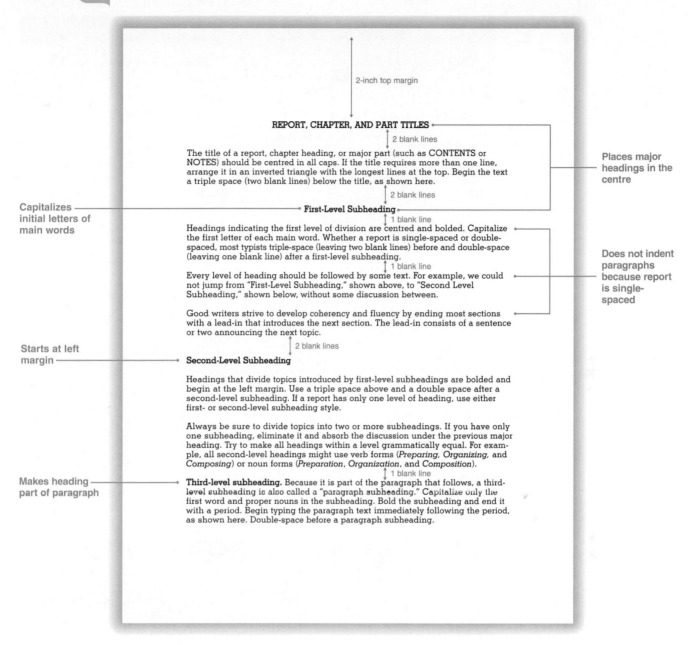

Places major headings in the centre

Capitalizes initial letters of main words

Does not indent paragraphs because report is single-spaced

Starts at left margin

Makes heading part of paragraph

2-inch top margin

REPORT, CHAPTER, AND PART TITLES

2 blank lines

The title of a report, chapter heading, or major part (such as CONTENTS or NOTES) should be centred in all caps. If the title requires more than one line, arrange it in an inverted triangle with the longest lines at the top. Begin the text a triple space (two blank lines) below the title, as shown here.

2 blank lines

First-Level Subheading

1 blank line

Headings indicating the first level of division are centred and bolded. Capitalize the first letter of each main word. Whether a report is single-spaced or double-spaced, most typists triple-space (leaving two blank lines) before and double-space (leaving one blank line) after a first-level subheading.

1 blank line

Every level of heading should be followed by some text. For example, we could not jump from "First-Level Subheading," shown above, to "Second Level Subheading," shown below, without some discussion between.

Good writers strive to develop coherency and fluency by ending most sections with a lead-in that introduces the next section. The lead-in consists of a sentence or two announcing the next topic.

2 blank lines

Second-Level Subheading

Headings that divide topics introduced by first-level subheadings are bolded and begin at the left margin. Use a triple space above and a double space after a second-level subheading. If a report has only one level of heading, use either first- or second-level subheading style.

Always be sure to divide topics into two or more subheadings. If you have only one subheading, eliminate it and absorb the discussion under the previous major heading. Try to make all headings within a level grammatically equal. For example, all second-level headings might use verb forms (*Preparing, Organizing,* and *Composing*) or noun forms (*Preparation, Organization,* and *Composition*).

1 blank line

Third-level subheading. Because it is part of the paragraph that follows, a third-level subheading is also called a "paragraph subheading." Capitalize only the first word and proper nouns in the subheading. Bold the subheading and end it with a period. Begin typing the paragraph text immediately following the period, as shown here. Double-space before a paragraph subheading.

Pictures? Figure 9.5 summarizes appropriate uses for each type of graphic. The following sections discuss each type in detail.

TABLES. Probably the most frequently used visual aid in reports is the table. A table presents quantitative information in a systematic order of columns and rows. Here are tips for designing good tables, one of which is illustrated in Figure 9.6:

- Provide clear heads for the rows and columns.
- Identify the units in which figures are given (percentages, dollars, units per worker-hour, and so forth) in the table title, in the column or row head, with the first item in a column, or in a note at the bottom.
- Arrange items in a logical order (alphabetical, chronological, geographical, highest to lowest) depending on what you need to emphasize.

> Tables permit systematic presentation of large amounts of data, while charts enhance visual comparisons.

FIGURE 9.5 Matching Graphics to Objectives

Graphic		Objective
Table	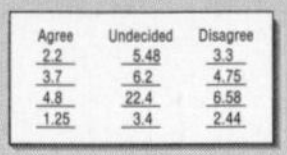	To show exact figures and values
Bar Chart	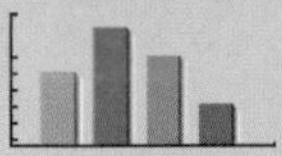	To compare one item with others
Line Chart	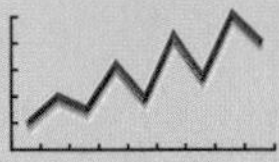	To demonstrate changes in quantitative data over time
Pie Chart		To visualize a whole unit and the proportions of its components
Flow Chart	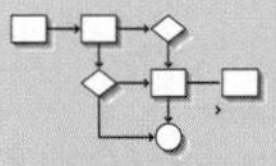	To display a process or procedure
Organization Chart	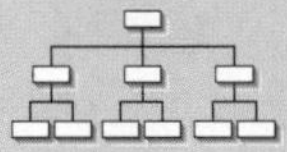	To define a hierarchy of elements
Photograph, Map, Illustration		To create authenticity, to spotlight a location, and to show an item in use

FIGURE 9.6 Table Summarizing Precise Data

FIGURE 1 SATSUNO COMPUTING NUMBER OF TABLETS SOLD, 2015					
REGION	1ST QTR.	2ND QTR.	3RD QTR.	4TH QTR.	YEARLY TOTALS
Atlantic	13 302	15 003	15 550	16 210	60 065
Central	12 678	11 836	10 689	14 136	49 339
Prairie	10 345	11 934	10 899	12 763	45 941
Pacific	9 345	8 921	9 565	10 256	38 087
Total	45 670	47 694	46 703	53 365	193 432

- Use *N/A* (not available) for missing data.
- Make long tables easier to read by shading alternate lines or by leaving a blank line after groups of five.

Bar charts enable readers to compare related items, see changes over time, and understand how parts relate to a whole.

BAR CHARTS. Although they lack the precision of tables, bar charts enable you to make emphatic visual comparisons. Bar charts can be used to compare related items, illustrate changes in data over time, and show segments as part of a whole.

FIGURE 9.7 Vertical Bar Chart

Figure 1

2014 MPM INCOME BY DIVISION

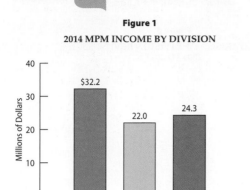

Source: *Industry Profiles* (New York: DataPro, 2012), p. 225.

FIGURE 9.8 Horizontal Bar Chart

Figure 2

TOTAL MPM INCOME, 2010 TO 2014*

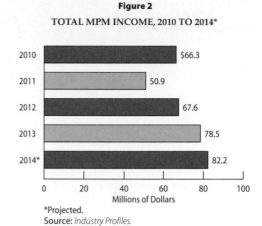

*Projected.
Source: *Industry Profiles.*

FIGURE 9.9 Grouped Bar Chart

Figure 3

**MPM INCOME BY DIVISION
2012, 2013, AND 2014**

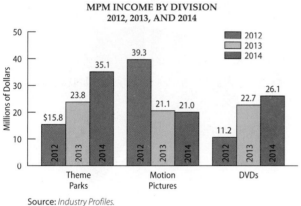

Source: *Industry Profiles.*

FIGURE 9.10 Segmented 100% Bar Chart

Figure 4

**PERCENTAGE OF TOTAL INCOME BY DIVISION
2012, 2013, AND 2014***

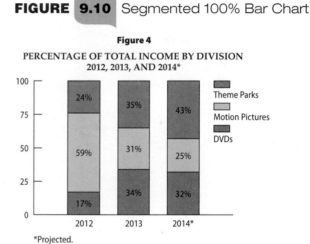

*Projected.
Source: *Industry Profiles.*

Figures 9.7 through 9.10 show vertical, horizontal, grouped, and segmented bar charts that highlight income for an entertainment company called MPM. Note how the varied bar charts present information in different ways.

Many suggestions for tables also hold true for bar charts. Here are a few additional tips:

- Keep the length of each bar and segment proportional.
- Include a total figure in the middle of a bar or at its end if the figure helps the reader and does not clutter the chart.
- Start dollar or percentage amounts at zero.

LINE CHARTS. The major advantage of line charts is that they show changes over time, thus indicating trends. Figures 9.11 through 9.13 show line charts that reflect revenue trends for the major divisions of MPM. Notice that line charts do not provide precise data. Instead, they give an overview or impression of the data. Experienced report writers use tables to list exact data; they use line charts or bar charts to spotlight important points or trends.

> Line charts illustrate trends and changes in data over time.

Simple line charts (Figure 9.11) show just one variable. Multiple line charts combine several variables (Figure 9.12). Segmented line charts (Figure 9.13), also called surface charts, illustrate how the components of a whole change over time.

FIGURE 9.11 Simple Line Chart

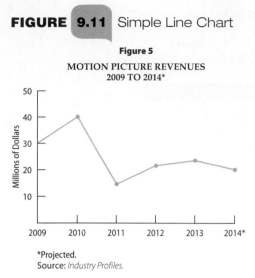

Figure 5

MOTION PICTURE REVENUES
2009 TO 2014*

*Projected.
Source: *Industry Profiles.*

FIGURE 9.12 Multiple Line Chart

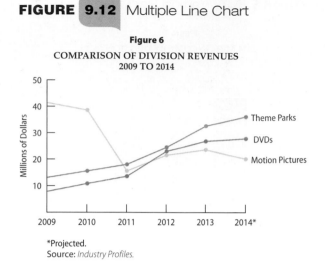

Figure 6

COMPARISON OF DIVISION REVENUES
2009 TO 2014

*Projected.
Source: *Industry Profiles.*

FIGURE 9.13 Segmented Line (Surface) Chart

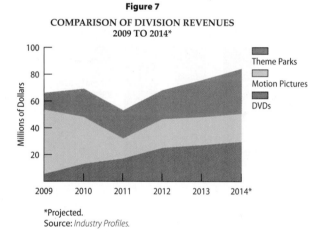

Figure 7

COMPARISON OF DIVISION REVENUES
2009 TO 2014*

*Projected.
Source: *Industry Profiles.*

FIGURE 9.14 Pie Chart

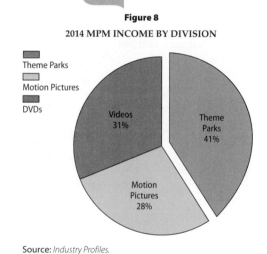

Figure 8

2014 MPM INCOME BY DIVISION

Source: *Industry Profiles.*

Here are tips for preparing line charts:

- Begin with a grid divided into squares.
- Arrange the time component (usually years) horizontally across the bottom; arrange values for the other variable vertically.
- Draw small dots at the intersections to indicate each value at a given year.
- Connect the dots and add colour if desired.
- To prepare a segmented (surface) chart, plot the first value (e.g., *DVD income*) across the bottom; add the next item (e.g., *motion picture income*) to the first figures for every increment; for the third item (e.g., *theme park income*) add its value to the total of the first two items. The top line indicates the total of the three values.

> Pie charts are most useful in showing the proportion of parts to a whole.

PIE CHARTS. Pie, or circle, charts help readers visualize a whole and the proportion of its components, or wedges. Pie charts, though less flexible than bar or line charts, are useful in showing percentages, as Figure 9.14 illustrates. For the most effective pie charts, follow these suggestions:

- Begin at the 12 o'clock position, drawing the largest wedge first. (Computer software programs don't always observe this advice, but if you're drawing your own charts, you can.)
- Include, if possible, the actual percentage or absolute value for each wedge.

FIGURE 9.15 Flow Chart

FLOW OF CUSTOMER ORDER THROUGH
ACME INC.

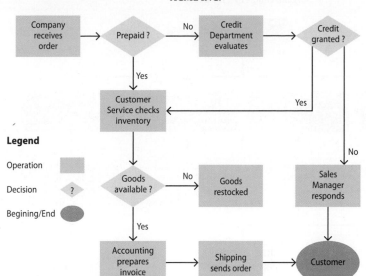

- Use four to eight segments for best results; if necessary, group small portions into one wedge called "Other."
- Distinguish wedges with colour, shading, or cross-hatching.
- Keep all labels horizontal.

FLOW CHARTS. Procedures are simplified and clarified by diagramming them in a flow chart, as shown in Figure 9.15. Whether you need to describe the procedure for handling a customer's purchase order or outline steps in solving a problem, flow charts help the reader visualize the process. Traditional flow charts use the following symbols:

- Ovals to designate the beginning and end of a process
- Diamonds to denote decision points
- Rectangles to represent major activities or steps

ORGANIZATION CHARTS. Many large organizations are so complex that they need charts to show the chain of command, from the boss down to managers and employees. Organization charts like the one in Figure 9.16 provide such information as who reports to whom, how many subordinates work for each manager (the span of control), and what channels of official communication exist. These charts may illustrate a company's structure—for example, by function, customer, or product. They may also be organized by the work being performed in each job or by the hierarchy of decision making.

USING SOFTWARE TO PRODUCE CHARTS. Designing effective bar charts, pie charts, figures, and other graphics is easy with today's software. Spreadsheet programs such as Excel as well as presentation graphics programs such as Microsoft PowerPoint allow even non-technical people to design quality graphics. These graphics can be printed directly on paper for written reports or used for transparency masters and slides for oral presentations. The benefits of preparing visual aids on a computer are near-professional quality, shorter preparation time, and substantial cost savings. To prepare computer graphics, follow these steps:

- Assemble your data, usually in table form (such as that in Figure 9.6, p. 276).
- Choose a chart type, such as a pie chart, grouped bar chart, vertical bar chart, horizontal bar chart, organization chart, or some other graphic.
- To make a pie chart, key in the data or select the data from an existing file.
- Add a title for the chart as well as any necessary labels.

FIGURE **9.16** Organization Chart

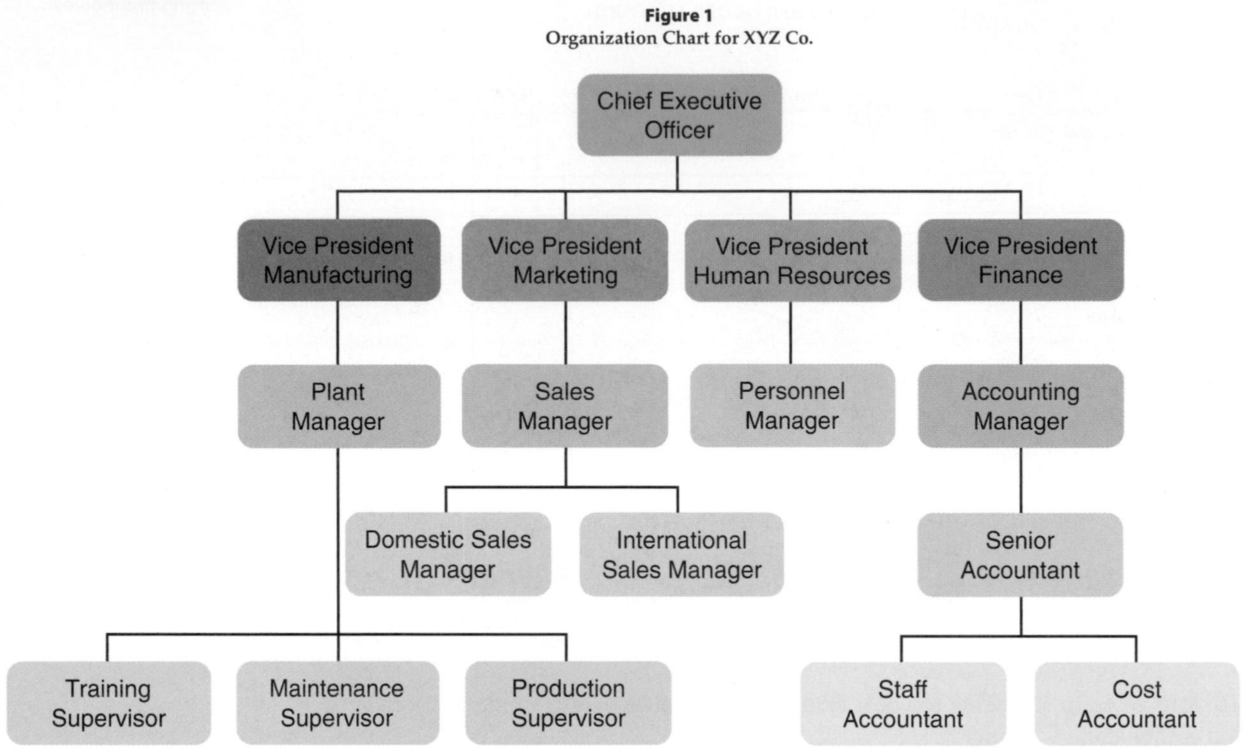

Figure 1
Organization Chart for XYZ Co.

- To make a bar or line chart, indicate the horizontal and vertical axes (reference lines or beginning points).
- Verify the legend, which your program may generate automatically.
- Print the final chart on paper or import into another program.

PHOTOGRAPHS, MAPS, AND ILLUSTRATIONS. Some business reports include photographs, maps, illustrations, and other graphics to serve specific purposes. Photos, for example, add authenticity and provide a visual record. An environmental engineer may use photos to document hazardous waste sites. Maps enable report writers to depict activities or concentrations geographically, such as dots indicating sales reps in states across the country. Illustrations and diagrams are useful in indicating how an object looks or operates. A drawing showing the parts of a printer with labels describing their functions, for example, is more instructive than a photograph or verbal description. With today's computer technology, photographs, maps, illustrations, and other graphics can be scanned and inserted directly into business reports. Treat them as you would tables, graphs, and charts, by giving them a figure number and title.

Presenting the Final Report

Business reports containing substantial research, analysis, and recommendations are generally organized into three major divisions: (1) prefatory parts, (2) body, and (3) supplementary parts. Following is a description of the order and content of each part. Refer to the model formal report in Figure 9.17 (starting on p. 283) for illustrations of most of these parts.

Prefatory Parts

Prefatory items (everything before the body of a report) and supplementary items (everything after the conclusions and recommendations) lengthen formal reports but enhance their professional tone and serve their multiple audiences. Formal reports may be read by many levels of managers, along with technical specialists and financial consultants. Therefore, breaking a long, formal report into small segments—and sometimes repeating the same information in different ways in these segments—makes a report more accessible and easier to understand.

- **Title page.** A report title page, as illustrated in the Figure 9.17 model report, begins with the name of the report typed in uppercase letters (no underscore and no quotation marks). Next comes *Prepared for* (or *Submitted to*) and the name, title, and organization of the individual receiving the report. Lower on the page is *Prepared by* (or *Submitted by*) and the author's name plus any necessary identification. The last item on the title page is the date of submission. All items after the title appear in a combination of upper- and lowercase letters. The information on the title page should be evenly spaced and balanced on the page for a professional look.
- **Letter or memo or e-mail of transmittal.** Generally written on organization letterhead (unless being sent via e-mail), a transmittal introduces a formal report. You will recall that letters are sent to external audiences; memos, to internal audiences. A transmittal follows the direct strategy and is usually less formal than the report itself. For example, the letter or memo may use contractions and the first-person pronouns *I* and *we*. The transmittal typically (a) announces the topic of the report and tells how it was authorized; (b) briefly describes the project; (c) highlights the report's findings, conclusions, and recommendations, if the reader is expected to be supportive; and (d) closes with appreciation for the assignment, instructions for the reader's follow-up actions, acknowledgment of help from others, or offers of assistance in answering questions. If a report is going to various readers, a special transmittal should be prepared for each, anticipating how each reader will use the report.

> A letter or memo of transmittal presents formally hands over the report to its recipient. It presents a brief summary of the report, expresses appreciation for the job, and offers to do more work if necessary.

- **Table of contents.** The table of contents shows the headings in a report and their page numbers. It gives an overview of the report topics and helps readers locate them. You should wait to prepare the table of contents until after you have completed the report. For short reports you should include all headings. For longer reports you might want to list only first- and second-level headings. Leaders (spaced or unspaced dots) help guide the eye from the heading to the page number. Items may be indented in outline form or typed flush with the left margin.
- **List of figures.** For reports with several figures or tables, you should include a list to help readers locate them. This list should appear on the same page as the table of contents, space permitting. For each figure or table, include a title and page number.
- **Executive summary or abstract.** As you learned in Chapter 8, the purpose of an executive summary is to present an overview of a longer report to people who may not have time to read the entire document. This time-saving device summarizes the purpose, key points, findings, and conclusions. An executive summary is usually no longer than 10 percent of the original document. Therefore, a twenty-page report might require a two-page executive summary. Chapter 8 discussed how to write an article summary and included an example (Figure 8.9 on page 244). An executive summary is part of Figure 9.17.

Body of Report

The main section of a report is the body. It generally begins with an introduction, includes a discussion of findings, and concludes with a summary and often with recommendations.

> The body of a report includes an introduction, a discussion of findings, and conclusions or recommendations.

INTRODUCTION. Formal reports start with an introduction that sets the scene and announces the subject. Because they contain many parts serving different purposes, the same information may be included in the letter or memo of transmittal, executive summary, and introduction. To avoid sounding repetitious, try to present the information slightly differently in each section.

A good report introduction typically covers the following elements, although not necessarily in this order:

1. **Background:** Describe the events leading up to the problem or need.
2. **Problem and purpose:** Explain the report topic and specify the problem or need that motivated the report.
3. **Significance:** Say why the topic is important. You may wish to quote experts or cite newspapers, journals, books, Web resources, and other secondary sources to establish the importance of the topic.
4. **Scope and limitations:** Clarify the boundaries of the report, defining what will be included or excluded.
5. **Sources and methods:** Describe your secondary sources (periodicals, books, databases). Also explain how you collected primary data, including survey size, sample design, and statistical programs used.
6. **Definitions:** Define any terms you'll use in your findings section that may not be clear to every reader.
7. **Organization:** Orient readers by giving them a road map that previews the structure of the report.

FINDINGS. This is the main section of the report and contains numerous headings and subheadings. It is unnecessary to use the title *Findings*; many business report writers prefer to begin immediately with the major headings into which the body of the report is divided. Present your findings objectively, avoiding the use of first-person pronouns (*I, we*). Include tables, charts, and graphs to illustrate findings. Analytic and scientific reports may include another section entitled *Implications of Findings*, in which the findings are analyzed and related to the problem. Less formal reports contain the author's analysis of the research findings within the findings section itself. In other words, most business research reports present data and follow the presentation by analyzing what the data means.

CONCLUSIONS AND RECOMMENDATIONS. If the report has been largely informational, it ends with a summary of the data presented. However, the report will usually also analyze its research findings; in that case it should end with conclusions drawn from the analyses. An analytic report frequently poses research questions. The conclusion to such a report reviews the major findings and answers the research questions. If a report seeks to determine a course of action, it may end with conclusions and recommendations. Recommendations regarding a course of action may be placed in a separate section or incorporated with the conclusions. Recommendations should be numbered in order of descending importance (i.e., the most important recommendation first) and should begin with a present-tense verb (e.g., *Purchase, Inform, Reduce*, etc.).

Supplementary Parts of a Report

A report doesn't end after the conclusion or recommendations. Readers will be looking for a few extras that should always be provided.

> Endnotes, a bibliography, and appendixes may appear after the body of the report.

- **Footnotes or endnotes.** See Appendix C for details on how to document sources. In the footnote method, the source notes appear at the foot of each page. In the endnote method, they are displayed immediately after the text on a page called "Notes." The trend today is away from the footnote or endnote method and toward the parenthetic method (either APA or MLA), which works all citations directly into the text of the report.
- **Works Cited.** Readers look here to locate the sources of ideas mentioned in a report. Your method of report documentation determines how this section is developed. If you use the Modern Language Association (MLA) referencing format, all citations would be listed alphabetically in the "Works Cited." If you use the American Psychological Association (APA) format, your list would be called "References." Regardless of the format, you must include the author, title, publication, date of

publication, page number, and other significant data for all sources used in your report. For electronic references include the URL and the date you accessed the information online. To see electronic and other citations, examine the list of references at the end of Figure 9.17, which follows the MLA documentation style. See Appendix C for more information on documentation formats.

- **Appendixes.** Incidental or supporting materials belong in appendixes at the end of a formal report. These materials are relevant to some readers but not

FIGURE 9.17 Model Formal Report

The title page is usually arranged in four evenly balanced areas. If the report is to be bound on the left, move the left margin and centre point 0.5 cm to the right. Notice that no page number appears on the title page, although it is counted as "page i." In designing the title page, be careful to avoid anything unprofessional, such as too many type fonts, italics, oversized print, and inappropriate graphics. Keep the title page simple and professional.

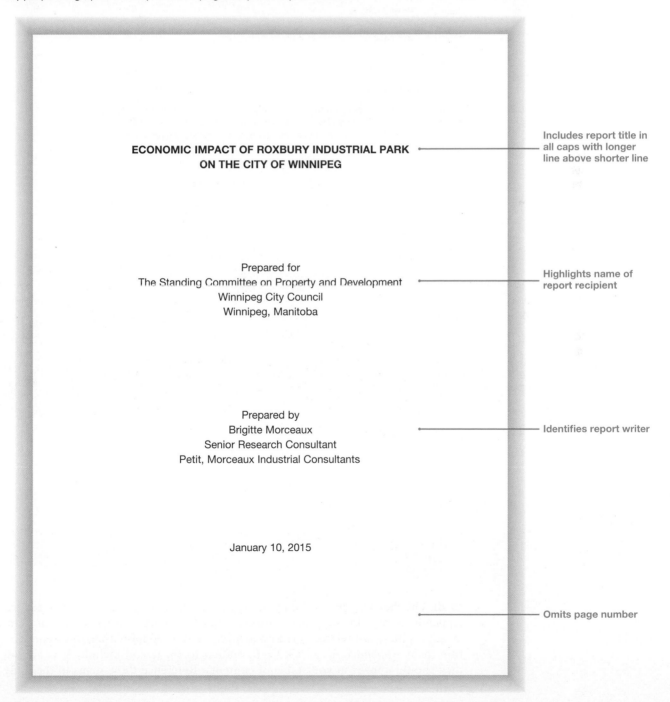

ECONOMIC IMPACT OF ROXBURY INDUSTRIAL PARK
ON THE CITY OF WINNIPEG

— Includes report title in all caps with longer line above shorter line

Prepared for
The Standing Committee on Property and Development
Winnipeg City Council
Winnipeg, Manitoba

— Highlights name of report recipient

Prepared by
Brigitte Morceaux
Senior Research Consultant
Petit, Morceaux Industrial Consultants

— Identifies report writer

January 10, 2015

— Omits page number

FIGURE 9.17 *(Continued)* Letter of Transmittal

A letter or memo of transmittal announces the report topic and explains who authorized it. It describes the project briefly and previews the conclusions, if the reader is supportive. Such messages generally close by expressing appreciation for the assignment, suggesting follow-up actions, acknowledging the help of others, or offering to answer questions. The margins for the transmittal should be the same as for the report, about 3 cm on all sides.

PETIT, MORCEAUX INDUSTRIAL CONSULTANTS

588 Main Street   www.petitmorceaux.com
Winnipeg, Manitoba R2L 1E6   (204) 549-1101

January 12, 2015

Councillor Richard Moody
Chairperson
Standing Committee on Property and Development
City of Winnipeg
Winnipeg, MB R2L 1E9

Dear Councillor Moody:

[Announces report and identifies authorization] The attached report, requested by the Standing Policy Committee on Property and Development in a letter dated May 20, describes the economic impact of Roxbury Industrial Park on the City of Winnipeg. We believe you will find the results of this study useful in evaluating future development of industrial parks within the city limits.

[Gives broad overview of report purposes] This study was designed to examine economic impact in three areas:

(1) Current and projected tax and other revenues accruing to the city from Roxbury Industrial Park

(2) Current and projected employment generated by the park

(3) Indirect effects on local employment, income, and economic growth

[Describes primary and secondary research] Primary research consisted of interviews with 15 Roxbury Industrial Park tenants and managers, in addition to a 2014 survey of over 5000 RIP employees. Secondary research sources included the Annual Budget of the City of Winnipeg, other government publications, periodicals, books, and online resources. Results of this research, discussed more fully in this report, indicate that Roxbury Industrial Park exerts a significant beneficial influence on the Winnipeg metropolitan economy.

[Offers to discuss report; expresses appreciation] I would be pleased to discuss this report and its conclusions with you at your request. My firm and I thank you for your confidence in selecting our company to prepare this comprehensive report.

Sincerely,

Brigitte Morceaux

Brigitte Morceaux
Senior Research Consultant

BM:mef

Attachment

---

to all. Or, they may be too bulky to include in the findings section of the report. Appendixes may include survey forms, copies of other reports, tables of data, large graphics, and related correspondence. If you need more than one appendix, title them *Appendix A, Appendix B,* and so forth. If you include Appendixes, they should appear in your table of contents. Reference these items in the body of the report.

FIGURE **9.17** *(Continued)* Table of Contents and List of Figures

Because the table of contents and the list of figures for this report are small, they are combined on one page. Notice that the titles of major report parts are in all caps, while other headings are a combination of upper- and lowercase letters. The style duplicates those within the report. Word processing programs enable you to generate a contents page automatically, including leaders and accurate page numbering—no matter how many times you revise.

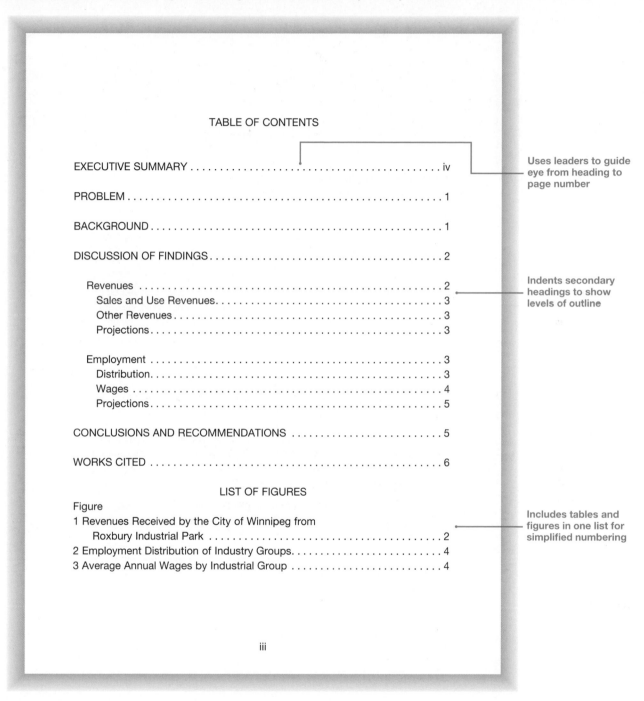

TABLE OF CONTENTS

EXECUTIVE SUMMARY iv

PROBLEM 1

BACKGROUND 1

DISCUSSION OF FINDINGS 2

    Revenues 2
        Sales and Use Revenues 3
        Other Revenues 3
        Projections 3

    Employment 3
        Distribution 3
        Wages 4
        Projections 5

CONCLUSIONS AND RECOMMENDATIONS 5

WORKS CITED 6

LIST OF FIGURES

Figure
1 Revenues Received by the City of Winnipeg from
   Roxbury Industrial Park 2
2 Employment Distribution of Industry Groups 4
3 Average Annual Wages by Industrial Group 4

Uses leaders to guide eye from heading to page number

Indents secondary headings to show levels of outline

Includes tables and figures in one list for simplified numbering

iii

Other Ways of Presenting Formal Reports

In today's busy workplace, formal reports are often presented in less formal ways, for example, as PowerPoint slides. Because a formal report is often presented orally to an audience, it makes sense that instead of creating a traditional formal report like the one in Figure 9.17, some business decision makers are fine if a copy of the PowerPoint slide deck is submitted in lieu of a traditional formal report. This is especially true for internal reports.

FIGURE 9.17 (*Continued*) Executive Summary

An executive summary or abstract highlights report findings, conclusions, and recommendations. Its length depends on the report it summarizes. A 100-page report might require a 10-page summary. Shorter reports may contain single-page summaries, as shown here. Unlike letters of transmittal (which may contain personal pronouns and references to the writer), summaries are formal and impersonal. They use the same margins as the body of the report.

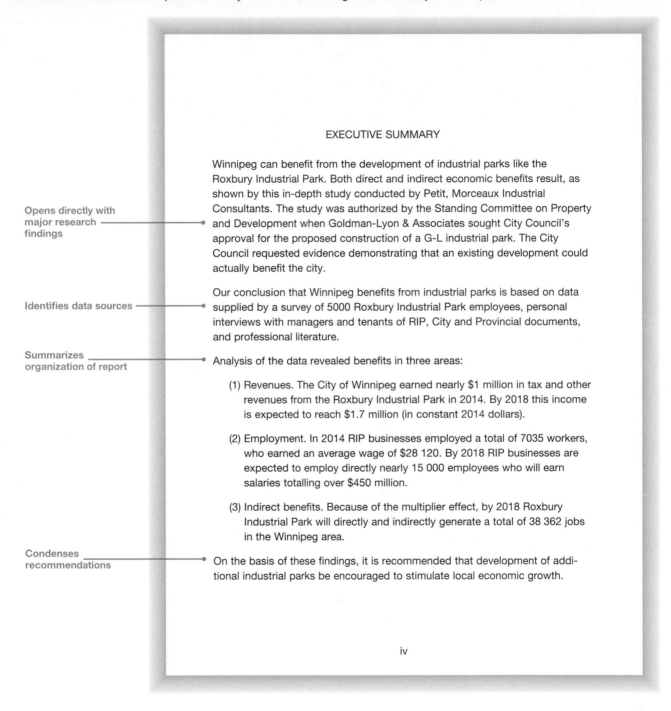

EXECUTIVE SUMMARY

Opens directly with major research findings

Winnipeg can benefit from the development of industrial parks like the Roxbury Industrial Park. Both direct and indirect economic benefits result, as shown by this in-depth study conducted by Petit, Morceaux Industrial Consultants. The study was authorized by the Standing Committee on Property and Development when Goldman-Lyon & Associates sought City Council's approval for the proposed construction of a G-L industrial park. The City Council requested evidence demonstrating that an existing development could actually benefit the city.

Identifies data sources

Our conclusion that Winnipeg benefits from industrial parks is based on data supplied by a survey of 5000 Roxbury Industrial Park employees, personal interviews with managers and tenants of RIP, City and Provincial documents, and professional literature.

Summarizes organization of report

Analysis of the data revealed benefits in three areas:

(1) Revenues. The City of Winnipeg earned nearly $1 million in tax and other revenues from the Roxbury Industrial Park in 2014. By 2018 this income is expected to reach $1.7 million (in constant 2014 dollars).

(2) Employment. In 2014 RIP businesses employed a total of 7035 workers, who earned an average wage of $28 120. By 2018 RIP businesses are expected to employ directly nearly 15 000 employees who will earn salaries totalling over $450 million.

(3) Indirect benefits. Because of the multiplier effect, by 2018 Roxbury Industrial Park will directly and indirectly generate a total of 38 362 jobs in the Winnipeg area.

Condenses recommendations

On the basis of these findings, it is recommended that development of additional industrial parks be encouraged to stimulate local economic growth.

iv

FIGURE 9.17 *(Continued)* Introduction

The introduction of a formal report contains the title printed 5 cm from the top edge. Titles for major parts of a report (such as Problem, Background, Findings, and Conclusions) are centred in all caps. First-level headings (such as Employment on page 3 of the report) are printed with bold upper- and lowercase letters. Second-level headings (such as Distribution on page 3 of the report) begin at the left side. See Figure 9.4 (page 275) for an illustration of heading formats.

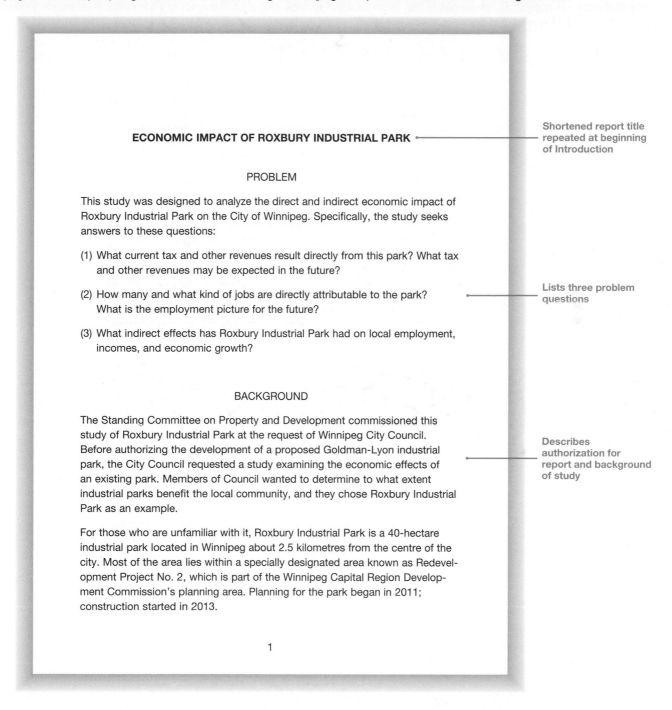

ECONOMIC IMPACT OF ROXBURY INDUSTRIAL PARK ⟵ Shortened report title repeated at beginning of Introduction

PROBLEM

This study was designed to analyze the direct and indirect economic impact of Roxbury Industrial Park on the City of Winnipeg. Specifically, the study seeks answers to these questions:

(1) What current tax and other revenues result directly from this park? What tax and other revenues may be expected in the future?

(2) How many and what kind of jobs are directly attributable to the park? What is the employment picture for the future? ⟵ Lists three problem questions

(3) What indirect effects has Roxbury Industrial Park had on local employment, incomes, and economic growth?

BACKGROUND

The Standing Committee on Property and Development commissioned this study of Roxbury Industrial Park at the request of Winnipeg City Council. Before authorizing the development of a proposed Goldman-Lyon industrial park, the City Council requested a study examining the economic effects of an existing park. Members of Council wanted to determine to what extent industrial parks benefit the local community, and they chose Roxbury Industrial Park as an example. ⟵ Describes authorization for report and background of study

For those who are unfamiliar with it, Roxbury Industrial Park is a 40-hectare industrial park located in Winnipeg about 2.5 kilometres from the centre of the city. Most of the area lies within a specially designated area known as Redevelopment Project No. 2, which is part of the Winnipeg Capital Region Development Commission's planning area. Planning for the park began in 2011; construction started in 2013.

1

FIGURE 9.17 (*Continued*) Introduction and Discussion

Notice that this formal report is single-spaced. Many businesses prefer this space-saving format. However, some organizations prefer double-spacing, especially for preliminary drafts. If you single-space, do not indent paragraphs. If you double-space, do indent the paragraphs. Page numbers may be centred near the bottom of the page or placed near the upper right corner at the margin. Strive to leave comfortable top, bottom, and side margins. References follow the MLA citation style. Notice that citations appear as references in the "Works Cited" section with a corresponding parenthetical reference to the author in the text of the report at the appropriate location.

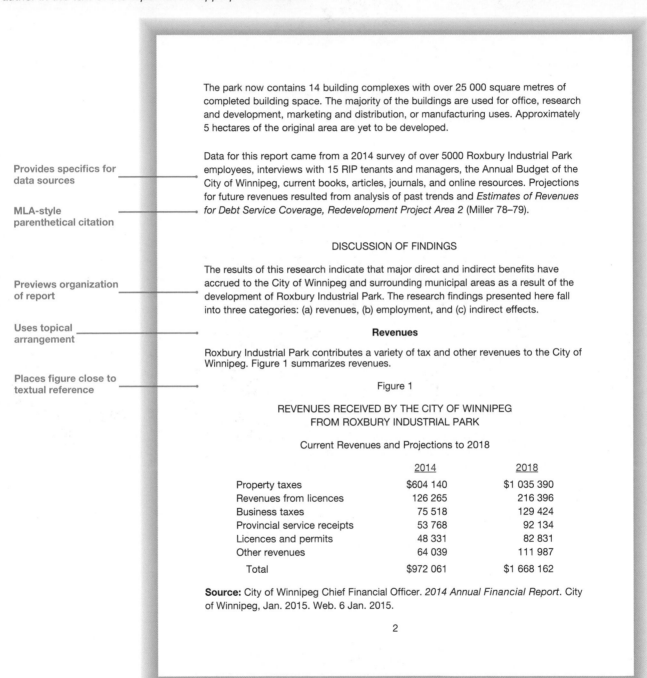

Provides specifics for
data sources

MLA-style
parenthetical citation

Previews organization
of report

Uses topical
arrangement

Places figure close to
textual reference

The park now contains 14 building complexes with over 25 000 square metres of completed building space. The majority of the buildings are used for office, research and development, marketing and distribution, or manufacturing uses. Approximately 5 hectares of the original area are yet to be developed.

Data for this report came from a 2014 survey of over 5000 Roxbury Industrial Park employees, interviews with 15 RIP tenants and managers, the Annual Budget of the City of Winnipeg, current books, articles, journals, and online resources. Projections for future revenues resulted from analysis of past trends and *Estimates of Revenues for Debt Service Coverage, Redevelopment Project Area 2* (Miller 78–79).

DISCUSSION OF FINDINGS

The results of this research indicate that major direct and indirect benefits have accrued to the City of Winnipeg and surrounding municipal areas as a result of the development of Roxbury Industrial Park. The research findings presented here fall into three categories: (a) revenues, (b) employment, and (c) indirect effects.

Revenues

Roxbury Industrial Park contributes a variety of tax and other revenues to the City of Winnipeg. Figure 1 summarizes revenues.

Figure 1

REVENUES RECEIVED BY THE CITY OF WINNIPEG
FROM ROXBURY INDUSTRIAL PARK

Current Revenues and Projections to 2018

	2014	2018
Property taxes	$604 140	$1 035 390
Revenues from licences	126 265	216 396
Business taxes	75 518	129 424
Provincial service receipts	53 768	92 134
Licences and permits	48 331	82 831
Other revenues	64 039	111 987
Total	$972 061	$1 668 162

Source: City of Winnipeg Chief Financial Officer. *2014 Annual Financial Report*. City of Winnipeg, Jan. 2015. Web. 6 Jan. 2015.

2

FIGURE 9.17 *(Continued)* Discussion

Only the most important research findings are interpreted and discussed for readers. The depth of discussion depends on the intended length of the report, the goal of the writer, and the expectations of the reader. Because the writer wants this report to be formal in tone, she avoids I and we in all discussions.

Sales and Use Revenues

As shown in Figure 1, the city's largest source of revenues from RIP is the property tax. Revenues from this source totalled $604 140 in 2014, according to the City of Winnipeg Standing Committee on Finance (City of Winnipeg 103). Property taxes accounted for more than half of the park's total contribution to the City of $972 061.

→ Continues interpreting figures in table

Other Revenues

Other major sources of City revenues from RIP in 2014 include revenues from licences such as motor vehicle in lieu fees, trailer coach licences ($126 265), business taxes ($75 518), and provincial service receipts ($53 768).

Projections

Total City revenues from RIP will nearly double by 2018, producing an income of $1.7 million. This projection is based on an annual growth rate of 1.4 percent in constant 2014 dollars.

Employment

One of the most important factors to consider in the overall effect of an industrial park is employment. In Roxbury Industrial Park the distribution, number, and wages of people employed will change considerably in the next five years.

→ Sets stage for next topics to be discussed

Distribution

A total of 7035 employees currently work in various industry groups at Roxbury Industrial Park, as shown below in Figure 2. The largest number of workers (58 percent) is employed in manufacturing and assembly operations. In the next largest category, the computer and electronics industry employs 24 percent of the workers. Some overlap probably exists because electronics assembly could be included in either group. Employees also work in publishing (9 percent), warehousing and storage (5 percent), and other industries (4 percent).

Although the distribution of employees at Roxbury Industrial Park shows a wide range of employment categories, it must be noted that other industrial parks would likely generate an entirely different range of job categories.

3

FIGURE **9.17** (*Continued*) Discussion

If you use figures or tables, be sure to introduce them in the text (for example, as shown below in Figure 3). Although it's not always possible, try to place them close to the spot where they are first mentioned. To save space, you can print the title of a figure at its side. Because this report contains few tables and figures, the writer named them all "Figures" and numbered them consecutively.

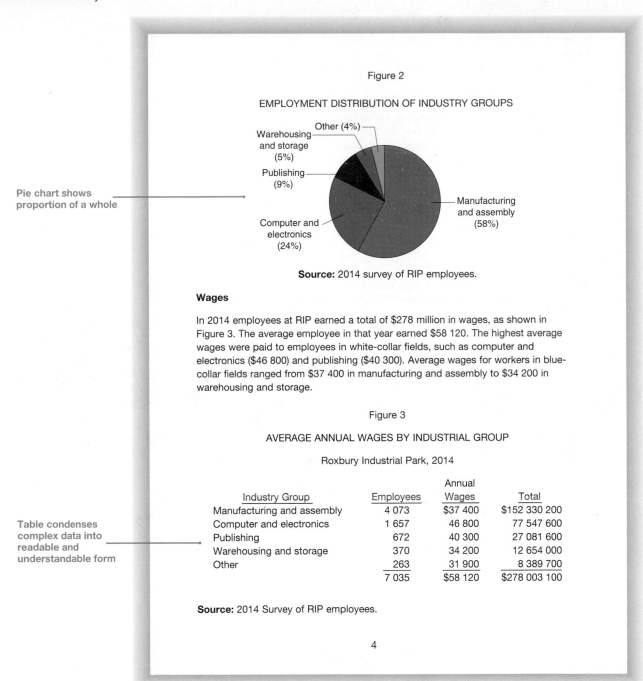

Figure 2

EMPLOYMENT DISTRIBUTION OF INDUSTRY GROUPS

Other (4%)

Warehousing and storage (5%)

Publishing (9%)

Computer and electronics (24%)

Manufacturing and assembly (58%)

Pie chart shows proportion of a whole

Source: 2014 survey of RIP employees.

Wages

In 2014 employees at RIP earned a total of $278 million in wages, as shown in Figure 3. The average employee in that year earned $58 120. The highest average wages were paid to employees in white-collar fields, such as computer and electronics ($46 800) and publishing ($40 300). Average wages for workers in blue-collar fields ranged from $37 400 in manufacturing and assembly to $34 200 in warehousing and storage.

Figure 3

AVERAGE ANNUAL WAGES BY INDUSTRIAL GROUP

Roxbury Industrial Park, 2014

Industry Group	Employees	Annual Wages	Total
Manufacturing and assembly	4 073	$37 400	$152 330 200
Computer and electronics	1 657	46 800	77 547 600
Publishing	672	40 300	27 081 600
Warehousing and storage	370	34 200	12 654 000
Other	263	31 900	8 389 700
	7 035	$58 120	$278 003 100

Table condenses complex data into readable and understandable form

Source: 2014 Survey of RIP employees.

4

FIGURE 9.17 (*Continued*) Discussion, Conclusions, and Recommendations

After discussing and interpreting the research findings, the writer articulates what she considers the most important conclusions and recommendations. Longer, more complex reports may have separate sections for conclusions and resulting recommendations. In this report they are combined. Notice that it is unnecessary to start a new page for the conclusions.

Projections

By 2018 Roxbury Industrial Park is expected to more than double its number of employees, bringing the total to over 15 000 workers. The total payroll in 2015 will also more than double, producing over $450 million (using constant 2014 dollars) in salaries to RIP employees. These projections are based on an 8 percent growth rate, along with anticipated increased employment as the park reaches its capacity (Miller 78–79).

> Clarifies information and explains what it means in relation to original research questions

Future development in the park will influence employment and payrolls. As Ivan Novak, RIP project manager, stated in an interview, much of the remaining five hectares is planned for medium-rise office buildings, garden offices, and other structures for commercial, professional, and personal services (September 2014). Average wages for employees are expected to increase because of an anticipated shift to higher-paying white-collar jobs. Industrial parks often follow a similar pattern of evolution (Badri 38–45). Like many industrial parks, RIP evolved from a warehousing centre into a manufacturing complex.

CONCLUSIONS AND RECOMMENDATIONS

> Summarizes conclusions and recommendations

Analysis of tax revenues, employment data, personal interviews, and professional literature leads to the following conclusions and recommendations about the economic impact of Roxbury Industrial Park on the City of Winnipeg:

1. Property tax and other revenues produced nearly $1 million in income to the City of Winnipeg in 2014. By 2018 revenues are expected to produce $1.7 million in city income.

2. RIP currently employs 7035 employees, the majority of whom are working in manufacturing and assembly. The average employee in 2014 earned $38 120.

3. By 2018 RIP is expected to employ more than 15 000 workers producing a total payroll of over $450 million.

4. Employment trends indicate that by 2018 more RIP employees will be engaged in higher-paying white-collar positions.

On the basis of these findings, we recommend that the City Council of Winnipeg authorize the development of additional industrial parks to stimulate local economic growth.

5

FIGURE 9.17 *(Continued)* Works Cited

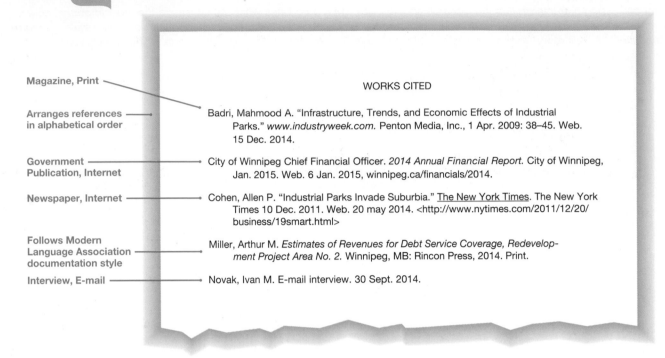

Magazine, Print

Arranges references in alphabetical order

Government Publication, Internet

Newspaper, Internet

Follows Modern Language Association documentation style

Interview, E-mail

WORKS CITED

Badri, Mahmood A. "Infrastructure, Trends, and Economic Effects of Industrial Parks." *www.industryweek.com.* Penton Media, Inc., 1 Apr. 2009: 38–45. Web. 15 Dec. 2014.

City of Winnipeg Chief Financial Officer. *2014 Annual Financial Report.* City of Winnipeg, Jan. 2015. Web. 6 Jan. 2015, winnipeg.ca/financials/2014.

Cohen, Allen P. "Industrial Parks Invade Suburbia." <u>The New York Times</u>. The New York Times 10 Dec. 2011. Web. 20 may 2014. <http://www.nytimes.com/2011/12/20/business/19smart.html>

Miller, Arthur M. *Estimates of Revenues for Debt Service Coverage, Redevelopment Project Area No. 2.* Winnipeg, MB: Rincon Press, 2014. Print.

Novak, Ivan M. E-mail interview. 30 Sept. 2014.

◼ SUMMING UP AND LOOKING FORWARD

Proposals are offers to solve problems, provide services, or sell equipment or goods. Today, both small and large businesses (as well as freelance consultants) must write proposals to generate income. Informal proposals may be as short as 2 pages; formal proposals may be 200 pages or more. Regardless of the size, proposals contain standard parts that must be developed persuasively.

Formal reports present well-organized information systematically. The information may be collected from primary or secondary sources. All ideas borrowed from others must be documented; otherwise plagiarism may occur. Good reports contain appropriate headings to help guide readers through the report. In addition, formal reports usually contain tables, charts, and graphs, and sometimes illustrations, to help make data more concrete.

Written reports are vital to decision makers, and they can be presented traditionally in manuscript format or as PowerPoint slides, especially if the report was first presented orally. And oral reports can be equally as important as written reports. In Chapters 10 and 11 you will learn how to conduct meetings and communicate effectively on the phone, as well as how to organize and give oral presentations.

◼ CRITICAL THINKING

1. Which type of proposal, solicited or unsolicited, is more likely to succeed and why?

2. Why is writing proposals an important function in many businesses?

3. Is information obtained on the Web as reliable as information obtained from journals, newspapers, and magazines? Explain.

4. Should all reports be written so that they follow the sequence of investigation—that is, description of the initial problem, analysis of issues, data collection, data analysis, and conclusions? Why or why not?

5. Distinguish between primary and secondary data. Which data are more likely to be useful in a business report?

6. Why is plagiarism a serious issue in the business world? Discuss.

7. Do graphic elements actually enhance a report or do they simply make its presentation more lively?

CHAPTER REVIEW

1. Who uses requests for proposals (RFPs) and why?
2. What are the principal parts and functions of an informal proposal?
3. How are formal proposals different from informal proposals?
4. Why is the budget section of a proposal especially important?
5. What is the first step in writing a formal report?
6. Why are formal reports written in business? Provide an original example of a recent business-related report.
7. List three sources of secondary report information, and be prepared to discuss how valuable each might be in writing a formal report about updating your company's travel policy.
8. Define these terms: *browser*, *URL*, *search tool*.
9. Explain plagiarism and how to avoid it.
10. What are the elements of a successful citation?
11. List four levels of headings, and explain how they are different.
12. Pie charts are most helpful in showing what?
13. Line graphs are most effective in showing what?
14. List three reasons for documenting data in a business report.
15. What are some patterns you can use to organize your report's findings?

 WRITING IMPROVEMENT EXERCISES

1. **Detecting and Eliminating Plagiarism.** A student doing business research comes across the *Canadian Business* article reprinted in Chapter 8 (p. 247). She uses the article's second paragraph in a report. The paragraph below is an extract from her report. Identify where and why she has plagiarized and revise her report so that no plagiarism exists.

   New Health Care Solutions
   One of the most exciting business opportunities in the field of health care is the provision of private consulting services. For example, NavaHealth, a for-profit, privately owned company, leads B.C. residents through the labyrinthine health care system by providing support and patient advocacy. The owner of this company has had to invest heavily, but she plans to make a profit in less than a year.

2. **Detecting and Eliminating Plagiarism.** A student doing business research comes across the *Toronto Star* article reprinted in Chapter 8 (p. 248). He uses the article's fifth paragraph in an essay. Below is an extract from his essay. Identify where and why he has plagiarized and revise his essay so that no plagiarism exists.

   As mentioned earlier, one of the fringe benefits of a hot economy is the spin-off effects it creates. One of the spin-off effects of the hot Canadian economy, especially in places like Alberta, is the corporate housing market. A study released recently by Royal LePage Relocation Services states that this market was worth $230 million in Canada in 2004. Another spin-off of the hot economy is corporate travel, corporate retreats, and corporate entertaining, which I will discuss below.

ACTIVITIES AND CASES

9.1 Doing Research

Like many business communication skills, research is one that only gets better when it is practised. In this activity you'll act as a consultant to your college or university, which needs some internal research done about the effectiveness of its policies, services, and procedures.

Your Task. Choose one of the research topics below and go through the following six-step procedure:

1. Create a five-question survey and a five-question follow-up interview.

2. After you've shown your survey and interview to your instructor, go out "into the field" and gather data. Try to get at least 15 completed surveys and two completed interviews.

3. Now that you have raw data, analyze the survey data by turning it into two or three of the types of illustration discussed in this chapter (e.g., bar chart, table, line chart).

4. Analyze your interview data by looking for similarities and differences between what the people you interviewed had to say.

5. Once you've completed your primary research and analysis, turn to secondary research. Find two newspaper or magazine articles, one academic article, one book, and one good Web site with information on your topic. How does this information compare with or help to illustrate the information you gathered in your primary research?

6. Finally, present all of the above in a two-page memo or e-mail to your instructor.

CRITICAL THINKING

Possible research topics:

- Is the cost of tuition at your institution too high?

- How well is your college/university doing in terms of customer service?

- Does your college/university career centre do a good job?

- Assess the usefulness of your college/university library.

- Examine the success of your institution's physical plant: washrooms, hallways, stairwells, elevators, etc.

- Choose a topic of your own in consultation with your instructor.

TEAM

9.2 Outlining

You work for a recruiting firm that helps businesses find candidates for jobs. Over the years, many clients have asked for suggestions on the best way to interview job candidates. Your supervisor asks you to write a short report on how to become a great interviewer. Here are some ideas you gathered from your own experience and that of other recruiters:

- One of the most important qualities of a successful interview is efficient use of the interview time. Most businesspeople hate the hiring process because it interrupts their daily routine and throws off their schedules. But if you block out an afternoon or a whole day, you don't feel so frustrated. In addition, shutting out all interruptions and setting aside 45 minutes for each interview can also be helpful.

- Interviewing is an inexact art because judging the talents and abilities of people is very subjective. To select the best candidate, you must begin with a list of all the job duties. Then you select the three duties with the highest priorities. Naturally, you would then ask questions to discover what candidate can perform those duties best.

- Every interview should have objectives. What do you want to achieve? One of the most important goals is uncovering the experience that qualifies the candidate to do the job. Another important element is the correlation you see between the candidate and your company's values. A major final objective is selling the candidate on the opportunity with your company.

Your Task. Select the most important information and organize it into an outline such as that shown in Figure 9.3 on page 274. You should have three main topics with three subdivisions under each. Assume that you would gather more information later. Add a title.

9.3 Selecting Visual Aids

Your Task. In teams, identify the best visual aid (table, bar chart, line chart, pie chart, flow chart, organization chart) to illustrate the following data:

a. Instructions for workers telling them how to distinguish between worker accidents that must be reported to appropriate provincial agencies and those that need not be reported

b. Figures showing what proportion of every provincial tax dollar is spent on education, social services, health care, debt, and other expenses

c. Data showing the academic, administrative, and operation divisions of a college, from the president to department chairs and deans

d. Figures showing the operating profit of a company for the past five years

e. Figures comparing the sales of PVRs, flat-screen TVs, and personal computers for the past five years

f. Percentages showing the causes of forest fires (lightning, 73 percent; arson, 5 percent; campfires, 9 percent; and so on) in the Canadian Rockies

g. Figures comparing the cost of basic TV cable service in five areas of Canada for the past ten years (the boss wants to see exact figures)

9.4 Evaluating Visual Aids

WEB

Your Task. From *Maclean's*, *Canadian Business*, *Businessweek*, *The Economist*, or some other publication, locate one example each of a table, a pie chart, a line chart, a bar chart, and an organization chart. Bring copies of these visual aids to class. How effectively could the data have been expressed in words, without the graphics? Is the appropriate graphic form used? How is the graphic introduced in the text? Your instructor may ask you to submit a short e-mail recommendation report discussing how to improve visual aids.

9.5 Visual Aids in Reports: Creating a Bar Chart and Writing a Title

Your Task. You've written a report that compares corporate tax rates in various countries, using data available at **www.kpmg.com/GLOBAL/EN/SERVICES/TAX/TAX-TOOLS -AND-RESOURCES/Pages/corporate-tax-rates-table.aspx**. To help illustrate your findings, prepare a bar chart comparing the tax rates in eight industrial countries: Canada, 26.5 percent; France, 33.3 percent; Germany, 29.6 percent; Japan, 35.6 percent; Netherlands, 25 percent; Sweden, 22 percent; United Kingdom, 21 percent; United States, 40 percent. Arrange the entries logically. Write two titles: a talking head and a functional head. What should you emphasize in the bar chart and title?

9.6 Annotated Bibliography: The Future of Tech

TEAM
EMAIL

Are you a member of the "thumb generation"? Can you work the keyboard of your smartphone faster than most people can speak? The term *thumb generation* was coined in South Korea and Japan and is applied to people under 25 who furiously finger their handheld devices to text at lightning speeds.

More technological innovations are coming that are likely to transform our lives. WiMAX is a new wireless supertechnology that will cover entire cities at cable speeds. Near field communication (NFC) takes the Bluetooth technology a step further to connect cellphones and other devices. Several pending technologies are purported to improve the lives of users and tech support pros alike.[16]

You are one of several marketing interns at MarketNet Global, a worldwide e-commerce specialist. Your busy boss, Jack Holden, wants to be informed of cutting-edge technical and communication trends, especially those that could be successfully used in selling and marketing. Individually or as a team, you will research one or several high-tech concepts found on the MIT Technology Review Web site at **www.technologyreview.com**. Focus on the tabs for Business, Computing, Web, and Communications. Chances are you will not find scholarly articles on these subjects because peer-reviewed publications take years to complete. Instead, you must rely on the Internet and on electronic databases to find up-to-date information. If you use search engines, you will retrieve many forum and discussion board contributions as well. Examine them critically.

Your Task. In teams or individually, write an e-mail or informational memo to Jack Holden (jack.holden@mnetglobal.com) complete with a short list of references in MLA or APA documentation style. Explain each new trend. Your instructor may ask you to complete this activity as a report assignment describing to Jack Holden what your sources suggest the new trends may mean for the future of business, specifically e-commerce and online marketing.

9.7 Proposal: Comparing Real Proposals

WEB

Many new companies with services or products to offer would like to land corporate or government contracts. However, they are intimidated by the request for proposal (RFP) process. You have been asked for help by your friend Mikayla, who has started her own catering business. Her goal is to deliver fresh sandwiches and salads to local offices and shops during lunch hour, either pre-ordered or ready-made. Before writing a proposal, however, she wants to see examples of RFPs and learn more about the process.

Your Task. Use the Internet to find at least two actual examples of business proposals. Then prepare a memo to Mikayla in which you do the following:

    a. Identify two sites with sample business proposals.
    b. Outline the parts of each proposal.
    c. Compare the strengths and weaknesses of each proposal.
    d. Draw conclusions on what Mikayla can learn from these examples.

9.8 Informal Proposal: Student Views Consulting Inc.

Imagine you are in your last semester of college or university. As part of your business program, there is a course you can take called "Consulting Business Simulation." This course allows students to simulate running a consulting business for a semester. You enroll in the course, and on the first day of class the instructor says, "There's only one requirement in this course and it's worth 100 percent of your grade. You will design, conduct, and write a research proposal and project of your choice for this institution. You won't get paid for it, but you'll have gained a lot of experience that will look good on your résumé." You choose to work with two other students and you call yourselves Student Views Consulting Inc. You decide to tackle the problem of poor customer service at your institution.

Your Task. Write a proposal to the Director of Student Services at your college or university. Propose that your consulting firm carry out a detailed study on current student satisfaction at your institution, which you understand has been problematic lately. For example, there have been questions about how effectively telephone, e-mail, and in-person queries are being handled in various college departments and offices. Also, how the service level at your institution compares to that of competing institutions in the same area has been questioned. Describe the background of this problem and draft a schedule of the work to be done. Cost out this research realistically. When it comes to describing the prior work of Student Views Consulting Inc., make up a realistic list of prior work. Format this proposal as a letter to the Director of Student Services.

TEAM

9.9 Unsolicited Proposal: Working From Home

You have been working as an administrative/virtual assistant for your company since its inception in 2001. Every day you commute from your home, almost two hours round trip. Most of your work is done at a computer terminal with little or no human contact. You would prefer to eliminate the commute time, which could be better spent working on your programming. You believe your job would be perfect for telecommuting. With a small investment in the proper equipment, you could do all of your work at home, perhaps reporting to the office once a week for meetings and other activities.

Your Task. Research the costs and logistics of telecommuting, and present your proposal to your supervisor, Sidney Greene. Because this is an unsolicited proposal, you will need to be even more persuasive. Convince your supervisor that the company will benefit from this telecommuting arrangement.

WEB

TEAM

9.10 Formal Report: The Savvy Buyer

Study a consumer product that you might consider buying. Are you or is your family or your business interested in purchasing a flat-screen TV, home theatre system, computer, digital camera, espresso machine, car, SUV, hot tub, or some other product?

Your Task. Use at least five primary and five secondary sources in researching your topic. Your primary research will be in the form of interviews with individuals (owners, users, salespeople, technicians) in a position to comment on the attributes of your product. Secondary research will be in the form of print or electronic sources, such as magazine articles, owner manuals, and Web sites. Be sure to use electronic databases and the Internet to find appropriate articles. Your report should analyze and discuss at least three comparable models or versions of the target product. Decide what criteria you will use to compare the models, such as price, features, warranty, service, and so forth. The report should include these components: transmittal, table of contents, executive summary, introduction (including background, purpose, scope of the study, and research methods), findings (organized by comparison criteria), summary of findings, conclusions, recommendations, and bibliography. Address the report to your instructor. You may work individually, in pairs, or in teams.

9.11 Formal Report: Is Vinyl Back?

Although you and fellow students were probably born long after the introduction of the CD in the early 1980s and regularly download music from iTunes to an MP3 player, something strange is afoot. Lately, sales of turntables and vinyl long-playing records (LPs) have been picking up. "Classic" bands such as the Beatles and Pink Floyd are not the only ones on vinyl. Contemporary artists such as the White Stripes, the Foo Fighters, and Metallica have released their music on vinyl to enthusiastic audiences. Listeners even claim that music sounds better on vinyl than it does on a CD.[17] Perhaps most surprising, many vinyl fans are not nostalgic baby boomers but their teenage or twenty-something children.

Major music retailers have caught on to the trend. Although Amazon.ca has been selling vinyl records since its founding in 1994, it has recently begun to offer a vinyl-only section on its site. Now, your employer, Best Buy Company, is eager to test vinyl sales at some of its stores. Your manager, José Martinez, was asked by headquarters to explore the feasibility of offering a vinyl selection in his store, and he left this research job to you.

Your Task. This assignment calls for establishing primary data using a survey. Devise a questionnaire and poll young music consumers in your area to find out whether they enjoy and, more important, purchase vinyl records. Examine attitudes toward LPs in the populations and age groups most likely to find them intriguing. After collecting your data, determine whether your Best Buy store could establish a profitable vinyl business. Support your recommendation with conclusions you draw from your survey but also from secondary research detailing the new trend. To illustrate your findings, use pie charts for percentages (e.g., how many LPs are sold in comparison to CDs and other media), line graphs to indicate trends over time (e.g., sales figures in various consumer segments), and other graphics. Prepare a formal report for José Martinez, who will share your report with upper management.

9.12 Formal Report: Quick-Service Restaurant Checkup

The national franchising headquarters for a quick-service chain has received complaints about the service, quality, and cleanliness of one of its restaurants in your area. You have been sent to inspect and to report on what you see.

Your Task. Select a quick-service restaurant in your area. Visit on two or more occasions. Make notes about how many customers were served, how quickly they received their food, and how courteously they were treated. Observe the number of employees and supervisors working. Note the cleanliness of observable parts of the restaurant. Inspect the washroom as well as the exterior and surrounding grounds. Sample the food. Your boss is a stickler for details; he has no use for general statements like *The washroom was not clean*. Be specific. Draw conclusions. Are the complaints justified? If improvements are necessary, make recommendations. Address your report to Lawrence C. Shymko, President.

9.13 Informal Proposal: Supporting a Charity

Your uncle recently sold his start-up software company for $53 million. He plans to invest a portion of his money and retire early. He also plans to donate $5 million to a philanthropic charity. He is especially concerned about the environment. He has asked you to prepare an informal proposal to recommend three possible charities that could make a positive impact on the environment with his contribution. He wants to be certain that he is supporting a charity that is stable, accountable, and productive.

Your Task. Research three environmental charities, looking at their mission, structure, financial statements, and achievements. In addtion to researching the charities' Web sites, consult other sites that monitor and evaluate charities, such as Charity Intelligence (**www.charityintelligence.ca**) and Charity Navigator (**www.charitynavigator.org**). Prepare an informal proposal for your uncle outlining your findings and recommendations.

9.14 Formal Report: Communication Skills on the Job

Collect information regarding communication skills used by individuals in a particular career field (accounting, management, marketing, office administration, paralegal, and so forth).

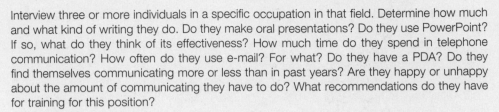

Interview three or more individuals in a specific occupation in that field. Determine how much and what kind of writing they do. Do they make oral presentations? Do they use PowerPoint? If so, what do they think of its effectiveness? How much time do they spend in telephone communication? How often do they use e-mail? For what? Do they have a PDA? Do they find themselves communicating more or less than in past years? Are they happy or unhappy about the amount of communicating they have to do? What recommendations do they have for training for this position?

Your Task. Write a report that discusses the findings from your interviews. What conclusions can you draw regarding communication skills in this field? What recommendations would you make for individuals entering this field? Your instructor may ask you to research the perception of businesspeople over the past ten years regarding the communication skills of employees. To gather such data, conduct library or online database research.

CRITICAL THINKING

9.15 Informal Proposal: Setting Up a Web Site

As a consultant, you have been asked to investigate the cost of setting up a Web site for Arni Arason, who owns a small wine distribution business in Stratford, Ontario, named Fruit of the Gods Inc. He hopes to begin with a simple, basic Web site, but he wants it to be user friendly, and he wants customers to be able to buy wine from the site with a credit card.

Your Task. Use search engines on the Internet to locate information. Try "Web site development" as a search term. Visit several sites that offer to build Web sites. Focus on those that seem most professional. Look to see when the site was last updated. Read the promotional material and decide whether it is well written. Remember, anyone can post a Web site. Investigate the general characteristics of a Web site, how to create and promote a site, and how to maintain a Web server. Mr. Arason wants a low-cost but high-quality site. Develop cost figures. Draw conclusions and make recommendations in a letter proposal to Mr. Arason.

Related Web site: Drinks Ontario (**www.drinksontario.com**), which Arni Arason hopes to join soon, has some brief background information about the wine distribution business.

WEB

TEAM

9.16 Formal Report: Selecting a Location for a Satellite Campus

The college or university you attend has recently been experiencing unprecedented growth. Student enrolment has been up for five years in a row, research and donation money has been on the increase, and the number of international students applying for admission is also up. The board of directors has asked the director of development to look into the idea of planning a small satellite campus in an outlying area of the city. The question is, where to locate the satellite?

Your Task. Using your own college or university as the example for this report, research and write a formal report offering a recommendation about where to locate a satellite campus. What components (e.g., locations) will you choose to structure your report? What criteria would be important to the board of directors? Price of land? Proximity to public transportation? Proximity to other institutions? Proximity to a large population base? Where will you find data on these criteria?

9.17 Formal Report: All About Wikis

As discussed earlier in this chapter, wikis are becoming increasingly important to businesses that rely on teamwork across time zones and national borders. Some educators also use wikis for collaboration in their college-level classes. You are part of a group of interns from your college working at a large financial institution, Home Bank. Your intern team has collaborated on your finance-related research using a wiki. Your informal wiki has also been helpful when you worked together on a team project for college credit. Your internship supervisor is impressed and would like you to collect more hard data so he can pilot wikis for wider application in collaborative settings at the bank. Your preliminary research suggests that quite a few companies are using wikis, such as Best Buy's Geek Squad, Xerox, and IBM. In fact, IBM conducted a massive online brainstorming session that took two 72-hour sessions and involved 100,000 employees, customers, and business partners in over 160 countries.[18] Your boss is interested in reading about such cases to decide whether to pilot a wiki, and if so, what kind would work for Home Bank. Your team of three to five will investigate.

Your Task. Keep in mind that your boss, Irving E. Pound, will share your report with other managers who may be computer-literate users but are no tech heads. Start with the brief definition of wikis earlier in this chapter. Expand the definition by searching the Web and electronic database articles. First explain what wikis are and how they work, which resources (cost, software, hardware) are needed, how much training is required, and so forth. Examine the use of wikis in business today. How are large and small companies benefiting from collaboration facilitated by wikis? If your instructor directs, the report (or a section thereof) could discuss wikis in education and how instructors harness this new tool. After collecting a amount of information and data, outline and then write a formal report with a recommendation at the end suggesting whether and how Home Bank would benefit from investing in wiki software.

 ## GRAMMAR/MECHANICS REVIEW 9—APOSTROPHES

Study each of the following statements. Underscore any inappropriate form. Write a correction in the space provided. If a sentence is correct, write *C*.

years'   **Example:** In just two years time, Marti earned her MBA degree.

_____ 1. Mark Hanleys smartphone was found in the conference room.

_____ 2. The severance package includes two weeks salary for each year worked.

_____ 3. In only one years time, her school loans totalled $5,000.

_____ 4. The board of directors strongly believed that John Petersons tenure as CEO was exceptionally successful.

_____ 5. Several employees records were accidentally removed from the files.

_____ 6. The last witness testimony was the most convincing to the jury members.

_____ 7. Everyone appreciated Robins careful editing of our report.

_____ 8. I always get my moneys worth at my favourite restaurant.

_____ 9. Three local companies went out of business last month.

_____ 10. In one months time, we hope to have our new Web site up and running.

_____ 11. I need my boss signature on this expense claim.

_____ 12. That legal secretarys credentials and years of experience qualified her for a higher salary.

_____ 13. In certain aerospace departments, new applicants must apply for security clearance.

_____ 14. Our companys stock price rose dramatically last year.

_____ 15. Several businesses opening hours will change in the next three months.

 ## GRAMMAR/MECHANICS CHALLENGE—9

Document for Revision

The following report executive summary has faults in grammar, punctuation, spelling, number form, wordiness, and word use. Use standard proofreading marks (see Appendix B) to correct the errors. When you finish, your instructor can show you the revised version of this summary.

Executive Summary

Problem

The Canadian salmon industry must expand it's markets abroad particularly in regard to Japan. Although consumption of salmon is decreasing in Canada they are increasing in Japan. The problem that is for the canadian salmon industry is developing apropriate marketing strategies to boost its current sale in Japanese markets.

Summary of Findings

This report analyzes the Japanese market which currently consumes six hundred thousand tons of salmon per year, and is growing rapidly. Much of this salmon is supplied by imports which at this point in time total about 35% of sales. Our findings indicate that not only will this expand, but the share of imports will continue to grow. The trend is alarming to Japanese salmon industry leaders, because this important market, close to a $billion a year, is increasingly subject to the influence of foreign imports. Declining catches by Japans own Salmon fleet as well as a sharp upward turn in food preference by affluent Japanese consumers, has contributed to this trend.

Recommendations

Based on our analisys we reccommend the following 5 marketing strategys for the Canadian Salmon industry.

1. Farm greater supplys of atlantic farmed salmon to export.

2. We should market our own value added products.

3. Sell fresh salmon direct to the Tokyo Central Wholesale market.

4. Sell to other Japanese markets also.

5. Direct sales should be made to Japanese Supermarket chains.

LAYING THE GROUNDWORK FOR TEAM WRITING PROJECTS

Chances are very good that you can look forward to some kind of team writing in your future career. You may collaborate voluntarily (seeking advice and differing perspectives) or involuntarily (through necessity or by assignment). Working with other people can be frustrating, particularly when some team members don't carry their weight or when conflict breaks out. Team projects, though, can be harmonious, productive, and rewarding when members establish ground rules at the outset and adhere to guidelines such as those presented here.

Preparing to Work Together

Before you discuss the project, talk about how your group will function.

- Limit the size of your team, if possible, to two to five members. Larger groups have more difficulties. An odd number is usually preferable to avoid ties in voting.
- Name a team leader (to plan and conduct meetings), a recorder (to keep a record of group decisions), and an evaluator (to determine whether the group is on target and meeting its goals).
- Decide whether your team will be governed by consensus (everyone must agree) or by majority rule.
- Compare schedules of team members, and set up the best meeting times. Plan to meet often. Avoid other responsibilities during meetings. Team meetings can take place face-to-face or virtually.
- Discuss the value of conflict. By bringing conflict into the open and encouraging confrontation, your team can prevent personal resentment and group dysfunction. Conflict can actually create better final documents by promoting new ideas and avoiding groupthink.
- Discuss how you will deal with members who are not doing their share of the work.

Planning the Document

Once you have established ground rules, you are ready to discuss the project and resulting document. Be sure to keep a record of the decisions your team makes.

- Establish the document's specific purpose and identify the main issues involved.
- Decide on the final form of the document. What parts will it have?
- Discuss the audience(s) for the document and what appeal would help it achieve its purpose.
- Develop a work plan. Assign jobs. Set deadlines.
- Decide how the final document will be written: individuals working separately on assigned portions, one person writing the first draft, the entire group writing the complete document together, or some other method.
- Discuss ways to ensure the accuracy and currency of the information collected.

Collecting Information

The following suggestions help teams gather accurate information:

- Brainstorm for ideas as a group.
- Decide who will be responsible for gathering what information.
- Establish deadlines for collecting information.

Organizing, Writing, and Revising

As the project progresses, your team may wish to modify some of its earlier decisions.

- Review the proposed organization of your final document, and adjust it if necessary.
- Write the first draft. If separate team members are writing segments, they should use the same word processing program to facilitate combining files.
- Meet to discuss and revise the draft(s).
- If individuals are working on separate parts, appoint one person (probably the best writer) to coordinate all the parts, striving for consistent style and format.

Editing and Evaluating

Before the document is submitted, complete these steps:

- Give one person responsibility for finding and correcting grammatical and mechanical errors.
- Meet as a group to evaluate the final document. Does it fulfill its purpose and meet the needs of the audience?

Option: Using a Collaboration Tool to Get the Job Done

Free software such as Google Drive/Google Docs and MediaWiki allow multiple team members to work on projects together. You can download these tools for free. In the case of the Google tools you'll need a Google account. In the case of Google, go to **https://drive .google.com/#** and start composing. For MediaWiki you'll need to download the software from **www.mediawiki.org/wiki/Download**.

Career Application

Select a report topic from this chapter or Chapter 8. Assume that you must prepare the report as a team project. If you are working on a long report, your instructor may ask you to prepare individual progress reports as you develop your topic.

YOUR TASK

- Form teams of two to five members.
- Plan your report by establishing its purpose, analyzing the audience, identifying the main issues, developing a work plan, and assigning tasks.
- Collect information, organize the data, and write the first draft (perhaps using MediaWiki).
- Decide how the document will be revised, edited, and evaluated (perhaps using GoogleDrive).

Tip: For revising and editing, consider using the Microsoft Word tools introduced in Chapter 3 to track changes and make comments.

Your instructor may assign grades not only on the final report but also on your team effectiveness and your individual contribution, as determined by fellow team members and, potentially, by tracking your activities if you are using a wiki or GoogleDrive.

Developing Speaking Skills

1. Opening
2. Key Points
3. Closing

CHAPTER 10
Communicating
in Person

CHAPTER 11
Business
Presentations

COMMUNICATION TECHNOLOGY IN THE NEWS

Finding the Right Words in Awkward Situations

Source: Danielle Harder, "Finding the right words in awkward situations," Canadian HR Reporter, January 31, 2011, pp. 22-23. Used with permission.

As a leadership and communications expert, Merge Gupta-Sunderji thought she had heard it all. But when her Calgary-based firm asked clients about the most difficult conversations they've had with employees, she was admittedly surprised.

Take, for example, the female manager who had to talk to a male employee about continually grabbing himself in his private area during meetings. The manager started by showing him Michael Jackson videos and footage of baseball players and asking, "What do you have in common with these guys?"

He didn't know so, eventually, the manager had to be more direct. It turns out he was a former baseball player and completely unaware of either his offensive habit or its impact on co-workers.

While conversations about sensitive issues—such as social habits, body odour, poor performance, gossip or workplace attire—are dreadful, they must happen, says Gupta-Sunderji.

"You have to make the first move," she said. "It's really uncomfortable but it won't go away. You're the manager and this is what you're paid to do."

Advance preparation

It helps to do some homework in advance. Before approaching an employee, be clear about the reason for having the conversation in the first place, says Mitch Fairrais, president of On the Mark, a Toronto consulting firm that offers workshops on navigating difficult talks.

"You need clarity," he says. "Get a clear sense from HR or your organization about what the hope is from you, and reflect back your intentions so everyone is clear."

Many conversations become stuck, says Fairrais, because managers forget the bigger picture: What impact is this poor performance or behaviour having on the company?

Ginger Brunner, president of Dynamic HR in Shawnigan Lake, B.C., once had to discuss personal attire, or lack thereof, with an employee. The woman was fit and wanted to show it off.

"I just had to keep bringing it back to our policies," says Brunner.

Having a productive talk starts by meeting one-on-one, says Fairrais.

"The only time a conversation like this can be good is if you're clear about the other party's view or frame of reference," he says. "You can't do that in a group."

Body language and seating also needs to be just right. It's best to sit—never stand—only a few feet apart with nothing between the two of you, says Fairrais. It's also important to lean in and be present—no checking email, taking a "quick" call or allowing others to butt into the conversation.

"You have to eliminate distractions," he says. "Otherwise, you will not be 'there.'"

It's also helpful to have a game plan, says Gupta-Sunderji. Employers should take a five-step approach, she says. This not only gives managers confidence, it also gives them a road map if the discussion goes off track. It can be helpful if you have the steps written down and mentally check them off as you go along.

First on the list, of course, is to have the conversation. Start by acknowledging any discomfort. A line such as, "I have something to discuss with you that I've really struggled with but it's something I'd want to know about if it were me," works well, says Gupta-Sunderji.

Then, you need to be direct.

"Be respectful, be empathetic, but get to the point," she says. "'There's a strong body odour coming from you' or 'I know you have a sick child but your work is falling behind.'"

The third step is to anticipate and be prepared for emotion, whether it's anger, defensiveness or tears.

"It's natural for people to be upset in these situations. Don't take it personally," says Gupta-Sunderji.

This leads to step four: Express your desire to resolve the issue rather than see it escalate.

"Try saying, 'I see how this has upset you. My goal is to see how we can turn this around so you come in on time so you don't face disciplinary action,'" she says.

How the conversation is framed sets the tone, says Fairrais, who tells clients to shift the talk from being a monologue to a dialogue.

"You could say, 'I have a challenge. It involves my perception of the practices you use in meetings. Here's what those perceptions are. What are your perceptions?'" he says. "It gets their guard down. When you make it about them alone, their guard goes up."

If there are tears or anger, it can help to take a break and resume the conversation later. It's a good idea to think through all potential reactions in advance of the meeting and to practise a response to them, says Fairrais. At the same time, consider what it would be like in the other person's situation.

"You have to be as sincere as possible," he says. "Bring as much clarity and transparency as you can. You don't want them to think you're trying to soft sell something."

Brunner brings a box of tissues and shows she cares.

"Don't forget you're dealing with a person," she says. "Sometimes we get caught up in all of the proper steps and we forget that there's a human on the other side of the table."

At the same time, to be effective, you have to stick to the facts and not get caught up in the emotion. These types of meetings should never go longer than 20 minutes, says Fairrais.

Wrapping it up

It's important to leave the meeting with a plan. That means laying out the problem, the desired change or outcome and the potential consequences as early as possible in the meeting, he says. This leaves time to work on a solution together.

"You really want to focus on the future, not what went wrong," he says. "Find a way to enlist their views. Unless they feel you truly understood them, and they are part of the solution, they will be back again."

As difficult as these discussions can be, if they're not dealt with, the consequences can be far worse, says Brunner.

"The rest of the employees see these things happening," she says. "If they're not being addressed, that sends a really loud message."

Summarize the article you've just read in a two- or three-sentence paragraph. Answer the following questions, either on your own or in a small group. Be prepared to present your answers in a short presentation or in an e-mail to your instructor.

QUESTIONS:

1. How does what you've learned in this article change your perception of business communication?

2. How might what you've learned in this article change your own communication style?

3. Come up with pro and con arguments for the following debate/discussion topic: It's better to not have difficult conversations at work and instead just get on with your job.

CHAPTER 10

Communicating in Person

LEARNING OBJECTIVES

1. Explain why employers appreciate professional and ethical behaviour and good business etiquette.

2. Demonstrate effective face-to-face workplace communication, including using your voice as a communication tool.

3. Explain how to promote positive workplace relations through conversation.

4. Review techniques for offering constructive criticism on the job, responding professionally to workplace criticism, and resolving workplace conflicts.

5. Identify ways to polish your phone skills.

6. Understand techniques for making the best use of voice mail.

7. Plan and participate in productive business and professional meetings.

© YURI ARCURS/SHUTTERSTOCK

Whether we call it *professionalism, business etiquette, ethical conduct, social intelligence, or soft skills*, we are referring to a whole range of desirable workplace behaviours.

The Importance of Professionalism, Business Etiquette, and Ethical Behaviour

You probably know that being professional is important. When you search for definitions, however, you will find a wide range of meanings. Related terms and synonyms, such as *business etiquette* or *protocol*, *soft skills*, *social intelligence*, *polish*, and *civility*, may add to the confusion. However, they all have one thing in common: they describe desirable workplace behaviour. Businesses have an interest in a workforce that gets along and delivers positive results that enhance profits and boost a company's image. As a budding business professional, you have a stake in acquiring skills that will make you a strong job applicant and a valuable, successful employee.

In this section you will learn which professional characteristics most businesspeople value in workplace relationships and will expect of you. Next you will be asked to consider the link between professional and ethical behaviour on the job. Finally, by knowing what recruiters want, you will have the power to shape yourself into the kind of professional they are looking to hire.

Defining Professional Behaviour

Smooth relations in the workplace and when interacting with business partners or the public are crucial for the bottom line. Therefore, many businesses have established protocol procedures or policies to encourage civility. They are responding to increasing incidents of "desk rage" in the workplace. Here are a few synonyms that attempt to define professional behaviour that will foster positive workplace relations:

CIVILITY. Management consultant Patricia M. Buhler defines rising incivility at work "as behaviour that is considered disrespectful and inconsiderate of others."[1] For an example of a policy encouraging civility, view Wikipedia's guidelines to its editors (**en.wikipedia.org/wiki/Wikipedia:Civility**), which offer principles to prevent rudeness and hateful responses on the Internet. The largest wiki ever created, the free encyclopedia must ensure that its more than 91,000 active collaborators get along and respect each other. Interestingly, Wikipedia admits that it is easier to define civility by its opposite: "[I]ncivility . . . consists of personally targeted, belligerent behaviour and persistent rudeness that result in an atmosphere of conflict and stress."[2]

POLISH. You may hear businesspeople refer to someone as being *polished* or displaying *polish* when dealing with others. In her book with the telling title *Buff and Polish: A Practical Guide to Enhance Your Professional Image and Communication Style*, Kathryn J. Volin focuses on nonverbal techniques and etiquette guidelines that are linked to career success. For example, she addresses making first impressions, shaking hands, improving one's voice quality, listening, and presentation skills.

BUSINESS AND DINING ETIQUETTE. Proper business attire, dining etiquette, and other aspects of your professional presentation can make or break your interview, as you will see in Chapter 13. Even a seemingly harmless act such as sharing a business meal can have a huge impact on your career. In the words of one executive, "Eating is not an executive skill . . . but it is especially hard to imagine why anyone negotiating a rise to the top would consider it possible to skip mastering the very simple requirements . . . . [W]hat else did they skip learning?"[3] This means that you will be judged on more than your college-bred expertise. You will need to hone your etiquette skills as a well-rounded future business professional.

SOCIAL INTELLIGENCE. Occasionally you may encounter the expression *social intelligence*. In the words of one of its modern proponents, it is "The ability to get along well with others and to get them to cooperate with you."[4] Social intelligence points to a deep understanding of culture and life that helps us negotiate interpersonal and social situations. This type of intelligence can be much harder to acquire than simple etiquette. Social intelligence requires us to interact well, be perceptive, show sensitivity toward others, and grasp a situation quickly and accurately.

SOFT SKILLS. Perhaps the most common term for important interpersonal habits is *soft skills*, as opposed to *hard skills*, a term for the technical knowledge in your field. Soft skills are a whole cluster of personal qualities, habits, attitudes (e.g., optimism and friendliness), communication skills, and social graces. Employers want managers and employees who are comfortable with diverse co-workers, who can listen actively to customers and colleagues, who can make eye contact, who display good workplace manners, and who possess a host of other interpersonal skills. *Dress for Success* guru John T. Molloy says that 99 out of 100 executives view social skills as prerequisites to success, whether over cocktails, during dinner, or in the boardroom.[5] These skills are immensely important not only to being hired but also to being promoted.

All attempts to explain proper behaviour at work aim at identifying traits that make someone a good employee and a compatible co-worker. You will want to achieve a positive image on the job and to maintain a solid reputation. For the sake of simplicity, in the discussion that follows, the terms *professionalism*, *business etiquette*, and *soft skills* will be used largely synonymously.

The Relationship Between Ethics and Professional Behaviour

The wide definition of professionalism also encompasses another crucial quality in a businessperson: *ethics* or *integrity*. Perhaps you subscribe to a negative view

of business after learning about companies such as the U.S.'s Enron or Canada's LiveEnt. The collapse of these businesses, along with fraud charges against their executives, has reinforced the cynical perception of business as unethical and greedy. However, for every company that captures the limelight for misconduct, hundreds or even thousands of others operate honestly and serve their customers and the public well. The overwhelming majority of businesses wish to recruit ethical and polished graduates.

The difference between ethics and etiquette is minimal in the workplace. Ethics suggest that no sharp distinction between ethics and etiquette exists. How we approach the seemingly trivial events of work life reflects our character and attitudes when we handle larger issues. Our conduct should be consistently ethical and professional. Harvard University Professor Douglas Chismar believes that "[w]e each have a moral obligation to treat each other with respect and sensitivity every day."[7] He calls on all of us to make a difference in the quality of life, morale, and even productivity at work. When employed appropriately in business, he says, professionalism brings greater good to society and makes for a better workplace.

Figure 10.1 summarizes the many components of professional workplace behaviour[8] and identifies six main dimensions that will ease your entry into the world of work. Follow these guidelines to ensure your success on the job and increase the likelihood of promotion.

Knowing What Employers Want

Professional polish is increasingly valuable in our knowledge-based economy and will set you apart in competition with others. Hiring managers expect you to have technical expertise in your field. A good résumé and interview may get you in the door. However, soft skills and professional polish will ensure your long-term success. Advancement and promotions will depend on your grasp of workplace etiquette and the ability to communicate with your boss, co-workers, and customers. You will also earn recognition on the job if you prove yourself as an effective and contributing team member—and as a well-rounded professional overall.

Even in technical fields such as accounting and finance, employers are looking for professionalism and soft skills. Based on a survey of international accounting

FIGURE **10.1** The Six Dimensions of Professional Behaviour

PROFESSIONAL DIMENSION	WHAT PROFESSIONALISM MEANS ON THE JOB
Courtesy and respect	• Be punctual. • Speak and write clearly and in language others can understand. • Apologize for errors or misunderstandings. • Notify the other person promptly when running late. • Accept constructive criticism. • Provide fair and gentle feedback. • Practise active listening.
Appearance and appeal	• Present yourself pleasantly with good hygiene and grooming. • Choose attractive, yet not distracting, business attire. • Understand that appropriate dress and behaviour are the first indication of professionalism and create lasting impressions. • Display proper business and dining etiquette.
Tolerance and tact	• Demonstrate self-control. • Stay away from public arguments and disagreements, including in written documents and e-mail. • Eliminate biases and prejudices in all business dealings. • Keep personal opinions of people private. • Avoid snap judgments, especially when collaborating with others.
Honesty and ethics	• Avoid even the smallest lies at all cost. • Steer clear of conflicts of interest. • Pay for services and products promptly. • Keep confidential information confidential. • Pass up opportunities to badmouth competitors—emphasize your company's benefits, not your competitors' flaws. • Take positive, appropriate actions; avoid resorting to vengeful behaviour when you feel wronged.
Reliability and responsibility	• Be dependable. • Follow through on commitments. • Keep promises and deadlines. • Perform work consistently and deliver effective results. • Make realistic promises about the quantity and quality of work output in a projected time frame.
Diligence and collegiality	• Deliver only work you can be proud of. • Strive for excellence at all times. • Give to customers more than they expect. • Be prepared before meetings and when presenting reports. • Do what needs to be done; do not leave work for others to do. • Show a willingness to share expertise. • Volunteer services to a worthy community or charity group. • Join networking groups and help their members.

executives, *CA Magazine* concluded that "the future is bright for the next generation of accounting and finance professionals provided they are armed with such soft skills as the ability to communicate, deal with change, and work in a team setting."[9] A survey of chief financial officers revealed that a majority believed that communication skills carry a greater importance today than in the past.[10] Increasingly, finance professionals must be able to interact with the entire organization and explain terms without using financial jargon.

Employment advertisements frequently mention team, communication, and people skills.

Employers want team players who can work together productively. If you look at current online or newspaper want ads, chances are you will find requirements such as the following examples:

- Proven team skills to help deliver on-time, on-budget results
- Strong verbal and written communication skills as well as excellent presentation skills
- Excellent interpersonal, organizational, and teamwork skills
- Interpersonal and team skills plus well-developed communication skills
- Good people skills and superior teamwork abilities

In addition, most hiring managers are looking for new hires who show enthusiasm, are eager to learn, volunteer to tackle even difficult tasks, and exhibit a positive attitude. You will not be hired to warm a seat.

This chapter focuses on developing interpersonal skills, telephone and voice mail etiquette, teamwork proficiency, and meeting management skills. These are some of the soft skills that employers seek in today's increasingly interconnected and competitive environments. You will learn many tips and techniques for becoming a professional communicator, valuable team player, and polished meeting participant.

Successful Face-to-Face Workplace Communication

One-dimensional communication technologies cannot replace the richness or effectiveness of face-to-face communication.

Because technology provides many alternate communication channels, you may think that face-to-face communication is no longer essential or even important in business and professional transactions. You've already learned that e-mail is now the preferred communication channel because it is faster, cheaper, and easier than telephone, mail, or fax. Yet, despite their popularity and acceptance, new communication technologies can't replace the richness or effectiveness of face-to-face communication.[11] Imagine that you want to tell your boss how you solved a problem. Would you settle for a one-dimensional e-mail when you could step into her office and explain in person?

Face-to-face conversation has many advantages. It allows you to be persuasive and expressive because you can use your voice and body language to make a point. You are less likely to be misunderstood because you can read feedback instantly and make needed adjustments. In conflict resolution, you can reach a solution more efficiently and cooperate to create greater levels of mutual benefit when communicating face to face.[12] Moreover, people want to see each other to satisfy a deep human need for social interaction. For numerous reasons, communicating in person remains the most effective of all communication channels. In this chapter you'll explore helpful business and professional interpersonal speaking techniques, starting with viewing your voice as a communication tool.

Using Your Voice as a Communication Tool

Like an actor, you can change your voice to make it a more powerful communication tool.

It's been said that language provides the words, but your voice is the music that makes words meaningful.[13] You may believe that a beautiful or powerful voice is unattainable. After all, this is the voice you were born with, and it can't be changed. Actually, the voice is a flexible instrument. For example, two of Canada's leading theatre companies, the Stratford and Shaw festivals in Ontario, both have speech coaches on staff to teach actors various accents and voice techniques. Celebrities, business executives, and everyday people consult voice and speech therapists to help them shake bad habits or help them speak so that they can be understood and not sound less intelligent than they are. Rather than consult a high-paid specialist, you can pick up useful tips for using your voice most effectively by learning how to control such elements as pronunciation, tone, pitch, volume, rate, and emphasis.

PRONUNCIATION. Pronunciation involves saying words correctly and clearly with the accepted sounds and accented syllables. You'll be at a distinct advantage in your job if, through training and practice, you learn to pronounce words correctly. Some of the most common errors, shown in Figure 10.2, include adding or omitting vowels, omitting consonants, reversing sounds, and slurring sounds. In casual conversation with your friends, correct pronunciation is not a big deal. But on the job you want to sound intelligent, educated, and competent. If you mispronounce words or slur phrases together, you risk being misunderstood as well as giving a poor impression of yourself. How can you improve your pronunciation skills? The best way is to listen carefully to educated people, read aloud from well-written newspapers like *The Globe and Mail* and the *National Post*, look up words in the dictionary, and avoid errors such as those in Figure 10.2.

TONE. The tone of your voice sends a nonverbal message to listeners. It identifies your personality and your mood. Some voices sound enthusiastic and friendly, conveying the impression of an upbeat person who is happy to be with the listener. But voices can also sound controlling, patronizing, slow-witted, angry, or childish. This doesn't mean that the speaker necessarily has that attribute. It may mean that the speaker is merely carrying on a family tradition or pattern learned in childhood. To check your voice tone, record your voice and listen to it critically. Is it projecting a positive quality about you?

PITCH. Effective speakers use a relaxed, controlled, well-pitched voice to attract listeners to their message. Pitch refers to sound vibration frequency; that is, it indicates the highness or lowness of a sound. In Canada, most speakers and listeners tend to prefer a variety of pitch patterns. Voices are most attractive when they rise and fall in conversational tones. Flat, monotone voices are considered boring and ineffectual. In business, communicators strive for a moderately low voice, which is thought to be pleasing and professional.

VOLUME AND RATE. Volume indicates the degree of loudness or the intensity of sound. Just as you adjust the volume on your MP3 player or television, you should adjust the volume of your speaking to the occasion and your listeners. When speaking face to face, you generally know whether you are speaking too loudly or softly by looking at your listeners. Are they straining to hear you? To judge what volume to

> Proper pronunciation means saying words correctly and clearly with the accepted sounds and accented syllables.

> Speaking in a moderately low-pitched voice at about 125 words a minute makes you sound pleasing and professional.

FIGURE 10.2 Pronunciation Errors to Avoid

Adding vowel sounds	*athlete* (NOT *ath-a-lete*) *disastrous* (NOT *disas-ter-ous*)
Omitting vowel sounds	*federal* (NOT *fed-ral*) *ridiculous* (NOT *ri-dic-lous*) *generally* (NOT *gen-rally*)
Substituting vowel sounds	*get* (NOT *git*) *separate* (NOT *sep-e-rate*)
Adding consonant sounds	*butter* (NOT *budder*) *statistics* (NOT *sta-stis-tics*) *especially* (NOT *ex-specially*)
Omitting consonant sounds	*library* (NOT *libery*) *perhaps* (NOT *praps*)
Confusing or distorting sounds	*ask* (NOT *aks*) *hundred* (NOT *hunderd*) *accessory* (NOT *assessory*)
Slurring sounds	*didn't you* (NOT *dint ya*) *going to* (NOT *gonna*)

use, listen carefully to the other person's voice. Use it as a guide for adjusting your voice. Rate refers to the pace of your speech. If you speak too slowly, listeners are bored and their attention wanders. If you speak too quickly, listeners can't understand you. Most people normally talk at about 125 words a minute. If you're the kind of speaker who speeds up when talking in front of a group of people, monitor the nonverbal signs of your listeners and adjust your rate as needed.

EMPHASIS. By emphasizing or stressing certain words, you can change the meaning you are expressing. For example, read these sentences aloud, emphasizing the italicized words:

> *Matt* said the hard drive failed again. (Matt knows what happened.)
>
> Matt *said* the hard drive failed again. (But he may be wrong.)
>
> Matt said the hard drive failed *again*? (Did he really say that?)

As you can see, emphasis affects the meaning of the words and the thought expressed. To make your message interesting and natural, use emphasis appropriately. You can raise your volume to sound authoritative and raise your pitch to sound disbelieving. Lowering your volume and pitch makes you sound professional or reasonable.

Some speakers today are prone to "uptalk." This is a habit of using a rising inflection at the end of a sentence that makes statements sound like questions. Once used exclusively by teenagers, uptalk is increasingly found in the workplace, with negative results. When statements sound like questions, speakers seem weak and tentative. Their messages lack conviction and authority. On the job, managers afflicted by uptalk may have difficulty convincing staff members to follow directions because their voice inflection implies that other valid options are available. If you want to sound confident and competent, avoid uptalk.

Promoting Positive Workplace Relations Through Conversation

In the workplace, conversations may involve giving and taking instructions, providing feedback, exchanging ideas on products and services, participating in performance appraisals, or engaging in small talk about such things as families and sports. Face-to-face conversation helps people work together harmoniously and feel that they are part of the larger organization. There are several guidelines that promote positive workplace conversations, starting with using correct names and titles.

USE CORRECT NAMES AND TITLES. Although the world seems increasingly informal, it's still wise to use titles and last names when addressing professional adults (*Mrs. Smith*, *Mr. Rivera*). In some organizations senior staff members will speak to junior employees on a first-name basis, but the reverse may not be encouraged. Probably the safest plan is to ask your superiors how they want to be addressed. Customers and others outside the organization should always be addressed by title and last name.

When you meet strangers, do you have trouble remembering their names? You can improve your memory considerably if you associate the person with an object, place, colour, animal, job, adjective, or some other memory hook. For example, *computer pro Kevin*, *Miami Kim*, *silver-haired Mr. Lee*, *bulldog Chris*, *bookkeeper Lynn*, *traveller Ms. Janis*. The person's name will also be more deeply embedded in your memory if you use it immediately after being introduced, in subsequent conversation, and when you part.

CHOOSE APPROPRIATE TOPICS. In some workplace activities, such as social gatherings or interviews, you will be expected to engage in small talk. Be sure to stay away from controversial topics with someone you don't know very well. Avoid politics, religion, or current events items that can start heated arguments until you know the person better. To initiate appropriate conversations, read newspapers and

"Uptalk," in which sentences sound like questions, makes speakers seem weak and tentative.

listen to radio and TV shows discussing current events. Make a mental note of items that you can use in conversation, taking care to remember where you saw or heard the news items so that you can report accurately and authoritatively. Try not to be defensive or annoyed if others present information that upsets you.

AVOID NEGATIVE REMARKS. Workplace conversations are not the place to complain about your colleagues, your friends, the organization, or your job. No one enjoys listening to whiners. And your criticism of others may come back to haunt you. A snipe at your boss or a complaint about a fellow worker may reach him or her, sometimes embellished or distorted with meanings you did not intend. Be careful about publicizing negative judgments. Remember, some people love to repeat statements that will stir up trouble or set off internal workplace wars. It's best not to give them the ammunition.

LISTEN TO LEARN. In conversations with colleagues, subordinates, and customers, train yourself to expect to learn something from what you are hearing. Being attentive is not only instructive but also courteous. Beyond displaying good manners, you'll probably find that your conversation partner has information that you don't have. Being receptive and listening with an open mind means not interrupting or prejudging. Let's say you very much want to be able to work at home for part of your workweek. You try to explain your ideas to your boss, but he cuts you off shortly after you start. He says, "It's out of the question; we need you here every day." Suppose instead he says, "I have strong reservations about your telecommuting, but maybe you'll change my mind," and he settles in to listen to your presentation. Even if your boss decides against your request, you will feel that your ideas were heard and respected.

"I had to spend the money I budgeted for your raise on a therapist after listening to your endless complaining."

GIVE SINCERE AND SPECIFIC PRAISE. A wise person once said, "Man does not live by bread alone. He needs to be buttered up once in a while." Probably nothing promotes positive workplace relationships better than sincere and specific praise. Whether the compliments and appreciation are travelling upward to management, downward to workers, or horizontally to colleagues, everyone responds well to recognition. Organizations run more smoothly and morale is higher when people feel appreciated. In your workplace conversations, look for ways to recognize good work and good people. And try to be specific. Instead of "You did a good job in leading that meeting," try something more specific, such as "Your leadership skills certainly kept that meeting focused and productive."

Offering Constructive Criticism at Work

No one likes to receive criticism, and most of us don't like to give it either. But in the workplace cooperative endeavours demand feedback and evaluation. How are we doing on a project? What went well? What failed? How can we improve our efforts? Today's workplace often involves team projects. As a team member, you will be called on to judge the work of others. In addition to working on teams, you can also expect to become a supervisor or manager one day. As such, you will need to evaluate your direct reports. Good employees seek good feedback from their supervisors. They want and need timely, detailed observations about their work to reinforce what they do well and help them overcome weak spots. But making that feedback palatable and constructive is not always easy. Depending on your

You will be most effective in workplace conversations if you use correct names and titles, choose appropriate topics, avoid negative and judgmental remarks, and give sincere and specific praise.

situation, you may find some or all of the following suggestions, in addition to the ones listed in the article that opens this unit (p. 304), helpful when you must deliver constructive criticism:

(p. 304)

- **Mentally outline your conversation.** Think carefully about what you want to accomplish and what you will say. Find the right words at the right time and in the right setting.
- **Generally, use face-to-face communication.** Most constructive criticism is better delivered in person rather than in e-mails or memos. Personal feedback offers an opportunity for the listener to ask questions and give explanations. Occasionally, however, complex situations may require a different strategy. You might prefer to write out your opinions and deliver them by telephone or in writing. A written document enables you to organize your thoughts, include all the details, and be sure of keeping your cool. Remember, though, that written documents create permanent records—for better or worse.
- **Focus on improvement.** Instead of attacking, use language that offers alternative behaviour. Use phrases such as "Next time, it would great if you could . . . ."
- **Offer to help.** Criticism is accepted more readily if you volunteer to help in eliminating or solving the problem.
- **Be specific.** Instead of a vague assertion such as "Your work is often late," be more specific: "The specs on the Riverside job were due Thursday at 5 p.m., and you didn't hand them in until Friday." Explain how the person's performance jeopardized the entire project.
- **Avoid broad generalizations.** Don't use words such as *should*, *never*, *always*, and other encompassing expressions. They may cause the listener to shut down and become defensive.
- **Discuss the behaviour, not the person.** Instead of "You seem to think you can come to work any time you want," focus on the behaviour: "Coming to work late means that we have to fill in with someone else until you arrive."
- **Use the word *we* rather than *you*.** "We need to meet project deadlines," is better than saying "You need to meet project deadlines." Emphasize organizational expectations rather than personal ones. Avoid sounding accusatory.
- **Encourage two-way communication.** Even if well-planned, criticism is still hard to deliver. It may surprise or hurt the feelings of the employee. Consider ending your message with, "It can be hard to hear this type of feedback. If you'd like to share your thoughts, I'm listening."
- **Avoid anger, sarcasm, and a raised voice.** Criticism is rarely constructive when tempers flare. Plan in advance what you will say and deliver it in low, controlled, and sincere tones.
- **Keep it private.** Offer praise in public; offer criticism in private. "Setting an example" through public criticism is never a wise management policy.

Responding Professionally to Workplace Criticism

As much as we hate giving criticism, we dislike receiving it even more. Yet the workplace requires that you not only provide it but also be able to accept it. When being criticized, you probably will feel that you are being attacked. You can't just sit back and relax. Your heart beats faster, your temperature increases, your face reddens, and you respond with the classic "fight or flight" syndrome. You feel that you want to instantly retaliate or escape from the attacker. But focusing on your feelings distracts you from hearing the content of what is being said, and it prevents you from responding professionally. Some or all of the following suggestions will guide you in reacting positively to criticism so that you can benefit from it:

- **Listen without interrupting.** Even though you might want to protest, make yourself hear the speaker out.
- **Determine the speaker's intent.** Unskilled communicators may throw "verbal bricks" with unintended negative-sounding expressions. If you think the intent

---

Sidebar 1:

Offering constructive criticism is easier if you plan what you will say, focus on improvement, offer to help, be specific, discuss the behaviour and not the person, speak privately face to face, and avoid anger.

Sidebar 2:

When being criticized, you should listen, paraphrase, and clarify what is said. If you agree that the criticism is valid, apologize or explain what you will do differently.

is positive, focus on what is being said rather than reacting to poorly chosen words.

- **Acknowledge what you are hearing.** Respond with a pause, a nod, or a neutral statement such as "I understand you have a concern." This buys you time. Do not disagree, counterattack, or blame, which may escalate the situation and harden the speaker's position.
- **Paraphrase what was said.** In your own words, restate objectively what you are hearing; for example, "So what you're saying is . . . ."
- **Ask for more information if necessary.** Clarify what is being said. Stay focused on the main idea rather than interjecting side issues.
- **Agree—if the comments are accurate.** If an apology is in order, give it. Explain what you plan to do differently. If the criticism is on target, the sooner you agree, the more likely you will engender respect from the other person.
- **Disagree respectfully and constructively—if you feel the comments are unfair.** After hearing the criticism, you might say, "May I tell you my perspective?" Or you could try to solve the problem by saying, "How can we improve this situation in a way you believe we can both accept?" If the other person continues to criticize, say "I want to find a way to resolve your concern. When do you want to talk about it next?"
- **Look for a middle position.** Search for a middle position or a compromise. Be genial even if you don't like the person or the situation.

If you feel you are being criticized unfairly, disagree respectfully and constructively; look for a middle position.

Resolving Workplace Conflicts

Conflict is a normal part of every workplace, but it is not always negative. When managed properly, conflict can improve decision making, clarify values, increase group cohesiveness, stimulate creativity, decrease tensions, and reduce dissatisfaction. Unresolved conflict, however, can destroy productivity and seriously reduce morale. You will be better prepared to resolve workplace conflict if you know the five most common response patterns as well as a six-step procedure for dealing with conflict.

COMMON CONFLICT RESPONSE PATTERNS. Imagine a time when you were very upset with a workplace colleague, boss, or a teammate. How did you respond? Experts who have studied conflict say that most of us deal with it in one of the following predictable patterns:

Although avoidance does not solve conflicts, it may be the best response for some situations, such as when the issue is trivial.

- **Avoidance/withdrawal.** Instead of trying to resolve the conflict, one person or the other simply withdraws. Avoidance of conflict generally results in a "lose-lose" situation because the problem festers and no attempt is made to understand the issues causing the conflict. On the other hand, avoidance may be the best response when the issue is trivial, when potential losses from an open conflict outweigh potential gains, or when insufficient time is available to work through the issue adequately.
- **Accommodation/smoothing.** When one person gives in quickly, the conflict is smoothed over and surface harmony results. This may be the best method when the issue is minor, when damage to the relationship would harm both parties, and when tempers are too hot for productive discussion.
- **Compromise.** In this pattern both people give up something of lesser importance to gain something more important. Compromise may be the best approach when both parties stand to gain, when a predetermined "ideal" solution is not required, and when time is short.
- **Competition/forcing.** This approach results in a contest in which one person comes out on top, leaving the other with a sense of failure. This method ends the conflict, but it may result in hurt feelings and potential future problems from the loser. This strategy is appropriate when a decision or action must be immediate and when the parties recognize the power relationship between themselves.

• **Collaboration/problem solving.** In this pattern both parties lay their cards on the table and attempt to reach consensus. This approach works when the involved people have common goals but they disagree over how to reach them. Conflict may arise from misunderstanding or a communication breakdown. Collaboration works best when all parties are trained in problem-solving techniques.[14]

SIX-STEP PROCEDURE FOR DEALING WITH CONFLICT. Probably the best pattern for resolving conflicts involves collaboration and problem-solving procedures. But this method requires a certain amount of training. Fortunately, experts in the field of negotiation have developed a six-step pattern that you can try the next time you need to resolve a conflict:

1. **Listen.** To be sure you understand the problem, listen carefully. If the other person doesn't seem to be listening to you, you need to set the example and be the first to listen.
2. **Understand the other point of view.** Once you listen, it's much easier to understand the other's position. Show your understanding by asking questions and paraphrasing. This will also verify what you think the other person means.
3. **Show a concern for the relationship.** By focusing on the problem, not the person, you can build, maintain, and even improve relationships. Show an understanding of the other person's situation and needs. Show an overall willingness to come to an agreement.
4. **Look for common ground.** Identify your interests and help the other side to identify its interests. Learn what you have in common, and look for a solution to which both sides can agree.
5. **Invent new problem-solving options.** Spend time identifying the interests of both sides. Then brainstorm to invent new ways to solve the problem. Be open to new options.
6. **Reach an agreement based on what's fair.** Seek to determine a standard of fairness that is acceptable to both sides. Then weigh the possible solutions, and choose the best option.[15]

Telephone, Smartphone, and Voice Mail Etiquette

The telephone is the most universal—and, some would say, the most important—piece of equipment in offices today.[16] For many businesspeople, it is a primary contact with the outside world. Some observers predicted that e-mail and faxes would "kill off phone calls."[17] In fact, the amazing expansion of wireless communication has given the telephone a new and vigorous lease on life. Telephones are definitely here to stay. But many of us do not use them efficiently or effectively. In this section we'll focus on traditional telephone techniques as well as voice mail efficiency.

Making Productive Phone Calls

Before making a phone call, decide whether the intended call is necessary. Could you find the information yourself? If you wait a while, would the problem resolve itself? Perhaps your message could be delivered more efficiently by some other means. One company found that phone interruptions consumed about 18 percent of staff members' workdays. Another study found that two thirds of all calls were less important than the work they interrupted.[18] Alternatives to phone calls include e-mail, texts, instant messages, or calls to voice mail systems. If a phone call must be made, use the following suggestions to make it fully productive.

• **Plan a mini-agenda.** Have you ever been embarrassed when you had to make a second phone call because you forgot an important item the first time? Before placing a call, jot down notes regarding all the topics you need to discuss. Following an agenda guarantees not only a complete call but also a quick one. You'll be less likely to wander from the business at hand while rummaging through your mind trying to remember everything.

- **Use a three-point introduction.** When placing a call, immediately (1) name the person you are calling, (2) identify yourself and your affiliation, and (3) give a brief explanation of your reason for calling. For example: "May I speak to Larry Levin? This is Hillary Dahl of Acme Ltd., and I'm seeking information about a software program called Power Presentations." This kind of introduction enables the receiving individual to respond immediately without asking further questions.

- **Be brisk if you are rushed.** For business calls when your time is limited, avoid questions such as "How are you?" Instead, say, "Lisa, I knew you'd be the only one who could answer these two questions for me." Another efficient strategy is to set a "contract" with the caller: "Hi, Lisa, I have only ten minutes, but I really wanted to get back to you."

- **Be cheerful and accurate.** Let your voice show the same kind of animation that you radiate when you greet people in person. In your mind try to envision the individual answering the phone. A smile can certainly affect the tone of your voice, so smile at that person. Moreover, be accurate about what you say. "Hang on a second; I'll be right back" is rarely true. Better to say, "It may take me two or three minutes to get that information. Would you prefer to hold or have me call you back?"

- **Bring it to a close.** The responsibility for ending a call lies with the caller. This is sometimes difficult to do if the other person rambles on. You may need to use suggestive closing language, such as "I've certainly enjoyed talking with you," "I've learned what I needed to know, and now I can proceed with my work," "Thanks for your help," or "I must go now, but may I call you again in the future if I need . . .?"

- **Avoid phone tag.** If you call someone who's not in, ask when it would be best for you to call again. State that you will call at a specific time—and do it. If you ask a person to call you, give a time when you can be reached—and then be sure you are in at that time.

- **Leave complete voice mail messages.** Remember that there's no rush when you leave a voice mail message. Always enunciate clearly. And be sure to provide a complete message, including your name, telephone number, and the time and date of your call. Explain your purpose so that the receiver can be ready with the required information when returning your call.

Receiving Phone Calls Professionally

With a little forethought, you can project a professional image and make your phone a productive, efficient work tool. Developing good phone manners also reflects well on you and on your organization. Try following the following phone etiquette guidelines for workplace success:

- **Identify yourself immediately.** In answering your phone or someone else's, provide your name, title or affiliation, and, possibly, a greeting. For example, "Larry Levin, Proteus Software. How may I help you?" Force yourself to speak clearly and slowly. Remember that the caller may be unfamiliar with what you are saying and fail to recognize slurred syllables.

- **Be responsive and helpful.** If you are in a support role, be sympathetic to callers' needs. Instead of "I don't know," try "That's a good question; let me investigate." Instead of "We can't do that," try "That's a tough one; let's see what we can do." Avoid "No" at the beginning of a sentence. It sounds especially abrasive and displeasing because it suggests total rejection.

- **Be cautious when answering calls for others.** Be courteous and helpful, but don't give out confidential information. Better to say, "She's away from her desk" or "He's out of the office" than to report a colleague's exact whereabouts.

- **Take messages carefully.** Few things are as frustrating as receiving a potentially important phone message that is illegible. Repeat the spelling of names and verify telephone numbers. Write messages legibly and record their time and date. Promise to give the messages to intended recipients, but don't guarantee return calls.

You can improve your telephone reception skills by identifying yourself, being responsive and helpful, and taking accurate messages.

- **Explain what you're doing when transferring calls.** Give a reason for transferring, and identify the extension to which you are directing the call in case the caller is disconnected.

Using Smartphones for Business

Today's smartphones are sophisticated mobile devices. They enable you to conduct business from virtually anywhere at any time. The smartphone has become an essential part of communication in the workplace. While the number of cellphone users in the U.S. has outpaced the number of landline telephone users (by more than 50 percent), the same trend is less evident in Canada, where 83 percent remain happier with their traditional landline. That said, the number of cellphone, netbook, and tablet computer users keeps growing in both countries, especially among those between the ages of 18 and 34.[19]

Today's smartphones can do much more than making and receiving calls. High-end smartphones function much like laptops or netbooks. They can be used to store contact information, make to-do lists, keep track of appointments and important dates, send and receive e-mail, send and receive text and multimedia messages, search the Web, get news and stock quotes from the Internet, take pictures and videos, synchronize with Outlook and other software applications, and many other functions. Whether businesspeople opt for BlackBerrys, Android phones, or the popular iPhone, thousands of applications ("apps") enable them to stay connected, informed, and entertained on the go.

Because so many people depend on their smartphones and cellphones, it is important to understand proper use and etiquette. How are these mobile devices best used? When is it acceptable to take calls? Where should calls be made? Most of us have experienced thoughtless and rude cellphone behaviour. Researchers say that the rampant use of technological devices has worsened workplace incivility. Some employees consider texting and compulsive e-mail checking while working and during meetings disruptive, even insulting. The message the "e-cruising" workers presumably send to their colleagues is that they value the gizmo over human interaction.[20] To avoid offending, smart business communicators practise cellphone etiquette, as outlined in Figure 10.3. In projecting a professional image, they are careful about location, time, and volume in relation to their cellphone calls.

"Do you mind? I happen to be on the phone!"

LOCATION. Use good judgment in placing or accepting cellphone calls. Some places are dangerous or inappropriate for cellphone use. Turn off your cellphone in your vehicle and when entering a conference room, interview, theatre, place of worship, or any other place where it could be distracting or disruptive to others. Taking a call in a crowded room or bar makes it difficult to hear and reflects poorly on you as a professional. A bad connection also makes a bad impression. Static or dropped signals create frustration and miscommunication. Don't sacrifice professionalism for the sake of a garbled phone call. It's smarter to turn off your phone in an area where the signal is weak and when you are likely to have interference. Use voice mail and return the call when conditions are better.

FIGURE 10.3 Practising Courteous and Responsible Cellphone Use

Business communicators find cellphones to be enormously convenient and real time-savers. But rude users have generated a backlash against inconsiderate callers. Here are specific suggestions for using cellphones safely and responsibly:

- **Be courteous to those around you.** Don't force those near you to hear your business. Don't step up to a service counter, such as at a restaurant, bank, or post office, while talking on your cellphone. Don't carry on a cellphone conversation while someone is waiting on you. Think first of those in close proximity instead of those on the other end of the phone. Apologize and make amends gracefully for occasional cellphone blunders.

- **Observe wireless-free quiet areas.** Don't allow your cellphone to ring in theatres, restaurants, museums, classrooms, important meetings, and similar places. Use the cellphone's silent/vibrating ring option. A majority of travellers prefer that cellphone conversations not be held on most forms of public transportation.

- **Speak in low, conversational tones.** Microphones on cellphones are quite sensitive, thus making it unnecessary to talk loudly. Avoid "cell yell."

- **Take only urgent calls.** Make full use of your cellphone's caller ID feature to screen incoming calls. Let voice mail take those calls that are not pressing.

- **Drive now, talk later.** Pull over if you must make a call. Talking while driving increases the chance of accidents fourfold. In most Canadian provinces, including British Columbia, Newfoundland and Labrador, Nova Scotia, Ontario, Quebec, and Saskatchewan, there are specific laws against driving and using handheld devices. Other provinces and territories are enacting similar laws.[21]

- **Choose a professional ringtone.** These days you can download a variety of ringtones, from classical to rap to the *Star Wars* theme. Choose a ringtone that will sound professional.

TIME. Often what you are doing is more important than whatever may come over the airwaves to you on your phone. For example, when you are having an important discussion with a business partner, customer, or superior, it is rude to allow yourself to be interrupted by an incoming call. It's also poor manners to practice multitasking while on the phone. What's more, it's dangerous. Although you might be able to read and print out e-mails, deal with a customer at the counter, and talk on your wireless phone simultaneously, it's impolite and risky. Lack of attention results in errors and a lack of respect. If a phone call is important enough to accept, then it's important enough to stop what you are doing and attend to the conversation.

> Avoid taking cellphone calls when you are talking with someone else, and avoid "cell yell."

VOLUME. Many people raise their voices when using their cellphones. "Cell yell" results, much to the annoyance of anyone nearby. Raising your voice is unnecessary since most phones have excellent microphones that can pick up even a whisper. If the connection is bad, louder volume will not improve the sound quality. As in face-to-face conversations, a low, modulated voice sounds professional and projects the proper image.

Making the Best Use of Voice Mail

Voice mail links a phone system to a computer that digitizes and stores incoming messages. Some systems also provide functions such as automated attendant menus, allowing callers to reach any associated extension by pushing specific buttons on a touch-tone telephone. For example, a ski resort in British Columbia uses voice mail to answer routine questions that once were routed through an operator: *Welcome to Panorama. For information on accommodations, press 1; for snow conditions, press 2; for ski equipment rental, press 3*, and so forth.

Because phone calls can be disruptive, many businesspeople are making extensive use of voice mail to intercept and screen incoming calls. Voice mail's popularity results from the many functions it serves, the most important of which is

> Voice mail eliminates telephone tag, inaccurate message taking, and time-zone barriers; it also allows communicators to focus on essentials.

message storage. Because as many as half of all business calls require no discussion or feedback, the messaging capabilities of voice mail can mean huge savings for businesses. Incoming information is delivered without interrupting potential receivers and without all the niceties that most two-way conversations require. Stripped of superfluous chitchat, voice mail messages allow communicators to focus on essentials. Voice mail also eliminates telephone tag, inaccurate message taking, and time-zone barriers.

However, voice mail should not be overused. Individuals who screen all incoming calls cause irritation, resentment, and needless phone tag. Both receivers and callers can use etiquette guidelines to make voice mail work most effectively for them.

RECEIVING VOICE MAIL MESSAGES. Your voice mail should project professionalism and should provide an efficient mechanism for your callers to leave messages for you. Here are some voice mail etiquette tips to follow:

- **Don't overuse voice mail.** Don't use voice mail to avoid taking phone calls. It is better to answer calls yourself than to let voice mail messages build up.
- **Set the number of rings appropriately.** Set your voice mail to ring as few times as possible before picking up. This shows respect for your callers' time.
- **Prepare a professional, concise, friendly greeting.** Make your mechanical greeting sound warm and inviting, both in tone and content. Your greeting should be in your own voice, not a computer-generated one. Identify yourself and your organization so that callers know they have reached the right number. Thank the caller and briefly explain that you are unavailable. Invite the caller to leave a message or, if appropriate, call back. Here's a typical voice mail greeting: *Hi! This is Larry Levin of Proteus Software, and I appreciate your call. You have reached my voice mailbox because I'm either working with customers or talking on another line at the moment. Please leave your name, number, and reason for calling so that I can be prepared when I return your call.* Give callers an idea of when you will be available, such as *I'll be back at 2:30* or *I'll be out of my office until Wednesday, May 20.* If you screen your calls as a time-management technique, try this message: *I'm not near my phone right now, but I should be able to return calls after 3:30.*
- **Test your message.** Call your number and assess your message. Does it sound inviting? Sincere? Professional? Understandable? Are you pleased with your tone? If not, record your message again until it conveys the professional image you want.
- **Change your message.** Update your message regularly, especially if you travel for your job.
- **Respond to messages promptly.** Check your messages regularly, and try to return all voice mail messages within one business day.
- **Plan for vacations and other extended absences.** If you will not be picking up voice mail messages for an extended period, let callers know how they can reach someone else if needed.

LEAVING VOICE MAIL MESSAGES. When leaving a voice mail message, you should follow these tips:

- **Be prepared to leave a message.** Before calling someone, be prepared for voice mail. Decide what you are going to say and what information you are going to include in your message. If necessary, write your message down before calling.
- **Leave a concise, thorough message.** When leaving a message, always identify yourself using your complete name and affiliation. Mention the date and time you called and a brief explanation of your reason for calling. Always leave a complete phone number, including the area code, even if you think the receiver already has it. Tell the receiver the best time to return your call. Don't ramble.

- **Use a professional and courteous tone.** When leaving a message, make sure that your tone is professional, enthusiastic, and respectful. Smile when leaving a message to add warmth to your voice.
- **Speak slowly and clearly.** You want to make sure that your receiver will be able to understand your message. Speak slowly and pronounce your words carefully, especially when providing your phone number. The receiver should be able to write information down without having to replay your message.
- **Be careful with confidential information.** Don't leave confidential or private information in a voice mail message. Remember that anyone could gain access to this information.
- **Don't make assumptions.** If you don't receive a call back within a day or two after leaving a message, don't get angry or frustrated. Assume that the message wasn't delivered or that it couldn't be understood. Call back and leave another message, or send the person an e-mail.

Becoming a Team Player in Professional Teams

As we discussed in Chapter 1, the workplace and economy are changing. One significant recent change is the emphasis on teamwork. You might find yourself a part of a work team, project team, customer support team, supplier team, design team, planning team, functional team, cross-functional team, or some other group. All of these teams are being formed to accomplish specific goals, and your career success will depend on your ability to function well in a team-driven professional environment.

Teams can be effective in solving problems and in developing new products. Take, for example, the creation of a unique two-engine digital printing system by a Xerox team. The company did not rely just on the expertise of its 30 engineers and scientists. Rather, Xerox involved more than 1,000 corporate customers who use its commercial printers. Chief Technology Officer Sophie V. Vandebroek named the goal of the collaboration: "Involving experts who know the technology with customers who know the main points."[22] Samsung, the world's largest technology company, used a 40-member task force several years ago to devise strategies and new products that would successfully compete with Apple's admired iPhone. The outcome of this team effort was the Android-based Galaxy smartphone, which so far is outselling the iPhone in the Korean market.[23] Perhaps you can now imagine why forming teams is important.

The Importance of Conventional and Virtual Teams in the Workplace

Businesses are constantly looking for ways to do jobs better at less cost. They are forming teams for the following reasons:

- **Better decisions.** Decisions are generally more accurate and effective because group and team members contribute different expertise and perspectives.
- **Faster response.** When action is necessary to respond to competition or to solve a problem, small groups and teams can act rapidly.
- **Increased productivity.** Because they are often closer to the action and to the customer, team members can see opportunities for improving efficiency.
- **Greater buy-in.** Decisions arrived at jointly are usually better received because members are committed to the solution and are more willing to support it.
- **Less resistance to change.** People who have input into decisions are less hostile, less aggressive, and less resistant to change.
- **Improved employee morale.** Personal satisfaction and job morale increase when teams are successful.
- **Reduced risks.** Responsibility for a decision is diffused, thus carrying less risk for any individual.

> Organizations are forming teams for better decisions, faster response, increased productivity, greater buy-in, less resistance to change, improved morale, and reduced risks.

Virtual teams are groups of people who work interdependently with a shared purpose across space, time, and organization boundaries using technology.

To connect with distant team members across borders and time zones, many organizations are creating *virtual teams*. These are groups of people who work interdependently with a shared purpose across space, time, and organization boundaries using technology.[24]

Virtual teams may be local or global. Many workers today complete their tasks from remote locations, thus creating local virtual teams. Hyundai Motors exemplifies virtual teaming at the global level. For its vehicles, Hyundai completes engineering in Korea, research in Tokyo and Germany, styling in California, engine calibration and testing in Michigan, and heat testing in the California desert.[25] Members of its virtual teams coordinate their work and complete their tasks across time and geographic zones. Work is increasingly viewed as what you do rather than a place you go.

In some organizations, remote co-workers may be permanent employees of the same company or may be specialists called together for temporary projects. Regardless of the assignment, virtual teams can benefit from shared views and skills.

Positive and Negative Team Behaviour

Professional team members follow team rules, analyze tasks, define problems, share information, listen actively to others, and try to involve quiet members.

Team members who are committed to achieving the group's purpose contribute by displaying positive behaviour. How can you be a professional team member? The most effective groups have members who are willing to establish rules and abide by those rules. Effective team members are able to analyze tasks and define problems so that they can work toward solutions. They offer information and try out their ideas on the group to stimulate discussion. They show interest in others' ideas by listening actively. Helpful team members also seek to involve silent members. They help to resolve differences, and they encourage a warm, supportive climate by praising and agreeing with others. When they sense that agreement is near, they review significant points and move the group toward its goal by synthesizing points of understanding.

Negative team behaviour includes insulting, criticizing, aggressing against others, wasting time, and refusing to participate.

Not all groups, however, have members who contribute positively. Negative behaviour is shown by those who constantly put down the ideas and suggestions of others. They insult, criticize, and aggress against others. They waste the group's time with unnecessary recounting of personal achievements or irrelevant topics. The team joker distracts the group with excessive joke telling, inappropriate comments, and disruptive antics. Also disturbing are team members who withdraw and refuse to be drawn out. They have nothing to say, either for or against ideas being considered. To be a productive and welcome member of a group, be prepared to perform the positive tasks described in Figure 10.4. Avoid the negative behaviours.

FIGURE 10.4 Positive and Negative Team Behaviours

POSITIVE TEAM BEHAVIOURS	NEGATIVE TEAM BEHAVIOURS
Setting rules and abiding by them	Blocking the ideas and suggestions of others
Analyzing tasks and defining problems	Insulting and criticizing others
Contributing information and ideas	Wasting the group's time
Showing interest by listening actively	Making inappropriate jokes and comments
Encouraging members to participate	Failing to stay on task
Synthesizing points of agreement	Withdrawing, failing to participate

Characteristics of Successful Professional Teams

The use of teams has been called the solution to many ills in the current workplace.[26] Someone even observed that as an acronym TEAM means "Together, Everyone Achieves More."[27] Yet, many teams do not work well together. In fact, some teams can actually increase frustration, lower productivity, and create employee dissatisfaction. Experts who have studied team workings and decisions have discovered that effective teams share some or all of the following characteristics.

SMALL SIZE, DIVERSE MAKEUP. Teams may range from 2 to 25 members, although 4 or 5 is optimum for many projects. Larger groups have trouble interacting constructively, much less agreeing on actions.[28] For the most creative decisions, teams generally have male and female members who differ in age, ethnicity, social background, training, and experience. Members should bring complementary skills to a team. The key business advantage of diversity is the ability to view a project and its context from multiple perspectives. Many of us tend to think that everyone in the world is like us because we know only our own experience.[29] Teams with members from a variety of ethnicities and cultures can look at projects beyond the limited view of one culture. Many organizations are finding that diverse teams can produce innovative solutions with broader applications than homogeneous teams can.

"Isn't this what teamwork is all about? You doing all my work for me?"

> Small, diverse teams often produce more creative solutions with broader applications than homogeneous teams do.

AGREEMENT ON PURPOSE. An effective team begins with a purpose. For example, a team at New Jersey–based Sealed Air Corporation developed its purpose when management instructed it to cut waste and reduce downtime.[30] Working from a general purpose to specific goals typically requires a huge investment of time and effort. Meaningful discussions, however, motivate team members to "buy in" to the project.

AGREEMENT ON PROCEDURES. The best teams develop procedures to guide them. They set up intermediate goals with deadlines. They assign roles and tasks, requiring all members to contribute equivalent amounts of real work. They decide how they will reach decisions using one of the strategies discussed earlier. Procedures are continually evaluated to ensure movement toward the attainment of the team's goals.

ABILITY TO CONFRONT CONFLICT. Poorly functioning teams avoid conflict, preferring sulking, gossiping, or backstabbing. A better plan is to acknowledge conflict and address the root of the problem openly. Although it may feel emotionally risky, direct confrontation saves time and enhances team commitment in the long run. To be constructive, however, confrontation must be task-oriented, not person-oriented. An open airing of differences, in which all team members have a chance to speak their minds, should centre on the strengths and weaknesses of the different positions and ideas—not on personalities. After hearing all sides, team members must negotiate a fair settlement, no matter how long it takes. Good decisions are based on consensus: most members must agree.

USE OF GOOD COMMUNICATION TECHNIQUES. The best teams exchange information and contribute ideas freely in an informal environment. Team members

OFFICE INSIDER

Teamwork is the ability to work together toward a common vision—to direct individual accomplishments toward organizational objectives. It is the fuel that allows common people to attain uncommon results.

speak clearly and concisely, avoiding generalities. They encourage feedback. Listeners become actively involved, read body language, and ask clarifying questions before responding. Tactful, constructive disagreement is encouraged. Although a team's task is taken seriously, successful teams are able to inject humour into their interactions.

<aside>
Effective teams exchange information freely and collaborate rather than compete.
</aside>

ABILITY TO COLLABORATE RATHER THAN COMPETE. Effective team members are genuinely interested in achieving team goals instead of receiving individual recognition. They contribute ideas and feedback unselfishly. They monitor team progress, including what is going right, what is going wrong, and what to do about it. They celebrate individual and team accomplishments.

SHARED LEADERSHIP. Effective teams often have no formal leader. Instead, leadership rotates to those with the appropriate expertise as the team evolves and moves from one phase to another. Many teams operate under a democratic approach. This approach can achieve buy-in to team decisions, boost morale, and create fewer hurt feelings and less resentment. But in times of crisis, a strong team member may need to step up as leader.

ACCEPTANCE OF ETHICAL RESPONSIBILITIES. Teams as a whole have ethical responsibilities to their members, to their larger organizations, and to society. Members have a number of specific responsibilities to each other, as shown in Figure 10.5. As a whole, teams have a responsibility to represent the organization's view and respect its privileged information. They should not discuss with outsiders any sensitive issues without permission. In addition, teams have a broader obligation to avoid advocating actions that would endanger members of society at large.

The skills that make you a valuable and ethical team player will serve you well when you run or participate in professional meetings.

FIGURE 10.5 Ethical Responsibilities of Team Members and Leaders

When people form a group or a team to achieve a purpose, they agree to give up some of their individual sovereignty for the good of the group. They become interdependent and assume responsibilities to one another and to the group. Here are important ethical responsibilities for members to follow:

- **Determine to do your best.** When you commit to the group process, you are obligated to offer your skills freely. Don't hold back, perhaps fearing that you will be repeatedly targeted because you have skills to offer. If the group project is worth doing, it is worth your best effort.

- **Decide to behave with the group's good in mind.** You may find it necessary to set aside your personal goals in favour of the group's goals. Decide to keep an open mind and to listen to evidence and arguments objectively. Strive to evaluate information carefully, even though it may contradict your own views or thwart your personal agendas.

- **Make a commitment to fair play.** Group problem solving is a cooperative, not a competitive, event. Decide that you cannot grind your private axe at the expense of the group project.

- **Expect to give and receive a fair hearing.** When you speak, others should give you a fair hearing. You have a right to expect them to listen carefully, provide you with candid feedback, strive to understand what you say, and treat your ideas seriously. Listeners do not have to agree with you, of course. However, all speakers have a right to a fair hearing.

- **Be willing to take on a participant/analyst role.** As a group member, it is your responsibility to pay attention, evaluate what is happening, analyze what you learn, and help make decisions.

- **As a leader, be ready to model appropriate team behaviour.** It is a leader's responsibility to coach team members in skills and teamwork, to acknowledge achievement and effort, to share knowledge, and to periodically remind members of the team's missions and goals.

Conducting Productive and Professional Business Meetings

As businesses become more team-oriented and management becomes more participatory, people are attending more meetings than ever. One survey of managers found that they were devoting as many as two days a week to various gatherings.[31] Yet meetings are almost universally disliked. Typical comments include "We have too many of them," "They don't accomplish anything," and "What a waste of time!" In spite of employee reluctance and despite terrific advances in communication and team technology, face-to-face meetings are not going to disappear. In discussing the future of meetings, Akio Morita, former chairman of Sony Corporation, said that he expects "face-to-face meetings will still be the number one form of communication in the twenty-first century."[32] So, get used to them. Meetings are here to stay. Our task, then, as business communicators, is to learn how to make them efficient, satisfying, and productive.

Meetings consist of three or more individuals who gather to pool information, solicit feedback, clarify policy, seek consensus, and solve problems. But meetings have another important purpose for you. They represent opportunities. Because they are a prime tool for developing staff, they are career-critical. According to one Canadian company's Web site, "It is . . . true that careers (rightly or wrongly) have been made or broken through performance at meetings."[33] At meetings judgments are formed and careers are made. Therefore, instead of treating them as thieves of your valuable time, try to see them as golden opportunities to demonstrate your leadership, communication, and problem-solving skills. Make the most of these opportunities with the following techniques for planning and conducting successful meetings.

Because you can expect to attend many workplace meetings, learn to make them efficient, satisfying, and productive.

Deciding Whether a Meeting Is Necessary

No meeting should be called unless the topic is important, can't wait, and requires an exchange of ideas. If the flow of information is strictly one way and no immediate feedback will result, then don't schedule a meeting. For example, if people are merely being advised or informed, send an e-mail, memo, or letter. Leave a telephone or voice mail message, but don't call a costly meeting. Remember, the real expense of a meeting is the lost productivity of all the people attending. To decide whether the purpose of the meeting is valid, it's a good idea to consult the key people who will be attending. Ask them what outcomes are desired and how to achieve those goals. This consultation also sets a collaborative tone and encourages full participation.

Call meetings only when necessary, and invite only key people.

Selecting Participants

The number of meeting participants is determined by the purpose of the meeting. If the meeting purpose is motivational, such as an employee awards ceremony for Bombardier, then the number of participants is unlimited. But to make decisions, according to studies at 3M Corporation, the best number is five or fewer participants.[34] Ideally, those attending should be people who will make the decision and people with information necessary to make the decision. Also attending should be people who will be responsible for implementing the decision and representatives of groups who will benefit from the decision.

Problem-solving meetings should involve five or fewer people.

Distributing an Agenda

At least one day in advance of a meeting, e-mail an agenda of topics to be discussed. Also include any reports or materials that participants should read in advance. For continuing groups, you might also include a copy of the minutes of the

Before a meeting, pass out a meeting agenda showing topics to be discussed and other information.

FIGURE 10.6 Typical Meeting Agenda

AGENDA
mAPP Dev™
Sales Department Meeting
November 15, 2016
9:30 a.m.–10:30 a.m.
Corporate Meeting Room

1. Sales update
   - Danny (10 mins.)
2. What's new and hot in the market
   - Monika (10 mins.)
3. Sales training tip of the week: Report on Mobile + WebDevCon 2015
   - Sasha (10 mins.)
4. Other updates: hires, products, etc.
   - Danny (5 mins.)
5. Morale boost: what's going well, where do we want to be, hero of the week
   - Danny + All (20 mins.)

previous meeting. To keep meetings productive, limit the number of agenda items. Remember, the narrower the focus, the greater the chances for success. A good agenda, as illustrated in Figure 10.6, covers the following information:

- Date and place of meeting
- Start time and end time
- Brief description of each topic, in order of priority, including the names of individuals who are responsible for performing some action
- Proposed allotment of time for each topic
- Any pre-meeting preparation expected of participants

Getting the Meeting Started

To avoid wasting time and irritating attendees, always start meetings on time—even if some participants are missing. Waiting for latecomers causes resentment and sets a bad precedent. For the same reasons, don't give a quick recap to anyone who arrives late. At the appointed time, open the meeting with a three- to five-minute introduction that includes the following:

- Goal and length of the meeting
- Background of topics or problems
- Possible solutions and constraints
- Tentative agenda
- Ground rules to be followed

A typical set of ground rules might include arriving on time, communicating openly, being supportive, listening carefully, participating fully, confronting conflict frankly, and following the agenda. More formal groups follow parliamentary procedures based on Robert's Rules. For example, in a meeting run using Robert's Rules, there is a way to stop a person from talking too long. It's called "calling the question," which means ending the current discussion and voting on the previous question (or motion) right away. Before you can call the question, however, you have to be recognized by the chair of the meeting, move the "previous question," have your motion seconded, and receive a two-thirds majority vote in favour of calling the question. Most business meetings do not follow Robert's Rules, except perhaps at the highest levels (board meetings), because of the specialized knowledge required to run a meeting in this way.

In most typical business meetings, after establishing basic ground rules, the leader should ask whether participants agree thus far. Ideally, the next step is to

> Start meetings on time and open with a brief introduction.

assign one attendee to take minutes and one to act as a recorder. The recorder stands at a flipchart or whiteboard and lists the main ideas being discussed and agreements reached.

Moving the Meeting Along

After the preliminaries, the leader should say as little as possible. Like a talk show host, an effective leader makes "sure that each panel member gets some air time while no one member steals the show."[35] Remember that the purpose of a meeting is to exchange views, not to hear one person, even the leader, do all the talking. If the group has one member who monopolizes, the leader might say, "Thanks for that perspective, Kurt, but please hold your next point while we hear how Ann would respond to that." This technique also encourages quieter participants to speak up.

> Keep the meeting moving by avoiding issues that sidetrack the group.

To avoid allowing digressions to sidetrack the group, try generating a "parking lot" list. This is a list of important but divergent issues that should be discussed at a later time. Another way to handle digressions is to say, "Folks, we are getting off track here. Forgive me for pressing on, but I need to bring us back to the central issue of . . . ."[36] It's important to adhere to the agenda and the time schedule. Equally important, when the group seems to have reached a consensus, is to summarize the group's position and check to see whether everyone agrees.

Dealing With Conflict

Conflict is natural and even desirable in workplaces, but it can cause awkwardness and uneasiness. In meetings, conflict typically develops when people feel unheard or misunderstood. If two people are in conflict, the best approach is to encourage each to make a complete case while group members give their full attention. Let each one question the other. Then, the leader should summarize what was said, and the group should offer comments. The group may modify a recommendation or suggest alternatives before reaching consensus on a direction to follow.

> When a conflict develops between two members, allow each to make a complete case before the group.

Handling Dysfunctional Group Members

When individuals are performing in a dysfunctional role (such as blocking discussion, attacking other speakers, joking excessively, or withdrawing), they should be handled with care and tact. The following specific techniques can help a meeting leader control some group members and draw others out:

> To control dysfunctional behaviour, team leaders should establish rules and seat problem people strategically.

- **Lay down the rules in an opening statement.** Give a specific overall summary of topics, time allotment, and expected behaviour. Warn that speakers who digress will be interrupted.
- **Seat potentially dysfunctional members strategically.** Experts suggest seating a difficult group member immediately next to the leader. It's easier to bypass a person in this position. Make sure the person with dysfunctional behaviour is not seated in a power point, such as at the end of table or across from the leader.
- **Avoid direct eye contact.** Direct eye contact is a nonverbal signal that encourages talking. Thus, when asking a question of the group, look only at those whom you wish to answer.
- **Assign dysfunctional members specific tasks.** Ask a potentially disruptive person, for example, to be the group recorder.
- **Ask members to speak in a specific order.** Ordering comments creates an artificial, rigid climate and should be done only when absolutely necessary. But such a system ensures that everyone gets a chance to participate.

- **Interrupt monopolizers.** If a difficult member dominates a discussion, wait for a pause and then break in. Summarize briefly the previous comments or ask someone else for an opinion.
- **Encourage non-talkers.** Give only positive feedback to the comments of reticent members. Ask them direct questions about which you know they have information or opinions.
- **Give praise and encouragement** to those who seem to need it, including the distracters, the blockers, and the withdrawn.[37]

Ending With a Plan

> End the meeting with a summary of accomplishments and a review of action items; follow up by reminding participants of their assigned tasks.

End the meeting at the agreed time or earlier if possible. The leader should summarize what has been decided, who is going to do what, and by what time. It may be necessary to ask people to volunteer to take responsibility for completing action items agreed to in the meeting. No one should leave the meeting without a full understanding of what was accomplished. One effective technique that encourages full participation is "once around the table." Everyone is asked to summarize briefly his or her interpretation of what was decided and what happens next. Of course, this closure technique works best with smaller groups. The leader should conclude by asking the group to set a time for the next meeting. He or she should also assure the group that a report will follow, and thank participants for attending.

"That's all very nice, Jefferson, but do you have any other new business?"

Following Up Actively

If minutes were taken, they should be distributed within a couple of days after the meeting. An example of a formal minutes report is found in Figure 8.10 on page 245. Figure 10.7 shows an informal minutes report, which is the kind you'll see more often in the business world today. It is up to the leader to see that what was decided at the meeting is accomplished. The leader may need to call or e-mail people to remind them of their assignments and also to volunteer to help them if necessary.

FIGURE 10.7 Informal Minutes of Meeting, E-mail Attachment Format

mAPP Dev™ Sales Department Meeting Minutes

November 15, 2016

Present: D. Usakli, M. Lin, S. Allen, J. Vitali, A. Ferretti, H. Ahmed

Regrets: J. Struth

What we discussed:

- Danny updated the team on current quarter sales: we're up 10% over Q2 but at the same time growth has slowed over Q2 last year; invited suggestions for how to increase growth
- Monika suggested forging a partnership with Bell — the one phone provider we haven't signed with yet; Monika also discussed current market stats: (a) Canadian smartphone sales predicted to rise 18% next year; tablets 15%; (b) Android leads industry with over 80% market penetration in Canada.
- Sasha reported on her attendance at Mobile + WebDevCon; said biggest trend/talking point was whether Apple would step in to fill BlackBerry's vacuum in corporate/enterprise — implications for what we do?
- No other department updates, though possible we will be hiring a sales coordinator for January 1; stay tuned for details
- Morale boost roundtable: John pointed out that anecdotally he's hearing that the trend toward free apps is cooling off and paid apps, especially in the travel and entertainment niches, are starting to take off

Decisions and actions:

- Approach Bell about partnership agreement (Monika and Danny – by next week)
- Send two team members to Mobile + WebDevCon 2016 (Danny to choose – by next meeting)

Next meeting:

- **December 1, 2016 9:30 a.m. – 10:30 a.m.** Corporate Meeting Room

 ## SUMMING UP AND LOOKING FORWARD

In this chapter you studied how to use professionalism to your advantage in the workplace. Professionalism is a type of ethical behaviour in which you consider the effects of your behaviour on other people before engaging in that behaviour. Also, the chapter discussed using your voice as a communication tool by focusing on pronunciation, tone, pitch, volume, rate, and emphasis. In workplace conversations, you should use correct names and titles, choose appropriate topics, avoid negative remarks, listen to learn, and be willing to offer sincere and specific praise.

You also learned how to give and take constructive criticism on the job. There are five common response patterns as well as a six-step plan for resolving interpersonal workplace conflicts. The chapter also presented techniques for polishing your professional phone and voice mail skills, including making and receiving productive phone calls. You then read about the importance of teamwork and best practices for achieving results when working with other people. Finally, you learned how to plan and participate in productive business and professional meetings.

This chapter focused on developing speaking skills in face-to-face workplace communication. The next chapter covers an additional element of oral communication: giving presentations. Learning to speak before groups is important to your career success because you will probably be expected to do so occasionally. You'll learn helpful techniques and practise applying them so that you can control stage fright and make polished presentations.

CRITICAL THINKING

1. How can we square the empathy needed for ethical professionalism with the individualistic, sometimes greedy, nature of private enterprise (e.g., profit, advancement, etc.)?

2. Is face-to-face communication always preferable to one-dimensional channels of communication such as e-mail? Why or why not?

3. In what ways can conflict be a positive force in the workplace?

4. Commentators often predict that new communications media will destroy old ones. Do you think e-mail, smart-phones, and instant messaging will replace phone calls? Why or why not?

5. Why do so many people hate voice mail when it is an efficient system for recording messages?

6. What's the right course of action when you're the only person on a team doing any actual work?

7. How can business meetings help you advance your career?

CHAPTER REVIEW

1. Define *soft skills* and list the qualities the term describes.

2. Describe some important aspects of professional behaviour.

3. Name five elements that you control in using your voice as a communication tool.

4. What topics should be avoided in workplace conversations?

5. List six techniques that you consider most important when delivering constructive criticism.

6. If you are criticized at work, what are eight ways in which you can respond professionally?

7. What are five common responses to workplace conflicts? Which response do you think is most constructive?

8. What is a three-point introduction for a phone call?

9. Name five ways in which callers can practise courteous and responsible cellphone use.

10. When should a business meeting be held?

11. What is an agenda and what should it include?

12. List eight tactics that a meeting leader can use in dealing with dysfunctional participants.

WRITING IMPROVEMENT EXERCISES

10.1 Constructive Criticism

You work for a large company that is organized into work teams. Your work team, in the company's marketing department, meets weekly for a quick half-hour meeting to review the week's activities and projects. The meetings are run by the team leader, Mandy Miller. The team leader is a position of extra responsibility with a higher salary than that of other marketing staffers. For the past three months, Mandy has been regularly missing or showing up late for meetings. No one has said anything but you. You had a conversation with Mandy in the cafeteria three weeks ago in which you relayed your concerns to her in as positive a way as possible. Mandy has again started to miss meetings. You feel it's appropriate to send an e-mail to the director of the marketing department, letting him know what's been happening, that you've talked to Mandy, and that things haven't improved.

Your Task. Draft an e-mail to your director about the situation with Mandy.

10.2 Meeting Agenda

It's now been two months since you sent your e-mail to the director of marketing. In the meantime, Mandy Miller has bween relieved of her extra responsibility as team leader. To your great surprise, your boss has asked you to be the new team leader. You are preparing for your first meeting and you decide to do something Mandy rarely did, which is to e-mail a meeting agenda to your colleagues. Besides discussing the changeover from Mandy to yourself at the meeting, activities to be discussed include the final proofreading of an important catalogue that is going to the printer on Friday and a conference call with your colleagues in the Toronto office on the rollout of 2015 Pan American Games merchandise. You are well liked by your colleagues, and you want to manage this meeting so that it doesn't look like you're "taking over" the department.

Your Task. Draft the agenda for the above meeting.

10.3 Meeting Minutes

TEAM

Because the weekly marketing team meetings happen so frequently, you're not sure whether it's important to send out formal meeting minutes. Instead, you decide to send out a weekly "Meeting Recap" e-mail after each meeting. At this morning's meeting—your first as team leader—things went well. Mandy made a point of congratulating you on your new position (without sarcasm). You appointed Tom Mavrogianis to be in charge of the catalogue proofread (deadline Thursday afternoon) and Mandy Miller to be in charge of running Friday's conference with the Toronto office. Mandy mentioned she needed the specs on the 2015 Pan American Games caps and T-shirts before the meeting, and you promised to get them to her. Also, an unexpected item of business came up at the meeting when Tom reminded you that it was time to start planning the annual department retreat. Besides Tom, Mandy, and you, Bill Brockton was at the meeting, while Nahla Karim was absent.

Your Task. Draft the minutes report from this meeting.

 ACTIVITIES AND CASES

10.1 Voice Rate

As discussed in this chapter, for business presentation purposes, you should be talking at roughly 125 words per minute. This is a different rate than the one you use when you're reading off a computer screen or talking to friends. A good way to practise achieving this ideal rate is to read aloud, as if you were telling a story.

Your Task. Choose an article reproduced at the beginning of one this book's Units and choose a partner or small group to work with. Stand up in front of your partner or group and read the article aloud as if you were presenting it to a group of people in a workplace setting. Have your partner or one member of your team time you for one minute. This person should say "Stop!" once the minute is over. Remember the last word you said, then go back and count how many words you managed to read in one minute. Is it higher or lower than 125? If it's lower, ask your partner or the people in your group if they thought you were reading too slowly. If it's higher than 125, you're probably reading too quickly; try reading one more time and consciously slow down the rate at which you're speaking. Once you're finished, it's the turn of your partner or someone else in the group to try. When everyone has had a try, let your instructor know. He or she may choose to have the students who come closest to 125 words per minute demonstrate their reading skills for the entire class.

10.2 Voice Quality

Recording your voice gives you a chance to learn how your voice sounds to others and provides an opportunity for you to improve its effectiveness. Don't be surprised if you fail to recognize your own voice.

Your Task. Record yourself reading a newspaper or magazine article.

a. If you think your voice sounds a bit high, practise speaking slightly lower.

b. If your voice is low or expressionless, practise speaking slightly louder and with more inflection.

c. Ask a colleague, teacher, or friend to provide feedback on your pronunciation, pitch, volume, rate, and professional tone.

10.3 Role Play: Delivering and Responding to Criticism

TEAM

Develop your skills in handling criticism by joining with a partner to role-play critical messages you might deliver and receive on the job.

Your Task. Designate one person "A" and the other "B." Person A should make a list of the kinds of critical messages she or he is likely to receive on the job (e.g., *We need you to be on time regularly*) and identify who might deliver them (e.g., the shift manager). In Scenario 1, Person B should take the role of the critic and deliver the criticism in an unskilled manner. Person A should then respond using techniques described in this chapter. In Scenario 2, Person B again is the critic but delivers the criticism using techniques described in this chapter. Person A responds again. Then A and B reverse roles and repeat Scenarios 1 and 2.

CRITICAL THINKING

10.4 Role Play: Discussing Workplace Criticism
In the workplace, criticism is often delivered thoughtlessly.

Your Task. In teams of two or three, describe a time when you were criticized by an untrained superior or colleague. What made the criticism painful? What goal do you think the critic had in mind? How did you feel? How did you respond? Considering techniques discussed in this chapter, how could the critic have improved his or her delivery? How does the delivery technique affect the way a receiver responds to criticism? Script the situation you've just discussed and present it to the rest of the class in a before-and-after scenario.

TEAM

10.5 Responding to Workplace Conflicts
Experts say that we generally respond to conflict in one of the following patterns: avoidance/withdrawal, accommodation/smoothing, compromise, competition/forcing, or collaboration/problem solving.

Your Task. For each of the following conflict situations, name the appropriate response pattern(s) and be prepared to explain your choice.

   a. A company policy manual is posted and updated at an internal Web page. Employees must sign that they have read and understand the manual. A conflict arises when one manager insists that employees should sign electronically. Another manager thinks that a paper form should be signed by employees so that better records may be kept. What conflict response pattern is most appropriate?

   b. Jeff and Mark work together but frequently disagree. Today they disagree on what tablets to purchase for an order that must be submitted immediately. Jeff insists on buying Brand X tablets. Mark knows that Brand X is made by a company that markets an identical tablet at a slightly lower price. However, Mark doesn't have stock numbers for the cheaper tablets at his fingertips. How should Mark respond?

   c. A manager and his assistant plan to attend a conference together at a resort location. Six weeks before the conference, the company announces a cutback and limits conference support to only one person. The assistant, who has developed a presentation specifically for the conference, feels that he should be the one to attend. Travel arrangements must be made immediately. What conflict response pattern will most likely result?

   d. Two vice presidents disagree on a company instant messaging policy. One wants to ban personal messaging totally. The other thinks that an outright ban is impossible to implement. He is more concerned with limiting Internet misuse, including visits to online game, pornography, and shopping sites. The vice presidents agree that they need a policy, but they disagree on what to allow and what to prohibit. What conflict response pattern is appropriate?

   e. Customer service rep Jackie comes to work one morning and finds Alexa sitting at Workstation 2. Although the customer service reps have no special workstation assigned to them, Jackie has the most seniority and has always assumed that Workstation 2 was hers. Other workstations were available, but the supervisor told Alexa to use Workstation 2 that morning because she didn't know that Jackie would be coming in. When Jackie arrives and sees "her" workstation occupied, she becomes angry and demands that Alexa vacate the station. What conflict response pattern might be most appropriate for Alexa and the supervisor?

10.6 Rules for Wireless Phone Use in Sales
As one of the managers of Wrigley Canada, a gum and confectionery company, you are alarmed at a newspaper article you just read. A stockbroker for BMO Nesbitt Burns was making cold calls on his personal phone while driving. His car hit and killed a motorcyclist. The brokerage firm was sued and accused of contributing to an accident by encouraging employees to use cellular telephones while driving. To avoid the risk of paying huge damages awarded by an emotional jury, the brokerage firm offered the victim's family a $500,000 settlement.

Your Task. Individually or in teams write an e-mail to Wrigley sales reps outlining company suggestions (or should they be rules?) for safe wireless phone use in cars. Check library databases for articles that discuss cellphone use in cars. Look for additional safety ideas. In your message to sales reps, try to suggest receiver benefits. How is safe cellphone use beneficial to the sales rep?

10.7 Role Play: Improving Telephone Skills

Acting out the roles of telephone caller and receiver is an effective technique for improving skills. To give you such practice, your instructor will divide the class into pairs.

Your Task. Read each scenario and rehearse your role silently. Then improvise the role with your partner. After improvising a couple of times, script one of the situations and present it to the rest of the class.

Partner 1	Partner 2
a. You are the HR manager of Datatronics, Inc. Call Elizabeth Franklin, office manager at Computers Plus. Inquire about a job applicant, Chelsea Chavez, who listed Ms. Franklin as a reference.	a. You are the receptionist for Computers Plus. The caller asks for Elizabeth Franklin, who is home sick today. You don't know when she will be able to return. Answer the call appropriately.
b. Call Ms. Franklin again the following day to inquire about the same job applicant, Chelsea Chavez. Ms. Franklin answers today, but she talks on and on, describing the applicant in great detail. Tactfully close the conversation.	b. You are now Ms. Franklin, office manager. Describe Chelsea Chavez, an imaginary employee. Think of someone with whom you've worked. Include many details, such as her ability to work with others, her appearance, her skills at computing, her schooling, her ambition, and so forth.
c. You are now the receptionist for Tom Wing, of Wing Imports. Answer a call for Mr. Wing, who is working in another office, at ext. 134, where he will accept calls.	c. You are now an administrative assistant for lawyer Michael Murphy. Call Tom Wing to verify a meeting date Mr. Murphy has with Mr. Wing. Use your own name in identifying yourself.
d. You are now Tom Wing, owner of Wing Imports. Call your lawyer, Michael Murphy, about a legal problem. Leave a brief, incomplete message.	d. You are now the receptionist for lawyer Michael Murphy. Mr. Murphy is skiing in Mont-Tremblant and will return in two days, but he doesn't want his clients to know where he is. Take a message.
e. Call Mr. Murphy again. Leave a message that will prevent telephone tag.	e. Take a message again.

10.8 Meetings: Managing Difficult or Reticent Team Members and Other Challenges

As you have learned, facilitating a productive meeting requires skills that may be critical to your career success.

Your Task. Individually or as a team describe how you would deal with the following examples of unproductive or dysfunctional behaviour and other challenges in a team meeting that you are running. Either report your recommendations verbally, or, if your instructor directs, summarize your suggestions in an e-mail or memo.

a. Jimmy, a well-known office clown, is telling racist jokes while others are discussing the business at hand.

b. Anna is quiet, although she is taking notes and seems to be following the discussion attentively.

c. Peter likes to make long-winded statements and often digresses to unrelated subjects.

d. Carla keeps interrupting other speakers and dominates the discussion.

e. Ron and Mark are hostile toward each other and clash over an agenda item.

f. Elena arrives 15 minutes late and noisily unpacks her briefcase.

g. Kristen, Shelley, and Paul are texting under the table.

h. The meeting time is up, but the group has not met the objective of the meeting.

10.9 Analyzing a Meeting

You've learned a number of techniques in this chapter for planning and participating in meetings. Here's your chance to put your knowledge to work.

Your Task. Attend a structured meeting of a college, social, business, or other organization. Compare the manner in which the meeting is conducted with the suggestions presented in this chapter. Why did the meeting succeed or fail? Prepare a brief recommendation report for your instructor or be ready to discuss your findings in class.

10.10 Planning a Meeting

Assume that at the next meeting of your Associated Students Organization (ASO), you will discuss preparations for a job fair in the spring. The group will hear reports from committees working on speakers, business recruiters, publicity, reservations of campus space, setup of booths, and any other matters you can think of.

Your Task. As president of your ASO, prepare an agenda for the meeting. Compose your introductory remarks to open the meeting. Your instructor may ask you to submit these two documents or use them in staging an actual meeting in class.

10.11 Running a Meeting

The best way to learn to run a meeting is to actually do it.

Your Task. Using the agenda your team wrote in Activity 10.10, run part of your next class as a meeting. Many decisions will have to be made. Who will chair the meeting? (It does not necessarily have to be your instructor—in fact it may be better if it's not.) What will the chair say to get the meeting started? What reports will be given at the meeting? How will you generate discussion at this meeting, considering that it's a mock meeting and the participants are your classmates, many of whom may be non-talkers? What will you do if the meeting gets off track? You may want to "plant" one of your team members as a disruptive meeting participant. Does the chair know how to deal with this disruptive person? Consider changing the normal seating arrangement of your class to more closely approximate that of a meeting. Who will take notes at this meeting? How will the meeting end and who will be in charge of following up?

10.12 Spoofing Meetings

One of the most popular ways to demonstrate to students the problems that can often occur in formal workplace meetings is to watch poorly run meetings on video.

Your Task. Search YouTube (**www.youtube.com**) for videos about poor meetings. You may also search Google using keywords like "spoof" "meetings" "bad business meetings." Screen five to ten of the videos you find. Make a list of the most commonly shown "bad" meeting behaviours. Why do you think the makers of the videos included these behaviours? Are there other, more subtle bad behaviours that might be hard to represent on the screen but that can have a serious impact in meetings? Share your results in a presentation to your class or your instructor.

GRAMMAR/MECHANICS REVIEW 10—OTHER PUNCTUATION

Insert any necessary punctuation and change any incorrect punctuation. In the space provided, indicate the number of changes you make. Count each mark separately; for example, a set of parentheses counts as two. If you make no changes, write *0*. Use the underscore to show italics.

__2__ **Example**   Current sales projections see page 11 in the attached report indicate a profitable year ahead.

____ 1. Three outstanding employees Santiago Wilson, Rae Thomas, and Charles Stoop will receive bonuses.

____ 2. Will you please Jonathon complete your assignment by six o'clock?

____ 3. To determine whether to spell e-mail with or without the hyphen be sure to consult our company style sheet.

____ 4. Cargill, Koch Industries, and Bechtel these are the most profitable private companies in North America.

____ 5. (De-emphasize) Today's employers regularly conduct three kinds of background checks drug, credit, and criminal before hiring employees.

____ 6. Was it Warren Buffet who said "The rearview mirror is always clearer than the windshield

____ 7. Did you see the article titled Wireless Riches From Serving the Poor that appeared in The Toronto Star

____ 8. (Emphasize) Three cities considered the best places in the world to live Vienna, Zurich, and Geneva are all in Europe.

____ 9. Did you send invitations to Dr Lisa Uhl, Ms Ginger Ortiz, and Mr Orrin T Tapia

____ 10. Our instructor recommended the chapter titled The Almost Perfect Meeting that appeared in Emily Post's book called The Etiquette Advantage in Business.

____ 11. Incredible Did you see the price of gold today

____ 12. Susan wondered what keywords would attract the most clicks in her Google ad?

____ 13. The owner of Smash Party Entertainment found that the best keyword for her online ad business was party.

____ 14. Is the reception scheduled to begin at 6 pm

____ 15. The term autoregressive is defined as using past data to predict future data.

GRAMMAR/MECHANICS CHALLENGE—10

Document for Revision

The following report showing meeting minutes has faults in grammar, punctuation, spelling, number form, wordiness, and word use. Use standard proofreading marks (see Appendix B) to correct the errors. When you finish, your instructor can show you the revised version of these minutes.

Canadian Federation of Small Business
Policy Board Committee
February 4, 2015

Present: Debra Chinnapongse, Tweet Jackson, Irene Kishita, Barry Knaggs, Kevin Poepoe, and Ralph Mason

Absent: Alex Watanabe

The meeting was call to order by Chair Kevin Poepo at 9:02 a.m. in the morning. Minutes from the January 6th meeting was read and approve.

Old Business

Debra Chinnapongse discussed the cost of the annual awards luncheon. That honours outstanding members. The ticket price ticket does not cover all the expenses incured. Major

NEL   Chapter 10: Communicating in Person   335

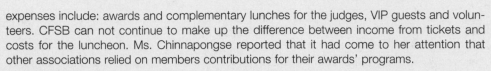

expenses include: awards and complementary lunches for the judges, VIP guests and volunteers. CFSB can not continue to make up the difference between income from tickets and costs for the luncheon. Ms. Chinnapongse reported that it had come to her attention that other associations relied on members contributions for their awards' programs.

MOTION: To send a Letter to board members asking for there contributions to support the annual awards luncheon. (Chinapongse/Kishita). PASSED 6-0.

Reports
Barry Knaggs reported that the media relations committee sponsored a get acquainted meeting in November. More than eighty people from various agencys attended.

The Outreach Committee reports that they have been asked to assist the Partnership for Small Business, an Ottawa-based organization in establishing a speakers bureau of Canadian small business owners. It would be available to speak at schools and colleges about small business and employment.

New Business
The chair announced a Planning Meeting to be held in March regarding revising the agri-business plan. In other New Business Ralph Mason reported that the staff had purchased fifty tickets for members, and our committees to attend the Zig Ziglar seminar in the month of March.

Next Meeting
The next meeting of the Policy Boare Committee will be held in early Aprl at the Lord Elgin hotel, Ottawa. At that time the meeting will conclude with a tour of the seaway Networks inc. offices in Kanata.

The meeting adjourned at 10:25 am by Keven Poepoe.

Respectfully submitted,

A GUIDE TO BUSINESS ETIQUETTE AND WORKPLACE MANNERS

Etiquette, civility, and goodwill efforts may seem out of place in today's fast-paced, high-tech offices. However, etiquette and courtesy are more important than ever if diverse employees want to work cooperatively and maximize productivity and workflow. Many organizations recognize that good manners are good for business. Some colleges and universities offer management programs that include a short course in manners. Companies are also conducting manners seminars for trainees and veteran managers. Why is politeness regaining legitimacy as a leadership tool? Primarily because courtesy works.

Good manners convey a positive image of an organization. We like to do business with people who show respect and treat others civilly. People also like to work in an environment that is pleasant. Considering how much time is spent at work, wouldn't an agreeable environment be preferable to one in which people are rude and uncivil?

You can brush up your workplace etiquette skills online at *Dr. Guffey's Guide to Business Etiquette and Workplace Manners* (**www.nelson.com/guffeyessentials8ce**). Of interest to both workplace newcomers and veterans, this guide covers the following topics:

Professional Image	Business Cards
Introductions and Greetings	Dealing With Angry Customers
Networking Manners	Telephone Manners
General Workplace Manners	Cellphone Etiquette
Coping With Cubicles	E-Mail Etiquette
Interacting With Superiors	Gender-Neutral Etiquette
Managers' Manners	Business Dining
Business Meetings	Avoiding Social Blunders When Abroad
Business Gifts	

To gauge your current level of knowledge of business etiquette, take the preview quiz at **www.nelson.com/guffeyessentials8ce**. Then, study all 17 business etiquette topics. These easy-to-read topics are arranged in bulleted lists of dos and don'ts. After you complete this etiquette module, your instructor may test your comprehension by giving a series of post-tests.

Career Application

As manager at OfficeTemps, a company specializing in employment placement and Human Resources information, you receive a request from a newspaper reporter. She is researching an article for the *Ottawa Citizen* about how workplace etiquette is changing in today's high-tech environment. The reporter asks for any other information you can share with her regarding her topic "Digital Age Etiquette."

Her voice mail lists the following questions:

- Are etiquette and workplace manners still important in today's fast-paced Digital Age work environment? Why or why not?
- Do workers need help in developing good business manners? Why or why not?
- Are the rules of office conduct changing? If so, how?
- What special manners do people working in shared workspaces need to observe?
- How does workplace diversity make etiquette challenging?

YOUR TASK

In teams or individually, prepare an information response e-mail addressed to Kara Cain, Education Reporter, Ottawa Citizen, kcain@citizen.ca. Use the data you learned in this workshop and conduct additional Web and database research if necessary (e.g., on workplace diversity). Remember that you will be quoted in her newspaper article, so make it interesting!

Business Presentations

© LAJOS REPASI/ISTOCKPHOTO.COM

1. Apply two important first steps in preparing effective oral presentations.

2. Explain the major elements in organizing the content of a presentation, including the introduction, body, and conclusion.

3. Identify techniques for gaining audience rapport, including using effective imagery, providing verbal signposts, and sending appropriate nonverbal messages.

4. Use visual aids, including PowerPoint and Prezi slides, handouts, and speaker's notes.

5. Explain how to design an impressive PowerPoint or Prezi presentation, including adapting text and colour schemes, and organizing, composing, and editing your slide show.

6. Use effective delivery techniques before, during, and after a presentation including use of voice and eye contact, rehearsal, and keeping audiences engaged.

Organizations today are interested in hiring people with good presentation skills. Why? The business world is changing. As you have seen, technical skills aren't enough to guarantee success. You also need to be able to communicate ideas effectively in presentations to customers, vendors, members of your team, and management. Your presentations will be made to inform, to influence, or to motivate action, or a combination of the three.

Speaking skills are useful at every career stage. A well-known study conducted by business communication researchers found that the number one competency hiring managers look for in new employees is strong oral communication skills, including presentation skills.[1] You might, for example, have to make a sales pitch before customers or speak to a professional gathering. You might need to describe your company's expansion plans to your banker, or you might need to persuade management to support your proposed marketing strategy. Speaking skills rank very high on recruiters' wish lists. As reported in an employer study, between 82 and 95 percent of executives consider oral communication skills very important for college and university graduates.[2]

This chapter prepares you to use speaking skills to give effective and professional oral presentations. You will learn what to do before, during, and after your presentation; and how to design effective visual aids including, PowerPoint and Prezi presentations.

◼ Getting Ready for an Oral Presentation

In getting ready for an oral presentation, you may feel a lot of anxiety. For many people fear of speaking before a group is almost as great as the fear of pain. We get butterflies in our stomachs just thinking about it. When you feel those butterflies, though, speech coach Dianne Booher advises getting them in formation and visualizing the swarm as a powerful push propelling you to a peak performance.[3] For any presentation, you can reduce your fears and lay the foundation for a professional performance by focusing on five areas: preparation, organization, audience rapport, visual aids, and delivery.

Know Your Purpose

> Preparing for an oral presentation means identifying your purpose and knowing the audience.

The most important part of your preparation is deciding on your purpose. Do you need to sell a group insurance policy to a prospective client? Do you need to persuade management to increase the marketing budget? Do you need to inform customer service reps of three important ways to prevent miscommunication? Whether your goal is to persuade or to inform, you must have a clear idea of where you are going. At the end of your presentation, what do you want your listeners to remember or do?

Erick Rosan, a finance manager at AutoFleet, a car brokerage company, faced such questions as he planned a talk for a class in business communication at his alma mater. His business communication professor had invited him back to school as a guest speaker. He was asked to talk about what happened after he graduated, how he uses his skills gained in college in his current job, and what a "day in the life" of his job entails. (You can see the outline for his talk in Figure 11.3, p. 343.) Because Eric obviously knows so much about this topic, he finds it difficult to extract a specific purpose statement for his presentation. After much thought he narrows his purpose to this: *To inform current business students about the realities of the post-college job market using my job as an example.* His entire presentation focuses on ensuring that the class members understand and remember three principal ideas.

Understand Your Audience

A second key element in preparation is analyzing your audience, anticipating its reactions, and making appropriate adaptations. Understanding four basic audience types, summarized in Figure 11.1, helps you decide how to organize your presentation. A friendly audience, for example, will respond to humour and personal experiences. A neutral audience requires an even, controlled delivery style. An uninterested audience that is forced to attend requires a brief presentation. Such an audience might respond best to humour, cartoons, colourful visuals, and startling statistics. A hostile audience demands a calm, controlled delivery style with objective data and expert opinions.

> Audience analysis issues include size, age, gender, experience, attitude, and expectations.

Other elements, such as age, education, experience, and size of audience will affect your style and message content. Erick's analysis tells him that while students are "forced" to attend, they will also probably be friendly and eager, because he'll be sharing information they may not be getting regularly from their professors. He decides he'll use some humour, but also maintain an even, professional tone. Answer the following questions to help you determine your organizational pattern, delivery style, and supporting material for any presentation.

- How will this topic appeal to this audience?
- How can I relate this information to their needs?
- How can I earn respect so that they accept my message?
- What would be most effective in making my point? Facts? Statistics? Personal experiences? Expert opinion? Humour? Cartoons? Graphic illustrations? Demonstrations? Case histories? Analogies?
- How can I ensure that this audience remembers my main points?

FIGURE 11.1 Succeeding With Four Audience Types

AUDIENCE MEMBERS	ORGANIZATIONAL PATTERN	DELIVERY STYLE	SUPPORTING MATERIAL
Friendly They like you and your topic.	Use any pattern. Try something new. Involve the audience.	Be warm, pleasant, and open. Use lots of eye contact and smiles.	Include humour, personal examples, and experiences.
Neutral They are calm, rational; their minds are made up, but they think they are objective.	Present both sides of the issue. Use pro/con or problem/solution patterns. Save time for audience questions.	Be controlled. Do nothing showy. Use confident, small gestures.	Use facts, statistics, expert opinion, and comparison and contrast. Avoid humour, personal stories, and flashy visuals.
Uninterested They have short attention spans; they may be there against their will.	Be brief—no more than three points. Avoid topical and pro/con patterns that seem lengthy to the audience.	Be dynamic and entertaining. Move around. Use large gestures.	Use humour, cartoons, colourful visuals, powerful quotations, and startling statistics.
	Avoid darkening the room, standing motionless, passing out handouts, using boring visuals, or expecting the audience to participate.		
Hostile They want to take charge or to ridicule the speaker; they may be defensive, emotional.	Organize using a noncontroversial pattern, such as a topical, chronological, or geographical strategy.	Be calm and controlled. Speak evenly and slowly.	Include objective data and expert opinion. Avoid anecdotes and humour.
	Avoid a question-and-answer period, if possible; otherwise, use a moderator or accept only written questions.		

Organizing Content for a Powerful Impact

Once you have determined your purpose and analyzed the audience, you're ready to collect information and organize it logically. Good organization and conscious repetition are the two most powerful keys to audience comprehension and retention. In fact, many speech experts recommend the following admittedly repetitious, but effective, plan:

> **Step 1:** Tell them what you're going to say.
> **Step 2:** Say it.
> **Step 3:** Tell them what you've just said.

In other words, repeat your main points in the introduction, body, and conclusion of your presentation. Although it sounds boring, this strategy works surprisingly well. This is because in an increasingly wired and mobile and distracting world, people may have trouble concentrating in face-to-face situations, and need to be reminded of important points more than once.[4] Let's examine how to construct the three parts of an effective presentation.

> Good organization and intentional repetition help your audience understand and retain what you say.

Capture Attention in the Introduction

How many times have you heard a speaker begin with *It's a pleasure to be here.* Or *I'm honoured to be asked to speak.* Boring openings such as these get speakers off to a dull start. Avoid such banalities by striving to accomplish three goals in the introduction to your presentation:

- Capture listeners' attention and get them involved.
- Identify yourself and establish your credibility.
- Preview your main points.

FIGURE 11.2 Gaining and Keeping Audience Attention

Experienced speakers know how to capture the attention of an audience and how to maintain that attention during a presentation. You can spruce up your presentations by trying these ten proven techniques.

- **A promise.** Begin with a realistic promise that keeps the audience expectant (e.g., *By the end of this presentation, you will know how you can increase your sales by 50 percent!*).

- **Drama.** Open by telling an emotionally moving story or by describing a serious problem that involves the audience. Throughout your talk include other dramatic elements, such as a long pause after a key statement. Change your vocal tone or pitch. Professionals use high-intensity emotions such as anger, joy, sadness, and excitement.

- **Eye contact.** As you begin, command attention by surveying the entire audience to take in all listeners. Give yourself two to five seconds to linger on individuals to avoid fleeting, unconvincing eye contact. Don't just sweep the room and the crowd.

- **Movement.** Leave the lectern area whenever possible. Walk around the conference table or down the aisles of your audience. Try to move toward your audience, especially at the beginning and end of your talk.

- **Questions.** Keep listeners active and involved with rhetorical questions. Ask for a show of hands to get each listener thinking. The response will also give you a quick gauge of audience attention.

- **Demonstrations.** Include a member of the audience in a demonstration (e.g., I'm going to show you exactly how to implement our four-step customer courtesy process, but I need a volunteer from the audience to help me).

- **Samples/props.** If you are promoting a product, consider using items to toss out to the audience or to award as prizes to volunteer participants. You can also pass around product samples or promotional literature. Be careful, though, to maintain control.

- **Visuals.** Give your audience something to look at besides yourself. Use a variety of visual aids in a single session. Also consider writing the concerns expressed by your audience on a flipchart or on the board as you go along.

- **Dress.** Enhance your credibility with your audience by dressing professionally for your presentation. Professional attire will help you look more competent and qualified, which will make your audience more likely to listen to you and take you seriously.

- **Self-interest.** Review your entire presentation to ensure that it meets the critical *What's-in-it-for-me* audience test. Remember that people are most interested in things that benefit them.

Attention-grabbing openers include questions, startling facts, jokes, anecdotes, and quotations.

"Please don't make me use another water balloon to keep your attention."

If you're able to appeal to listeners and involve them in your presentation right from the start, you're more likely to hold their attention until the finish. Consider some of the same techniques that you used to open sales messages: a question, a startling fact, a joke, a story, or a quotation. Some speakers achieve involvement by opening with a question or command that requires audience members to raise their hands or stand up. You'll find additional techniques for gaining and keeping audience attention in Figure 11.2.

To establish your credibility, you need to describe your position, knowledge, or experience—whatever qualifies you to speak. Try also to connect with your audience. Listeners are particularly drawn to and identify with speakers who reveal something of themselves. This is why Erick Rosan plans to talk a bit about his former extracurricular activities at the beginning of his upcoming "visiting alumnus" presentation at his old college, in Figure 11.3. Similarly, a consultant addressing office workers might reminisce about how he started as a temporary worker; a CEO might tell a funny story in which the joke is on herself.

After capturing attention and establishing yourself, you'll want to preview the main points of your topic, perhaps with a visual aid. You may wish to put off actually writing your introduction until after you have organized the rest of the presentation and crystallized your principal ideas.

Take a look at Erick Rosan's introduction, shown in Figure 11.3, to see how he integrated all the elements necessary for a good opening.

FIGURE 11.3 Oral Presentation Outline

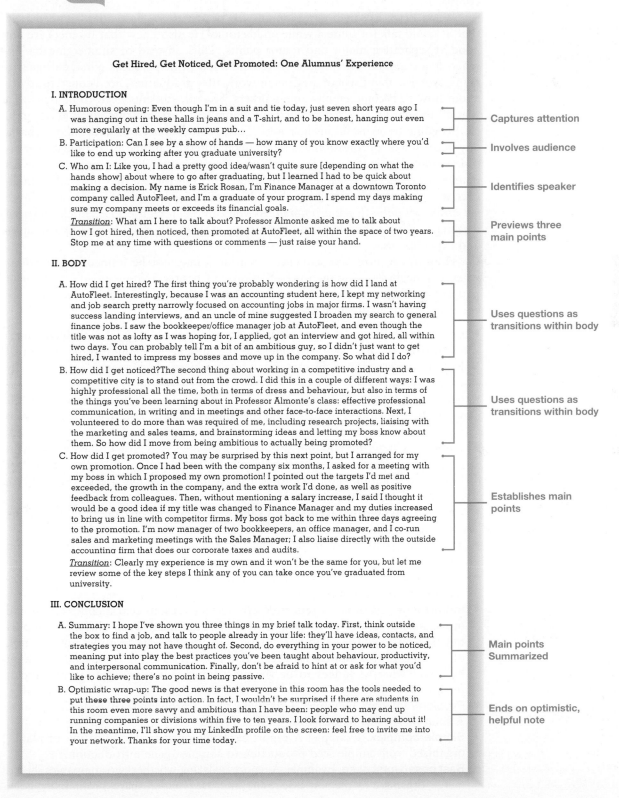

Get Hired, Get Noticed, Get Promoted: One Alumnus' Experience

I. INTRODUCTION

A. Humorous opening: Even though I'm in a suit and tie today, just seven short years ago I was hanging out in these halls in jeans and a T-shirt, and to be honest, hanging out even more regularly at the weekly campus pub… — Captures attention

B. Participation: Can I see by a show of hands — how many of you know exactly where you'd like to end up working after you graduate university? — Involves audience

C. Who am I: Like you, I had a pretty good idea/wasn't quite sure [depending on what the hands show] about where to go after graduating, but I learned I had to be quick about making a decision. My name is Erick Rosan, I'm Finance Manager at a downtown Toronto company called AutoFleet, and I'm a graduate of your program. I spend my days making sure my company meets or exceeds its financial goals. — Identifies speaker

Transition: What am I here to talk about? Professor Almonte asked me to talk about how I got hired, then noticed, then promoted at AutoFleet, all within the space of two years. Stop me at any time with questions or comments — just raise your hand. — Previews three main points

II. BODY

A. How did I get hired? The first thing you're probably wondering is how did I land at AutoFleet. Interestingly, because I was an accounting student here, I kept my networking and job search pretty narrowly focused on accounting jobs in major firms. I wasn't having success landing interviews, and an uncle of mine suggested I broaden my search to general finance jobs. I saw the bookkeeper/office manager job at AutoFleet, and even though the title was not as lofty as I was hoping for, I applied, got an interview and got hired, all within two days. You can probably tell I'm a bit of an ambitious guy, so I didn't just want to get hired, I wanted to impress my bosses and move up in the company. So what did I do? — Uses questions as transitions within body

B. How did I get noticed? The second thing about working in a competitive industry and a competitive city is to stand out from the crowd. I did this in a couple of different ways: I was highly professional all the time, both in terms of dress and behaviour, but also in terms of the things you've been learning about in Professor Almonte's class: effective professional communication, in writing and in meetings and other face-to-face interactions. Next, I volunteered to do more than was required of me, including research projects, liaising with the marketing and sales teams, and brainstorming ideas and letting my boss know about them. So how did I move from being ambitious to actually being promoted? — Uses questions as transitions within body

C. How did I get promoted? You may be surprised by this next point, but I arranged for my own promotion. Once I had been with the company six months, I asked for a meeting with my boss in which I proposed my own promotion! I pointed out the targets I'd met and exceeded, the growth in the company, and the extra work I'd done, as well as positive feedback from colleagues. Then, without mentioning a salary increase, I said I thought it would be a good idea if my title was changed to Finance Manager and my duties increased to bring us in line with competitor firms. My boss got back to me within three days agreeing to the promotion. I'm now manager of two bookkeepers, an office manager, and I co-run sales and marketing meetings with the Sales Manager; I also liaise directly with the outside accounting firm that does our corporate taxes and audits. — Establishes main points

Transition: Clearly my experience is my own and it won't be the same for you, but let me review some of the key steps I think any of you can take once you've graduated from university.

III. CONCLUSION

A. Summary: I hope I've shown you three things in my brief talk today. First, think outside the box to find a job, and talk to people already in your life: they'll have ideas, contacts, and strategies you may not have thought of. Second, do everything in your power to be noticed, meaning put into play the best practices you've been taught about behaviour, productivity, and interpersonal communication. Finally, don't be afraid to hint at or ask for what you'd like to achieve; there's no point in being passive. — Main points Summarized

B. Optimistic wrap-up: The good news is that everyone in this room has the tools needed to put these three points into action. In fact, I wouldn't be surprised if there are students in this room even more savvy and ambitious than I have been: people who may end up running companies or divisions within five to ten years. I look forward to hearing about it! In the meantime, I'll show you my LinkedIn profile on the screen: feel free to invite me into your network. Thanks for your time today. — Ends on optimistic, helpful note

Organize the Body

The best oral presentations focus on a few key ideas.

The biggest problem with most oral presentations is a failure to focus on a few principal ideas. Thus, the body of your short presentation (20 or fewer minutes) should include a limited number of main points, say, two to four. Develop each main point with adequate, but not excessive, explanation and details. Too many details can obscure the main message, so keep your presentation simple and logical. Remember, listeners have no pages to leaf back through should they become confused.

When Erick Rosan began planning his presentation, he realized immediately that he could talk for quite a while on his topic. He also knew that listeners are not good at separating major and minor points. Thus, instead of submerging his listeners in a sea of information, he sorted out a few principal ideas. First, college students, worried about where they might work after graduating, need concrete advice about how to become employable workers. Second, students need to be reassured that all the hard work they're currently doing (e.g., assignments, exams, research, etc.) is going to be useful in their jobs. Third, students need to understand what a day in the life of a professional is like: how it differs from that of a student or part-time worker (an experience most students already have). These would become his main points, but Erick wanted to streamline them further so that his student audience would be sure to remember them. He summarized the three points as follows: *get hired, get noticed, get promoted.* As you can see in Figure 11.3, Erick prepared a sentence outline showing these three main ideas. Each is supported by examples and explanations.

Organize your report by time, geography, function, importance, or some other method that is logical to the receiver.

How to organize and sequence main ideas may not be immediately obvious when you begin working on a presentation. In Chapter 9 you studied a number of patterns for organizing written reports. Those patterns, and a few new ones, are equally appropriate for oral presentations:

- **Chronology.** Example: A presentation describing the history of a problem, organized from the first sign of trouble to the present. We could argue that Erick Rosan's presentation is chronological: first get hired, then get noticed, and finally get promoted.
- **Geography/space.** Example: A presentation about the changing diversity of the workforce, organized by regions in the country (East Coast, West Coast, and so forth).
- **Topic/function/conventional grouping.** Example: A report discussing mishandled airline baggage, organized by names of airlines. We could also argue that Erick's presentation is topical: topic 1 is getting hired, topic 2 is getting noticed, and topic 3 is getting promoted.
- **Comparison/contrast (pro/con).** Example: A report comparing organic farming methods with those of modern industrial farming.
- **Journalism pattern.** Example: A report describing how identity thieves can ruin your good name, organized by *who, what, when, where, why,* and *how.*
- **Value/size.** Example: A report describing fluctuations in housing costs, organized by prices of homes.
- **Importance.** Example: A report describing five reasons that a company should move its headquarters to a specific city, organized from the most important reason to the least important (using some criteria to judge importance, of course). Erick's presentation can also be seen as being organized this way; he leaves what he judges to be the most important topic (getting promoted) for last.
- **Problem/solution.** Example: A company faces a problem such as declining sales. A solution such as reducing the staff is offered.
- **Simple/complex.** Example: A report explaining genetic modification of plants, organized from simple seed production to complex gene introduction.
- **Best case/worst case.** Example: A report analyzing whether two companies should merge, organized by the best-case result (improved market share, profitability, good

employee morale) as opposed to the worst-case result (devalued stock, lost market share, poor employee morale).

When organizing any presentation, prepare a little more material than you think you will actually need. Savvy speakers always have something useful in reserve (such as an extra handout, transparency, or idea)—just in case they finish early.

Summarize in the Conclusion

Nervous speakers often rush to wrap up their presentations because they can't wait to flee the stage. But listeners will remember the conclusion more than any part of a speech. That's why you should spend some time to make it most effective. Strive to achieve two goals:

- Summarize the main themes of the presentation, for example "Today, we've attempted to show you/explain for you . . ."
- Include a statement that allows you to leave the podium gracefully, such as "Thanks, ladies and gentlemen, for your time and attention. If you have any other questions . . ."

Some speakers end limply with comments such as "I guess that's about all I have to say." This leaves bewildered audience members wondering whether they should continue listening. Skilled speakers alert the audience that they are finishing. They use phrases such as *In conclusion, As I end this presentation*, or *It's time for me to stop*. Then they proceed immediately to the conclusion. Audiences become justly irritated with a speaker who announces the conclusion but then digresses with one more story or talks on for ten more minutes.

A straightforward summary should review major points and focus on what you want the listeners to do, think, or remember. You might say, *In bringing my presentation to a close, I'll briefly repeat my main idea . . .*; or *In summary, my major purpose has been to . . .*; or *In support of my purpose, I have presented three major points. They are (a) . . ., (b) . . ., and (c) . . . .* Notice how Erick Rosan, in the conclusion shown in Figure 11.3, summarized his three main points and provided a final focus to his audience.

If you are promoting a recommendation, you might end as follows: *In conclusion, I recommend that we consider Moncton as the most appropriate home for our new customer service call centre. I make this recommendation using the criteria I've outlined, namely (a) there is an experienced, bilingual workforce available in Moncton, (b) the city is home to other call centres, fostering resource synergies, and (c) Moncton offers the most attractive tax and other municipal and provincial incentives among the cities we've considered.*

In your conclusion you might want to use an anecdote, an inspiring quotation, or a statement that ties in the attention-capturing opener and offers a new insight. Whatever strategy you choose, be sure to include a closing thought that indicates you are finished. For example, *This concludes my presentation. After investigating three qualified Canadian cities in detail, we are convinced that Moncton suits our customer service needs best. Your authorization of my recommendation will enable us to move forward quickly with this important infrastructure and productivity goal. Thank you.*

> Effective conclusions summarize main points and allow the speaker to exit gracefully.

◼ Building Audience Rapport Like a Pro

Good speakers are adept at building audience rapport. Rapport is the bond formed with an audience; speakers with good rapport entertain as well as inform. How do they do it? Based on observations of successful and unsuccessful speakers, we can see that the good ones use a number of verbal and nonverbal techniques to connect with the audience. Some of their helpful techniques include providing effective imagery, supplying verbal signposts such as transitions and repetition, and using body language strategically.

Effective Imagery

You'll lose your audience quickly if your talk is filled with abstractions, generalities, and dry facts. To enliven your presentation and enhance comprehension, try using some of these techniques:

- **Analogies.** A comparison of similar traits between dissimilar things can be effective in explaining and drawing connections. For example, *Good customer service is akin to hosting a good dinner party: people should leave the customer service interaction happier than when they arrived, wanting to come back again.* Or, *Downsizing and restructuring are similar to an overweight person dieting, changing habits, and exercising: painful but necessary.*
- **Metaphors.** A comparison between otherwise dissimilar things without using the words *like* or *as* results in a metaphor. For example, *Those new drill sergeants in Accounting won't let me submit expense claims late, even by five minutes!* or *My desk is a garbage dump.*
- **Similes.** A comparison that includes the words *like* or *as* is a simile. For example, *Building a business team is like building a sports team—you want people not only with the right abilities, but also with the willingness to work together.* Or, *Change management can be about as difficult as converting people to a new religion!*
- **Personal anecdotes.** Nothing connects you faster or better with your audience than a good personal story. In a talk about e-mail best practices, you could reveal your own blunders that became painful learning experiences. In a talk to potential "angel" investors, the creator of a new app could talk about the "cool" factor of seeing a prior app he developed being used widely by young people.
- **Personalized statistics.** Although often misused, statistics stay with people— particularly when they relate directly to the audience. A speaker discussing job retraining might say, *If this is a typical workplace I can safely say that half of the people in this room won't be here within three years—that's the rate of job change these days.* If possible, simplify and personalize facts. For example, *The sales of Creemore Springs Brewery totalled 5 million cases last year. That's a full case of Creemore for every man, woman, and child in the Greater Toronto Area.*
- **Worst- and best-case scenarios.** Hearing the worst that could happen can be effective in driving home a point. For example, *I don't want to sound alarmist, but if we don't listen more closely to consumers in terms of what products they want, we could be the next tech company to land in the graveyard of has-beens.*
- **Examples.** If all else fails, remember that an audience likes to hear specifics. If you're giving a presentation on interpersonal communication, for example, instead of just saying, *Rudeness in the workplace is a growing problem*, it's always better to say something like *Rudeness in the workplace is a growing problem. For example, we've heard from some of our clients that our customer service representatives are using an inappropriate tone of voice.*

Verbal Signposts

Speakers must remember that listeners, unlike readers of a report, cannot control the rate of presentation or flip back through pages to review main points. As a result, listeners get lost easily. Knowledgeable speakers help the audience recognize the organization and main points in an oral message with verbal signposts. They keep listeners on track by including helpful previews, summaries, and transitions, such as these:

- **Previewing**
  The next segment of my talk presents three reasons for . . .
  I'll pass things off to Alia, who'll consider the causes of . . .
- **Switching directions**
  So far we've talked solely about . . .; now let's move to . . .
  I've argued that . . . and . . ., but an alternate view holds that . . .
- **Summarizing**
  Let me review with you the major problems I've just discussed.
  You can see, then, that the most significant factors are . . .

Knowledgeable speakers provide verbal signposts to indicate when they are previewing, summarizing, or switching directions.

You can further improve any oral presentation by including appropriate transitional expressions such as *first, second, next, then, therefore, moreover, on the other hand, on the contrary*, and *in conclusion*. These expressions lend emphasis and tell listeners where you are headed. Notice in Erick Rosan's outline, in Figure 11.3, that the specific transitional questions and other elements are designed to help listeners recognize each new principal point.

Nonverbal Messages

Although what you say is most important, the nonverbal messages you send can also have a potent effect on how well your message is received. How you look, how you move, and how you speak can make or break your presentation. The following suggestions focus on nonverbal tips to ensure that your verbal message is well received.

The way you look, how you move, and how you speak affect the success of your presentation.

- **Look professional.** Like it or not, you will be judged by your appearance. For everything but small, in-house presentations, be sure you dress professionally. The rule of thumb is that you should dress at least as well as the best-dressed person in the company.
- **Animate your body.** Be enthusiastic and let your body show it. Emphasize ideas to enhance points about size, number, and direction. Use a variety of gestures, but try not to consciously plan them in advance.
- **Punctuate your words.** You can keep your audience interested by varying your tone, volume, pitch, and pace. Use pauses before and after important points. Allow the audience to take in your ideas.
- **Get out from behind the podium/table/desk.** Avoid being planted behind the furniture. Movement makes you look natural and comfortable. You might pick a few places in the room to walk to. Even if you must stay close to your visual aids, make a point of leaving them occasionally so that the audience can see your whole body.
- **Vary your facial expression.** Begin with a smile, but change your expressions to correspond with the thoughts you are voicing. You can shake your head to show disagreement, roll your eyes to show disdain, look heavenward for guidance, or wrinkle your brow to show concern or dismay. To see how speakers convey meaning without words, mute the sound on your TV and watch the facial expressions of any well-known talk show host.

Planning Visual Aids

Before you give a business presentation, consider this wise Chinese proverb: "Tell me, I forget. Show me, I remember. Involve me, I understand." Your goals as a speaker are to make listeners understand, remember, and act on your ideas. To get them interested and involved, include effective visual aids. Some experts say that we acquire 85 percent of all our knowledge visually. Therefore, an oral presentation that incorporates visual aids is far more likely to be understood and retained than one lacking visual enhancement.

Good visual aids have many purposes. They emphasize and clarify main points, thus improving comprehension and retention. They increase audience interest, and they make the presenter appear more professional, better prepared, and more persuasive. Furthermore, research by Joline Morrisson and Doug Vogel, published in the journal *Information & Management*, shows that the use of visual aids during presentations leads to "a strong improvement in comprehension and retention."[5] Visual aids are particularly helpful for inexperienced speakers because the audience concentrates on the aid rather than on the speaker. Good visuals also serve to jog the memory of a speaker, thus improving self-confidence, poise, and delivery.

Types of Visual Aids

Fortunately for today's speakers, many forms of visual media are available to enhance a presentation. Figure 11.4 describes a number of visual aids and compares their degree of formality and other considerations. Some of the most popular visuals are PowerPoint or Prezi slides, a blackboard/whiteboard, and handouts.

SLIDES. With today's excellent software programs—such as PowerPoint and Prezi—you can create dynamic, colourful presentations with your laptop or tablet. The output from these programs is shown on a computer monitor, a TV monitor, or, in professional and academic settings, on a screen. With a little expertise and advanced equipment, you can create a slide presentation that includes professional sound, videos, and hyperlinks, as described in the discussion of slide presentations below. Slides can also be uploaded to a Web site or turned into podcasts to be broadcast live over the Internet.

FLIPCHART/WHITEBOARD/BLACKBOARD. Even though it may seem old-fashioned, effective use of a blackboard and chalk, a whiteboard and magic markers,

FIGURE 11.4 Presentation Enhancers

MEDIUM	PROS	CONS
PowerPoint or other slides	Create professional appearance with many colour, art, graphic, and font options. Easy to use and transport via removable storage media, Web download, or e-mail attachment. Inexpensive to update.	Present potential incompatibility issues. Require costly projection equipment and practice for smooth delivery. Tempt user to include razzle-dazzle features that may fail to add value.
Flipcharts or whiteboards	Provide inexpensive option available at most sites. Easy to (a) create, (b) modify or customize on the spot, (c) record comments from the audience, and (d) combine with more high-tech visuals in the same presentation.	Require graphics talent. Difficult for larger audiences to see. Prepared flipcharts are cumbersome to transport and easily worn with use.
Handouts or speaker's notes	Encourage audience participation. Easy to maintain and update. Enhance recall because audience keeps reference material.	Increase risk of unauthorized duplication of speaker's material. Can be difficult to transport. May cause speaker to lose audience's attention.
Video	Gives an accurate representation of the content; strong indication of forethought and preparation.	Creates potential for compatibility issues related to computer video formats. Expensive to create and update.
Props	Offer a realistic reinforcement of message content. Increase audience participation with close observation.	Lead to extra work and expense in transporting and replacing worn objects. Limited use with larger audiences.

or a paper flipchart and magic markers is one of the best ways to teach a relatively small audience something so that it sticks in people's minds. If you think about it, the reason for this effectiveness is clear. Instead of just using your voice and assuming people will listen, understand, and take notes, if you write down major headings, important concepts, new vocabulary words, and so on, the audience gets a double dose of information: orally through your voice and visually by your writing things on the board. Another reason why using these boards is effective? It makes you look dynamic. You are *doing* something besides just talking.

HANDOUTS. You can enhance and complement your presentations by distributing pictures, outlines, brochures, articles, charts, summaries, or other supplements. Speakers who use slide programs often prepare a set of their slides (sometimes called a "deck") along with notes to hand out to viewers, with mixed results. Often, the audience doesn't pay attention to the speaker but noisily flips through the printed-out pages of the slides. Timing the distribution of any handout, though, is tricky. If given out during a presentation, your handouts tend to distract the audience, causing you to lose control. Thus, it's probably best to discuss most handouts during the presentation but delay distributing them until after you finish.

Designing an Impressive Slide Presentation

Imagine all the people who sit through the more than 30 million PowerPoint presentations that Microsoft estimates are given each day.[6] No doubt, many of them would say this "disease" has reached epidemic proportions. PowerPoint, say its detractors, dictates the way information is structured and presented. They say that the program is turning the nation's businesspeople into a "mindless gaggle of bullet-pointed morons."[7] If you looked up *death by PowerPoint* in your favourite search engine, you would score hundreds of thousands of hits. Writing in *Canadian Business* magazine, Andrew Wahl paints an all-too-familiar picture: "We've all been there, sitting in some dark, airless space, straining to keep our eyes open during a presentation that drones on and on. A screen glows with a seemingly endless series of slides and charts, bullet points and words streaking and spinning round. But it's all in vain. Befuddled by the barrage of information, you fail to glean anything of use. The presentation ends, the lights come up, and you stumble away in a haze, thirsty for comprehension."[8] Wahl goes on to describe a number of problems with relying too heavily on PowerPoint, but without a doubt the greatest two are the curse of too many words on slides, which leads to audience exhaustion and divided attention, and the curse of the presenter who merely reads his or her slides, often turned away from the audience.

However, text-laden, amateurish slides that distract and bore audiences are the fault of their creator and not the software program itself. The ease with which most of us use PowerPoint has led to a false sense of security. We seem to have forgotten that to be effective, presenters using PowerPoint must first be effective presenters, period. And effective presenters do not overwhelm an audience by assuming it will be happy to read multiple slides with multiple lines or paragraphs of text, nor do they rely so heavily on a screen image that no one is paying attention to or listening to them. In other words, smart business presenters have to keep the attention of their audience by deploying the skills discussed above and in Chapter 10. They cannot assume that simply because they have a well-designed PowerPoint presentation, their actual *presentation* will go well.

Of course, learning how to use templates, working with colour, building bullet points, and add multimedia effects are valuable skills. In the sections that follow, you will learn to create an impressive slide presentation using the most widely used presentation software program, PowerPoint. We'll also discuss an up-and-coming rival to PowerPoint, Prezi. With any software, of course, gaining expertise requires your investment of time and effort. You could take a course or you could teach

yourself through an online tutorial such as that at **http://office.microsoft.com/en-us/powerpoint-help/training-courses-for-powerpoint-2013-HA104015465.aspx** or one of the many user-generated tutorial videos on YouTube. If used by a proficient slide preparer and a skillful presenter, slides can add a distinct visual impact to any presentation.

Preparing a Visually Appealing Slide Presentation

Some presenters prefer to create their slides first and then develop the narrative around their slides. Others prepare their content first and then create the visual component. The risk associated with the first approach is that you may be tempted to spend too much time making your slides look good and not enough time preparing your content. Remember that great-looking slides never compensate for thin content. In the following discussion, you will learn how to adjust the content and design of your slides to the situation or purpose and your audience. You will also receive how-to instructions for composing a PowerPoint and Prezi slide show.

ANALYZE THE SITUATION AND PURPOSE. Making the best content and design choices for your slides depends greatly on your analysis of the presentation situation and the purpose of your slide show. Will your slides be used during a live presentation? Will they be part of a self-running presentation such as in a store kiosk? Will they be saved on a server so that those with Internet access can watch the presentation at their convenience? Will they be sent as an attachment—to a client instead of a hard-copy report? Are you converting slide shows into video podcasts using a program like Jing or Camtasia for viewing on the Internet via a laptop, tablet, or smartphone?

If you are e-mailing the presentation or posting it online as a self-contained file, the slides will typically feature more text than if they were delivered orally. If, on the other hand, you are creating slides for a live presentation, your analysis will include answering questions such as these: *Should I prepare speaker's notes pages for my own use during the presentation? Should I distribute hard copies of my slides* to my audience?

> Slide presentations are economical, flexible, professional, and easy to prepare.

> Critics say that PowerPoint is too regimented and produces "bullet-pointed morons."

"My presentation lacks power and it has no point. I assumed the software would take care of that!"

ANTICIPATE YOUR AUDIENCE. Think about how you can design your slides to get the most positive response from your audience. Audiences respond, for example, to the colours you use. Because the messages that colours convey can vary from culture to culture, colours must be chosen carefully. In the Western world, blue and white are the colours of credibility, transparency, tranquility, conservatism, and trust. Therefore, they are the background colour of choice for many business presentations. Green relates to interaction, growth, money, and stability. It can work well as a background or an accent colour. Purple can be used as a background or accent colour. It conveys spirituality, aspirations, or humour.[9] As for slide text, adjust the colour so it provides high contrast and is readable. Black or blue, for example, usually work well on a white background.

Just as you anticipate audience members' reactions to colour, you can usually anticipate their reactions to special effects. Using animation and sound effects—flying objects, swirling text, and the like—only because they are available is not a good idea. This is a concern especially in Prezi, because zooming in and out of frames is at the core of this software.[10] Special effects may distract your audience, drawing attention away from your main points. Add animation features only if doing so helps to convey your message or adds interest to the content. When your audience members leave, they should be commenting on the ideas you conveyed—not the cool swivels and sound effects.

ADAPT TEXT AND COLOUR SELECTIONS. Adapt the amount of text on your slide to how your audience will use the slides. As a general guideline, most graphic designers encourage the 6-x-6 rule: "Six bullets per screen, max; six words per bullet, max."[11] You may find, however, that breaking this rule is sometimes necessary, particularly when your users will be viewing the presentation on their own with no speaker assistance.

Adjust the colours based on where the presentation will be given. Use light text on a dark background for presentations in darkened rooms. Use dark text on a light background for presentations in lighted rooms. Avoid using a dark font on a dark background, such as red text on a dark blue background. In the same way, avoid using a light font on a light background, such as white text on a pale blue background. Dark on dark or light on light results in low contrast, making the slides difficult to read.

> Follow the 6-x-6 rule and select background and text colours based on the lightness of the room.

ORGANIZE YOUR SLIDES. When you prepare your slides, you'll most probably translate the major headings in your presentation outline into titles for slides. So, you'll have an introduction slide, body slides, and a conclusion slide. In each of these five or so slides, you'll then paste from Word or write bullet points under each slide title using short phrases. In Chapter 4 you learned to improve readability by using graphic highlighting techniques, including bullets, numbers, and headings. In preparing a slide presentation, you will put those techniques into practice.

COMPOSE YOUR SLIDE SHOW. All presentation software requires you to (a) select or create a template that will serve as the background for your presentation and (b) add content (i.e., text, images, or links) that best conveys your message. In both PowerPoint and Prezi, you can use one of the templates provided with the software (see examples in Figure 11.5), download templates from Web sites, or create a template from scratch.

Most business users (unless they are in creative fields like design, advertising, or performing arts) usually choose existing templates because they are designed by professionals who know how to combine harmonious colours, borders, bullet styles, and fonts for pleasing visual effects. If you prefer, you can alter existing templates so they better suit your needs. Adding a corporate logo, adjusting the colour scheme to better match the colours used on your organization's Web site, and selecting a different font are just some of the ways you can customize existing templates.

FIGURE 11.5 Selecting a Slide Layout in PowerPoint and Prezi

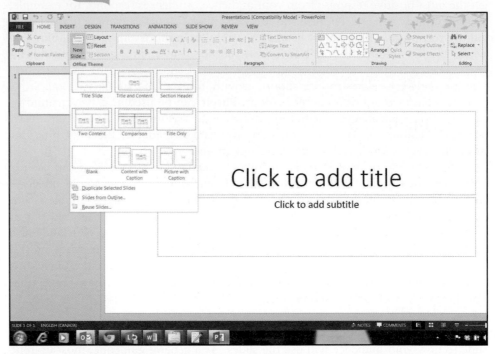

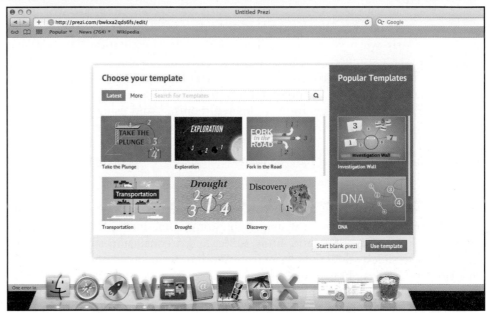

Overused templates and clip art produce "visual clichés" that may bore audiences.

Be careful, though, of what one expert labels "visual clichés."[12] Overused templates and even clip art that come with slide software can weary viewers who have seen them repeatedly in presentations. Instead of using a standard template, search for "PowerPoint template" in Google. You will see hundreds of template options available as free downloads. Unless your employer requires that presentations all have the same look, your audience may appreciate fresh templates that complement the purpose of your presentation and provide visual variety. That said, there's an argument to be made for consistency of slide appearance; for example, that consistency connotes professionalism.

As Figure 11.6 shows, you should experiment with graphic elements that will enhance your presentation by making your slides visually more appealing and memorable. One of the simplest but most effective lessons to learn is to try to avoid long, boring bulleted lists like the one in the left-hand slide of Figure 11.6.

FIGURE **11.6** Revising and Enhancing Slides for Greater Impact

Reasons for Selling Online

- Your online business can grow globally.
- Customer convenience.
- Conduct business 24/7.
- No need for renting a retail store or hiring employees.
- Reduce inquiries by providing policies and a privacy statement.
- Customers can buy quickly and easily.

Why You Should Sell Online

- Grow your business globally.
- Provide convenience for customers.
- Conduct business 24/7.
- Save on rent and hiring.
- Provide policies to reduce inquiries.

The slide on the left contains bullet points that are not parallel and that overlap meaning. The second and sixth bullet points say the same thing. Moreover, some bullet points are too long. After revision, the slide on the right has a more convincing title illustrating the "you" view. The bullet points are shorter, and each begins with a verb for parallelism. The photo adds interest. Note that the revised slide features a more lively and readable colour scheme, starting with the title.

If you look more closely at Figure 11.6, you will notice that the listed items on the first slide are not parallel. The slide looks as if the author had been brainstorming or freewriting a first draft. The second and sixth bullet points express the same thought, that shopping online is convenient and easy for customers. Some bullet points are too long. The bullets on the improved slide (right-hand side) are short, well within the 6-x-6 rule, although they are complete sentences, and easy to read (due to the use of the bullets). The photograph in the revised slide also adds interest and helps illustrate the point. You may use free stock photos that you can download from the Web for personal or school use without penalty, or consider taking your own pictures with a digital camera or smartphone.

Another effective and simple lesson about using slides is illustrated in Figure 11.7. The figure shows the same "reasons for online selling" from Figure 11.6, but has used

FIGURE 11.7 Converting a Bulleted Slide into a Diagram

Revised With a SmartArt Graphic

SmartArt Graphics Options

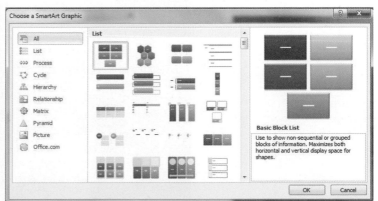

The same content that appears in the Figure 11.6 slides takes on a totally different look when arranged as spokes radiating from a central idea. Add a 3-D effect and a muted background image to the middle shape, for example, and you depart from the usual boring template look. When presenting this slide, you can animate each item and control when it is revealed, further enlivening your presentation. PowerPoint 2013 provides SmartArt graphics with many choices of diagrams and shapes for arranging information.

a spoke diagram to add variety and pizzazz to the presentation. This spoke diagram is just one of six common diagram possibilities available in PowerPoint's Diagram Gallery. Similar diagram options exist in Prezi. You can also animate each item in the diagram. As a best practice, try occasionally (e.g., once per presentation) to convert pure text and bullet points to diagrams, charts, and other images to add punch to your slide show. You will keep your audiences interested and help them retain the information you are presenting.

Numeric information is more easily grasped in charts or graphs than in a listing of numbers. In most programs, you can also animate your graphs and charts. Say, for instance, you have four columns in a bar chart. You can control when each column appears to your audience by determining in what order and how each column appears on the screen. The idea is to use animation strategically to introduce elements of the presentation simultaneously as they are mentioned in your spoken remarks, as a way of adding suspense to your presentation. Figure 11.8 shows how a chart can be used in PowerPoint to illustrate the concept of selling online, which is being discussed in a presentation.

During the design stage many slide users fall into the trap of excessive formatting. They fritter away precious time fine-tuning their slides and don't spend enough time on what they are going to say and how they will say it. To avoid this trap, set a limit on how much time you will spend making your slides visually appealing. Your time limit will be based on how many "bells and whistles" your audience expects and your content requires to make it understandable. Remember that not every point or every thought requires a visual. In fact, it is smart to switch off the slides occasionally and direct the focus to yourself. Darkening the screen while you discuss a point, tell a story, give an example, or involve the audience will add variety to your presentation.

Create a slide only if the slide accomplishes at least one of the following purposes:

- Generates interest in what you are saying and helps the audience follow your ideas
- Highlights points you want your audience to remember
- Introduces or reviews your key points

> Use animation to introduce elements of a presentation as they unfold in your spoken remarks.

FIGURE 11.8 Using a Bar Chart (Column Chart) to Illustrate a Concept

> This slide was created using PowerPoint's Insert, Chart function. The information presented here is more exciting and easier to comprehend than if it had been presented in a bulleted list.

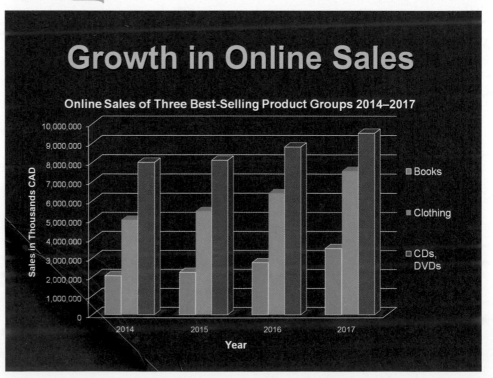

- Provides a transition from one major point to the next
- Illustrates and simplifies complex ideas

In a later section of this chapter, you will find specific steps to follow as you create your presentation.

REVISE, PROOFREAD, AND EVALUATE YOUR SLIDE SHOW. Well before actually giving the presentation, you should build in time to focus on making your presentation as clear and concise as possible. In other words, just as you were taught in earlier chapters to revise written messages, you also need to revise visual messages. For example, if you are listing items in a slide, be sure that all items use parallel grammatical form. If you created your own slide template, be sure all slides have the same background colour. If you quickly created the presentation from scratch, make sure the slides are in the right order so they don't confuse your audience. If you haven't yet proofread the slides, do so to make sure there are no spelling, punctuation, or grammar and style errors. Nothing is as embarrassing as projecting errors on a huge screen in front of your audience. Also check for consistency in how you capitalize and punctuate throughout the presentation. Finally, do a quick scan to ensure that basic slide best practices, such as number of bullet points per slide and length of sentence per bullet, are appropriate, so as not to overwhelm your audience.

Figure 11.9 shows how to revise a typical slide to improve it for conciseness, parallelism, and other features. Look closely at the design tips described in the first slide and determine which suggestions were not followed. Then compare it with the revised slide.

Notice that both slides in Figure 11.9 feature a blue background. This calming colour is the colour of choice for many business presentations (though white is just as popular an option for its elegance and ease of reading). However, the background swirls on the first slide are distracting. In addition, the uppercase white font is hard to read and contributes to making the image look busy. Inserting a transparent overlay and choosing a dark font to mute the distracting waves create a cleaner-looking slide.

As a last step before presenting, critically evaluate your slide show. Consider whether you have done all you can to use the tools PowerPoint or Prezi provide to communicate your message in a visually appealing way. In addition, test your slides on the equipment and in the room you will be using during your presentation. Do

FIGURE 11.9 Designing More Effective Slides

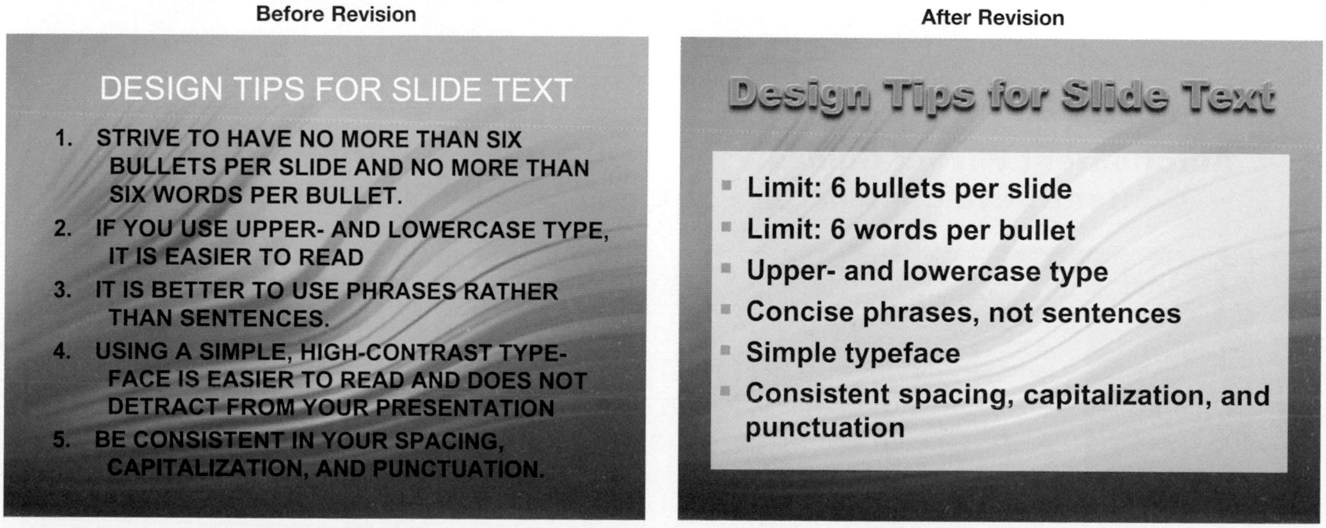

The slide on the left is difficult to read and understand because it violates many slide-making rules. How many violations can you detect? The slide on the right illustrates an improved version of the same information. Which slide do you think viewers would rather read?

the colours you selected work in this new setting? Are the font styles and sizes readable from the back of the room? Figure 11.10 shows a number of examples of slides that incorporate best slide practices from the above discussion.

As you look at the six PowerPoint slides in Figure 11.10 and the six Prezi frames in Figure 11.11, you'll notice that a white background has been chosen for

FIGURE 11.10 PowerPoint Slides That Demonstrate Best Practices in Multimedia Presentations

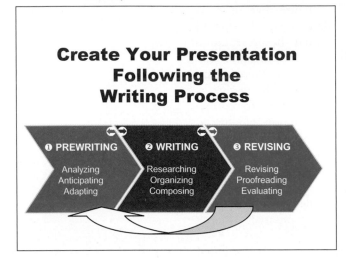

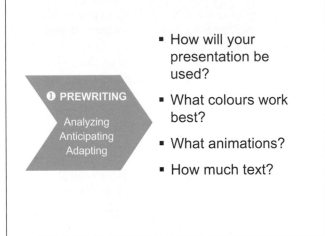

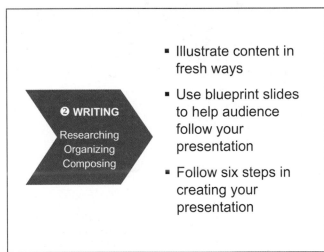

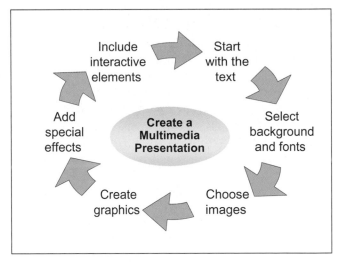

FIGURE 11.11 Choosing a Prezi Template

Much like PowerPoint, Prezi offers users numerous professional templates to choose from when creating a presentation.

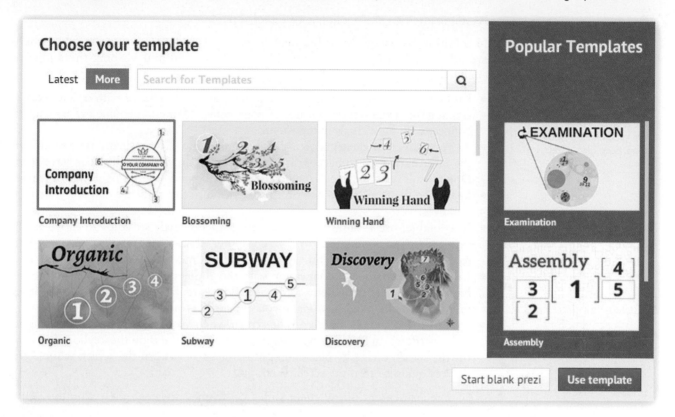

simplicity and professionalism. You'll also see that spare amounts of bulleted text are often paired with one simple image to create audience interest. Notice also their consistency: titles are in the same font and size, for example.

Using Slides Effectively in Front of an Audience

It's worth remembering that many promising presentations have been sabotaged by technology glitches or by the presenter's unfamiliarity with the equipment. Fabulous slides are of value only if you can manage the technology expertly. The late Apple CEO Steve Jobs was famous for his ability to wow his audiences during his keynote addresses. A journalist described his approach as follows: "Jobs unveils Apple's latest products as if he were a particularly hip and plugged-in friend showing off inventions in your living room. Truth is, the sense of informality comes only after gruelling hours of practice."[13] At one of his Macworld rehearsals, for example, he spent more than four hours on stage practising and reviewing every technical and performance aspect of his product launch.

> A fabulous slide show can be ruined if you are unfamiliar with the equipment.

Practising and Preparing

Allow plenty of time before your presentation to set up and test your equipment.[14] Confirm that the places you plan to stand are not in the line of the projected image. Audience members don't appreciate having part of the slide displayed on your body. Make sure that all video or Web links are working, that the sound level is appropriate (if audio is part of the slides), and that you know how to operate all features the first time you try. No matter how much time you put into pre-show setup and testing, you still have no guarantee that all will go smoothly. Therefore, you should always bring backups of your presentation. Handouts of your presentation provide a good substitute. Transferring your presentation to a USB flash drive that can run from any available laptop might prove useful as well.

Keeping Your Audience Engaged

In addition to using the technology to enhance and enrich your message, here are additional tips for performing like a professional and keeping the audience engaged:

- Know your material, so you are free to look at your audience with only the occasional gaze at the screen, but not at your notes. Maintain genuine eye contact to connect with individuals in the room.
- As you show new elements on a slide or frame, allow the audience time to absorb the information. Then paraphrase and elaborate on what the listeners have seen. Don't insult your audience's intelligence by reading verbatim from a slide or frame.
- Leave the lights as bright as you can. Make sure the audience can see your face and eyes.
- If available, use a radio remote control (not infrared) so you can move freely rather than remain tethered to your computer. Radio remotes allow you to be up to 15 metres away from your laptop.
- Consider maintaining a connection with the audience by using a laser pointer to highlight slide or frame items to discuss. Be aware, however, that a dancing laser point in a shaky hand may make you appear nervous. Steady your hand.
- Don't leave a slide or frame on the screen when you are no longer discussing it. In PowerPoint, in Slide Show, View Show mode, strike *B* on the keyboard to turn off the screen image by blackening it (or press *W* to turn the screen white). Hit the key again to turn the screen back on.

Some presenters allow their slides or frames to steal their thunder. One expert urges speakers to "use their PowerPresence in preference to their PowerPoint."[15] Although good slide presentations supply terrific sizzle, they cannot replace the steak. In developing a presentation, don't expect your slides to carry the show.

You can avoid being upstaged by not relying totally on your slides. Help the audience visualize your points by using other techniques. For example, drawing a diagram on a whiteboard or flipchart can be more engaging than showing slide after slide of static drawings. Demonstrating or displaying real objects or props is a welcome relief from slides. Remember that slides should be used only to help your audience understand the message and to add interest. You are still the main attraction!

Giving Powerful Slide Presentations in Eight Steps

We have now discussed many suggestions for designing effective slide presentations, but you may still be wondering how to put it all together. Here is a step-by-step process for creating a powerful multimedia presentation:

1. **Start with the text.** The text is the foundation of your presentation. Express your ideas using words that are clear, concise, and understandable. Once the entire content of your presentation is in place (for example, in a Word document), you are ready to begin choosing slide templates, colour, and all the other elements that will make your slides visually appealing. In this stage you'll also paste your text from a Word file into your slides (or, if you're confident, type your text directly onto your slides).

2. **Select background and fonts.** Select a template that will provide consistent font styles, font sizes, and a background for your slides. You can create your own template or use one included with PowerPoint or Prezi. You can also download free templates or pay for templates from many online sites. You can't go wrong selecting a basic template design with an easy-to-read font, such

as Times New Roman or Arial. As a general rule, use no more than two font styles in your presentation. The point size should be between 24 and 36. Title fonts should be larger than text font. The more you use PowerPoint and Prezi and find out what works and doesn't work, the more you can experiment with bolder, more innovative background and font options that effectively convey your message.

3. **Choose images that help communicate your message.** Images, such as clip art, photographs, and maps, should complement the text. Never use an image that is not immediately relevant. Microsoft Office Online is accessed in PowerPoint and contains thousands of clip art images and photographs, most of which are in the public domain and require no copyright permissions. Prezi allows you to easily insert images from Google Images or the Internet. Before using images from the Internet, however, determine whether permission from the copyright holder is required. At the very least, if pasting an image from the Internet, include a source line such as "Source: Google Images." Bear in mind that some people consider clip art amateurish, and given that clip art and Google Images are available to almost any user, they tend to become stale fast.

4. **Create graphics.** PowerPoint and Prezi include a variety of tools to help you simplify complex information or to transform a boring bulleted list into a visually appealing graphic. You can use PowerPoint's Draw and AutoShapes tools to create a time line or a flow chart. The Diagram Gallery will help you create an organization chart or a cycle, radial, pyramid, Venn, or target diagram, as well as over a dozen other chart types including line, pie, and bar charts. Prezi includes an easy-to-use Insert menu that allows you to insert not only diagrams, but also PDF and Excel files. All of these tools require practice before you can create effective graphics. When you're using either software for the first time, give yourself at least five times as long as you think you'll need to create a functioning presentation. Remember that graphics should be easy to understand without overloading your audience with unnecessary details or too much text. In fact, consider putting such details in handouts rather than cluttering your slides with them.

> Learn to simplify complex information in visually appealing graphics.

5. **Add special effects.** To keep your audience focused on what you are discussing, use PowerPoint's Custom Animation feature to control when objects or text appear on the screen. Animate points in a bulleted list to appear one at a time, for example, or the boxes in a radial diagram to appear as each is discussed. Keep in mind that the first thing your audience sees on every slide should present the slide's content. With motion paths and other animation options, you can move objects to various positions on the slide; or to minimize clutter, you can dim or remove them once they have served their purpose.

In addition, as you move from slide to slide in a presentation, you can select transition effects, such as Wipe Down. The animation and transition options range from subtle to flashy—choose them with care so that the visual delivery of your presentation doesn't distract from the content of your message.

6. **Create hyperlinks to approximate the Web-browsing experience.** Make your presentation more interactive and intriguing by connecting your slide presentation, via hyperlinks, to Internet sources that provide content that will enhance your presentation. You can hyperlink to other slides within the presentation or in other files; other programs that will open a second window that displays items such as spreadsheets, documents, or videos; and if you have an Internet connection, to Web sites.

Once you have finished discussing the hyperlinked source or watching the video that opened in a second window, close that window and your hyperlinked slide will be back in view. In this way, you can break up the monotony of typical linear slide presentations. Instead, your hyperlinked show approximates the viewing experience of a Web user who enters a site through a main page or portal and then navigates at will to reach second- and third-level pages.

7. **Engage your audience by asking for interaction.** When audience response and feedback are needed, interactive tools are useful. Audience response systems such as the iResponse App (iresponseapp.com) allow teachers or managers to pose questions, and students and employees and clients (who've paid for and downloaded the "app") to respond—with their answers immediately appearing on screen in front of the class or meeting. Options that are free but not as immediately interactive include creating free surveys in SurveyMonkey .com; sending a link to the survey to students, employees, or clients; asking them to fill it out; then showing the results on screen. Of course, interactivity can be generated even more simply by displaying a multiple-choice question on screen, asking students to vote for their response, and then displaying the correct response.

8. **Move your presentation to the Internet.** You can easily turn your PowerPoint or Prezi file into an engaging video by using a free tool like Techsmith's Jing software (**www.techsmith.com/download/jing**). Jing allows you to record your slide presentation as a video and record your voice over it. The resulting file can be posted on YouTube or on your company's intranet, assuming you have permission to do so. (Watch Professor Robert Kelley's YouTube video for a quick tutorial on how to turn a basic PowerPoint presentation into a free Jing video at **www.youtube.com/watch?v=npMuCWOvmVE.**) Web-based presentations and videos can have many applications, including marketing and promoting a business, or providing access to updated training or sales data whenever needed.

Some businesses convert their PowerPoint or Prezi presentations to PDF documents or send PowerPoint slide shows (file extension *.pps), which open directly in Slide Show View and are ready to run. Both types of documents are highly suitable for e-mailing. They start immediately, can't be easily changed, and typically result in smaller, less memory-hogging files.

> Internet options for slide presentations range from posting slides online to conducting a live Web conference with slides, narration, and speaker control.

Polishing Your Delivery and Following Up

Once you've organized your presentation and prepared visuals, you're ready to practise delivering it. Here are suggestions for selecting a delivery method, along with specific techniques to use before, during, and after your presentation.

Delivery Method

Inexperienced speakers often feel that they must memorize an entire presentation to be effective. Unless you're a professional performer, however, you will sound wooden and unnatural; and forgetting your place can be embarrassing. Therefore, memorizing an entire oral presentation is not recommended. However, memorizing significant parts—the introduction, the conclusion, and perhaps a meaningful quotation—can be dramatic and impressive.

If memorizing won't work, is reading your presentation the best plan? Definitely not. Reading to an audience is boring and ineffective. Because reading suggests that you don't know your topic well, the audience loses confidence in your expertise. Reading also prevents you from maintaining eye contact. You can't see audience reactions; consequently, you can't benefit from feedback.

Neither the memorizing nor the reading method creates convincing presentations. The best plan, by far, is a "cue-card" method. As Erick Rosan, the guest speaker from earlier in this chapter did, plan your presentation carefully and talk from cue cards containing key sentences and major ideas. One of Erick's cue cards is shown below in Figure 11.12. By preparing and then practising with your cue cards, you can talk to your audience in a conversational manner. Your cards should

FIGURE 11.12 Sample Cue Card for Presentation

A. How did I get hired at AutoFleet?

- Looked at accounting jobs
- Talked to uncle; broadened search
- Applied, was interviewed, and hired at AutoFleet
- Wanted to impress boss

So what did I do?...

include neither entire paragraphs nor single words. Instead, they should contain phrases that help you introduce each major idea. Cue cards will keep you on track and prompt your memory, but only if you have rehearsed the presentation thoroughly.

Delivery Techniques

Nearly everyone experiences some degree of stage fright when speaking before a group. "If you hear someone say he or she isn't nervous before a speech, you're talking either to a liar or a very boring speaker," says corporate speech consultant Dianna Booher.[16] In other words, you can capitalize on the adrenaline that is coursing through your body by converting it to excitement and enthusiasm for your performance. But you can't just walk in and "wing it." People who don't prepare suffer the most anxiety and give the worst performances. You can learn to make effective oral presentations by focusing on four areas: preparation, organization, visual aids, and delivery.

Being afraid is quite natural and results from actual physiological changes occurring in your body. Faced with a frightening situation, your body responds with the fight-or-flight response, discussed more fully in Figure 11.13. You can learn to control and reduce stage fright, as well as to incorporate techniques for effective speaking, by using the following strategies and techniques before, during, and after your presentation.

"In this seminar we'll discuss a simple technique for overcoming your fear of speaking in public."

The best method for delivering your presentation is speaking from carefully prepared note cards.

Stage fright is both natural and controllable.

Thorough preparation, extensive rehearsal, and stress-reduction techniques can lessen stage fright.

BEFORE YOUR PRESENTATION

- **Prepare thoroughly.** One of the most effective strategies for reducing stage fright is knowing your subject thoroughly. Research your topic diligently and prepare a careful sentence outline. Those who try to "wing it" usually suffer the worst butterflies—and make the worst presentations.
- **Rehearse repeatedly.** When you rehearse, practise your entire presentation, not just the first half. Place your outline sentences on separate cards. You may also wish to include transitional sentences to help you move to the next topic. Use these cards as you practise, and include your visual aids in your rehearsal. Rehearse alone or before friends and family. Also try rehearsing on audio- or videotape so that you can evaluate your effectiveness.
- **Time yourself.** Most audiences tend to get restless during longer talks. Thus, try to complete your presentation in no more than 20 minutes. Set a timer during your rehearsal to measure your speaking time.
- **Request a lectern.** Every beginning speaker needs the security of a high desk or lectern from which to deliver a presentation. It serves as a note holder and a convenient place to rest wandering hands and arms.
- **Check the room.** Before you talk, make sure that a lectern has been provided. If you are using sound equipment or a projector, be certain they are operational.

FIGURE 11.13 Conquer Stage Fright With These Techniques

Ever get nervous before giving a speech? Everyone does! And it is not all in your head, either. When you face something threatening or challenging, your body reacts in what psychologists call the fight-or-flight response. This physical reflex provides your body with increased energy to deal with threatening situations. It also creates those sensations—dry mouth, sweaty hands, increased heartbeat, and stomach butterflies—that we associate with stage fright. The fight-or-flight response arouses your body for action—in this case, making a presentation.

Because everyone feels some form of apprehension before speaking, it is impossible to eliminate the physiological symptoms altogether.

However, you can reduce their effects with the following techniques:

- **Breathe deeply.** Use deep breathing to ease your fight-or-flight symptoms. Inhale to a count of ten, hold this breath to a count of ten, and exhale to a count of ten. Concentrate on your counting and your breathing; both activities reduce your stress.

- **Convert your fear.** Don't view your sweaty palms and dry mouth as evidence of fear. Interpret them as symptoms of exuberance, excitement, and enthusiasm to share your ideas.

- **Know your topic and come prepared.** Feel confident about your topic. Select a topic that you know well and that is relevant to your audience. Test your equipment and arrive with time to spare.

- **Use positive self-talk.** Remind yourself that you know your topic and are prepared. Tell yourself that the audience is on your side—because it is! Moreover, most speakers appear to be more confident than they feel. Make this apparent confidence work for you.

- **Take a sip of water.** Drink some water to alleviate your dry mouth and constricted voice box, especially if you are talking for more than 15 minutes.

- **Shift the spotlight to your visuals.** At least some of the time the audience will be focusing on your slides, transparencies, handouts, or whatever you have prepared—and not totally on you.

- **Ignore any stumbles.** Don't apologize or confess your nervousness. If you keep going, the audience will forget any mistakes quickly.

- **Don't admit you are nervous.** Never tell your audience that you are nervous. They will probably never notice!

- **Feel proud when you finish.** You will be surprised at how good you feel when you finish. Take pride in what you have accomplished, and your audience will reward you with applause and congratulations. Your body, of course, will call off the fight-or-flight response and return to normal!

Check electrical outlets and the position of the viewing screen. Ensure that the seating arrangement is appropriate to your needs.

- **Greet members of the audience.** Try to make contact with a few members of the audience when you enter the room, while you are waiting to be introduced, or when you walk to the podium. Your body language should convey friendliness, confidence, and enjoyment.

- **Practise stress reduction.** If you feel tension and fear while you are waiting your turn to speak, use stress-reduction techniques, such as deep breathing. Additional techniques to help you conquer stage fright are presented in Figure 11.13.

DURING YOUR PRESENTATION

- **Begin with a pause.** When you first approach the audience, take a moment to adjust your notes and make yourself comfortable. Establish your control of the situation.

- **Present your first few sentences from memory.** By memorizing your opening, you can immediately establish rapport with the audience through eye contact. You'll also sound confident and knowledgeable.

- **Maintain eye contact.** If the size of the audience overwhelms you, pick out two individuals on the right and two on the left. Talk directly to these people.

- **Control your voice and vocabulary.** This means speaking in moderated tones but loudly enough to be heard. Eliminate verbal static, such as *ah*, *er*, *you know*, and *um*. Silence is preferable to meaningless fillers when you are thinking of your next idea.

- **Put the brakes on.** Many novice speakers talk too rapidly, displaying their nervousness and making it difficult for audience members to understand their ideas. Slow down and listen to what you are saying.

- **Move naturally.** You can use the lectern to hold your notes so that you are free to move about casually and naturally. Avoid fidgeting with your notes, your clothing, or items in your pockets. Learn to use your body to express a point.

> Eye contact, a moderate tone of voice, and natural movements enhance a presentation.

- **Use visual aids effectively.** Discuss and interpret each visual aid for the audience. Move aside as you describe it so that it can be seen fully. Use a pointer if necessary.
- **Avoid digressions.** Stick to your outline and notes. Don't suddenly include clever little anecdotes or digressions that occur to you on the spot. If it's not part of your rehearsed material, leave it out so that you can finish on time. Remember, too, that your audience may not be as enthralled with your topic as you are.
- **Summarize your main points.** Conclude your presentation by reiterating your main points or by emphasizing what you want the audience to think or do. Once you have announced your conclusion, proceed to it directly.

AFTER YOUR PRESENTATION

- **Distribute handouts.** If you prepared handouts with data the audience will need, pass them out when you finish.
- **Encourage questions.** If the situation permits a question-and-answer period, announce it at the beginning of your presentation. Then, when you finish, ask for questions. Set a time limit for questions and answers.
- **Repeat questions.** Although the speaker may hear the question, audience members often do not. Begin each answer with a repetition of the question. This also gives you thinking time. Then, direct your answer to the entire audience.
- **Reinforce your main points.** You can use your answers to restate your primary ideas (*I'm glad you brought that up because it gives me a chance to elaborate on . . .*). In answering questions, avoid becoming defensive or debating the questioner.
- **Keep control.** Don't allow one individual to take over. Keep the entire audience involved.
- **Avoid "Yes, but" answers.** The word "but" immediately cancels any preceding message. Try replacing it with "and". For example, *Yes, X has been tried. And Y works even better because . . .*
- **End with a summary and appreciation.** To signal the end of the session before you take the last question, say something like *We have time for just one more question.* As you answer the last question, try to work it into a summary of your main points. Then, express appreciation to the audience for the opportunity to talk with them.

> The time to answer questions, distribute handouts, and reiterate main points is after a presentation.

SUMMING UP AND LOOKING FORWARD

This chapter presented techniques for giving effective oral presentations. Good presentations begin with analysis of your purpose and your audience. Organizing the content involves preparing an effective introduction, body, and closing. The introduction should capture the audience's attention, identify the speaker, establish credibility, and preview the main points. The body should discuss two to four main points, with appropriate explanations, details, and verbal signposts to guide listeners. The conclusion should review the main points, provide a final focus, and allow the speaker to leave the podium gracefully.

You can improve audience rapport by using effective imagery including examples, analogies, metaphors, similes, personal anecdotes, statistics, and worst/best-case scenarios. In illustrating a presentation, use simple, easily understood visual aids to emphasize and clarify main points. If you employ PowerPoint or Prezi, you can enhance the presentation by using templates, layout designs, and bullet points, and by not letting your slides overwhelm you and your audience.

In delivering your presentation, outline the main points on cue cards and rehearse at least once if not more. During the presentation consider beginning with a pause and presenting your opening from memory. Make eye contact, control your voice, speak and move naturally, and avoid digressions. After your talk distribute handouts and answer questions. End gracefully and express appreciation.

The final two chapters of this book focus on your ultimate goal—getting a job or advancing in your career. You'll learn how to write a persuasive résumé and how to succeed in an employment interview.

CRITICAL THINKING

1. Why is repetition always a good idea in writing, but an excellent idea when presenting?

2. Which of the visual aid options you learned about in this chapter is the most effective? Is using the same visual aid as everyone else necessarily the best choice in a presentation?

3. If PowerPoint and Prezi are so effective, why are people critical of their use in presentations?

4. How can speakers prevent electronic presentation software from overtaking the presentation?

5. To what degree is stage fright real, as opposed to an excuse we make because of our discomfort?

CHAPTER REVIEW

1. The planning of a business presentation should begin with serious thinking about what two factors?

2. Name three goals to be achieved in the introduction of a business presentation.

3. What should the conclusion to a business presentation include?

4. Name three ways for a speaker to use verbal signposts in a presentation. Illustrate each.

5. List seven techniques for creating effective imagery in a presentation. Be prepared to discuss each.

6. List ten ways that a business presentation can be organized.

7. Name specific advantages and disadvantages of slide software.

8. Why is a PowerPoint or Prezi slide with less text preferable to one with more text?

9. What delivery method is most effective for speakers?

WRITING IMPROVEMENT EXERCISES

1. **PowerPoint Practice.**

Your Task: Using the summary you wrote in Chapter 8 for Writing Improvement Exercise 1 (p. 247), develop two electronic presentations to go along with this summary. In the first presentation, make the mistake of having too many words on your slides. In the second presentation, correct this mistake. Give both presentations to your class, and see if students can identify the problematic presentation and tell you why it's problematic.

2. **PowerPoint Practice.**

Your Task: Using the summary you wrote in Chapter 8 for Writing Improvement Exercise 2 (p. 247), develop two electronic presentations to go along with this summary. In the first presentation, make the mistake of having too busy or tasteless a design for your slides. In the second presentation, correct this mistake. Give both presentations to your class, and see if students can identify the problematic presentation and tell you why it's problematic.

3. **PowerPoint Practice.**

Your Task: Using the summary you wrote in Chapter 8 for Writing Improvement Exercise 3 (p. 247), develop an electronic presentation to go along with this summary. Make your presentation twice, first making the mistake of reading from the screen or slides, and second, correcting this mistake. See if students can identify the problematic presentation and tell you why it's problematic.

ACTIVITIES AND CASES

11.1 It's All About the Audience

As we saw at the beginning of this chapter, it's vital to think about your audience before developing a presentation. Depending on the type of audience, certain elements of your presentation will be emphasized, while others will be downplayed or eliminated altogether.

Your Task. Choose one of the presentation topics below and one of the audience sets below. Spend 15 minutes brainstorming what each presentation will look like; then, in front of a partner, a group, or the entire class, deliver a short improvised presentation in two different ways. Once you're done, see if your partner/group/class can figure out what you've done differently and why you chose to do so.

Topics	Audience sets
Surviving your first year of college/university	a) Your institution's board of governors b) Your institution's orientation day
The pros and cons of a particular piece of technology	a) A prospective customer b) Your parents
Your recent work experience	a) Your best friend b) A prospective employer
Choose a topic of your own with your instructor's permission	a) A formal audience b) An informal audience

11.2 Twitter: Follow Your Favourite Entrepreneur or Tycoon

Your Task. Go to **http://twitter.com** and sign up for a Twitter account (if you don't have one yet) so that you can follow businesspeople and examine the topics they like to tweet about. In the Search window on top of the page, enter the name of the businessperson whose tweets you wish to follow. Donald Trump, Richard Branson, Chris Hadfield, Suze Orman, Guy Kawasaki, Kevin O'Leary, and other well-known businesspeople are avid Twitter users. Over the course of a few days, read the tweets of your favourite expert. After a while, you should be able to discern certain trends and areas of interest. Note whether and how your subject responds to queries from followers. What are his or her favourite topics? Report your findings to the class, using notes or PowerPoint. If you find particularly intriguing tweets and links, share them with the class.

WEB

TEAM

11.3 Preparing, Rehearsing, and Critiquing an Oral Presentation

Just as this book's chapters on business writing stress the importance of a revision stage, so too oral communication must be revised if it is to be effective. In other words, until you are a seasoned veteran, you should get into the habit of rehearsing your oral presentations. Likewise, you should get into the habit of offering constructive criticism to your peers and colleagues when they solicit it, and of accepting the same criticism when it is offered to you.

Your Task. In groups of four or five, select an issue with business ramifications that interests you. For example, people have strongly held views on the issue of whether or not Canada should allow privatized health care. Investigate your chosen issue in a couple of newspaper or magazine articles found through library online databases, and prepare an oral presentation based on your research. Rehearse the complete oral presentation in front your group. Your audience members will politely raise their hand and interrupt your presentation each time they believe there needs to be improvement (e.g., your voice trails off, you mispronounce a word, you fidget nervously, your body language is sending the wrong signal, you've lost your train of thought, etc.). Accept their constructive criticism and keep rehearsing. Appoint someone to be note taker each time a presentation is being rehearsed so that at the end each of you has a list of "notes"—much like a theatre director would give to actors during rehearsal—that you can use to improve future presentations. Are there any common elements among the group members' notes?

11.4 Exploring the New World of Web Conferencing

Your boss at Home Realty Company is interested in learning more about Web conferencing but doesn't have time to do the research herself. She asks you to find out the following:

WEB

a. In terms of revenue, how big is the Web conferencing industry?

b. Who are the leading providers of Web conferencing tools?

c. What are the typical costs associated with holding a Web conference?

d. What kind of equipment does Web conferencing usually require?

e. How are other realtors using Web conferencing?

Your Task. Using electronic databases and the Internet, locate articles and Web sites that will provide the information your boss has outlined. Be prepared to role-play an informal presentation to your boss in which you begin with an introduction, answer the five questions in the body, and present a conclusion.

11.5 Critiquing a Speech

Your Task. Go to the CBC Digital Archives at **www.cbc.ca/archives**, and in the search box type the word "speech." Look through the four pages of speeches from Canadian history and choose one that interests you. Then, read up on speech critiques and how the pros review speeches; read Andrew Dlugan's blog at **http://sixminutes .dlugan.com/speech-evaluation-1-how-to-study-critique-speech** or Google "speech critiques." Write a memo report to your instructor critiquing the speech you've chosen in terms of the following:

a. Effectiveness of the introduction, body, and conclusion

b. Evidence of effective overall organization

c. Use of verbal signposts to create coherence

d. Emphasis of two to four main points

e. Effectiveness of supporting facts (use of examples, statistics, quotations, and so forth)

f. Focus on audience benefits

g. Enthusiasm for the topic

11.6 Investigating Oral Presentations in Your Field

One of the best sources of career information is someone in your field.

Your Task. Interview one or two individuals in your professional field. How are oral presentations important in this profession? Does the frequency of oral presentations change as one advances? What suggestions can these people make to newcomers to the field for developing proficient oral presentation skills? What are the most common reasons for giving oral presentations in this profession? Discuss your findings with your class.

11.7 Outlining an Oral Presentation

For many people the hardest part of preparing an oral presentation is developing the outline.

Your Task. Select an oral presentation topic from the list in Activity 11.10 (p. 367) or suggest an original topic. Prepare an outline for your presentation using the following format.

Title
Purpose

                        I. INTRODUCTION

Gain attention of audience   A.
Involve audience   B.
Establish credibility   C.
Preview main points   D.

Transition

                        II. BODY

Main point   A.
Illustrate, clarify, contrast   1.
                        2.
                        3.

Transition

Main point   B.
Illustrate, clarify, contrast   1.
                        2.
                        3.

Transition

Main point   C.
Illustrate, clarify, contrast   1.
                        2.
                        3.

Transition

Summarize main points
Provide final focus
Encourage questions

III. CONCLUSION
   A.
   B.
   C.

11.8 Discovering New Presentation Tips

Your Task. Using your library's online databases, perform a subject search for *business presentations*. Read at least three articles that provide suggestions for giving business presentations. If possible, print the most relevant findings. Select at least eight good tips or techniques that you did *not* learn from this chapter. Your instructor may ask you to bring them to class for discussion or to submit a short e-mail or memo report outlining your tips.

11.9 Researching Job-Application Information

Your Task. Using your library's online databases, perform a subject search for one of the following topics. Find as many articles as you can. Then organize and present a five-to-ten-minute informative talk to your class.

a. Do recruiters prefer one- or two-page résumés?

b. How do applicant tracking systems work?

c. How are inflated résumés detected, and what are the consequences?

d. What's new in writing cover letters in job applications?

e. What is online résumé fraud?

f. What are some new rules for résumés?

11.10 Choosing a Topic for an Oral Presentation

Your Task. Select a topic from the list below. Prepare a five- to ten-minute oral presentation. Consider yourself an expert who has been called in to explain some aspect of the topic before a group of interested people. Since your time is limited, prepare a concise yet forceful presentation with effective visual aids.

a. What is the career outlook in a field of your choice?

b. How has the Internet changed job searching?

c. What are the advantages and disadvantages of instant messaging as a method of workplace communication?

d. How do employees use online services?

e. What is telecommuting, and for what kind of workers is it an appropriate work alternative?

f. How much choice should parents have in selecting schools for their young children (parochial, private, and public)?

g. What travel location would you recommend for college students at March Break (or another holiday period, or in summer)?

h. What is the economic outlook for a given product (such as domestic cars, laptop computers, digital cameras, fitness equipment, or a product of your choice)?

i. How can your organization or institution improve its image?

j. Why should people invest in a company or scheme of your choice?

k. What brand and model of computer and printer represent the best buy for college students today?

l. What franchise would offer the best investment opportunity for an entrepreneur in your area?

m. How should a job candidate dress for an interview?

n. What should a guide to proper cellphone use include?

o. Are internships worth the effort?

p. How is an administrative assistant different from a secretary?

q. Where should your organization hold its next convention?

r. What is your opinion of the statement "Advertising steals our time, defaces the landscape, and degrades the dignity of public institutions"?[17]

s. How can businesspeople reduce the amount of e-mail spam they receive?

t. What is the outlook for real estate (commercial or residential) investment in your area?

u. What are the pros and cons of videoconferencing for [name an organization]?

v. Are today's communication technologies (e-mail, instant messaging, text messaging, PDAs, etc.) making us more productive or just more stressed out?

w. What kinds of gifts are appropriate for businesses to give clients and customers during the holiday season?

x. How are businesses and conservationists working together to protect the world's dwindling tropical forests?

y. Should employees be able to use computers in a work environment for anything other than work-related business?

11.11 Creating a PowerPoint Presentation

You are a consultant who has been hired to improve the effectiveness of corporate trainers. These trainers frequently make presentations to employees on topics such as conflict management, teamwork, time management, problem solving, performance appraisals, and employment interviewing. Your goal is to teach these trainers how to make better presentations.

Your Task. Create six visually appealing slides. Base the slides on the following content, which will be spoken during the presentation titled "Effective Employee Training." The comments shown here are only a portion of a longer presentation.

Trainers have two options when they make presentations. The first option is to use one-way communication, where the trainer basically dumps the information on the employees and leaves. The second option is to use a two-way audience-involvement approach. The two-way approach can accomplish many purposes, such as helping the trainer connect with the employees, helping the trainer reinforce key points, increasing the employees' retention rates, and changing the pace and adding variety. The two-way approach also encourages employees to get to know each other better. Because today's employees demand more than just a "talking head," trainers must engage their audiences by involving them in a two-way dialogue.

When you include interactivity in your training sessions, choose approaches that suit your delivery style. Also, think about which options your employees would be likely to respond to most positively. Let's consider some interactivity approaches now. Realize, though, that these ideas are presented to help you get your creative juices flowing. After I present the list, we will think about situations in which these options might be effective. We will also brainstorm to come up with creative ideas we can add to this list.

- Ask employees to guess at statistics before revealing them.
- Ask an employee to share examples or experiences.
- Ask a volunteer to help you demonstrate something.
- Ask the audience to complete a questionnaire or worksheet.
- Ask the audience to brainstorm or list something as fast as possible.
- Ask a variety of question types to achieve different purposes.
- Invite the audience to work through a process or examine an object.
- Survey the audience.
- Pause to let the audience members read something to themselves.
- Divide the audience into small groups to discuss an issue.

11.12 Improving the Design and Content of PowerPoint Slides

Your Task. Identify ways to improve the design and content of the three slides presented in Figure 11.14. Classify your comments under the following categories: (a) colour choices, (b) font choice including style and point size, (c) 6-x-6 rule, (d) listings in parallel grammatical form, (e) consistent capitalization and punctuation, and (f) graphics and images. Identify what needs to be improved and exactly how you would improve it. For example, if you identify category (d) as an area needing improvement, your answer would include a revision of the listing. When you finish, your instructor may show you a revised set of slides.

FIGURE 11.14 PowerPoint Slides Needing Revision

Webcasting Basics

- Inexpensive way to hold conferences and meetings.
- Presenter broadcasts via one of many Webcast platforms available today.
- Participants access meeting from anywhere via Internet connection and free software.
- Capabilities include live Q&A sessions and live polls of audience members.
- Those who missed the event can access stored presentations when convenient.

Voice Quality During Webcast

- The Three Ps are critical
  - Pacing
  - Pausing
  - Passion

Webcasting Pointers

- To engage audience early on, tell personal stories.
- Standing while webcasting adds energy to your voice.
- Remember, smiles are audible.
- Change slides frequently.
- Prepare a brief summary conclusion to follow Q&A session.

■ GRAMMAR/MECHANICS REVIEW 11—CAPITALIZATION

Study each of the following statements. Draw three underlines below any letter that should be capitalized. Draw a slash (/) through any capital letter that you wish to change to lowercase. Indicate in the space provided the number of changes you made in each sentence. If you made no changes, write *0*.

5 **Example** The consumer product safety act was revised specifically to ensure the safety of Children's toys.

___ 1. Employees of bank of montreal had to evacuate their Headquarters in suite 200 after the renfrew fire department units arrived.

___ 2. Canadians are reluctant to travel to europe because of the weak dollar; however, more british and french citizens are travelling to Canada, according to Maurice Dubois, Vice President at Hilton hotels.

___ 3. Once the Management Team and the Union members finally agreed, mayor Faria signed the Agreement.

___ 4. The boston marathon is an annual sporting event hosted by the city of boston on patriot's day.

___ 5. Luis was disappointed when he learned that the university of new mexico eliminated italian from its curriculum; now he must take history, geography, and political science classes to learn about italy.

___ 6. The most popular sites on the internet are those operated by google, facebook, and youtube.

___ 7. According to a Federal Government report issued in january, any regulation of State and County banking must receive local approval.

___ 8. The position of director of research must be filled before summer.

___ 9. The Vice President of MegaTech Industries reported to the President that the securities and exchange commission was beginning an investigation of their Company.

___ 10. My Uncle, who lives near wasaga beach in simcoe county, says that the Moon and Stars are especially brilliant on cool, clear nights.

___ 11. Our marketing director met with Adrienne Hall, Manager of our advertising media department, to plan an Adwords campaign for google.

___ 12. During the Fall our Faculty Advisor explored new exchange and semester-abroad opportunities in asia, australia, and china.

___ 13. Last february my Father and I headed south to visit the summer waves water park located on jekyll island in georgia.

___ 14. On page 6 of my report, you will find a list of all instructors in our business division with Master's degrees.

___ 15. Please consult figure 5.1 in chapter 5 of the book *analysis of population growth* for the latest Canadian census figures regarding non-english-speaking residents.

■ GRAMMAR/MECHANICS CHALLENGE—11

Document for Revision
The following executive summary of a report has faults in grammar, punctuation, spelling, number form, wordiness, and word use. Use standard proofreading marks (see Appendix B) to correct the errors. When you finish, your instructor can show you the revised version of this abstract.

Executive Summary

Purpose of Report
The purposes of this report is (1) To determine the Sun coast university campus communitys awareness of the campus recycling program and (2) To recommend ways to increase participation. Sun Coasts recycling program was intended to respond to the increasing problem of waste disposal, to fulfil it's social responsibility as an educational institution, and to meet the demands of legislation that made it a requirement for individuals and organizations to recycle.

A Survey was conducted in an effort to learn about the campus communities recycling habits and to make an assessment of the participation in the recycling program that is current. 220 individuals responded to the Survey but twenty-seven Surveys could not be used. Since Sun coast universitys recycling program include only aluminum, glass, paper and plastic at this point in time these were the only materials considered in this Study.

Recycling at Sun coast
Most Survey respondants recognized the importance of recycling, they stated that they do recycle aluminum, glass, paper and plastic on a regular basis either at home or at work. However most respondants displayed a low-level of awareness, and use of the on campus program. Many of the respondants was unfamilar with the location of the bins around campus; and therefore had not participated in the Recycling Program. Other responses indicated that the bins were not located in convenent locations.

Reccommendations for increasing recycling participation
Recommendations for increasing participation in the Program include the following;

1. relocating the recycling bins for greater visability

2. development of incentive programs to gain the participation of on campus groups

3. training student volunteers to give on campus presentations that give an explanation of the need for recycling, and the benefits of using the Recycling Program

4. we should increase Advertising in regard to the Program

COMMUNICATION WORKSHOP

TECHNIQUES FOR TAKING PART IN EFFECTIVE AND PROFESSIONAL TEAM PRESENTATIONS

In the classroom or on the job, it is likely that you will join a team to prepare and deliver an oral presentation. If you have been part of a team before, you know that such projects can be frustrating—particularly when some team members don't carry their weight or when members cannot resolve conflict. Team projects, however, can be harmonious and productive when members establish ground rules and follow these steps:

- **Prepare to work together.** First, you should (a) compare schedules of team members in order to set up the best meetings times, (b) plan to meet often, and (c) discuss how you will deal with team members who are not contributing to the project.
- **Plan the presentation.** Your team will need to agree on (a) the specific purpose of the presentation, (b) your audience, (c) the length of the presentation, (d) the types of visuals to include, and (e) the basic structure and content of the presentation.
- **Assign work.** Once you decide what your presentation will cover, each team member should have a written assignment that details his or her responsibilities for researching content, producing visuals, developing handouts, building transitions between segments, and showing up for team meetings and rehearsals.
- **Collect information.** To gather or generate information, teams can brainstorm together, conduct interviews, or search the Web for information. The team should decide on deadlines for collecting information and discuss how to ensure its accuracy and currency. Team members should exchange periodic reports on how their research is progressing.
- **Organize and develop the presentation.** Once your team has gathered all research, you will start working on the presentation. Determine the organization of the presentation, compose a draft in writing, and prepare PowerPoint slides and other visual aids. Meet often to discuss the presentation and decide which team member will be responsible for delivering what parts of the presentation. Be sure to build transitions between each presenter's topic and strive for logical connections between segments.
- **Edit, rehearse, and evaluate.** Before you deliver the presentation, rehearse several times as a team. Make sure that transitions from speaker to speaker are smooth. For example, you might say, *Now that I have discussed . . ., Ashley is going to present . . . .* Decide who will be responsible for advancing slides during the presentation. Practice fielding questions if you plan to have a question-and-answer session. Decide how you are going to dress to look professional and competent. Run a spell check and proofread your PowerPoint slides to ensure that the design, format, and vocabulary are consistent.
- **Deliver the presentation.** Show up on time for your presentation and wear appropriate attire. Deliver your part of the presentation with professionalism and enthusiasm. Remember that your audience is judging the team on its performance, not the individuals. Do what you can to make your team shine!

Career Application

Your boss assigns you to a team that is to produce an organizational five-year plan for your company. You know this assignment will end with an oral presentation to management and stockholders. Your first reaction is dismay because you have been on teams before in the classroom, and you know how frustrating they can be. However, you want to give your best, and you resolve to contribute positively to this team effort.

YOUR TASK

In small groups, discuss effective collaboration. How can one contribute positively to a team? What does research say about how teams should deal with members who aren't contributing or who have negative attitudes? What should team members do to ensure that the final presentation is professional and well coordinated? Present your group's answers in front of your class, making sure everyone in the group has a chance to speak. Ask the class for feedback on your impromptu presentation.

Communicating for Employment

CHAPTER 12
The Job Search:
Résumés, Social
Media, and
Cover Letters

CHAPTER 13
Interviews and
Follow-Up

COMMUNICATION TECHNOLOGY IN THE NEWS

Freshen Up That Online Resume With Original "Keywords"

Source: Jenny Lee, "Freshen up that online resume with original 'keywords,'" Vancouver Sun, Jan. 3, 2011, pg. C1.

If you are looking for work, using an online resume can be a good idea, but use it wisely. Online profiles and resumes show a clear pattern of overused employment buzzwords, and while at first these words might sound professional, they do little to set you apart, life coach Phyllis Reardon says.

Canadian and U.S. job hunters highlight their "extensive experience," while most of Europe hopes to be seen as "innovative," South Americans want to be seen as "dynamic," as do folks in Spain and India, while the Brits stand alone in their desire to appear "motivated," according to a LinkedIn study of the most overused words and phrases in member profiles.

Are the words extensive experience, innovative, dynamic, motivated, team player, results-oriented, fast-paced, proven track record, multitasker and entrepreneurial liberally sprinkled through your resume? These are Canada's top 10 employment buzzwords according to LinkedIn's records.

"Most Canadians are using the same 10 words in their profiles, and their profile on LinkedIn is playing the role of the modern resume," Reardon said. "While those words are okay in themselves, they can appear a little bit tired. If I was coaching a client, I would say use words which are more descriptive of your working behaviour."

An online resume can reach millions of people, but using it successfully requires savvy.

LinkedIn alone has 85 million members. "Hundreds, if not thousands, of other professionals have those words in their profile, so if you're including them in the hope they will make you stand out, it isn't going to work, said Krista Canfield, LinkedIn's senior PR manager for the Americas.

It's important to use keywords in your summary and descriptions of positions you've held, Canfield said.

An employer looking for an accountant is more likely searching for certain types of accountants rather than a "dynamic" accountant, Canfield said.

And someone seeking a corporate tax accountant won't find you if your profile doesn't include the words "corporate" and "tax," she said.

Make sure you're connected to at least 50 people, Canfield said.

"That's the magic number where people start having more of those network effects, first-, second- and third-degree connections," she said. "The starting point could be co-workers, clients, professors if you're a new professional, college classmates, family members—primarily people you know and trust who are vested in your career."

Canfield tells the story of older, established airlines advertising their "low-cost airfare" online when faced with competition from younger airlines such as Virgin, Southwest and JetBlue.

"But no one was searching for that," she said. "They were searching for 'cheap tickets.'"

Put two lenses on your profile, Canfield said. Look at the industry terms you may be proficient at, and then flip to the terms your clients are using.

If you were in sales, you might want to talk about the size of your deals and how frequently you hit your quota, she said.

While some believe employers will search words like "dynamic" in a resume or profile, Reardon said job hunters are better off using words that best describe their behaviour.

Think about how unique you are, Reardon said. "There's no one else like you in the world. Think about what makes you.

"Write a list of the words that describe you and sometimes some of those tired words just may spill out on the page. Let them stay there. Then find synonyms that are more lively that better suit you."

In place of "dynamic," are you adaptable, persuasive, flexible, proactive, enthusiastic? Instead of listing words, describe your behaviours at work, Reardon said. Write up some of your work tasks. Alternatives to "innovative" include entrepreneurial, imaginative, enterprising, open-minded or insightful.

One good exercise is to search your job by title and take a look at your competition.

More and more people are using social media to find work. "Research has shown time and time again people procure work more easily through contacts than an employment office. Work has changed and people seeking work must change," Reardon said.

"Networking is the key to success in work. It's a key to success in life and LinkedIn offers the ultimate in networking," said Reardon, noting that she is not paid by LinkedIn.

"Any employer can go right into your name and they have all that information that [at] one time would probably [have been] sitting in somebody's file cabinet."

Reardon sets aside time in the morning and afternoon to blog and post in life-coaching groups. She used to go to conferences to make contacts, but now that is less important to her. "At LinkedIn and the groups I'm in, it's like going into a big conference centre, and every single morning I have access to some of the best minds in the world."

Small-business professionals are among LinkedIn's most active users, Canfield said.

"More than 65 per cent of Fortune 100 companies use LinkedIn's hiring solutions to find talent," she said.

Summarize the article you've just read in a two- or three-sentence paragraph. Answer the following questions, either on your own or in a small group. Be prepared to present your answers in a short presentation or in an e-mail to your instructor.

QUESTIONS:

1. How does what you've learned in this article change your perception of business communication?

2. How might what you've learned in this article change your own communication style or strategy?

3. Come up with pro and con arguments for the following debate/discussion topic: All you need to do to get a job today is have a profile posted on LinkedIn.

CHAPTER
12

The Job Search: Résumés, Social Media, and Cover Letters

LEARNING OBJECTIVES

1. Prepare for employment by identifying your interests, evaluating your assets, recognizing the changing nature of jobs, and choosing a career path.

2. Use traditional and online job search techniques.

3. Compare and contrast chronological, functional, and combination résumés.

4. Organize and format the parts of a résumé to produce a persuasive product.

5. Use LinkedIn and video resumes effectively to produce a persuasive adjunct to your traditional resume.

6. Write a persuasive cover letter to accompany your résumé.

Finding a satisfying career means learning about oneself, the job market, and the employment process.

Whether you are applying for your first permanent position, competing for promotion, or changing careers, you'll be more successful if you understand employment strategies and how to promote yourself with a winning résumé. This chapter provides up-to-date advice on preparing for employment, searching the job market, writing a persuasive résumé, and developing an effective cover letter.

Preparing for Employment

You may think that the first step in finding a job is writing a résumé, but the job search process actually begins long before you are ready to prepare one. Regardless of the kind of employment you seek, you must invest time and effort getting ready. You can't hope to find the position of your dreams without knowing yourself, knowing the job market, and knowing the employment process.

In addition to searching for career information and choosing a specific job objective, you should study the job market and be aware of the substantial changes in the nature of work. You'll also want to understand how to use the latest online resources like LinkedIn in your job search, as the quote and the article at the beginning of this chapter makes clear. When you have finished all this preparation, you're ready to design a persuasive résumé and job application letter and an online profile. These documents should be appropriate for small businesses as well as for larger organizations that may be using résumé-scanning programs. Following the above steps, summarized in Figure 12.1 and described in this chapter, gives you a master plan for getting the interview you really want.

FIGURE 12.1 The Employment Search

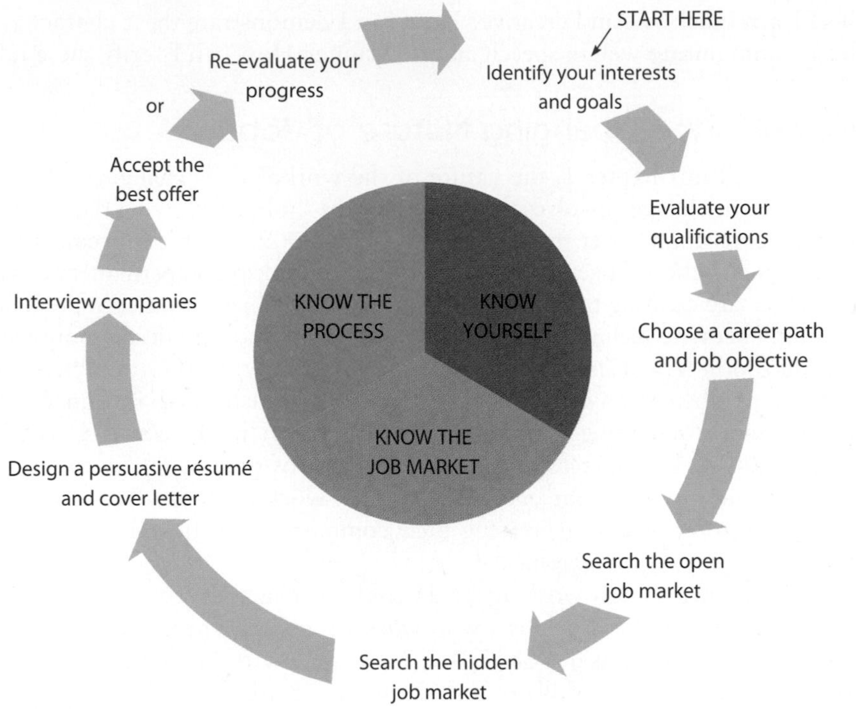

Identify Your Interests

The employment process begins with looking inside yourself to analyze what you like and dislike so that you can make good employment choices. Career counsellors at your college or university can help you with this process. You can also do a self-examination—without making an appointment. For guidance in choosing a field that eventually proves to be satisfying, answer the following questions. You can use your responses to match the description of opportunities you come across in your job search. If a number of your responses appear in a particular job description, there's a good chance it might be a good fit for you.

- Do I enjoy working with people, data, or things?
- How important is it to be my own boss?
- How important are salary, benefits, and job stability?
- What type of working conditions, colleagues, and job stimulation am I looking for?
- Would I rather work for a large or small company?
- Must I work in a specific city, geographical area, or climate?
- Am I looking for security, travel opportunities, money, power, or prestige?
- How would I describe the perfect job, boss, and co-workers?

> Analyzing your likes and dislikes helps you make wise employment decisions.

> Answering specific questions can help you choose a career.

Evaluate Your Qualifications

In addition to your interests, assess your qualifications. Employers today want to know what assets you have to offer them. Your responses to the following questions will target your thinking as well as prepare a foundation for your résumé. As you'll see later in this chapter, there is room in a résumé to include answers to most of the questions below. Remember that employers seek more than empty assurances; they will want proof of your qualifications.

- What computer skills can I offer? (Name specific software programs.)
- What other hard skills have I acquired in school, on the job, or through activities? How can I demonstrate these skills?
- Do I work well with people? What proof can I offer? (Consider extracurricular activities, clubs, and jobs.)

> Assessing your skills and experience prepares you to write a persuasive résumé.

- Am I a leader, self-starter, or manager? What evidence can I offer?
- Do I speak, write, or understand another language?
- Do I learn quickly? Am I creative? How can I demonstrate these characteristics?
- Do I communicate well in speech and in writing? How can I verify these talents?

Recognize the Changing Nature of Jobs

As you learned in Chapter 1, the nature of the workplace is changing. One of the most significant changes involves the concept of the "job." Following the downsizing in many organizations after the recession of 2008–2009, and the movement toward flattened organizations in general, fewer people are employed in permanent positions. More people are creating their own work through freelancing and entrepreneurship. Many employees are feeling less job security, although they are doing more work.

In his book *The Canadian Workplace in Transition*, Gordon Betcherman describes a number of ways in which work is being transformed. In Canada, "non-standard" work, including temporary and short-term work, contract work, and self-employed work, is increasing, as is the amount of time people work in a week and the amount of work done outside traditional working hours. At the same time, Canadian corporations are increasing their commitment to flexible work arrangements and employee empowerment.[1]

People are increasingly working for themselves or smaller companies, or they are becoming consultants or specialists who work on tasks or projects under arrangements too fluid to be called "jobs." And because new technologies can spring up overnight, making today's skills obsolete, employers are less willing to hire people into jobs with narrow descriptions.

What do these changes mean for you? For one thing, you should no longer think in terms of a lifelong career with a single company. In fact, you can't even expect reasonably permanent employment for work well done. This social contract between employer and employee is no longer a given. And predictable career paths within companies have largely disappeared. In the new workplace you can expect to work for multiple employers on flexible job assignments associated with teams and projects.

Because of this changing nature of work, you can never become complacent about your position or job skills. Be prepared for constant retraining and updating of your skills. People who learn quickly and adapt to change are valued individuals who will always be in demand, especially in a climate of surging change.

Choose a Career Path

Today's job market is vastly different from that of a decade or two ago. As a result of job trends and personal choices, the average Canadian can expect to change careers at least three times and change jobs at least seven times in a lifetime. As a student you may not have yet settled on your first career choice; others are embarking on a second or perhaps third career. Although you may be changing jobs in the future, you still need to train for a specific career area now. In choosing an area, you'll make the best decisions when you can match your interests and qualifications with the requirements of specific careers. But where can you find career information? Here are some suggestions:

- **Visit your school career or counselling centre.** Most centres will have literature on job search techniques, workshops on résumé and cover-letter writing, information about local job fairs, and Internet connections that allow you to investigate any field you may be interested in.
- **Search the Internet.** Many job search Web sites (e.g., Workopolis, Monster, and Charity Village) offer career planning information and resources. For example, Workopolis.com helps you link to various career search resources in its Career Resources link, such as Resume Rescue and Salary Calculator. A sample online job site list of opportunities is shown in Figure 12.2.

Downsizing and flatter organizations have resulted in people feeling less secure in their jobs.

"Jobs" are becoming more flexible and less permanent.

People can expect to have eight to ten jobs in three or more different careers in a lifetime.

Career information can be obtained at school career centres and libraries, from the Internet, in classified ads, and from professional organizations.

FIGURE 12.2 Results from Online Searches

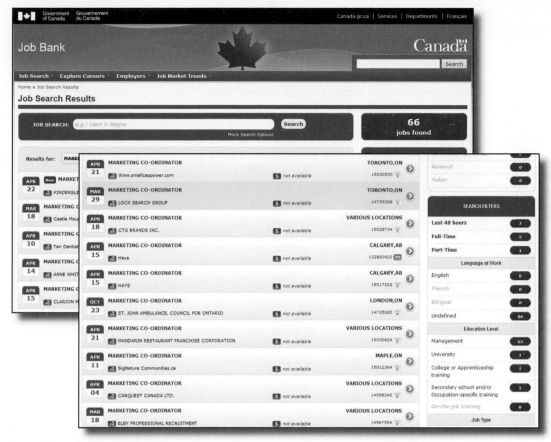

Source: Government of Canada Job Bank search results
URL: http://www.jobbank.gc.ca/job_search_results.do:jsessionid=70B1BC28180A2852A768194992CF7B49.imna
v2?searchstring=Canada&button.submit=Search
Employment and Social Development Canada, 2014. Reproduced with the permission of the Minister of Employment and Social Development Canada, 2014.

- **Use your library.** Consult the latest edition of the *Index of Occupational Titles*, the U.S. government's *Occupational Outlook Handbook* (**www .bls.gov/oco**), and the Canadian government's National Occupational Classification (**www5.hrsdc.gc.ca/NOC/English/NOC/2011/Welcome.aspx**) for information about career duties, qualifications, salaries, and employment trends.
- **Take a summer job, internship, or part-time position in your field.** Nothing is better than trying out a career by actually working in it or in a similar area. Many companies offer internships, or may be open to you creating your own internship via networking. They may also offer temporary jobs to begin training students and to develop relationships with them (e.g., Walmart hires thousands of holiday-season workers—a possible entry to a retail management career). These relationships sometimes blossom into permanent positions.
- **Volunteer with a nonprofit organization.** Many colleges and universities encourage service learning opportunities. In volunteering their services to non-profit organizations in their city or town, students gain valuable experience. Nonprofits, in turn, appreciate the expertise and fresh ideas that students bring and are often happy to provide free training.
- **Interview someone in your chosen field.** People are usually flattered when asked to describe their careers. Once you've settled on your intended career or sector, use LinkedIn and the Internet to find names of leaders within organizations. Then, send a polite e-mail or voice mail in which you request an informational interview. In the interview, politely inquire about needed skills, required courses,

> Summer and part-time jobs and internships are good opportunities to learn about different careers.

financial and other rewards, benefits, working conditions, future trends, and entry requirements.

- **Monitor job ads.** Early in your postsecondary education career, begin monitoring newspaper ads and job Web sites for listings by companies in your career area. Check job availability, qualifications sought, duties, and salary range. Don't wait until you're about to graduate to see how the job market looks.

- **Join professional organizations in your field.** Organizations like the Canadian Marketing Association (CMA) and the Human Resources Professionals Association (HRPA) are fantastic places to find out about your intended career. Frequently, these organizations offer student membership status and reduced rates for conferences and workshops. You'll get inside information on issues, career news, and possible jobs, as well as the opportunity to meet people who are working in the field you've identified as your future goal.

Searching for a Job Online

Another significant change in the workplace involves the way we find jobs. Prior to the early 2000s, a job seeker browsed the local newspaper's classified ads, found a likely sounding job listing, prepared a résumé on paper, and sent it out by mail (and later by fax). All that has long since changed. Today, searching for a job online has become a common, but not always fruitful, approach. With all the publicity given to Internet employment sites (e.g., in the quote at the beginning of this chapter) you might think that online job searching has totally replaced traditional methods. Not so! Although Web sites such as Workopolis and Monster list millions of jobs (see Figure 12.3 on the next page), actually landing a job is much harder than just clicking a mouse. In addition, these job boards are facing competition from social networking sites such as LinkedIn and Facebook.[2]

Both recruiters and job seekers complain about employment sites. Corporate recruiters say that the big sites can bring a flood of candidates, many of whom are not suited for the listed jobs. Workplace experts estimate that the average large corporation can be inundated with up to 2,000 résumés a day.[3] Job candidates grumble that listings are frequently out of date and fail to produce leads. Some career advisors call these sites *black holes*[4] into which résumés vanish without a trace. Some applicants worry about the privacy of information posted at big sites. All that said, experts in source of hire (i.e., the study of where and how new hires come about) say that although internal referrals are still the greatest source of hires at about 25 percent, employment sites account for just under 20 percent.[5] Clearly, a successful job search will come about through a combination of networking with people who already work inside companies, searching employment sites, and searching career sites on company and organization websites.

> Employment Web sites list many jobs, but finding a job electronically requires more work than simply clicking a mouse.

USING THE BIG EMPLOYMENT SITES. Whether or not you end up landing an interview from a referral, corporate site, or employment site, you should definitely learn to use employment sites if you haven't already to gather job search information, such as résumé, interviewing, and salary tips. These sites serve as a jumping-off point in most people's searches. They can inform you about the kinds of jobs that are available, the skill sets required, and the current vocabulary of both job searching and the area you're looking in. Start your search at a few of the best-known online job sites:

- **Workopolis (www.workopolis.com).** Workopolis is probably Canada's leading employment site. It includes thousands of jobs in all major industries. A useful feature on this site is a separate area for Student Jobs, as well as the blog-style "Latest News and Advice" area that offers timely advice and stories about issues in job search. Take some time to learn how to navigate Workopolis if you've not already done so—everyone else has!

FIGURE 12.3 Three Leading Internet Job Sites

- **Monster (www.monster.ca)**. Monster is similar to Workopolis, but its website is not as effectively designed. Like Workopolis it includes thousands of jobs in all major industries. A differentiator between Monster and Workopolis is that Monster allows you, via Facebook, to access instant, real-time career counselling. Of specific interest to students is Monster College (**http://college .monster.com**) with specific (but often U.S.-based) help for student job seekers.
- **Charity Village (www.charityvillage.com)**. Charity Village advertises jobs solely in the nonprofit sector. Often overlooked by students and graduates, this site offers a wealth of opportunities in traditional business areas such as accounting, finance, customer service, and marketing.

- **Other employment sites.** If you Google "Canadian employment sites," you'll get a number of interesting hits. For example, the site Career Builder is a professional, current site that lists jobs by type and by geographical location. Another site with a simple interface is Wow Jobs. You may also, in Google, try a more specific search, such as "Hospitality Jobs Canada." The first hit is Hcareers (**www.hcareers.ca**), a reputable employment site exclusively targeted to jobs in the hospitality, tourism, and leisure industry. From this site you can also link to job boards in the public service, federally and provincially.

BEYOND THE BIG EMPLOYMENT SITES. As the source-of-hire study cited above shows, savvy candidates also know how to use the Internet to search for jobs at Web sites such as the following:

- **Corporate/Organization Web sites.** Next to internal referrals, probably the best way to find a job online is at a company's own Web site. Usually jobs are found at a link with the name "Employment" or "Jobs" or "Work for us." One poll found that 70 percent of job seekers felt they were more likely to obtain an interview if they posted their résumés on corporate sites. In addition to finding a more direct route to decision makers, job seekers thought that they could keep their job searches more private at corporate Web sites than at big job board sites.[6]
- **Association Web sites.** Online job listings have proved to be the single most popular feature of many professional organizations such as the Canadian Apparel Federation. If you go to the association's Web site at **www.apparel.ca** you'll see that one of the six squares on the home page is the job board. Clicking on this link takes you to a job board with positions in apparel (clothing) companies across the country. Even if you have no interest in a career in apparel, why not try a search for your geographical area and see what jobs exist? You may be surprised. To find a list of the many trade associations in Canada, go to the Government of Canada's site on this topic, at **www.ic.gc.ca/eic /site/ccc_bt-rec_ec.nsf/eng/h_00001.html**. Sometimes job boards at association Web sites are open only to fee-paying members, and you'll have to decide whether it's a good idea to join your target association, perhaps as a student member.
- **Professional networking sites.** Perhaps you use Twitter or Facebook to chat with friends. However, users are increasingly tapping into social networking sites to prospect for jobs. Facebook and other sites have started professional offshoots. LinkedIn boasts more than 13 million active users, but smaller sites, such as by-invitation-only Doostang, may have an edge in specialized fields.[7] Finally, international networking sites—Chinese Wealink and German Xing—can help candidates who seek a global reach.

Thousands of employment sites listing millions of jobs now flood the Internet. The sobering reality, however, is that landing a job still depends largely on personal contacts. Stanford University sociologist Mark Granovetter found that 70 percent of jobs are discovered through networking.[8] One employment expert believes that overreliance on technology may have made job seekers lazy: "At the end of the day, the job hunt is largely about people and it is about networking—looking at who you know and where they work."[9] Job-search consultant Debra Feldman concurs: "More important than what you know is who knows what you know. Make sure you are on the radar of people who have access to the kind of job leads you want."[10]

Using Traditional Job Search Techniques

Finding your ideal job requires an early start and a determined effort. Whether you use traditional or online job search techniques, you should be prepared to launch an aggressive campaign. And you can't start too early. Students are told early on that a degree or diploma alone doesn't guarantee a good job. They are cautioned that final grades make a difference to employers, as does proficiency in "soft skills" like customer service,

> Job prospects may be more promising at the Web sites of corporations, professional associations, employers' organizations, niche fields, and, most recently, professional networking sites.

> A traditional job search campaign might include checking classified ads and announcements in professional publications, contacting companies, and developing a network of contacts.

teamwork, and communication. And they are advised of the importance of experience and networking. Here are some traditional steps that job candidates can take:

- **Contact companies in which you're interested, even if you know of no current opening.** Write an unsolicited e-mail or letter and include your résumé. Follow up with a phone call. Check the company's Web site for employment possibilities and procedures.
- **Sign up for school interviews with visiting company representatives.** Campus recruiters may open your eyes to exciting jobs and locations.
- **Attend career fairs.** Job fairs are invaluable in your quest to learn about specific companies and your future career options. Recruiters say that the more you know about the company and its representatives, the more comfortable you will be in an interview.[11]
- **Ask for advice from your instructors.** They often have contacts and ideas for expanding your job search.
- **Develop your own network of contacts.** Networking still accounts for most of the jobs found by candidates. Therefore, plan to spend a considerable portion of your job search time developing a personal network, including online through LinkedIn, but also in person by meeting people and talking to them. The Communication Workshop at the end of this chapter provides hints about how to network effectively.
- **Look at classified ads in local and national newspapers.** Although traditional paper-based job ads are a rapidly disappearing category, they are still there. But be aware that classified ads are only one small source of jobs. Nearly two-thirds of all jobs, representing the "hidden" job market, are unadvertised. These days, paper-based job ads are more apt to give you ideas about companies, jobs, and requirements than to actually landing you an interview.
- **Check announcements in publications of professional organizations.** If you do not have a student membership, ask your professors to share (or a librarian to locate) current copies of professional journals, newsletters, and so on. Also, find the Web site of the professional organization you'd like to eventually join and see if there are job listings on it.

Creating a Persuasive Résumé

After reviewing traditional and online employment ads, you will focus on writing a persuasive résumé. Such a résumé does more than merely list your qualifications; it packages your assets into a convincing advertisement that sells you for a specific job. The goal of a persuasive résumé is getting an interview. Even if you are not in the job market at this moment, preparing a résumé now has advantages. Having a current résumé makes you look well organized and professional should an unexpected employment opportunity arise. Moreover, preparing a résumé early can help you recognize weak areas and give you time to bolster your credentials.

Choose a Résumé Style

Your qualifications and career goal will help you choose between three basic résumé styles: chronological, functional, or combination chronological/functional.

CHRONOLOGICAL. Most popular with recruiters is the chronological résumé, shown in Figure 12.7 (p. 390). It lists work history job by job, starting with the most recent position (i.e., starting in the present and working back to older jobs). Recruiters are familiar with the chronological résumé, and as many as three-quarters of them prefer to see a candidate's résumé in this format.[12] The chronological style works well for candidates who have experience in their field of employment and for those who show steady career growth. It's also the most honest form: it clearly shows what your work experience includes. Some students or recent immigrants who lack extensive experience may want to try the functional format, which is described below.

> Chronological résumés focus on past employment; functional résumés focus on skills.

FUNCTIONAL. The functional résumé, shown in Figure 12.8 (p. 391), focuses attention on a candidate's skills rather than on past employment. Like a chronological résumé, the functional résumé begins with the candidate's name, address, telephone number, job objective, and education. Instead of listing jobs, though, the functional résumé lists skills and accomplishments, such as *Supervisory and Management Skills* or *Retail and Customer Service Experience*. This résumé style highlights accomplishments and can de-emphasize a negative or negligible employment history. People who have changed jobs frequently or who have gaps in their employment history (in addition to the students and immigrants mentioned above) may prefer the functional résumé. Be aware, though, that online employment sites may insist on chronological format. In addition, some recruiters may be suspicious of functional résumés, thinking the candidate is hiding something.

Although the functional résumé of Kevin Touhy shown in Figure 12.8 concentrates on skills, it does include a short employment section because he recognizes that recruiters expect it. Notice that Kevin breaks his skills into three categories. An easier method is to make one large list, perhaps with a title such as *Areas of Accomplishment*, *Summary of Qualifications*, or *Areas of Expertise and Ability*.

COMBINATION. A third style of résumé, shown in Figure 12.9 (p. 392), combines the main two types just described. In a combination résumé, you begin with your skills as you would in a functional résumé, and follow this up with the employment history that's typical of a chronological résumé. The trick with the combination style is recognizing that many human resources and hiring managers have gone on record stating they won't look at a résumé that's more than two pages long. A word of caution, then, that when choosing the combination method, you'll need to be brief as well as make smart use of graphic highlighting techniques (e.g., headings, spacing, bullets, numbering) in your descriptions.

Decide on Length

Conventional wisdom has always held that recruiters prefer one-page résumés. A controlled study of 570 recruiters, however, revealed that while they *claimed* they preferred one-page résumés, they actually *chose* to interview the applicants with two-page résumés.[13] Recruiters who are serious about candidates often prefer a fuller picture with the kind of details that can be provided in a two-page résumé. On the other hand, recruiters are extremely busy, and concise résumés help speed up their work.

> Recruiters may say they prefer one-page résumés, but many choose to interview those with longer résumés.

Perhaps the best advice is to make your résumé as long as needed to sell your skills to recruiters and hiring managers. Individuals with more experience will naturally have longer résumés. Those with fewer than ten years of experience, those making a major career change, and those who have had only one or two employers will likely have a one-page résumé. Finally, some senior-level managers and executives with a lengthy history of major accomplishments might have a résumé that is three pages or longer.[14] A recent survey by a global staffing firm found that 61 percent of hiring managers now prefer to receive two-page résumés from experienced candidates for management jobs; 31 percent stated that they would accept three pages. Even applicants for low-level staff jobs may opt for two pages, 44 percent of recruiters said.[15]

Arrange the Parts

> The parts of résumés should be arranged with the most important qualifications first.

A customized résumé emphasizes skills and achievements aimed at a particular job or company. It shows a candidate's most important qualifications first, and it de-emphasizes any weaknesses. In arranging your information and qualifications, try to create as few headings as possible; more than six generally looks cluttered. No two résumés are ever exactly alike, but many job applicants include all or some of these items: main heading, career objective, summary of qualifications, education, experience, capabilities and skills, awards and activities, personal information, and references.

MAIN HEADING. Keep the main heading of your résumé, whether chronological or functional, as uncluttered and simple as possible. (Don't include the word résumé; it's like putting the word e-mail in the subject line of an e-mail; i.e., it's redundant.) Begin with your name, adding your middle initial for a professional look, and formatting it so that it stands out on the page. Following your name, list your contact information, including your complete address, area code and phone number (voice-mail enabled), and e-mail address. Some people today are adding links to their LinkedIn page or to a video resume they've posted on a site like YouTube. If you do this, make sure these links lead to professional-looking and professional-sounding sites.

The recorded message at the phone number you list should be in your voice, mention your full name, and be concise and professional (e.g., "Thanks for your call. You've reached Casey Jepson. Please leave a message after the beep. I'll reply shortly."). If you are expecting an important recruiting call on your cellphone, pick up only when you are in a quiet environment and can concentrate.

Make sure your e-mail address sounds professional instead of something like *1foxylady@yahoo.com* or *hotdaddy@hotmail.com*. Also be sure that you are using a personal e-mail address. Putting your work e-mail address on your résumé announces to prospective employers that you are using your current employer's resources to look for another job. See Figure 12.7 (p. 390) for an example of an effective main heading.

CAREER OBJECTIVE. Recruiters claim that career objective statements can indicate that a candidate has made a commitment to a career and is sure about what he or she wants to do. Career objectives, of course, make the recruiter's life easier by quickly classifying the résumé. But such declarations may also disqualify a candidate if the stated objective doesn't match a company's job description.[16] A well-written objective customized for the job opening can add value to a chronological or functional résumé.

> Career objectives are most appropriate for specific, targeted positions, but they may limit a broader job search.

A person applying for an auditor position might include the following objective: *Seeking an auditor position in an internal corporate accounting department where my accounting skills, computer experience, knowledge of GAAP, and attention to detail will help the company run efficiently and ensure that its records are kept accurately.*

Your objective should also focus on the employer's needs. Therefore, it should be written from the employer's perspective, not your own. Focus on how you can contribute to the organization, not on what the organization can do for you. A typical self-serving objective is *To obtain a meaningful and rewarding position that enables me to learn more about the graphic design field and allows for advancement.* Instead, show how you will add value to the organization with an objective such as *Position with advertising firm designing Web sites, publications, logos, and promotional displays for clients, where creativity, software knowledge, and proven communication skills can be used to build client base and expand operations.*

Also be careful that your career objective doesn't downplay your talents. For example, some consultants warn against using the words *entry level* in your objective, as they emphasize lack of experience or show poor self-confidence. Finally, your objective should be concise. Try to limit your objective to no more than two or three lines. Avoid using complete sentences and the pronoun "I." A good example of a career objective can be found in Figure 12.9 (p. 392).

If you choose to omit the career objective, be sure to discuss your objectives and goals in your cover letter. Savvy job seekers are also incorporating their objectives into a summary of qualifications, which is discussed next.

SUMMARY OF QUALIFICATIONS. "The biggest change in résumés over the last decade has been a switch from an objective to a summary at the top," says career expert Wendy Enelow.[17] Recruiters are busy, and smart job seekers add a summary of qualifications to their résumés to save the time of recruiters and hiring managers. Once a job is advertised, a hiring manager may get hundreds or even thousands of résumés in response. A summary at the top of your résumé makes it easier to read and ensures that your most impressive qualifications are not overlooked by a recruiter, who may be skimming résumés quickly. A well-written summary motivates the recruiter to read further.

> A Summary of Qualifications section lists your most impressive accomplishments and qualifications in one concise bulleted list.

A summary of qualifications will include three to eight bulleted statements that prove you are the ideal candidate for the position. When formulating these statements, consider your experience in the field, your education, your unique skills, awards you have won, certifications, and any other accomplishments that you want to highlight. Include quantifiable accomplishments wherever possible (e.g., *Over five years' experience in ...*). Target the most important qualifications an employer will be looking for in the person hired for this position. Examples of summaries of qualifications appear in Figures 12.7 (p. 390) and 12.9 (p. 392).

EDUCATION. The next component in a chronological résumé is your education—if it is more noteworthy than your work experience. In this section you should include the name and location of schools, dates of attendance, major fields of study, and certifications received (e.g., diplomas, degrees). By the way, once you have attended college, you don't need to list high-school information on your résumé.

> The education section shows degrees and grades but does not list all courses a job applicant has taken.

Your grades and/or class ranking may be important to prospective employers. Sixty-six percent of employers screen candidates by GPA (grade point average), a recent survey found, and 58 percent of survey respondents stated that they would be less likely to hire candidates with GPAs below 3.0. One way to enhance your GPA is to calculate it in your major courses only (for example, *3.6/4.0 in major*). It is not unethical to showcase your GPA in your major—as long as you clearly indicate what you are doing. Although some hiring managers may think that applicants are hiding something if they omit a poor record of grades, consultant Terese Corey Blanck suggests leaving out a poor GPA. Instead, she advises that students try to excel in internships, show extracurricular leadership, and target smaller, lesser-known companies to offset low grades.[18]

Under "Education" you might be tempted to list all the courses you took, but such a list makes for very dull reading. Refer to courses only if you can relate them to the position sought. When relevant, include certificates earned, seminars attended, workshops completed, and honours earned. If your education is incomplete, include such statements as *B.S. degree expected May 2015* or *80 units completed in 120-unit program*. Title this section *Education, Academic Preparation,* or *Professional Training*. If you are preparing a functional résumé, you will probably put the education section below your skills summaries, as Kevin Touhy has done in Figure 12.8 (p. 391).

WORK EXPERIENCE OR EMPLOYMENT HISTORY. If your work experience is significant and relevant to the position sought, this information should appear before your education information. List your most recent employment first and work backwards, including only those jobs that you think will help you win the targeted position. A job application form may demand a full employment history, but your résumé may be selective. Be aware, though, that time gaps in your employment history will probably be questioned in the interview. For each position show the following:

> The work experience section of a résumé should list specifics and quantify achievements.

- Employer's name, city/town, and province
- Dates of employment (month and year)
- Most important job title
- Significant duties, activities, accomplishments, and promotions

Describe your employment achievements concisely but concretely to make what résumé consultants call "a strong value proposition."[19] Avoid generalities such as *Worked with customers*. Be more specific, with statements such as *Served 40 or more retail customers a day*; *Successfully resolved problems about custom stationery orders*; or *Acted as intermediary among customers, printers, and suppliers*. If possible, quantify your accomplishments, such as *Conducted study of equipment needs of 100 small businesses in Hamilton, ON*; *Personally generated orders for sales of $90,000 annually*; or *Keyed all the production models for a 250-page employee procedures manual*. One professional recruiter said, "I spend a half hour every day screening 50 résumés or more, and if I don't spot some [quantifiable] results in the first 10 seconds, the résumé is history."[20]

FIGURE 12.4 Sample Action Verbs to Strengthen a Résumé

accelerated	enabled	introduced	reviewed
achieved	encouraged	managed	revitalized
analyzed	engineered	organized	screened
collaborated	established	originated	served
conceptualized	expanded	overhauled	spearheaded
constructed	expedited	pioneered	spurred
converted	facilitated	reduced	strengthened
designed	grew	resolved	targeted
directed	increased	restructured	transformed

Your employment achievements and job duties will be easier to read if you place them in a bulleted list. When writing these bullet points, don't try to list every single thing you have done on the job; instead, customize your information so that it relates to the target job. Make sure your list of job duties shows what you have to contribute and how you are qualified for the position you are applying for. Do not make your bullet points complete sentences, and avoid using personal pronouns (*I*, *me*, *my*) in them. If you have performed a lot of the same duties for multiple employers, you don't have to repeat them.

In addition to technical skills, employers seek individuals with developed soft skills. This means you will want to select work experiences and achievements that illustrate your initiative, dependability, responsibility, resourcefulness, flexibility, creativity, leadership, and interpersonal communication strengths. One soft skills employers repeatedly ask for is people who can work together in teams. Therefore, include statements like *Collaborated with interdepartmental task force in developing ten page handbook for temporary workers* and *Headed student government team that conducted most successful voter registration in campus history*.

Statements describing your work experience can be made forceful and persuasive by using action verbs, such as those listed in Figure 12.4 and illustrated in Figure 12.5. Starting each of your bullet points with an action verb will help ensure that your bulleted lists are parallel.

FIGURE 12.5 Use Action Verbs to Quantify Achievements

Identified weaknesses in internships and **researched** five alternate programs accelerated

Reduced delivery delays by an average of three days per order

Streamlined filing system, thus reducing 400-item backlog to zero

Organized holiday awards program for 1,200 attendees and 140 workers

Designed customer feedback form for company Web site

Represented 2,500 students on committee involving university policies and procedures

Calculated shipping charges for overseas deliveries and **recommended** most economical rates

Managed 24-station computer network linking data in three departments

Distributed and **explained** voter registration forms to over 500 prospective voters

Praised by top management for enthusiastic teamwork and achievement

Secured national recognition from Tree Canada for tree project

CAPABILITIES AND SKILLS. Recruiters want to know specifically what you can do for their companies. Therefore, list your skills, such as *Proficient in preparing federal, state, and local payroll tax returns as well as franchise and personal property tax returns*. Include any special ability you have with the Internet, mobile apps, software programs, office equipment, and communication technology tools. If you can speak a foreign language or use sign language, include it on your résumé. Describe proficiencies you have acquired through training and experience, such as *Certified in computer graphics and Web design through an intensive 350-hour classroom program*. Use expressions such as *competent in, skilled in, proficient with, experienced in,* and *ability to;* for example, *Competent in writing, editing, and proofreading reports, tables, letters, memos, manuscripts, and business forms.*

You will also want to highlight exceptional aptitudes, such as working well under stress, learning computer programs quickly, and interacting with customers. If possible, provide details and evidence that back up your assertions; for example, *Led Conflict Resolution workshop through staff development department on 10 occasions for over 200 employees*. Search for examples of your writing, speaking, management, organizational, and interpersonal skills—particularly those talents that are relevant to your targeted job. For recent graduates, this section can be used to give recruiters evidence of your potential. Instead of *Capabilities*, the section might be called *Skills and Abilities*.

Those job hunters preparing a functional résumé will place more focus on skills than on any other section. A well-written functional résumé groups skills into categories such as *Accounting/Finance Skills, Management/Leadership Skills, Communication/Teamwork Skills,* and *Computer/Technology Skills*. Each skills category includes a bulleted list of achievements and experience that demonstrate the skill, including specific quantifiable amounts (e.g., *20 seminars*) whenever possible. These skills categories should be placed at the beginning of the résumé where they will be highlighted, followed by education and work experience. The action verbs shown in Figures 12.4 and 12.5 can also be used when constructing a functional résumé.

AWARDS, HONOURS, AND ACTIVITIES. If you have three or more awards or honours, highlight them by listing them under a separate heading. If not, put them with *Activities* or in the *Education* or *Work Experience* section if appropriate. Include awards, scholarships (financial and other), fellowships, dean's list, sports or other team affiliations, and so on. Instead of saying *Recipient of King Scholarship*, give more details: *Recipient of King Scholarship given by Macdonald College to outstanding graduates who combine academic excellence and extracurricular activities.*

It is also appropriate to include school, community, volunteer, and professional activities. Employers are interested in evidence that you are a well-rounded person. This section provides an opportunity to demonstrate leadership and interpersonal skills. Strive to use specific action statements. For example, instead of saying *Treasurer of business club*, explain more fully: *Collected dues, kept financial records, and paid bills while serving as treasurer of 35-member business management club.*

PERSONAL DATA. Today's résumés omit personal data, such as birth date, marital status, height, weight, national origin, health, and religious affiliation. Such information doesn't relate to genuine occupational qualifications, and recruiters are legally barred from asking for such information. Some job seekers do, however, include hobbies or interests (such as skiing or photography) that might grab the recruiter's attention or serve as conversation starters. You could also indicate your willingness to travel or to relocate, since many companies will be interested.

FIGURE **12.6** Sample Reference List

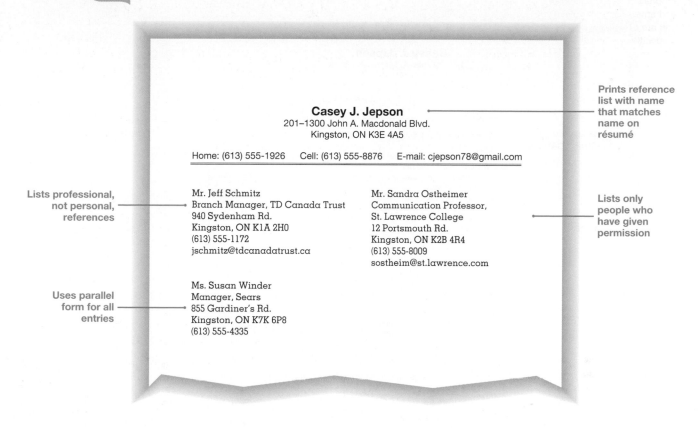

Casey J. Jepson
201–1300 John A. Macdonald Blvd.
Kingston, ON K3E 4A5

Home: (613) 555-1926   Cell: (613) 555-8876   E-mail: cjepson78@gmail.com

Prints reference list with name that matches name on résumé

Mr. Jeff Schmitz
Branch Manager, TD Canada Trust
940 Sydenham Rd.
Kingston, ON K1A 2H0
(613) 555-1172
jschmitz@tdcanadatrust.ca

Mr. Sandra Ostheimer
Communication Professor,
St. Lawrence College
12 Portsmouth Rd.
Kingston, ON K2B 4R4
(613) 555-8009
sostheim@st.lawrence.com

Ms. Susan Winder
Manager, Sears
855 Gardiner's Rd.
Kingston, ON K7K 6P8
(613) 555-4335

Lists professional, not personal, references

Uses parallel form for all entries

Lists only people who have given permission

REFERENCES. Listing references directly on a résumé takes up valuable space. Moreover, references are not normally instrumental in securing an interview—most companies don't check them until after the interview. Instead, recruiters prefer that you bring to the interview a list of individuals willing to discuss your qualifications. Therefore, you should prepare a separate list, such as that in Figure 12.6, when you begin your job search. Ask three of your professors, your current employer or previous employers, colleagues or subordinates, or other professional contacts whether they would be willing to answer inquiries regarding your qualifications for employment. Be sure, however, to provide them with an opportunity to refuse. No reference at all is better than a negative one. Better yet, to avoid rejection and embarrassment, ask only those contacts who you can be sure will give you a glowing endorsement.

> References are unnecessary for the résumé, but they should be available for the interview.

Do not include personal references, such as friends, family, or neighbours, because recruiters will rarely consult them. Companies are more interested in the opinions of objective individuals who know how you perform professionally and academically. One final note: most recruiters see little reason for including the statement *References available upon request* at the end of your résumé. It is unnecessary and takes up precious space.

In Figures 12.7 through 12.9, you will find three models corresponding to the three main resume types: chronological, functional, and combination. Notice as you study the models that the chronological résumé (Figure 12.7) is for a current student with only one type of experience; the functional résumé (Figure 12.8) is for a recent graduate with largely unrelated work experience; and the third combination-style résumé (Figure 12.9) is for a graduate with significant related experience following her postsecondary education. Use the appropriate model to help you organize the content and format of your own persuasive résumé.

FIGURE **12.7** Chronological Résumé: Current Student

Casey J. Jepson
201–1300 John A. Macdonald Blvd.
Kingston, ON K3E 4A5

E-mail: cjepson82@gmail.com
Phone: 613–555-8876   http://www.youtube.com/watch?v=a2L8DHECtNj   •—— Casey has posted a video resume on YouTube

SUMMARY OF QUALIFICATIONS	• Over two years' experience in customer service positions in major organizations • Excellent customer service skills including oral communication, listening, and written communication • Proven teamwork and interpersonal skills including leadership, cooperation, and on-time delivery • Mastery of computer skills (MOS certification) • Strengths in research, proofreading, coaching, and math
EXPERIENCE	Customer Service Representative, Co-op placement St. Lawrence College, Kingston, ON September 2015 – present • Provide friendly, helpful service via face–to–face, phone, e-mail, and messaging channels at a large urban college • File weekly incident/outlier reports • Work effectively in team of 15–20 co-op students and fulltime CSRs Front Desk Representative, part-time TD Canada Trust, Kingston, ON May 2013–June 2014 • Provide friendly, helpful face–to–face service at busy urban bank branch • Replace lost and stolen credit and debit cards for clients • Liaise with branch manager and tellers to increase branch profitability Customer Associate, part-time Sears, Kingston, ON May 2012–June 2012; December 2012 • Manage busy cash desk in women's clothing department • Provide friendly, helpful face–to–face answers to customer queries
EDUCATION	St. Lawrence College, Kingston, ON Major: Retail Management Advanced Diploma Graduation expected June 2016 Current average: A-
ACTIVITIES AND AWARDS	• Member of St. Lawrence Enactus team • Nominated for SLC Ambassador Award (recognizes outstanding students for excellence in and out of classroom) • Volunteer leader at annual student orientation (2014 & 2015)

Using LinkedIn and Video to Bolster the Traditional Résumé

Professional recruiters are increasingly interested in candidates whose job application is supported by multimedia. A profile on the social media site LinkedIn, and a video version of a cover letter uploaded to your personal channel on YouTube, for example, are two ways of adding a multimedia facet to your job application.

LinkedIn: The "Professional" Social Media Site

In the past decade, the task of searching for a job and of recruiting people into jobs has changed radically with the arrival of the social media site LinkedIn. The article by Jenny Lee at the beginning of this chapter discusses this reality in more

Recent graduate Kevin Touhy chose this functional format to de-emphasize his meagre work experience and emphasize his potential in sales and marketing. This version of his résumé is more generic than one targeted for a specific position. Nevertheless, it emphasizes his strong points with specific achievements and includes an employment section to satisfy recruiters. The functional format presents ability-focused topics. It illustrates what the job seeker can do for the employer instead of narrating a history of previous jobs. Although recruiters prefer chronological résumés, the functional format is a good choice for new graduates, career changers, and those with employment gaps.

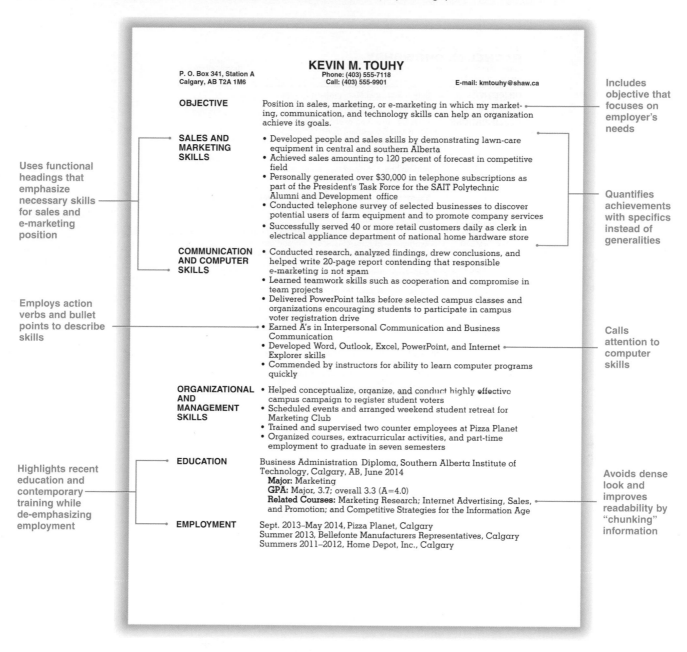

Uses functional headings that emphasize necessary skills for sales and e-marketing position

Employs action verbs and bullet points to describe skills

Highlights recent education and contemporary training while de-emphasizing employment

KEVIN M. TOUHY

P. O. Box 341, Station A
Calgary, AB T2A 1M6

Phone: (403) 555-7118
Call: (403) 555-9901

E-mail: kmtouhy@shaw.ca

OBJECTIVE
Position in sales, marketing, or e-marketing in which my marketing, communication, and technology skills can help an organization achieve its goals.

SALES AND MARKETING SKILLS
- Developed people and sales skills by demonstrating lawn-care equipment in central and southern Alberta
- Achieved sales amounting to 120 percent of forecast in competitive field
- Personally generated over $30,000 in telephone subscriptions as part of the President's Task Force for the SAIT Polytechnic Alumni and Development office
- Conducted telephone survey of selected businesses to discover potential users of farm equipment and to promote company services
- Successfully served 40 or more retail customers daily as clerk in electrical appliance department of national home hardware store

COMMUNICATION AND COMPUTER SKILLS
- Conducted research, analyzed findings, drew conclusions, and helped write 20-page report contending that responsible e-marketing is not spam
- Learned teamwork skills such as cooperation and compromise in team projects
- Delivered PowerPoint talks before selected campus classes and organizations encouraging students to participate in campus voter registration drive
- Earned A's in Interpersonal Communication and Business Communication
- Developed Word, Outlook, Excel, PowerPoint, and Internet Explorer skills
- Commended by instructors for ability to learn computer programs quickly

ORGANIZATIONAL AND MANAGEMENT SKILLS
- Helped conceptualize, organize, and conduct highly effective campus campaign to register student voters
- Scheduled events and arranged weekend student retreat for Marketing Club
- Trained and supervised two counter employees at Pizza Planet
- Organized courses, extracurricular activities, and part-time employment to graduate in seven semesters

EDUCATION
Business Administration Diploma, Southern Alberta Institute of Technology, Calgary, AB, June 2014
Major: Marketing
GPA: Major, 3.7; overall 3.3 (A=4.0)
Related Courses: Marketing Research; Internet Advertising, Sales, and Promotion; and Competitive Strategies for the Information Age

EMPLOYMENT
Sept. 2013–May 2014, Pizza Planet, Calgary
Summer 2013, Bellefonte Manufacturers Representatives, Calgary
Summers 2011–2012, Home Depot, Inc., Calgary

Includes objective that focuses on employer's needs

Quantifies achievements with specifics instead of generalities

Calls attention to computer skills

Avoids dense look and improves readability by "chunking" information

detail. The traditional methods of posting jobs discussed earlier in this chapter (e.g., classified ads in newspapers, Internet job sites) are still important resources. However, if you Google "LinkedIn popularity recruiters," you'll find numerous media articles proclaiming that LinkedIn is in fact becoming indispensable in recruiting. What this means to you as a college or university student is that, if you haven't done so already, you need to become aware of this new platform for finding jobs. In fact, at a recent workshop the social media manager from Monster.ca proclaimed that within a year,

Because Rachel has many years of experience and seeks executive-level employment, she highlighted her experience by placing it before her education. Her summary of qualifications highlighted her most impressive experience and skills. This chronological two-page résumé shows the steady progression of her career to executive positions, a movement that impresses and reassures recruiters.

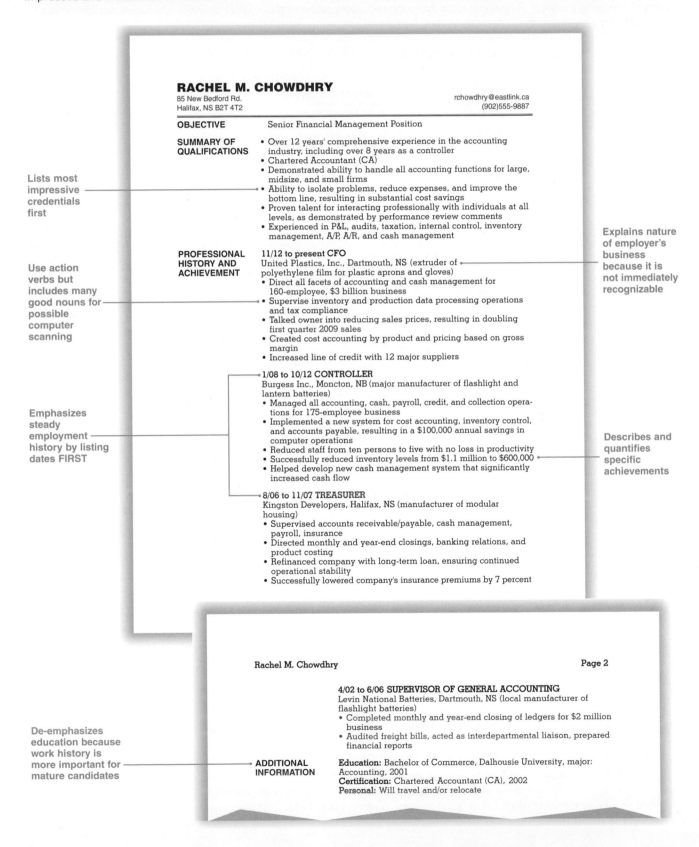

RACHEL M. CHOWDHRY
85 New Bedford Rd.
Halifax, NS B2T 4T2

rchowdhry@eastlink.ca
(902)555-9887

OBJECTIVE — Senior Financial Management Position

SUMMARY OF QUALIFICATIONS
- Over 12 years' comprehensive experience in the accounting industry, including over 8 years as a controller
- Chartered Accountant (CA)
- Demonstrated ability to handle all accounting functions for large, midsize, and small firms
- Ability to isolate problems, reduce expenses, and improve the bottom line, resulting in substantial cost savings
- Proven talent for interacting professionally with individuals at all levels, as demonstrated by performance review comments
- Experienced in P&L, audits, taxation, internal control, inventory management, A/P, A/R, and cash management

Lists most impressive credentials first

PROFESSIONAL HISTORY AND ACHIEVEMENT

11/12 to present CFO
United Plastics, Inc., Dartmouth, NS (extruder of polyethylene film for plastic aprons and gloves)
- Direct all facets of accounting and cash management for 160-employee, $3 billion business
- Supervise inventory and production data processing operations and tax compliance
- Talked owner into reducing sales prices, resulting in doubling first quarter 2009 sales
- Created cost accounting by product and pricing based on gross margin
- Increased line of credit with 12 major suppliers

Use action verbs but includes many good nouns for possible computer scanning

Explains nature of employer's business because it is not immediately recognizable

1/08 to 10/12 CONTROLLER
Burgess Inc., Moncton, NB (major manufacturer of flashlight and lantern batteries)
- Managed all accounting, cash, payroll, credit, and collection operations for 175-employee business
- Implemented a new system for cost accounting, inventory control, and accounts payable, resulting in a $100,000 annual savings in computer operations
- Reduced staff from ten persons to five with no loss in productivity
- Successfully reduced inventory levels from $1.1 million to $600,000
- Helped develop new cash management system that significantly increased cash flow

Emphasizes steady employment history by listing dates FIRST

Describes and quantifies specific achievements

8/06 to 11/07 TREASURER
Kingston Developers, Halifax, NS (manufacturer of modular housing)
- Supervised accounts receivable/payable, cash management, payroll, insurance
- Directed monthly and year-end closings, banking relations, and product costing
- Refinanced company with long-term loan, ensuring continued operational stability
- Successfully lowered company's insurance premiums by 7 percent

Rachel M. Chowdhry

Page 2

4/02 to 6/06 SUPERVISOR OF GENERAL ACCOUNTING
Levin National Batteries, Dartmouth, NS (local manufacturer of flashlight batteries)
- Completed monthly and year-end closing of ledgers for $2 million business
- Audited freight bills, acted as interdepartmental liaison, prepared financial reports

De-emphasizes education because work history is more important for mature candidates

ADDITIONAL INFORMATION
Education: Bachelor of Commerce, Dalhousie University, major: Accounting, 2001
Certification: Chartered Accountant (CA), 2002
Personal: Will travel and/or relocate

FIGURE 12.10 LinkedIn Sign-up Page

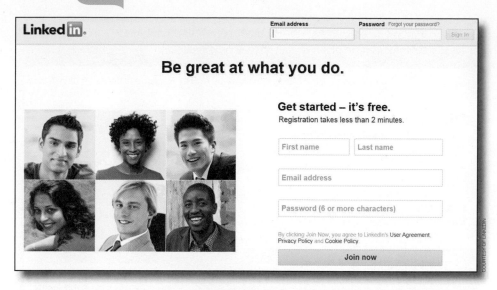

two Canadian banks would be moving to recruiting all their employees *only* from LinkedIn.[21]

Clearly, LinkedIn is a social media site you can no longer ignore. Even if you have an active Facebook account, you'll need to create an account on LinkedIn if you want to be taken seriously in the new world of recruiting. This is because while employers may check your Facebook site to make sure you're not posting damaging, embarrassing, or poorly chosen material, they won't hire you because of it. On the other hand, a fantastic LinkedIn site may get you a job.[22] In other words, in the world of social media, Facebook is considered a "personal" social media site while LinkedIn is considered the "professional" social media site. So how does it work?

Once you sign up for a free account on LinkedIn (see Figure 12.10 for a screen capture of what the sign-up page looks like), you will be prompted to begin creating your LinkedIn profile. Like the traditional résumé discussed earlier in this chapter, this profile tells the world who you are, what you've done, and what you're good at. However, it does one more thing that a résumé can't: it tells others who you know and who knows you—this is the social media difference.

A traditional résumé is only effective once it's been e-mailed or sent to a recruiter. Once you've created your LinkedIn profile, however, the site itself does a lot of work for you. It allows you to be Googled and found; and it allows the people you are "connected" with or who have been "added to your network" (this is LinkedIn vocabulary) to look at your profile, to comment on it, and to potentially search you out as a possible new employee. In addition, having an active LinkedIn profile with the right keywords (e.g., *creative*, *innovative*) and experience can draw the attention of professional recruiters. A screen capture of Richard Almonte's public LinkedIn profile is shown in Figure 12.11, or you can view it at **www.linkedin.com/pub/ richard-almonte/4b/961/b37**.

As you can see from Richard's LinkedIn profile, like a traditional résumé, the profile has a number of standard elements that you fill in when you create an account.

- **A personalized heading.** Include your picture, your name, your current job title, and place of employment.
- **A brief summary.** Analogous to the career objective from a traditional résumé, this summary allows you to encapsulate yourself in a few words.
- **Your employment experience.** List the details of your previous jobs and responsibilities as you would in a traditional résumé.

FIGURE **12.11** Typical LinkedIn Public Profile

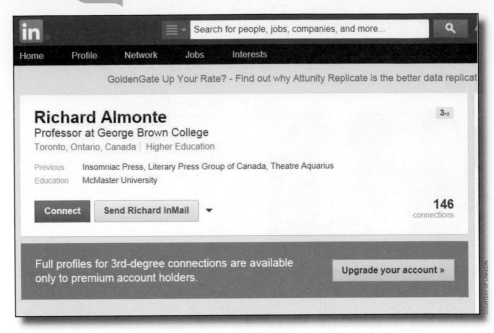

- **Your education experience.** List your completed postsecondary certificates, degrees, or diplomas.
- **Extra details.** Round out your experience by mentioning languages in which you're proficient, publications, projects managed, and personal interests.

A healthy debate rages on the blogosphere about how to make your LinkedIn page useful and visible instead of a dud. If you Google a phrase like "LinkedIn best practices job seeker," you'll find a number of bloggers and writers offering advice about how to craft your profile (including what words to use and who to invite to link with you) to optimize the chances that your profile will get you a job.

> LinkedIn is considered a professional social media site, while Facebook is considered a primarily personal site.

Video Résumés

Another way of bolstering your traditional résumé and cover letter is to upload a video that profiles you and your skills to a site like YouTube or Vimeo. These video-sharing sites allow you to broadcast yourself and are incredibly powerful tools—a well-produced video résumé may open doors and secure an interview where other techniques have failed.[23] However, some recruiters are skeptical about video résumés because they fear that such applications will take more time to view than paper-based résumés do. Moreover, a lack of professionalism when creating video résumés can lead to embarrassment. For example, Aleksey Vayner's video résumé ended up on YouTube in late 2006, causing him to be widely ridiculed. The Yale University student and budding investment banker created a six-minute video titled *Impossible Is Nothing*, showing him lifting weights, ballroom dancing, and playing tennis, all the while engaging in shameless puffery.[24]

People who blog and write about video résumés suggest incorporating a number of best practices. These practices include ensuring excellent video quality; taking advantage of multiple, realistic locations; using effective language; offering something unique from a traditional résumé; editing the sound and lighting so that there are no distractions; limiting video length to between three and five minutes.[25] Also, if you're satisfied with your video résumé, we suggest that you include a link to it in the heading of your traditional résumé, under your e-mail address.

Applying the Final Touches to Your Résumé

Because your résumé is probably one of the most important documents you will ever write, you should revise it many times. With so much information in concentrated form, and with so much riding on its outcome, your résumé demands careful polishing, proofreading, and critiquing.

As you revise, be certain to verify all the facts, particularly those involving your previous employment and education. Don't be caught in a mistake, or worse, a distortion of previous jobs and dates of employment. These items likely will be checked, and the consequences of puffing up a résumé with deception or flat-out lies are simply not worth the risk.

Be Honest and Ethical

A résumé is expected to showcase a candidate's strengths and minimize weaknesses. For this reason, recruiters expect a certain degree of self-promotion. Some résumé writers, however, step over the line that separates honest self-marketing from deceptive half-truths and blatant lies. Distorting facts on a résumé is unethical; lying is illegal. Either practice can destroy a career.

Given the competitive job market, it might be tempting to puff up your résumé. What's more, you wouldn't be alone in telling fibs or outright whoppers. One study found that 44 percent of applicants lied about their work histories, 23 percent fabricated licences or credentials, and 41 percent falsified their educational backgrounds.[26] A more recent U.S. study found a comparable rate of resume fraud of 33 percent.[27]

Although recruiters can't check everything, most will verify previous employment and education before hiring candidates. Over half will require official transcripts. BackCheck, a Canadian background checking company, has performed over 3 million reference checks on prospective employees in Canada and around the world.[28]

After hiring, the checking process may continue. If hiring managers find a discrepancy in grades or prior experience and the error is an honest mistake, they meet with the new hire to hear an explanation. If the discrepancy wasn't a mistake, they will likely fire the person immediately. No job seeker wants to be in the unhappy position of explaining résumé errors or defending misrepresentation. Avoiding the following common problems can keep you off the hot seat:

- **Inflated education, grades, or honours.** Some job candidates claim degrees from colleges or universities when in fact they merely attended classes. Others increase their grade point averages or claim fictitious honours. Any such dishonest reporting is grounds for dismissal when discovered.
- **Enhanced job titles.** Wishing to elevate their status, some applicants misrepresent their titles. For example, one technician called himself a programmer when he had actually programmed only one project for his boss. A customer service representative who assumed added responsibilities conferred upon herself the title of supervisor. Even when the description seems accurate, it is unethical to list any title not officially granted.
- **Puffed-up accomplishments.** Some job seekers inflate their employment experience or achievements. One entry-level employee, eager to make her photocopying duties sound more important, said that she assisted the *vice president in communicating and distributing employee directives*. A university graduate who spent the better part of six months watching movies on his iPhone described the activity as *Independent Film Study*. That statement may have helped win an interview, but it lost him the job. In addition to avoiding puffery, guard against taking sole credit for achievements that required the efforts of many people. When recruiters suspect dubious claims on résumés, they ask applicants specific—and often embarrassing—questions during their interviews.
- **Altered employment dates.** Some candidates extend the dates of employment to hide unimpressive jobs or to cover up periods of unemployment and illness.

> Deception on a résumé, even if discovered much later, can result in firing.

Let's say that several years ago Cindy was unemployed for 14 months between working for Company A and being hired by Company B. To make her employment history look better, she adds seven months to her tenure with Company A and seven months to Company B. Now her employment history has no gaps, but her résumé is dishonest and represents a potential booby trap for her.

- **Hidden keywords.** One of the latest sneaky tricks involves inserting invisible keywords in digital résumé files. To fool scanning programs into ranking their résumés higher, some job hunters use white type on a white background or they use Web coding to pack their résumés with target keywords. However, newer recruiter search tools detect such mischief, and those résumés can be tossed.[29]

If your actual qualifications aren't good enough to get you the job you want, start working now to improve them.

Polishing Your Résumé

While you continue revising, look for other ways to improve your résumé. For example, consider consolidating headings. By condensing your information into as few headings as possible, you will produce a clean, professional-looking document. Study other résumés for valuable formatting ideas. Ask yourself what graphic highlighting techniques you can use to improve readability: capitalization, underlining, indenting, and bulleting. Experiment with headings and styles to achieve a pleasing, easy-to-read message. Moreover, look for ways to eliminate wordiness. For example, instead of *Supervised two employees who worked at the counter*, try *Supervised two counter employees*. Review Chapter 3 for more tips on writing concisely.

In addition to making your résumé concise, make sure that you haven't included any of the following information, which doesn't belong on a résumé:

- Any basis for discrimination (age, marital status, gender, national origin, religion, race, number of children, disability)
- A photograph

Study résumé models for ideas on improving your format.

OFFICE INSIDER

It sounds basic, but make sure that your résumé is free of typos and other errors. When applying by e-mail, there is more of a tendency to rush and make careless mistakes. For many employers, this shows a lack of attention to detail and is an easy way to eliminate someone from consideration.

- Reasons for leaving previous jobs
- The word "résumé"
- Social insurance number
- Salary history or requirements
- High-school information
- References
- Full addresses of schools or employers (include city and province only)

Above all, make sure your résumé look professional. Avoid anything humorous or "cute," such as a help-wanted poster with your name or picture inside. Eliminate the personal pronoun "I" to ensure an objective style. If printing out your résumé to hand in in person, use a laser printer.

Proofreading Your Résumé

After revising, you must proofread, proofread, and proofread again for spelling, mechanics, content, and format. Then have a knowledgeable friend or relative proofread it yet again. This is one document that must be perfect. Because the job market is so competitive, one typo, misspelled word, or grammatical error could eliminate you from consideration.

By now you may be thinking that you'd like to hire someone to write your résumé. Don't! First, you know yourself better than anyone else. Second, you will end up with a generic or a one-time résumé. A generic résumé in today's highly competitive job market will lose out to a customized résumé nine times out of ten. Equally useless is a one-time résumé aimed at a single job. What if you don't get that job? Because you will need to revise your résumé many times as you seek a variety of jobs, be prepared to write (and rewrite) it yourself.

> In addition to being well written, a résumé must be carefully formatted and meticulously proofread.

Submitting Your Résumé

If you are responding to a job posting on a company Web site or a job site like Workopolis.com, be sure to read the listing carefully to make sure you know how the employer wants you to submit your résumé. Not following the prospective employer's instructions can eliminate you from consideration before your résumé is even reviewed. Employers will probably ask you to submit your résumé in one of the following ways:

> Send or post your résumé in the format the employer requests.

- **Word document.** Recruiters will probably ask applicants to attach their résumés as Word documents to an e-mail. Alternatively, you may be asked to upload your Word file directly onto the recruiter's site.
- **PDF document.** For the sake of safety, many hiring managers prefer PDF (portable document format) files. A PDF résumé will look exactly like the original and cannot be easily altered. Save your Word résumé file as a PDF file (check for PDF under Format when you click Save As) and keep it in the same folder as your Word version.
- **Company database.** Some organizations prefer that you complete an online form with your résumé information. This enables them to plug your data into their formats for rapid searching. You might be able to cut and paste your information into the form.
- **Fax.** In rare cases, you may still be asked to fax your résumé. If you must fax your résumé, use at least a 12-point font to improve readability. Thinner fonts—such as Times, Palatino, New Century Schoolbook, Arial, and Bookman—are clearer than thicker ones. Avoid underlines, which may look broken or choppy when faxed.

Whether you are submitting your résumé by e-mail, or uploading it onto a site, don't send it on its own. Regardless of the submission format, in almost all cases a résumé is accompanied by a cover letter, which is discussed in the next section.

The Persuasive Cover Letter

To accompany your résumé, you'll need a persuasive cover letter. The cover letter has three purposes: (1) introducing the résumé, (2) highlighting ways your strengths will benefit the reader, and (3) obtaining an interview. In many ways your cover letter is a sales letter; it sells your talents and tries to beat the competition. It will, accordingly, include many of the techniques you learned for sales letters in Chapter 6.

Human resource professionals disagree on how long to make cover letters. Many prefer short letters with no more than four paragraphs; instead of concentrating on the letter, these readers focus on the résumé. Others desire longer letters that supply more information, thus giving them a better opportunity to evaluate a candidate's qualifications and gauge his or her personality. They argue that hiring and training new employees is expensive and time-consuming; extra data can guide them in making the best choice the first time. Use your judgment; if you feel, for example, that you need space to explain in more detail what you can do for a prospective employer, do so.

Regardless of its length, a cover letter should have three primary parts: (1) an opening that gets attention, (2) a body that builds interest and reduces resistance by explaining why you're the right candidate for the role, and (3) a closing that motivates action.

> Cover letters introduce résumés, relate writer strengths to reader benefits, and seek an interview.

Gaining Attention in the Opening

The first step in gaining the interest of your reader is addressing that individual by name. Rather than sending your letter to the "Human Resources Department," try to obtain the name of the appropriate individual. Make it a rule to call the organization for the correct spelling and the complete address. This personal touch distinguishes your letter and demonstrates your serious interest.

> The opening in a cover letter gets attention by addressing the receiver by name.

How you open your cover letter depends largely on whether your résumé is for a position that is solicited or unsolicited. If an employment position has been announced and applicants are being solicited, you can use a direct approach. If you do not know whether a position is open and you are prospecting for a job, use an indirect approach. Whether direct or indirect, the opening should attract the attention of the reader. Strive for openings that are more imaginative than *I would like to apply for . . . .* Instead, you could say *I'm pleased to submit my application for the X position to which I will be able to bring significant related experience.*

OPENINGS FOR SOLICITED JOBS. Here are some of the best techniques to open a letter of application for a job that has been announced:

- **Refer to the name of an employee in the company.** Remember that employers always hope to hire known quantities rather than complete strangers:
  - Mitchell Sims, a member of your Customer Service Department, told me that DataTech is seeking an experienced customer service representative. The attached summary of my qualifications demonstrates my preparation for this position.
  - At the suggestion of Ms. Claudette Guertin of your Human Resources Department, I submit my qualifications for the position of personnel assistant.
- **Refer to the source of your information precisely.** If you are answering an advertisement, include the exact position advertised and the name and date of the publication. For large organizations it's also wise to mention the section of the newspaper where the ad appeared:
  - Your listing on Workopolis for a junior accountant (competition 15-003) greatly appeals to me. With my accounting training and computer experience, I believe I could serve the City of Richmond well.

> Openings for solicited jobs refer to the source of the information, the job title, and qualifications for the position.

- The September 10 issue of the *National Post* reports that you are seeking a mature, organized, and reliable administrative assistant (position15-A54) with excellent communication skills.
- Susan Butler, placement director at Carleton University, told me that Open Text Corporation has an opening for a technical writer with knowledge of Web design and graphics.
- **Refer to the job title and describe how your qualifications fit the requirements.** Human Resources directors are looking for a match between an applicant's credentials and the job needs:
  - Will an honours graduate with a degree in recreation studies and two years of part-time experience organizing social activities for a retirement community qualify for your position of activity director?
  - Because of my specialized training in accounting at Simon Fraser University, I feel confident that I have the qualifications you described in your advertisement for an accountant trainee.

OPENINGS FOR UNSOLICITED JOBS. If you are unsure whether a position actually exists, you may wish to use a more persuasive opening. Since your goal is to convince this person to read on, try one of the following techniques:

- **Demonstrate interest in and knowledge of the reader's business.** Show the Human Resources director that you have done your research and that this organization is more than a mere name to you:

  > Since the Canadian Automobile Association is organizing a new IT team for its recently established group insurance division, could you use the services of a well-trained information systems graduate who seeks to become a professional underwriter?

- **Show how your special talents and background will benefit the company.** Human Resources directors need to be convinced that you can do something for them:

  > Could your rapidly expanding publications division use the services of an editorial assistant who offers exceptional language skills, an honours degree from Brandon University, and two years' experience in producing a school literary publication?

In applying for an advertised job, Kendra Hawkins wrote the solicited cover letter shown in Figure 12.12. Notice that her opening identifies the position and the newspaper completely so that the reader knows exactly what advertisement Kendra refers to. Using features of Microsoft Word, Kendra designed her own letterhead that uses her name and looks professionally printed.

More challenging are unsolicited letters of application, such as Donald Vinton's, shown in Figure 12.13. Because he's writing a cover letter where no advertised job exists, he is essentially hoping to create a job. For this reason his opening must grab the reader's attention immediately. To do this, he capitalizes on company information appearing in an online news story. Donald purposely keeps his application letter short and to the point because he anticipates that a busy executive will be unwilling to read a long, detailed letter. Donald's unsolicited letter "prospects" for a job. Some job candidates feel that such letters may be even more productive than efforts to secure advertised jobs, since "prospecting" candidates face less competition. Donald's letter uses a standard return address format, placing his name, street, city, province, and postal code above the date.

Building Interest in the Body

Once you have captured the attention of the reader, you can use the body of the letter to build interest and reduce resistance. Keep in mind that your résumé emphasizes

> Openings for unsolicited jobs show interest in and knowledge of the company, as well as spotlighting reader benefits.

> The body of a cover letter should build interest, reduce resistance, and discuss relevant personal traits.

> Spotlighting reader benefits means matching your personal strengths to an employer's needs.

FIGURE **12.12** Solicited Cover Letter

Uses personally designed letterhead

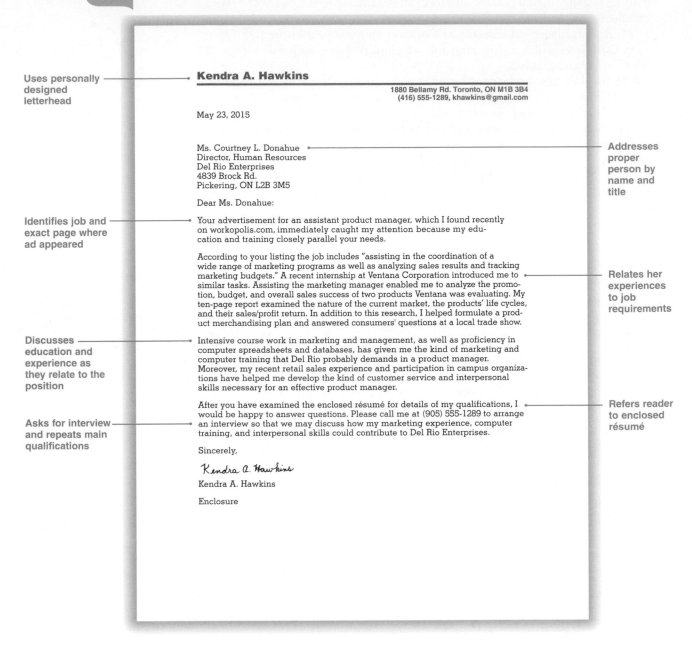

Kendra A. Hawkins

1880 Bellamy Rd. Toronto, ON M1B 3B4
(416) 555-1289, khawkins@gmail.com

May 23, 2015

Ms. Courtney L. Donahue
Director, Human Resources
Del Rio Enterprises
4839 Brock Rd.
Pickering, ON L2B 3M5

Addresses proper person by name and title

Dear Ms. Donahue:

Your advertisement for an assistant product manager, which I found recently on workopolis.com, immediately caught my attention because my education and training closely parallel your needs.

Identifies job and exact page where ad appeared

According to your listing the job includes "assisting in the coordination of a wide range of marketing programs as well as analyzing sales results and tracking marketing budgets." A recent internship at Ventana Corporation introduced me to similar tasks. Assisting the marketing manager enabled me to analyze the promotion, budget, and overall sales success of two products Ventana was evaluating. My ten-page report examined the nature of the current market, the products' life cycles, and their sales/profit return. In addition to this research, I helped formulate a product merchandising plan and answered consumers' questions at a local trade show.

Relates her experiences to job requirements

Discusses education and experience as they relate to the position

Intensive course work in marketing and management, as well as proficiency in computer spreadsheets and databases, has given me the kind of marketing and computer training that Del Rio probably demands in a product manager. Moreover, my recent retail sales experience and participation in campus organizations have helped me develop the kind of customer service and interpersonal skills necessary for an effective product manager.

After you have examined the enclosed résumé for details of my qualifications, I would be happy to answer questions. Please call me at (905) 555-1289 to arrange an interview so that we may discuss how my marketing experience, computer training, and interpersonal skills could contribute to Del Rio Enterprises.

Refers reader to enclosed résumé

Asks for interview and repeats main qualifications

Sincerely,

Kendra A. Hawkins

Kendra A. Hawkins

Enclosure

what you have done in the past; your cover letter stresses what you can do in the future for the employer.

Your first goal is to relate your letter to a specific position. If you are responding to a listing, you'll want to explain how your preparation and experience fill the stated requirements. If you are prospecting for a job, you may not know the exact requirements. Your employment research and knowledge of your field, however, should give you a reasonably good idea of what is expected for this position.

It's also important to emphasize reader benefits. In other words, you should describe your strong points in relation to the needs of the employer. In one employment survey many human resources professionals expressed the same view: "I want you to tell me what you can do for my organization. This is much more important to me than telling me what courses you took in college or what 'duties' you performed on your previous jobs."[30] Instead of simply saying what you've done—*I have completed*

FIGURE **12.13** Unsolicited Cover Letter

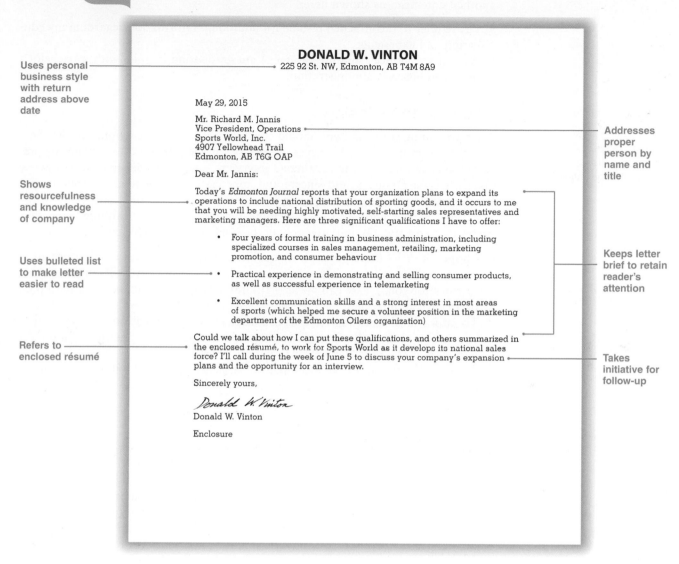

Uses personal business style with return address above date

Shows resourcefulness and knowledge of company

Uses bulleted list to make letter easier to read

Refers to enclosed résumé

Addresses proper person by name and title

Keeps letter brief to retain reader's attention

Takes initiative for follow-up

DONALD W. VINTON
225 92 St. NW, Edmonton, AB T4M 8A9

May 29, 2015

Mr. Richard M. Jannis
Vice President, Operations
Sports World, Inc.
4907 Yellowhead Trail
Edmonton, AB T6G OAP

Dear Mr. Jannis:

Today's *Edmonton Journal* reports that your organization plans to expand its operations to include national distribution of sporting goods, and it occurs to me that you will be needing highly motivated, self-starting sales representatives and marketing managers. Here are three significant qualifications I have to offer:

- Four years of formal training in business administration, including specialized courses in sales management, retailing, marketing promotion, and consumer behaviour
- Practical experience in demonstrating and selling consumer products, as well as successful experience in telemarketing
- Excellent communication skills and a strong interest in most areas of sports (which helped me secure a volunteer position in the marketing department of the Edmonton Oilers organization)

Could we talk about how I can put these qualifications, and others summarized in the enclosed résumé, to work for Sports World as it develops its national sales force? I'll call during the week of June 5 to discuss your company's expansion plans and the opportunity for an interview.

Sincerely yours,

Donald W. Vinton

Donald W. Vinton

Enclosure

---

courses in business communication, report writing, and technical writing—say how what you've done will be useful in the position for which you're applying:

> Courses in business communication, report writing, and technical writing have helped me develop the research and writing skills required of your technical writers.

Choose your strongest qualifications and show how they fit the targeted job. And remember, students with little experience are better off spotlighting their education and its practical applications, as these candidates did:

- Because you're looking for an architect's apprentice with proven ability, I've submitted a drawing of mine that won second place in the Algonquin College drafting contest last year.
- Successfully transcribing over 100 letters and memos in my college transcription class gave me experience in converting the spoken word into the written word, an exacting communication skill demanded of your legal assistants.

In the body of your letter, you'll also want to discuss relevant personal traits. Employers are looking for candidates who, among other things, are team players, take responsibility, show initiative, and learn easily. Finally, in this section or the next, you should refer the reader to your résumé. Do so directly or as part of another statement, as shown here:

- Please refer to the attached résumé for additional information regarding my education and experience.
- As you will notice from my résumé, I am graduating in June with a bachelor's degree in business administration.

Action in the Closing

The closing of a cover letter should include a request for an interview.

After presenting your case, you should conclude with a spur to action. This is where you ask for an interview. However, never ask for the job. To do so would be presumptuous and naive. In requesting an interview, suggest reader benefits or review your strongest points. Sound sincere and appreciative. Remember to make it easy for the reader to agree by supplying your phone number, e-mail address, and the best times to call you. And keep in mind that some human resources managers prefer that you take the initiative to call them. Here are possible endings:

- I hope this brief description of my qualifications and the additional information on my résumé indicate to you my genuine desire to put my skills in accounting to work for you. Please call me at (416) 488-2291 before 10 a.m. or after 3 p.m. to arrange an interview.
- To add a hard-working, experienced strategic communications practitioner to your team, please call me at (604) 492-1433 to arrange an interview. I can meet with you at any time convenient to your schedule.
- Next week, after you have examined the attached résumé, I will call you to discuss the possibility of arranging an interview.

Avoiding "I" Dominance

As you revise your cover letter, notice how many sentences begin with "I". Although it's impossible to talk about yourself without using "I", you can reduce the number of sentences beginning with this pronoun by using two techniques. First, place "I" in the middle of sentences instead of dominating the opening. Instead of *I was the top salesperson in my department*, try *While working in X department, I did Y and Z*, or *Among 15 co-workers, I received top ratings from my managers*. Incorporating *I* into the middle of sentences considerably reduces its domination.

Another technique for avoiding "I" dominance involves making activities and outcomes, not yourself, the subjects of sentences. For example, rather than *I took classes in business communication and data mining*, say *Classes in business communication and data mining prepared me to . . . .* Instead of *I enjoyed helping customers*, say *Helping customers taught me to be patient under stress*.

Sending Your Cover Letter by E-Mail

Serious job candidates send a professional cover letter even if the résumé is submitted online, by e-mail, or by fax.

More than 90 percent of résumés at Fortune 500 companies arrive by e-mail or are submitted through the corporate Web site.[31] Some applicants make the mistake of not including cover letters with their résumés when they submit them by e-mail. An application submitted electronically should contain two separate files: a cover letter file and a résumé file. An application that arrives without a cover letter makes the receiver wonder what it is and why it was sent. Recruiters want you to introduce yourself, and they also are eager to see some evidence that you can write. Some candidates either skip the cover letter or think they can get by with one-line e-mail cover notes such as this: *Please see attached résumé, and thanks for your consideration.*

A cover letter should look professional and suggest quality.

If you are serious about landing the job, take the time to prepare a professional cover letter. As illustrated in Figure 12.14, an application should include a brief cover note, plus the two files mentioned above, as attachments.

FIGURE 12.14 Job Application Sent Electronically

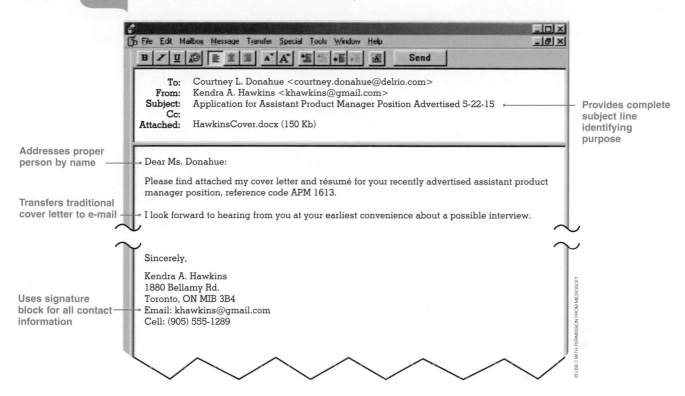

Provides complete subject line identifying purpose

Addresses proper person by name

Transfers traditional cover letter to e-mail

Uses signature block for all contact information

© USED WITH PERMISSION FROM MICROSOFT

The email reads:

To: Courtney L. Donahue <courtney.donahue@delrio.com>
From: Kendra A. Hawkins <khawkins@gmail.com>
Subject: Application for Assistant Product Manager Position Advertised 5-22-15
Cc:
Attached: HawkinsCover.docx (150 Kb)

Dear Ms. Donahue:

Please find attached my cover letter and résumé for your recently advertised assistant product manager position, reference code APM 1613.

I look forward to hearing from you at your earliest convenience about a possible interview.

Sincerely,

Kendra A. Hawkins
1880 Bellamy Rd.
Toronto, ON M1B 3B4
Email: khawkins@gmail.com
Cell: (905) 555-1289

SUMMING UP AND LOOKING FORWARD

In today's competitive job market, an employment search begins with identifying your Interests, evaluating your qualifications, considering your network, and choosing a career path. Finding the perfect job will mean a concentrated effort devoted to checking online job sites, having an up-to-date LinkedIn profile, and ensuring that your other social media sites are "clean" and don't hurt your application. It also helps to check traditional classified advertisements in newspapers, association magazines, and so forth.

In applying for jobs, you'll want to submit (via e-mail or uploading directly to a site) a persuasive cover letter and résumé that sell your skills and experience and your fit for the job. Whether you choose a chronological, functional, or combination résumé style, you should tailor your assets to fit the position sought. A persuasive cover letter should introduce your résumé and describe how your skills and experiences match those required.

If your résumé and cover letter have been successful, you'll proceed to the employment interview. For some people this is one of life's most stressful experiences, while for others it's an exhilarating experience. The last chapter in this book provides helpful suggestions for successful interviewing and follow-up communication.

CRITICAL THINKING

1. How has the concept of the job changed, and how will this affect your employment search?

2. To what degree is a social media profile (e.g., on LinkedIn or Twitter) a replacement for or an adjunct to the traditional cover letter/résumé package?

3. How is a résumé different from a job application form?

4. If a combination résumé combines the chronological and functional types, shouldn't a combination resume be the style everyone uses?

5. Some job candidates think that applying for unsolicited jobs can be more fruitful than applying for advertised openings. Discuss the advantages and disadvantages of letters that "prospect" for jobs.

6. **Ethical Issue:** At work, fellow employee Karl confesses that he did not complete the degree he claims on his résumé. You have never liked Karl, but he does satisfactory work. You are both competing for the same promotion. You are considering writing an anonymous note to the boss telling him to verify Karl's degree. Use Google or your library database to research Canadian guidelines for whistle-blowing at work. Based on your research, do you think your plan is a good one?

7. A cover letter is a persuasive letter, but do you really want to reduce a potential employer's resistance? Why might this be dangerous?

1. List at least five questions that you should ask yourself to identify your employment interests.
2. List some job sites that are useful when looking for work.
3. How are most jobs likely to be found? Through the classified ads? Employment agencies? Networking? Explain.
4. What is the goal of your résumé?
5. What are the advantages and disadvantages of the three résumé types?
6. When does it make sense to include a career objective on your résumé?
7. In a chronological résumé, what information should you include for the jobs you list?
8. In addition to technical skills, what traits and characteristics do employers seek?
9. How might a LinkedIn profile lead to landing a job?
10. What distinguishes a LinkedIn profile from a résumé and cover letter?
11. When sending an application package by e-mail, what needs to be included?
12. What are the three purposes of a cover letter?
13. How can you make it easy for a recruiter to reach you?
14. What is a video résumé, and why might it be useful?

WRITING IMPROVEMENT EXERCISES

1. Cover Letter Opening.

Your Task. James Nickson has just graduated from college with a three-year diploma in accounting. With the help of his college's career centre, James has begun applying for full-time employment. Below is the opening of one of James's cover letters. Analyze the letter, identify any problems, and rewrite this section of the letter following the guidelines in this chapter.

To whom it may concern,

It was a stroke of luck to find the job advertisement in the local newspaper last week for your company. I've always wanted to work for a company like yours, and this job opening may now give me the opportunity! My name is Jim Nickson and I just graduated in Accounting at a local college.

2. Cover Letter Body.

Your Task. Below is the body of James Nickson's cover letter. Analyze the letter, identify any problems, and rewrite this section of the letter following the guidelines in this chapter.

As you can see from my enclosed résumé, I am a strong student, and I am also a good team player. I think these skills would be useful to me in your company. For example, I took a course in Auditing in which I received the highest GPA in the program. Finally, I have worked as a bookkeeper for the past two summers.

3. Cover Letter Closing.

Your Task. The closing of James Nickson's cover letter is found below. Analyze the letter, identify any problems, and rewrite this section of the letter following the guidelines in this chapter.

In closing, permit me to be blunt and say that there's nothing I'd like more than the opportunity to work for your company. I know I would be an asset to your organization. I look forward to hearing from you at your earliest convenience.

Best,

Jim Nickson

ACTIVITIES AND CASES

12.1 Interests and Qualifications Inventory

It's often surprising what kind of information you can find out about your fellow classmates in a classroom setting. Imagine you are conducting a study for your college's co-op office or student association about future aspirations of students. The co-op office or student association wants to know the future career interests of the college's students as well as their current qualifications.

Your Task. Choose three people in your class (preferably classmates you don't know very well) and interview them. Ask them the questions listed on page 377 under "Identify Your Interests" and then the questions on page 377 under "Evaluate Your Qualifications." Develop a profile of each of your interviewees, and e-mail this profile to your instructor. Your instructor may choose to share the "inventory" with you in a later class. How might you use this inventory for future networking purposes?

12.2 Evaluating Your Qualifications

Prepare four worksheets that inventory your own qualifications in the areas of employment, education, capabilities and skills, and honours and activities. Use active verbs when appropriate.

a. *Employment.* Begin with your most recent job or internship. For each position list the following information: employer; job title; dates of employment; and three to five duties, activities, or accomplishments. Emphasize activities related to your job goal. Strive to quantify your achievements.

b. *Education.* List degrees, certificates, diplomas, and training accomplishments. Include courses, seminars, or skills that are relevant to your job goal. Calculate your GPA in your major.

c. *Capabilities and skills.* List all capabilities and skills that recommend you for the job you seek. Use words such as *skilled, competent, trained, experienced*, and *ability to*. Also list five or more qualities or interpersonal skills necessary for a successful individual in your chosen field. Write action statements demonstrating that you possess some of these qualities. Empty assurances aren't good enough; try to show evidence (*Developed teamwork skills by working with a committee of eight to produce a . . .*).

d. *Awards, honours, and activities.* Explain any awards so that the reader will understand them. List school, community, and professional activities that suggest you are a well-rounded individual or possess traits relevant to your target job.

12.3 Choosing a Career Path

WEB

Visit your school library, local library, or employment centre. Select an appropriate resource such as Human Resources and Skills Development Canada's *National Occupational Classification* (**www5.hrsdc.gc.ca/NOC/English/NOC/2011/Welcome.aspx**) to find a description for a position for which you could apply in two to five years. Photocopy or print the pages from the resource you chose that describe employment in the area in which you are interested. If your instructor directs, attach these copies to the cover letter you will write in Activity 12.10. Were you able to find the job that interests you? If not, where else can you find information on this job?

12.4 Using Social Media in a Job Search

WEB

One of the fastest-growing trends in employment is using social media sites during a job search.

Your Task. Locate one social media site and set up an account. Explore the site to discover how job seekers can use it to search for a job and how employers can use it to find job candidates. If it's not immediately apparent how this site can be used to find a job, research this question using a search engine or library database. Be prepared to share your findings in class.

12.5 Résumé Research

WEB

By reading this chapter, you've learned about a number of different types of résumé. But what's reality like on the ground? Do employers care what the résumé looks like as long as it's well written? Or do they care a lot and have particular things they're looking for?

Your Task. Using the material from this chapter, develop a five- to ten-question survey about résumés. For example, do employers care what type of résumé applicants submit? What do employers look for in a résumé? What in a résumé turns them off a prospective candidate? Then identify three to five employers (people you know or who live in your area) and ask them to respond to your survey (this might be easier to do in person than over the phone or by e-mail). Present the results of your primary research in a short memo or e-mail or a presentation. Do your results corroborate or challenge what you learned in this chapter?

12.6 Posting a Résumé on the Web

WEB

Learn about the procedure for posting résumés at job boards on the Web.

Your Task. Prepare a list of at least three online employment sites where you could post your résumé. Describe the procedure involved and the advantages of each site.

12.7 Draft Document: Résumé

Analyze the following résumé. Discuss its strengths and weaknesses. Your instructor may ask you to revise sections of this résumé before showing you an improved version.

Winona Skudra
5349 Main Street
Saskatoon, SK S2N 0B4
Phone: (306) 834-4583 skudraw@lycos.ca.

Seeking to be hired at Meadow Products as an intern in Accounting

SKILLS: Accounting, Internet, MS Office 2007, Excel, PowerPoint, Freelance Graphics

EDUCATION

Now working on B.Comm. in Business Administration. Major, Management and Accounting; GPA is 3.5. Expect to graduate in June, 2016.

EXPERIENCE:

Assistant Accountant, 2007 to present. March and McLennan, Inc., Bookkeeping/Tax Service, Saskatoon. I keep accounting records for several small businesses accurately. I prepare 150 to 200 individual income tax returns each year. For Hill and Hill Trucking I maintain accurate and up-to-date A/R records. And I prepare payroll records for 16 employees at three firms.

Peterson Controls Inc., Saskatoon. Data Processing Internship, 2009 to present. I design and maintain spreadsheets and also process weekly and monthly information for production uptime and downtime. I prepare graphs to illustrate uptime and downtime data.

Saskatoon Curling Club. Accounts Payable Internship, 2008 to 2009. Took care of accounts payable including filing system for the club. Responsible for processing monthly adjusting entries for general ledger. Worked closely with treasurer to give the Board budget/disbursement figures regularly.

Saskatoon High School, Saskatoon. I marketed the VITA program to students and organized volunteers and supplies. Official title: Coordinator of Volunteer Income Tax Assistance Project.

COMMUNITY SERVICE: March of Dimes Drive, Central High School; All Souls Lutheran Church, coordinator for Children's Choir

12.8 Draft Document: Cover Letter

Analyze each section of the following cover letter written by an accounting major about to graduate.

Dear Human Resources Director:

Please consider this letter as an application for the position of staff accountant that I saw advertised in the Saskatoon *Star Phoenix*. Although I have had no paid work experience in this field, accounting has been my major in college and I'm sure I could be an asset to your company.

For four years I have studied accounting, and I am fully trained for full-charge bookkeeping as well as electronic accounting. I have completed 36 credits of college accounting and courses in business law, economics, statistics, finance, management, and marketing. In addition to my course work, during the tax season I have been a student volunteer for VITA. This is a project to help individuals in the community prepare their income tax returns, and I learned a lot from this experience. I have also received some experience in office work and working with figures when I was employed as an office assistant for Copy Quick, Inc.

I am a competent and responsible person who gets along pretty well with others. I have been a member of some college and social organizations and have even held elective office.

I feel that I have a strong foundation in accounting as a result of my course work and my experience. Along with my personal qualities and my desire to succeed, I hope that you will agree that I qualify for the position of staff accountant with your company.

Sincerely,

12.9 Résumé

Using the data you developed in Activity 12.2, write your résumé. Aim it at a full-time job, part-time position, or internship. Attach a job listing for a specific position (from Activity 12.4). Revise your résumé until it is perfect.

12.10 Cover Letter

WEB

Write an application letter introducing your résumé from Activity 12.9. Revise your application letter until it is perfect.

12.11 Unsolicited Cover Letter

As you read in this chapter, job applications are not always solicited. As part of your college education, you have no doubt come into contact with periodicals related to your field. For example, you may have read articles in *Canadian Business*, *Report on Business*, *HR Reporter*, *Marketing*, or any number of other magazines. In these magazines, you've come across the names of various businesspeople, either because they were featured in an article or because they were quoted as experts.

Your Task. Using your college library or local public library, read through an issue of a business-related periodical or your local newspaper's business section. Look for a businessperson who is mentioned, quoted, or featured in that periodical. Write that person an unsolicited cover letter asking for an entry-level position or internship either for the summer or upon graduation. Make sure to revise this letter sufficiently, and hand it in to your instructor for comments before actually mailing it.

12.12 Being Wary of Career Advisory Firms With Big Promises and Big Prices

Not long ago employment agencies charged applicants 5 percent of their annual salaries to find jobs. Most agencies have quit this unethical practice, but unscrupulous firms still prey on vulnerable job seekers. Some career advisory firms claim to be legitimate, but they make exaggerated promises and charge inflated fees—an up-front payment of $4,000 is typical, with a typical hourly honorarium of $90 to $125.

Your Task. Using databases and the Web, find examples of current employment scams or danger areas for job seekers. In a presentation to the class or in team discussions, describe three examples of disreputable practices candidates should recognize. Make recommendations to job seekers for avoiding employment scams and disappointment with career advisory services.

12.14 E-Portfolios: Job Hunting in the Twenty-First Century

In high-tech fields digital portfolios have been steadily gaining in popularity and now seem to be going mainstream as universities are providing space for student job seekers to profile their qualifications in e-portfolios online. Although it is unlikely that digital portfolios will become widely used very soon, you would do well to learn about them by viewing many samples—good and bad.

Your Task. Conduct a Google search using the search term *student e-portfolios* or *student digital portfolios*. You will see long lists of hits, some of which will be actual digital document samples on the Web or instructions for creating an e-portfolio. Your instructor may assign individual students or teams to visit specific digital portfolio sites and ask them to summarize their findings in a memo or in a brief oral presentation. If this is your task, you could focus on the composition of the site, page layout, links provided, colours used, types of documents included, and so forth. A fine site to start from that offers many useful links is maintained by the Center for Excellence in Teaching (CET) at the University of Southern California. Visit **www.usc.edu** and type "student e-portfolios" to search the USC Web pages. Click the link to the CET site.

Alternatively, single groups or the whole class could study sites that provide how-to instructions and combine the advice of the best among them to create practical tips for making a digital portfolio. This option would lend itself to team writing, for example, with the help of a wiki.

GRAMMAR/MECHANICS REVIEW 12—NUMBER STYLE

Study each of the following pairs. Assume that these expressions appear in the context of letters, reports, or memos. In the answer spaces provided, write the preferred number style.

__three__ **Example:** He had (three, 3) cellphones.

_____ 1. At least (20, twenty) candidates applied for the opening.

_____ 2. The interview was on (Fourth, 4th) Street.

_____ 3. Angelica saw (12, twelve) possible jobs listed on the Web.

_____ 4. One job started on (June 1, June 1st).

_____ 5. She filled her gas tank for ($40, forty dollars).

_____ 6. She hoped to have a job by the (15th, fifteenth) of June.

_____ 7. Her interview started at (3 p.m., 3:00 p.m.).

_____ 8. The assistant edited (4 three-page, four 3-page) memos.

_____ 9. She founded her company over (40, forty) years ago.

_____ 10. About (3 million; 3,000,000) people visited Monster.com.

_____ 11. (16, Sixteen) candidates applied for one open position.

_____ 12. I need (50, fifty) cents for the machine.

_____ 13. She graduated at the age of (21, twenty-one).

_____ 14. The interest rate on her loan was (7, seven) percent.

_____ 15. Only (4, four) of the 35 e-mail messages were undelivered.

GRAMMAR/MECHANICS CHALLENGE—12

Document for Revision

The following résumé (shortened for this exercise) has faults in grammar, punctuation, spelling, number form, verb form, wordiness, and word use. Use standard proofreading marks (see Appendix B) to correct the errors. When you finish, your instructor can show you the revised version of this résumé.

MEGAN A. Kozlov
245 Topsail Street
St. John's, Newfoundland A1B 3Z4
makozlov@hotmail.com

EDUCATION

Memorial University, St. John's, Newfoundland. Bachelor of Arts Degree expected in June 2015. Major English.

EXPERIENCE:

- Administrative Assistant. Host Systems, St. John's. 2012 too pressent. Responsible for entering data on the computer. I had to insure accuracy and completness of data that was to be entered. Another duty was maintaining a clean and well-organized office. I also served as Office Courier.
- Lechter's Housewares. Outlook Newfoundland. 2010-2011. 2nd Asst. Mgr I managed store in absence of mgr. and asst. mgr. I open and close registers. Ballanced daily reciepts. Ordered some mds. I also had to supervise 2 employes, earning rabid promotion.
- Office Assistant. Sunshine Travel Outlook. 2009–2010. (part time) Entered travel information onto a spreadsheet. Did personalized followup emails to customer inquirys. Was responsible for phones. I also handled all errands as courier.

STRENGTHS

Microsoft Office Applications, transcription, poofreading.

Can input 50 words/per/minute.

I am a fast learner, and very accurate.

Msoffice 2013 including Excell, Access, and Outlook,

COMMUNICATION WORKSHOP

 ## NETWORK YOUR WAY TO A JOB IN THE HIDDEN MARKET

Not all jobs are advertised on job sites. The "hidden" job market, according to some estimates, accounts for as much as two thirds of all positions available. Companies don't always announce openings publicly because it's time-consuming to interview all the applicants, many of whom are not qualified. But the real reason that companies resist announcing a job is that they dislike hiring "strangers." One recruiter says that when she needs to hire, she first looks around among her friends and acquaintances. If she can't find anyone suitable, she then turns to advertising.[32] It's clear that many employers are more comfortable hiring a person they know.

The key to finding a good job, then, is converting yourself from a "stranger" into a known quantity. One way to become a known quantity is by networking. You can use either traditional or online networking methods.

Traditional Networking

- **Step 1: Develop a list.** Make a list of anyone who would be willing to talk with you about finding a job. List your friends, relatives, former employers, former co-workers, classmates from grade school and high school, college friends, members of your religious group, people in social and athletic clubs, present and former teachers, neighbours, and friends of your parents.

- **Step 2: Make contacts.** Call the people on your list or, even better, ask to meet with them in person for an informational interview. To set up a meeting, say (or write), "Hi, Aunt Martha! I'm looking for a job and I wonder if you could help me out. When could I come over to talk about it?" During your visit be friendly, well organized, polite, and interested in what your contact has to say. Provide a copy of your résumé, and try to keep the conversation centred on your job search area. Your goal is to get two or more referrals. In pinpointing your request, ask two questions. "Do you know of anyone who might have an opening for a person with my skills?" If not, "Do you know of anyone else who might know of someone who would?"

- **Step 3: Follow up on your referrals.** Call the people whose names are on your referral list. You might say something like, "Hello. I'm Carlos Ramos, a friend of Connie Cole. She suggested that I call and ask you for help. I'm looking for an internship position in product management, and she thought you might be willing to see me and give me a few ideas." Don't ask for a job. During your referral interview ask how the individual got started in this line of work, what he or she likes best (or least) about the work, what career paths exist in the field, and what problems must be overcome by a newcomer. Most important, ask how a person with your background and skills might get started in the field. Send an informal thank-you e-mail to anyone who helps you in your job search, and stay in touch with the most promising contacts. Ask whether you may call every three weeks or so during your job search.

Online Networking

As with traditional networking, the goal is to make connections with people who are advanced in their fields. Ask for their advice about finding a job. Most people like talking about themselves, and asking them about their experiences is an excellent way to begin an online correspondence that might lead to "electronic mentoring" or a letter of recommendation from an expert in the field. Making online connections with industry professionals is a great way to keep tabs on the latest business trends and potential job leads. Here are possible online networking sources:

- **Get on LinkedIn.** Build your own professional network by joining LinkedIn, as discussed earlier in this chapter. Once you are satisfied with your profile, start inviting people you know to be your contacts. Once you've sent out invitations to this initial group, and received some accepted invitations, you'll have your own LinkedIn network. This will allow you to see the contacts of the people in your network, thereby broadening it. If you think it's appropriate, you might decide to send a few "cold" invitations to people you don't know, but who know one of your contacts. These invitations need to be written carefully (don't use LinkedIn's template invitation). Be personal: "Hi, my name's Richard. My cousin Brad Atossa suggested I get in touch with you …" Once you have five or ten people in your LinkedIn network who you don't yet know personally, you can start contacting them to ask for an informational interview. Do this twice a year.
- **Participate in a discussion groups and mailing lists.** Two good discussion group resources for beginners are Yahoo! Groups (**http://groups.yahoo.com**) and Google Groups (**http://groups.google.com**). You may choose from groups in a variety of fields including business and computer technology. For example, if you click the Business/Finance listing, you will see links leading to more specialized groups. Click Employment and Work, and you will find career groups including construction, customer service, office administration, court reporting, and interior design.
- **Locate relevant blogs.** Blogs are the latest trend for networking and sharing information. A quick Web search will result in hundreds of career-related blogs and blogs in your field of study. Many companies, such as Microsoft, also maintain employment-related blogs. A good list of career blogs can be found at **www.quintcareers.com/career -related_blogs.html**. Once you locate a relevant blog, you can read recent postings, search archives, and post replies.
- **Get out there.** There's no substitute for meeting with people in person. The best way to do this is to attend workshops, seminars, meetings, professional development opportunities, and by volunteering. If you're a human resources student, find the relevant association in your area and go online to see what events they are holding. Attend one of these events. Make a point of introducing yourself to three people. Have a business card (or a card that lists your LinkedIn profile) with you to hand out. After the event, follow up with the person by e-mail or by phone, and request an informational interview or ask if you can invite this person to join your LinkedIn network.

Career Application

Everyone who goes out into the job market needs to develop his or her own network. Assume you are ready to change jobs or look for a permanent position. Begin developing your personal network.

YOUR TASK

- Conduct at least one informational interview and report on it to your class.
- Join one professional networking site or discussion group, or attend one event. Takes notes on the discussion or event, and describe your reactions and findings to your class.
- Find a blog related to your career or your major. After monitoring the blog for several days, describe your experience to your class.
- Create an Excel file called "My Network." In it, list all the people you know who are working, their job title, and their place of employment. Then ask each of the people in your spreadsheet to recommend one person they work with (and whom you don't yet know) that you could contact and potentially add to your spreadsheet. Maintain your spreadsheet by reviewing it twice a year, and adding to it at least once per year. Ask for informational interviews with 10 percent of the new people in your spreadsheet.

Interviews and Follow-Up

LEARNING OBJECTIVES

1. Explain the purposes and kinds of job interviews, including screening, one-on-one, panel, group, sequential, stress, and online interviews.

2. Describe what to do before the interview to make an impressive initial contact.

3. Explain how to prepare for employment interviews, including researching the target company.

4. Recognize how to control nonverbal messages and fight interview fears.

5. Be prepared to answer common interview questions and close an interview positively.

6. Be prepared to engage in post-interview communication, including thanking the interviewer and contacting references.

7. Write follow-up and other employment messages.

Employment Interviews

Whether you are completing your education and searching for your first full-time position or in the workforce and striving to change jobs, a job interview can be life changing. Because employment is a major part of everyone's life, job interviews take on enormous importance.

Most people consider job interviews to be extremely stressful. However, the more you learn about the process and the more prepared you are, the less stress you will feel. Also, a job interview is a two-way street. It's not just about being judged by the employer. You, the candidate, will be using the job interview to evaluate the employer and find out if you really want to work for this organization.

This chapter will increase your interviewing effectiveness and confidence by explaining the purposes and kinds of interviews and how to prepare for them. You will learn how to project a professional image throughout the interview process, gather information about an employer, and reduce nervousness. You will receive advice on how to send positive nonverbal messages that will help you stay in control during your interview. You will pick up tips for responding to recruiters' favourite questions and learn how to cope with illegal questions and salary matters. In addition, you will receive pointers on significant questions you can ask during an interview. Finally, you will learn what you should do as a successful follow-up to an interview.

Clearly, job interviews are intimidating for most of us. No one enjoys being judged and possibly rejected. Should you expect to be nervous about an upcoming job interview? Of course. Everyone is uneasy about being scrutinized and questioned. But think of how much more nervous you would be if you had no idea what to expect in the interview and were unprepared.

Yes, you can expect to be nervous. But you can also expect to succeed in an interview when you know what's coming and when you prepare thoroughly. Remember, it's often the degree of preparation as well as the appearance of confidence that determines who gets the job.

Purposes of Employment Interviews

An interview has several purposes for you as a job candidate. It is an opportunity to (a) convince the employer of your potential, (b) learn more about the job and the company, and (c) expand on the information in your résumé. This is the time for you to gather information about whether you would fit into the company culture. You should also be thinking about whether this job suits your career goals.

From the employer's perspective, the interview is an opportunity to (a) assess your abilities in relation to the requirements for the position; (b) discuss your training, experience, knowledge, and abilities in more detail; (c) see what drives and motivates you; and (d) decide whether you would fit into the organization.

Kinds of Employment Interviews

Job applicants generally face two kinds of interviews: screening interviews and hiring/placement interviews. You must succeed in the first to proceed to the second. Once you make it to the hiring/placement interview, you will find a variety of interview styles, including one-on-one, panel, group, sequential, stress, and online interviews. You will be better prepared if you know what to expect in each type of interview.

SCREENING INTERVIEWS. Screening interviews do just that—they screen candidates to eliminate those who fail to meet minimum requirements. Companies use screening interviews to save time and money by weeding out lesser qualified candidates before scheduling face-to-face interviews. Although some screening interviews are conducted during job fairs or on college campuses, many screening interviews take place on the telephone, and some take place online.[1]

Some companies conduct their screening interviews using technology. For example, Lowe's Home Improvement has applicants access a Web site where they answer a series of ethics-related questions. Retail giant Walmart screens cashiers, stockers, and customer service representatives with a multiple-choice questionnaire that applicants answer by pushing buttons on a phone keypad.[2] Even more cutting edge, some employers, such as Hewlett-Packard, Microsoft, Sodexo, and Verizon, are using Second Life, an online virtual community, to hold virtual job fairs and to screen job applicants.[3]

During a screening interview, the interviewer will probably ask you to provide details about the education and experience listed on your résumé; therefore, you must be prepared to promote your qualifications. Remember that the person conducting the screening interview is trying to determine whether you should move on to the next step in the interview process.

A screening interview may be as short as five minutes. Even though it may be short, don't treat it casually. If you don't perform well, it may be your last interview with that organization. You can use the tips that follow in this chapter to succeed during the screening process.

HIRING/PLACEMENT INTERVIEWS. The most promising candidates selected from screening interviews will be invited to hiring/placement interviews. Hiring managers want to learn whether candidates are motivated, qualified, and a good fit for the position. Their goal is to learn how the candidate would fit into their organization. Conducted in depth, hiring/placement interviews may take many forms.

> Screening interviews are intended to eliminate those who fail to meet minimum requirements.

> In hiring/placement interviews, recruiters try to learn how the candidate might fit into their organization.

ONE-ON-ONE INTERVIEWS. This is the most common interview type. You can expect to sit down with a company representative (or two) and talk about the job and your qualifications. If the representative is the hiring manager, questions will be specific and job-related. If the representative is from the human resources department, the questions will probably be more general.

PANEL INTERVIEWS. Panel interviews are typically conducted by people who will be your supervisors and colleagues. Usually seated around a table, interviewers may take turns asking questions. Panel interviews are advantageous because they save time and show you how the staff works together. For these interviews, you can prepare basic biographical information about each panel member. When answering questions, maintain eye contact with the questioner as well as with the other team members. Try to take notes during the interview so that you can remember each person's questions and what was important to that individual.[4]

GROUP INTERVIEWS. Group interviews occur when a company interviews several candidates for the same position at the same time. Some employers use this technique to measure leadership skills and communication styles. During a group interview, stay focused on the interviewer and treat the other candidates with respect. Even if you are nervous, try to remain calm, take your time when responding, and express yourself clearly. The key during a group interview is to make yourself stand out from the other candidates in a positive way.[5]

SEQUENTIAL INTERVIEWS. In a sequential interview, you meet individually with two or more interviewers over the course of several hours or days. For example, you may meet separately with human resources representatives, your hiring manager, and potential future supervisors and colleagues in your division or department. You must listen carefully and respond positively to all interviewers. Promote your qualifications to each one; don't assume that any interviewer knows what was said in a previous interview. Keep your responses fresh, even when repeating yourself many times over. Subsequent interviews also tend to be more in-depth than first interviews, which means that you need to be even more prepared and know even more about the company. According to Chantal Verbeek-Vingerhoed, head of enterprise talent for ING, during subsequent interviews employers "dig deeper into your technical skills, and make connections about how you'd add value and solve issues in the department. If you know the exact job requirements and expectations, you can really shine."[6]

STRESS INTERVIEWS. This interview type, rarely used, is meant to test your reactions in difficult situations. In a stress interview, you may, for example, be forced to wait a long time before being greeted by the interviewer, or you may be given a test with an impossible time limit, or you may be treated rudely (all on purpose, of course).

If asked rapid-fire questions from many directions, take the time to slow things down. For example, *I would be happy to answer your question, Ms. X, but allow me to finish responding to Mr. Z.* If greeted with silence, another stress technique, you might say *Would you like me to begin the interview? Let me tell you about myself.* Or ask a question such as *Can you give me more information about the position?* The best way to handle stress interview situations is to remain calm and give carefully considered answers. One career expert says, "The key to surviving stress interviews is to remain calm, keep a sense of humor, and avoid getting angry or defensive."[7]

ONLINE INTERVIEWS. Many companies today use technology to interview job candidates from a distance. Although conference call interviews have a long tradition, today's savvy companies such as Zappos.com use webcams and

> Hiring interview types include one-on-one, panel, group, sequential, stress, and online.

videoconferencing software to conduct interviews. If an applicant doesn't have a webcam, Zappos sends one with a return label.[8]

Using the free Skype service and a webcam saves job applicants and companies time and money, especially when applicants are not in the same geographic location as the company. Even though your interview may be online, conducted with videoconferencing software and a webcam, don't take it any less seriously than a face-to-face interview.

Despite the technical ability to conduct interviews online through videoconferencing, there is evidence that, although flexible and time-saving, these types of interviews are not viewed in as positive a light (by both employers and candidates) as traditional, in-person interviews.[9]

Before the Interview

Once you have sent out at least one résumé or filled out at least one job application, you must consider yourself an active job seeker. Being active in the job market means that you must be prepared to be contacted by potential employers. As discussed earlier, employers use screening interviews to narrow the list of candidates. If you do well in the screening interview, you will be invited to an in-person or online meeting. Below are tips for how to prepare yourself before an interview.

Use Professional Phone Techniques

Even with the popularity of e-mail, most employers contact job applicants by phone to set up interviews. Employers can judge how well applicants communicate by hearing their voices and expressions and tone over the phone. Therefore, once you are actively looking for a job, any time the phone rings, it could be a potential employer. Don't make the mistake of letting an unprofessional voice mail message or a lazy roommate ruin your chances. Here's how you can avoid such problems:

- Make sure that your voice mail instructions are concise and professional, with no distracting background sounds. If your home voice mail instructions are for your entire family, consider offering only your personal cellphone number on your résumé. The instructions should be in your own voice and include your full name for clarity. You will find more tips for creating professional voice mail instructions in Chapter 10.
- Tell anyone who might answer your phone about your job search. Explain to them the importance of acting professionally and taking complete messages. Family members or roommates can affect the first impression an employer has of you.
- If your cellphone number is on your résumé, don't answer it unless you are in a quiet enough location to have a conversation with an employer. It is hard to pay close attention when you are in a noisy restaurant or on a crowded bus. That said, if you do answer the phone in a noisy situation and find an employer on the other end, say hello politely, identify yourself, apologize for the noise, and ask whether the employer wants to continue the conversation or have you call back shortly.

Make the First Conversation Impressive

Whether you answer the phone directly or return an employer's call, make sure you are prepared for the conversation. Remember that this is the first time the employer has heard your voice. How you conduct yourself on the phone will create a lasting impression. To make that first impression a positive one, follow these tips:

- Keep a list near or in your phones of the positions for which you have applied.
- Treat any call from an employer just like an interview. Use a professional tone and appropriate language. Be polite and enthusiastic, and sell your qualifications.
- If caught off guard by the call, ask whether you can call back in a few minutes. Organize your materials and yourself.

While it's technically possible to interview online via videoconferencing, a study finds that this channel is not favourably viewed by employers or candidates.

After submitting a resume, you may be contacted by phone by potential employers for a screening interview.

Sounding flustered, unprepared, or unprofessional when an employer calls may ruin a job seeker's chances with that company.

- Have a copy of your résumé available so that you can answer any questions that come up. Also have your list of references, a calendar, and a notepad handy. If you're talking on a smartphone, you'll be able to access a calendar and notepad on the phone itself.
- Be prepared to undergo a screening interview. As discussed earlier, this might occur during the first phone call.
- Take notes during the phone conversation. Obtain accurate directions, and verify the spelling of your interviewer's name. If you will be interviewed by more than one person, get all of their names.
- Before you hang up, reconfirm the date and time of your interview. You could say something like *I look forward to meeting with you next Wednesday at 2 p.m.*

Research the Target Company

Once you have scheduled an in-person or online interview, you need to start preparing for it. One of the most important steps in effective interviewing is gathering detailed information about a prospective employer. Never enter an interview cold. Recruiters are impressed by candidates who have done their homework.

Search the potential employer's Web site, news sources, trade journals, and industry directories. Unearth information about the job, the company, and the industry. Don't forget to Google the interviewer.[10] Learn all you can about the company's history, mission and goals, size, geographic locations, number of employees, customers, competitors, culture, management structure, reputation in the community, financial condition, strengths and weaknesses, and future plans, as well as the names of its leaders. Also, learn what you can about the industry in which the company operates. Visit the library and explore your campus career centre to find additional information about the target company and its field, service, or product.

Analyze the company's advertising, including sales and marketing brochures. One candidate, a marketing major, spent a great deal of time poring over brochures from an aerospace contractor. During his initial interview, he shocked and impressed the recruiter with his knowledge of the company's guidance systems. The candidate had, in fact, relieved the interviewer of his least-favourite task— explaining the company's complicated technology.

Talking with company employees is always a good idea, if you can manage it. They are probably the best source of inside information. Try to speak to someone who is currently employed there, but not working in the immediate area where you wish to be hired. You may be able to find this person by using LinkedIn. Remember, however, that asking favours of someone who doesn't know you is a risky proposition and is best handled with complete transparency.

Blogs are also good sources for company research. One marketing specialist calls them "job posting gold mines."[11] Many employees maintain both formal and informal blogs, where they share anecdotes and information about their employers. You can use these blogs to learn about a company's culture, its current happenings, and its future plans. Many job seekers find that they can get a more realistic picture of a company's day-to-day culture by reading blogs than they would by reading news articles or company Web site information. Blogs written by employees and ex-employees can be particularly informative. If you can bring up a suitable post on the company blog in your cover letter or mention it in the interview, you may have an advantage over the competition.

Finally, you may also want to connect with the company through social media. "Like" the company on Facebook and comment shrewdly on the organization's status updates and other posts. You may hear about vacancies before they are advertised. If you follow the company and its key people on Twitter, you may draw some positive attention to yourself and perhaps even hear about up-to-the-minute job openings. If you know the interviewers' names, look up their profiles on LinkedIn but don't try to connect with them before actually meeting them. You may find more in-depth information about these individuals on LinkedIn than on Facebook.[12]

> Before your interview, take time to research the target company and learn about its goals, customers, competitors, reputation, branding, and so forth.

> Blogs can provide authentic information about a company's culture, current happenings, and future plans.

Researching an organization enlightens candidates and impresses recruiters.

The best source of inside information is company employees.

In learning about a company, you may uncover information that convinces you that this is not the company for you. It is always better to learn about negatives early in the process. More likely, though, the information you collect will help you tailor your interview responses to the organization's needs. You know how flattered you feel when an employer knows about you and your background. That feeling works both ways. Employers are pleased when job candidates take an interest in them. Be ready to put in plenty of effort in investigating a target employer because this effort really pays off at interview time.

In addition, one of the best things a job seeker can do is to get into the habit of reading the newspaper regularly. The best place to go for current information on Canadian companies is the business section of the two national newspapers, the *National Post* and *The Globe and Mail*, including these newspapers' Web sites. Your local city or town newspaper will occasionally profile local businesses.

Prepare and Practise

After you have learned about the target organization, study the job description or job listing. The most successful job candidates never go into interviews cold. They prepare success stories and practise answers to typical questions. They also plan their responses to any problem areas on their résumés. As part of their preparation before the interview, they decide what to wear, and they gather the items they plan to take with them, such as a portfolio of projects completed.

Practise success stories that emphasize your most strategic skills, areas of knowledge, strongest personality traits, and key accomplishments.

PREPARE AND REHEARSE SUCCESS STORIES. To feel confident and be able to sell your qualifications, prepare and practise success stories. These stories are specific examples of your educational and work-related experience that demonstrate your qualifications and achievements. Look over the job description and your résumé to determine what skills, training, personal characteristics, and experience you want to emphasize during the interview. Then prepare a success story for each one. Incorporate numbers, such as dollars saved or percentage of sales increased, whenever possible. Your success stories should be detailed but brief. Think of them as 30-second sound bites.

Practise telling your success stories until they fluently roll off your tongue and sound natural. Then in the interview be certain to find places to insert them. Tell stories about (a) dealing with a crisis, (b) handling a tough interpersonal situation, (c) successfully juggling many priorities, (d) changing course to deal with changed circumstances, (e) learning from a mistake, (f) working on a team, and (g) going above and beyond expectations.[13]

PRACTISE ANSWERS TO POSSIBLE QUESTIONS. Imagine the kinds of questions you may be asked and work out sample answers. Although you can't anticipate precise questions, you can expect to be asked about your education, skills, experience, and availability. Practise answering some typical interview questions aloud, either into a mirror, with a friend, while driving in your car, or before going to bed. Keep practising until you have the best responses down pat. Consider recording a practice session to see and hear how you answer questions. Do you look and sound enthusiastic?

CLEAN UP ANY DIGITAL DIRT. A study showed that 45 percent of employers screen candidates using Google and social networking sites such as Facebook, LinkedIn, MySpace, and Twitter.[14] Even more important, 70 percent of recruiters have found something online that caused them not to hire a candidate.[15] The top reasons cited for not considering an applicant after an online search were that the candidate (a) posted provocative or inappropriate photographs or information; (b) posted content about drinking or doing drugs; (c) talked negatively about current or previous employers, colleagues, or clients; (d) exhibited poor communication skills; (e) made discriminatory comments; (f) lied about qualifications; or (g) revealed a current or previous employer's confidential information.[16]

For example, the president of a small consulting company was about to hire a summer intern when he discovered the student's Facebook page. The candidate described his interests as "smokin' blunts [cigars hollowed out and stuffed with marijuana], shooting people and obsessive sex."[17] The executive quickly lost interest in this candidate. Even if the student was merely posturing, it showed poor judgment. Teasing photographs and provocative comments about drinking, drug use, and sexual exploits make students look immature and unprofessional. You should, therefore, follow these steps to clean up your online presence:

- **Remove questionable content.** Remove any incriminating, provocative, or distasteful photos, content, and links that could make you look unprofessional to potential employers.
- **Stay positive.** Don't complain about things in your professional or personal life online. Even negative reviews you have written on sites such as Amazon.com can turn employers off.
- **Be selective about who is on your list of friends.** You don't want to miss out on an opportunity because you seem to associate with negative, immature, or unprofessional people. Your best bet is to make your personal social networking pages private.
- **Avoid joining groups or pages that may be viewed negatively.** Remember that online searches can turn up your online activities, including group memberships, blog postings, and so on. If you think any activity you are involved in might show poor judgment, remove yourself immediately.
- **Don't discuss your job search if you are still employed.** Employees can find themselves in trouble with their current employers by writing status updates or sending tweets about their job search.
- **Set up a professional social networking page or create your own personal Web site.** Use Facebook, LinkedIn, or other social networking sites to create a professional page. Many employers actually find information during their online searches that convinces them to hire candidates. Make sure your professional page demonstrates creativity, strong communication skills, and well-roundedness.[18]

> Make sure everything posted about you online is professional and positive.

WORKPLACE IN FOCUS

How can you protect your career prospects online? Imagine that your search using Google, 123people .com, Snitch.name, or PeekYou.com unearthed negative information about you. What can you do? Look for contact information on the Web site and ask the owner to remove any offensive information about you. In serious cases, you may need legal advice. Understand that digital dirt can persist on other Web sites even after it is removed on the one you found. To prevent future problems, consider using nicknames or pseudonyms when starting a new profile on a social network. Know the privacy policy and understand who can view your profile before posting any text, images, or videos. Start with the strictest privacy settings. Finally, accept "friend" requests only from people you know, never from strangers. *What else can you do to impress curious recruiters in cyberspace?*

Chapter 13: Interviews and Follow-Up

EXPECT TO EXPLAIN PROBLEM AREAS ON YOUR RÉSUMÉ. Interviewers are certain to question you about problem areas on your résumé. If you have little or no experience, you might emphasize your recent training and up-to-date skills. If you have gaps in your résumé, be prepared to answer questions about them positively and truthfully. If you were fired from a job, accept some responsibility for what happened and explain what you gained from the experience. Don't criticize a previous employer, and don't hide the real reasons. If you received low grades for one term, explain why and point to your improved grades in subsequent terms.

DECIDE HOW TO DRESS. What you wear to a job interview still matters. Even if some employees in the organization dress casually, you should look qualified, competent, and successful. One young applicant complained to his girlfriend about having to wear a suit for an interview when everyone at the company dressed casually. She replied, "You don't get to wear the uniform, though, until you make the team!"

If uncertain, call the company and ask about the dress code. When in doubt, a business suit is a good idea as it will probably be expected. Avoid loud colours; strive for a coordinated, natural appearance. Favourite colours for interviews are gray and dark blue. Cover tattoos and conceal body piercings; these can be a turnoff or at least a distraction or many interviewers. Don't overdo jewellery, and make sure that what you do wear is clean, pressed, odour-free, and lint-free. Shoes should be polished and scuff-free, and they should be "dress" shoes, not casual running shoes

To summarize, ensure that what you wear projects professionalism and shows your respect for the interview situation.

GATHER ITEMS TO BRING. Decide what you should bring with you to the interview, and get everything ready the night before. You should plan to bring copies of your résumé, your reference list, a pad of paper and pen, money for parking and tolls or for public transit, and samples of your work, if appropriate. If you deem the workplace to be tech savvy, bring along your smartphone or tablet if you own one, just in case. Place everything in a businesslike briefcase or folder to add that final professional touch to your look.

Travelling to and Arriving at Your Interview

The big day has arrived! Ideally you are fully prepared for your interview. Now you need to make sure that everything goes smoothly. That means arriving on time and handling that fear you are likely to feel.

On the morning of your interview, give yourself plenty of time to groom and dress. Then give yourself ample time to get to the employer's office. If something unexpected happens that will to cause you to be late, such as an accident or transit issue, call the interviewer right away to explain what is happening. Most interviewers will be understanding, and your call will show that you are responsible. On the way to the interview, don't smoke, don't eat anything messy or smelly, and don't load up on perfume or cologne. Arrive at the interview five or ten minutes early. If possible, check your appearance before going in.

When you enter the office, be courteous and congenial to everyone. Remember that you are being judged not only by the interviewer but by the receptionist and anyone else who sees you before and after the interview. They will notice how you sit, what you read, and how you look. Introduce yourself to the receptionist if there is one, and to whoever else you may bump into, and wait to be invited to sit. You may be asked to fill out a job application while you are waiting. You will find tips for doing this effectively later in this chapter.

Greet the interviewer confidently, and don't be afraid to initiate a handshake. Doing so exhibits professionalism and confidence. Extend your hand, look the

> Allow ample time to arrive unflustered, and be congenial to everyone who greets you.

interviewer directly in the eye, smile pleasantly, and say, *I'm pleased to meet you, Mr. Thomas. I'm Constance Ferraro.* In this culture a firm, not crushing, handshake sends a nonverbal message of poise and assurance. Once introductions have taken place, wait for the interviewer to offer you a chair. Make small talk with upbeat comments, such as *This is a beautiful headquarters* or *I'm very impressed with the facilities you have here.* Don't immediately begin rummaging in your briefcase, bag, or folder for your résumé. Being at ease and unrushed suggest that you are self-confident.

Fighting Fear

Expect to be nervous before and during the interview. It is natural! Other than public speaking, employment interviews are some of the most anxiety-inducing events in people's lives. One of the best ways to overcome fear is to know what happens in a typical interview. You can further reduce your fears by following these suggestions:

> Fight fear by practising, preparing thoroughly, breathing deeply, and knowing that you are in charge for part of the interview.

- **Practise interviewing.** Try to get as much interviewing practice as you can—especially with real companies. The more times you experience the interview situation, the less nervous you will be. If offered, campus mock interviews also provide excellent practice, and the interviewers will offer tips for improvement.
- **Prepare thoroughly.** Research the company. Know how you will answer the most frequently asked questions. Be ready with success stories. Rehearse your closing statement. One of the best ways to reduce butterflies is to know that you have done all you can to be ready for the interview.
- **Understand the process.** Find out ahead of time how the interview will be structured. Will you be meeting with an individual, or will you be interviewed by a panel? Is this the first of a series of interviews? Don't be afraid to ask about these details before the interview so that an unfamiliar situation won't catch you off guard.
- **Dress professionally.** If you know you look sharp, you will feel more confident.
- **Breathe deeply.** Take deep breaths, particularly if you feel anxious while waiting for the interviewer. Deep breathing makes you concentrate on something other than the interview and also provides much-needed oxygen.
- **Know that you are not alone.** Everyone feels some level of anxiety during a job interview. Interviewers expect some nervousness, and a skilled interviewer will try to put you at ease.
- **Remember that an interview is a two-way street.** The interviewer isn't the only one who is gleaning information. You have come to learn about the job and the company. In fact, during some parts of the interview, you will be in charge. This should give you courage.

During the Interview

During the interview you will be answering questions and asking some of your own. Your behaviour, body language, and other nonverbal cues will also be on display. The interviewer will be trying to learn more about you, and you should learn more about the job and the organization. Although you may be asked some unique questions, many interviewers ask standard, time-proven questions, which means that you can prepare your answers ahead of time.

Sending Positive Nonverbal Messages and Acting Professionally

You have already sent nonverbal messages to your interviewer by arriving on time, being courteous, dressing professionally, and greeting the receptionist confidently.

An old adage of interviewing says, "You never get a second chance to make a first impression." Until recently, image consultants differed on how much time individuals have to put their best face forward. But a study conducted by two psychologists has concluded that it takes only one-tenth of a second to form judgments about the key character traits of others. In practical terms, this means employers will make inferences about one's likableness, competence, trustworthiness, and aggressiveness in the blink of an eye. *What should job candidates do to make a good first impression during an interview?*

> Send positive nonverbal messages by arriving on time, being courteous, dressing professionally, greeting the interviewer confidently, controlling your body movements, making eye contact, listening attentively, and smiling.

You will continue to send nonverbal messages throughout the interview. Remember that what comes out of your mouth and what is written on your résumé are not the only messages an interviewer receives from you. Nonverbal messages also create powerful impressions. Here are suggestions that will help you send the right nonverbal messages during interviews:

- **Control your body movements.** Keep your hands, arms, and elbows to yourself. Don't lean on a desk. Keep your feet on the floor. Don't cross your arms in front of you. Keep your hands out of your pockets.
- **Exhibit good posture.** Sit erect, leaning forward slightly. Don't slouch in your chair; at the same time, don't look too stiff and uncomfortable. Good posture demonstrates confidence and interest.
- **Practise appropriate eye contact.** A direct eye gaze, at least in North America, suggests interest and trustworthiness. If you are being interviewed by a panel, remember to maintain eye contact with all interviewers.
- **Use gestures effectively.** Nod to show agreement and interest. Gestures should be used as needed, but don't overdo it.
- **Smile enough to convey a positive attitude.** Have a friend give you honest feedback on whether you generally smile too much or not enough.
- **Listen attentively.** Show the interviewer you are interested and attentive by listening carefully to the questions being asked. This will also help you answer questions appropriately.
- **Turn off your devices.** Avoid the embarrassment of allowing your phone or other device to ring, or even to buzz, during an interview. Turn devices off completely; don't just switch them to vibrate.
- **Don't chew gum.** Chewing gum during an interview is distracting and unprofessional.
- **Sound enthusiastic and interested—but sincere.** The tone of your voice has an enormous effect on the words you say. Avoid sounding bored, frustrated, or sarcastic during an interview. Employers want employees who are enthusiastic and interested.
- **Avoid "empty" words.** Filling your answers with verbal pauses such as *um*, *uh*, *like*, and *basically* communicates that you are not prepared. Also avoid annoying distractions such as clearing your throat repeatedly or sighing deeply.

Above all, remember that employers want to hire people who have confidence in their own abilities. To put yourself into an employer's shoes, so to speak, think of the interview from his or her point of view, as explained below in Figure 13.1. Then, let your body language, posture, dress, and vocal tone prove that you are self-assured.

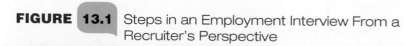

FIGURE 13.1 Steps in an Employment Interview From a Recruiter's Perspective

Before the Interview

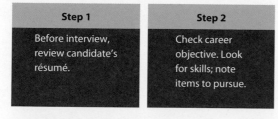

Step 1	Step 2
Before interview, review candidate's résumé.	Check career objective. Look for skills; note items to pursue.

During the Interview

Step 3	Step 4	Step 5
Greet candidate. Introduce self. Make candidate feel comfortable.	Describe open position. Confirm candidate's interest in position.	Give brief overview of organization.

Step 6	Step 7	Step 8
Using résumé, probe for evidence of relevant skills and traits.	Solicit questions from candidate.	Close interview by promoting organization and explaining next step.

After the Interview

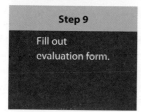

Step 9
Fill out evaluation form.

ANSWERING TYPICAL QUESTIONS CONFIDENTLY. The way you answer questions can be almost as important as what you say. Use the interviewer's name and title from time to time when you answer: *Ms. Lyon, I would be pleased to tell you about . . . .* People like to hear their own names. But be sure you are pronouncing the name correctly. Avoid answering questions with a simple *yes or no*; elaborate on your answers to better promote yourself and your assets. Keep answers positive; try not to criticize anything or anyone.

> How you answer questions can be as important as the answers themselves.

Occasionally it may be necessary to re-focus and clarify vague questions. Some interviewers are inexperienced and ill at ease in the role. You may even have to ask your own question to understand what was asked: *By . . . do you mean . . .?*

Consider closing some of your responses with *Does that answer your question?* or *Would you like me to elaborate on any particular experience?*

Always aim your answers at the key characteristics interviewers seek: expertise and competence, motivation, interpersonal skills, decision-making skills, enthusiasm for the job, and a pleasing personality. And remember to stay focused on your strengths. Don't reveal weaknesses, even if you think they make you look human. You won't be hired for your weaknesses, only for your strengths.

> Stay focused on the skills and traits that employers seek; don't reveal weaknesses.

Use proper English and enunciate clearly. Remember, you will definitely be judged by how well you communicate. Avoid slurred words such as *gonna*

FIGURE 13.2 Interview Actions to Avoid

1. Don't ask for the job. It's naive, undignified, and unprofessional. Wait to see how the interview develops.

2. Don't be negative about your previous employer, supervisors, or colleagues. The tendency is for interviewers to wonder if you would speak about their companies similarly.

3. Don't be a threat to the interviewer. Avoid suggesting directly or indirectly that your goal is to become head honcho, a path that might include the interviewer's job.

4. Don't be late or too early for your appointment. Arrive five minutes before you are scheduled.

5. Don't discuss controversial subjects, and don't use profanity.

6. Don't emphasize salary or benefits. If the interview goes well and these subjects have not been addressed, you may mention them toward the end of the interview.

7. Don't be negative about yourself or others. Never dwell on your liabilities.

8. Don't interrupt. Not only is it impolite but it also prevents you from hearing a complete question or remark.

9. Don't accept an offer until you have completed all your interviews.

and *y'know*, as well as slangy expressions such as *yeah*, *like*, and *whatever*. Also eliminate verbal static (*ah*, *and*, *uhm*). As you practise for the interview, a good idea is to record answers to expected interview questions. Is your speech filled with verbal static?

You can't expect to be perfect in an employment interview. No one is. But you can increase your chances of success by avoiding certain topics and behaviours such as those described in Figure 13.2.

Employment interviews are all about questions. And most of the questions are not new. You can actually anticipate 90 to 95 percent of all questions that will be asked before you ever walk into an interview room.[19]

The following section presents questions that are often asked during employment interviews. You'll find get-acquainted questions, experience and accomplishment questions, future-oriented questions, squirm questions, and money questions. The employer may also use situational/behavioural questions.

To get you thinking about how to respond, we've provided an answer or discussion for the first question in each group. As you read the remaining questions in each group, think about how you could respond most effectively.

QUESTIONS TO GET ACQUAINTED. After opening introductions, recruiters generally try to start the interviewing questioning period with personal questions that put the candidate at ease. They are also striving to gain a picture of the candidate to see if he or she will fit into the organization's culture.

1. Tell me about yourself.

   Experts agree that you must keep this answer short (one to two minutes, tops) but on target. Try practising this formula: "My name is _____. I have completed a _____ degree with a major in _____. Recently I worked for _____ as a _____. Before that I worked for _____ as a _____. My strengths are _____ (interpersonal) and _____ (technical)." Try rehearsing your response in 30-second segments devoted to your education, your work experience, and your qualities/skills. Some candidates end with "Now that I've told you about myself, can you tell me a little more about the position?"

> Prepare for get-acquainted questions by practising a short formula response.

2. What are your greatest strengths?
3. Do you prefer to work by yourself or with others? Why?
4. What was your major in college, and why did you choose it?
5. What are some things you do in your spare time?

"Yes, I think I have good people skills.
What kind of idiot question is that?"

QUESTIONS TO GAUGE YOUR INTEREST. Interviewers want to understand your motivation for applying for a position. Although they will realize that you are probably interviewing for other positions, they still want to know why you are interested in this particular position with this organization. These types of questions help them determine your level of interest.

> Recruiters want to know how interested you are in this organization and in this specific position.

1. Why do you want to work for (*name of company*)?

   Questions like this illustrate why you must research an organization thoroughly before the interview. The answer to this question must prove that you understand the company and its culture. This is the perfect place to bring up the company research you did before the interview. Show what you know about the company, and discuss why you would like to become a part of this organization. Describe your desire to work for this organization not only from your perspective but also from its point of view. What do you have to offer?

2. Why are you interested in this position?
3. What do you know about our company?
4. Why do you want to work in the _____ industry?
5. What interests you about our products (services)?

QUESTIONS ABOUT YOUR EXPERIENCE AND ACCOMPLISHMENTS. After questions about your background and education, the interview generally becomes more specific, with questions about your experience and accomplishments.

> Employers will hire a candidate with less experience and fewer accomplishments if he or she can demonstrate the skills required.

1. Why should we hire you when we have applicants with more experience or better credentials?

   In answering this question, remember that employers often hire people who present themselves well instead of others with better credentials. Emphasize your personal strengths that could be an advantage with this employer. Are you a hard worker? How can you demonstrate it? Have you had recent training? Some people have had more years of experience but actually have less knowledge because they have done the same thing over and over. Stress your experience using new technologies and equipment. Be sure to mention any software you can use effectively. Emphasize that you are open to new ideas and learn quickly.

2. Describe the most rewarding experience of your career so far.
3. How have your education and professional experiences prepared you for this position?
4. What were your major accomplishments in each of your past jobs?
5. What was a typical workday like?
6. What job functions did you enjoy most? Least? Why?
7. Tell me about your computer skills.
8. Who was the toughest boss you ever worked for and why?
9. What were your major achievements in college?
10. Why did you leave your last position? OR: Why are you leaving your current position?

QUESTIONS ABOUT THE FUTURE. Questions that look into the future tend to stump some candidates, especially those who have not prepared adequately. Some of these questions give you a chance to discuss your personal future goals, while others require you to think on your feet and explain how you would respond in hypothetical situations.

1. Where do you expect to be five (or ten) years from now?

When asked about the future, show ambition and interest in succeeding with this company.

Formulate a realistic plan with respect to your present age and situation. The important thing is to be prepared for this question. It is a sure kiss of death to respond that you would like to have the interviewer's job! Instead, show an interest in the current job and in making a contribution to the organization. Talk about the levels of responsibility you would like to achieve. One employment counsellor suggests showing ambition but not committing to a specific job title. Suggest that you hope to have learned enough to have progressed to a position in which you will continue to grow. Keep your answer focused on educational and professional goals, not personal goals.

2. If you got this position, what would you do to be sure you fit in?
3. This is a large (or small) organization. Do you think you would like that environment?
4. Do you plan to continue your education?
5. What do you predict for the future of the _____ industry?
6. How do you think you can contribute to this company?
7. What would you most like to accomplish if you get this position?
8. How do you keep current with what is happening in your profession?

CHALLENGING QUESTIONS. The following questions may make you uncomfortable, but the important thing to remember is to answer truthfully without dwelling on your weaknesses. As quickly as possible, convert any negative response into a discussion of your strengths.

1. What are your greatest weaknesses?

Strive to convert discussion of your weaknesses to topics that show your strengths.

It's amazing how many candidates knock themselves out of the competition by answering this question poorly. Actually, you have many choices. You can present a strength as a weakness (*Some people complain that I'm a workaholic or too attentive to details*). You can mention a corrected weakness (*I found that I really needed to learn about the Internet, so I took a course*). You can cite an unrelated skill (*I really need to brush up on my French*). You can cite a learning objective (*One of my long-term goals is to learn more about international management. Does your company have any plans to expand overseas?*). Another possibility is to reaffirm your qualifications (*I have no weaknesses that affect my ability to do this job*). Be careful that your answer doesn't sound like a cliché (*I tend to be a perfectionist*) and instead shows careful analysis of your abilities.

2. What type of people do you have little patience for?
3. If you could live your life over, what would you change and why?
4. How would your former (or current) supervisor describe you as an employee?
5. What do you want the most from your job?
6. What is your grade point average, and does it accurately reflect your abilities?
7. Have you ever used drugs?
8. Who in your life has influenced you the most and why?
9. What are you reading right now?
10. Describe your ideal work environment.
11. Is the customer always right?
12. How do you define success?

SITUATIONAL QUESTIONS. Questions related to situations help employers test your thought processes and logical thinking. When using situational questions, interviewers describe a hypothetical situation and ask how you would handle it. Situational questions differ based on the type of position for which you are interviewing. Knowledge of the position and the company culture will help you respond favourably to these questions. Even if the situation sounds negative, keep your response positive. Here are just a few examples:

Employers find that situational and behavioural interview questions give them useful information about job candidates.

1. You receive a call from an irate customer who complains about the service she received last night at your restaurant. She is demanding her money back. How would you handle the situation?

   When answering situational questions, it's always a good idea to tie your answer to a real experience from your past. You could say, for example, that you experienced a similar situation in one of your retail positions, and then explain the similarity. Tell the interviewer that you learned to first agree with the complaining customer in order to validate her complaint. Your next step would be to remedy the complaint, which does not necessarily mean giving the complaining customer what she is asking for. For example, in this case, based on restaurant policy, you could say politely that while you cannot refund her money, you can offer a two-for-one coupon valid for a year and a promise that service will be exemplary next time.

2. If you were aware that a co-worker was falsifying data, what would you do?
3. Your supervisor has just told you that she is dissatisfied with your work, but you think it is acceptable. How would you resolve the conflict?
4. Your supervisor has told you to do something a certain way, and you think that way is wrong and that you know a far better way to complete the task. What would you do?
5. Assume that you are hired for this position. You soon learn that one of the staff is extremely resentful because she applied for your position and was turned down. As a result, she is being unhelpful and obstructive. How would you handle the situation?
6. A colleague has told you in confidence that she suspects another colleague of stealing. What would your actions be?
7. You have noticed that communication between upper management and entry-level employees is eroding. How would you solve this problem?

BEHAVIOURAL QUESTIONS. Instead of traditional interview questions, you may be asked to tell stories. The interviewer may say, *Describe a time when . . .* or *Tell me about a situation in which . . . .* To respond effectively, learn to use the storytelling or STAR technique. Ask yourself, what the Situation or Task was, what Action you took, and what the Results were.[20] Practise using this method to recall specific examples of your skills and accomplishments. To be fully prepared, develop a coherent and articulate STAR narrative for every bullet point on your résumé. When answering behavioural questions, describe only educational and work-related situations or tasks, and try to keep them as current as possible. Here are a few examples of behavioural questions:

1. Tell me about a time when you solved a difficult problem.

   Tell a concise story explaining the situation or task, what you did, and the result. For example, *When I was at Ace Products, we continually had a problem of excessive back orders. After analyzing the situation, I discovered that orders went through many unnecessary steps. I suggested that we eliminate much of the paperwork. As a result, we reduced back orders by 30 percent.* Go on to emphasize what you learned and how you can apply that learning to this job. Practise your success stories in advance so that you will be ready.

2. Describe a situation in which you were able to use persuasion to successfully convince someone to see things your way.

"Apart from being a CEO and a job bagging bagels, what other work experience do you have?"

3. Describe a time when you had to analyze information and make a recommendation.
4. Describe a time that you worked successfully as part of a team.
5. Tell me about a time you dealt with confidential information.
6. Give me an example of a time when you were under stress to meet a deadline.
7. Tell me about a time when you had to go above and beyond the call of duty in order to get a job done.
8. Tell me about a time you were able to successfully deal with another person even when that person may not have personally liked you (or vice versa).
9. Give me an example of an occasion when you showed initiative and took the lead.
10. Tell me about a recent situation in which you had to deal with an upset customer or co-worker.

Illegal and Inappropriate Questions

Because human rights legislation protects job applicants from discrimination, interviewers may not ask questions such as those in the following list. Nevertheless, you may face an inexperienced or unscrupulous interviewer who does ask some of these questions. How should you react? If you find the question harmless and if you want the job, go ahead and answer. If you think that answering would damage your chance to be hired, try to deflect the question tactfully with a response such as *Could you tell me how my marital status relates to the responsibilities of this position?* Or you could use the opportunity to further emphasize your strengths. An older worker responding to a question about age might mention experience, fitness, knowledge, maturity, stability, or extensive business contacts. You might also wish to reconsider working for an organization that sanctions such procedures.

> You may respond to an illegal question by asking tactfully how it relates to the responsibilities of the position.

Here are some illegal or inappropriate questions that you may or may not want to answer:

1. Are you married, divorced, separated, single, or living common-law?
2. Is your spouse subject to transfer in his/her job? Tell me about your spouse's job.
3. What is your corrected vision? (But it is legal to ask about quality of vision if visual acuity is directly related to safety or some other factor of the job.)
4. Do you have any disabilities? Do you drink or take drugs? Have you ever received psychiatric care or been hospitalized for emotional problems? Have you ever received workers' compensation? (But it is legal to ask if you have any condition that could affect your ability to do the job or if you have any condition that should be considered during selection.)
5. Have you ever been arrested? Have you ever been convicted of a crime? Do you have a criminal record? (But if bonding is a requirement of the job, it is legal to ask if you are eligible.)
6. How old are you? What is your date of birth? Can I see your birth certificate? (But it is legal to ask *Are you eligible to work under Canadian laws pertaining to age restrictions?*)
7. In what other countries do you have a current address? (But it is legal to ask *What is your current address, and how long have you lived there?*)
8. What is your maiden name? (But it is legal to ask *What is your full name?*)
9. What is your religion? How often do you attend religious services? Would you work on a specific religious holiday? Can you provide a reference from a clergyperson or religious leader?
10. Do you have children? What are your child care arrangements? (But it is legal to ask *Can you work the required hours?* and *Are you available for overtime?*)

11. Where were you born? Were you born in Canada? Can you provide proof of citizenship? (But it is legal to ask *Are you legally entitled to work in Canada?*)
12. Were you involved in military service in another country? (But it is legal to ask about Canadian military service.)
13. What is your first language? Where did you receive your language training? (But it is legal to ask if you understand, read, write, and/or speak the language[s] required for the job.)
14. How much do you weigh? How tall are you?
15. What is your sexual orientation?
16. Are you under medical care? Who is your family doctor? Are you receiving therapy or counselling? (But it is legal to make offers of employment conditional on successful completion of a medical exam that is relevant to that job.)

Asking Your Own Questions

At some point in the interview, you will be asked if you have any questions. The worst thing you can say is no. Instead, ask questions that will help you gain information and will impress the interviewer with your thoughtfulness and interest in the position. Remember that the interview is an opportunity for you to see how you would fit with the company. You must be happy with the prospect of working for this organization. You want a position that matches your skills and personality. Use this opportunity to find out whether this job is right for you. Be aware that you don't have to wait for the interviewer to ask you for questions. You can ask your own questions throughout the interview to learn more about the company and position. Here are some questions you might ask:

> Your questions should impress the interviewer but also draw out valuable information about the job.

1. What will my duties be (if not already discussed)?
2. Tell me what it's like working here in terms of the people, management practices, work loads, expected performance, and rewards.
3. What training programs are available from this organization? What specific training will be given for this position?
4. Who would be my immediate supervisor?
5. What is the organizational structure, and where does this position fit in?
6. Is travel required in this position?
7. How is job performance evaluated?
8. Assuming my work is excellent, where do you see me in five years?
9. How long do employees generally stay with this organization?
10. What are the major challenges for a person in this position?
11. What do you see in the future for this organization?
12. What do employees say they like best about working for this organization?
13. May I have a tour of the facilities?
14. When do you expect to make a decision?

Do not ask about salary or benefits, especially during the first interview. It is best to let the interviewer bring those topics up first.

Ending Positively

After you have asked your questions, the interviewer will signal the end of the interview, usually by standing up or by expressing appreciation that you came. If not addressed earlier, you should at this time find out what action will follow. Demonstrate your interest in the position by asking when it will be filled or what the next step will be. Too many candidates leave the interview without knowing their status or when they will hear from the recruiter. Don't be afraid to say that you want the job!

Before you leave, summarize your strongest qualifications, show your enthusiasm for obtaining this position, and thank the interviewer for a constructive interview and for considering you for the position. Ask the interviewer for a business card, which will provide the information you need to write a thank-you letter, which is discussed below. Shake the interviewer's hand with confidence, and acknowledge anyone else you see on the way out. Be sure to thank the receptionist if there is one. Leaving the interview gracefully and enthusiastically will leave a lasting impression on those responsible for making the final hiring decision.

After the Interview

End the interview by thanking the interviewer, reviewing your strengths for this position, and asking what action will follow.

After leaving the interview, immediately make notes of what was said in case you are called back for a second interview. Write down key points that were discussed, the names of people you spoke with, and other details of the interview. Ask yourself what went really well and what could have been improved. Note your strengths and weaknesses during the interview so that you can work to improve in future interviews. Next, write down your follow-up plans. To whom should you send thank-you messages? Will you contact the employer by phone? If so, when? Then be sure to follow up on those plans, beginning with writing a thank-you message and contacting your references.

Thank Your Interviewer

A follow-up thank-you message shows your good manners and your enthusiasm for the job.

After a job interview you should always send a thank-you message, also called a follow-up message. This courtesy sets you apart from other applicants, some of whom will not bother. Your message also reminds the interviewer of your visit as well as suggesting your good manners and genuine enthusiasm for the job.

Follow-up messages are most effective if sent immediately after the interview. Experts believe that a thoughtful follow-up note carries as much weight as the cover letter does. Almost nine out of ten senior executives admit that in their evaluation of a job candidate they are swayed by a written thank you.[21] In your thank-you message refer to the date of the interview, the exact job title for which you were interviewed, and specific topics discussed. "An effective thank-you message should hit every one of the employer's hot buttons," author and career consultant Wendy Enelow says.[22] Don't get carried away after a successful interview and send an poorly planned thank-you e-mail that reads like a text message or sounds too chummy. Smart interviewees don't ruin their chances by communicating with recruiters in hasty text messages.

In addition to being respectful when following up after an interview, try to avoid worn-out phrases, such as *Thank you for taking the time to interview me.* There are better ways of expressing the same idea. Try *Today's interview was enjoyable; thank you for the opportunity.* Be careful, too, about overusing *I*, especially to begin sentences. Most important, show that you really want the job and that you are qualified for it. Notice how the thank-you e-mail in Figure 13.3 conveys both enthusiasm and confidence.

If you have been interviewed by more than one person, send a separate message to the two most important people in the room (e.g., hiring manager; human resources recruiter). These days most follow-up messages are sent by e-mail, so make sure to get the correct addresses before you leave the interview. One job candidate summarizes her method for sending follow-up e-mails in this way: thank the employer for the interview opportunity, very briefly summarize what was discussed during the face-to-face interview, and add a bit of information you didn't get to mention during the interview.[23]

Contact Your References

Once you have thanked your interviewer, it is time to alert your references that they may be contacted by the employer. You might also have to request a letter of recommendation to be sent to the employer by a certain date. As discussed in Chapter 12, you should have already asked permission to use these individuals as references, and you should have supplied them with a copy of your résumé and information about the types of positions you are seeking.

FIGURE **13.3** Interview Follow-up E-Mail

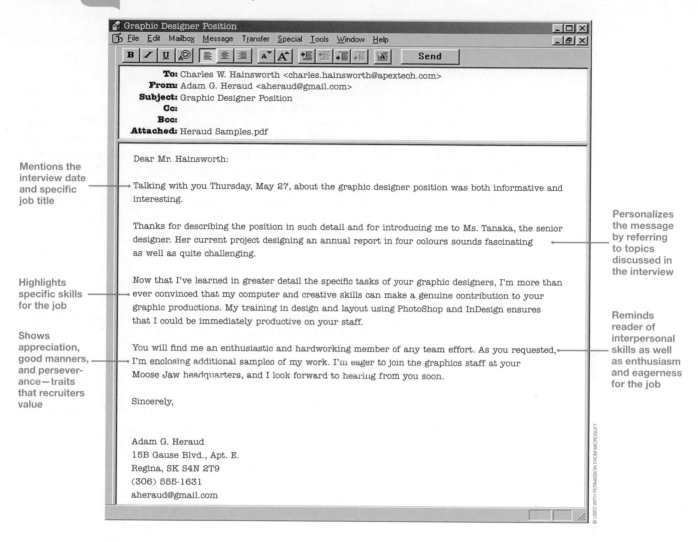

Mentions the interview date and specific job title

Highlights specific skills for the job

Shows appreciation, good manners, and perseverance—traits that recruiters value

Personalizes the message by referring to topics discussed in the interview

Reminds reader of interpersonal skills as well as enthusiasm and eagerness for the job

To: Charles W. Hainsworth <charles.hainsworth@apextech.com>
From: Adam G. Heraud <aheraud@gmail.com>
Subject: Graphic Designer Position
Cc:
Bcc:
Attached: Heraud Samples.pdf

Dear Mr. Hainsworth:

Talking with you Thursday, May 27, about the graphic designer position was both informative and interesting.

Thanks for describing the position in such detail and for introducing me to Ms. Tanaka, the senior designer. Her current project designing an annual report in four colours sounds fascinating as well as quite challenging.

Now that I've learned in greater detail the specific tasks of your graphic designers, I'm more than ever convinced that my computer and creative skills can make a genuine contribution to your graphic productions. My training in design and layout using PhotoShop and InDesign ensures that I could be immediately productive on your staff.

You will find me an enthusiastic and hardworking member of any team effort. As you requested, I'm enclosing additional samples of my work. I'm eager to join the graphics staff at your Moose Jaw headquarters, and I look forward to hearing from you soon.

Sincerely,

Adam G. Heraud
15B Gause Blvd., Apt. E.
Regina, SK S4N 2T9
(306) 555-1631
aheraud@gmail.com

To provide the best possible recommendation, your references need information. What position have you applied for and with what company? What should they stress to the prospective employer? Let's say you are applying for a specific job that requires a letter of recommendation. Professor Orenstein has already agreed to be a reference for you. To get the best letter of recommendation from Professor Orenstein, help her out. Send her an e-mail telling her about the position, its requirements, and the recommendation deadline. Attach a copy of your résumé. You might remind her of a positive experience with you that she could use in the recommendation. Remember that recommenders need evidence to support generalizations. Give them appropriate ammunition, as the student has done in the following request:

Dear Professor Orenstein:

Recently I interviewed for the position of administrative assistant in the Human Resources Department of Host International. Because you kindly agreed to help me, I'd like to ask you to be available by phone to provide a recommendation to Host.

The position calls for good organizational, interpersonal, and writing skills, as well as computer experience. To help you review my skills and training, I enclose my résumé. As you may recall, I earned an A in your business communication class last fall; and you commended my research report for its clarity and organization.

In a reference request message, explain immediately why you are writing. Identify the target position and company.

Specify the job requirements so that the recommender knows what to stress.

You can expect to hear from James Jenkins at Host International (jjenkins@hinternational.com) before July 1. He said he'd call in the morning before 10 a.m. I'm grateful for your support, and I promise to let you know the results of my job search.

Follow Up

If you don't hear from the interviewer within five days, or at the specified time, consider following up. The standard advice to job candidates is to call to follow up a few days after the interview. However, some experts suggest that cold calling a hiring manager is fraught with risk. You may be putting a busy recruiter on the spot and forcing him or her to search for your application. In addition, remember that you are not the only candidate; multiply your phone call by the 200 applicants whom some hiring managers interview.[24] Therefore, you don't want to be a pest. Sending an e-mail to find out how the decision process is going may be best because such a message is much less intrusive.

However, if you believe it is safe to follow up by phone, or if the recruiter suggested it, practise saying something like, *I'm wondering what else I can do to convince you that I'm the right person for this job*, or *I'm calling to find out the status of your search for the _____ position*. When following up, it is important to sound professional and courteous. Sounding desperate, angry, or frustrated because you have not been contacted can ruin your chances. The following follow-up e-mail message would impress the interviewer:

> Dear Ms. Kahn:
>
> I enjoyed my interview with you last Thursday for the receptionist position. You should know that I'm very interested in this opportunity with Coastal Enterprises. Because you mentioned that you might have an answer this week, I'm eager to know how your decision process is coming along. I look forward to hearing from you.
>
> Sincerely,

Depending on the response you get to your first follow-up request, you may have to follow up additional times.[25] Keep in mind, though, that some employers won't tell you about their hiring decision unless you are the one hired. Don't harass the interviewer, and don't force a decision. If you don't hear back from an employer within several weeks after following up, it is best to assume that you didn't get the job and to continue with your job search.

> A follow-up message inquires courteously and does not sound angry or desperate.

Other Employment Documents and Follow-Up Messages

Although the résumé and cover letter are your major tasks, other important documents and messages are often required during the employment process. You may need to complete an employment application form and write follow-up messages. You might also have to write a letter of resignation when leaving a job. Because each of these tasks reveals something about you and your communication skills, you will want to put your best foot forward. These documents often subtly influence company officials to offer a job.

Application Form

Some organizations require job candidates to fill out job application forms instead of, or in addition to, submitting résumés. This practice permits them to gather and store standardized data about each applicant. Whether the application is on paper or online, follow the directions carefully and provide accurate information. The following suggestions can help you be prepared:

- Put your resume on your smartphone. If you don't have a smartphone, carry a card that has some basic information written on it, such as graduation dates; beginning and ending dates of all employment; salary history; full names, titles, and present work addresses of former supervisors; full addresses and phone numbers of current and previous employers; and full names, occupational titles, occupational addresses, and telephone numbers of persons who have agreed to serve as references.
- Look over all the questions before starting.
- Fill out the form neatly, using blue or black ink. Career counsellors recommend printing your responses.
- Answer all questions honestly. Write *Not applicable* or *N/A* if appropriate.
- Use accurate spelling, grammar, and punctuation.
- If asked for the position desired, give a specific job title or type of position. Don't say, *Anything* or *Open*. These answers will make you look unfocused; moreover, they make it difficult for employers to know what you are qualified for or interested in.
- Be prepared for a salary question. Unless you know what comparable employees are earning in the company, the best strategy is to suggest a salary range or to write *Negotiable* or *Open*. See the Communication Workshop at the end of this chapter for tips on dealing with money matters while interviewing.
- Be prepared to explain the reasons for leaving previous positions. Use positive or neutral phrases such as *Relocation*, *Seasonal*, *To accept a position with more responsibility*, *Temporary position*, *To continue education*, or *Career change*. Avoid words or phrases such as *Fired*, *Quit*, *Didn't get along with supervisor*, or *Pregnancy*.
- Look over the application before submitting to make sure it is complete and that you have followed all instructions. Sign and date the application.

Application or Résumé Follow-Up Message

If your résumé or application generates no response within a reasonable time, you may decide to send a short follow-up email such as the following. Doing so (a) jogs the memory of the personnel officer, (b) demonstrates your serious interest, and (c) allows you to emphasize your qualifications or to add new information.

> Dear Ms. Lavecchia:
>
> Please know I am still interested in becoming an administrative support specialist with Quad, Inc.
>
> Since submitting my application [*or* résumé] in May, I have completed my degree and have been employed as a summer replacement for office workers in several downtown offices. This experience has honed my communication and project management skills. It has also introduced me to a wide range of office procedures.
>
> Please keep my application in your active file and let me know when I may put my formal training, technical skills, and practical experience to work for you.
>
> Sincerely,

Open by reminding the reader of your interest.

Review your strengths or add new qualifications.

Rejection Follow-Up Message

If you didn't get the job and you think it was perfect for you, don't give up. Employment specialists encourage applicants to respond to a rejection. The candidate who was offered the position may decline, or other positions may open up. In a rejection follow-up e-mail, it is okay to admit you are disappointed. Be sure to add, however, that you are still interested and will contact the company again in a month in case a job opens up. Then follow through for a couple of months—but don't overdo it. You should be professional and persistent, but not a pest. Here's an example of an effective rejection follow-up message:

Subordinate your disappointment to your appreciation at being notified promptly and courteously.

> Dear Mr. O'Neal:
>
> Although I'm disappointed that someone else was selected for your accounting position, I appreciate your promptness and courtesy in notifying me.
>
> Because I firmly believe that I have the technical and interpersonal skills needed to work in your fast-paced environment, I hope you will keep my résumé in your active file. My desire to become a productive member of Deloitte staff remains strong.
>
> I enjoyed our interview, and I especially appreciate the time you and Ms. Goldstein spent describing your company's presence in international markets. To enhance my qualifications, I have enrolled in a CFA program.
>
> If you have an opening for which I am qualified, please reach me at (519) 555-3901. In the meantime, I will call you in a month to discuss employment possibilities.
>
> Sincerely,

Refer to specifics of your interview.

Take the initiative; say when you will call for an update.

Job Acceptance and Rejection Messages

When all your hard work pays off, you will be offered the position you want. Although you will likely accept the position over the phone, it is a good idea to follow up with an acceptance e-mail to confirm the details and to formalize the acceptance. Your acceptance message might look like this:

Confirm your acceptance of the position with enthusiasm.

> Dear Ms. Madhumali:
>
> It was a pleasure talking with you earlier today. As I mentioned, I am delighted to accept the position of Web designer with Innovative Creations, Inc., in your Richmond office. I look forward to becoming part of the IC team and to starting work on a variety of exciting and innovative projects.
>
> As we agreed, my starting salary will be $46,000, with a benefits package including health and life insurance, retirement plan, stock options, and three weeks of vacation per year.
>
> I look forward to starting my position with Innovative Creations on September 15, 2015. Before that date I will send you the completed tax and insurance forms you need. Thanks again for everything, Ms. Madhumali.
>
> Sincerely,

Review salary and benefits details.

Include the specific starting date.

If you must turn down a job offer, show your professionalism by writing a sincere e-mail. This message should thank the employer for the job offer and explain briefly that you are turning it down. Taking the time to extend this courtesy could help you in the future if this employer has a position you really want. Here's an example of a job rejection message:

Thank the employer for the job offer and decline the offer without giving specifics. Express gratitude and best wishes for the future.

> Dear Mr. Opperman:
>
> Thank you very much for offering me the position of sales representative with Bendall Pharmaceuticals. It was a difficult decision to make, but I have accepted a position with another company.
>
> I appreciate your taking the time to interview me, and I wish Bendall much success in the future.
>
> Sincerely,

Resignation Letter

After you have been in a position for a period of time, you may find it necessary to leave. Perhaps you have been offered a better position, or maybe you have decided to return to school full time. Whatever the reason, you should leave your position gracefully and tactfully. Although you will likely discuss your resignation in person with your supervisor, it is a good idea to document your resignation by writing a formal letter. Some resignation letters are brief, while others contain great detail. Remember that many resignation letters are placed in human resources files; therefore, it should be formatted and written using the professional business letter-writing techniques you learned earlier. Here is an example of the body of a basic letter of resignation:

> Dear Ms. Patrick:
>
> This letter serves as formal notice of my resignation from Allied Corporation, effective Friday, August 15. I have enjoyed working as your office assistant for the past two years, and I am grateful for everything I have learned during my employment with Allied.
>
> Please let me know what I can do over the next two weeks to help you prepare for my departure. I would be happy to help with finding and training my replacement.
>
> Thanks again for providing such a positive employment experience.
>
> Sincerely,

> **Confirm exact date of resignation. Remind employer of your contributions.**

> **Offer assistance to prepare for your resignation. Offer thanks and end with a forward-looking statement.**

Although this employee gave a standard two-week notice, you may find that a longer notice is necessary. The higher and more responsible your position, the longer the notice you should give your employer. You should, however, always give some notice as a courtesy.

Writing job acceptance, job rejection, and resignation messages requires effort. That effort, however, is worth it because you are building bridges that later may carry you to even better jobs in the future.

▌ SUMMING UP AND LOOKING FORWARD

Whether you face a screening interview or a hiring/placement interview, you must be well prepared. You can increase your chances of success and reduce your anxiety considerably by knowing how interviews are typically conducted and by researching the target company thoroughly. Practise answering typical questions, including situational, behavioural, and challenging ones. Consider audio- or video-recording a mock interview so that you can check your body language and improve your answering techniques.

At the end of the interview, thank the interviewer, review your main strengths for the position, and ask what the next step is. Follow up with a thank-you letter and a follow-up call or message, if appropriate. Prepare other employment-related documents as needed, including application forms, application and résumé follow-up messages, rejection follow-up letters, job acceptance and rejection letters, and resignation letters.

You have now completed 13 chapters of instruction aimed at developing your skills so that you can be a successful business communicator in today's rapidly changing world of information. Remember that this is but a starting point. Your skills as a business communicator will continue to grow on the job as you apply the principles you have learned and expand your expertise.

▌ CRITICAL THINKING

1. Why do you think so many employers search for information about job applicants online using Google, Facebook, Twitter, and other online tools? Do you think these kinds of searches are ethical or appropriate? Is this similar to snooping?

2. Is it normal to be nervous about an employment interview? What can be done to overcome this fear?

3. What can you do to improve the first impression you make at an interview?

4. In employment interviews, do you think that behavioural questions (such as *Tell me about a business problem you have had and how you solved it*) are more effective than traditional questions (such as *Tell me what you are good at and why*)?

5. If you are asked an illegal interview question, why is it important to first assess the intentions of the interviewer?

6. Why is it important to ask one's own questions of the interviewer?

7. Why is it a smart strategy to thank an interviewer, to follow up, and even to send a rejection follow-up message? Are any risks associated with this strategy?

CHAPTER REVIEW

1. Name the main purposes of interviews—for job candidates as well as for employers.

2. If you have sent out your résumé to many companies, what information should you keep handy and why?

3. Briefly describe the types of hiring/placement interviews you may encounter.

4. How can you address problem areas on your résumé such as lack of experience, getting fired, or earning low grades?

5. Name at least six interviewing behaviours you can exhibit that send positive nonverbal messages.

6. What is your greatest fear of what you might do or what might happen to you during an employment interview? How can you overcome your fears?

7. Should you be candid with an interviewer when asked about your weaknesses?

8. How can you clarify vague questions from recruiters?

9. How should you respond to questions you believe to be illegal?

10. List the steps you should take immediately following your job interview.

11. Explain the various kinds of follow-up letters.

WRITING IMPROVEMENT EXERCISES

1. **Scripting Answers to Typical Interview Questions.**

Your Task: You've probably already been through a number of job interviews in your life, but they may not have been formal like the interviews you will go through when you start applying for post-college jobs. Script a one- to two-minute answer to the following interview question, and memorize it. Do not use the template on page 422. Then practise speaking the answer in a natural voice so that you don't appear to have memorized it.

Question: Tell me about yourself and your previous work experience.

2. **Scripting Answers to Typical Interview Questions.**

Your Task: Script a one- to two-minute answer to the following typical interview question, and memorize it. Then practise speaking the answer in a natural voice so that you don't appear to have memorized it.

Question: Tell me about a time in a previous job when you faced a difficulty or a criticism or a problem and how you dealt with it.

Follow-Up Question: What would you do differently if this problem happened again?

3. **Scripting Answers to Typical Interview Questions.**

Your Task: Script a one- to two-minute answer to the following typical interview question, and memorize it. Then practise speaking the answer in a natural voice so that you don't appear to have memorized it.

Question: Tell me about a former boss or co-worker whom you admire a lot and why you admire him or her.

Now that you've memorized these three answers, practise interviewing a partner. As you ask each other questions, surprise each other by slightly modifying the questions so they're not exactly as printed above. This modification will force you to improvise on the spot, a valuable interviewing skill.

 ACTIVITIES AND CASES

13.1 Researching an Organization

WEB

Select an organization where you would like to be employed. Assume you've been selected for an interview. Using resources described in this chapter, locate information about the organization's leaders and their business philosophy. Find out about the organization's accomplishments, setbacks, finances, products, customers, competition, and advertising. Prepare a summary report documenting your findings.

13.2 Learning What Jobs Are Really About Through Blogs

WEB

Blogs are becoming an important tool in the employment search process. By accessing blogs, job seekers can learn more about a company's culture and day-to-day activities.

Your Task. Using the Web, locate a blog that is maintained by an employee of a company where you would like to work. Monitor the blog for at least a week. Prepare a short report that summarizes what you learned about the company through reading the blog postings. Include a statement of whether this information would be valuable during your job search.

13.3 Building Interview Skills

Successful interviews require diligent preparation and repeated practice. To be best prepared, you need to know what skills are required for your targeted position. In addition to computer and communication skills, employers generally want to know whether a candidate works well with a team, accepts responsibility, solves problems, is efficient, meets deadlines, shows leadership, saves time and money, and is a hard worker.

Your Task. Consider a position for which you are eligible now or one for which you will be eligible when you complete your education. Identify the skills and traits necessary for this position. If you prepared a résumé in Chapter 12, be sure that it addresses these targeted areas. Now prepare interview worksheets listing at least ten technical and other skills or traits you think a recruiter will want to discuss in an interview for your targeted position.

13.4 Preparing Success Stories

You can best showcase your talents if you are ready with your own success stories that show how you have developed the skills or traits required for your targeted position.

Your Task. Using the worksheets you prepared in Activity 13.3, prepare success stories that highlight the required skills or traits. Select three to five stories to develop into answers to potential interview questions. For example, here's a typical question: "How does your background relate to the position we have open?" A possible response: "As you know, I have just completed an intensive training program in _____. In addition, I have over three years of part-time work experience in a variety of business settings. In one position I was selected to manage a small business in the absence of the owner. I developed responsibility and customer-service skills in filling orders efficiently, resolving shipping problems, and monitoring key accounts. I also inventoried and organized products worth over $200,000. When the owner returned from a vacation trip to Florida, I was commended for increasing sales and was given a bonus in recognition of her gratitude." People relate to and remember stories. Try to shape your answers into memorable stories.

13.5 Digging for Digital Dirt: Keeping a Low Profile Online

WEB

Before embarking on your job hunt, you may want to know what employers might find if they searched your personal life in cyberspace, specifically on Facebook, MySpace, Twitter, and so forth. Running your name through Google and other search engines, particularly enclosed in quotation marks to lower the number of hits, is usually the first step. Assembling a digital portrait of an applicant is easier than ever thanks to new spy-worthy Web sites such as Snitch.name (**http://snitch.name**) that collect information from a number of search engines, Web sites, and social networks. Self-titled "The Social White Pages," Snitch.name not only looks for people's profiles in social networks, but also compiles publicly available data found on services such as 123people.com, PeekYou.com, and so forth.

Your Task. Use Google, Snitch.name, Bing, or Dogpile to search the Web for your full name, enclosed in quotation marks. In Google, don't forget to run an *Image* search at **www.google .com/images** to find any photos of questionable taste. If your instructor requests, share your insights with the class—not the salacious details, but general observations—or write a short memo summarizing the results.

WEB

13.6 Exploring Appropriate Interview Attire

As you prepare for your interview by learning about the company and the industry, don't forget a key component of interview success: creating a favourable first impression by wearing appropriate business attire. Job seekers often have nebulous ideas about proper interview wear. Some wardrobe mishaps include choosing a conservative "power" suit but accessorizing it with beat-up casual shoes or a shabby bag. Grooming glitches include dandruff on dark suit fabric, dirty fingernails, or mothball odour. Women sometimes wrongly assume that any black clothing items are acceptable, even if they are too tight, revealing, sheer, or made of low-end fabrics. Most image consultants agree that workplace attire falls into three main categories: business formal, business casual, and casual. Only business formal is considered proper interview apparel.

Your Task. To prepare for your big day, search your library databases and the Web for descriptions and images of *business formal*. You may research *business casual* and *casual* styles, but for an interview, always dress on the side of caution—conservatively. Compare prices and look for suit sales to buy one or two attractive interview outfits. Share your findings (notes, images, and price ranges for suits, shoes, and accessories) with the class and your instructor.

13.7 Polishing Answers to Interview Questions

Practice makes perfect in interviewing. The more often you rehearse responses to typical interview questions, the closer you are to getting the job.

Your Task. Select three questions from each of the five question categories discussed in this chapter (pp. 422–426). Write your answers to each set of questions. Try to incorporate skills and traits required for the targeted position. Polish these answers and your delivery technique by practising in front of a mirror or with a video or audio recorder.

13.8 Creating an Interview "Cheat Sheet"

Even the best-rehearsed applicants sometimes forget to ask the questions they prepared, or they fail to stress their major accomplishments in job interviews. Sometimes applicants are so rattled they even forget the interviewer's name. To help you keep your wits during an interview, make a "cheat sheet" that summarizes key facts, answers, and questions. Review it before the interview and again as the interview is ending to be sure you have covered everything that is critical.

Your Task. Prepare a cheat sheet with the following information:

- Day and time of interview:
- Meeting with: [Name of interviewer(s), title, company, city, province, postal code, telephone, cell, e-mail]
- Major accomplishments: (four to six)
- Management or work style: (four to six)
- Things you need to know about me: (three to four items)
- Reason I left my last job:
- Answers to difficult questions: (four to five answers)
- Questions to ask interviewer:
- Things I can do for you:

TEAM

13.9 Role Play: Practising Answering Interview Questions

One of the best ways to understand interview dynamics and to develop confidence is to role-play the parts of interviewer and candidate.

Your Task. Choose a partner from your class. Make a list of five interview questions from those presented in this chapter. In team sessions you and your partner will role-play an actual interview. One acts as interviewer, the other as the candidate. Prior to the interview, the candidate tells the interviewer what job he/she is applying for, at which company. For the interview, the interviewer and candidate should dress appropriately and sit in chairs facing each other. The interviewer greets the candidate and makes him/her comfortable. The candidate gives the interviewer a copy of his/her résumé. The interviewer asks three (or more, depending on your instructor's time schedule) questions from the candidate's list. The interviewer may also ask follow-up questions if appropriate. When finished, the interviewer ends the meeting graciously. After one interview, reverse roles and repeat.

13.10 Learning to Answer Situational Interview Questions

WEB

TEAM

Situational interview questions can vary widely from position to position. You should know enough about a position to understand some of the typical situations you would encounter on a regular basis.

Your Task. Use your favourite search tool to locate typical job descriptions of a position in which you are interested. Based on these descriptions, develop a list of six to eight typical situations someone in this position would face; then write situational interview questions for each of these scenarios. In pairs of two students, role-play interviewer and interviewee alternating with your listed questions.

13.11 Developing Skill with Behavioural Interview Questions

WEB

TEAM

Behavioural interview questions are increasingly popular, and you will need a little practice before you can answer them easily.

Your Task. Use your favourite search tool to locate lists of behavioural questions on the Web. Select five skills areas such as communication, teamwork, and decision making. For each skills area find three behavioural questions that you think would be effective in an interview. In pairs of two students, role-play interviewer and interviewee alternating with your listed questions. You goal is to answer effectively in one or two minutes. Remember to use the STAR method when answering.

13.12 Answering Puffball and Killer Questions in a Virtual Interview

WEB

Two Web sites offer excellent interview advice. At Monster Career Advice (**http://career -advice.monster.com/interview-tips/home.aspx**) you can improve your interviewing skills in virtual interviews. You will find questions, answers, and explanations for interviews in job fields ranging from administrative support to human resources to technology. At WetFeet (**www.wetfeet.com**) you can learn how to answer résumé-based questions and how to handle pre-interview jitters, and see dozens of articles filled with helpful tips.

Your Task. Visit one or both of the targeted Web sites and briefly summarize the best piece of advice you find on the site. (If the URLs have been changed, use your favourite search tool to locate *Monster Interviews* and *WetFeet Interviews*.)

13.13 Video-Recording an Interview

Seeing how you look during an interview can help you improve your body language and presentation style. Your instructor may act as interviewer, or an outside businessperson may be asked to conduct mock interviews in your classroom.

Your Task. Engage a student or campus specialist to video-record each interview. Review your performance and critique it, looking for ways to improve. Your instructor may ask class members to offer comments and suggestions on individual interviews.

13.14 Handling Difficult Interview Questions

CRITICAL THINKING

Although some questions are not appropriate in job interviews, many interviewers will ask them anyway—whether intentionally or unknowingly. Being prepared is important.

Your Task. How would you respond in the following scenario? Let's assume you are being interviewed at one of the top companies on your list of potential employers. The interviewing committee consists of a human resources manager and the supervising manager of the department where you would work. At various times during the interview the supervising manager has asked questions that made you feel uncomfortable. For example, he asked whether

Chapter 13: Interviews and Follow-Up

you were married. You know this question is illegal, but you saw no harm in answering it. But then he asked how old you were. Since you started college early and graduated in two years, you are worried that you may not be considered mature enough for this position. But you have most of the other qualifications required and you are convinced you could succeed on the job. How should you answer this question?

13.15 Saying Thanks for the Interview
You've just completed an exciting employment interview, and you want the interviewer to remember you.

Your Task. Write a follow-up thank-you e-mail to Ronald T. Ranson, Human Resources Manager, Electronic Data Sources, ranson@eds.ca (or a company of your choice).

13.16 Refusing to Take No for an Answer
After an excellent interview with Electronic Data Sources (or a company of your choice), you're depressed to learn that it hired someone else. But you really want to work for the company.

Your Task. Write a follow-up e-mail to Ronald T. Ranson, Human Resources Manager, Electronic Data Sources, ranson@eds.ca (or a company of your choice). Indicate that you are disappointed but still interested.

WEB
13.17 Answering Difficult Questions in a Virtual Interview
The Monster Web site offers an entertaining online practice interview with questions ranging from easy to challenging. Even an experienced interviewee is unlikely to get all of these questions right the first time.

Your Task. Visit Monster's Interview section at the URL below. Craft responses to the five bolded questions (without reading Monster's suggestions). After you've crafted your responses, read Monster's suggestions. What do you think of these suggestions?

Related Web site: **http://career-advice.monster.ca/job-interview/interview-questions/common-interview-questions-canada/article.aspx.**

WEB
13.18 Following Up After Submitting Your Résumé
A month has passed since you sent your résumé and cover letter in response to a job advertisement. You are still interested in the position and would like to find out whether you still have a chance.

Your Task. Write a follow-up letter that won't offend the reader or damage your chances of employment.

13.19 Requesting a Reference
Your favourite professor has agreed to be one of your references. You have just arrived home from a job interview that went well, and you must ask your professor to write a letter of recommendation.

Your Task. Write to the professor requesting that a letter of recommendation be sent to the company where you were interviewed. Explain that the interviewer asked that the letter be sent directly to him. Provide data about the job description and about yourself so that the professor can target its content.

13.20 Saying Yes to a Job Offer
Your dream has come true: you have just been offered an excellent position. Although you accepted the position on the phone, you want to send a formal acceptance letter.

Your Task. Write a job acceptance letter to an employer of your choice. Include the specific job title, your starting date, and details about your compensation package. Make up any necessary details.

EMAIL
13.21 Grounding Helicopter Parents
Overprotective couples hovering over their Millennial offspring have been dubbed "helicopter parents" by some human resources specialists. These take-charge parents seem to extend

their involvement into managing their adult children's job searches. Recruiters and career counsellors are reporting that parents accompany their kids to job fairs and job interviews. Some don't think twice about attempting to arrange interview appointments for their kids. Others go as far as calling hiring managers to ask why their 24-year-old didn't get the job. Experts explain that the Millennials grew up on an electronic leash. When in trouble, they could rely on a cell phone, IM or text messages, or e-mail to contact their parents for help and advice. Millennials view their parents as trusted advisors. Second, the skyrocketing costs of a postsecondary education have prompted parents to become more hands-on to protect their investment.

Most hiring managers are troubled by this trend. After all, they want to employ mature, independent individuals. Whereas most recruiters frown on parental involvement and would not hire a recent graduate who brings mom or dad to a job interview, some employers are beginning to reach out to parents. Merrill Lynch, Office Depot, and others may hold a parents' day, send a letter of introduction to parents of recent hires, or instruct parents on the corporate Web site on how to strike a balance between support and meddling.[26]

Your Task. Ponder this information about helicopter parents in light of what you learned in this chapter. Consider the following questions: How do you feel about parents who hover around their kids and intervene in their job searches? Can you name benefits of parental involvement? What are the advantages of the opposite—the hands-off approach? Do hands-on parents improve or hurt their children's job prospects? What specific problems do helicopter parents pose for hiring managers and their companies? How involved are your parents in your education? Are they supportive? Intrusive? After jotting down answers to these and similar questions, discuss parental involvement with your peers in class. Your instructor may ask you to summarize your thoughts in a memo or e-mail.

13.21 Humour and Job Interviews

Job interviews can be stressful occasions, so it's no surprise that comedians have for a long time used job interviews in their routines. The popular Web site YouTube (**www.youtube.com**) has a number of postings under the category "Job Interview Funny."

Your Task. Do some research on YouTube by watching a few funny interview clips. Decide whether there's anything new and useful to be learned from these clips, or whether it has all been covered, and more usefully, by this chapter. If you think there's something new to be learned from the clips you've seen, develop a three- to five-minute presentation in which you use part of a YouTube clip to illustrate your point. Remember, humour has to be used carefully in a classroom or workplace situation. You're using the humour to make a point, not just to get laughs from your audience.

 # GRAMMAR/MECHANICS REVIEW 13—TOTAL REVIEW

The following sentences contain errors in grammar, punctuation, capitalization, number style, usage, and spelling. Write a corrected version of each sentence.

1. In the evening each of the female nurses are escorted to there cars.

2. It must have been him who received the highest score although its hard to understand how he did it.

3. Our Office Manager asked Rachel and I to fill in for him for 4 hours on Saturday morning.

4. Working out at the Gym and jogging twenty miles a week is how she stays fit.

5. 3 types of costs must be considered for proper inventory controll, holding costs, ordering costs and stockout costs.

6. If I was him I would fill out the questionaire immediately so that I would qualify for the drawing.

7. Higher engine revolutions per mile mean better acceleration, however lower revolutions mean the best fuel economy.

8. Our teams day to day operations include: setting goals, improving customer service, manufacturing quality products and hitting sales targets.

9. If I had saw the shippers bill I would have payed it immediately.

10. When convenent will you please send me 3 copys of the companys color logo?

11. Do you think it was him who left the package on the boss desk.

12. About 1/2 of Pizza Huts six thousand outlets will make deliverys, the others concentrates on walk in customers.

13. Every thing accept labor is covered in this five year warranty.

14. Our Director of Human Resources felt nevertheless that the applicant should be given a interview.

15. When Keisha completes her degree she plans to apply for employment in: Calgary, Toronto and Halifax

GRAMMAR/MECHANICS CHALLENGE—13

Document for Revision

The following interview thank-you e-mail (Figure 13.4) has faults in grammar, punctuation, spelling, wordiness, and word use. Use standard proofreading marks (see Appendix B) to correct the errors. When you finish, your instructor can show you the revised version of this e-mail.

FIGURE 13.4 Follow-Up E-Mail

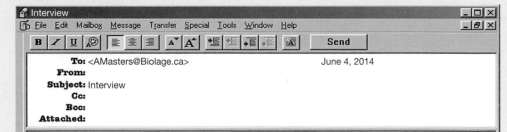

Dear Mr. Masters:

I appriciate the opportunity for the interview yesterday for the newly-listed Position of Sales Trainee. It was really a pleasure meeting yourself and learning more about Biolage Enterprises, you have a fine staff and a sophisticated approach to marketing.

You're organization appears to be growing in a directional manner that parralels my interests' and career goals. The interview with yourself and your staff yesterday confirmed my initale positive impressions of Biolage Enterprises and I want to reiterate my strong interest in working with and for you. My prior Retail sales experience as a sales associate with Sears; plus my recent training in Microsoft Word and Excel would enable me to make progress steadily through your programs of training and become a productive member of your sales team in no time at all.

Again, thank-you for your kind and gracius consideration. In the event that you need any additional information from me, all you have to do is give me a call me at (405) 391-7792.

Sincerly yours,

LET'S TALK MONEY: NEGOTIATING A SALARY

The question of when to talk about salary causes concern for many job applicants. Some advisors recommend bringing the issue up immediately; others suggest avoiding the topic entirely. What happens if the company asks for salary expectations in the job advertisement? The best plan is to be prepared to discuss salary when required, but not to force the issue. The important thing to remember is that almost all salaries are negotiable.

Suggestion No. 1: Avoid discussing salary for as long as possible in the interview process

The longer you delay salary discussion, the more time you will have to convince the employer that you are worth what you are asking for. Ideally, you should try to avoid discussing salary until you know for sure that the interviewing company is making a job offer. The best time for you to negotiate your salary is between the time you are offered the position and the time you accept it. Wait for the employer to bring salary up first. If salary comes up and you are not sure whether the job is being offered to you, it is time for you to be blunt. Here are some things you could say:

- Are you making me a job offer?
- What salary range do you pay for positions with similar requirements?
- I'm very interested in the position, and my salary would be negotiable.
- Tell me what you have in mind for the salary range.

Suggestion No. 2: Know the salary range for similar jobs in similar organizations, but be aware of an amount that would motivate you

Remember that if you provide an amount that is too high you will price yourself out of the market. If the amount is too low you might be sorry. Everyone wants to make money, but salary by itself should not be a reason to take or reject a job. The important thing here is to think in terms of a wide range. Let's say you are hoping to start at between $40,000 and $50,000. To an interviewer, you might say, *I was looking for a salary in the low to high forties.* This technique is called bracketing. In addition, stating your salary range in an annual dollar amount sounds more professional than asking for an hourly wage. Be sure to consider such things as geographic location, employer size, industry standards, the strength of the economy, and other factors to make sure that the range you come up with is realistic.

Suggestion No. 3: When negotiating, focus on what you are worth, not on what you need

Throughout the interview and negotiation process, focus continually on your strengths. Make sure that the employer knows everything of value that you will bring to the organization. You have to prove that you are worth what you are asking for. Employers pay salaries based on what you will accomplish on the job and contribute to the organization. When discussing your salary, focus on how the company will benefit from these contributions. Don't bring personal issues into the negotiation process. No employer will be willing to pay you more because you have bills to pay, mouths to feed, or debt to get out of.

Suggestion No. 4: Never say no to a job before it is offered

Why would anyone refuse a job offer before it's made? It happens all the time. Let's say you were hoping for a salary of $45,000. The interviewer tells you that the salary scheduled for this job is $39,000. You respond, *Oh, that's out of the question!* Before being offered the job, you have, in effect, refused it. Instead, wait for the job offer; then start negotiating your salary.

Suggestion No. 5: Ask for a higher salary first, and consider benefits

Within reason, always try to ask for a higher salary first. This will leave room for this amount to decrease during negotiations until it is closer to your original expectations. Remember to consider the entire compensation package when negotiating. You may be willing to accept a lower salary if benefits such as insurance, flexible hours, time off, and retirement are attractive.

Suggestion No. 6: Be ready to bargain if offered a low starting salary

Many salaries are negotiable. Companies are often willing to pay more for someone who interviews well and fits their culture. If the company seems right to you and you are pleased with the sound of the open position but you have been offered a low salary, say *That is somewhat lower than I had hoped but this position does sound exciting. If I were to consider this, what sorts of things could I do to quickly become more valuable to this organization?* Also discuss such things as bonuses based on performance or a shorter review period. You could say something like, *Thanks for the offer. The position is very much what I wanted in many ways, and I am delighted at your interest. If I start at this salary, may I be reviewed within six months with the goal of raising the salary to _____?*

Another possibility is to ask for more time to think about the low offer. Tell the interviewer that this is an important decision, and you need some time to consider the offer. The next day you can call and say, *I am flattered by your offer but I cannot accept, because the salary is lower than I would like. Perhaps you could reconsider your offer or keep me in mind for future openings.*

Suggestion No. 7: Be honest

Be honest throughout the entire negotiation process. Don't inflate the salaries of your previous positions to try to get more money. Don't tell an employer that you have received other job offers unless it is true. These lies can be grounds for being fired later on.

Suggestion No. 8: Get the final offer in writing

Once you have agreed on a salary and compensation package, get the offer in writing. You should also follow up with a position acceptance letter, as discussed earlier in this chapter.

Career Application

You've just passed the screening interview and have been asked to come in for a personal interview with the human resources representative and the hiring manager of a company where you are very eager to work. Although you are delighted with the company, you have promised yourself that you will not accept any position that pays less than $45,000 to start.

YOUR TASK

- In teams of two, role-play the position of interviewer and interviewee.
- Interviewer: Set the interview scene. Discuss preliminaries, and then offer a salary of $39,000.
- Interviewee: Respond to preliminary questions and then counter with a salary request for $42,500.
- Reverse roles so that the interviewee becomes the interviewer. Repeat the scenario.

Business communicators produce documents and messages that have standardized formats. Becoming familiar with these formats is important because documents and messages actually say two things about the writer. Meaning is conveyed by the words chosen to express the writer's ideas. A sense of trust and credibility is conveyed by the appearance of a document and its adherence to recognized formats.

To ensure that what you write and send out speaks favourably about you and your organization, you'll want to give special attention to the appearance and formatting of your e-mails, letters, envelopes, memos, and fax cover sheets. While we don't cover texts, social media posts, and instant messages in this appendix, as you learned earlier, these short messages should have a professional tone when sent at work, meaning they should not contain slang or other inappropriate language, they should be short and to the point, and they should deal with one issue at a time.

🗨 E-MAILS

E-mail has been around now for about 20 years; as a result, certain formatting and usage norms have developed. The following suggestions, illustrated in Figure A.1 and also in Figure 4.2 on page 95, can guide you in setting up the parts of an e-mail. Always check, however, with your organization so that you can observe its practices.

TO LINE. Type the receiver's e-mail address after To. If replying to an e-mail, your software will fill in the address once you click on Reply. If responding to someone you once were in touch with, you can either click Reply in an old saved e-mail from him or her, or type in the address once again.

CC AND BCC. Insert the e-mail address of anyone who is to receive a copy of the message. Cc stands for *carbon copy* or *courtesy copy*. Don't be tempted, though, to send needless copies just because it's so easy. Some organizations develop an internal style in which anyone cc'd on an original e-mail should be cc'd on the response. Other organizations ask employees to only cc when it's necessary. Check with your manager or experienced co-worker.

Bcc stands for *blind carbon copy*. Some writers use bcc to send a copy of the message without the addressee's knowledge. Writers also use the bcc line for mailing lists. When a message is being sent to a number of people and their e-mail addresses should not be revealed, the bcc line works well to conceal the names and addresses of all receivers.

SUBJECT. Identify the subject of the e-mail with a brief but descriptive summary of the topic. Be sure to include enough information to be clear and compelling. Capitalize the initial letters of principal words.

SALUTATION. Include a brief greeting, if you like. Some writers use a salutation such as *Dear Selina* followed by a comma or a colon. Others are more informal with *Hi, Selina!* or *Good morning* or *Greetings*. Some writers simulate a salutation by including the name of the receiver in an abbreviated first line, as shown in Figure A.1. Others writers treat an e-mail like a memo and skip the salutation entirely or include only a brief salutation consisting of the recipient's name, such as *Dave*.

FIGURE A.1 Effective E-Mail

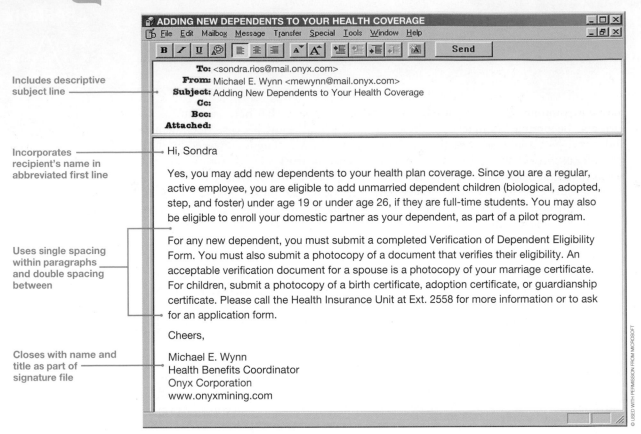

Includes descriptive subject line

Incorporates recipient's name in abbreviated first line

Uses single spacing within paragraphs and double spacing between

Closes with name and title as part of signature file

MESSAGE. Cover just one topic in your e-mail, and try to keep your total message under one screen in length. Single-space and be sure to use both upper- and lowercase letters. Double-space between paragraphs, and use graphic highlighting (bullets, numbering) whenever you are listing three or more items.

CLOSING. Conclude your e-mails with a short expression such as *Cheers* or *Best wishes* or *Regards* followed by your name. If the recipient is unlikely to know you, it's not a bad idea to include your title and organization. In order not to have to type all this information with every e-mail sent out, most professional e-mail users prepare an e-mail signature that includes name, title, and department/company name, and that can also be embellished with an electronic business card, hyperlink (e.g., to the company's Web site), and a picture. Use restraint, however, because e-mail signatures take up precious space. Writers of e-mail sent within organizations may omit a closing and even skip their names at the ends of messages because receivers will recognize them from their identification in the opening lines.

LETTERS

Business communicators write business letters primarily to correspond with people outside the organization. Letters may go to customers, vendors, other businesses, and the government, as discussed earlier in this book. The following information will help you format your letters following conventional guidelines.

Letter Parts

Professional-looking business letters are arranged in a conventional sequence with standard parts. Following is a discussion of how to use these letter parts properly. Figure A.2 illustrates the parts in a block-style letter.

LETTERHEAD. Most business organizations use 8.5-by-11-inch paper printed with a letterhead displaying their official name, street address, Web site address, e-mail address, and telephone and fax numbers. The letterhead may also include a logo and an advertising tag line such as *Ebank: A new way to bank.*

DATELINE. On letterhead paper you should place the date two blank lines below the last line of the letterhead or 5 centimetres from the top edge of the paper (line 13). On plain paper, place the date immediately below your return address. Since the date goes on line 13, start the return address an appropriate number of lines above it. The most common dateline format is as follows: *June 9, 2015.* Don't use *th* (or *rd*) when the date is written this way. For European or military correspondence, use the following dateline format: *9 June 2012.* Notice that no commas are used.

ADDRESSEE AND DELIVERY NOTATIONS. Delivery notations such as *FAX TRANSMISSION, FEDERAL EXPRESS, MESSENGER DELIVERY, CONFIDENTIAL,* or *CERTIFIED MAIL* are typed in all capital letters two blank lines above the inside address.

INSIDE ADDRESS. Type the inside address—that is, the address of the organization or person receiving the letter—single-spaced, starting at the left margin. The number of lines between the dateline and the inside address depends on the size of the letter body, the type size (point or pitch size), and the length of the typing lines. Generally, two to ten lines is appropriate.

Be careful to duplicate the exact wording and spelling of the recipient's name and address on your documents. Usually, you can copy this information from the letterhead of the correspondence you are answering. If, for example, you are responding to *Jackson & Perkins Company,* don't address your letter to *Jackson and Perkins Corp.*

Always be sure to include a courtesy title such as *Mr., Ms., Mrs., Dr.,* or *Professor* before a person's name in the inside address—for both the letter and the envelope. Although many women in business today favour *Ms.,* you'll want to use whatever title the addressee prefers.

In general, avoid abbreviations (such as *Ave.* or *Co.*) unless they appear in the printed letterhead of the document being answered.

ATTENTION LINE. An attention line allows you to send your message officially to an organization but to direct it to a specific individual, officer, or department. However, if you know an individual's complete name, it's always better to use it as the first line of the inside address and avoid an attention line. Here are two common formats for attention lines:

MultiMedia Enterprises	MultiMedia Enterprises
931 Calkins Avenue	Attention: Marketing Director
Toronto, ON M3W 1E6	931 Calkins Road
	Toronto, ON M3W 1E6
Attention Marketing Director	

Attention lines may be typed in all caps or with upper- and lowercase letters. The colon following *Attention* is optional. Notice that an attention line may be placed two lines below the address block or printed as the second line of the inside address. You'll want to use the latter format if you're composing on a word processor, because the address block may be copied to the envelope and the attention line will not interfere with the last-line placement of the postal code. (Mail can be sorted more easily if the postal code appears in the last line of a typed address.)

FIGURE A.2 Block and Modified Block Letter Styles

Letterhead → *peerless* **graphics**
893 Dillingham Boulevard Stony Plain, AB
Phone (403) 667-8880 Fax (403) 667-8830 www.peergraph.com

↓ line 13, or 2 blank lines below letterhead

Dateline → September 13, 2015

↓ 2 to 10 blank lines

Inside address →
Mr. T. M. Wilson, President
Visual Concept Enterprises
1256 Lumsden Avenue
Nordegg, AB T0M 3T0

↓ 1 blank line

Salutation → Dear Mr. Wilson

↓ 1 blank line

Subject line → SUBJECT: BLOCK LETTER STYLE

↓ 1 blank line

Body →

This letter illustrates block letter style, about which you asked. All typed lines begin at the left margin. The date is usually placed 5 cm from the top edge of the paper or two lines below the last line of the letterhead, whichever position is lower.

This letter also shows open punctuation. No colon follows the salutation, and no comma follows the complimentary close. Although this punctuation style is efficient, we find that most of our customers prefer to include punctuation after the salutation and the complimentary close.

If a subject line is included, it appears two lines below the salutation. The word SUBJECT is optional. Most readers will recognize a statement in this position as the subject without an identifying label. The complimentary close appears two lines below the end of the last paragraph.

↓ 1 blank line

Complimentary close and signature block →

Sincerely

Mark H. Wong

↓ 3 to 4 blank lines

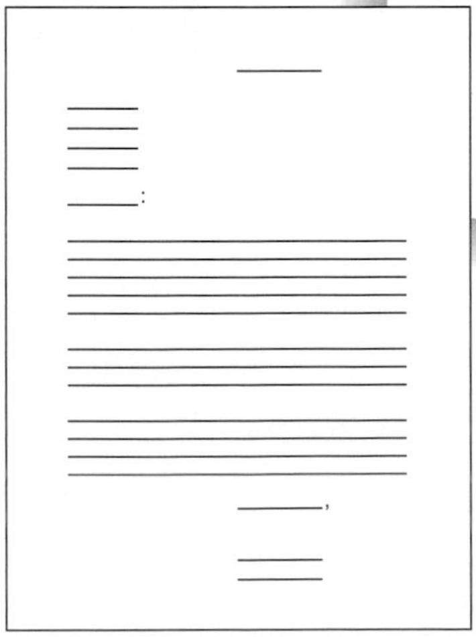

Mark H. Wong
Graphics Designer

↓ 1 blank line

MHW:pil

Modified block style, mixed punctuation

In block-style letters, as shown above, all lines begin at the left margin. In modified block-style letters, as shown at the left, the date is centred or aligned with the complimentary close and signature block, which start at the centre. The date may also be backspaced from the right margin. Paragraphs may be blocked or indented. Mixed punctuation includes a colon after the salutation and a comma after the complimentary close. Open punctuation, shown above, omits the colon following the salutation and omits the comma following the complimentary closing.

SALUTATION. Place the letter greeting, or salutation, two lines below the last line of the inside address or the attention line (if used). If the letter is addressed to an individual, use that person's courtesy title and last name (*Dear Mr. Lanham*). Even if you are on a first-name basis (*Dear Leslie*), be sure to add a colon (not a comma or a semicolon) after the salutation, unless you are using open punctuation. Do not use an individual's full name in the salutation (not *Dear Mr. Leslie Lanham*) unless you are unsure of gender (*Dear Leslie Lanham*).

SUBJECT AND REFERENCE LINES. Although traditionally the subject line is placed one blank line below the salutation, many businesses actually place it above the salutation. Use whatever style your organization prefers. Reference lines often show policy or file numbers; they generally appear two lines above the salutation.

BODY. Most business letters and memos are single-spaced, with double line spacing between paragraphs. Very short messages may be double-spaced with indented paragraphs.

COMPLIMENTARY CLOSE. Typed two lines below the last line of the letter, the complimentary close may be formal (*Yours truly*) or informal (*Sincerely* or *Respectfully*). The simplified letter style omits a complimentary close.

SIGNATURE BLOCK. In most letter styles, the writer's typed name and optional identification appear three to four blank lines below the complimentary close. The combination of name, title, and organization information should be arranged to achieve a balanced look. The name and title may appear on the same line or on separate lines, depending on the length of each. Use commas to separate categories within the same line, but not to conclude a line.

Sincerely,   Respectfully,

Jeremy M. Wood   *Casandra Baker-Murillo*

Jeremy M. Wood, Manager   Casandra Baker-Murillo
Technical Sales and Services   Executive Vice President

Some organizations include their names in the signature block. In such cases the organization name appears in all caps two lines below the complimentary close, as shown here:

Sincerely,
LITTON COMPUTER SERVICES

Shelina A. Simpson

Ms. Shelina A. Simpson
Executive Assistant

REFERENCE INITIALS. If used, the initials of the typist and writer are typed two lines below the writer's name and title. Generally, the writer's initials are capitalized and the typist's are lowercased, but this format varies.

ENCLOSURE NOTATION. When an enclosure or attachment accompanies a document, a notation to that effect appears two lines below the reference initials. This notation reminds the typist to insert the enclosure in the envelope, and it reminds the recipient to look for the enclosure or attachment. The notation may be spelled out (*Enclosure, Attachment*), or it may be abbreviated (*Enc., Att.*). It may indicate the number of enclosures or attachments, and it may also identify a specific enclosure (*Enclosure: Form 1099*).

COPY NOTATION. If you make copies of correspondence for other individuals, you may use cc to indicate carbon copy, pc to indicate photocopy, or merely c for any kind of copy. A colon following the initial(s) is optional.

SECOND-PAGE HEADING. When a letter extends beyond one page, use plain paper of the same quality and colour as the first page. Identify the second and succeeding pages with a heading consisting of the name of the addressee, the page number, and the date. Use either of the following two formats:

Ms. Rachel Ruiz   2   May 3, 2012

Ms. Rachel Ruiz
Page 2
May 3, 2012

Both headings appear on line 7, followed by two blank lines to separate them from the continuing text. Avoid using a second page if you have only one line or the complimentary close and signature block to fill that page.

PLAIN-PAPER RETURN ADDRESS. If you prepare a personal or business letter on plain paper, place your address immediately above the date. Do not include your name; you will type (and sign) your name at the end of your letter. If your return address contains two lines, begin typing it on line 11 so that the date appears on line 13. Avoid abbreviations other than the two-letter province/territory abbreviation.

580 East Leffels Street
Dartmouth, NS B6R 2F3
December 14, 2012

Ms. Ellen Siemens
Retail Credit Department
Union National Bank
1220 Dunsfield Boulevard
Halifax, NS B4L 2E2

Dear Ms. Siemens:

For letters prepared in the block style, type the return address at the left margin. For modified block-style letters, start the return address at the centre to align with the complimentary close.

Letter and Punctuation Styles

Business letters are generally prepared in either block or modified block style, and they generally use mixed punctuation.

BLOCK STYLE. In the block style, shown in Figure A.2, all lines begin at the left margin. This style is a favourite because it is easy to format.

MODIFIED BLOCK STYLE. The modified block style differs from block style in that the date and closing lines appear in the centre, as shown at the bottom of Figure A.2. The date may be (1) centred, (2) begun at the centre of the page (to align with the closing lines), or (3) backspaced from the right margin. The signature block—including the complimentary close, writer's name and title, or organization identification—begins at the centre. The first line of each paragraph may begin at the left margin or may be indented five or ten spaces. All other lines begin at the left margin.

Most businesses today use mixed punctuation, shown with the modified block-style letter at the bottom left of Figure A.2. This style requires a colon after the salutation and a comma after the complimentary close. Even when the salutation is a first name, the colon is appropriate.

◖ ENVELOPES

An envelope should be of the same quality and colour of stationery as the letter it carries. Because the envelope introduces your message and makes the first impression, you need to be especially careful in addressing it. Moreover, how you fold the letter is important.

RETURN ADDRESS. The return address is usually printed in the upper left corner of an envelope, as shown in Figure A.3. In large companies some form of identification (the writer's initials, name, or location) may be typed or handwritten above the company name and return address. This identification helps return the letter to the sender in case of non-delivery.

On an envelope without a printed return address, single-space the return address in the upper left corner. Beginning on line 3 on the fourth space (approximately 12 millimetres or 0.5 inch) from the left edge, type the writer's name, title, company, and mailing address.

MAILING ADDRESS. On legal-sized No. 10 envelopes (10.5 by 24 centimetres), begin the address on line 13 about 11.5 centimetres from the left edge, as shown in Figure A.3. For small envelopes (7.5 by 15 centimetres), begin typing on line 12 about 6.2 centimetres from the left edge.

Canada Post recommends that addresses be typed in all caps without any punctuation. This Postal Service style, shown in the small envelope in Figure A.3, was originally developed to facilitate scanning by optical character readers (OCRs). Today's OCRs, however, are so sophisticated that they scan upper- and lowercase letters easily. Many companies today prefer to use the same format for the envelope as for the inside address. If the same format is used, writers can take advantage of

FIGURE A.3 Envelope Formats

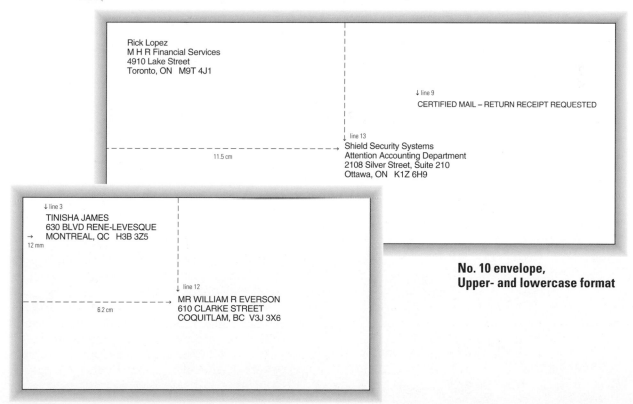

No. 10 envelope,
Upper- and lowercase format

No. 6¾ envelope, uppercase format

word processing programs to copy the inside address to the envelope, thus saving keystrokes and reducing errors. Having the same format on both the inside address and the envelope also looks more professional and consistent. For these reasons you may choose to use the familiar upper- and lowercase combination format. But you will want to check with your organization to learn its preference.

In addressing your envelopes for delivery in North America, use the two-letter province, territory, and state abbreviations shown in Figure A.4. Notice that these abbreviations are in capital letters without periods.

FIGURE A.4 Abbreviations of Provinces, Territories, and States

PROVINCE OR TERRITORY	TWO-LETTER ABBREVIATION	PROVINCE OR TERRITORY	TWO-LETTER ABBREVIATION
Alberta	AB	Nova Scotia	NS
British Columbia	BC	Nunavut	NU
Manitoba	MB	Ontario	ON
New Brunswick	NB	Prince Edward Island	PE
Newfoundland and Labrador		Quebec	QC
	NL	Saskatchewan	SK
Northwest Territories	NT	Yukon Territory	YT

STATE OR TERRITORY	TWO-LETTER ABBREVIATION	STATE OR TERRITORY	TWO-LETTER ABBREVIATION
Alabama	AL	Missouri	MO
Alaska	AK	Montana	MT
American Samoa	AS	Nebraska	NE
Arizona	AZ	Nevada	NV
Arkansas	AR	New Hampshire	NH
California	CA	New Jersey	NJ
Colorado	CO	New Mexico	NM
Connecticut	CT	New York	NY
Delaware	DE	North Carolina	NC
District of Columbia	DC	North Dakota	ND
Florida	FL	North Mariana Islands	MP
Georgia	GA	Ohio	OH
Guam	GU	Oklahoma	OK
Hawaii	HI	Oregon	OR
Idaho	ID	Palau	PW
Illinois	IL	Pennsylvania	PA
Indiana	IN	Puerto Rico	PR
Iowa	IA	Rhode Island	RI
Kansas	KS	South Carolina	SC
Kentucky	KY	South Dakota	SD
Louisiana	LA	Tennessee	TN
Maine	ME	Texas	TX
Marshall Islands	MH	Utah	UT
Maryland	MD	Vermont	VT
Massachusetts	MA	Virgin Islands	VI
Michigan	MI	Virginia	VA
Micronesia	FM	Washington	WA
Minnesota	MN	West Virginia	WV
Minor Outlying Islands	UM	Wisconsin	WI
Mississippi	MS	Wyoming	WY

FOLDING. The way a letter is folded and inserted into an envelope sends an additional credibility signal about a writer's professionalism and carefulness. Your goal in following the procedures shown here is to produce the least number of creases that may distract readers.

For traditional business letter envelopes, begin with the letter face up. Fold slightly less than one third of the sheet toward the top, as shown in the diagram. Then fold down the top third to within 6 to 7 millimetres of the bottom fold. Insert the letter into the envelope with the last fold toward the bottom of the envelope.

For smaller personal note envelopes, begin by folding the bottom up to within 6 to 7 millimetres of the top edge. Then fold the right third over to the left. Fold the left third to within 6 to 7 millimetres of the last fold. Insert the last fold into the envelope first.

MEMOS

Memos are still important business documents where they are used, but they are being replaced by mass e-mails in many organizations. For example, in the past if a company wanted to announce an important policy change to its employees, it would send out a hard-copy memo to each employee's mailbox (or desk or workstation). Today, it's increasingly rare to receive hard-copy memos. Nevertheless, you may still find it necessary to create a memo on occasion.

The easiest route is to choose a memo template in Microsoft Word, but if you'd like to design your own memo, follow these instructions:

- Open a Word document and begin typing 3 centimetres from the top of the page.
- Right and left margins may be set at 1.5 inches (4 centimetres).
- Include an optional company name and the word MEMO or MEMORANDUM as a heading. Leave two blank spaces after this heading.
- Create four subheadings on the left side of the page, each separated by one blank line: DATE, TO, FROM, and SUBJECT. The information that comes after each of these subheadings should be stated as clearly and succinctly as possible.
- After the SUBJECT subheading, leave one or two blank lines and begin typing the content of your memo. Single-space between lines and double-space between paragraphs.
- Do not include a closing salutation or signature. This is one of the major differences between, on the one hand, e-mails and letters, and on the other, faxes and memos. Because you've included the FROM subheading at the top, you don't need to repeat your name again at the end of a memo or fax.

FAX COVER SHEET

Documents transmitted by fax are usually introduced by a cover sheet, such as that shown in Figure A.5. As with memos, the format can vary considerably, but most

FAX TRANSMISSION

DATE: _____

TO: _____   FAX
NUMBER:_____
           _____
           _____

FROM:_____   FAX
NUMBER:_____
         _____
         _____

NUMBER OF PAGES TRANSMITTED INCLUDING THIS COVER SHEET: ___

MESSAGE:

If any part of this fax transmission is missing or not clearly received, please contact:

NAME: _____

PHONE:_____

E-MAIL:_____

important items are incorporated into Microsoft Word's fax templates. Important items in a fax cover sheet are (1) the name and fax number of the receiver, (2) the name and fax number of the sender, (3) the number of pages being sent, and (4) the name, telephone number, and e-mail address of the person to notify in case of unsatisfactory transmission.

When the document being transmitted requires little explanation, you may prefer to attach an adhesive note (such as a Post-it fax transmittal form) to your document instead of a full cover sheet. These notes carry essentially the same information as shown in our printed fax cover sheet. They are perfectly acceptable in most business organizations and can save paper and transmission costs.

Correction Abbreviations and Proofreading Marks

APPENDIX

B

When marking your hard-copy assignments, your instructor may use the following symbols or abbreviations to indicate writing areas for improvement. You may also see them in the workplace when proofreading written documents.

The abbreviations refer to style issues discussed in Appendix D or in the Grammar/Mechanics Handbook at the end of this book. The symbols are proofreading marks used by professional editors (although their usage is diminishing due to the acceptance of electronic tools such as Microsoft Word's Track Changes feature and Adobe's Comment feature). Knowing this information is valuable, because part of your career may involve reviewing documents for others.

CORRECTION ABBREVIATIONS

For an explanation of the errors covered by the 11 abbreviations below, consult either Chapter 3, the G/M Handbook, or Appendix D.

ART   An article has been used incorrectly or is missing.

AWK   Your sentence is awkwardly written (see also PREC below).

PA   A pronoun does not agree with its antecedent (the noun it replaces).

PREC   Your sentence is imprecise.

PUNCT   A punctuation mark has been used incorrectly or is missing.

RO   Your sentence has two or more independent clauses without a conjunction or semi-colon, or it uses a comma to join the clauses.

SF   Your sentence is actually a fragment of a sentence; either a subject or a verb is missing.

SV   The subject and verb in your sentence do not agree.

WORDY   Your sentence includes repetition or redundancy.

VPR   A pronoun in your sentence is vague.

VT   One of your verbs is in the wrong tense, or you have shifted its tense unnecessarily.

PROOFREADING MARKS

PROOFREADING MARK	DRAFT COPY	FINAL COPY
⹀ Align horizontally	TO: Rick Munoz	TO: Rick Munoz
‖ Align vertically	‖166.32 132.45	166.32 132.45
≡ Capitalize	Coca-çola runs on android	Coca-Cola runs on Android
◡ Close up space	meeting at 3 p. m.	meeting at 3 p.m.
⸥ ⸤ Centre	⸥Recommendations⸤	Recommendations
ℛ Delete	in my final judgement	in my judgment
ⱽ Insert apostrophe	our companys product	our company's product
⋀ Insert comma	you will of course	you will, of course,
⋏ Insert semicolon	value therefore, we feel	value; therefore, we feel
⹀ Insert hyphen	tax free income	tax-free income
⨀ Insert period	Ms Holly Hines	Ms. Holly Hines
ⱽⱽ Insert quotation mark	shareholders receive a bonus	shareholders receive a "bonus"
# Insert space	downloadapps	download apps
/ Lowercase (remove capitals)	the Vice-President	the vice-president
⊏ Move to left	HUMAN RESOURCES	Human Resources
⊐ Move to right	⊏I. Labour costs	I. Labour costs
○ Spell out	A. Findings of study ⊐ aimed at 2 depts	A. Findings of study aimed at two departments
¶ Start new paragraph	¶Keep the screen height at eye level.	Keep the screen height at eye level.
⋯⋯ Stet (don't delete)	officials talked openly	officials talked openly
∿ Transpose	accounts recievable	accounts receivable
∿∿∿ Use boldface	Conclusions	**Conclusions**
⎯ Use italics	The Perfect Résumé	*The Perfect Résumé*
⌐ Start new line	Globex, 23 Acorn Lane	Globex 23 Acorn Lane
⌇ Run lines together	Invoice No., 122059	Invoice No. 122059

Careful writers make sure they properly document any data appearing in reports or messages, for many reasons. Citing sources strengthens a writer's argument, as you learned earlier in this book. Acknowledging sources also shields writers from charges of plagiarism and the loss of reputation that may follow. Moreover, clear references help readers pursue further research. Fortunately, word processing software has taken much of the pain out of documenting data, particularly for footnotes and endnotes.

SOURCE NOTES AND CONTENT NOTES

Before we discuss specific documentation formats, you should know the difference between source notes and content notes. Source notes (also called in-text citations) identify quotations, paraphrased passages, and author references. They lead readers to the sources of cited information, and they must follow a consistent format. Content notes, on the other hand, allow writers to add comments, explain information not directly related to the text, or refer readers to other sections of a report.

TWO DOCUMENTATION METHODS FOR SOURCE NOTES

For years researchers have struggled to develop the perfect documentation system—one that is efficient for the writer and crystal-clear to the reader. Most of these systems can be grouped into two methods: the footnote/endnote method and the parenthetic method.

Footnote/Endnote Method

Writers using footnotes or endnotes insert a small superscript (raised) figure into the text close to the place where a reference is mentioned. This number leads the reader to a footnote at the bottom of the page or to an endnote at the end of the document. Footnotes or endnotes contain a complete description of the source document. In this book we have used the endnote method. We chose this style because it least disrupts the text. Most of the individual citation formats in this book follow the traditional style suggested in *The Chicago Manual of Style*, 16th ed. (Chicago: The University of Chicago Press, 2010). Here are some of the most frequently used endnotes, styled in accordance with the *Chicago Manual*. They are numbered here with full-sized numbers; endnotes with superscript figures are also acceptable.

Book, One Author

1. Sara White, *Profiting in the Knowledge Age: A Canadian Guide to the Future* (Toronto: McKnight Publishing, 2015), 25.

Book, Many Authors

2. Manny Colver, Dan Smith, and Jeremy Devport, *Careers in the 21st Century* (Scarborough, ON: Nelson Education, 2014), 356–58.

Academic Journal Article

3. John Drovich, "Peace in the Middle East," *Canadian Journal of International Studies* 19, no. 10 (2011): 23–45.

Monthly Magazine Article

4. Bill Safer, "Future Leadership," *Canadian Management,* April 2012, 45.

Newspaper Article

5. Trisha Khan, "Beyond Hard Skills: Emotional Intelligence in the Workplace," *Winnipeg Free Press,* August 22, 2015, B3.

Government Publication

6. Employment and Social Development Canada, *Labour Market Bulletin: Ontario* (Ottawa: Queen's Printer, 2013), 5.

Online Services

7. Loblaw Companies Ltd., *2012 Annual Report,* http://www.loblaw.ca/files/4.%20Investor%20Centre/Financial%20Reports/2012/Q4/2012%20Annual%20Report_v002_c4xn04.pdf, 14 (accessed January 18, 2014).

Interview

8. Jonathan Ross (Senior Director, Investor Relations, Loblaw Companies Ltd.), personal interview, May 25, 2015.

In referring to a previously mentioned footnote, cite the page number along with the author's last name or a shortened form of the title if no author is given. The Latin forms *ibid., op. cit.,* and *et al.* are rarely seen in business reports today. A portion of a business report using the endnote method for source citation is found in Figure C.1.

Parenthetic Method

Many academic writers prefer to use a parenthetic style to cite references. In this method a reference to the author appears in parentheses close to the place where it is mentioned in the text. Some parenthetic styles show the author's last name and date of publication (e.g., *Cook 2000*), while others show the author's last name and page cited (e.g., *Cook 24*). One of the best-known parenthetic systems is the Modern Language Association (MLA) format. The long report shown in Chapter 9 illustrates this format. Below we'll discuss both MLA and American Psychological Association (APA) formats.

Which Method for Business?

Students frequently ask, "What documentation system is most used in business?" While we can't know which style is used in all businesses, anecdotal evidence shows that MLA format is considered more appropriate for humanities subjects, and that for business (both academic and real-world), the APA format, in which the year of publication is mentioned along with the author name, is becoming more generally accepted and expected.

 ## APA STYLE—AMERICAN PSYCHOLOGICAL ASSOCIATION

Popular in the social and physical sciences, and increasingly the standard in business writing, the American Psychological Association (APA) documentation style uses parenthetic citations. That is, each author reference is shown in parentheses when cited in the text. Following are selected features of the APA style. For more

These changes are introducing challenges to companies operating both in Canada and abroad. Obviously, all of these employees need specific business and technology skills, but they also need to be aware of, and be sensitive to, the cultures in which they are living and working.[1] The Bank of Montreal has targeted several of these areas in which to enhance services. Chinese-Canadian business has increased 400 percent in the last five years.[2]

Women are increasing their role as both customer and worker. By the year 2011 women are expected to compose 48 percent of the labour force in Canada, as compared with 27 percent in 1961.[3] However, women hold only about 20 percent of the top management positions in organizations in the industrialized world.[4]

Companies that focus on diversity are improving their bottom line. Recently, Federal Express was named in the *Financial Post* as one the 100 best companies to work for in Canada. Canadian Pacific Forest Products received recognition for ensuring that selection committees had diverse membership, for their development of antiharassment policies, and for other diversity initiatives.[5]

Notes

1. Brenda Lynn, "Diversity in the Workplace: Why We Should Care," *CMA Management Accounting Magazine* 70, no. 5 (June 2010): 9–12.

2. Richard Sommer, "Firms Gain Competitive Strength from Diversity (Says Report by Conference Board of Canada)," *Financial Post,* 9 May 2011, 31.

3. British Columbia, Ministry of Education, Skills and Training, *The Impact of Demographic Change* (Victoria: Ministry of Education, Skills, and Training, 2012), 35.

4. R. J. Burke and C. A. McKeen, "Do Women at the Top Make a Difference? Gender Proportions and the Experiences of Managerial and Professional Women," *Human Relations* 49, no. 8 (2012): 1093–1104.

5. British Columbia, 36.

information see the *Publication Manual of the American Psychological Association,* 6th ed. (Washington, DC: American Psychological Association, 2010).

In-Text Citation

In-text citations consist of the author's last name, year of publication, and pertinent page number(s). These items appear in parentheses, usually at the end of a clause or end of a sentence in which material is cited. This parenthetic citation, as shown in the following illustration, directs readers to a reference list at the end of the report where complete bibliographic information is recorded.

The strategy of chicken king Don Tyson was to expand aggressively into other "center-of-the-plate" proteins, such as pork, fish, and turkey (Berss, 2010, p. 64).

One of the paragraphs from the report in Figure C1, with the citation style changed from Chicago to APA, would look like this:

These changes are introducing challenges to companies operating both in Canada and abroad. Obviously, as Brenda Lynn (2010) argues, all of these employees need specific business and technology skills, but they also need to be aware of, and be sensitive to, the cultures in which they are living and working. The Bank of Montreal has targeted several of these areas in which to enhance services. Chinese-Canadian business has increased 400 percent in the last five years (Sommer, 2011).

Bibliography

All reference sources are alphabetized in a bibliography entitled "References." Below are selected guidelines summarizing important elements of the APA bibliographic format:

- Include authors' names with the last name first followed by initials, such as: **Smith, M. A.** First and middle names are not used.
- Show the date of publication in parentheses, such as: **Smith, M. A. (2011).**
- Italicize the titles of books and use "sentence-style" (sometimes called *down style*) capitalization. This means that only the first word of a title, proper nouns, and the first word after an internal colon are capitalized. Book titles are followed by the place of publication and publisher's name, such as: **Smith, M. A. (2011).** *Communication for managers.* **Elmsford, NY: Pergamon Press.**
- Type the titles of magazine and journal articles without italics or quotation marks. Use sentence-style capitalization for article titles. However, italicize the names of magazines and journals and capitalize the initial letters of all important words. Also italicize the volume number, such as: **Cheung, H. K., & Burn, J. M. (2004). Distributing global information systems resources in multinational companies—a contingency model.** *Journal of Global Information Management,* **2(3), 14–27.** ["2(3), 14–27" indicates volume 2, issue 3, pages 14 to 27.]
- Space only once following periods and colons.
- Do not include personal communications (such as interviews, telephone conversations, e-mail, and messages from non-archived discussion groups and online forums) in the reference list, since they are not retrievable.

Electronic References

When print information is available, APA suggests placing it first followed by online information. For example, a newspaper article: **Schellhardt, T. D. (2009, March 4). In a factory schedule, where does religion fit in?** *The Wall Street Journal,* **pp. B1, B12. Retrieved March 5, 2009, from http://interactive.wsj.com.** For additional discussion and examples, visit the APA Web site (**http://www.apastyle.org/elecref.html**).

Figure C.2 shows the format of an APA References List.

MLA Style—Modern Language Association

The MLA citation style uses parenthetic author references in the text. These in-text citations guide the reader to a bibliography called "Works Cited." Following are selected characteristics of the MLA style. For more information, consult The Modern Language Association of America, *MLA Handbook for Writers of Research Papers,* 7th ed. (New York: The Modern Language Association of America, 2009).

In-Text Citations

Within the text the author's last name and relevant page reference appear in parentheses, such as "(Chartrand 310)." In-text citations should be placed close to the reference they cite. Notice that no separating comma appears. If the author's name is mentioned in the text, cite only the page number in parentheses. If you don't know the author's name (e.g., when quoting from a Web site or blog), use the title of the Web site section or blog entry you took the information from in your in-text citation. Your goal is to avoid interrupting the flow of your writing. Thus, you should strive

FIGURE C.2 Model APA Bibliography of Sample References

References

Online annual report
> Air Canada. (2014). *2014 annual report*. Retrieved May 26, 2015, from http://www .aircanada.com/en/about/investor/index.html#reports

Magazine article
> Berss, M. (2010, October 24). Protein man. *Forbes, 154*, 64–66.

Newspaper article, no author
> Globalization often means that the fast track leads overseas. (2012, June 16). *The Financial Post*, p. A10.

Online research database magazine article
> Jahl, A. (2013, November 24). PowerPoint of no return. *Canadian Business*, 14–15. Retrieved May 27, 2014, from CBCA Current Affairs, George Brown College Library.

Newspaper article, one author
> Lancaster, H. (2012, February 7). When taking a tip from a job network, proceed with caution. *The Wall Street Journal*, p. B1.

Online newspaper article
> Markoff, J. (2009, June 5). Voluntary rules proposed to help ensure privacy for Internet users. *The New York Times*. Retrieved June 9, 2009, from http://www.nytimes.com/library/cyber/week/y05dat.html

Online magazine article
> Murphy, H. L. (2008, August 31). Saturn's orbit still high with consumers. *Marketing News Online*. Retrieved September 1, 2009, from http://www.ama.org/pubs/mn/0818n1.htm

Brochure
> Pinkerton Investigation Services. (2008). *The employer's guide to investigation services* (3rd ed.) [Brochure]. Atlanta, GA: Pinkerton Information Center.

Book, two authors
> Rose, R. C., & Garrett, E. M. (2008). *How to make a buck and still be a decent human being*. New York: HarperCollins.

Government publication
> Statistics Canada. (2005). *A portrait of persons with disabilities: Target groups project*. Ottawa, ON: Department of Industry, Science and Technology.

Web site, no author
> Transmission models—criticism. (2010). *Communication, Culture and Media Studies*. Retrieved May 23, 2012, from http://www.cultshock.ndirect.co.uk/MUHome/cshtml/

Journal article with volume and issue numbers
> Wetherbee, J. C., Vitalari, N. P., & Milner, A. (2010). Key trends in systems development in Europe and North America. *Journal of Global Information Management, 3*(2), 5–20.

to place the parenthetical reference where a pause would naturally occur, but as near as possible to the material documented. Note the following examples:

Author's Name in Text

Peters also notes that stress could be a contributing factor in the health problems reported thus far (135).

Author's Name Unknown

One Web site goes so far as to claim that new communication technologies such as BlackBerrys and multi-purpose cell phones will soon make in-person conversations "a thing of the past" ("Talking Not Cool").

Author's Name in Reference

The study was first published in 1958 (Peters 127–35).

Authors' Names in Text

Others, like Bergstrom and Voorhees (243–51), support a competing theory.

Authors' Names in Reference

Others support a competing theory (e.g., Bergstrom and Voorhees 243–51).

When citing an entire work—whether a print source, a non-print source such as a film, a television program, or a Web source that has no pagination or any other reference numbers—MLA style recommends that you include in the text, rather than in a parenthetical reference, the name of the person or organization that begins the corresponding entry in the works-cited list.

Electronic Source With Author

William J. Kennedy's *Bits and Bytes* discusses new computer technologies in the context of the digital telecommunications revolution. (In the "Works Cited" list, the reader would find a complete reference under the author's name.)

Electronic Source Without Author

More companies today are using data mining to unlock hidden value in their data. The data mining program "TargetSource," described at the Tener Solutions Group Web site, helps organizations predict consumer behaviour. (In the "Works Cited" list, the reader would find a complete reference under "Tener Solutions Group," the organization that owns the Web site.)

Works Cited List

In-text citations lead the reader to complete bibliographical citations in the "Works Cited." This alphabetical listing may contain all works consulted or only those mentioned in the text. Check with your instructor or editor to learn what method is preferred. Below are selected guidelines summarizing important elements of the MLA format for "Works Cited," as shown in Figure C.3.

- **Medium of publication.** The seventh edition of the *MLA Handbook* mandates that every entry in the works-cited list indicate the medium of publication. For print periodicals (journals, newspapers, magazines), the medium appears after the page numbers. For non-periodical print publications (such as books and pamphlets), the medium appears after the date of publication; however, if the item being cited is only part of a larger work (e.g., an essay, poem, or short story in an anthology or an introduction, preface, foreword, or afterword in a book), give the inclusive page numbers of the piece you are citing after the publication date, then list the medium of publication. For Web publications, the medium appears between the date of publication and the date of access.
- **Hanging indented style.** Indent the second and succeeding line for each item. MLA format suggests double-spacing for the entire paper, including the works-cited list. However, Figure C.3 is single-spaced to represent preferred business usage.
- **Book and Web site titles.** Italicize the titles of books and use "headline style" for capitalization. This means that the initial letters of all main words are capitalized:

> Lewe, Glenda, and Carol D. MacLeod. *Step Into the World of Workplace Learning: A Collection of Authentic Workplace Materials.* Scarborough, ON: Nelson Thomson Learning, 2011. Print.

> "ACE Aviation to Take Minority Stake in Merged U.S. Airline." *CBC.* *ca.* 19 May 2015. Web. 23 May 2015.

FIGURE C.3 Model MLA Bibliography of Sample References

Works Cited

Air Canada. *2014 Annual Report*. Air Canada, Feb. 2005. Web. 26 May 2015. — Online annual report

Beresford, Marcia. "The Shift in Profit." *Maclean's* 24 Oct. 2011: 25–26. Print. — Magazine article

British Columbia Ministry of Education, Skills and Training, *The Impact of Demographic Change*. Victoria: Ministry of Education, Skills and Training, 2012. Print. — Government publication

"Globalization Often Means That the Fast Track Leads Overseas." *Globe and Mail* 16 June 2012: A10. Print. — Newspaper article, no author

Jahl, Andrew. "PowerPoint of No Return." *Canadian Business*. 24 Nov. 2013: 14–15. *CBCA Current Affairs*. George Brown College Library. Web. 27 May 2015. — Online research database magazine article, where "CBCA Current Affairs" is the research database

Lancaster, Hal. "When Taking a Tip From a Job Network, Proceed With Caution." *Wall Street Journal* 7 Feb. 2012: B1. Print. — Newspaper article, one author

Mark, John. "Feds Provide Summary of New Privacy Legislation for Internet Users." *globeandmail.com*. Globe and Mail, 5 June 2012. Web. 9 June 2014. — Online newspaper article

"Message Treatment." *Communication, Culture and Media Studies*. N.p., n.d. Web. 23 May 2015 <http://www.cultsock.ndirect.co.uk/>. — Web site, no author

Murdry, Henry. "Consumers Still Driving the Economy." *Marketing News Online*. Canadian Marketing Association, 31 Aug. 2011. Web. 1 Sept. 2014. — Online magazine article

Pinnacle Security Services. *What Employers Should Know About Employees*. 2nd ed. Toronto: Pinnacle Information Centre, 2012. Print. — Brochure

Rivers, John. Personal interview. 16 May 2015. — Interview

Rose, Richard C., and Echo Montgomery Garrett. *How to Make a Buck and Still Be a Decent Human Being*. New York: HarperCollins, 2008. Print. — Book, two authors

SPSS Inc. "Clementine@work." *SPSS.com*. 15 May 2014. Web. 7 Sept. 2014. <http://www.spss.com/customer/clem_stories/>. — Company Web site, no author

Weathers, Nicholas. "Key Trends in Systems Development." *Journal of Information Management* 3.2 (2010): 5–20. Print. — Journal article with volume and issue numbers

- **Magazine titles.** For the titles of magazine articles, include the date of publication but omit volume and issue numbers:

  Lee, Mary M. "Investing in International Relationships." *Business Monthly* 18 Feb. 2010: 25–27. Print.

- **Journal articles.** For journal articles, follow the same format as for magazine articles except include the volume number, issue number, and the year of publication (inside parentheses):

  Collier, Roger. "Morals, Medicine, and Geography." *Canadian Medical Association Journal* 179.10 (2014): 996–98. Print. ["179.10" indicates volume 179, issue 10.]

- **Italics and underscoring.** MLA style now recommends italicizing book, magazine, and journal titles (instead of underscoring).

Electronic References

The objective in citing sources, whether print publications or electronic publications, is to provide enough information so that your reader can locate your sources. In addition to the information provided for all print sources (e.g., author's name if available, title, date of publication, medium of publication, etc.), a citation for an electronic source requires at least three other kinds of information. First, you must provide the publisher or sponsor of the site (if not available, use "N.p."). Second, you must provide the date when you accessed the source. Finally, the medium of publication ("Web") must appear between the two dates (date of publication and date of access), reducing the potential for confusion.

The seventh edition of the MLA Handbook makes the following recommendations for citing Web publications:

- Give the same information for electronic sources as you would if you were citing a print publication (e.g., author name, title, page number).
- Give all relevant dates. Because electronic sources can change or move, cite the date the document was produced (if available; if not, use "n.d.") as well as the date you accessed the information. The date of access is required because multiple versions of an electronic work may be available, and any version may vary from previous or future versions.
- Include the electronic address or universal resource locator (URL) only when requested by your instructor or if the reader could not locate your source without it. The MLA used to recommend the inclusion of URLs of Web sources in works-cited-list entries. However, URLs change frequently and may be of little value; readers are more likely to use a search engine to find titles and authors' names. If you insert a URL, it should appear immediately after the date of access, followed by a period and a space. It should be the complete address, if possible (include "http://"), and must be enclosed in angle brackets (<, >) and followed by a period. If the URL needs to be divided at the end of a line, do so only after the double slashes or a single slash. Never add a hyphen (or allow your word processor to add one) to mark a break in the address.
- Download or print (for future reference) any Web material you use, as online resources frequently move or even disappear.

Article in an Online Journal

Chrisman, Laura, and Laurence Phillips. "Postcolonial Studies and the British Academy." *Jouvert* 3.3 (1999). Web. 10 June 2015.

Brown, Ronnie R. "Photographs That Should Have Been Taken." *Room of One's Own* 18.2 (Summer 1995). Web. 26 May 2014.

Article in an Online Newspaper or on a Newswire

These sites change very frequently—in some cases daily—so it is a good idea to download or record citation information (and URL, if needed) immediately.

Scarth, Deborah. "Many Top University Students Use Tutors to Keep an Edge." *globeandmail.com*. Globe and Mail, 4 June 2000. Web. 5 October 2013.

"Canada's Unemployment Rate Dips." *CBCnews.ca*. Canadian Broadcasting Corporation, 4 June 2000. Web. 5 Aug. 2015.

Article in an Online Magazine

Campbell, Colin. "Making Bad Times Good." *Macleans.ca*. Maclean's Magazine, 26 Feb. 2009. Web. 4 Mar. 2013.

Professional or Personal Web Site

List the publication information in the following order: the name of the creator of the site, the title of the site (italicized), a description (for example: Home page—neither italicized nor enclosed in quotation marks), publisher or sponsor of the site (if not available, use "N.p."), the date of publication (day, month, year, as available; if no date is available, use "n.d."), the medium of publication, the date you accessed the information, and the electronic address (if needed). If some of this information is unavailable, cite whatever is available.

> Canadian Tire Corporation Ltd. *Canadiantire.ca.* Investors page. N.p., n.d. Web. 28 May 2015.

> Ellison, Sara. *Sara's Home Page.* Home page. U of Victoria, n.d. Web. 29 July 2015. <http://orca.phys.uvic.ca/~sara/>.

Online Book

Many books are now available electronically, either independently or as part of a scholarly project. Some have appeared previously in print, while others exist only on the Web. Follow the general recommendations for citing books in print, but include the additional information required for electronic citations, as outlined below.

If a book that you are citing has appeared in print, it may be important to include the print version of the publication information (e.g., if the book was scanned as part of an online database). In that case, give the name of the author first, if it is available; if not, give the name of the editor, translator, or compiler, followed by a comma and then the appropriate abbreviation *(ed., trans.,* or *comp.)*. Next give the title of the work (italicized if the work is independent; in quotation marks if the work is part of a larger work); the name of the editor, translator, or compiler (if relevant); the edition or version used; followed by the publication information for the printed version (city of publication, name of the publisher, and year of publication). Then, instead of listing "Print" as the medium of publication at the end of the citation, add the following information: the title of the Web site or database (italicized), the medium of publication (Web), the date you accessed the information, and the URL (if needed).

If the book you are citing has not been previously published, follow the instructions above regarding the name of the author, editor, translator, or compiler, and the title of the work. Follow that information with the title of the Web site (italicized); the edition or version used; the publisher or sponsor of the Web site (if available; if not, use *"N.p."*); the date of publication (day, month, year, if available; if not, use *"n.d."*); the medium of publication (Web); the date you accessed the information; and the URL (if needed).

> Montgomery, Lucy Maud. *Anne of Green Gables.* 1908. *The Literature Network.* Web. 30 May 2015.

> Dewey, John. *Democracy and Education.* London: Macmillan, 1916. *ILT Web.* Web. 22 Nov. 2015.

Other Non-print Sources

The citations for other non-print sources will follow the recommendations for print versions, with some additional required information. Be sure to include the type of source you are citing (for example, *Transcript, Online posting,* or *E-mail*); this information will appear either before or after the date of publication/broadcast, depending on the type of source (see examples below). If you are citing an online posting, you may need to include the URL, as it could otherwise be difficult for your reader to find the posting.

Television/Radio

> "Sears Saga." Narr. Peter Mansbridge. *The National.* Canadian Broadcasting Corp. CBLT, Toronto, 4 June 2014. Television.

Transcript of Television/Radio Program

"Sears Saga." Narr. Peter Mansbridge. *The National*. Canadian Broadcasting Corp. CBLT, Toronto, n.p., 4 June 2014. Transcript.

E-Mail Communication

Pen Canada. "Your Inquiries to PEN." E-mail to author. 3 July 2016.

Online Posting

Matus, Roger. "Another University Sends False Admission Emails." Online posting. *Robert Matus' Death By Email*. InBoxer Inc., 6 Apr. 2009. Web. 7 April 20014.

Material From an Online Research Database

Online services such as ProQuest and LexisNexis provide a variety of databases that your college library will have. Give the name of the service (in italics) before the medium of publication (Web) and the date you accessed the information.

Golden, Anne. "Do Our Foreign Investment Laws Still Have Legs?" *The Globe and Mail*. 1 Dec. 2004: A23. *CBCA Current Affairs*. Web. 2 March 2015.

Careful writers work hard over time to develop an effective style. While all business writers should be able to write simple declarative sentences (*The stock market is down today*) or even more complex sentences (*The stock market is down today, despite the higher employment numbers*), more experienced writers recognize certain "tricks of the trade" that lend their writing an even more professional, persuasive tone. Some of these tricks are discussed below. Try incorporating them into your work as you progress through your course and your future career.

EMPHASIS

When you are talking with someone, you can emphasize your main ideas by saying them loudly or by repeating them slowly. You could pound the table if you wanted to show real emphasis. Another way you can signal the relative importance of an idea is by raising your eyebrows, shaking your head, or whispering. But when you write, you must rely on other means to tell your readers which ideas are more important than others. Emphasis in writing can be achieved in two ways: mechanically and stylistically.

Emphasis Through Mechanics

To emphasize an idea, a writer may use any of the following devices:

Underlining	<u>Underlining</u> draws the eye to a word.
Italics and boldface	Use *italics* or **boldface** for special meaning and emphasis.
Font changes	Changing from a large font to a smaller font or to a different font adds interest and emphasis.
All caps	Printing words in ALL CAPS is like shouting them.
Dashes	Dashes—if used sparingly—can be effective in capturing attention.
Tabulation	Listing items vertically makes them stand out:

    1. First item
    2. Second item
    3. Third item

Other means of achieving mechanical emphasis include the arrangement of space, colour, lines, boxes, columns, titles, headings, and subheadings. Today's software and colour printers provide a wide choice of capabilities for emphasizing ideas.

> You can emphasize an idea mechanically by using underlining, italics, boldface, font changes, all caps, dashes, and tabulation.

> You can emphasize ideas stylistically by using vivid words, labelling the main idea, and positioning the main idea strategically.

Emphasis Through Style

Although mechanical means are occasionally appropriate, a good writer more often achieves emphasis stylistically. That is, the writer chooses words carefully and constructs sentences skillfully to emphasize main ideas and de-emphasize minor or negative ideas. Here are four suggestions for emphasizing ideas stylistically:

- **Use vivid words.** Vivid words are emphatic because the reader can picture ideas clearly.
  > **General** One business uses personal selling techniques.
  > **Vivid** Avon uses face-to-face selling techniques.

  > **General** A customer said that he wanted the contract returned soon.
  > **Vivid** Mr. LeClerc insisted that the contract be returned by July 1.

- **Label the main idea.** If an idea is significant, tell the reader.
  > **Unlabelled** Explore the possibility of leasing a site, but also hire a consultant.
  > **Labelled** Explore the possibility of leasing a site, but most important, hire a consultant.

- **Place the important idea first or last in the sentence.** Ideas have less competition from surrounding words when they appear first or last in a sentence. Observe how the concept of productivity is emphasized in the first and second examples:
  > **Emphatic** Productivity is more likely to be increased when profit-sharing plans are linked to individual performance rather than to group performance.
  > **Emphatic** Profit-sharing plans linked to individual performance rather than to group performance are more effective in increasing productivity.
  > **Unemphatic** Profit-sharing plans are more effective in increasing productivity when they are linked to individual performance rather than to group performance.

- **Place the important idea in a simple sentence or in an independent clause.** Don't dilute the effect of the idea by making it share the spotlight with other words and clauses.
  > **Emphatic** You are the first trainee we have hired for this program. (Use a simple sentence for emphasis.)
  > **Emphatic** Although we considered many candidates, you are the first trainee we have hired for this program. (Independent clause contains main idea.)
  > **Unemphatic** Although you are the first trainee we have hired for this program, we had many candidates and expect to expand the program in the future. (Main idea is lost in a dependent clause.)

When to De-emphasize

To de-emphasize something, such as bad news, try one of the following stylistic devices:

> You can de-emphasize ideas through word choice and placement.

- **Use general words.**
  > **Vivid** Our records indicate that you were recently fired.
  > **General** Our records indicate that your employment status has changed recently.

- **Place the bad news in a dependent clause connected to an independent clause with something positive.** In sentences with dependent clauses, the main emphasis is always on the independent clause.
  > **Emphasizes bad news** We cannot issue you credit at this time, but we do have a plan that will allow you to fill your immediate needs on a cash basis.
  > **De-emphasizes bad news** We have a plan that will allow you to fill your immediate needs on a cash basis since we cannot issue credit at this time.

■ ACTIVE AND PASSIVE VOICE

> Active-voice sentences are direct and easy to understand.

In sentences with active-voice verbs, the subject is the doer of the action. In passive-voice sentences, the subject is acted upon.

Active verb Mr. Wong completed the tax return before the April 30 deadline. (The subject, *Mr. Wong*, is the doer of the action.)
Passive verb The tax return was completed before the April 30 deadline. (The subject, *tax return*, is acted upon.)

In the first sentence, the active-voice verb emphasizes Mr. Wong. In the second sentence, the passive-voice verb emphasizes the tax return. In sentences with passive-voice verbs, the doer of the action may be revealed or left unknown. In business writing, and in personal interactions, some situations demand tact and sensitivity. Instead of using a direct approach with active verbs, we may prefer the indirectness that passive verbs allow. Rather than making a blunt announcement with an active verb (*Gunnar made a major error in the estimate*), we can soften the sentence with a passive construction (*A major error was made in the estimate*).

Here's a summary of the best use of active- and passive-voice verbs:

- **Use the active voice for most business writing.** It clearly tells what the action is and who is performing that action.
- **Use the passive voice to emphasize an action or the recipient of the action.** *You have been selected to represent us.*
- **Use the passive voice to de-emphasize negative news.** *Your watch has not been repaired.*
- **Use the passive voice to conceal the doer of an action.** *A major error was made in the estimate.*

How can you tell if a verb is active or passive? Identify the subject of the sentence and decide whether the subject is doing the acting or being acted upon. For example, in the sentence *An appointment was made for January 1*, the subject is *appointment*. The subject is being acted upon; therefore, the verb (was made) is passive. Another clue in identifying passive-voice verbs is that they generally include a "to be" helping verb, such as *is*, *are*, *was*, *were*, *being*, or *been*.

> Although active-voice verbs are preferred in business writing, passive-voice verbs perform useful functions.

◼ PARALLELISM

Parallelism is a writing technique that creates balanced writing. Sentences written so that their parts are balanced or parallel are easy to read and understand. To achieve parallel construction, use similar structures to express similar ideas. For example, the words *computing*, *coding*, *recording*, and *storing* are parallel because they all end in "ing". To express the list as *computing*, *coding*, *recording*, *and storage* is disturbing because the last item is not what the reader expects. Try to match nouns with nouns, verbs with verbs, and clauses with clauses. Avoid mixing active-voice verbs with passive-voice verbs. Your goal is to keep the wording balanced in expressing similar ideas.

> Balanced wording helps the reader anticipate and comprehend your meaning.

Lacks parallelism The market for industrial goods includes manufacturers, contractors, wholesalers, and those concerned with the retail function.
Revision The market for industrial goods includes manufacturers, contractors, wholesalers, and retailers. (Parallel construction matches nouns.)

Lacks parallelism Our primary goals are to increase productivity, reduce costs, and the improvement of product quality.
Revision Our primary goals are to increase productivity, reduce costs, and improve product quality. (Parallel construction matches verbs.)

Lacks parallelism We are scheduled to meet in Toronto on January 5, we are meeting in Montreal on the 15th of March, and in Burlington on June 3.
Revision We are scheduled to meet in Toronto on January 5, in Montreal on March 15, and in Burlington on June 3. (Parallel construction matches phrases.)

Lacks parallelism Mrs. Chorney audits all accounts lettered A through L; accounts lettered M through Z are audited by Mr. Faheem.
Revision Mrs. Chorney audits all accounts lettered A through L; Mr. Faheem audits accounts lettered M through Z. (Parallel construction matches active-voice verbs in balanced clauses.)

In presenting lists of data, whether printed horizontally or tabulated vertically, be certain to express all the items in parallel form.

Parallelism in vertical list Three primary objectives of advertising are as follows:
1. Increase the frequency of product use.
2. Introduce complementary products.
3. Enhance the corporate image.

💬 UNITY

> Unified sentences contain only related ideas.

Unified sentences contain thoughts that are related to only one main idea. The following sentence lacks unity because the first clause has little or no relationship to the second clause:

Lacks unity Our insurance plan is available in all provinces, and you may name anyone as a beneficiary for your coverage.
Revision Our insurance plan is available in all provinces. What's more, you may name anyone as a beneficiary for your coverage.

The ideas in a sentence are better expressed by separating the two dissimilar clauses and adding a connecting phrase. Three writing faults that destroy sentence unity are imprecise writing, mixed constructions, and misplaced modifiers.

Imprecise Writing

> Imprecise sentences often should be broken into two sentences.

Sentences that twist or turn unexpectedly away from the main thought are examples of imprecise writing. Such confusing writing may result when too many thoughts are included in one sentence or when one thought does not relate to another. To rectify an imprecise sentence, revise it so that the reader understands the relationship between the thoughts. If that is impossible, move the unrelated thoughts to a new sentence.

Imprecise writing I appreciate the time you spent with me last week, and I have purchased a computer and software that generate graphics.
Revision I appreciate the time you spent with me last week. As a result of your advice, I have purchased a computer and software that generate graphics.

Imprecise writing The stockholders of a corporation elect a board of directors, although the chief executive officer is appointed by the board and the CEO is not directly responsible to the stockholders.
Revision The stockholders of a corporation elect a board of directors, who in turn appoint the chief executive officer. The CEO is not directly responsible to the stockholders.

Mixed Constructions

> Mixed constructions confuse readers.

Writers who fuse two different grammatical constructions destroy sentence unity and meaning.

Mixed construction The reason I am late is because my car battery is dead.
Revision The reason I am late is that my car battery is dead. (The construction introduced by *the reason is* should be a noun clause beginning with that, not an adverbial clause beginning with because.)

Mixed construction When the stock market index rose five points was our signal to sell.

Revision When the stock market index rose five points, we were prepared to sell. Or: Our signal to sell was an increase of five points in the stock market index.

Dangling and Misplaced Modifiers

For clarity, modifiers must be close to the words they describe or limit. A modifier dangles when the word or phrase it describes is missing from the sentence. A modifier is misplaced when the word or phrase it describes is not close enough for the relationship to be clear. In both instances, the solution is to position the modifier closer to the word(s) it describes or limits. Introductory verbal phrases are particularly dangerous; be sure to follow them immediately with the words they logically describe or modify.

> Modifiers must be close to the words they describe or limit.

Dangling modifier To win the lottery, a ticket must be purchased. (Purchased by whom? The verbal phrase must be followed by a subject.)
Revision To win the lottery, you must purchase a ticket.

Dangling modifier Driving through Tetrahedron Plateau, the ocean suddenly came into view. (Is the ocean driving through Tetrahedron Plateau?)
Revision Driving through Tetrahedron Plateau, we saw the ocean suddenly come into view.

Try this trick for detecting and remedying dangling modifiers. Ask the question "Who or what?" after any introductory phrase. The words immediately following should tell the reader who or what is performing the action. Try the test on the previous danglers.

Misplaced modifier Seeing his error too late, the envelope was immediately re-sealed by Adrian. (Did the envelope see the error?)
Revision Seeing his error too late, Adrian immediately re-sealed the envelope.

Misplaced modifier A wart appeared on my left hand that I want removed. (Is the left hand to be removed?)
Revision I want to remove the wart that appeared on my left hand.

Misplaced modifier The busy human resources director interviewed only candidates who had excellent computer skills in the morning. (Were the candidates skilled only in the morning?)
Revision In the morning the busy human resources director interviewed only candidates who had excellent computer skills.

💬 PARAGRAPH COHERENCE

A paragraph is a group of sentences with a controlling idea, usually stated first. Paragraphs package similar ideas into meaningful groups for readers. Effective paragraphs are coherent; that is, they hold together. But coherence does not happen accidentally. It is achieved through effective organization and (1) repetition of key ideas, (2) use of pronouns, and (3) use of transitional expressions.

> Three ways to create paragraph coherence are (1) repetition of key ideas, (2) use of pronouns, and (3) use of transitional expressions.

- **Repetition of key ideas or key words.** Repeating a word or key thought from a preceding sentence helps guide a reader from one thought to the next. This redundancy is necessary to build cohesiveness into writing.

Effective repetition Quality problems in production are often the result of inferior raw materials. Some companies have strong programs for ensuring the quality of incoming production materials and supplies.

The second sentence of the preceding paragraph repeats the key idea of quality. Moreover, the words incoming production materials and supplies refer to the raw materials mentioned in the preceding sentence. Good writers find similar

Appendix D: Style in Writing

words to describe the same idea, thus using repetition to clarify a topic for the reader.

- **Use of pronouns.** Pronouns such as this, *that*, *they*, *these*, and *those* promote coherence by connecting the thoughts in one sentence to the thoughts in a previous sentence. To make sure that the pronoun reference is clear, consider joining the pronoun with the word to which it refers, thus making the pronoun into an adjective.

Pronouns with clear antecedents can improve coherence.

Pronoun repetition Xerox has a four-point program to assist suppliers. This program includes written specifications for production materials and components.

Be very careful, though, in using pronouns. A pronoun without a clear antecedent can be annoying. That's because the reader doesn't know precisely to what the pronoun refers.

Faulty: When company profits increased, employees were given either a cash payment or company stock. This became a real incentive to employees. (Is This the cash or the stock or both?)

Revision: When company profits increased, employees were given either a cash payment or company stock. This profit-sharing plan became a real incentive to employees.

- **Use of transitional expressions.** One of the most effective ways to achieve paragraph coherence is through the use of transitional expressions. These expressions act as road signs: they indicate where the message is headed and they help the reader anticipate what is coming. Here are some of the most effective transitional expressions. They are grouped according to use.

Transitional expressions build paragraph coherence.

TIME ASSOCIATION	CONTRAST	ILLUSTRATION
before, after	although	for example
first, second	but	in this way
meanwhile	however	
next	instead	
until	nevertheless	
when, whenever	on the other hand	
CAUSE, EFFECT	**ADDITIONAL IDEA**	
consequently	furthermore	
for this reason	in addition	
hence	likewise	
therefore	moreover	

PARAGRAPH LENGTH

Although no rule regulates the length of paragraphs, business writers recognize the value of short paragraphs. Paragraphs with eight or fewer printed lines look inviting and readable. Long, solid chunks of print appear formidable. If a topic can't be covered in eight or fewer printed lines (not sentences), consider breaking it into smaller segments.

The most readable paragraphs contain eight or fewer printed lines.

WRITING IMPROVEMENT EXERCISES

EMPHASIS. For each of the following sentences, circle (a) or (b). Be prepared to justify your choice.

1. Which is more emphatic?
   a. We need a faster, more efficient distribution system.
   b. We need a better distribution system.
2. Which is more emphatic?
   a. Increased advertising would improve sales.
   b. Adding $50,000 in advertising would double our sales.
3. Which is more emphatic?
   a. The committee was powerless to act.
   b. The committee was unable to take action.
4. Which sentence puts more emphasis on product loyalty?
   a. Product loyalty is the primary motivation for advertising.
   b. The primary motivation for advertising is loyalty to the product, although other purposes are also served.
5. Which sentence places more emphasis on the seminar?
   a. An executive training seminar that starts June 1 will include four candidates.
   b. Four candidates will be able to participate in an executive training seminar that we feel will provide a valuable learning experience.
6. Which sentence puts more emphasis on the date?
   a. The deadline is December 30 for applications for overseas jobs.
   b. December 30 is the deadline for applications for overseas jobs.
7. Which is less emphatic?
   a. Lily Takahashi said that her financial status had worsened.
   b. Lily Takahashi said that she had lost her job and owed $2,000.
8. Which sentence de-emphasizes the credit refusal?
   a. We are unable to grant you credit at this time, but we will reconsider your application later.
   b. Although we welcome your cash business, we are unable to offer you credit at this time; but we will be happy to reconsider your application later.
9. Which sentence gives more emphasis to judgment?
   a. He has many admirable qualities, but most important is his good judgment.
   b. He has many admirable qualities, including good judgment and patience.
10. Which is more emphatic?
    a. Three departments are involved: (1) Legal, (2) Accounting, and (3) Distribution.
    b. Three departments are involved:
       1. Legal
       2. Accounting
       3. Distribution

ACTIVE-VOICE VERBS. Business writing is more forceful if it uses active-voice verbs. Revise the following sentences so that the verbs are in the active voice. Put the emphasis on the doer of the action. Add subjects if necessary.

Example The computers were powered up each day at 7 a.m.

Revision Kamal powered up the computers each day at 7 a.m.

11. Initial figures for the bid were submitted before the June 1 deadline.
12. New spices and cooking techniques were tried by Lick's to improve its hamburgers.
13. Substantial sums of money were earned by employees who enrolled early in our stock option plan.
14. A significant financial commitment has been made by us to ensure that our customers can take advantage of our discount pricing.

PASSIVE-VOICE VERBS. When indirectness or tact are required, use passive-voice verbs. Revise the following sentences so that they are in the passive voice.

Example   Sade did not submit the accounting statement on time.

Revision   The accounting statement was not submitted on time.

15. Andreas made a computational error in the report.
16. We cannot ship your order for 10 monitors until June 15.
17. The government first issued a warning regarding the use of this pesticide over 15 months ago.
18. We will notify you immediately if we make any changes in your travel arrangements.
19. We cannot allow a cash refund unless you provide a receipt.

PARALLELISM. Revise the following sentences so that their parts are balanced.

20. (Hint: Match verbs.) Some of our priorities include linking employee compensation to performance, keeping administrative costs down, the expansion of computer use, and the improvement of performance review skills of supervisors.
21. (Hint: Match active voice of verbs.) Yin Huang, of the Red River office, will now supervise our Western Division; and the Eastern Division will be supervised by our Ottawa office manager, David Ali.
22. (Hint: Match nouns.) Word processing software is used extensively in the fields of health care, by lawyers, by secretaries in insurance firms, for scripts in the entertainment industry, and in the banking field.
23. If you have decided to cancel our service, please cut your credit card in half, and the card pieces should be returned to us.
24. We need more laboratory space, additional personnel is required, and we also need much more capital.
25. The application for a grant asks for this information: funds required for employee salaries, how much we expect to spend on equipment, and what is the length of the project.
26. To lease a car is more expensive than buying one.
27. To use the copier, insert your account card, the paper trays must be loaded, indicate the number of copies needed, and your original sheet should be inserted through the feeder.

SENTENCE UNITY. The following sentences lack unity. Rewrite, correcting the identified fault.

Example   (Dangling modifier) By advertising extensively, all the open jobs were filled quickly.

Revision   By advertising extensively, we were able to fill all the open jobs quickly.

28. (Dangling modifier) To open a money market account, a deposit of $3,000 is required.
29. (Mixed construction) The reason why Ms. Rutulis is unable to travel extensively is because she has family responsibilities.
30. (Misplaced modifier) Identification passes must be worn at all times in offices and production facilities showing the employee's picture.
31. (Misplaced modifier) The editor-in-chief's rules were to be observed by all staff members, no matter how silly they seemed.
32. (Imprecise sentence) The business was started by two engineers, and these owners worked in a garage, which eventually grew into a million-dollar operation.

COHERENCE. Revise the following paragraphs to improve coherence. Be aware that the transitional expressions and key words selected depend largely on the emphasis desired. Many possible revisions exist.

Example   Computer style checkers rank somewhere between artificial intelligence and artificial ignorance. Style checkers are like clever children: smart but not wise. Business writers should be cautious. They should be aware of the usefulness of style checkers. They should know their limitations.

Revision   Computer style checkers rank somewhere between artificial intelligence and artificial ignorance. For example, they are like clever children: smart but not wise. For this reason, business writers should be cautious. Although they should be aware of the usefulness of these software programs, business writers should also know their limitations.

33. Our computerized file includes all customer data. It provides space for name, address, and other vital information. It has an area for comments. The area for comments comes in handy. It requires more time and careful keyboarding, though.

34. No one likes to turn out poor products. We began highlighting recurring problems. Employees make a special effort to be more careful in doing their work right the first time. It doesn't have to be returned to them for corrections.

35. Service was less than perfect for many months. We lacked certain intangibles. We didn't have the customer-specific data that we needed. We made the mistake of removing all localized, person-to-person coverage. We are returning to decentralized customer contacts.

INTRODUCTION

Because many students need a quick review of basic grammar and mechanics, we provide a number of resources in condensed form. The Grammar/Mechanics Handbook, which offers you a rapid systematic review, consists of four parts:

- **Grammar/Mechanics Diagnostic Test.** This 65-point pretest helps you assess your strengths and weaknesses in eight areas of grammar and mechanics. Your instructor may later give you a post-test to assess your improvement.
- **Grammar/Mechanics Profile.** The G/M Profile enables you to pinpoint specific areas in which you need remedial instruction or review.
- **Grammar/Mechanics Review.** Provided here is a concise review of basic principles of grammar, punctuation, capitalization, and number style. The review also provides reinforcement and quiz exercises that help you interact with the principles of grammar and test your comprehension. The guidelines not only provide a study guide for review but will also serve as a reference manual throughout the course. The grammar review can be used for classroom-centred instruction or for self-guided learning.
- **Confusing Words and Frequently Misspelled Words.** A list of selected confusing words, along with a list of 160 frequently misspelled words, completes the Grammar/Mechanics Handbook.

The first step in your systematic review of grammar and mechanics involves completing the following diagnostic pretest.

 ## GRAMMAR/MECHANICS DIAGNOSTIC PRETEST

Name _____

This diagnostic pretest is intended to reveal your strengths and weaknesses in using the following:

plural nouns	adjectives	punctuation
possessive nouns	adverbs	capitalization style
pronouns	prepositions	number style
verbs	conjunctions	

The pretest is organized into sections corresponding to the preceding categories. In Sections A through H, each sentence is either correct or has one error related to the category under which it is listed. If a sentence is correct, write C. If it has an error, underline the error and write the correct form in the space provided. When you finish, check your answers with your instructor and fill out the Grammar/Mechanics Profile at the end of the test.

A. Plural Nouns

<u>companies</u> **Example:** Large <u>companys</u> hire numerous CPAs and accountants.

_____ 1. All job candidates are asked whether they can work on Saturday's.

_____ 2. Two students discussed the pro's and con's of using laptops and cell phones in their classes.

_____ 3. Both of Jeff's sister-in-laws worked as secretaries at different facilities.

_____ 4. Neither the Parvezes nor the Harris's knew about the changes in beneficiaries.

_____ 5. Since the early 2000s, most judicial systems and lawyers have invested in packages that detect computer viruses.

B. Possessive Nouns

_____ 6. We sincerely hope that the jurys judgment reflects the stories of all the witnesses.

_____ 7. In a little over two months time, the analysts finished their reports.

_____ 8. Ms. Porters staff is responsible for all accounts receivable for customers purchasing electronics parts.

_____ 9. At the next stockholders meeting, we will discuss benefits for employees and dividends for shareholders.

_____ 10. For the past 90 days, employees in the sales department have complained about Mr. Navetta smoking.

C. Pronouns

<u>me</u> **Example:** Whom did you ask to replace Francisco and <u>I</u>?

_____ 11. The chief and myself were quite willing to send copies to whoever requested them.

_____ 12. Much of the project assigned to Samantha and I had to be reassigned to Matt and them.

_____ 13. Although it's CPU was noisy, the computer worked for Jeremy and me.

_____ 14. Just between you and me, only you and I know that she will be transferred.

_____ 15. My friend and I applied at Loblaw because of their excellent benefits.

D. Verb Agreement

<u>has</u> **Example:** The list of payments <u>have</u> to be approved by the boss.

_____ 16. This cell phone and its calling plan costs much less than I expected.

_____ 17. A description of the property, together with several other legal documents, were submitted by my lawyer.

_____ 18. There are a wide range of proposals for reducing e-mail overload.

_____ 19. Neither the manager nor the employees in the office think the solution is fair.

_____ 20. Because of the holiday, our committee were unable to meet.

E. Verb Mood, Voice, and Tense

_____ 21. If I was in charge, I would certainly change things.

_____ 22. To make a copy, first open the disk drive door and then you insert the disk.

_____ 23. If I could chose any city, I would select Hong Kong.

_____ 24. Those contracts have laid on his desk for more than two weeks.

_____ 25. The auditors have went over these accounts carefully, and they have found no discrepancies.

F. Adjectives and Adverbs

_____ 26. Until we have a more clearer picture of what is legal, we will proceed cautiously.

_____ 27. Britney thought she had done good in her job interview.

_____ 28. A recently appointed official was in charge of monitoring peer to peer file-sharing systems.

_____ 29. Robert only has two days before he must submit his end-of-the-year report.

_____ 30. The architects submitted their drawings in a last-minute attempt to beat the deadline.

G. Prepositions and Conjunctions

_____ 31. Can you tell me where the meeting is scheduled at?

_____ 32. It seems like we have been taking this pretest forever.

_____ 33. Our investigation shows that cell phones may be cheaper then landlines.

_____ 34. My courses this semester are totally different than last semester's.

_____ 35. Do you know where this shipment is going to?

H. Commas

For each of the following sentences, insert any necessary commas. Count the number of commas that you added. Write that number in the space provided. All punctuation must be correct to receive credit for the sentence. If a sentence requires no punctuation, write C.

__1__   **Example:** Because of developments in theory and computer applications⌃ management is becoming more of a science.

_____ 36. For example management determines how orders assignments and responsibilities are delegated to employees.

_____ 37. Your order Ms. Lee will be sent from Niagara Falls Ontario on July 3.

_____ 38. When you need service on any of your equipment we will be happy to help you Mr. Lemieux.

_____ 39. Michelle Wong who is the project manager at TeleCom suggested that I call you.

_____ 40. You have purchased from us often and your payments in the past have always been prompt.

I. Commas and Semicolons 1

Add commas and semicolons to the following sentences. In the space provided, write the number of punctuation marks that you added.

_____ 41. The salesperson turned in his report however he did not indicate the time period it covered.

_____ 42. Interest payments on bonds are tax deductible dividend payments are not.

_____ 43. We are opening a branch office in Brandon and hope to be able to serve all your needs from that office by the middle of January.

_____ 44. As suggested by the committee we must first secure adequate funding then we may consider expansion.

_____ 45. When you begin to research a report consider many sources of information namely think about using the Internet, books, periodicals, government publications, and databases.

J. Commas and Semicolons 2

_____ 46. After our chief had the printer repaired it jammed again within the first week although we treated it carefully.

_____ 47. Our experienced courteous staff has been trained to anticipate your every need.

_____ 48. In view of the new law that went into effect on April 1 our current liability insurance must be increased therefore we need to adjust our budget.

_____ 49. As stipulated in our contract your agency will develop a social media program and supervise our media budget.

_____ 50. As you know Ms. Okui we aim for long-term business relationships not quick profits.

K. Other Punctuation

Each of the following sentences may require colons, question marks, quotation marks, periods, parentheses, and underscores, as well as commas and semicolons. Add the appropriate punctuation to each sentence. Then in the space provided, write the total number of marks that you added or changed.

<u>3</u>   **Example:** Fully recharging your digital camera's battery (see page 6 of the instruction manual) takes only 90 minutes.

_____ 51. The following members of the department volunteered to help on Saturday Kim Carlos Dan and Sylvia.

_____ 52. Mr Phillips, Miss Reed, and Mrs. Garcia usually arrived at the office by 8:30 a m.

_____ 53. We recommend that you use hearing protectors see the warning on page 8 when using this electric drill.

_____ 54. Did the CEO really say "All employees may take Friday off

_____ 55. We are trying to locate an edition of *Canadian Business* that carried an article titled Who Is Reading Your E-Mail

L. Capitalization

For each of the following sentences, underline any letter that should be capitalized. In the space provided, write the number of words you marked.

<u>4</u>   **Example:** <u>v</u>ice president <u>k</u>umar devised a procedure for expediting purchase orders from <u>a</u>rea 4 warehouses.

_____ 56. although english was his native language, he also spoke spanish and could read french.

_____ 57. on a trip to the east coast, uncle henry visited peggy's cove.

_____ 58. karen enrolled in classes in history, german, and sociology.

_____ 59. the business manager and the vice president each received a new dell computer.

_____ 60. james lee, the president of kendrick, inc., will speak to our conference in the spring.

M. Number Style

Decide whether the numbers in the following sentences should be written as words or as figures. Each sentence either is correct or has one error. If it is correct, write C. If it has an error, underline it and write the correct form in the space provided.

<u>five</u>   **Example:** The bank had <u>5</u> branches in three suburbs.

_____ 61. More than 3,000,000 people have visited the Parliament Buildings in the past five years.

_____ 62. Of the 28 viewer comments we received regarding our online commercial, only three were negative.

_____ 63. We set aside forty dollars for petty cash, but by December 1 our fund was depleted.

_____ 64. The meeting is scheduled for May fifth at 3 p.m.

_____ 65. In the past five years, nearly fifteen percent of the population changed residences at least once.

GRAMMAR/MECHANICS PROFILE

In the spaces at the right, place a check mark to indicate the number of correct answers you had in each category of the Grammar/Mechanics Diagnostic Pretest.

		NUMBER CORRECT*				
		5	4	3	2	1
1–5	Plural Nouns	__	__	__	__	__
6–10	Possessive Nouns	__	__	__	__	__
11–15	Pronouns	__	__	__	__	__
16–20	Verb Agreement	__	__	__	__	__
21–25	Verb Mood, Voice, and Tense	__	__	__	__	__
26–30	Adjectives and Adverbs	__	__	__	__	__
31–35	Prepositions and Conjunctions	__	__	__	__	__
36–40	Commas	__	__	__	__	__
41–45	Commas and Semicolons 1	__	__	__	__	__
46–50	Commas and Semicolons 2	__	__	__	__	__
51–55	Other Punctuation	__	__	__	__	__
56–60	Capitalization	__	__	__	__	__
61–65	Number Style	__	__	__	__	__

*Note: *5 = have excellent skills; 4 = need light review; 3 = need careful review; 2 = need to study rules; 1 = need serious study and follow-up reinforcement.*

GRAMMAR/MECHANICS REVIEW

Parts of Speech (1.01)

1.01 Functions. English has eight parts of speech. Knowing the functions of the parts of speech helps writers better understand how words are used and how sentences are formed.

a. **Nouns.** Name persons, places, things, qualities, concepts, and activities (e.g., *Kevin, Lethbridge, computer, joy, work, banking*)

b. **Pronouns.** Substitute for nouns (e.g., *he, she, it, they*)

c. **Verbs.** Show the action of a subject or join the subject to words that describe it (e.g., *walk, heard, is, was jumping*)

d. **Adjectives.** Describe or limit nouns and pronouns and often answer the questions *what kind? how many?* and *which one?* (e.g., *red* car, *ten* items, *good* manager)

e. **Adverbs.** Describe or limit verbs, adjectives, or other adverbs and frequently answer the questions *when? how? where?* or *to what extent?* (e.g., *tomorrow, rapidly, here, very*)

f. **Prepositions.** Join nouns or pronouns to other words in sentences (e.g., desk *in* the office, ticket *for* me, letter *to* you)

g. **Conjunctions:** Connect words or groups of words (e.g., you *and* I, Mark *or* Jill)

h. **Interjections.** Express strong feelings (e.g., *Wow! Oh!*)

Nouns (1.02–1.06)

Nouns name persons, places, things, qualities, concepts, and activities. Nouns may be classified into a number of categories.

1.02 Concrete and Abstract. Concrete nouns name specific objects that can be seen, heard, felt, tasted, or smelled. Examples of concrete nouns are *telephone, dollar, IBM,* and *tangerine.* Abstract nouns name generalized ideas such as qualities or concepts that are not easily pictured. *Emotion, power,* and *tension* are typical examples of abstract nouns.

Business writing is most effective when concrete words predominate. It is clearer to write *We need 16-pound copy paper* than to write *We need office supplies.* Chapter 4 provides practice in developing skill in the use of concrete words.

1.03 Proper and Common. Proper nouns name specific persons, places, or things and are always capitalized *(Lululemon Athletica, Kamloops, Jennifer).* All other nouns are common nouns and begin with lowercase letters *(company, city, student).* Rules for capitalization are presented in Sections 3.01–3.16.

1.04 Singular and Plural. Singular nouns name one item; plural nouns name more than one. From a practical view, writers seldom have difficulty with singular nouns. They may need help, however, with the formation and spelling of plural nouns.

1.05 Guidelines for Forming Noun Plurals

a. Add *s* to most nouns *(chair, chairs; mortgage, mortgages; Monday, Mondays).*

b. Add *es* to nouns ending in *s, x, z, ch,* or *sh (bench, benches; boss, bosses; box, boxes; Parvez, Parvezes).*

c. Change the spelling in irregular noun plurals *(man, men; foot, feet; mouse, mice; child, children).*

d. Add *s* to nouns that end in *y* when *y* is preceded by a vowel *(journey, journeys; valley, valleys).*

e. Drop the *y* and add *ies* to nouns ending in *y* when *y* is preceded by a consonant *(company, companies; city, cities; secretary, secretaries).*

f. Add *s* to the principal word in most compound expressions *(editors in chief, fathers-in-law, bills of lading, runners-up).*

g. Add *s* to most numerals, letters of the alphabet, words referred to as words, degrees, and abbreviations *(5s, 2000s, Bs, ands, CPAs, lbs.).*

h. Add *'s* only to clarify letters of the alphabet that might be misread, such as *A's*, *I's*, *M's*, and *U's* and *i's*, *p's*, and *q's*. An expression like *c.o.d.s* requires no apostrophe because it would not easily be misread.

1.06 Collective Nouns. Nouns such as *staff, faculty, committee, group,* and *herd* refer to a collection of people, animals, or objects. Collective nouns may be considered singular or plural depending on their action. See Section 1.10i for a discussion of collective nouns and their agreement with verbs.

Review Exercise A—Nouns

In the space provided for each item, write *a* or *b* to complete the following statements accurately. When you finish, compare your responses with those provided. Answers are provided for odd-numbered items. Your instructor has the remaining answers. For each item on which you need review, consult the numbered principle shown in parentheses.

_____ 1. Two of the contest (a) *runner-ups*, (b) *runners-up* protested the judges' choice.

_____ 2. Several (a) *journeys*, (b) *journies* together proved that we could work well as a team.

_____ 3. Please write to the (a) *Davis's*, (b) *Davises* about the missing contract.

_____ 4. The industrial complex has space for nine additional (a) *companys*, (b) *companies*.

_____ 5. That accounting firm employs two (a) *secretaries*, (b) *secretarys* for five CPAs.

_____ 6. Four of the wooden (a) *benches*, (b) *benchs* must be repaired.

_____ 7. The home was constructed with numerous (a) *chimneys*, (b) *chimnies*.

_____ 8. Tours of the production facility are made only on (a) *Tuesdays*, (b) *Tuesday's*.

_____ 9. We asked the (a) *Parvez's*, (b) *Parvezes* to contribute to the fund-raising drive.

_____ 10. Both my (a) *sister-in-laws*, (b) *sisters-in-law* agreed to the settlement.

_____ 11. The stock market is experiencing abnormal (a) *ups and downs*, (b) *up's and down's*.

_____ 12. Three (a) *mouses*, (b) *mice* were seen near the trash cans.

_____ 13. This office is unusually quiet on (a) *Sundays*, (b) *Sunday's*.

_____ 14. Several news (a) *dispatchs*, (b) *dispatches* were released during the strike.

_____ 15. Two major (a) *countries*, (b) *countrys* will participate in arms negotiations.

_____ 16. Some young children have difficulty writing their (a) *bs and ds*, (b) *b's and d's*.

_____ 17. The (a) *board of directors*, (b) *boards of directors* of all the major companies participated in the surveys.

_____ 18. In their letter the (a) *Metzes*, (b) *Metzs* said they intended to purchase the property.

_____ 19. In shipping we are careful to include all (a) *bill of sales*, (b) *bills of sale*.

_____ 20. Over the holidays many (a) *turkies*, (b) *turkeys* were consumed.

1. b (1.05f) 3. b (1.05b) 5. a (1.05e) 7. a (1.05d) 9. b (1.05b) 11. a (1.05g) 13. a (1.05a) 15. a (1.05e) 17. b (1.05f) 19. b (1.05f) (Only odd-numbered answers are provided. Consult your instructor for the others.)

◼ GRAMMAR/MECHANICS CHECKUP—1

Nouns

Review Sections 1.01–1.06 above. Then study each of the following statements. Underline any mistakes and write a correction in the space provided. Record the appropriate Handbook section and letter that illustrates the principle involved. If a sentence is correct, write C. When you finish, compare your responses with those provided on page 538. If your answers differ, carefully study again the principles shown in parentheses.

Companies (1.05e) Example: Two surveys revealed that many <u>companys</u> will move to the new industrial park.

_____ 1. Several attornies worked on the three cases simultaneously.

_____ 2. Counter business is higher on Saturday's, but telephone business is greater on Sundays.

_____ 3. Some of the citys in Kevin's report offer excellent opportunities.

_____ 4. Frozen chickens and turkies are kept in the company's lockers.

_____ 5. All secretaries were asked to check supplies and other inventorys.

_____ 6. Only the Nashs and the Lopezes brought their entire families.

_____ 7. In the 1980s profits grew rapidly; in the 1990's investments lagged.

_____ 8. Both editor in chiefs instituted strict proofreading policies.

_____ 9. Luxury residential complexs are part of the architect's plan.

_____ 10. Trustees in three municipalitys are likely to approve increased school taxes.

_____ 11. The instructor was surprised to find three Jennifer's in one class.

_____ 12. Andre sent descriptions of two valleys in France to us via the Internet.

_____ 13. How many copies of the statements showing your assets and liabilitys did you make?

_____ 14. My monitor makes it difficult to distinguish between *o*'s and *a*'s.

_____ 15. Both runner-ups complained about the winner's behaviour.

Pronouns (1.07–1.09)

Pronouns substitute for nouns. They are classified by case.

1.07 Case. Pronouns function in three cases, as shown in the following chart.

Nominative Case	Objective Case	Possessive Case
(Used for subjects of verbs and subject complements)	*(Used for objects of prepositions and objects of verbs)*	*(Used to show possession)*
I	me	my, mine
we	us	our, ours
you	you	your, yours
he	him	his
she	her	her, hers
it	it	its
they	them	their, theirs
who, whoever	whom, whomever	whose

1.08 Guidelines for Selecting Pronoun Case

a. Pronouns that serve as subjects of verbs must be in the nominative case:

> *He* and *I* (not *Him* and *me*) decided to apply for the jobs.

b. Pronouns that follow linking verbs (such as *am, is, are, was, were, be, being, been*) and rename the words to which they refer must be in the nominative case.

> It must have been *she* (not *her*) who placed the order. (The nominative-case pronoun *she* follows the linking verb *been* and renames *it*.)

> If it was *he* (not *him*) who called, I have his number. (The nominative-case pronoun *he* follows the linking verb *was* and renames *it*.)

c. Pronouns that serve as objects of verbs or objects of prepositions must be in the objective case:

> Mr. Andrews asked *them* to complete the proposal. (The pronoun *them* is the object of the verb *asked*.)

> All computer printouts are sent to *him*. (The pronoun *him* is the object of the preposition *to*.)

> Just between you and *me*, profits are falling. (The pronoun *me* is one of the objects of the preposition *between*.)

d. Pronouns that show ownership must be in the possessive case. Possessive pronouns (such as *hers, yours, ours, theirs,* and *its*) require no apostrophes:

> I bought a cheap cell phone, but *yours* (not *your's*) is expensive.

> All parts of the machine, including *its* (not *it's*) motor, were examined.

> The house and *its* (not *it's*) contents will be auctioned.

Don't confuse possessive pronouns and contractions. Contractions are shortened forms of subject–verb phrases (such as *it's* for *it is, there's* for *there is,* and *they're* for *they are*).

e. When a pronoun appears in combination with a noun or another pronoun, ignore the extra noun or pronoun and its conjunction. In this way pronoun case becomes more obvious:

> The manager promoted Jeff and *me* (not I). (Ignore *Jeff and*.)

f. In statements of comparison, mentally finish the comparative by adding the implied missing words:

> Next year I hope to earn as much as *she*. (The verb *earns* is implied here: . . . *as much as she earns*.)

g. Pronouns must be in the same case as the words they replace or rename. When pronouns are used with appositives, ignore the appositive:

> A new contract was signed by *us* (not *we*) employees. (Temporarily ignore the appositive *employees* in selecting the pronoun.)

> *We* (not us) citizens have formed our own organization. (Temporarily ignore the appositive *citizens* in selecting the pronoun.)

h. Pronouns ending in *self* should be used only when they refer to previously mentioned nouns or pronouns:

> The CEO *himself* answered the telephone.

> Robert and *I* (not *myself*) are in charge of the campaign.

i. Use objective-case pronouns as objects of the prepositions *between, but, like* and *except:*

> Everyone but John and *him* (not *he*) qualified for the bonus.

> Employees like Miss Gillis and *her* (not *she*) are hard to replace.

j. Use *who* or *whoever* for nominative-case constructions and *whom* or *whomever* for objective-case constructions. In making the correct choice, it's sometimes helpful to substitute *he* for *who* or *whoever* and *him* for *whom* or *whomever:*

> For *whom* was this book ordered? *(This book was ordered for him/whom?)*

> *Who* did you say would drop by? *(Who/He ... would drop by?)*

> Deliver the package to *whoever* opens the door. (In this sentence the clause *whoever opens the door* functions as the object of the preposition *to.* Within the clause itself, *whoever* is the subject of the verb *opens.* Again, substitution of *he* might be helpful: *He/Whoever opens the door.)*

1.09 Guidelines for Making Pronouns Agree With Their Antecedents.
Pronouns must agree with the words to which they refer (their antecedents) in gender and in number.

a. Use masculine pronouns to refer to masculine antecedents, feminine pronouns to refer to feminine antecedents, and neuter pronouns to refer to antecedents without gender:

> The man opened *his* office door. (Masculine gender applies.)

> A woman sat at *her* desk. (Feminine gender applies.)

> This computer and *its* programs fit our needs. (Neuter gender applies.)

b. Use singular pronouns to refer to singular antecedents:

> Common-gender pronouns (such as *him* or *his*) traditionally have been used when the gender of the antecedent is unknown. Sensitive writers today, however, prefer to recast such constructions to avoid gender-biased pronouns. Study these examples for bias-free pronouns:

> Each student must submit *a* report on Monday.

> All students must submit *their* reports on Monday.

> Each student must submit *his or her* report on Monday. (This alternative is least acceptable since it is wordy and calls attention to itself.)

c. Use singular pronouns to refer to singular indefinite subjects and plural pronouns for plural indefinite subjects. Words such as *anyone, something,* and *anybody* are considered indefinite because they refer to no specific person or object. Some indefinite pronouns are always singular; others are always plural.

Always Singular		Always Plural	
anybody	either	nobody	both
anyone	everyone	no one	few
anything	everything	somebody	many
each	neither	someone	several

> Somebody in the group of touring women left *her* (not *their*) purse in the museum.

Either of the companies has the right to exercise *its* (not *their*) option to sell stock.

d. Use singular pronouns to refer to collective nouns and organization names:

The engineering staff is moving *its* (not *their*) facilities on Friday. (The singular pronoun *its* agrees with the collective noun *staff* because the members of *staff* function as a single unit.)

Jones, Cohen, & Chavez, Inc., *has* (not *have*) cancelled *its* (not *their*) contract with us. (The singular pronoun *its* agrees with *Jones, Cohen, & Chavez, Inc.,* because the members of the organization are operating as a single unit.)

e. Use a plural pronoun to refer to two antecedents joined by *and*, whether the antecedents are singular or plural:

Our company president and our vice president will be submitting *their* expenses shortly.

f. Ignore intervening phrases—introduced by expressions such as *together with, as well as,* and *in addition to*—that separate a pronoun from its antecedent:

One of our managers, along with several salespeople, is planning *his* retirement. (If you wish to emphasize both subjects equally, join them with *and*: One of our managers *and* several salespeople are planning *their* retirements.)

g. When antecedents are joined by *or* or *nor*, make the pronoun agree with the antecedent closest to it.

Neither Jackie nor Kim wanted *her* (not *their*) desk moved.

Review Exercise B—Pronouns

In the space provided for each item, write *a, b,* or *c* to complete the statement accurately. When you finish, compare your responses with those provided. For each item on which you need review, consult the numbered principle shown in parentheses.

_____ 1. Send e-mail copies of the policy to the manager or (a) *me*, (b) *myself*.

_____ 2. James promised that he would call; was it (a) *him*, (b) *he* who left the message?

_____ 3. Much preparation for the seminar was made by Mrs. Cho and (a) *I*, (b) *me* before the brochures were sent out.

_____ 4. The Employee Benefits Committee can be justly proud of (a) *its*, (b) *their* achievements.

_____ 5. A number of inquiries were addressed to Jeff and (a) *I*, (b) *me*, (c) *myself*.

_____ 6. (a) *Who*, (b) *Whom* did you say the letter was addressed to?

_____ 7. When you visit Western Financial, inquire about (a) *its*, (b) *their* GICs.

_____ 8. All e-mail messages for Taylor and (a) *I*, (b) *me*, (c) *myself* will become part of the lawsuit.

_____ 9. Apparently one of the applicants forgot to sign (a) *her*, (b) *their* application.

_____ 10. Both the printer and (a) *it's*, (b) *its* cover are missing.

_____ 11. I've never known any man who could work as fast as (a) *him*, (b) *he*.

_____ 12. Just between you and (a) *I*, (b) *me*, the stock price will fall by afternoon.

_____ 13. Give the supplies to (a) *whoever,* (b) *whomever* ordered them.

_____ 14. (a) *Us,* (b) *We* employees have been given an unusual voice in choosing benefits.

_____ 15. When he finally found a job, Dante, along with many other recent graduates, described (a) *his,* (b) *their* experience in an employment blog.

_____ 16. Either Mohamed or Robert must submit (a) *his,* (b) *their* report next week.

_____ 17. Any woman who becomes a charter member of this organization will be able to have (a) *her,* (b) *their* name inscribed on a commemorative plaque.

_____ 18. We are certain that (a) *our's,* (b) *ours* is the smallest camera phone available.

_____ 19. Everyone has completed the reports except Debbie and (a) *he,* (b) *him.*

_____ 20. Lack of work disturbs Mr. Thomas as much as (a) *I,* (b) *me.*

1. a (1.08h)   3. b (1.08c)   5. b (1.08c, 1.08e)   7. a (1.09d)   9. a (1.09b)   11. b (1.08f)
13. a (1.08j)   15. a (1.09f)   17. a (1.09b)   19. b (1.08i)

◼ GRAMMAR/MECHANICS CHECKUP—2

Pronouns

Review Sections 1.07–1.09 above. Then study each of the following statements. In the space provided, write the word that completes the statement correctly and the number of the Handbook principle illustrated. When you finish, compare your responses with those provided on page 538 again. If your responses differ, carefully study again the principles in parentheses.

its (1.09d) Example: The Recreation and Benefits Committee will be submitting (its, their) report soon.

_____ 1. I was expecting the manager to call. Was it (he, him) who left the message?

_____ 2. Every one of the members of the men's soccer team had to move (his car, their cars) before the game could begin.

_____ 3. A serious disagreement between management and (he, him) caused his resignation.

_____ 4. Does anyone in the office know for (who, whom) this stationery was ordered?

_____ 5. It looks as if (her's, hers) is the only report that cites electronic sources.

_____ 6. Ms. Simmons asked my colleague and (I, me, myself) to help her complete the work.

_____ 7. My friend and (I, me, myself) were also asked to work on Saturday.

_____ 8. Both printers were sent for repairs, but (yours, your's) will be returned shortly.

_____ 9. Give the budget figures to (whoever, whomever) asked for them.

_____ 10. Everyone except the broker and (I, me, myself) claimed a share of the commission.

_____ 11. No one knows that problem better than (he, him, himself).

_____ 12. Investment brochures and information were sent to (we, us) shareholders.

_____ 13. If any one of the tourists has lost (their, her) scarf, she should see the driver.

_____ 14. Neither the glamour nor the excitement of the position had lost (its, it's, their) appeal.

_____ 15. Any new subscriber may cancel (their, his or her) subscription within the first month.

■ CUMULATIVE EDITING QUIZ 1

Use proofreading marks (see Appendix B) to correct errors in the following sentences. All errors must be corrected to receive credit for the sentence. Check with your instructor for the answers.

Example: Max and ~~her~~ *she* started ~~there~~ *their* own company in early 2000′s.

1. Neither the citys nor the countys would take responsibility for there budget overruns.
2. Can we keep this matter just between you and I?
3. Only a few secretarys took the day off, despite the storm.
4. Our staff committee gave their recommendation to the president and I as soon as they finished deliberating.
5. Theres really no excuse for we citizens to have no voice in the matter.
6. The manager and myself will deliver supplies to whomever ordered them.
7. Many basketball and hockey star's earn huge salarys.
8. Are you sure that this apartment is their's?
9. Each student must submit their report on Monday.
10. Both the network administrator and myself are concerned about the increase in personal Web use and it's tendency to slow productivity.

Verbs (1.10–1.15)
Verbs show the action of a subject or join the subject to words that describe it.

1.10 Guidelines for Agreement With Subjects. One of the most troublesome areas in English is subject–verb agreement. Consider the following guidelines for making verbs agree with subjects.

a. A singular subject requires a singular verb:

> The stock market *opens* at 10 a.m. (The singular verb *opens* agrees with the singular subject *market*.)

> He *doesn't* (not *don't*) work on Saturday.

b. A plural subject requires a plural verb:

> On the packing slip several items *seem* (not *seems*) to be missing.

c. A verb agrees with its subject regardless of prepositional phrases that may intervene:

> This list of management objectives *is* extensive. (The singular verb *is* agrees with the singular subject *list*.)

> Every one of the letters *shows* (not *show*) proper form.

d. A verb agrees with its subject regardless of intervening phrases introduced by *as well as, in addition to, such as, including, together with,* and similar expressions:

> An important memo, together with several contracts, *is* missing. (The singular verb *is* agrees with the singular subject *memo.*)

> The president as well as several other top-level executives *approves* of our proposal. (The singular verb *approves* agrees with the subject *president.*)

e. A verb agrees with its subject regardless of the location of the subject:

> Here *is* one of the contracts about which you asked. (The verb *is* agrees with its subject *one,* even though it precedes *one.* The adverb *here* cannot function as a subject.)

> There *are* many problems yet to be resolved. (The verb *are* agrees with the subject *problems.* The word *there* does not function as a subject.)

> In the next office *are* several printers. (In this inverted sentence, the verb *are* must agree with the subject *printers.*)

f. Subjects joined by *and* require a plural verb:

> Analyzing the reader and organizing a strategy *are* the first steps in message writing. (The plural verb *are* agrees with the two subjects, *analyzing* and *organizing.*)

> The tone and the wording of the message *were* persuasive. (The plural verb *were* agrees with the two subjects, *tone* and *wording.*)

g. Subjects joined by *or* or *nor* may require singular or plural verbs. Make the verb agree with the closer subject:

> Neither the memo nor the report *is* ready. (The singular verb *is* agrees with *report,* the closer of the two subjects.)

h. The following indefinite pronouns are singular and require singular verbs: *anyone, anybody, anything, each, either, every, everyone, everybody, everything, many a, neither, nobody, nothing, someone, somebody,* and *something*:

> Either of the alternatives that you present *is* acceptable. (The verb *is* agrees with the singular subject *either.*)

i. Collective nouns may take singular or plural verbs, depending on whether the members of the group are operating as a unit or individually:

> Our management team *is* united in its goal.

> The faculty *are* sharply divided on the tuition issue. (Although acceptable, this sentence sounds better recast: The faculty *members* are sharply divided on the tuition issue.)

j. Organization names and titles of publications, although they may appear to be plural, are singular and require singular verbs.

> Bergeron, Anderson, and Horne, Inc., *has* (not *have*) hired a marketing consultant.

> *Thousands of Investment Tips is* (not *are*) again on the best-seller list.

1.11 Voice. Voice is that property of verbs that shows whether the subject of the verb acts or is acted upon. Active-voice verbs direct action from the subject toward the object of the verb. Passive-voice verbs direct action toward the subject.

Active voice: Our employees *send* many e-mails.
Passive voice: Many e-mails *are sent* by our employees.

Business writers generally prefer active-voice verbs because they are specific and forceful. However, passive-voice constructions can help a writer be tactful. Chapter 3 presents strategies for effective use of active- and passive-voice verbs.

1.12 Mood. Three verb moods express the attitude or thought of the speaker or writer toward a subject: (a) the **indicative** mood expresses a fact; (b) the **imperative** mood expresses a command; and (c) the **subjunctive** mood expresses a doubt, a conjecture, or a suggestion.

Indicative: I am looking for a job.
Imperative: Begin your job search by networking.
Subjunctive: I wish I were working.

Only the subjunctive mood creates problems for most speakers and writers. The most common use of subjunctive mood occurs in clauses including *if* or *wish*. In such clauses substitute the subjunctive verb *were* for the indicative verb *was*:

If he *were* (not *was*) in my position, he would understand.

Mr. Simon acts as if he *were* (not *was*) the boss.

We wish we *were* (not *was*) able to ship your order.

The subjunctive mood can maintain goodwill while conveying negative information. The sentence *We wish we were able to ship your order* sounds more pleasing to a customer than *We cannot ship your order*. However, for all practical purposes, both sentences convey the same negative message.

1.13 Tense. Verbs show the time of an action by their tense. Speakers and writers can use six tenses to show the time of sentence action; for example:

Present tense: I *work*; he *works*.
Past tense: I *worked*; she *worked*.
Future tense: I *will work*; he *will work*.
Present perfect tense: I *have worked*; he *has worked*.
Past perfect tense: I *had worked*; she *had worked*.
Future perfect tense: I *will have worked*; he *will have worked*.

1.14 Guidelines for Verb Tense

a. Use present tense for statements that, although introduced by past-tense verbs, continue to be true:

What did you say his name *is*? (Use the present tense *is* if his name has not changed.)

b. Avoid unnecessary shifts in verb tenses:

The manager *saw* (not *sees*) a great deal of work yet to be completed and *remained* to do it herself.

Although unnecessary shifts in verb tense are to be avoided, not all the verbs within one sentence have to be in the same tense; for example:

She *said* (past tense) that she *likes* (present tense) to work late.

1.15 Irregular Verbs. Irregular verbs cause difficulty for some writers and speakers. Unlike regular verbs, irregular verbs do not form the past tense and past participle by adding *-ed* to the present form. Here is a partial list of selected troublesome irregular verbs. Consult a dictionary if you are in doubt about a verb form.

Troublesome Irregular Verbs

Present	Past	Past Participle (*always use helping verbs*)
begin	began	begun
break	broke	broken
choose	chose	chosen
come	came	come
drink	drank	drunk
go	went	gone
lay (to place)	laid	laid
lie (to rest)	lay	lain
ring	rang	rung
see	saw	seen
write	wrote	written

a. Use only past-tense verbs to express past tense. Notice that no helping verbs are used to indicate simple past tense:

> The auditors *went* (not *have went*) over our books carefully.

> He *came* (not *come*) to see us yesterday.

b. Use past-participle forms for actions completed before the present time. Notice that past-participle forms require helping verbs:

> Steve *had gone* (not *had went*) before we called. (The past-participle *gone* is used with the helping verb *had*.)

c. Avoid inconsistent shifts in subject, voice, and mood. Pay particular attention to this problem area because undesirable shifts are often characteristic of student writing.

Inconsistent: When Mrs. Thobani read the report, the error was found. (The first clause is in the active voice; the second, passive.)

Improved: When Mrs. Thobani read the report, she found the error. (Both clauses are in the active voice.)

Inconsistent: The clerk should first conduct an inventory. Then supplies should be requisitioned. (The first sentence is in the active voice; the second, passive.)

Improved: The clerk should first conduct an inventory. Then he or she should requisition supplies. (Both sentences are in the active voice.)

Inconsistent: All workers must wear security badges, and you must also sign a daily time card. (This sentence contains an inconsistent shift in subject from *all workers* in the first clause to *you* in the second clause.)

Improved: All workers must wear security badges, and they must also sign a daily time card.

Inconsistent: Begin the transaction by opening an account; then you enter the customer's name. (This sentence contains an inconsistent shift from the imperative mood in the first clause to the indicative mood in the second clause.)

Improved: Begin the transaction by opening an account; then enter the customer's name. (Both clauses are now in the imperative mood.)

Review Exercise C—Verbs

In the space provided for each item, write *a* or *b* to complete the statement accurately. When you finish, compare your responses with those provided. For each item on which you need review, consult the numbered principle shown in parentheses.

_____ 1. Our directory of customer names and addresses (a) *was* (b) *were* out-of-date.

_____ 2. There (a) *is,* (b) *are* a customer-service engineer and two salespeople waiting to see you.

_____ 3. Improved communication technologies and increased global competition (a) *is,* (b) *are* changing the world of business.

_____ 4. Crews, Meliotes, and Mishra, Inc., (a) *has,* (b) *have* opened an office in Boston.

_____ 5. Yesterday Mrs. Phillips (a) *choose,* (b) *chose* a new office on the second floor.

_____ 6. The man who called said that his last name (a) *is,* (b) *was* Panagiotis.

_____ 7. Our management team and our lawyer (a) *is,* (b) *are* researching the privacy issue.

_____ 8. Either of the flight times (a) *appears,* (b) *appear* to fit my proposed itinerary.

_____ 9. If you had (a) *saw,* (b) *seen* the rough draft, you would better appreciate the final copy.

_____ 10. Across from our office (a) *is,* (b) *are* the parking structure and the information office.

_____ 11. Although we have (a) *began,* (b) *begun* to replace outmoded equipment, the pace is slow.

_____ 12. Specific training as well as ample experience (a) *is,* (b) *are* important for that position.

_____ 13. Changing attitudes and increased job opportunities (a) *is,* (b) *are* resulting in increased numbers of working women.

_____ 14. Neither the organizing nor the staffing of the program (a) *has been,* (b) *have been* completed.

_____ 15. If I (a) *was,* (b) *were* you, I would ask for a raise.

_____ 16. If you had (a) *wrote,* (b) *written* last week, we could have sent a brochure.

_____ 17. The hydraulic equipment that you ordered (a) *is,* (b) *are* packed and will be shipped Friday.

_____ 18. One of the reasons that sales have declined in recent years (a) *is,* (b) *are* a lack of effective online advertising.

_____ 19. Either of the proposed laws (a) *is,* (b) *are* going to affect our business negatively.

_____ 20. Merger statutes (a) *requires,* (b) *require* that a failing company accept bids from several companies before merging with one.

1. a (1.10c)   3. b (1.10f)   5. b (1.15a)   7. b (1.10f)   9. b (1.15b)   11. b (1.15b)   13. b (1.10f)
15. b (1.12)   17. a (1.10a)   19. a (1.10h)

Review Exercise D—Verbs

In the following sentence pairs, choose the one that illustrates consistency in use of subject, voice, and mood. Write *a* or *b* in the space provided. When you finish, compare your responses with those provided. For each item on which you need review, consult the numbered principle shown in parentheses.

_____ 1. (a) You need more than a knowledge of technology; one also must be able to interact well with people.

(b) You need more than a knowledge of technology; you also must be able to interact well with people.

_____ 2. (a) Tim and Jon were eager to continue, but Bob wanted to quit.

(b) Tim and Jon were eager to continue, but Bob wants to quit.

_____ 3. (a) The salesperson should consult the price list; then you can give an accurate quote to a customer.

(b) The salesperson should consult the price list; then he or she can give an accurate quote to a customer.

_____ 4. (a) Read all the instructions first; then you install the printer program.

(b) Read all the instructions first, and then install the printer program.

_____ 5. (a) She was an enthusiastic manager who always had a smile for everyone.

(b) She was an enthusiastic manager who always has a smile for everyone.

1. b (1.15c)   3. b (1.15c)   5. a (1.14b)

■ GRAMMAR/MECHANICS CHECKUP—3

Verbs

Review Sections 1.10–1.15 above. Then study each of the following statements. Underline any verbs that are used incorrectly. In the space provided, write the correct form (or C if correct) and the number of the Handbook principle illustrated. When you finish, compare your responses with those provided on page 538. If your responses differ, carefully study again the principles in parentheses.

was (1.10c) Example: Our inventory of raw materials were presented as collateral for a short-term loan.

_____ 1. Located across town is a research institute and our product-testing facility.

_____ 2. Can you tell me whether a current list with all customers' names and addresses have been sent to marketing?

_____ 3. The credit union, along with 20 other large national banks, offer a variety of savings plans.

_____ 4. Neither the plans that this bank offers nor the service just rendered by the teller are impressive.

_____ 5. Locating a bank and selecting a savings/chequing plan often require considerable research and study.

_____ 6. The budget analyst wants to know whether the Equipment Committee are ready to recommend a printer.

_____ 7. Either of the printers that the committee selects is acceptable to the budget analyst.

_____ 8. If Mr. Tutchone had chose the Maximizer Plus savings plan, his money would have earned maximum interest.

_____ 9. Although the applications have laid there for two weeks, they may still be submitted.

_____ 10. Nadia acts as if she was the manager.

_____ 11. One of the reasons that our Nunavut sales branches have been so costly are the high cost of living.

In the space provided, write the letter of the sentence that illustrates consistency in subject, voice, and mood.

_____ 12. (a) If you will read the instructions, the answer can be found.

(b) If you will read the instructions, you will find the answer.

_____ 13. (a) All employees must fill out application forms; only then will you be insured.

(b) All employees must fill out application forms; only then will they be insured.

_____ 14. (a) First, take an inventory of equipment; then, order supplies.

(b) First, take an inventory of equipment; then, supplies must be ordered.

_____ 15. (a) Select a savings plan that suits your needs; deposits may be made immediately.

(b) Select a savings plan that suits your needs; begin making deposits immediately.

■ CUMULATIVE EDITING QUIZ 2

Use proofreading marks (see Appendix B) to correct errors in the following sentences. All errors must be corrected to receive credit for the sentence. Check with your instructor for the answers.

1. The production cost and the markup of each item is important in calculating the sale price.

2. Sheila acts as if she was the manager, but we know she is not.

3. The committee are reconsidering their decision in view of recent health care legislation.

4. My all-in-one computer and it's lightweight keyboard is attractive but difficult to use.

5. Waiting in the outer office is a job applicant and a sales representative who you told to stop by.

6. Each applicant could have submitted his application online if he had went to our Web site.

7. One of the reasons she applied are that she seen the salarys posted at our Web site.

8. Either of the options that you may chose are acceptable to Jake and myself.

9. Although there anger and frustration is understandable, both editor in chiefs decided to apologize and reprint the article.

10. The Lopez'es, about who the article was written, accepted the apology graciously.

Adjectives and Adverbs (1.16–1.17)

Adjectives describe or limit nouns and pronouns. They often answer the questions *what kind? how many?* or *which one?* Adverbs describe or limit verbs, adjectives, or other adverbs. They often answer the questions *when? how? where?* or *to what extent?*

1.16 Forms. Most adjectives and adverbs have three forms, or degrees: *positive, comparative,* and *superlative.*

	Positive	**Comparative**	**Superlative**
Adjective:	clear	clearer	clearest
Adverb:	clearly	more clearly	most clearly

Some adjectives and adverbs have irregular forms:

	Positive	**Comparative**	**Superlative**
Adjective:	good	better	best
	bad	worse	worst
Adverb:	well	better	best

Adjectives and adverbs composed of two or more syllables are usually compared by the use of *more* and *most*; for example:

> The Payroll Department is *more efficient* than the Shipping Department.

> Payroll is the *most efficient* department in our organization.

1.17 Guidelines for Use

a. Use the comparative degree of the adjective or adverb to compare two persons or things; use the superlative degree to compare three or more:

> Of the two plans, which is *better* (not *best*)?

> Of all the plans, we like this one *best* (not *better*).

b. Do not create a double comparative or superlative by using *-er* with *more* or *-est* with *most*:

> His explanation couldn't have been *clearer* (not *more clearer*).

c. A linking verb (*is, are, look, seem, feel, sound, appear,* and so forth) may introduce a word that describes the verb's subject. In this case be certain to use an adjective, not an adverb:

> The characters on the monitor look *bright* (not *brightly*). (Use the adjective *bright* because it follows the linking verb *look* and modifies the noun *characters.*)

> The company's letter made the customer feel *bad* (not *badly*). (The adjective *bad* follows the linking verb *feel* and describes the noun *customer.*)

d. Use adverbs, not adjectives, to describe or limit the action of verbs:

> The business is running *smoothly* (not *smooth*). (Use the adverb *smoothly* to describe the action of the verb *is running*. *Smoothly* explains how the business is running.)

> Don't take his remark *personally* (not *personal*). (The adverb *personally* describes the action of the verb *take*.)

> Drishti said she did *well* (not *good*) on the test. (Use the adverb *well* to tell how she did.)

e. Two or more adjectives that are joined to create a compound modifier before a noun should be hyphenated:

> The *four-year-old* child was tired.

> Our agency is planning a *coast-to-coast* campaign.

Hyphenate a compound modifier following a noun only if your dictionary shows the hyphen(s):

> Our speaker is very *well-known*. (Include the hyphen because most dictionaries do.)

The tired child was four years old. (Omit the hyphens because the expression follows the word it describes, *child*, and because dictionaries do not indicate hyphens.)

f. Keep adjectives and adverbs close to the words they modify:

She asked for *a cup of hot coffee* (not *a hot cup of coffee*).

Patty *had only two days* of vacation left (not *only had two days*).

Students may sit in the *first five rows* (not *in five first rows*).

He *has saved almost* enough money for the trip (not *has almost saved*).

g. Don't confuse *there* with the possessive pronoun *their* or the contraction *they're*:

Put the documents *there*. (The adverb *there* means "at that place or at that point.")

There are two reasons for the change. (The pronoun *there* is used as function word to introduce a sentence or a clause.)

We already have *their* specifications. (The possessive pronoun *their* shows ownership.)

They're coming to inspect today. (The contraction *they're* is a shortened form of *they are*.)

Review Exercise E—Adjectives and Adverbs

In the space provided for each item, write *a, b,* or *c* to complete the statement accurately. If two sentences are shown, select *a* or *b* to indicate the one expressed more effectively. When you finish, compare your responses with those provided. For each item on which you need review, consult the numbered principle shown in parentheses.

_____ 1. After the interview, Yoshi looked (a) *calm*, (b) *calmly*.

_____ 2. If you had been more (a) *careful*, (b) *carefuler*, the box might not have broken.

_____ 3. Because we appointed a new manager, the advertising campaign is running (a) *smooth*, (b) *smoothly*.

_____ 4. To avoid a (a) *face to face*, (b) *face-to-face* confrontation, she sent an e-mail.

_____ 5. Darren completed the employment test (a) *satisfactorily*, (b) *satisfactory*.

_____ 6. I felt (a) *bad*, (b) *badly* that he was not promoted.

_____ 7. Which is the (a) *more*, (b) *most* dependable of the two cars?

_____ 8. Can you determine exactly what (a) *there*, (b) *their*, (c) *they're* company wants us to do?

_____ 9. Of all the copiers we tested, this one is the (a) *easier*, (b) *easiest* to operate.

_____ 10. (a) Mr. Aldron almost was ready to accept the offer.

(b) Mr. Aldron was almost ready to accept the offer.

_____ 11. (a) We only thought that it would take two hours for the test.

(b) We thought that it would take only two hours for the test.

_____ 12. (a) Please bring me a glass of cold water.

(b) Please bring me a cold glass of water.

_____ 13. (a) The committee decided to retain the last ten tickets.

(b) The committee decided to retain the ten last tickets.

_____ 14. New owners will receive a (a) *60-day,* (b) *60 day* trial period.

_____ 15. The time passed (a) *quicker,* (b) *more quickly* than we expected.

_____ 16. We offer a (a) *money back,* (b) *money-back* guarantee.

_____ 17. Today the financial news is (a) *worse,* (b) *worst* than yesterday.

_____ 18. Please don't take his comments (a) *personal,* (b) *personally.*

_____ 19. You must check the document (a) *page by page,* (b) *page-by-page.*

_____ 20. (a) We try to file only necessary paperwork.

(b) We only try to file necessary paperwork.

1. a (1.17c) 3. b (1.17d) 5. a (1.17d) 7. a (1.17a) 9. b (1.17a) 11. b (1.17f) 13. a (1.17f)
15. b (1.17d) 17. a (1.17a) 19. a (1.17e)

◼ GRAMMAR/MECHANICS CHECKUP—4

Adjectives and Adverbs

Review Sections 1.16 and 1.17 above. Then study each of the following statements. Underline any inappropriate forms. In the space provided, write the correct form (or *C* if correct) and the number of the Handbook principle illustrated. You may need to consult your dictionary for current practice regarding some compound adjectives. When you finish, compare your responses with those provided on page 538. If your answers differ, carefully study again the principles in parentheses.

live-and-let-live (1.17e) Example: He was one of those individuals with <u>a live and let live</u> attitude.

_____ 1. Most of our long time customers have credit card accounts.

_____ 2. Many subscribers considered the $50 per year charge to be a bargain.

_____ 3. Other subscribers complained that $50 per year was exorbitant.

_____ 4. The Internet supplied the answer so quick that we were all amazed.

_____ 5. He only had $5 in his pocket.

_____ 6. Some experts predict that double digit inflation may return.

_____ 7. Jeremy found a once in a lifetime opportunity.

_____ 8. Although the car was four years old, it was in good condition.

_____ 9. Of the two colours, which is best for a Web background?

_____ 10. Professor Candace Carbone is well known in her field.

_____ 11. Channel 12 presents up to the minute news broadcasts.

_____ 12. Lower tax brackets would lessen the after tax yield of some bonds.

_____ 13. The conclusion drawn from the statistics couldn't have been more clearer.

_____ 14. This new investment fund has a better than fifty fifty chance of outperforming the older fund.

_____ 15. If you feel badly about the transaction, contact your portfolio manager.

Prepositions (1.18)

Prepositions are connecting words that join nouns or pronouns to other words in a sentence. The words *about, at, from, in,* and *to* are examples of prepositions.

1.18 Guidelines for Use

a. Include necessary prepositions:

> What type *of* software do you need (not *What type software*)?

> I graduated *from* high school two years ago (not *I graduated high school*).

b. Omit unnecessary prepositions:

> Where is the meeting? (Not *Where is the meeting at?*)

> Both printers work well. (Not *Both of the printers...*)

> Where are you going? (Not *Where are you going to?*)

c. Avoid the overuse of prepositional phrases.

> **Weak:** We have received your application for credit at our branch in the Windsor area.
>
> **Improved:** We have received your Windsor credit application.

d. Repeat the preposition before the second of two related elements:

> Applicants use the résumé effectively by summarizing their most important experiences and *by* relating their education to the jobs sought.

e. Include the second preposition when two prepositions modify a single object:

> George's appreciation *of* and aptitude *for* computers led to a promising career.

Conjunctions (1.19)

Conjunctions connect words, phrases, and clauses. They act as signals, indicating when a thought is being added, contrasted, or altered. Coordinate conjunctions (such as *and, or, but*) and other words that act as connectors (such as *however, therefore, when, as*) tell the reader or listener in what direction a thought is heading. They are like road signs signalling what's ahead.

1.19 Guidelines for Use

a. Use coordinating conjunctions to connect only sentence elements that are parallel or balanced.

> **Weak:** His report was correct and written in a concise manner.
>
> **Improved:** His report was correct and concise.

> **Weak:** Management has the capacity to increase fraud, or reduction can be achieved through the policies it adopts.
>
> **Improved:** Management has the capacity to increase or reduce fraud through the policies it adopts.

b. Do not use the word *like* as a conjunction:

> It seems *as if* (not *like*) this day will never end.

c. Avoid using *when* or *where* inappropriately. A common writing fault occurs in sentences with clauses introduced by *is when* and *is where*. Written English ordinarily requires a noun (or a group of words functioning as a noun) following the linking verb *is*. Instead of acting as conjunctions in these constructions, the words *where* and *when* function as adverbs, creating faulty grammatical equations (adverbs cannot complete equations set up by linking verbs). To avoid the problem, revise the sentence, eliminating *is when* or *is where*.

> **Weak:** A bullish market is when prices are rising in the stock market.
>
> **Improved:** A bullish market is created when prices are rising in the stock market.

Weak: A flow chart is when you make a diagram showing the step-by-step progression of a procedure.

Improved: A flow chart is a diagram showing the step-by-step progression of a procedure.

Weak: A podcast is where a pre-recorded audio program is posted to a Web site.

Improved: A podcast is a pre-recorded audio program posted to a Web site.

A similar faulty construction occurs in the expression *I hate when*. English requires nouns, noun clauses, or pronouns to act as objects of verbs, not adverbs.

Weak: I hate when we're asked to work overtime.

Improved: I hate it when we're asked to work overtime.

Improved: I hate being asked to work overtime.

d. Don't confuse the adverb *then* with the conjunction *than*. *Then* means "at that time"; *than* indicates the second element in a comparison:

We would rather remodel *than* (not *then*) move.

First, the equipment is turned on; *then* (not *than*) the program is loaded.

Review Exercise F—Prepositions and Conjunctions

In the space provided for each item, write *a* or *b* to indicate the sentence that is expressed more effectively. When you finish, compare your responses with those provided. For each item on which you need review, consult the numbered principle shown in parentheses.

_____ 1. (a) The chief forgot to tell everyone where today's meeting is.

(b) The chief forgot to tell everyone where today's meeting is at.

_____ 2. (a) She was not aware of nor interested in the company insurance plan.

(b) She was not aware nor interested in the company insurance plan.

_____ 3. (a) Josh Samuels graduated college last June.

(b) Josh Samuels graduated from college last June.

_____ 4. (a) "Flextime" is when employees arrive and depart at varying times.

(b) "Flextime" is a method of scheduling worktime in which employees arrive and depart at varying times.

_____ 5. (a) Both employees enjoyed setting their own hours.

(b) Both of the employees enjoyed setting their own hours.

_____ 6. (a) I hate when my cell loses its charge.

(b) I hate it when my cell loses its charge.

_____ 7. (a) What style of typeface should we use?

(b) What style typeface should we use?

_____ 8. (a) Business letters should be concise, correct, and written clearly.

(b) Business letters should be concise, correct, and clear.

_____ 9. (a) Mediation in a labour dispute occurs when a neutral person helps union and management reach an agreement.

(b) Mediation in a labour dispute is where a neutral person helps union and management reach an agreement.

_____ 10. (a) It looks as if the plant will open in early January.

(b) It looks like the plant will open in early January.

_____ 11. (a) We expect to finish up the work soon.

(b) We expect to finish the work soon.

_____ 12. (a) At the beginning of the program in the fall of the year at the central office, we experienced staffing difficulties.

(b) When the program began last fall, the central office experienced staffing difficulties.

_____ 13. (a) Your client may respond by e-mail or a telephone call may be made.

(b) Your client may respond by e-mail or by telephone.

_____ 14. (a) A résumé is when you make a written presentation of your education and experience for a prospective employer.

(b) A résumé is a written presentation of your education and experience for a prospective employer.

_____ 15. (a) Sara exhibited both an awareness of and talent for developing innovations.

(b) Sara exhibited both an awareness and talent for developing innovations.

_____ 16. (a) This course is harder then I expected.

(b) This course is harder than I expected.

_____ 17. (a) An ombudsman is an individual hired by management to investigate and resolve employee complaints.

(b) An ombudsman is when management hires an individual to investigate and resolve employee complaints.

_____ 18. (a) I'm uncertain where to take this document to.

(b) I'm uncertain where to take this document.

_____ 19. (a) By including accurate data and by writing clearly, you will produce effective messages.

(b) By including accurate data and writing clearly, you will produce effective messages.

_____ 20. (a) We need computer operators who can load software, monitor networks, and files must be duplicated.

(b) We need computer operators who can load software, monitor networks, and duplicate files.

---

1. a (1.18b)   3. b (1.18a)   5. a (1.18b)   7. a (1.18a)   9. a (1.19c)   11. b (1.18b)   13. b (1.19a)
15. a (1.18e)   17. a (1.19c)   19. a (1.18d)

◼ GRAMMAR/MECHANICS CHECKUP—5

Prepositions and Conjunctions

Review Sections 1.18 and 1.19 above. Then study each of the following statements. Write *a* or *b* to indicate the sentence in which the idea is expressed more effectively. Also record the number of the Handbook principle illustrated. When you finish, compare your responses with those provided on page 538. If your answers differ, carefully study again the principles shown in parentheses.

b (1.18a) Example: (a) Raoul will graduate college this spring.

(b) Raoul will graduate from college this spring.

_____ 1. (a) DataTech enjoyed greater profits this year then it expected.

(b) DataTech enjoyed greater profits this year than it expected.

_____ 2. (a) I hate it when we have to work overtime.

(b) I hate when we have to work overtime.

_____ 3. (a) Dr. Simon has a great interest and appreciation for the study of robotics.

(b) Dr. Simon has a great interest in and appreciation for the study of robotics.

_____ 4. (a) Gross profit is where you compute the difference between total sales and the cost of goods sold.

(b) Gross profit is computed by finding the difference between total sales and the cost of goods sold.

_____ 5. (a) We advertise to increase the frequency of product use, to introduce complementary products, and to enhance our corporate image.

(b) We advertise to have our products used more often, when we have complementary products to introduce, and we are interested in making our corporation look better to the public.

_____ 6. (a) What type printer do you prefer?

(b) What type of printer do you prefer?

_____ 7. (a) Where are you going to?

(b) Where are you going?

_____ 8. (a) The sale of our Halifax office last year should improve this year's profits.

(b) The sale of our office in Halifax during last year should improve the profits for this year.

_____ 9. (a) Do you know where the meeting is at?

(b) Do you know where the meeting is?

_____ 10. (a) The cooling-off rule is a provincial government rule that protects consumers from making unwise purchases at home.

(b) The cooling-off rule is where the provincial government has made a rule that protects consumers from making unwise purchases at home.

_____ 11. (a) Meetings can be more meaningful if the agenda is stuck to, the time frame is followed, and if someone keeps follow-up notes.

(b) Meetings can be more meaningful if you stick to the agenda, follow the time frame, and keep follow-up notes.

_____ 12. (a) They printed the newsletter on yellow paper like we asked them to do.

(b) They printed the newsletter on yellow paper as we asked them to do.

_____ 13. (a) A code of ethics is a set of rules indicating appropriate standards of behaviour.

(b) A code of ethics is where a set of rules indicates appropriate standards of behaviour.

_____ 14. (a) We need an individual with an understanding and serious interest in black-and-white photography.

(b) We need an individual with an understanding of and serious interest in black-and-white photography.

_____ 15. (a) The most dangerous situation is when employees ignore the safety rules.

(b) The most dangerous situation occurs when employees ignore the safety rules.

CUMULATIVE EDITING QUIZ 3

Use proofreading marks (see Appendix B) to correct errors in the following sentences. All errors must be corrected to receive credit for the sentence. Check with your instructor for the answers.

1. Her new tablet is definitely more faster then her previous tablet.
2. Max said that he felt badly that he missed his appointment with you and myself.
3. Neither the managers nor the union are happy at how slow the talks are progressing.
4. Just between you and I, we have learned not to take the boss's criticism personal.
5. After completing a case by case search, the consultant promised to send his report to Carlos and I.
6. If you was me, which of the two job offers do you think is best?
7. Did your team members tell you where there meeting is at?
8. Jason felt that he had done good on the three hour certification exam.
9. It seems like our step by step instructions could have been more clearer.
10. I hate when I'm expected to finish up by myself.

PUNCTUATION REVIEW

Commas 1 (2.01–2.04)

2.01 Series. Commas are used to separate three or more equal elements (words, phrases, or short clauses) in a series. To ensure separation of the last two elements, careful writers always use a comma before the conjunction in a series:

> Business letters usually contain a dateline, address, salutation, body, and closing. (This series contains words.)

> The job of an ombudsman is to examine employee complaints, resolve disagreements between management and employees, and ensure fair treatment. (This series contains phrases.)

> Interns complete basic office tasks, marketing coordinators manage author events, and editors proofread completed projects. (This series contains short clauses.)

2.02 Direct Address. Commas are used to set off the names of individuals being addressed:

> Your inquiry, *Mrs. Johnson,* has been referred to me.

> We genuinely hope that we may serve you, *Mr. Zhou.*

2.03 Parenthetical Expressions. Skilled writers use parenthetical words, phrases, and clauses to guide the reader from one thought to the next. When these expressions interrupt the flow of a sentence and are unnecessary for its grammatical completeness, they should be set off with commas. Examples of commonly used parenthetical expressions follow:

all things considered	however	needless to say
as a matter of fact	in addition	nevertheless
as a result	incidentally	no doubt
as a rule	in fact	of course

at the same time	in my opinion	on the contrary
consequently	in the first place	on the other hand
for example	in the meantime	therefore
furthermore	moreover	under the circumstances

> *As a matter of fact,* I wrote to you just yesterday. (Phrase used at the beginning of a sentence.)

> We will, *in the meantime,* send you a replacement order. (Phrase used in the middle of a sentence.)

> Your satisfaction is our first concern, *needless to say.* (Phrase used at the end of a sentence.)

Do not use commas if the expression is necessary for the completeness of the sentence:

> Kimberly had *no doubt* that she would finish the report. (Omit commas because the expression is necessary for the completeness of the sentence.)

2.04 Dates, Addresses, and Geographical Items. When dates, addresses, and geographical items contain more than one element, the second and succeeding elements are normally set off by commas.

a. Dates:

> The conference was held February 2 at our home office. (No comma is needed for one element.)

> The conference was held February 2, 2014, at our home office. (Two commas set off the second element.)

> The conference was held Tuesday, February 2, 2014, at our home office. (Commas set off the second and third elements.)

> In February 2014 the conference was held. (This alternate style omitting commas is acceptable if only the month and year are written.)

b. Addresses:

> The letter addressed to Jim W. Ellman, 600 Ellerby Trail, Calgary, AB T4E 8N9, should be sent today. (Commas are used between all elements except the province and postal code, which in this special instance act as a single unit.)

c. Geographical items:

> She moved from Whitehorse, Yukon, to Toronto, Ontario. (Commas set off the province/territory unless it appears at the end of the sentence, in which case only one comma is used.)

In separating cities from provinces/territories and days from years, many writers remember the initial comma but forget the final one, as in the examples that follow:

> The package from Sydney, Nova Scotia{,} was lost.

> We opened June 1, 2009{,} and have grown steadily since.

Review Exercise G—Commas 1

Insert necessary commas in the following sentences. In the space provided, write the number of commas that you add. Write C if no commas are needed. When you finish, compare your responses with those provided. For each item on which you need review, consult the numbered principle shown in parentheses.

_____ 1. As a rule, we do not provide complimentary tickets.

_____ 2. You may be certain Mr. Mobuto that your policy will be issued immediately.

_____ 3. I have no doubt that your calculations are correct.

_____ 4. The safety hazard on the contrary can be greatly reduced if workers wear rubber gloves.

_____ 5. Every accredited TV newscaster radio broadcaster and blogger had access to the media room.

_____ 6. Deltech's main offices are located in Ottawa Ontario and Vancouver British Columbia.

_____ 7. The employees who are eligible for promotions are Terry Evelyn Vicki Rosanna and Steve.

_____ 8. During the warranty period of course you are protected from any parts or service charges.

_____ 9. Many of our customers include architects engineers attorneys and others who are interested in database management programs.

_____ 10. I wonder Dr. Stevens if you would send my letter of recommendation as soon as possible.

_____ 11. The new book explains how to choose appropriate legal protection for ideas trade secrets copyrights patents and restrictive covenants.

_____ 12. The factory is scheduled to be moved to 2250 North Main Street Cambridge Ontario N2F 8V7 within two years.

_____ 13. You may however prefer to be in touch directly with the manufacturer in China.

_____ 14. Are there any alternatives in addition to those that we have already considered?

_____ 15. The rally has been scheduled for Monday January 12 in the campus stadium.

_____ 16. A cheque for the full amount will be sent directly to your home Mr. Jefferson.

_____ 17. Goodstone Tire & Rubber for example recalled 400,000 steelbelted radial tires because some tires failed their rigorous tests.

_____ 18. Kevin agreed to unlock the office open the mail and check all the equipment in my absence.

_____ 19. In the meantime thank you for whatever assistance you are able to furnish.

_____ 20. Research facilities were moved from St. John's Newfoundland to Hamilton Ontario.

---

1. rule, (2.03)   3. C (2.03)   5. newscaster, radio broadcaster, (2.01)   7. Terry, Evelyn, Vicki, Rosanna, (2.01)   9. architects, engineers, attorneys, (2.01)   11. ideas, trade secrets, copyrights, patents, (2.01)   13. may, however, (2.03)   15. Monday, January 12, (2.04a)   17. Rubber, for example, (2.03)   19. meantime, (2.03)

◼ GRAMMAR/MECHANICS CHECKUP—6

Commas 1

Review Sections 2.01–2.04 above. Then study each of the following statements and insert necessary commas. In the space provided, write the number of commas that you add; write 0 if no commas are needed. Also record the number of the Handbook principle illustrated. When you finish, compare your responses with those on page 538. If your answers differ, carefully study again the principles shown in parentheses.

2 (2.01) Example: In this class students learn to write clear and concise business letters, memos, and reports.

_____ 1. We do not as a rule allow employees to take time off for dental appointments.

_____ 2. You may be sure Ms. Schwartz that your car will be ready by 4 p.m.

_____ 3. Anyone who is reliable conscientious and honest should be very successful.

_____ 4. A conference on sales motivation is scheduled for May 5 at the Plainsview Hotel beginning at 2 p.m.

_____ 5. As a matter of fact I just called your office this morning.

_____ 6. We are relocating our distribution centre from Calgary Alberta to La Salle Quebec.

_____ 7. In the meantime please continue to send your orders to the regional office.

_____ 8. The last meeting recorded in the minutes was on February 4 2011 in Windsor.

_____ 9. Ms. Horne Mr. Hae Mrs. Andorra and Mr. Baker are our new representatives.

_____ 10. The package mailed to Ms. Leslie Holmes 3430 Larkspur Lane Regina Saskatchewan S5L 2E2 arrived three weeks after it was mailed.

_____ 11. The manager feels needless to say that the support of all employees is critical.

_____ 12. Eric was assigned three jobs: checking supplies replacing inventories and distributing delivered goods.

_____ 13. We will work diligently to retain your business Mr. Fuhai.

_____ 14. The vice president feels however that all sales representatives need training.

_____ 15. The name selected for a product should be right for that product and should emphasize its major attributes.

Commas 2 (2.05–2.09)

2.05 Independent Clauses. An independent clause is a group of words that has a subject and a verb and that could stand as a complete sentence. When two such clauses are joined by _and, or, nor,_ or _but,_ use a comma before the conjunction:

> We can ship your merchandise July 12, but we must have your payment first.

> Net income before taxes is calculated, and this total is then combined with income from operations.

Notice that each independent clause in the preceding two examples could stand alone as a complete sentence. Do not use a comma unless each group of words is a complete thought (that is, has its own subject and verb).

> Our accountant calculates net income before taxes _and_ then combines that figure with income from operations. (No comma is needed because no subject follows _and._)

2.06 Dependent Clauses. Dependent clauses do not make sense by themselves; for their meaning they depend on independent clauses.

a. **Introductory clauses.** When a dependent clause precedes an independent clause, it is followed by a comma. Such clauses are often introduced by *when*, *if*, and *as:*

> *When your request came,* we responded immediately.

> *As I mentioned earlier,* Clementine James is the manager.

b. **Terminal clauses.** If a dependent clause falls at the end of a sentence, use a comma only if the dependent clause is an afterthought:

> We have rescheduled the meeting for October 23, *if this date meets with your approval.* (Comma used because dependent clause is an afterthought.)

> We responded immediately *when we received your request.* (No comma is needed.)

c. **Essential versus nonessential clauses.** If a dependent clause provides information that is unneeded for the grammatical completeness of a sentence, use commas to set it off. In determining whether such a clause is essential or nonessential, ask yourself whether the reader needs the information contained in the clause to identify the word it explains:

> Our district sales manager, *who just returned from a trip to the Northern Ontario District,* prepared this report. (This construction assumes that there is only one district sales manager. Because the sales manager is clearly identified, the dependent clause is not essential and requires commas.)

> The salesperson *who just returned from a trip to the Northern Ontario District* prepared this report. (The dependent clause in this sentence is necessary to identify which salesperson prepared the report. Therefore, use no commas.)

> The position of assistant sales manager, *which we discussed with you last week,* is still open. (Careful writers use *which* to introduce nonessential clauses. Commas are also necessary.)

> The position *that we discussed with you last week* is still open. (Careful writers use *that* to introduce essential clauses. No commas are used.)

2.07 Phrases. A phrase is a group of related words that lacks both a subject and a verb. A phrase that precedes a main clause is followed by a comma if the phrase contains a verb form or has five or more words:

> *Beginning November 1,* Worldwide Savings will offer two new combination chequing/savings plans. (A comma follows this introductory phrase because the phrase contains the verb form *beginning.*)

> *To promote our plan,* we will conduct an extensive social media advertising campaign. (A comma follows this introductory phrase because the phrase contains the verb form *to promote.*)

> *In a period of only one year,* we were able to improve our market share by 30 percent. (A comma follows the introductory phrase—actually two prepositional phrases—because its total length exceeds five words.)

> *In 2014* our organization installed a multiuser system that could transfer programs easily. (No comma needed after the short introductory phrase.)

2.08 Two or More Adjectives. Use a comma to separate two or more adjectives that equally describe a noun. A good way to test the need for a comma is this: Mentally insert the word *and* between the adjectives. If the resulting phrase sounds natural, a comma is used to show the omission of *and:*

> We're looking for a *versatile, error-free* operating system. (Use a comma to separate *versatile* and *error-free* because they independently describe *operating system. And* has been omitted.)

Our *experienced, courteous* staff is ready to serve you. (Use a comma to separate *experienced* and *courteous* because they independently describe *staff*. *And* has been omitted.)

It was difficult to refuse the *sincere young* caller. (No commas are needed between *sincere* and *young* because *and* has not been omitted.)

2.09 Appositives. Words that re-name or explain preceding nouns or pronouns are called *appositives*. An appositive that provides information not essential to the identification of the word it describes should be set off by commas:

James Wilson, *the project director for Sperling's,* worked with our architect. (The appositive, *the project director for Sperling's,* adds nonessential information. Commas set it off.)

Review Exercise H—Commas 2

Insert only necessary commas in the following sentences. In the space provided, indicate the number of commas that you add for each sentence. If a sentence requires no commas, write C. When you finish, compare your responses with those provided. For each item on which you need review, consult the numbered principle shown in parentheses.

_____ 1. A corporation must register in the province in which it does business and it must operate within the laws of that province.

_____ 2. The manager offered a point-by-point explanation of the distribution dilemma and then presented his plan to solve the problem.

_____ 3. If you will study the cost analysis you will see that our company offers the best system at the lowest price.

_____ 4. Molly Epperson who amassed the greatest number of sales points won a bonus trip to Montreal.

_____ 5. The salesperson who amasses the greatest number of sales points will win a bonus trip to Montreal.

_____ 6. To promote goodwill and to generate international trade we are opening offices in South Asia and in Europe.

_____ 7. On the basis of these findings I recommend that we retain Jane Rada as our counsel.

_____ 8. Scott Cook is a dedicated hardworking employee for our company.

_____ 9. The bright young student who worked for us last summer will be able to return this summer.

_____ 10. When you return the completed form we will be able to process your application.

_____ 11. We will be able to process your application when you return the completed form.

_____ 12. The employees who have been with us over ten years automatically receive additional insurance benefits.

_____ 13. Knowing that you wanted this merchandise immediately I took the liberty of sending it by FedEx.

_____ 14. The central processing unit requires no scheduled maintenance and has a self-test function for reliable performance.

_____ 15. A tax credit for energy-saving homes will expire at the end of the year but Ottawa might extend it if pressure groups prevail.

_____ 16. Katisha Smith our newly promoted office manager has made a number of worthwhile suggestions.

_____ 17. For the benefit of employees recently hired we are offering a two-hour seminar regarding employee benefit programs.

_____ 18. Please bring your suggestions and those of Mr. Mason when you attend our meeting next month.

_____ 19. The meeting has been rescheduled for September 30 if this date meets with your approval.

_____ 20. Some of the problems that you outline in your recent e-mail could be rectified through more stringent purchasing procedures.

1. business, (2.05) 3. analysis, (2.06a) 5. C (2.06c) 7. findings, (2.07) 9. C (2.08)
11. C (2.06b) 13. immediately, (2.07) 15. year, (2.05) 17. hired, (2.07) 19. September 30, (2.06b)

◼ GRAMMAR/MECHANICS CHECKUP—7

Commas 2

Review Sections 2.05–2.09 above. Then study each of the following statements and insert necessary commas. In the space provided, write the number of commas that you add; write _0_ if no commas are needed. Also record the number of the Handbook principle(s) illustrated. When you finish, compare your responses with those provided on page 538. If your answers differ, carefully study again the principles shown in parentheses.

<u>1 (2.06a)</u> Example: When businesses encounter financial problems,they often reduce their administrative staffs.

_____ 1. As stated in the warranty this printer is guaranteed for one year.

_____ 2. Today's profits come from products currently on the market and tomorrow's profits come from products currently on the drawing boards.

_____ 3. Companies introduce new products in one part of the country and then watch how the product sells in that area.

_____ 4. One large automobile manufacturer which must remain nameless recognizes that buyer perception is behind the success of any new product.

_____ 5. The imaginative promising agency opened its offices April 22 in Cambridge.

_____ 6. The sales associate who earns the highest number of recognition points this year will be honoured with a bonus vacation trip.

_____ 7. Ian Sims our sales manager in the North Bay area will present the new sales campaign at the June meeting.

_____ 8. Our new product has many attributes that should make it appealing to buyers but it also has one significant drawback.

_____ 9. Although they have different technical characteristics and vary considerably in price and quality two or more of a firm's products may be perceived by shoppers as almost the same.

_____ 10. To motivate prospective buyers we are offering a cash rebate of $25.

Review of Commas 1 and 2

_____ 11. When you receive the application please fill it out and return it before Monday January 3.

_____ 12. On the other hand we are very interested in hiring hard-working conscientious individuals.

_____ 13. In March we expect to open a new branch in Bragg Creek which is an area of considerable growth.

_____ 14. As we discussed on the telephone the ceremony is scheduled for Thursday June 9 at 3 p.m.

_____ 15. Dr. Adams teaches the morning classes and Ms. Miori is responsible for evening sections.

Commas 3 (2.10–2.15)

2.10 Degrees and Abbreviations. Degrees following individuals' names are set off by commas. Abbreviations such as *Jr.* and *Sr.* are also set off by commas unless the individual referred to prefers to omit the commas:

> Anne G. Turner, *MBA*, joined the firm.

> Michael Migliano, *Jr.*, and Michael Migliano, *Sr.*, work as a team.

> Anthony A. Gensler *Jr.* wrote the report. (The individual referred to prefers to omit commas.)

The abbreviations *Inc.* and *Ltd.* are set off by commas only if a company's legal name has a comma just before this kind of abbreviation. To determine a company's practice, consult its stationery or a directory listing:

> Firestone and Blythe, *Inc.*, is based in Waterloo. (Notice that two commas are used.)

> Computers *Inc.* is extending its franchise system. (The company's legal name does not include a comma before *Inc.*)

2.11 Omitted Words. A comma is used to show the omission of words that are understood:

> On Monday we received 15 applications; on Friday, only 3. (Comma shows the omission of *we received.*)

2.12 Contrasting Statements. Commas are used to set off contrasting or opposing expressions. These expressions are often introduced by such words as *not, never, but,* and *yet:*

> The prime minister suggested cutbacks, *not* layoffs, to ease the crisis.

> Our budget for the year is reduced, *yet* adequate.

> The greater the effort, the greater the reward.

If increased emphasis is desired, use dashes instead of commas, as in *Only the sum of $100—not $1,000—was paid on this account.*

2.13 Clarity. Commas are used to separate words repeated for emphasis. Commas are also used to separate words that may be misread if not separated:

> The building is a long, long way from completion.

> Whatever is, is right.

> No matter what, you know we support you.

2.14 Quotations and Appended Questions

a. A comma is used to separate a short quotation from the rest of a sentence. If the quotation is divided into two parts, two commas are used:

> The manager asked, "Shouldn't the managers control the specialists?"

> "Perhaps the specialists," replied Tim, "have unique information."

b. A comma is used to separate a question appended (added) to a statement:

> You will confirm the shipment, won't you?

2.15 Comma Overuse. Do not use commas needlessly. For example, commas should not be inserted merely because you might drop your voice if you were speaking the sentence:

> One of the reasons for expanding our East Coast operations is{,} that we anticipate increased sales in that area. (Do not insert a needless comma before a clause.)

> I am looking for an article entitled{,} "State-of-the-Art Communications." (Do not insert a needless comma after the word *entitled*.)

> Customers may purchase many food and nonfood items in convenience stores *such as*{,} 7-Eleven and Couche-Tard. (Do not insert a needless comma after *such as*.)

> We have{,} at this time{,} an adequate supply of parts. (Do not insert needless commas around prepositional phrases.)

Review Exercise I—Commas 3

Insert only necessary commas in the following sentences. Remove unnecessary commas with the delete sign ($\mathscr{o}$). In the space provided, indicate the number of commas inserted or deleted in each sentence. If a sentence requires no changes, write C. When you finish, compare your responses with those provided. For each item on which you need review, consult the numbered principle shown in parentheses.

_____ 1. We expected Anna Wisniowska not Tyler Rosen to conduct the audit.

_____ 2. Brian said "We simply must have a bigger budget to start this project."

_____ 3. "We simply must have" said Brian "a bigger budget to start this project."

_____ 4. In August customers opened at least 50 new accounts; in September only about 20.

_____ 5. You returned the merchandise last month didn't you?

_____ 6. In short employees will now be expected to contribute more to their own retirement funds.

_____ 7. The better our advertising and recruiting the stronger our personnel pool will be.

_____ 8. Mrs. Delgado investigated selling her stocks not her real estate to raise the necessary cash.

_____ 9. "On the contrary" said Kamal Stevens "we will continue our present marketing strategies."

_____ 10. Our company will expand into surprising new areas such as, women's apparel and fast foods.

_____ 11. What we need is more not fewer suggestions for improvement.

_____ 12. Randall Clark Esq. and Jonathon Georges MBA joined the firm.

_____ 13. "Canada is now entering" said Minister Saunders "the Age of Innovation."

_____ 14. One of the reasons that we are inquiring about the publisher of the software is, that we are concerned about whether that publisher will be in the market five years from now.

_____ 15. The talk by D. A. Spindler PhD was particularly difficult to follow because of his technical and abstract vocabulary.

_____ 16. The month before a similar disruption occurred in distribution.

_____ 17. We are very fortunate to have, at our disposal, the services of excellent professionals.

_____ 18. No matter what you can count on us for support.

_____ 19. Emily Sandoval was named legislative counsel; Sam Freeman executive advisor.

_____ 20. The data you are seeking can be found in an article entitled, "The 100 Fastest Growing Games in Computers."

1. Cortez, Rosen, (2.12) 3. have," said Brian, (2.14a) 5. month, (2.14b) 7. recruiting, (2.12)
9. contrary," Stevens, (2.14a) 11. more, not fewer, (2.12) 13. entering," Saunders, (2.14a)
15. Spindler, PhD, (2.10) 17. have at our disposal (2.15) 19. Freeman, (2.11)

■ GRAMMAR/MECHANICS CHECKUP—8

Commas 3

Review Sections 2.10–2.15 above. Then study each of the following statements and insert necessary commas. In the space provided, write the number of commas that you add; write *0* if no commas are needed. Also record the number of the Handbook principle(s) illustrated. When you finish, compare your responses with those provided on page 538. If your answers differ, carefully study again the principles shown in parentheses.

<u>2 (2.12)</u> **Example:** It was Lucia Bosano, not Melinda Ho, who was given the Kirkland account.

_____ 1. "The choice of a good name" said President Etienne "cannot be overestimated."

_____ 2. Hanna H. Cox Ph.D. and Katherine Meridian M.B.A. were hired as consultants.

_____ 3. Their August 15 order was shipped on Monday wasn't it?

_____ 4. The Web is most useful in providing customer service such as online catalogue information and verification of shipping dates.

_____ 5. The bigger the investment the greater the profit.

Review Commas 1, 2, 3

_____ 6. As you requested your order for cartridges file folders and copy paper will be sent immediately.

_____ 7. We think however that you should reexamine your Web site and that you should consider redesigning its navigation system.

_____ 8. Within the next eight-week period we hope to hire Mina Vidal who is currently CEO of a small consulting firm.

_____ 9. Our convention will attract more participants if it is held in a resort location such as Collingwood the Laurentians or Banff.

_____ 10. If everyone who applied for the position were interviewed we would be overwhelmed.

_____ 11. In the past ten years we have employed over 30 well-qualified individuals many of whom have selected banking as their career.

_____ 12. Kimberly Johansson who spoke to our class last week is the author of a book entitled *Writing Winning Résumés*.

_____ 13. A recent study of productivity that was conducted by authoritative researchers revealed that Canadian workers are more productive than workers in Europe or Japan.

_____ 14. The report concluded that Canada's secret productivity weapon was not bigger companies more robots or even brainier managers.

_____ 15. As a matter of fact the report said that Canada's productivity resulted from the rigours of unprotected hands-off competition.

▋ CUMULATIVE EDITING QUIZ 4

Use proofreading marks (see Appendix B) to correct errors and omissions in the following sentences. All errors must be corrected to receive credit for the sentence. Check with your instructor for the answers.

1. E-mails must be written clear and concise, to ensure that receivers comprehend the message quick.

2. Our next sales campaign of course must target key decision makers.

3. In the meantime our online sales messages must include more then facts testimonials and guarantees.

4. The Small Business Administration which provide disaster loans are establishing additional offices in High River Calgary and Lethbridge.

5. Because we rely on e-mail we have reduced our use of faxes, and voice messages.

6. In business time is money.

7. "The first product to use a bar code" said Alice Beasley "was Wrigley's gum."

8. In 1912, the Model 41 Touring went into production in Sam McLaughlin's plant in Oshawa Ontario.

9. As Professor Payne predicted the resourceful well trained graduate was hired quick.

10. The company's liability insurance in view of the laws that went into effect January 1 need to be increased.

Semicolons (2.16)

2.16 Independent Clauses, Series, Introductory Expressions

a. **Independent clauses with conjunctive adverbs.** Use a semicolon before a conjunctive adverb that separates two independent clauses. Some of the most common conjunctive adverbs are *therefore, consequently, however,* and *moreover:*

> Business messages should sound conversational; *therefore,* writers often use familiar words and contractions.

> The bank closes its doors at 5 p.m.; *however,* the ATM is open 24 hours a day.

Notice that the word following a semicolon is *not* capitalized (unless, of course, that word is a proper noun).

b. **Independent clauses without conjunctive adverbs.** Use a semicolon to separate closely related independent clauses when no conjunctive adverb is used:

> RRSPs are taxed upon redemption; TFSAs are not.

> Ambient lighting fills the room; task lighting illuminates each workstation.

Use a semicolon in *compound* sentences, not in *complex* sentences:

> After one week the paper feeder jammed; we tried different kinds of paper. (Use a semicolon in a compound sentence.)

> After one week the paper feeder jammed, although we tried different kinds of paper. (Use a comma in a complex sentence. Do not use a semicolon after *jammed.*)

The semicolon is very effective for joining two closely related thoughts. Don't use it, however, unless the ideas are truly related.

c. **Independent clauses with other commas.** Normally, a comma precedes *and, or,* and *but* when those conjunctions join independent clauses. However, if either clause contains commas, the writer may elect to change the comma preceding the conjunction to a semicolon to ensure correct reading:

> Our primary concern is financing; and we have discovered, as you warned us, that capital sources are quite scarce.

d. **Series with internal commas.** Use semicolons to separate items in a series when one or more of the items contains internal commas:

> Delegates from Charlottetown, Prince Edward Island; Moncton, New Brunswick; and Truro, Nova Scotia, attended the conference.

> The speakers were Kevin Lang, manager, Riko Enterprises; Henry Holtz, vice president, Trendex, Inc.; and Margaret Woo, personnel director, West Coast Productions.

e. **Introductory expressions.** Use a semicolon when an introductory expression such as *namely, for instance, that is,* or *for example* introduces a list following an independent clause:

> Switching to computerized billing are several local companies; namely, Ryson Electronics, Miller Vending Services, and Black Home Heating.

> The author of a report should consider many sources; for example, books, periodicals, databases, and newspapers.

Colons (2.17–2.19)

2.17 Listed Items

a. **With colon.** Use a colon after a complete thought that introduces a formal list of items. A formal list is often preceded by such words and phrases as *these, thus, the following,* and *as follows.* A colon is also used when words and phrases like these are implied but not stated:

> Additional costs in selling a house involve *the following*: title examination fee, title insurance costs, and closing fee. (Use a colon when a complete thought introduces a formal list.)

> Collective bargaining focuses on several key issues: cost-of-living adjustments, fringe benefits, job security, and work hours. (The introduction of the list is implied in the preceding clause.)

b. **Without colon.** Do not use a colon when the list immediately follows a *to be* verb or a preposition:

> The employees who should receive the preliminary plan are James Sears, Monica Spears, and Rose Lopretti. (No colon is used after the verb *are*.)

> We expect to consider equipment for Accounting, Legal Services, and Payroll. (No colon is used after the preposition *for*.)

2.18 Quotations. Use a colon to introduce long one-sentence quotations and quotations of two or more sentences:

> Our consultant said: "This system can support up to 32 users. It can be used for decision support, computer-aided design, and software development operations at the same time."

2.19 Salutations. Use a colon after the salutation of a business letter:

> Dear Mrs. Seaman:
>
> Dear Jamie:

Review Exercise J—Semicolons, Colons

In the following sentences, add semicolons, colons, and necessary commas. For each sentence indicate the number of punctuation marks that you add. If a sentence requires no punctuation, write C. When you finish, compare your responses with those provided. For each item on which you need review, consult the numbered principle shown in parentheses.

_____ 1. Technological advances make full-motion video viewable on small screens consequently mobile phone makers and carriers are rolling out new services and phones.

_____ 2. Our branch in Brampton specializes in industrial real estate our branch in Oakville concentrates on residential real estate.

_____ 3. The sedan version of the automobile is available in these colours Olympic red metallic silver and Aztec gold.

_____ 4. If I can assist the new manager please call me however I will be gone from June 10 through June 15.

_____ 5. The individuals who should receive copies of this announcement are Jeff Wong Alicia Green and Kim Doogan.

_____ 6. We would hope of course to send personal letters to all prospective buyers however we have not yet decided just how to do this.

_____ 7. Many of our potential customers are in Southern Ontario therefore our promotional effort will be strongest in that area.

_____ 8. Since the first of the year we have received inquiries from one lawyer two accountants and one information systems analyst.

_____ 9. Three dates have been reserved for initial interviews January 15 February 1 and February 12.

_____ 10. Several staff members are near the top of their salary ranges and we must reclassify their jobs.

_____ 11. Several staff members are near the top of their salary ranges we must reclassify their jobs.

_____ 12. Several staff members are near the top of their salary ranges therefore we must reclassify their jobs.

_____ 13. If you apply for an Advantage Express card today we will waive the annual fee moreover you will earn 10,000 bonus miles and reward points for every $1 you spend on purchases.

_____ 14. Monthly reports from the following departments are missing Legal Department Human Resources Department and Engineering Department.

_____ 15. Monthly reports are missing from the Legal Department Human Resources Department and Engineering Department.

_____ 16. Since you became director of that division sales have tripled therefore I am recommending you for a bonus.

_____ 17. The convention committee is considering Victoria British Columbia Whistler British Columbia and Canmore Alberta.

_____ 18. Several large companies allow employees access to their personnel files namely Bank of Montreal Sobeys Inc. and Infodata.

_____ 19. Sherry first asked about salary next she inquired about benefits.

_____ 20. Sherry first asked about the salary and she next inquired about benefits.

1. screens; consequently, (2.16a)   3. colors: Olympic red, metallic silver, (2.01, 2.17a)
5. Doogan, Alicia Green, (2.01, 2.17b)   7. Ontario; therefore, (2.16a)   9. interviews: January 15, February 1, (2.01, 2.17a)   11. ranges; (2.16b)   13. today, fee; moreover, (2.06a, 2.16a)
15. Department, Human Resources Department, (2.01, 2.17b)   17. Victoria, British Columbia; Whistler, British Columbia; Canmore, (2.16d)   19. salary; (2.16b)

 GRAMMAR/MECHANICS CHECKUP—9

Semicolons and Colons

Review Sections 2.16–2.19 above. Then study each of the following statements. Insert any necessary punctuation. Use the delete symbol to omit unnecessary punctuation. In the space provided, indicate the number of changes you made and record the number of the Handbook principle(s) illustrated. (When you replace one punctuation mark with another, count it as one change.) If you make no changes, write *0*. This exercise concentrates on semicolon and colon use, but you will also be responsible for correct comma use. When you finish, compare your responses with those shown on page 538. If your responses differ, carefully study again the specific principles shown in parentheses.

2 (2.16a) Example: The job of Mr. Wellworth is to make sure that his company has enough cash to meet its obligations moreover he is responsible for locating credit when needed.

_____ 1. Short-term financing refers to a period of under one year long-term financing on the other hand refers to a period of ten years or more.

_____ 2. Cash resulting from product sales does not arrive until December therefore our cash flow becomes critical in October and November.

_____ 3. We must negotiate short-term financing during the following months September October and November.

_____ 4. Large corporations that offer huge amounts of trade credit are, automobile dealers, utility companys, oil companys, and computer hardware manufacturers.

_____ 5. Although some firms rarely, if ever, need to borrow short-term money many businesses find that they require significant credit to pay for current production and sales costs.

_____ 6. A grocery store probably requires no short-term credit, a greeting card manufacturer however typically would need considerable short-term credit.

_____ 7. We offer three basic types of credit loans promissory notes and floating lines of credit.

_____ 8. Speakers at the conference on credit include the following businesspeople Mary Ann Mahan financial manager Ritchie Industries Terry L. Buchanan comptroller International Bank and Edmée Cavalier operations Business Bank of Canada.

_____ 9. The prime interest rate is set by the Bank of Canada and this rate goes up or down as the cost of money to the bank itself fluctuates.

_____ 10. Most banks are in business to lend money to commercial customers for example retailers service companies manufacturers and construction firms.

_____ 11. Avionics, Inc. which is a small electronics firm with a solid credit rating recently applied for a loan but the Federal Business

Development Bank refused the loan application because the risk was too great.

_____ 12. When Avionics, Inc., was refused by Federal Business Development Bank its financial managers submitted applications to the following Worldwide Investments, Dominion Securities, and Mid Mountain Group.

_____ 13. The cost of financing capital investments at the present time is very high therefore Avionics' managers may elect to postpone certain expansion projects.

_____ 14. If interest rates reach as high as 18 percent the cost of borrowing becomes prohibitive and many businesses are forced to reconsider or abandon projects that require financing.

_____ 15. Several investors decided to pool their resources then they could find attractive investments.

Apostrophes (2.20–2.22)

2.20 Basic Rule. The apostrophe is used to show ownership, origin, authorship, or measurement.

Ownership:	We are looking for *Brian's keys.*
Origin:	At the *president's suggestion,* we doubled the order.
Authorship:	The *accountant's annual report* was questioned.
Measurement:	In *two years' time* we expect to reach our goal.

a. **Ownership words not ending in s.** To place the apostrophe correctly, you must first determine whether the ownership word ends in an *s* sound. If it does not, add an apostrophe and an *s* to the ownership word. The following examples show ownership words that do not end in an *s* sound:

the employee's file	(the file of a single employee)
a member's address	(the address of a single member)
a year's time	(the time of a single year)
a month's notice	(notice of a single month)
the company's building	(the building of a single company)

b. **Ownership words ending in s.** If the ownership word does end in an *s* sound, usually add only an apostrophe:

several employees' files	(files of several employees)
ten members' addresses	(addresses of ten members)
five years' time	(time of five years)
several months' notice	(notice of several months)
many companies' buildings	(buildings of many companies)

A few singular nouns that end in *s* are pronounced with an extra syllable when they become possessive. To these words, add *'s*.

my boss's desk	the waitress's table	the actress's costume

Use no apostrophe if a noun is merely plural, not possessive:

All the sales representatives, as well as the assistants and managers, had their names and telephone numbers listed in the directory.

2.21 Names Ending in *s* or an *s* Sound. The possessive form of names ending in *s* or an *s* sound follows the same guidelines as for common nouns. If an extra syllable can be pronounced without difficulty, add *'s* . If the extra syllable is hard to pronounce, end with an apostrophe only.

Add apostrophe and *s*	Add apostrophe only
Russ's computer	New Orleans' cuisine
Bill Gates's business	Los Angeles' freeways
Mrs. Jones's home	the Morrises' family
Mr. Lopez's desk	the Lopezes' pool

Individual preferences in pronunciation may cause variation in a few cases. For example, some people may prefer not to pronounce an extra *s* in examples such as *Bill Gates' business*. However, the possessive form of plural names is consistent: *the Joneses' home, the Burgesses' children, the Bushes' car*. Notice that the article *the* is a clue in determining whether a name is singular or plural.

2.22 Gerunds. Use *'s* to make a noun possessive when it precedes a gerund, a verb form used as a noun:

> Ken Smith's smoking prompted a new office policy. (Ken *Smith* is possessive because it modifies the gerund *smoking*.)

> It was Betsy's careful proofreading that revealed the discrepancy.

Review Exercise K—Apostrophes

Insert necessary apostrophes and corrections in the following sentences. In the space provided for each sentence, write the corrected word. If none were corrected, write C. When you finish, compare your responses with those provided. For each item on which you need review, consult the numbered principle shown in parentheses.

———— 1. In five years time, Lisa hopes to repay all of her student loans.

———— 2. If you go to the third floor, you will find Mr. Londons office.

———— 3. All the employees personnel folders must be updated.

———— 4. In a little over a years time, that firm was able to double its sales.

———— 5. The Harrises daughter lived in Halifax for two years.

———— 6. A patent protects an inventors invention for 17 years.

———— 7. Both companies headquarters will be moved within the next six months.

———— 8. That position requires at least two years experience.

———— 9. Some of their assets could be liquidated; therefore, a few of the creditors received funds.

———— 10. All secretaries workstations were equipped with Internet access.

———— 11. The package of electronics parts arrived safely despite two weeks delay.

———— 12. Many nurses believe that nurses notes are not admissible evidence.

———— 13. According to Mr. Parvez latest proposal, all employees would receive an additional holiday.

———— 14. Many of our members names and addresses must be checked.

———— 15. His supervisor frequently had to correct Jacks financial reports.

———— 16. We believe that this firms service is much better than that firms.

———— 17. Mr. Jackson estimated that he spent a years profits in reorganizing his staff.

———— 18. After paying six months rent, we were given a receipt.

———— 19. The contract is not valid without Mrs. Harris signature.

———— 20. It was Mr. Smiths signing of the contract that made us happy.

---

1. years' (2.20b) 3. employees' (2.20b) 5. Harrises' (2.21) 7. companies' (2.20b)
9. C (2.20b) 11. weeks' (2.20b) 13. Parvez's (2.21) 15. Jack's (2.21) 17. year's (2.20a)
19. Harris's (2.21)

GRAMMAR/MECHANICS CHECKUP—10

Possessives

Review Sections 2.20–2.22 above. Then study each of the following statements. Underline any inappropriate form. Write a correction in the space provided, and record the number of the Handbook principle(s) illustrated. If a sentence is correct, write C. When you finish, compare your responses with those on page 538. If your answers differ, carefully study again the principles shown in parentheses.

years' (2.20b) Example: In just two <u>years</u> time, the accountants and managers devised an entirely new system.

_____ 1. Two supervisors said that Mr. Ruskins work was excellent.

_____ 2. In less than a years time, the offices of both lawyers were moved.

_____ 3. None of the employees in our Electronics Department had taken more than two weeks vacation.

_____ 4. All the secretaries agreed that Ms. Lanhams suggestions were practical.

_____ 5. After you obtain your boss approval, send the application to Human Resources.

_____ 6. We tried to sit in our favourite server section, but all her tables were filled.

_____ 7. Despite Kaspar grumbling, his wife selected two bonds and three stocks for her investments.

_____ 8. The apartment owner requires two months rent in advance from all applicants.

_____ 9. Four companies buildings were damaged in the fire.

_____ 10. In one months time we hope to be able to complete all the address files.

_____ 11. One secretaries desk will have to be moved to make way for the computer.

_____ 12. Several sellers permits were issued for two years.

_____ 13. Marks salary was somewhat higher than David.

_____ 14. Latikas job in accounts receivable ends in two months.

CUMULATIVE EDITING QUIZ 5

Use proofreading marks (see Appendix B) to correct errors and omissions in the following sentences. All errors must be corrected to receive credit for the sentence. Check with your instructor for the answers.

1. Mark Zuckerberg worked for years to build Facebook however it was years' before the company made a profit.

2. E-businesses has always been risky, online companys seem to disappear as quick as they appear.

3. According to a leading data source three of the top European entertainment companys are the following Double Fusion, Jerusalem, Israel, Echovoc, Geneva, Switzerland, and IceMobile, Amsterdam, The Netherlands.

4. By the way Tess e-mail was forwarded to Mr. Lopezes incoming box in error and she was quite embarrassed.

5. The OSCs findings and ruling in the securitys fraud case is expected to be released in one hours time.

6. Only one hospitals doctors complained that they were restricted in the time they could spend listening to patients comments.

7. Any one of the auditors are authorized to conduct an independent action however only the CEO can change the councils directives.

8. Charles and Les mountain bicycles were stole from there garage last night.

9. Five of the worst computer passwords are the following your first name, your last name, the Enter key, *Password,* and the name of a sports' team.

10. On January 15 2015 we opened an innovative full equipped fitness center.

Other Punctuation (2.23–2.29)

2.23 Periods

a. **Ends of sentences.** Use a period at the end of a statement, command, indirect question, or polite request. Although a polite request may have the same structure as a question, it ends with a period:

> Corporate legal departments demand precise skills from their workforce. (End a statement with a period.)

> Get the latest data by reading current periodicals. (End a command with a period.)

> Mr. Rand wondered whether we had sent any follow-up literature. (End an indirect question with a period.)

> Would you please re-examine my account and determine the current balance. (A polite request suggests an action rather than a verbal response.)

b. **Abbreviations and initials.** Use periods after initials and after many abbreviations.

R. M. Johnson	c.o.d.	Ms.
p.m.	a.m.	Mr.
Inc.	i.e.	Mrs.

The latest trend is to omit periods in degrees and professional designations: BA, PhD, MD, RN, DDS.

Use just one period when an abbreviation falls at the end of a sentence:

> Guests began arriving at 5:30 p.m.

2.24 Question Marks. Direct questions are followed by question marks:

> Did you send your proposal to Datatronix, Inc.?

> Statements with questions added are punctuated with question marks.

> We have completed the proposal, haven't we?

2.25 Exclamation Points. Use an exclamation point after a word, phrase, or clause expressing strong emotion. In business writing, however, exclamation points should be used sparingly:

> Incredible! Every terminal is down.

2.26 Dashes. The dash (constructed at a keyboard by striking the hyphen key twice in succession) is a legitimate and effective mark of punctuation when used according to accepted conventions. As a connecting punctuation mark, however, the dash loses effectiveness when overused.

a. **Parenthetical elements.** Within a sentence a parenthetical element is usually set off by commas. If, however, the parenthetical element itself contains internal commas, use dashes (or parentheses) to set it off:

> Three top salespeople—Tom Judkins, Gary Templeton, and Mona Yashimoto—received bonuses.

Grammar/Machanics Handbook

b. **Sentence interruptions.** Use a dash to show an interruption or abrupt change of thought:

> News of the dramatic merger—no one believed it at first—shook the financial world.

> Ship the materials Monday—no, we must have them sooner.

Sentences with abrupt changes of thought or with appended afterthoughts can usually be improved through rewriting.

c. **Summarizing statements.** Use a dash (not a colon) to separate an introductory list from a summarizing statement:

> Sorting, merging, and computing—these are tasks that our data processing programs must perform.

2.27 Parentheses. One means of setting off nonessential sentence elements involves the use of parentheses. Nonessential sentence elements may be punctuated in one of three ways: (a) with commas, to make the lightest possible break in the normal flow of a sentence; (b) with dashes, to emphasize the enclosed material; and (c) with parentheses, to de-emphasize the enclosed material. Parentheses are frequently used to punctuate sentences with interpolated directions, explanations, questions, and references:

> The cost analysis (which appears on page 8 of the report) indicates that the copy machine should be leased.

> Units are lightweight (approximately 1 kg) and come with a leather case and operating instructions.

> The latest laser printer (have you heard about it?) will be demonstrated for us next week.

A parenthetical sentence that is not embedded within another sentence should be capitalized and punctuated with end punctuation:

> The Model 20 has stronger construction. (You may order a Model 20 brochure by circling 304 on the reader service card.)

2.28 Quotation Marks

a. **Direct quotations.** Use double quotation marks to enclose the exact words of a speaker or writer:

> "Keep in mind," Kelly Frank said, "that you'll have to justify the cost of networking our office."

> The boss said that automation was inevitable. (No quotation marks are needed because the exact words are not quoted.)

b. **Quotations within quotations.** Use single quotation marks (apostrophes on the keyboard) to enclose quoted passages within quoted passages:

> In her speech, Marge Deckman remarked, "I believe it was the poet Robert Frost who said, 'All the fun's in how you say a thing.'"

c. **Short expressions.** Slang, words used in a special sense, and words following *stamped* or *marked* are often enclosed within quotation marks:

> Jeffrey described the damaged shipment as "gross." (Quotation marks enclose slang.)

> Students often have trouble spelling the word "separate." (Quotation marks enclose words used in a special sense.)

> Jobs were divided into two categories: most stressful and least stressful. The jobs in the "most stressful" list involved high risk or responsibility. (Quotation marks enclose words used in a special sense.)

The envelope marked "Confidential" was put aside. (Quotation marks enclose words following *marked*.)

In the four preceding sentences, the words enclosed within quotation marks can be set in italics, if italics are available.

d. **Definitions.** Double quotation marks are used to enclose definitions. The word or expression being defined should be underscored or set in italics:

> The term *penetration pricing* is defined as "the practice of introducing a product to the market at a low price."

e. **Titles.** Use double quotation marks to enclose titles of literary and artistic works, such as magazine and newspaper articles, chapters of books, movies, television shows, poems, lectures, and songs. Names of major publications—such as books, magazines, pamphlets, and newspapers—are set in italics (underscored).

> Particularly helpful was the chapter in Smith's *Effective Writing Techniques* entitled "Right Brain, Write On!"

> John's article, "E-Mail Blunders," appeared in *The Globe and Mail*; however, we could not locate it online.

f. **Additional considerations.** Periods and commas are always placed inside closing quotation marks. Semicolons and colons, on the other hand, are always placed outside quotation marks:

> Mrs. James said, "I could not find the article entitled 'Cell Phone Etiquette.'"

> The director asked for "absolute security": All written messages were to be destroyed.

Question marks and exclamation points may go inside or outside closing quotation marks, as determined by the form of the quotation:

> Sales Manager Martin said, "Who placed the order?" (The quotation is a question.)

> When did the sales manager say, "Who placed the order?" (Both the incorporating sentence and the quotation are questions.)

> Did the sales manager say, "Ryan placed the order"? (The incorporating sentence asks a question; the quotation does not.)

> "In the future," shouted Bob, "ask me first!" (The quotation is an exclamation.)

2.29 Brackets. Within quotations, brackets are used by the quoting writer to enclose his or her own inserted remarks. Such remarks may be corrective, illustrative, or explanatory:

> My professor said that "CSIS [the Canadian Security Intelligence Service] is becoming one of the most controversial and secretive of the federal government agencies."

Review Exercise L—Other Punctuation

Insert necessary punctuation in the following sentences. In the space provided for each item, indicate the number of punctuation marks that you added. Count sets of parentheses, dashes, and quotation marks as two marks. Emphasis or de-emphasis will be indicated for some parenthetical elements. When you finish, compare your responses with those provided. For each item on which you need review, consult the numbered principle shown in parentheses.

_____ 1. Will you please send me your latest catalogue

_____ 2. (Emphasize) Three of my friends Irina Volodyeva, Stan Meyers, and Ivan Sergo were promoted.

_____ 3. Mr Lee, Miss Evans, and Mrs Rivera have not responded.

_____ 4. We have scheduled your interview for 4 45 p m

_____ 5. (De-emphasize) The appliance comes in limited colours black, ivory, and beige, but we accept special orders.

_____ 6. The expression de facto means exercising power as if legally constituted.

_____ 7. Who was it who said "This, too, will pass

_____ 8. Should this package be marked Fragile

_____ 9. Did you see the Macleans article titled How Far Can Wireless Go

_____ 10. Amazing All sales reps made their targets

1. catalogue. (2.23a)   3. Mr.; Mrs. (2.23)   5. colours (black, ivory, and beige) (2.26a)
7. said,; pass"? (2.28f)   9. _Maclean's_; "How Go?" (2.28e)

GRAMMAR/MECHANICS CHECKUP—11

Other Punctuation

Although this checkup concentrates on Sections 2.23–2.29 above, you may also refer to other punctuation principles. Insert any necessary punctuation. In the space provided, indicate the number of changes you make and record the number of the Handbook principle(s) illustrated. Count each mark separately; for example, a set of parentheses counts as 2. If you make no changes, write 0. When you finish, compare your responses with those provided on page 538. If your responses differ, carefully study again the specific principles shown in parentheses.

2 (2.27) Example: (De-emphasize.) The consumption of cereal products is highest in certain provinces (Manitoba, Saskatchewan, Alberta, and Newfoundland), but this food trend is spreading to other parts of the country.

_____ 1. (Emphasize.) The convention planning committee has invited three managers Yu Wong, Frank Behr, and Yvette Sosa to make presentations.

_____ 2. Would you please Miss Fundy use your computer to recalculate these totals.

_____ 3. (De-emphasize.) A second set of demographic variables see Figure 13 on page 432 includes nationality, religion, and race.

_____ 4. Because the word recommendation is frequently misspelled we are adding it to our company style book.

_____ 5. Recruiting, hiring, and training these are three important functions of a human resources officer.

_____ 6. The office manager said, Who placed an order for two dozen printer cartridges

_____ 7. Have any of the research assistants been able to locate the article entitled How Tax Reform Will Affect You

_____ 8. (Emphasize.) The biggest oil-producing provinces Alberta, Newfoundland, and Ontario are experiencing significant tax cuts.

_____ 9. Have you sent invitations to Mr Kieran E Manning, Miss Kathy Tanguay, and Ms Petra Bonaventura?

_____ 10. Dr. Y. W. Yellin wrote the chapter entitled Trading on the Options Market that appeared in a book called Securities Markets.

_____ 11. James said, "I'll be right over" however he has not appeared yet.

_____ 12. In business the word liability may be defined as any legal obligation requiring payment in the future.

_____ 13. Because the work was scheduled to be completed June 10 we found it necessary to hire temporary workers to work June 8 and 9.

_____ 14. Did any c o d shipments arrive today

_____ 15. Hooray I have finished this checkup haven't I

■ GRAMMAR/MECHANICS CHECKUP—12

Punctuation Review

Review Sections 1.19 and 2.01–2.29. Study the groups of sentences below. In the space provided write the letter of the one that is correctly punctuated. When you finish, compare your responses with those on page 538. If your responses differ, carefully study again the principles in parentheses.

_____ 1. a. Our accounting team makes a point of analyzing your business operations, and getting to know what's working for you and what's not.

b. We are dedicated to understanding your business needs over the long term, and taking an active role when it comes to creating solutions.

c. We understand that you may be downsizing or moving into new markets, and we want to help you make a seamless transition.

_____ 2. a. If you are growing, or connecting to new markets, our team will help you accomplish your goals with minimal interruptions.

b. When you look at our organization chart, you will find the customer at the top.

c. Although we offer each customer a dedicated customer account team we also provide professional general services.

_____ 3. a. The competition is changing; therefore, we have to deliver our products and services more efficiently.

b. Although delivery systems are changing; the essence of banking remains the same.

c. Banks will continue to be available around the corner, and also with the click of a mouse.

_____ 4. a. One of the reasons we are decreasing the number of our ABMs, is that two thirds of the bank's customers depend on customer care representatives for transactions.

b. We are looking for an article entitled, "Online Banking."

c. Banks are at this time competing with non-traditional rivals that can provide extensive financial services.

_____ 5. a. We care deeply about the environment; but we also care about safety and good customer service.

b. The president worked with environmental concerns; the vice president focused on customer support.

c. Our Web site increases our productivity, it also improves customer service.

Grammar/Machanics Handbook

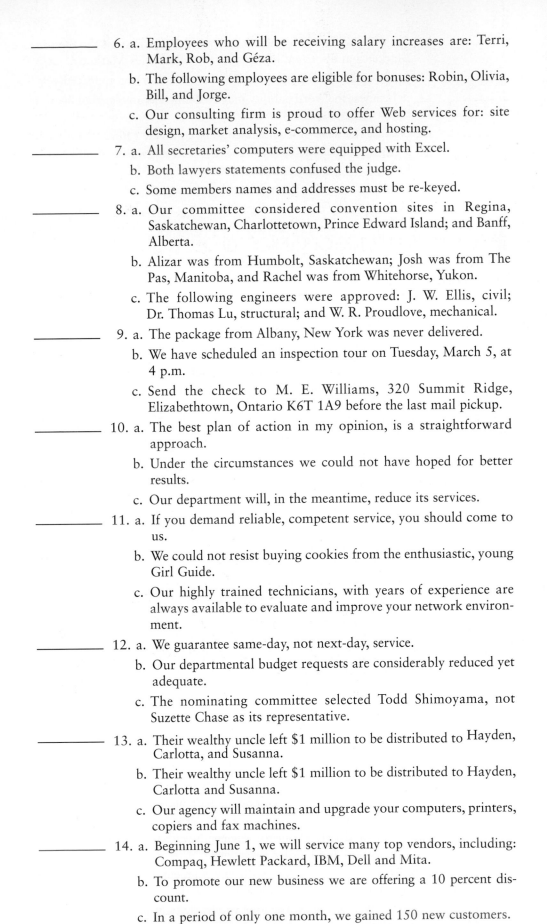

_____ 6. a. Employees who will be receiving salary increases are: Terri, Mark, Rob, and Géza.

b. The following employees are eligible for bonuses: Robin, Olivia, Bill, and Jorge.

c. Our consulting firm is proud to offer Web services for: site design, market analysis, e-commerce, and hosting.

_____ 7. a. All secretaries' computers were equipped with Excel.

b. Both lawyers statements confused the judge.

c. Some members names and addresses must be re-keyed.

_____ 8. a. Our committee considered convention sites in Regina, Saskatchewan, Charlottetown, Prince Edward Island; and Banff, Alberta.

b. Alizar was from Humbolt, Saskatchewan; Josh was from The Pas, Manitoba, and Rachel was from Whitehorse, Yukon.

c. The following engineers were approved: J. W. Ellis, civil; Dr. Thomas Lu, structural; and W. R. Proudlove, mechanical.

_____ 9. a. The package from Albany, New York was never delivered.

b. We have scheduled an inspection tour on Tuesday, March 5, at 4 p.m.

c. Send the check to M. E. Williams, 320 Summit Ridge, Elizabethtown, Ontario K6T 1A9 before the last mail pickup.

_____ 10. a. The best plan of action in my opinion, is a straightforward approach.

b. Under the circumstances we could not have hoped for better results.

c. Our department will, in the meantime, reduce its services.

_____ 11. a. If you demand reliable, competent service, you should come to us.

b. We could not resist buying cookies from the enthusiastic, young Girl Guide.

c. Our highly trained technicians, with years of experience are always available to evaluate and improve your network environment.

_____ 12. a. We guarantee same-day, not next-day, service.

b. Our departmental budget requests are considerably reduced yet adequate.

c. The nominating committee selected Todd Shimoyama, not Suzette Chase as its representative.

_____ 13. a. Their wealthy uncle left $1 million to be distributed to Hayden, Carlotta, and Susanna.

b. Their wealthy uncle left $1 million to be distributed to Hayden, Carlotta and Susanna.

c. Our agency will maintain and upgrade your computers, printers, copiers and fax machines.

_____ 14. a. Beginning June 1, we will service many top vendors, including: Compaq, Hewlett Packard, IBM, Dell and Mita.

b. To promote our new business we are offering a 10 percent discount.

c. In a period of only one month, we gained 150 new customers.

_____ 15. a. We specialize in network design, however we also offer troubleshooting and consulting.

b. We realize that downtime is not an option; therefore, you can count on us for reliable, competent service.

c. Our factory-trained and certified technicians perform repair at your location, or in our own repair depot for products under warranty and out of warranty.

CUMULATIVE EDITING QUIZ 6

Use proofreading marks (see Appendix B) to correct errors and omissions in the following sentences. All errors must be corrected to receive credit for the sentence. Check with your instructor for the answers.

1. We wondered whether Ellen Hildago PhD would be the speaker at the Kingston Ontario event?

2. Our operating revenue for 2014 see Appendix A exceeded all the consultants expectations.

3. Four features, camera, text messaging, Web access, and voice mail—are what Canadians want most on there cell phones.

4. Serge Laferia CEO of Imperial Tobacco said "We're being socially responsible in a rather controversial industry.

5. Kym Andersons chapter titled Subsidies and Trade Barriers appears in the book How to Spend $50 Billion to Make the World a Better Place.

6. Wasnt it Zack Tesar not Ellen Trask who requested a 14 day leave.

7. Was it Oprah Winfrey who said that the best jobs are those we'd do even if we didn't get paid.

8. The word mashup is a technology term that is defined as a Web site that uses content from more then one source to create a completely new service.

9. Miss. Rhonda Evers is the person who the employees council elected as there representative.

10. Would you please send a current catalog to Globex, Inc?

⬛ STYLE AND USAGE

Capitalization (3.01–3.16)
Capitalization is used to distinguish important words. However, writers are not free to capitalize all words they consider important. Rules or guidelines governing capitalization style have been established through custom and use. Mastering these guidelines will make your writing more readable and more comprehensible.

3.01 Proper Nouns. Capitalize proper nouns, including the *specific* names of persons, places, schools, streets, parks, buildings, holidays, months, agreements, Web sites, software programs, historical periods, and so forth. Do not capitalize common nouns that make only *general* references.

Proper nouns	Common nouns
Peter Mansbridge	well-known news anchor
Mexico, U.S.A.	Canadian trading partners
Algonquin College	a community college
Parc Lafontaine	a park in the city
Rideau Room, Royal York Hotel	a meeting room in the hotel

Proper nouns	Common nouns
Family Day, New Year's Day	two holidays
Google, Facebook, Wikipedia	popular Web sites
Burlington Skyway	a bridge
Consumer Protection Act	a law to protect consumers
Halifax Chamber of Commerce	a chamber of commerce
Billy Bishop Airport	a municipal airport
January, February, March	months of the year

3.02 Proper Adjectives. Capitalize most adjectives that are derived from proper nouns:

Greek symbol	British thermal unit
Roman numeral	Freudian slip
Xerox copy	Hispanic markets

Do not capitalize the few adjectives that, although originally derived from proper nouns, have become common adjectives through usage. Consult your dictionary when in doubt:

manila folder	diesel engine
venetian blinds	china dishes

3.03 Geographic Locations. Capitalize the names of *specific* places such as continents, countries, provinces, mountains, valleys, lakes, rivers, oceans, and geographic regions:

Quebec City	Lake Athabasca
Rocky Mountains	Pacific Ocean
Annapolis Valley	Bay of Fundy
the East Coast	the Prairie provinces

3.04 Organization Names. Capitalize the principal words in the names of all business, civic, educational, governmental, labour, military, philanthropic, political, professional, religious, and social organizations:

Bombardier	Board of Directors, Scotiabank
The Montreal Gazette*	Vancouver Art Gallery
Toronto Stock Exchange	Bank of Canada
United Way	Canadian Union of Public Employees
Al Purdy A-Frame Association	Canadian Association of Retired Persons

3.05 Academic Courses and Degrees. Capitalize particular academic degrees and course titles. Do not capitalize general academic degrees and subject areas:

Professor Bernadette Ordian, *PhD,* will teach *Accounting* 221 next fall.

Mrs. Snyder, who holds *bachelor's* and *master's degrees,* teaches *marketing* classes.

Jim enrolled in classes in *history, business English,* and *management.*

3.06 Personal and Business Titles

a. Capitalize personal and business titles when they precede names:

Vice President Ames	Uncle Edward
Board Chairman Frazier	Councillor Herbert

---

*Note: Capitalize *the* only when it is part of the official name of an organization, as printed on the organization's stationery.

Premier Thurmond	Sales Manager Klein
Professor Mahfouz	Dr. Samuel Washington

b. Capitalize titles in addresses, salutations, and closing lines:

Mr. Juan deSanto	Very truly yours,
Director of Purchasing	
Space Systems, Inc.	Clara J. Smith
Madoc, ON K0K 2K0	Supervisor, Marketing

c. Generally, do not capitalize titles of high government rank or religious office when they stand alone or follow a person's name in running text.

> The prime minister conferred with the armed forces council and many senators.

> Meeting with the chief justice of the Supreme Court were the senator from British Columbia and the mayor of Vancouver.

> Only the cardinal from Montréal had an audience with the pope.

d. Do not capitalize most common titles following names:

> The speech was delivered by Robert Lynch, *president,* Academic Publishing.

> Lois Herndon, *chief executive officer,* signed the order.

e. Do not capitalize common titles appearing alone:

> Please speak to the *supervisor* or to the *office manager.*

> Neither the *president* nor the *vice president* could attend.

However, when the title of an official appears in that organization's minutes, bylaws, or other official document, it may be capitalized.

f. Do not capitalize titles when they are followed by appositives naming specific individuals:

> We must consult our *director of research*, Ronald E. West, before responding.

g. Do not capitalize family titles used with possessive pronouns:

my mother	your father
our aunt	his cousin

h. Capitalize titles of close relatives used without pronouns:

> Both *Mother* and *Father* must sign the contract.

3.07 Numbered and Lettered Items. Capitalize nouns followed by numbers or letters (except in page, paragraph, line, and verse references):

Flight 34, Gate 12	Plan No. 2
Volume I, Part 3	Warehouse 33-A
Invoice No. 55489	Figure 8.3
Model A5673	Serial No. C22865404-2
Provincial Highway 10	page 6, line 5

3.08 Points of the Compass. Capitalize *north, south, east, west,* and their derivatives when they represent *specific* geographical regions. Do not capitalize the points of the compass when they are used in directions or in general references.

Specific Regions	General References
from the South	heading north on the highway
living in the West	west of the city
Easterners, Westerners	western Ontario, southern Saskatchewan
going to the Middle East	the northern part of province
from the East Coast	the east side of the street

3.09 Departments, Divisions, and Committees. Capitalize the names of departments, divisions, or committees within your own organization. Outside your organization capitalize only *specific* department, division, or committee names:

> The inquiry was addressed to the *Legal Department* in our *Consumer Products Division.*

> John was appointed to the *Employee Benefits Committee.*

> Send your resume to their *human resources division.*

> A *planning committee* will be named shortly.

3.10 Governmental Terms. Do not capitalize the words *federal, government, nation,* or *province* unless they are part of a specific title:

> Unless *federal* support can be secured, the *provincial* project will be abandoned.

> The *Council of the Federation* promotes inter-provincial cooperation.

3.11 Product Names. Capitalize product names only when they refer to trademarked items. Except in advertising, common names following manufacturers' names are not capitalized:

Magic Marker	Lululemon pants
Kleenex tissues	Swingline stapler
Q-tip swab	ChapStick lip balm
Levi 501 jeans	Excel spreadsheet
DuPont Teflon	Roots sweatshirt

3.12 Literary Titles. Capitalize the principal words in the titles of books, magazines, newspapers, articles, movies, plays, songs, poems, and reports. Do *not* capitalize articles (*a, an, the*), short conjunctions *(and, but, or, nor)*, and prepositions of fewer than four letters (*in, to, by, for*) unless they begin or end the title:

> Jackson's *What Job Is for You?* (Capitalize book titles.)

> Gant's "Software for the Executive Suite" (Capitalize principal words in article titles.)

> "Performance Standards to Go By" (Capitalize article titles.)

> "The Improvement of Fuel Economy With Alternative Fuels" (Capitalize report titles.)

3.13 Beginning Words. In addition to capitalizing the first word of a complete sentence, capitalize the first word in a quoted sentence, independent phrase, item in an enumerated list, and formal rule or principle following a colon:

> The business manager said, "*All* purchases must have requisitions." (Capitalize first word in a quoted sentence.)

> Yes, if you agree. (Capitalize an independent phrase.)

Some of the duties of the position are as follows:

1. *Editing* and formatting Word files

2. *Arranging* video and teleconferences

3. *Verifying* records, reports, and applications (Capitalize items in a vertical enumerated list.)

One rule has been established through the company: *No* smoking is allowed in open offices. (Capitalize a rule following a colon.)

3.14 Celestial Bodies. Capitalize the names of celestial bodies such as *Mars, Saturn,* and *Neptune.* Do not capitalize the terms *earth, sun,* or *moon* unless they appear in a context with other celestial bodies:

Where on *earth* did you find that manual typewriter?

Venus and *Mars* are the closest planets to *Earth.*

3.15 Ethnic References. Capitalize terms that refer to a particular culture, language, or race:

Asian	Hebrew
Caucasian	Indian
Latino	Japanese
Persian	Judeo-Christian

3.16 Seasons. Do not capitalize seasons:

In the *fall* it appeared that *winter* and *spring* sales would increase.

Review Exercise M—Capitalization

In the following sentences, correct any errors that you find in capitalization. Underscore any lowercase letter that should be changed to a capital letter. Draw a slash (/) through a capital letter that you wish to change to a lowercase letter. In the space provided, indicate the total number of changes you have made in each sentence. If you make no changes, write *0.* When you finish, compare your responses with those provided.

<u>5</u>   **Example**   Bill McAdams, currently A̸ssistant M̸anager in our Compensation <u>d</u>ivision, will be promoted to M̸anager of the Employee Services <u>d</u>ivision.

_____ 1. The copyright modernization act, passed in 2011, has been seen as taking away rights from content creators.

_____ 2. Our company will soon be moving its operations to the west coast.

_____ 3. Marilyn Hunter, mba, received her bachelor's degree from Queen's university in kingston.

_____ 4. The President of Datatronics, Inc., delivered a speech entitled "Taking off into the future."

_____ 5. Please ask your Aunt and your Uncle if they will come to the Lawyer's office at 5 p.m.

_____ 6. Your reservations are for flight 32 on WestJet leaving from gate 14 at 2:35 p.m.

_____ 7. Once we establish an organizing committee, arrangements can be made to rent holmby hall.

_____ 8. Bob was enrolled in history, french, business communications, and physical education courses.

_____ 9. Either the President or the Vice President of the company will make the decision about purchasing xerox copiers.

_____ 10. Rules for hiring and firing Employees are given on page 7, line 24, of the Contract.

_____ 11. Some individuals feel that canadian companies do not have the sense of loyalty to their employees that japanese companies do.

_____ 12. Where on Earth can we find better workers than Robots?

_____ 13. The prime minister recently said, "we must protect our domestic economy from foreign competition."

_____ 14. After crossing the sunshine skyway bridge, we drove to Southern Florida for our vacation.

_____ 15. All marketing representatives of our company will meet in the empire room of the red lion motor inn.

_____ 16. Richard Elkins, phd, has been named director of research for spaceage strategies, inc.

_____ 17. The special keyboard for the Dell Computer must contain greek symbols for Engineering equations.

_____ 18. After she received a master's degree in electrical engineering, Joanne Dudley was hired to work in our product development department.

_____ 19. In the Fall our organization will move its corporate headquarters to the franklin building in downtown winnipeg.

_____ 20. Dean Amador has one cardinal rule: always be punctual.

1. Copyright Modernization Act (3.01)   3. MBA University Kingston (3.01, 3.05)
5. aunt uncle lawyer's (3.06e, 3.06g)   7. Holmby Hall (3.01)   9. president vice president
Xerox (3.06e, 3.11)   11. Canadian Japanese (3.02)   13. We foreign (3.10, 3.13)
15. Empire Room Red Lion Motor Inn (3.01)   17. computer Greek engineering (3.01, 3.02, 3.11)
19. fall Franklin Building Halifax (3.01, 3.03, 3.16)

■ GRAMMAR/MECHANICS CHECKUP—13

Capitalization

Review Sections 3.01–3.16 above. Then study each of the following statements. Circle any lowercase letter that should be capitalized. Draw a slash (/) through any capital letter that you wish to change to lowercase. Indicate in the space provided the number of changes you made in each sentence and record the number of the Handbook principle(s) illustrated. If you made no changes, write _0_. When you finish, compare your responses with those provided on page 538. If your responses differ, carefully study again the principles in parentheses.

4 (3.01, 3.06a) **Example:** After consulting our /Attorneys for /Legal advice, Vice Ⓟresident Fontaine signed the /Contract.

_____ 1. All canadian passengers from Flight 402 must pass through Customs Inspection at Gate 17 upon arrival at Pearson international airport.

_____ 2. Personal tax rates for japanese citizens are low by International standards; rates for japanese corporations are high, according to Iwao Nakatani, an Economics Professor at Osaka university.

_____ 3. In the end, Business passes on most of the burden to the Consumer: What looks like a tax on Business is really a tax on Consumption.

_____ 4. Abel enrolled in courses in History, Sociology, Spanish, and Computer Science.

_____ 5. Did you see the *Maclean's* article entitled "Careers in horticulture are nothing to sneeze at"?

_____ 6. Although I recommend Minex Printers sold under the brandname MPLazerJet, you may purchase any Printers you choose.

_____ 7. According to a Federal Government report, any development of Provincial waterways must receive an environmental assessment.

_____ 8. The deputy prime minister of canada said, "this country continues to encourage Foreign investment."

_____ 9. The Comptroller of Ramjet International reported to the President and the Board of Directors that canada revenue agency was beginning an investigation of their Company.

_____ 10. My Mother, who lives near Plum Coulee, reports that protection from the Sun's rays is particularly important when travelling to the South.

_____ 11. Our Managing Editor met with Leslie Hawkins, Manager of the Advertising Sales Department, to plan an Ad Campaign for our special issue.

_____ 12. Next week, Editor in Chief Mercredi plans an article detailing the astounding performance of the euro.

_____ 13. To reach Terrasee Vaudreuil park, which is located on an Island in the St. Lawrence river, tourists pass over the vanier bridge.

_____ 14. On page 6 of the catalogue you will see that the computer science department is offering a number of courses in programming.

_____ 15. Please consult figure 3.2 in chapter 5 for statistics Canada figures regarding non-english-speaking residents.

◼ CUMULATIVE EDITING QUIZ 7

Use proofreading marks (see Appendix B) to correct errors and omissions in the following sentences. All errors must be corrected to receive credit for the sentence. Check with your instructor for the answers.

1. I wonder whether ceo Jackson invited our Marketing Vice President to join the upcoming three hour training session?

2. Our Sales Manager said that you attending the two day seminar is fine however we must find a replacement.

3. The boston marathon is an annual Sporting Event hosted by the City of Boston, Massachusetts on the third monday of April.

4. Steve Chen one of the founders of YouTube hurried to gate 44 to catch flight 246 to north carolina.

5. Jake noticed that the english spoken by asians in hong kong sounded more british than north american.

6. Good Friday is a Statutory holiday therefore banks will be closed.

7. Because the package was marked fragile the mail carrier handled it careful.

8. Money traders watched the relation of the american dollar to the chinese yuan, the european euro and the canadian dollar.

9. My Aunt and me travel South each Winter to vacation in the okanagan with our friends the Perry's.

10. Jim Balsillie former Co-CEO of Research in motion now serves as Chair of the Board of the centre for Interntional Governance Innovation in waterloo.

Number Style (4.01–4.13)

Usage and custom determine whether numbers are expressed in the form of figures (e.g., *5, 9*) or in the form of words (e.g., *five, nine*). Numbers expressed as figures are shorter and more easily understood, yet numbers expressed as words are necessary in certain instances. The following guidelines are observed in expressing numbers in written sentences. Numbers that appear on business forms—such as invoices, monthly statements, and purchase orders—are always expressed as figures.

4.01 General Rules

a. The numbers *one* through *ten* are generally written as words. Numbers above *ten* are written as figures:

> The bank had a total of *nine* branch offices in *three* suburbs.

> All *58* employees received benefits in the *three* categories shown.

> A shipment of *45,000* lightbulbs was sent from *two* warehouses.

b. Numbers that begin sentences are written as words. If a number beginning a sentence involves more than two words, however, the sentence should be revised so that the number does not fall at the beginning.

> *Fifteen* different options were available in the annuity programs.

> A total of 156 companies participated in the promotion (not *One hundred fifty-six companies participated in the promotion*).

4.02 Money.
Sums of money $1 or greater are expressed as figures. If a sum is a whole dollar amount, omit the decimal and zeros (whether or not the amount appears in a sentence with additional fractional dollar amounts):

> We budgeted *$300* for a digital camera, but the actual cost was *$370.96*.

> On the invoice were items for *$6.10, $8, $33.95,* and *$75*.

Sums less than $1 are written as figures that are followed by the word *cents:*

> By shopping carefully, we can save *15 cents* per unit.

4.03 Dates.
In dates, numbers that appear after the name of the month are written as cardinal figures *(1, 2, 3,* etc.). Those that stand alone or appear before the name of a month are written as ordinal figures *(1st, 2nd, 3rd,* etc.):

> The Workplace Safety Committee will meet *May 7*.

> On the *5th* day of February and again on the *25th*, we placed orders.

In Canadian business documents, dates generally take the following form: *January 4, 2012*. An alternative form, used primarily in military and foreign correspondence, begins with the day of the month and omits the comma: *4 January 2012*.

4.04 Clock Time.
Figures are used when clock time is expressed with *a.m.* or *p.m.* Omit the colon and zeros in referring to whole hours. When exact clock time is expressed with the contraction *o'clock*, either figures or words may be used:

> Mail deliveries are made at *11 a.m.* and *3:30 p.m.*

> At *four* (or *4*) *o'clock* employees begin to leave.

4.05 Addresses and Telephone Numbers

a. Except for the number *one*, house numbers are expressed in figures:

> 540 Queen Street   17802 8th Avenue NW

> One Rene-Levesque Boulevard   2 Highland Street

b. Street names containing numbers *ten* or lower are written entirely as words. For street names involving numbers greater than *ten,* figures are used:

330 Third Street	3440 Seventh Avenue
6945 East 32nd Avenue	4903 West 23rd Street

c. Telephone numbers are expressed with figures. When used, the area code is placed in parentheses preceding the telephone number:

> Please call us at *(519) 347-0551* to place an order.

> Mr. Sims asked you to call *(604) 554-8923,* Ext. 245, after 10 a.m.

4.06 Related Numbers. Numbers are related when they refer to similar items in a category within the same reference. All related numbers should be expressed as the largest number is expressed. Thus if the largest number is greater than *ten,* all the numbers should be expressed in figures:

> Only *5* of the original *25* applicants completed the processing. (Related numbers require figures.)

> The *two* plans affected *34* employees working in *three* sites. (Unrelated numbers use figures and words.)

> Beaver Drilling operated *14* rigs, of which *3* were rented. (Related numbers require figures.)

> The company hired *three* accountants, *one* customer service representative, and *nine* sales representatives. (Related numbers under ten use words.)

4.07 Consecutive Numbers. When two numbers appear consecutively and both modify a following noun, generally express the first number in words and the second in figures. If, however, the first number cannot be expressed in one or two words, place it in figures also (*120 70-cent* stamps). Do not use commas to separate the figures.

> Historians divided the era into *four 25-year* periods. (Use word form for the first number and figure form for the second.)

> We ordered *ten 30-page* colour brochures. (Use word form for the first number and figure form for the second.)

> Did the manager request *150 100-watt* bulbs? (Use figure form for the first number since it would require more than two words.)

4.08 Periods of Time. Seconds, minutes, days, weeks, months, and years are treated as any other general number. Numbers above ten are written in figure form. Numbers below ten are written in word form unless they represent a business concept such as a discount rate, interest rate, or warranty period.

> This business was incorporated over *50* years ago. (Use figures for a number above ten.)

> It took *three* hours to write this short report. (Use words for a number under ten.)

> The warranty period is limited to *2* years. (Use figures for a business term.)

4.09 Ages. Ages are generally expressed in word form unless the age appears immediately after a name or is expressed in exact years and months:

> At the age of *twenty-one*, Elizabeth inherited the business.

> Wanda Tharp, *37*, was named acting president.

> At the age of *4 years and 7 months*, the child was adopted.

4.10 Round Numbers. Round numbers are approximations. They may be expressed in word or figure form, although figure form is shorter and easier to comprehend:

> About *600* (or *six hundred*) stock options were sold.

> It is estimated that *1,000* (or *one thousand*) people will attend.

For ease of reading, round numbers in the millions or billions should be expressed with a combination of figures and words:

> At least *1.5 million* readers subscribe to the ten top magazines.

> Deposits in money market accounts totalled more than *$115 billion*.

4.11 Weights and Measurements. Weights and measurements are expressed with figures:

> The new deposit slip measures *2* by *6 inches*.

> Her new suitcase weighed only *2 pounds 4 ounces*.

> Toronto is *60 kilometres* from Oshawa.

4.12 Fractions. Simple fractions are expressed as words. Complex fractions may be written either as figures or as a combination of figures and words:

> Over *two thirds* of the stockholders have already voted.

> This microcomputer will execute the command in *1 millionth* of a second. (A combination of words and numbers is easier to comprehend.)

> She purchased a *one-fifth* share in the business.[1]

4.13 Percentages and Decimals. Percentages are expressed with figures that are followed by the word *percent*. The percent sign (%) is used only on business forms or in statistical presentations:

> We had hoped for a *7 percent* interest rate, but we received a loan at *8 percent*.

> Over *50 percent* of the condo owners supported the plan.

Decimals are expressed with figures. If a decimal expression does not contain a whole number (an integer) and does not begin with a zero, a zero should be placed before the decimal point:

> The actuarial charts show that *1.74* out of *1,000* people will die in any given year.

> Inspector Norris found the setting to be *.005* centimetre off. (Decimal begins with a zero and does not require a zero before the decimal point.)

> Considerable savings will accrue if the unit production cost is reduced *0.1* percent. (A zero is placed before a decimal that neither contains a whole number nor begins with a zero.)

---

[1] *Note:* Fractions used as adjectives require hyphens.

Quick Chart—Expression of Numbers

Use Words	Use Figures
Numbers *ten* and under	Numbers *11* and over
Numbers at beginning of sentence	Money
Ages	Dates
Fractions	Addresses and telephone numbers
	Weights and measurements
	Percentages and decimals

Review Exercise N—Number Style

Write the preferred number style on the lines provided. Assume that these numbers appear in business correspondence. When you finish, compare your responses with those provided. For each item on which you need review, consult the numbered principle shown in parentheses.

_____ 1. (a) 2 alternatives   (b) two alternatives

_____ 2. (a) Seventh Avenue   (b) 7th Avenue

_____ 3. (a) sixty sales reps   (b) 60 sales reps

_____ 4. (a) November ninth   (b) November 9

_____ 5. (a) forty dollars   (b) $40

_____ 6. (a) on the 23d of May   (b) on the twenty-third of May

_____ 7. (a) at 2:00 p.m.   (b) at 2 p.m.

_____ 8. (a) 4 two-hundred-page books   (b) four 200-page books

_____ 9. (a) at least 15 years ago   (b) at least fifteen years ago

_____ 10. (a) 1,000,000 viewers   (b) 1 million viewers

_____ 11. (a) twelve cents   (b) 12 cents

_____ 12. (a) a sixty-day warranty   (b) a 60-day warranty

_____ 13. (a) ten percent interest rate   (b) 10 percent interest rate

_____ 14. (a) 4/5 of the voters   (b) four fifths of the voters

_____ 15. (a) the rug measures four by six feet   (b) the rug measures 4 by 6 feet

_____ 16. (a) about five hundred people attended   (b) about 500 people attended

_____ 17. (a) at eight o'clock   (b) at 8 o'clock

_____ 18. (a) located at 5 Yonge Street   (b) located at Five Yonge Street

_____ 19. (a) three computers for twelve people   (b) three computers for 12 people

_____ 20. (a) 4 out of every 100 licences   (b) four out of every 100 licences

---

1. b (4.01a) 3. b (4.01a) 5. b (4.02) 7. b (4.04) 9. a (4.08) 11. b (4.02) 13. b (4.13)
15. b (4.11) 17. a or b (4.04) 19. b (4.06)

◼ GRAMMAR/MECHANICS CHECKUP—14

Number Style

Review Sections 4.01–4.13 above. Then study each of the following pairs. Assume that these expressions appear in the context of letters, reports, or e-mails. Write *a* or *b* in the space provided to indicate the preferred number style and record the number of the Handbook principle illustrated. When you finish, compare your responses with those on page 539. If your responses differ, carefully study again the principles in parentheses.

__a (4.01)__ **Example:** (a) six investments (b) 6 investments

———— 1. (a) sixteen credit cards   (b) 16 credit cards
———— 2. (a) Fifth Avenue   (b) 5th Avenue
———— 3. (a) 34 newspapers   (b) thirty-four newspapers
———— 4. (a) July eighth   (b) July 8
———— 5. (a) twenty dollars   (b) $20
———— 6. (a) on the 15th of June   (b) on the fifteenth of June
———— 7. (a) at 4:00 p.m.   (b) at 4 p.m.
———— 8. (a) 3 200-page reports   (b) three 200-page reports
———— 9. (a) over 18 years ago   (b) over eighteen years ago
———— 10. (a) 2,000,000 people   (b) 2 million people
———— 11. (a) fifteen cents   (b) 15 cents
———— 12. (a) a thirty-day warranty   (b) a 30-day warranty
———— 13. (a) 2/3 of the e-mails   (b) two thirds of the e-mails
———— 14. (a) two telephones for   (b) 2 telephones for
             15 employees   15 employees
———— 15. (a) 6 of the 130 letters   (b) six of the 130 letters

▮ CUMULATIVE EDITING QUIZ 8

Use proofreading marks (see Appendix B) to correct errors and omissions in the following sentences. All errors must be corrected to receive credit for the sentence. Check with your instructor for the answers.

1. My partner and myself will meet at our lawyers office at three p.m. on June ninth to sign our papers of incorporation.

2. Emily prepared 2 forty page business proposals to submit to the Senior Account Manager.

3. Of the 235 e-mail messages sent yesterday only seven bounced back.

4. Your short term loan for twenty-five thousand dollars covers a period of sixty days.

5. Each new employee must pick up their permanent parking permit for lot 3-A before the end of the 14 day probationary period.

6. 259 identity theft complaints were filed with the Competition bureau on November second alone.

7. Robertas 11 page report was more easier to read then Davids because her's was better organized and had good headings.

8. Every morning on the way to the office Tatiana picked up 2 lattes that cost a total of six dollars.

9. Taking 7 years to construct the forty thousand square foot home of Olexiy Karpolin reportedly cost more then fifty million dollars.

10. Many companys can increase profits nearly ninety percent by retaining only 5% more of there current customers.

Confusing Words

accede:	to agree or consent
exceed:	over a limit
accept:	to receive
except:	to exclude; (prep) but
adverse:	opposing; antagonistic
averse:	unwilling; reluctant
advice:	suggestion, opinion
advise:	to counsel or recommend
affect:	to influence
effect:	(n.) outcome, result; (v.) to bring about, to create
all ready:	prepared
already:	by this time
all right:	satisfactory
alright:	unacceptable variant spelling
altar:	structure for worship
alter:	to change
appraise:	to estimate
apprise:	to inform
ascent:	(n.) rising or going up
assent:	(v.) to agree or consent
assure:	to promise
ensure:	to make certain
insure:	to protect from loss
capital:	(n.) city that is seat of government; wealth of an individual; (adj.) chief
capitol:	building that houses U.S. state or national lawmakers
cereal:	breakfast food
serial:	arranged in sequence
cite:	to quote; to summon
site:	location
sight:	a view; to see
coarse:	rough texture
course:	a route; part of a meal; a unit of learning
complement	that which completes
compliment:	(n.) praise, flattery; (v.) to praise or flatter
conscience:	regard for fairness
conscious:	aware
council:	governing body

counsel:	(n.) advice, lawyer; (v.) to give advice
credible:	believable
creditable:	good enough for praise or esteem; reliable
desert:	arid land; to abandon
dessert:	sweet food
device:	invention or mechanism
devise:	to design or arrange
disburse:	to pay out
disperse:	to scatter widely
elicit:	to draw out
illicit:	unlawful
envelop:	(v.) to wrap, surround, or conceal
envelope:	(n.) a container for a written message
every day:	each single day
everyday:	ordinary
farther:	a greater distance
further:	additional
formally:	in a formal manner
formerly:	in the past
grate:	(v.) to reduce to small particles; to cause irritation; (n.) a frame of crossed bars blocking a passage
great:	(adj.) large in size; numerous; eminent or distinguished
hole:	an opening
whole:	complete
imply:	to suggest indirectly
infer:	to reach a conclusion
lean:	(v.) to rest against; (adj.) not fat
lien:	(n.) a legal right or claim to property
liable:	legally responsible
libel:	damaging written statement
loose:	not fastened
lose:	to misplace
miner:	person working in a mine

minor:	a lesser item; person under age	*principle:*	rule of action
patience:	calm perseverance	*stationary:*	immovable
patients:	people receiving medical treatment	*stationery:*	writing material
personal:	private, individual	*than:*	conjunction showing comparison
personnel:	employees	*then:*	adverb meaning "at that time"
plaintiff:	(n.) one who initiates a lawsuit	*their:*	possessive form of *they*
plaintive:	(adj.) expressive of suffering or woe	*there:*	at that place or point
		they're:	contraction of *they are*
populace:	(n.) the masses; population of a place	*to:*	a preposition; the sign of the infinitive
populous:	(adj.) densely populated	*too:*	an adverb meaning "also" or "to an excessive extent"
precede:	to go before		
proceed:	to continue	*two:*	a number
precedence:	priority	*waiver:*	abandonment of a claim
precedents:	events used as an example	*waver:*	to shake or fluctuate
principal:	(n.) capital sum; school official; (adj.) chief		

160 Frequently Misspelled Words

absence	desirable	independent	prominent
accommodate	destroy	indispensable	qualify
achieve	development	interrupt	quantity
acknowledgment	disappoint	irrelevant	questionnaire
across	dissatisfied	itinerary	receipt
adequate	division	judgment	receive
advisable	efficient	knowledge	recognize
analyze	embarrass	legitimate	recommendation
annually	emphasis	library	referred
appointment	emphasize	license	regarding
argument	employee	maintenance	remittance
automatically	envelope	manageable	representative
bankruptcy	equipped	manufacturer	restaurant
becoming	especially	mileage	schedule
beneficial	evidently	miscellaneous	secretary
budget	exaggerate	mortgage	separate
business	excellent	necessary	similar
calendar	exempt	nevertheless	sincerely
cancelled	existence	ninety	software
catalogue	extraordinary	ninth	succeed
changeable	familiar	noticeable	sufficient
column	fascinate	occasionally	supervisor
committee	feasible	occurred	surprise
congratulate	February	offered	tenant
conscience	fiscal	omission	therefore
conscious	foreign	omitted	thorough
consecutive	forty	opportunity	though
consensus	fourth	opposite	through

consistent	friend	ordinarily	truly
control	genuine	paid	undoubtedly
convenient	government	pamphlet	unnecessarily
correspondence	grammar	permanent	usable
courteous	grateful	permitted	usage
criticize	guarantee	pleasant	using
decision	harass	practical	usually
deductible	height	prevalent	valuable
defendant	hoping	privilege	volume
definitely	immediate	probably	weekday
dependent	incidentally	procedure	writing
describe	incredible	profited	yield

Key to Grammar/ Mechanics Checkups

Checkup 1
1. attorneys (1.05d) 2. Saturdays (1.05a) 3. cities (1.05e)
4. turkeys (1.05d) 5. inventories (1.05e) 6. Nashes (1.05b)
7. 1990s (1.05g) 8. editors in chief (1.05f) 9. complexes (1.05b)
10. counties (1.05e) 11. Jennifers (1.05a) 12. C (1.05d)
13. liabilities (1.05e) 14. C (1.05h) 15. runners-up (1.05f)

Checkup 2
1. he (1.08b) 2. his car (1.09b) 3. him (1.08c) 4. whom (1.08j)
5. hers (1.08d) 6. me (1.08c) 7. I (1.08a) 8. yours (1.08d)
9. whoever (1.08j) 10. me (1.08i) 11. he (1.08f) 12. us (1.08g)
13. her (1.09c) 14. its (1.09g) 15. his or her (1.09b)

Checkup 3
1. *are* for *is* (1.10e) 2. *has* for *have* (1.10c) 3. *offers* for *offer* (1.10d)
4. *is* for *are* (1.10g) 5. C (1.10f) 6. *is* for *are* (1.10i) 7. C (1.10h)
8. chosen (1.15) 9. *lain* for *laid* (1.15) 10. *were* for *was* (1.12)
11. *is* for *are* (1.10c) 12. b (1.15c) 13. b (1.15c) 14. a (1.15c)
15. b (1.15c)

Checkup 4
1. long-time (1.17e) 2. $50-per-year (1.17e) 3. C (1.17e)
4. quickly (1.17d) 5. had only (1.17f) 6. double-digit (1.17e)
7. once-in-a-lifetime (1.17e) 8. C (1.17e) 9. better (1.17a)
10. well-known (1.17e) 11. up-to-the-minute (1.17e)
12. after-tax (1.17e) 13. couldn't have been clearer (1.17b)
14. fifty-fifty (1.17e) 15. feel bad (1.17c)

Checkup 5
1. b (1.19d) 2. a (1.19d) 3. b (1.18e) 4. b (1.19c) 5. a (1.19a)
6. b (1.18a) 7. b (1.19d) 8. a (1.18c) 9. b (1.18b) 10. a (1.19c)
11. b (1.19a) 12. b (1.19b) 13. a (1.19c) 14. b (1.18c)
15. b (1.19c)

Checkup 6
1. (2) not, as a rule, (2.03) 2. (2) sure, Mrs. Schwartz, (2.02)
3. (2) reliable, conscientious, (2.01) 4. (0) 5. (1) fact, (2.03)
6. (3) Calgary, Alberta, La Salle, (2.04c) 7. (1) meantime, (2.03)
8. (2) February 4, 2011, (2.04a) 9. (2) Ms. Horne, Mr. Hae,
(2.01) 10. (4) Holmes, Lane, Regina, Saskatchewan S5L 2E2,
(2.04b) 11. (2) feels, needless to say, (2.03) 12. (2) supplies,
replacing inventories, (2.01) 13. (1) business, (2.02) 14. (2) feels,
however, (2.03) 15. 0

Checkup 7
1. (1) warranty, (2.06a) 2. (1) market, (2.05) 3. (0) (2.05)
4. (2) manufacturer, nameless, (2.06c) 5. (1) imaginative, (2.08)
6. (0) (2.06c) 7. (2) Sims, area, (2.09) 8. (1) buyers, (2.05)
9. (1) quality, (2.06a) 10. (1) buyers, (2.07) 11. (2) application,
Monday, (2.06a, 2.04a) 12. (2) hand, hard-working, (2.03, 2.08)
13. (1) Bragg Creek, (2.06c) 14. (3) telephone, Thursday, June 9,
(2.06a, 2.04a) 15. (1) classes, (2.05)

Checkup 8
1. (2) name," Etienne, (2.14a) 2. (4) Cox, Ph.D., Meridian,
M.B.A., (2.10) 3. (1) Monday, (2.14b) 4. (0) (2.15) 5. (1) investment, (2.12) 6. (3) requested, cartridges, folders, (2.06a, 2.01)
7. (2) think, however, (2.03) 8. (2) period, Vidal, (2.07, 2.06c)
9. (2) Collingwood, Laurentians, (2.01, 2.15) 10. (1) interviewed,
(2.06a, 2.06c) 11. (2) years, individuals, (2.07, 2.09) 12. (2)
Johansson, week, (2.05c, 2.15) 13. (0) (2.06c) 14. (2) companies,
robots, (2.01) 15. (2) act, unprotected, (2.03, 2.08)

Checkup 9
1. (3) one year; long-term financing, hand, (2.03, 2.16b)
2. (2) December; therefore, (2.16a) 3. (3) months: September,
October, (2.01, 2.17a) 4. (1) are [omit comma] (2.17b)
5. (1) money, (2.06a, 2.16b) 6. (3) short-term credit; manufacturer, however, (2.03, 2.16a) 7. (3) credit: loans, promissory
notes, (2.03, 2.16a) 8. (8) businesspeople: Mary Ann Mahan,
financial manager, Ritchie Industries; Buchanan, comptroller,
Edmée Cavalier, operations, (2.16d, 2.17) 9. (1) Canada, (2.05)
10. (5) customers; for example, retailers, service companies,
manufacturers, (2.16e) 11. (2) Inc., rating, (2.06c, 2.16c)
12. (2) Bank, applications to the following: (2.06a, 2.17a)
13. (2) high; therefore, (2.16) 14. (2) 18 percent, prohibitive;
(2.06a, 2.16c) 15. (1) resources; (2.16b)

Checkup 10
1. Mr. Ruskin's (2.20a, 2.21) 2. year's (2.20a) 3. weeks' (2.20b)
4. Ms. Lanham's (2.21) 5. boss's (2.20b) 6. server's (2.20b)
7. Kaspar's (2.22) 8. months' (2.20b) 9. companies' (2.20b)
10. month's (2.20a) 11. secretary's (2.20b) 12. sellers' (2.20b)
13. Mark's, David's (2.20a) 14. Latika's (2.20a)

Checkup 11
1. (2) managers—Yu Sosa—(2.26a, 2.27) 2. (3) please, Miss
Fundy, totals? (2.20, 2.23a) 3. (2) variables (see Figure 13 on
page 432) (2.27) 4. (3) "recommendation" misspelled, (2.06a,
2.28c) 5. (1) training— (2.26c) 6. (2) said, "Who cartridges?"
(2.28f) 7. (3) "How You"? (2.28e, 2.28f) 8. (2) provinces—
Alberta, Newfoundland, and Ontario— (2.26a) 9. (4) Mr. Kieran
E. Manning, Miss Kathy Tanguay, and Ms. Petra (2.23b,
2.24) 10. (3) "Trading Market" <u>Securities Markets</u> (2.28e)
11. (2) over"; however, (2.16, 2.28f) 12. (3) <u>liability</u> defined as
"any future." (2.28d) 13. (1) June 10; (2.06) 14. (4) c.o.d. today?
(2.23b, 2.24) 15. (3) Hooray! checkup, haven't I? (2.24, 2.25)

Checkup 12
1. c (2.05) 2. b (2.06) 3. a (2.16a) 4. c (2.15) 5. b (2.16b)
6. b (2.17a) 7. a (2.20) 8. c (2.16d) 9. b (2.04a) 10. c (2.03)
11. a (2.08) 12. a (2.12) 13. a (2.01) 14. c (2.07) 15. b (2.16)

Checkup 13
1. (5) Canadian customs inspection International Airport (3.01,
3.02, 3.07) 2. (6) Japanese international Japanese economics
professor University (3.01, 3.02, 3.04, 3.06d) 3. (4) business consumer business consumption (3.01, 3.13) 4. (4) history sociology
computer science (3.05) 5. (5) Horticulture Are Nothing Sneeze
At (3.12) 6. (2) printers printers (3.11) 7. (3) federal government

provincial (3.10) **8.** (3) Canada This foreign (3.01, 3.06c, 3.13) **9.** (8) comptroller president board directors Canada Revenue Agency company (3.01, 3.04, 3.06c) **10.** (2) mother sun's (3.03, 3.06g, 3.08, 3.14) **11.** (5) managing editor manager ad campaign (3.01, 3.06d, 3.06e, 3.09) **12.** (3) Austrian German Italian (3.02, 3.06a, 3.16) **13.** (4) Park island Vanier Bridge (3.01, 3.03)

14. (3) Computer Science Department (3.05, 3.07, 3.09) **15.** (4) Figure Chapter Statistics English (3.02, 3.04, 3.07)

Checkup 14

1. b (4.01a) **2.** a (4.05b) **3.** a (4.01a) **4.** b (4.03) **5.** b (4.02) **6.** a (4.03) **7.** b (4.04) **8.** b (4.07) **9.** b (4.08) **10.** b (4.10) **11.** b (4.02) **12.** b (4.08) **13.** b (4.12) **14.** a (4.06) **15.** a (4.06)

Notes

Chapter 1

[1] Backdraft Corporation. (n.d.). History & clients. Retrieved July 3, 2013, http://www.backdraft.org/history.htm

[2] Statistics Canada predicts that by 2031, foreign-born workers will make up one-third of the Canadian labour force. See Statistics Canada. (2011, August 17). *The Daily*. Retrieved from http://www.statcan.gc.ca/daily-quotidien/110817/dq110817b-eng.htm

[3] Marotte, B. (2013, April 26). Out of office reply: Canadian firms split on value of telecommuting. *The Globe and Mail*. Retrieved June 26, 2014, from http://www.theglobeandmail.com/report-on-business/careers/the-future-of-work/out-of-office-reply-canadian-firms-split-on-value-of-telecommuting/article11566700

[4] Beckstead, D., & and Tara Vinodrai, T. (2003). Dimensions of occupational changes in Canada's knowledge economy, 1971–1996. The Canadian Economy in Transition Series (Catalogue no. 11-622-MIE—No. 004). *Statistics Canada*. Retrieved July 2, 2013, from http://publications.gc.ca/Collection/Statcan/11-622-M/11-622-MIE2003004.pdf

[5] O'Toole, M., & Selley, C. (2013, January 11). "You can't be the director of education and plagiarizing": Chris Spence resigns as head of school board. *National Post*. Retrieved from http://news.nationalpost.com/2013/01/11/you-cant-be-the-director-of-education-and-plagiarizing-apparent-serial-plagiarist-resigns-as-head-of-school-board

[6] Gabriele, S., & Stober, J. (n.d.). Old messengers, new media: The legacy of Innis and McLuhan. Retrieved July 2, 2013, from http://www.collectionscanada.gc.ca/innis-mcluhan/index-e.html

[7] Burgoon, J., Coker, D., & Coker, R. (1986). Communicative explanations. *Human Communication Research, 12*, 463–94.

[8] Birdwhistell, R. (1970). *Kinesics and context*. Philadelphia: University of Pennsylvania Press, p. 8.

[9] Hall, E. T. (1966). *The hidden dimension*. Garden City, NY: Doubleday, pp. 107–22.

[10] Bell, C. (n.d.). Customized corporate seminars, Image consulting: Telecoaching. Retrieved July 2, 2013, from http://www.prime-impressions.com

[11] Mitchell, G. A., Skinner, L. B., & White, B. J. (2010). Essential soft skills for success in the twenty-first-century workforce as perceived by business educators. *The Delta Pi Epsilon Journal, 52*(1). Retrieved from http://www.faqs.org/periodicals/201001/2036768821.html

[12] McEwen, B. C. (2010). Cross-cultural and international career exploration and employability skills. *National Business Education Association Yearbook 2010: Cross-Cultural and International Business Education, 48*, 142.

[13] Wilson-Smith, A. (1995, July 1). A quiet passion. *Maclean's*, pp. 8–12.

[14] Alston, J. P., & Morris, T. M. Comparing Canadian and American values: New evidence from national surveys. *Canadian Review of American Studies, 26*(3), 301–15.

[15] Davis, T., Ward, D. A., & Woodland, D. (2010). Cross-cultural and international business communication—verbal. *National Business Education Association Yearbook: Cross-Cultural and International Business Education*, p. 3; and Hall, E. T., & Hall, M. R. (1990). *Understanding cultural differences*. Yarmouth, ME: Intercultural Press, pp. 183–84.

[16] Chaney, L. H., & Martin, J. S. (2000). *Intercultural business communication* (2nd ed.). Upper Saddle River, NJ: Prentice Hall, p. 83.

[17] Lipset, S. M. (1991). *Continental divide: The values and institutions of the United States and Canada*. New York: Routledge.

[18] Jarvis, S. S. (1990, June). Preparing employees to work south of the border. *Personnel*, p. 763.

[19] Gallois, C., & Callan, V. (1997). *Communication and culture*. New York: Wiley, p. 29.

[20] Ian Austin, I. (2007, October 19). Canucks polite, Vancouverites more so, Readers Digest finds. *The Vancouver Province*. Retrieved July 2, 2013, from http://www.canada.com/theprovince/news/story.html?id=b3610ee8-156f-4d46-aa69-d53c89bdc740

[21] McGuinness, N., & Campbell, N. (1991). Selling machinery to China: Chinese perceptions of strategies and relationships. *Journal of International Business Studies, 22*(3), 187.

[22] Axtell quoted in Elfatihi, M. (n.d.). The role of nonverbal communication in beginners' EFL classrooms. Retrieved from http://uqu.edu.sa/files2/tiny_mce/plugins/filemanager/files/4281947/a5.pdf, p. 4.

[23] Statistics Canada. (2010). Labour force characteristics by age and sex. Retrieved November 8, 2010, from http://www40.statcan.ca/l01/cst01/labor20a-eng.htm

[24] Ibid.

[25] Galt, V. (2004, November 23). Western Union remakes Canadian image: Profits from overseas hiring, staff diversity. *The Globe and Mail*, p. B1.

[26] Adler quoted in Lee Gardenswartz, L., & Rowe, A. (1998). *Managing diversity: A complete desk reference and planning guide*. New York: McGraw-Hill, p. 124.

[27] Makower, J. (1995). Managing diversity in the workplace. *Business & Society Review, 92*, 48–54. Retrieved February 2, 2008, from Business Source Premier database.

Chapter 2

[1] Canadian Management Centre. (2013, May 7). Businesses ignore communications at their peril during times of change. *Canada Newswire*. Retrieved July 5, 2013, from http://www.newswire.ca/en/story/1159755/businesses-ignore-communications-at-their-peril-during-times-of-change

[2] Tapscott, D. (2003, October). R U N2 It? *enRoute*, pp. 35–36.

[3] Marron, K. (2001, November 1). Instant messaging comes of age. *The Globe and Mail*, p. B30.

4 Harbert, E. N. (1986). Knowing your audience. In J. L. Digaetani (Ed.), *The handbook of executive communication*. Homewood, IL: Dow Jones/Irwin, p. 17.

Chapter 3

1 Department of English, University of Victoria. (1995). The UVic writer's guide: The first draft. *UVic English*. Retrieved May 25, 2011, from http://web.uvic.ca/wguide/Pages/EssayWritingFirstDraft.html

2 Piotrowski, M. V. (1996). *Effective business writing*. New York: Harper Perennial, p. 12.

Chapter 4

1 Thomas, J. (1999). Business writing in history: What caused the dictamen's demise? *Journal of Business Communication, 36*(1), 40–54.

2 Guillory, J. (2004). The memo and modernity. *Critical Inquiry, 31*(1), 108–32.

3 BrandSpeak. (2012). Did you know 144.8 billion emails are sent every day. *Mashable.com*. Retrieved July 10, 2013, from http://mashable.com/2012/11/27/email-stats-infographic

4 Statistics Canada. (2010). Business and government use of information communication technologies. Retrieved January 24, 2011, from http://www40.statcan.ca/l01/cst01/econ146a-eng.htm

5 Stewart, S. (2005, February 17). CIBC turns up heat as fight with Genuity hits home. *The Globe and Mail*, p. B4.

6 Muchmore, M. (2010, August 11). The best IM clients. *PC Mag*. Retrieved from http://www.pcmag.com/article2/0,2817,2367620,00.asp

7 Living the fast, young life in Asia. (2008, April). *Change Agent*. Retrieved from http://www.synovate.com/changeagent/index.php

8 Baker, S., & Green, H. (2008, June 2). Beyond blogs: What business needs to know. *BusinessWeek Online*. Retrieved from http://www.businessweek.com/magazine/content/08_22/b4086044617865.htm?chan=technology_technology+index+page_top+stories

9 The wisdom of crowds: Understanding your customers better through social media. (2010, October). *PwC*. Retrieved from http://www.pwc.com/en_GX/gx/retail-consumer/pdf/NY-11-0206_RC_Worlds_Social_Media_digital_v5final.pdf

10 Conlin, M., & MacMillan, D. (2009, June 1). Managing the tweets. *BusinessWeek*, p. 21.

11 Baker, S., & Green, H. (2008, June 2). Beyond blogs. *BusinessWeek*, pp. 46, 48.

12 Conlin, M., & MacMillan, D. (2009, June 1). Managing the tweets. *BusinessWeek*, p. 20.

13 Ibid., pp. 20–21.

14 Irvine, M. (2009, July 12). Young workers push employers for wider Web access. *USA Today*. Retrieved from http://www.usatoday.com /tech/webguide/internetlife/2009-07-13-blocked-internet_N.htm

15 Villano, M. (2009, April 25). The online divide between work and play. *The New York Times*. Retrieved from http://www.nytimes.com/2009/04/26/jobs/26career.html?module=Search&mabReward=relbias%3Ar%2C[%22RI%3A5%22%2C%22RI%3A16%22

16 Ibid.

17 Ibid.

18 Hanson, A. (2013, April 12). What do the best corporate blogs do well? Retrieved from http://www.arikhanson.com/2013/04/05/what-do-the-best-corporate-blogs-do-well

19 BlogPulse Stats. (2011, June 1). Retrieved from http://www.blogpulse.com

20 Brown, M. (2011, January 31). Southwest Airlines social media strategy—Lessons for all organizations. *Social Media Today*. Retrieved from http://socialmediatoday.com/mikebrown-brainzooming/266092/southwest-airlines-social-media-strategy-lessons-all-organizations

21 Gardner, T. (2009, September 13). It may pay to Twitter. *Los Angeles Times*, p. L8.

22 Scott, C. (2010, February 20). The best blogging sites and platforms. *Blogtap*. Retrieved from http://www.blogtap.net/the-best-blogging-sites-and-platforms-top-blog-sites

23 FON Wiki. (2010, January 26). Retrieved from http://wiki.fon.com/wiki/Join_FON_Wiki_Team

24 Brown, P. B. (2008, January 26). Same office, different planets. *New York Times*, p. B5.

25 Nova Scotia Human Rights Commission. (n.d.). Rights on religion or creed. Retrieved April 27, 2005, from http://www.gov.ns.ca/humanrights/human-rights-act.asp

26 Office of the Privacy Commissioner of Canada. (2009). Fact sheet: Privacy and social networking in the workplace. Retrieved July 12, 2013, from http://www.priv.gc.ca/resource/fs-fi/02_05_d_41_sn_e.asp

27 Gross, G. (2012, May 29). Gartner predicts huge rise in monitoring of employees' social media use. *PCWorld*. Retrieved July 12, 2013, from http://www.pcworld.com/article/256420/gartner_predicts_huge_rise_in_monitoring_of_employees_social_media_use.html

28 Office of the Privacy Commisioner of Canada.

29 Wood, C., & Branswell, B. (2001, February 19). Do you know who's watching you? *Maclean's*, p. 18.

30 Ibid.

Chapter 5

1 Business News Daily. (2012, June 7). Most work emails not important [Study]. *Mashable.com*. Retrieved July 17, 2013, from http://mashable.com/2012/06/07/most-work-emails-not-important-study

2 Kellerman, B. (2006, April). When should a leader apologize—and when not? *Harvard Business Review*. Retrieved July 17, 2013, from http://hbr.org/2006/04/when-should-a-leader-apologize-and-when-not/ar/1

3 Baer, J. (2011, December 10). 70% of companies ignore customer complaints on Twitter. Retrieved July 17, 2013, from http://www.convinceandconvert.com/social-media-monitoring/70-of-companies-ignore-customer-complaints-on-twitter

4 Emily Post Institute. (2008). Conveying sympathy Q & A. Retrieved from http://ww31.1800flowers.com

5 Canadian Business for Social Responsibility. (2010, June). CSR governance guidelines. *CBSR*. Retrieved May 26, 2011, from http://www.cbsr.ca/resources/cbsr-publications

6 CBC. Irving Oil not charged after refinery problems. (2011, January 12). *CBC News*. Retrieved July 17, 2013, from http://www.cbc.ca/news/canada/new-brunswick/story/2011/01/12/nb-irving-oil-refinery-catalyst-958.html

Chapter 6

1 Chambers, D. (1998). *The agile manager's guide to writing to get action*. Bristol, VT: Velocity Press, p. 86.

2 Lowenstein, M. Make both an emotional and rational appeal to your customers: Inside-out and outside-in commitment and advocacy. *Customer Think*. Retrieved July 22, 2013, from http://www.digitalmarketingone.com/article/make_emotional_rational_appeal_customers

3 Interactive Advertising Bureau. (2013, June 3). First quarter 2013 Internet ad revenues set new high, at $9.6 billion. *IAB*.

Retrieved July 22, 2013, from http://www.iab.net/about_the
_iab/recent_press_releases/press_release_archive/press_release/
pr-060313

4 Segal, B., & Duong, K. (2013, February). 2012 digital advertising Highlights. Prepared for IAB Canada. Retrieved July 22,
2013, from http://www.slideshare.net/IABCanada/comscore
-2012-digital-advertising-highlights

5 Cited in Rubel, S. (2010, August 9). Hot or not: E-mail marketing vs. social-media marketing. *Advertising Age*. Retrieved
July 22, 2013, from http://adage.com/digital/article?article
_id=145285

6 Stone, B. (2010, September 22). Facebook sells your friends.
BusinessWeek. Retrieved July 22, 2013, from http://www
.businessweek.com/magazine/content/10_40/b4197064860826
.htm

7 Sumit, R. (2010, February 25). The global social media checkup. Burson-Marsteller Blog. Retrieved July 22, 2013, from
http://www.slideshare.net/sumitkroy/burson-marsteller-2010
-global-social-media-check-up-white-paper

8 Burson-Marsteller Asia-Pacific. (2010, October 28). Asia-
Pacific corporate social media study 2011. Burson-Marsteller
Blog. Retrieved July 22, 2013, from http://www.slideshare
.net/bmasia/burson-marsteller-asiapacific-corporate-social
-media-study-2011

9 To learn more about HP's blogs, go to http://h30507.www3
.hp.com

10 *PR Week* and Burson-Marsteller study cited in Rubel, S.
(2005, November 7). Study: 47% of CEOs say blogs useful
for PR. *WebPro News*. Retrieved July 22, 2013, from http://
www.webpronews.com/study-of-ceos-say-blogs-useful-for
-pr-2005-11

11 Friberg, M. (2006). GigaSpaces: A conversation with Gilad
David Mayaan, technical writer at GigaSpaces. Atlassian Case
Studies. *Atlassian*. Retrieved July 22, 2013, from https://www
.atlassian.com/software/confluence/casestudies/gigaspaces.jsp

12 Pilgrim, M. (n.d.). What is RSS? *O'Reilly About*. Retrieved
July 22, 2013, from http://oreilly.com/feeds

13 Weinberg, T. (2009). *The new community rules: Marketing
on the social Web*. Sebastopol, CA: O'Reilly Media, pp. 127,
128–29.

14 See note 5 above.

15 Canadian Fitness and Lifestyle Research Institute. (2003,
January 1). 2002 Physical Activity Monitor. *Canadian Fitness
and Lifestyle Research Institute*. Retrieved July 28, 2011,
from http://72.10.49.94/node/595

16 Rogers false advertising case heads towards close. (2013, May
14). *The Huffington Post Canada*. Retrieved July 22, 2013,
from http://www.huffingtonpost.ca/2013/05/14/rogers-false
-advertising-_n_3274774.html

Chapter 7

1 Rodger, R. (2011, June 30). Communicating in a Crisis. *Step
Two Designs*. Retrieved July 23, 2013, from http://www
.steptwo.com.au/papers/kmc_crisis/index.html

2 Webber, L. (2013, July 18). Text from the boss: U R fired.
The Wall Street Journal. Retrieved July 23, 2013, from http://
blogs.wsj.com/atwork/2013/07/18/text-from-the-boss-u-r
-fired

3 Credit Guru Inc. (n.d.). Collection letters. *CreditGuru.com*.
Retrieved July 23, 2013, from http://www.creditguru.com/
collectionletters.htm

4 Mascolini, M. (1994, June). Another look at teaching the
external negative message. *Bulletin of the Association for
Business Communication*, p. 47.

5 Schweitzer, M. E. (2006, December). Wise negotiators know
when to say "I'm sorry." *Negotiation*, 4. PDF file retrieved
from http://search.ebscohost.com

6 Brodkin, J. (2007, March 19). Rating apologies.
Networkworld, 24(11), 14. Retrieved from http://search
.ebscohost.com

7 Neeleman, D. (2007). An apology from David Neeleman.
JetBlue. Retrieved from http://www.jetblue.com/about/
ourcompany/apology/index.html

8 Letters to Lands' End. (1991, February). *1991 Lands' End
Catalogue*. Dodgeville, WI: Lands' End, p. 100.

9 Forbes, M. (1999). How to write a business letter. In K. Harty
(Ed.), *Strategies for business and technical writing*. Boston:
Allyn and Bacon, p. 108.

10 Dorn, E. M. (1999, March). Case method instruction in
the business writing classroom. *Business Communication
Quarterly*, 51–52.

11 Browning, M. (2003, November 24). Work dilemma:
Delivering bad news a good way. *Government Computer
News*, p. 41; and Mowatt, J. (2002, February). Breaking bad
news to customers. *Agency Sales*, p. 30.

12 Engels, J. (2007, July). Delivering difficult messages. *Journal
of Accountancy*, 204(1), 50–52. Retrieved from http://search
.ebscohost.com; see also Lewis, B. (1999, September 13). To
be an effective leader, you need to perfect the art of delivering
bad news. *InfoWorld*, p. 124. Retrieved from http://books
.google.com

13 Granberry, M. (1992, November 14). Lingerie chain fined
$100,000 for gift certificates. *Los Angeles Times*, p. D3.

14 Bristol-Smith, D. (2003, November). Quoted in Need to
deliver bad news? How & why to tell it like it is. *HR Focus*,
p. 3. Retrieved from http://search.ebscohost.com

15 See note 10 above.

16 Gartner identifies top ten disruptive technologies for 2008 to
2012 [Press release]. (2008, May 28). Retrieved from http://
www.gartner.com/it/page.jsp?id=68117

17 Based on SUV surprise. (2004, June 15). *The Wall Street
Journal*, p. W7.

18 Based on Bonavita, C. V. (2010, August 5). Employers should
eye telecommuting's benefits, pitfalls. *The Legal Intelligencer*.
Retrieved from http://www.law.com/jsp/lawtechnologynews/
PubArticleLTN.jsp?id=1202464268970

Chapter 8

1 Klie, S. (2009, July 13). LGBT employees still face barriers.
Canadian HR Reporter, p. 13. Retrieved February 4, 2011,
from CBCA Business (Proquest).

2 Farries, M. T., II, Maes, J. D., & Bunz, U. K. (1998, Summer).
References and bibliography: Citing the Internet. *Journal of
Applied Business Research*, 33–36.

Chapter 9

1 Holtz, H. (1990). *The consultant's guide to proposal writing*.
New York: John Wiley, p. 188.

2 Union Pearson Express. (n.d.). *Metrolinx*. Retrieved August 6,
2013, from http://www.metrolinx.com/en/projectsandprograms/
upexpress/upexpress.aspx

3 Bort, J. (2012, March 8). How many Web sites are there?
Business Insider. Retrieved August 6, 2013, from http://www
.businessinsider.com/how-many-web-sites-are-are-there-2012-3

4 Suzukamo, L. B. (2002, July 3). Search engines become popular
for fact-finding, game playing. *Knight-Ridder/Tribune News
Service*, p. K6110.

5 Bulkeley, W. M. (2005, June 23). Marketers scan blogs for brand insights. *The Wall Street Journal*, p. B1.

6 Sobel, J. (2010, November 3). State of the blogosphere 2010. *Technorati*. Retrieved from http://technorati.com/blogging/article/who-bloggers-brands-and-consumers-day/page-3

7 Pimentel, B. (2001, June 13). Writing the codes on blogs: Companies figure out what's OK, what's not in online realm. *San Francisco Chronicle*, p. E1. Retrieved June 6, 2008, from http://www.sfgate.com/cgi-bin/article.cgi?file=/c/a/2005/06/13/BLOG.TMP

8 BlogPulse stats. (2011, January 6). Retrieved from BlogPulse Web site: http://www.blogpulse.com and Beutler, W. (2007, April 10). Yes, but how many blogs are there really? Blog, P. I. Retrieved from http://www.blogpi.net/yes-but-how-many-blogs-are-there-really

9 Pew Research Center. (2010, May). Online activities, 2000–2009. *Pew Research Internet Project*. Retrieved from http://www.pewinternet.org/Static-Pages/Trend-Data/Online-Activites-Total.aspx

10 Petouhoff, N. L. (2010, January 26). How Carphone Warehouse uses Twitter and social media to transform customer service. *Forrester*. Retrieved from http://www.forrester.com/rb/Research/how_carphone_warehouse_uses_twitter_and_social/q/id/55956/t/2

11 Berfield, S. (2009, August 17). Howard Schultz versus Howard Schultz. *BusinessWeek*, p. 31.

12 Writing Tutorial Services, Indiana University. (2011) Plagiarism: What it is and how to recognize and avoid it. Retrieved from http://www.indiana.edu/~wts/pamphlets/plagiarism.shtml

13 Census 2011: Canada's 10 fastest growing cities. (2012, August 2). *The Huffington Post Canada*. Retrieved August 6, 2012, from http://www.huffingtonpost.ca/2012/02/08/census-2011-canadas-fastest-growing-cities_n_1262436.html

14 Brady, D. (2006, December 4). *!#?@ the e-mail. Can we talk? *BusinessWeek*, p. 109.

15 Schmidt, S. (2006, October 21). Older profs more worried about Net-savvy cheaters. *Ottawa Citizen*. Retrieved July 3, 2008, from http://www.canada.com/ottawacitizen/story.html?id=030b0bdb-2b0d-4ccd-9260-f4b7ce328f93&k=83050

16 Tynan-Wood, C. (2010, August 17). The (better) future of tech support. Adventures in IT. Retrieved from http://infoworld.com/d/adventures-in-it/the-better-future-tech-support-066?page=0,0; and Edwards, C., & Ihlwan, M. (2006, December 4). Upward mobility. *BusinessWeek*, pp. 68–82.

17 Based on Skidmore, S. (2008, June 10). Some retailers give vinyl records a spin. *Los Angeles Times*, p. C6.

18 Tapscott, D., & Williams, A. D. (2007, March 26). The wiki workplace. *Business Week Online*. Retrieved June 10, 2008, from http://www.businessweek.com/innovate/content/mar2007/id20070326_237620.htm

Chapter 10

1 Buhler, P. M. (2003, April 20). Workplace civility: Has it fallen by the wayside? *SuperVision*. Retrieved June 24, 2008, from ProQuest database.

2 Civility. (n.d.). *Wikipedia*. Retrieved June 20, 2008, from http://en.wikipedia.org/wiki/Wikipedia:CIV

3 Johnson, D. (n.d.). Dine like a diplomat [Seminar script]. The Protocol School of Washington, 1998–2006.

4 Albrecht, K. (2005). *Social intelligence: The new science of success*. San Francisco: Pfeiffer, p. 3.

5 Molloy, J. T. (1988). *New dress for success*. New York: Warner Books, pp. 13–14.

6 Evans, L. (2013, June 21). Will work for biscuits: Celebrating Take Your Dog to Work Day. *Canadian Business*. Retrieved March 30, 2014, from http://www.canadianbusiness.com/lifestyle/will-work-for-biscuits

7 Chismar, D. (2001). "Vice and virtue in everyday (business) life. *Journal of Business Ethics, 29*, 169–76.

8 Hughes, T. (n.d.). Being a professional. *Word Constructions*. Retrieved June 16, 2008, from http://www.wordconstructions.com/articles/business/professional.html; and Grove, C., & Hallowell, W. (n.d.). The seven balancing acts of professional behavior in the United States: A cultural values perspective. *Grovewell*. Retrieved July 18, 2008, from http://www.grovewell.com/pub-usa-professional.html

9 Brent, P. (2006, November). Soft skills speak volumes. *CA Magazine, 139*, 112. Retrieved June 16, 2008, from ProQuest database.

10 Laff, M. (2006, December). Wanted: CFOs with communications skills. *T+D, 60*(12), 20. Retrieved July 28, 2011, from http://www.pecktraining.com/articles.html

11 Duke, S. (2001, Winter). E-Mail: Essential in media relations, but no replacement for face-to-face communication. *Public Relations Quarterly*, 19; and Flaherty, L. M., Pearce, K. J., & Rubin, R. B. (1998, Summer). Internet and face-to-face communication: Not functional alternatives. *Communication Quarterly*, 250.

12 Drolet, A. L., & Morris, M. W. (2000, January). Rapport in conflict resolution: Accounting for how face-to-face contact fosters mutual cooperation in mixed-motive conflicts. *Journal of Experimental Social Psychology*, 26.

13 Miculka, J. (1999). *Speaking for success*. Cincinnati: South-Western, p. 19.

14 Hamilton, C., with C. Parker. (2001). *Communicating for success* (6th ed.). Belmont, CA: Wadsworth, pp. 100–104.

15 Miculka, *Speaking*, p. 127.

16 Fire up your phone skills. (2000, November). *Successful Meetings*, p. 30.

17 Fletcher, W. (2000, February). How to make sure it's a good call. *Management Today*, p. 34.

18 Did you know that . . . . (1992, August 15). *Boardroom Reports*.

19 McHugh, E. (2013, March 11). Canadians still love their landlines—But for how long? *The Chronicle Herald* (Halifax). Retrieved August 7, 2013, from http://thechronicleherald.ca/bcw/942869-mchugh-canadians-still-love-their-landlines-but-for-how-long; Smith, A. (2010, July 7). Mobile access 2010. *Pew Research Internet Project*. Retrieved from http://www.pewinternet.org/Reports/2010/Mobile-Access-2010.aspx; and Lanman, S. (2005, July 9). Mobile-phone users become a majority. *San Francisco Chronicle*, p. C1.

20 Pearson, C. (2010, May 16). Sending a message that you don't care. *The New York Times*. Retrieved from http://www.nytimes.com/2010/05/16/jobs/16pre.html?_r=0

21 CBC. (2014, March 19). Distracted driving laws across Canada. *CBC News*. Retrieved July 8, 2014, from http://www.cbc.ca/news/canada/distracted-driving-laws-across-canada-1.2576880

22 Xerox' new design team: Customers. (2007, May 6). *Bloomberg Businessweek*. Retrieved from http://www.businessweek.com/magazine/content/07_19/b4033087.htm

23 Glionna, J. M., & Choi, J. (2011, January 22). Apple grows on Samsung's soil. *Los Angeles Times*, p. B3.

24 Brown, M. K., Huettner, B., & James-Tanny, C. (2007). *Managing virtual teams: Getting the most of wikis, blogs, and other collaborative tools*. Plano, TX: Wordware Publishing; and Lipnack, J., & Stamps, J. (2000). *Virtual teams: People*

working across boundaries with technology (2nd ed.). New York: Wiley, p. 18.

25 Cutler, G. (2007, January/February). Mike leads his first virtual team. *Research-Technology Management, 50*(1), 66. Retrieved June 17, 2008, from ABI/INFORM database.

26 Amason, A. C., Hochwarter, W. A., Thompson, K. R., & Harrison, A. W. (1995, Autumn). Conflict: An important dimension in successful management teams. *Organizational Dynamics, 24*(2), 1. Retrieved June 17, 2008, from EBSCO database; and Romando, R. (2006, November 9). Advantages of corporate team building. *Ezine Articles.* Retrieved June 17, 2008, from http://ezinearticles.com/?Advantages-of-Corporate-Team-Building&id=352961

27 Ruffin, B. (2006, January). T.E.A.M. work: Technologists, educators, and media specialists collaborating. *Library Media Connection, 24*(4), 49. Retrieved June 20, 2008, from EBSCO database.

28 Katzenbach, J. R., & Smith, D. K. (1994). *The wisdom of teams.* New York: HarperBusiness, p. 45.

29 Gale, S. F. (2006, July). Common ground. *PM Network*, p. 48. Retrieved June 17, 2008, from EBSCO database.

30 Lancaster, H. (1998, May 26). Learning some ways to make meetings slightly less awful. *The Wall Street Journal*, p. B1.

31 Katzenbach & Smith, *The wisdom*, p. 50.

32 McDonald, T. (1996, June). Minimizing meetings. *Successful Meetings*, p. 24.

33 I've got to go to another . . . meeting. (2000, November). *Interventions: The EFAP Journal of CMR Canada.* Retrieved May 25, 2005, from http://www.cmrcanada.ca/InterventionsNov2000.html

34 Bruening, J. C. (1996, July). There's good news about meetings. *Managing Office Technology*, pp. 24–25.

35 Schabacker, K. (1991, June). A short, snappy guide to meaningful meetings. *Working Women*, p. 73.

36 Cook, J. K. (1995, April). Try these eight guidelines for more effective meetings. *Communication Briefings*, Bonus Item, p. 8a. See also Stettner, M. (1998, October 8). How to manage a corporate motormouth. *Investor's Business Daily*, p. A1.

37 Hamilton & Parker, *Communicating*, pp. 311–12.

Chapter 11

1 Maes, J. D., Weldy, T. G., & Icenogle, M. L. (1997, January). A managerial perspective: Oral communication competency is most important for business students in the workplace. *The Journal of Business Communication, 34*(1), 67–80. Retrieved October 6, 2013, from http://home.bi.no/fgl96053/orgcom/oral.pdf

2 Barrington, L., & Casner-Lotto, J. (2008, May). *Are they really ready to work?* Report of The Conference Board. Retrieved October 6, 2013, from http://www.p21.org/storage/documents/FINAL_REPORT_PDF09-29-06.pdf

3 Booher, D. (1992). *Executive's portfolio of model speeches for all occasions.* Upper Saddle River, NJ: Prentice Hall, p. 260.

4 Dassanayake, D. (2013, October 2). Just Google it: Britons lose ability to remember key dates because of search engines. Retrieved October 6, 2013, from http://www.express.co.uk/news/science-technology/433898/Just-Google-it-Britons-lose-ability-to-remember-key-dates-because-of-search-engines

5 Morrison, J., & Vogel, D. (1998). The impacts of presentation visuals on persuasion. *Information & Management, 33*(3), 125–35. Retrieved October 6, 2013, from ScienceDirect database.

6 P., K. (2013, May 31). Question: How many PowerPoint presentations are given daily worldwide? [Discussion group comment]. *Microsoft Community.* Retrieved October 6, 2013, from http://answers.microsoft.com/en-us/office/forum/officeversion_other-powerpoint/how-many-powerpoint-presentations-are-given-daily/aabe6b3a-a8f5-4e26-bb4c-1da213186a9c?msgId=44ad9416-8d94-4467-adb5-3a8d1668a6b6

7 Nass quoted in Simons, T. (2001, July). When was the last time PowerPoint made you sing? *Presentations*, p. 6. See also Tufte, E. R. (2006). *The cognitive style of PowerPoint: Pitching out corrupts within.* Cheshire, CT: Graphics Press.

8 Wahl, A. (2003, November). PowerPoint of no return. *Canadian Business.* Retrieved July 28, 2011, from www.sociablemedia.com/PDF/press_canadian_business_11_11_03.pdf

9 Booher, D. (2003). *Speak with confidence: Powerful presentations that inform, inspire, and persuade.* New York: McGraw-Hill Professional, p. 126. See also Paradi, D. (2009, March 3). Choosing colors for your presentation slides. Retrieved from http://www.indezine.com/ideas/prescolors.html

10 Arts and Science Support of Education through Technology (ASSETT), University of Colorado. (n.d.). Prezi vs. SlideShare. Retrieved October 6, 2013, from http://assett.colorado.edu/prezi-vs-slideshare

11 Bates, S. (2005). *Speak like a CEO: Secrets for commanding attention and getting results.* New York: McGraw-Hill Professional, p. 113.

12 Sommerville, J. (n.d.). The seven deadly sins of PowerPoint presentations. *About.com: Entrepreneurs.* Retrieved October 6, 2013, from http://entrepreneurs.about.com/cs/marketing/a/7sinsofppt.htm

13 Burrows, P., & Grover, R., with H. Green. (2006, February 6). Steve Jobs' magic kingdom. *BusinessWeek.* Retrieved October 6, 2013, from http://www.businessweek.com/stories/2006-02-05/steve-jobs-magic-kingdom; see also Gallo, C. (2006, April 6). How to wow 'em like Steve Jobs. *BusinessWeek.* Retrieved October 6, 2013, from http://www.businessweek.com/stories/2006-04-05/how-to-wow-em-like-steve-jobs

14 See TLC Creative Services Inc. (n.d.). PowerPoint pre-show checklist. Retrieved October 6, 2013, from http://www.tlccreative.com/images/tutorials/PreShowChecklist.pdf

15 Ellwood, J. (2004, August 4). Less PowerPoint, more powerful points. *The Times* (London), p. 6.

16 Booher, *Executive's portfolio*, p. 259.

17 Jackson, M., quoted in (1992, December). Garbage in, garbage out. *Consumer Reports*, p. 755.

Chapter 12

1 Betcherman, G. (1994). *The Canadian workplace in transition.* Kingston, ON: IRC Press, p. 11.

2 Kharif, O. (2007, January 3). Online job sites battle for share. *BusinessWeek.* Retrieved October 10, 2013, from http://www.businessweek.com/technology/content/jan2007/tc20070103_369308.htm

3 Korkki, P. (2007, July 1). So easy to apply, so hard to be noticed. *The New York Times.* Retrieved October 10, 2013, from LexisNexis database.

4 Marquardt, K. (2008, February 21). 5 tips on finding a new job. *U.S. News & World Report.* Retrieved October 10, 2013, from http://www.usnews.com/articles/business/careers/2008/02/21/5-tips-on-finding-a-new-job.html

5 Haun, L. (2013, March 22). Source of hire report: Referrals, career sites, job boards dominate. *ERE.net.* Retrieved October 10, 2013, from http://www.ere.net/2013/03/22/source-of-hire-report-referrals-career-sites-job-boards-dominate

6 Farquharson, L. (2003, September 15). Technology special report: The best way to find a job. *The Wall Street Journal*, p. R8. Retrieved October 10, 2013, from http://articles.chicagotribune.com/2003-09-24/business/0309240303_1_sites-focus-on-particular-industries-job-boards

7 McConnon, A. (2007, August 30). Social networking graduates and hits the job market. *Business Week*. Retrieved October 10, 2013, from http://www.businessweek.com/stories/2007-08-30/social-networking-graduates-and-hits-the-job-marketbusinessweek-business-news-stock-market-and-financial-advice

8 Ibid.

9 Cheesman quoted in Wolgemuth, L. (2008, February 25). Using the Web to search for a job. *U.S. News & World Report*. Retrieved October 10, 2013, from http://money.usnews.com/money/careers/articles/2008/02/25/using-the-web-to-search-for-a-job

10 Feldman quoted in Marquardt, 5 Tips.

11 Black quoted in Brandon, E. (2007, January 31). Tips for getting that first job. *U.S. News & World Report*. Retrieved October 10, 2013, from http://www.usnews.com/usnews/biztech/articles/070131/31firstjob.htm

12 Burns, K. (2009, September 30). Chronological vs. functional resumes. *U.S. News & World Report*. Retrieved October 10, 2013, from http://money.usnews.com/money/blogs/outside-voices-careers/2009/09/30/chronogical-vs-functional-resumes

13 Blackburn-Brockman, E., & Belanger, K. (2001, January). One page or two? A national study of CPA recruiters' preferences for résumé length. *The Journal of Business Communication*, 29–57. Retrieved October 10, 2013, from Sage Journals Database.

14 Isaacs, K. (n.d.). How to decide on résumé length. *Monster*. Retrieved October 10, 2013, from http://career-advice.monster.com/resumes-cover-letters/resume-writing-tips/how-to-decide-on-resume-length/article.aspx

15 Fisher, A. (2007, March 29). Does a resume have to be one page long? *CNNMoney.com*. Retrieved October 10, 2013, from http://money.cnn.com/2007/03/28/news/economy/resume.fortune/index.htm

16 Hansen, K. (n.d.). Should you use a career objective on your résumé? *Quintessential Careers*. Retrieved October 22, 2013, from http://www.quintcareers.com/resume_objectives.html

17 Quoted in Korkki, So easy to apply.

18 Koeppel, D. (2006, December 31). Those low grades in college may haunt your job search. *The New York Times*, p. 1. Retrieved October 22, 2013, from Academic Search Premier (EBSCO) database.

19 Locke, A. (2008, June 18). Is your resume telling the wrong story? *Bryant Associates, Inc.* Retrieved October 22, 2013, from http://www.bryantassociates.com/candidates/career_resources/articles/resume_considerations.html

20 Washington, T. (n.d.). Effective resumes bring results to life. *CareerJournalEurope.com/WallStreetJournal.com*. Retrieved October 22, 2013, from http://www.careerjournaleurope.com/jobhunting/resumes/20000913-washington.html

21 George, G. (2013). *Employability in the 21st century*. Paper presented at panel, George Brown College, Toronto, ON, October 24.

22 Sylvestre-Williams, R. (2012, May 31). How recruiters use Linkedin. *Forbes*. Retrieved October 29, 2013, from http://www.forbes.com/sites/reneesylvestrewilliams/2012/05/31/how-recruiters-use-linkedin

23 Saltpeter, M. (2012, August 17). How a good video resume leads to a good job. *U.S. News & World Report*. Retrieved October 29, 2013, from http://money.usnews.com/money/blogs/outside-voices-careers/2012/08/17/how-a-good-video-resume-leads-to-a-good-job

24 Peter, T. A. (2007, March 26). Résumés get a technology makeover. *Christian Science Monitor*, p. 13. Retrieved October 29, 2013, from LexisNexis database.

25 Nale, M. (2008, February 8). 10 things that make up a good video resume. *ERE.net*. Retrieved October 29, 2013, from http://www.ere.net/2008/02/08/10-things-that-make-up-a-good-video-resume

26 Kidwell, R. E., Jr. (2004, May). "Small" lies, big trouble: The unfortunate consequences of résumé padding from Janet Cooke to George O'Leary. *Journal of Business Ethics*, 175.

27 Wallace, K. (2009, September 2). Resume cheating soars in tough economy. *CBS Evening News*. Retrieved October 29, 2013, from http://www.cbsnews.com/8301-18563_162-5283689.html

28 BackCheck. (n.d.). Corporate profile. Retrieved October 29, 2013, from http://backcheck.net/about.htm

29 Needleman, S. E. (2007, March 6). Why sneaky tactics may not help résumé. *The Wall Street Journal*, p. B8.

30 Augustin, H. (1991, September). The written job search: A comparison of the traditional and a nontraditional approach. *The Bulletin of the Association for Business Communication*, p. 13.

31 Korkki, So easy to apply.

32 Schroer, J. (1990, November 19). Seek a job with a little help from your friends. *USA Today*, p. B1.

Chapter 13

1 Bergey, B. (2009, December 10). Online job interviews becoming more popular. *WKOW.com*. Retrieved November 19, 2013, from http://www.wkowtv.com/Global/story.asp?S=11655389; and Kennedy, J. L. (2008). *Job interviews for dummies*. Hoboken, NJ: Wiley Publishing, p. 20.

2 Wilmott, N. (n.d.). Interviewing styles: Tips for interview approaches. *About.com*. Retrieved November 19, 2013, from http://humanresources.about.com/cs/selectionstaffing/a/interviews.htm

3 Mease, B. (2010, June 4). Employers using Second Life to scout out job candidates. *Ezine Articles*. Retrieved November 19, 2013, from http://ezinearticles.com/?Employers-Using-Second-Life-to-Scout-Out-Job-Candidates&id=4422448; and Athavaley, A. (2007, June 20). A job interview you don't have to show up for. *The Wall Street Journal*. Retrieved November 19, 2013, from http://online.wsj.com/article/SB118229876637841321.html#articleTabs%3Darticle

4 Ziebarth, B. (2009, December 10). Tips to ace your panel job interview. *Yahoo! Voices*. Retrieved November 19, 2013, from http://voices.yahoo.com/tips-ace-panel-job-interview-5036880.html

5 Cristante, D. (n.d.). How to succeed in a group interview. *Career FAQs*. Retrieved November 19, 2013, from http://www.careerfaqs.com.au/careers/interview-questions-and-tips/how-to-succeed-in-a-group-interview

6 Weiss, T. (2009, May 12). Going on the second interview. *Forbes*. Retrieved November 19, 2013, from http://www.forbes.com/2009/05/12/second-interview-advice-leadership-careers-basics.html

7 Hansen, R. (n.d.). Situational interviews and stress interviews: What to make of them and how to succeed in them. *Quintessential Careers*. Retrieved November 19, 2013, from http://www.quintcareers.com/situational_stress_interviews.html

8 Bergey, B. (2009, December 10). Online job interviews becoming more popular. *WKOW.com*. Retrieved November 19, 2013, from http://www.wkowtv.com/Global/story.asp?S=11655389

9 Dobson, S. (2013, September 23). Videoconferencing interviews viewed unfavourably—by both sides. *Canadian HR Reporter*,

p. 2. Retrieved November 19, 2013, from http://www
.hrreporter-digital.com/hrreporter/20130923?pg=2#pg2

10 Rossheim, J. (n.d.). Do your homework before the big interview. *Monster*. Retrieved November 21, 2013, from http://
career-advice.monster.com/job-interview/interview
-preparation/do-your-homework-before-interview/article.aspx

11 Gold, T. (2010, October 28). How social media can get you a
job. *Right Source Marketing*. Retrieved November 21, 2013,
from http://www.marketingtrenches.com/marketing-careers/
how-social-media-can-get-you-a-job

12 Bowles, L. (n.d.). How to research a company for a job
search. *eHow*. Retrieved November 21, 2013, from http://
www.ehow.com/how_7669153_research-company-job-search
.html; and Gold, How social media can get you a job.

13 Ryan, L. (2006, February 9). Job-seekers: Prepare your stories.
Ezine Articles. Retrieved November 21, 2013, from http://
ezinearticles.com/?Job-Seekers:-Prepare-Your-Stories
&id=142327

14 Haefner, R. (2009, October 6). More employers screening can-
didates via social networking sites. *CareerBuilder*. Retrieved
November 21, 2013, from http://www.careerbuilder.com/
Article/CB-1337-Getting-Hired-More-Employers-Screening
-Candidates-via-Social-Networking-Sites

15 Guiseppi, M. (2010, April 30). Microsoft study finds online
reputation management not optional. *Executive Career
Brand*. Retrieved November 21, 2013, from http://
executivecareerbrand.com/microsoft-study-finds-online
-reputation-management-not-optional

16 Haefner, More employers screening candidates.

17 Finder, A. (2006, June 11). For some, online persona under-
mines a résumé. *The New York Times*. Retrieved November 21,
2013, from http://www.nytimes.com/2006/06/11/us/11recruit
.html?pagewanted=all&_r=0

18 Haefner, More employers screening candidates.

19 Krannich, C. R., & Krannich, R. L. (1994). *Dynamite
answers to interview questions*. Manassas Park, VA: Impact
Publications, p. 46.

20 Wright, D. (2002, August/September). Tell stories, get hired.
OfficePro, 64(6), 32–33. Retrieved November 29, 2013, from
Business Source Premier (EBSCO).

21 Lublin, J. (2008, February 5). Notes to interviewers should go
beyond a simple thank you. *The Wall Street Journal*, p. B1.
Retrieved November 29, 2013, from ProQuest database.

22 Enelow quoted in Lublin, Notes to interviewers, p. B1.

23 Needleman, S. E. (2006, February 7). Be prepared when
opportunity calls. *The Wall Street Journal*, p. B4.

24 Green, A. (2010, December 27). How to follow up after
applying for a job. *U.S. News & World Report*. Retrieved
November 29, 2013, from http://money.usnews.com/money/
blogs/outside-voices-careers/2010/12/27/how-to-follow
-up-after-applying-for-a-job

25 Korkki, P. (2009, August 25). No response after an interview?
What to do. *The New York Times*. Retrieved November 29,
2013, from http://www.nytimes.com/2009/08/23/jobs/
25searchweb.html?_r=0

26 Based in part on Weiss, T. (2006, November 9). Are parents
killing their kids' careers? *Forbes*. Retrieved from http://www
.forbes.com/2006/11/08/leadership-careers-jobs-lead-careers
-cx_tw_1109kids.html

A

Abbreviations, 23
  errors/corrections, 453
  provinces, 450f
  punctuation, 507
  states, 450f
  territories, 450f
Abstract, 281, 286f
Abstract noun, 72, 479
Academic journals, 264
accede, exceed, 535
accept, except, 535
Accommodation/smoothing
  (conflict response), 314
Accounting firms, 44
Acronym, 23
Action-specific verbs, 23
Action verbs, 387
Active listening, 13
Active voice, 71, 466–467,
  487, 488
Adaptive techniques, 41
Adjective, 72, 492–495
Adjustment message, 136–141
  apologizing, 140
  body, 140
  closing, 140–141
  examples, 139f
  goals, 138
  negative words, 140
  opening, 138–140
  rebuilding customer confidence, 140
  revealing good news, 138
  writing plan, 138
Adler, Nancy, 24
Adobe Acrobat, 77
Adobe's Portable Document Format
  (PDF), 5–6, 77, 78f, 228, 397
Adverb, 66, 492–495
adverse, averse, 535
advice, advise, 535
affect, effect, 535
Age-biased language, 46
Agreement
  pronoun-antecedent, 483–484
  subject-verb, 486–487
AIDA, 171
  action, 171–172
  attention, 169–170
  desire, 171
  interest, 170–171
Airline industry, 136
AirLinx Partners, 261
all ready, already, 535
all right, alright, 535
altar, alter, 535
Ambiguous wording, 23
American Psychological Association
  (APA). *See* APA style
American spelling *vs.* Canadian
  spelling, 7
Analogies, 346
Analytical report, 224, 225f
Anecdotes, 346
Angry e-mails, 87
Antecedent, 483–484
Anticipating the audience, 39
APA style, 456–458

  electronic references, 458
  in-text citation, 457–458
  justification/recommendation
    report, 238–239f
  References List, 458, 459f
  when used, 456
Apology/apologizing
  adjustment letter, 140
  bad-news message, 194, 195
  poor/improved apology, 195
Apology culture, 140
Apostrophe, 514–515
Appearance
  business documents, 15
  employment interview, 418
  oral presentation, 342f
  people, 16
  professionalism, 309f
Appendixes, 283–284
Application form, 430–431
Application or résumé follow-up
  message, 431
Appositive, 482, 505
appraise, apprise, 535
Appreciation letter, 144–146
ascent, assent, 535
Association of Proposal Management
  Professionals, 262
Association web sites, 382
assure, ensure, insure, 535
Attention-grabbing techniques, 162,
  258, 342f
Attention line, 445
Attentive listening, 24
Audacity, 105
Audience
  blog, 108
  direct strategy, 59f, 225f
  indirect strategy, 59f, 225f
  oral presentations, 340, 341f, 351,
    358, 360
  profiling, 39–41
  report organization, 225f
  secondary, 41
Audience benefits, 41
Audience-focused message, 43
Audience response systems, 360
Audience types, 341f
Audioconferencing, 9f
Avoidance/withdrawal (conflict
  response), 314
Axtell, Roger, 22

B

Baby boomers, 23
BackCheck, 395
Backdraft Corporation, 4
Bad-news messages. *See* Negative
  writing situations
Bar chart, 276–277, 277f, 354f
Barriers to listening, 12
BBY, Best Buy Community, 107
Bcc, 443
Beckstead, Desmond, 5
Beehive, 101
Behavioural interview questions,
  425–426

Bell, Catherine, 16
Best- and worst-case scenarios, 346
Best Buy, 101, 107
Best case/worst case (organizational
  pattern), 273f
Betcherman, Gordon, 378
Bias, 24
Bias-free language, 45–46
Bibliography (References), 458, 459f
Bing, 265
Biometric thumbprint scanning, 8f
Bishop, Buzz, 106
Black holes, 380
BlackBerry, 8f, 265
"Blackberry etiquette has yet to be
  defined" (Baum), 221
Blackboard, 348
Bloch, Michael, 100
Block style letter, 446f, 448
Blog, 9f, 38f, 105–109
  audience, 108
  blogrolling, 108
  crisis communication, 107
  customer relations, 107
  defined, 105
  employment-related, 410
  inappropriate topics, 108
  internal communication and
    recruiting, 108
  market research, 108
  marketing tool, 176
  McCain Foods (*The All Good Blog*),
    107f
  monitor traffic to your site,
    108–109
  online communities, 108
  public relations, 107
  search engines/keywords, 108
  secondary research, 267
  tips/pointers, 108–109
Bloglines, 103
Blogrolling, 108
Blue Shirt Nation, 101
Body (of message)
  adjustment message, 140
  business letters, 113, 447
  complaint or claim message, 135
  cover letter, 399–402
  e-mail, 92
  information response, 132
  memo, 112
  recommendation message, 142
  report, 281–282
Body language, 14. *See also*
  Nonverbal communication
Boeing, 105
Booher, Dianne, 340, 361
Bookmarks, 267
Books, 264
"Boom in housing for executives on
  move" (Wong), 248
Bouton, Daniel, 196
BP Deepwater Horizon oil
  explosion, 60
Brackets, 519
Brainstorming, 58
Broad generalizations, 314
BT Group, 101, 109

*Buff and Polish: A Practical Guide
  to Enhance Your Professional
  Image and Communication Style*
  (Volin), 307
Buffer, 193
Buhler, Patricia M., 307
Bulleted list, 73
Business and dining etiquette, 307, 337
Business letters, 90, 444–451
  attention line, 445
  block style, 446f, 448
  body, 113, 447
  closing salutation and signature, 113
  collection letter, 190–191, 192f
  complimentary close, 446f, 447
  confidentiality, 113
  copy notation, 448
  date and address, 113, 445
  delivery notations, 445
  enclosure notation, 447
  envelope, 449–451
  examples, 446f
  formality, 113
  formatting, 113, 114f
  inside address, 445, 446f
  letter proposal, 258–261
  letter report, 225, 226–227f
  letterhead, 113, 445
  modified block style, 446f, 448
  open/closed punctuation, 446f
  permanent record, 112
  persuasiveness, 113
  plain-paper return address, 448
  reference initials, 447
  salutation, 446f, 447
  sample letter, 114f
  second-page heading, 448
  sensitivity, 113
  signature block, 446f, 447
  subject and reference lines, 446f, 447
  template, 113
  when used, 38f
Business meetings, 325–329
  agenda, 325–326, 326f
  are they necessary?, 325
  closing, 328
  conflict, 327
  dysfunctional group members,
    327–328
  following up, 328, 329
  ground rules, 326
  informal minutes, 329f
  minutes, 233, 245, 245f, 329f
  monopolizers, 328
  non-talkers, 328
  "parking lot" list, 327
  Robert's Rules, 326
  selecting participants, 325
  wikis, 110
Business presentations, 339–372
  attention-grabbing techniques, 342f
  audience, 340, 341f, 351, 358, 360
  audience types, 341f

conclusion, 345
cue-card method, 360–361, 361f
delivery method, 360–361
digressions, 363
eye contact, 362
imagery, 346
nonverbal messages, 347
organization, 341, 343–344
outline, 343f
post-presentation activities, 363
preparation, 361–362
previewing, 347
purpose, 340
question-and-answer period, 363
questions to ask, 340
slide presentation. See Slide presentation
stage fright, 361, 362f
summarizing, 347, 363
switching directions, 347
team presentations, 371
transitional expressions, 347
verbal signposts, 346–347
verbal static (fillers), 362
visual aids, 347–349
Business reports. See Report writing
Business trends, 4–5
Business writing, 34–85
active/passive voice, 71
audience benefits, 41
bias-free language, 45–46
communication channels, 37–39
concise wording, 64–68
conversational, professional tone, 43–44
courteous language, 45
direct/indirect pattern, 59–61
first draft, 63–64
forms. See Forms of business writing
goals, 34–35
plain language and familiar words, 47
positive language, 44–45
precise, vigorous words, 47–49
profiling the audience, 39–41
proofreading, 75–78
purpose, 36–37
readability, 71–75
research, 56–58
scheduling the writing process, 35–36, 35f
sentence structure. See Sentence
sprint writing, 63
steps in writing process, 35–36, 35f
style. See Style in writing
tone, 41
word choice, 68–72
"you" view, 42–43

C

Callebaut, Vincent, 262
Canadian spelling vs. American spelling, 7
Canadian Workplace in Transition, The (Betcherman), 378
capital, capitol, 535
Capitalization, 523–529
academic courses and degrees, 524
beginning words, 526–527
celestial bodies, 527
departments, divisions, committees, 526
ethnic references, 527
geographic locations, 524
governmental terms, 526
literary titles, 526
numbered and lettered items, 525
organization names, 524
personal and business titles, 524–525

points of the compass, 525–526
product names, 526
proper adjectives, 524
proper nouns, 523–524
seasons, 527
Career advisory firms, 407
Career blogs, 410
Career counsellors, 377
Career fairs, 383
Cc, 443
Celebrity endorsements, 186
"Cell yell," 319
Cellphones and smartphones, 106, 318–319
basic guidelines, 319f
e-cruising, 318
location, 318
professionalism, 17f
ringtone, 319f
time, 319
use of, during meetings, presentations, etc., 221–222, 318, 319f
volume, 319
wireless-free quiet zones, 319f
cereal, serial, 535
CERN, 263
Changing world of work, 4–5
Channel noise, 10
Channels of communication, 37–39
Charity Village, 381, 381f
Charts. See Graphics
Chatr, 186
China, 22
Chismar, Douglas, 308
Chiu, Kevin, 39
Chronological order, 272, 273f
Chronological résumé, 383, 390f
Circle chart, 278. See also Pie chart
Citations, 271
documentation. See also Documenting your sources
electronic references. See Electronic references, citing
in-text, 271, 457–458, 458–460
cite, site, sight, 535
Civility, 307, 337
Claim letter. See Complaint or claim message
Claim refusal, 201–203
Classified job ads, 383
Cliché, 69–70
Clip art, 7
Clock time, 530
Closing
adjustment message, 140–141
complaint or claim message, 135–136
cover letter, 402
e-mail, 93, 444
information response, 132
meetings, 328
memo, 112
negative writing situations, 198
recommendation message, 142
Cloud computing, 87, 228
coarse, course, 535
Coca-Cola, 102f, 174
Collaboration/problem solving (conflict response), 315
Collaboration software, 302
Collaboration technologies, 9f
Collaborative writing, 7
Collective noun, 480, 487
Collectivism, 20
Colon, 511–512
Column chart, 354f. See also Bar chart
Combination résumé, 384, 392f

Comma, 500–510
abbreviations, 507
addresses, 501
appended questions, 507
appositives, 505
clarity, 507
contrasting statements, 507
dates, 501
degrees, 507
dependent clauses, 503–504
direct address, 500
essential/nonessential clauses, 504
geographical items, 501
independent clauses, 503
introductory clauses, 504
omitted words, 507
overuse, 508
parenthetical expressions, 500–501
phrases, 504
quotations, 507
series, 500
terminal clauses, 504
two or adjectives, 504–505
Comma splice, 63
Common-gender pronoun, 483
Common ground, 24–25, 315
Common noun, 479, 523–524
Communicating in person, 306–338
appropriate topics, 312–313
conflict, 315–316
criticism, 313–315
face-to-face communication, 310–316
listening, 313
meetings, 325–329
names and titles, 312
negative remarks, 313
praise, 313
smartphones, 318–319
teamwork, 321–324
telephone, 316–318
voice mail, 319–321
voice quality, 310–312
Communication
defined, 10
face-to-face. See Communicating in person
intercultural, 21–23
nonverbal. See Nonverbal communication
process, 10–11, 10f
seeking employment. See Job search
synchronous, 10
teams, 323–324
Communication channels, 37–39
Communication coaches, 4
Communication process, 10–11, 10f
Communication style, 20
Communication technologies, 4–5, 8f
Communication technology in the news
angry e-mails, 87
cellphone use during meetings, presentations, etc., 221–222
finding the right words in awkward situations, 304–305
online resume, 374–375
texting lingo, 2
Web 2.0, 32–33
Company intranet, 8f
Company records, 229
Comparative degree (adjective/adverb), 493
Compare/contrast (organizational pattern), 273f
Competition/forcing (conflict response), 314
Complaint or claim message, 133–136
body, 135
closing, 135–136

complex claim/complaint, 164–165, 166f
examples, 137f
opening, 135
refusing the claim, 201–203
resolving the problem and following up, 203–204, 204f
writing plan, 135
Complaints.com, 203
complement, compliment, 535
Complex fractions, 532
Complex sentence, 61–62
Complimentary close, 446f, 447
Compound-complex sentence, 62
Compound modifier, 493–494
Compound sentence, 61
Compromise (conflict response), 314
Concise wording, 64–68
e-mail, 96
fillers, 66
long lead-ins, 65
needless adverbs, 66
outdated expressions, 65–66
parallelism, 68
redundant words, 67
repetitious words, 66–67
wordy expressions, 64–65
Concrete noun, 72, 479
Condolence message, 147
Conference calling, 9f
Conflict
teams, 323
workplace, 315–316
Conformity, 24
Confusing words, 535–536
Congratulatory note, 144, 146
Conjunction, 496–497
Conjunctive adverb, 510
connect.MetLife, 101
conscience, conscious, 535
Consumer Reports, 264
Consumers Union, 264
Content notes, 455
Contraction, 482
Convention (organizational pattern), 273f
Conversational, professional tone, 43–44
Coordinate conjunction, 496
Copy notation, 448
Corporate social responsibility (CSR), 159
Corporate twitter feed, 106f
Corporation/organization web sites, 382
Correction abbreviations, 453
council, counsel, 535
Courteous language, 45
Courtesy and respect, 309f
Cover letter, 398–403
body, 399–402
closing, 402
e-mail, sending letter by, 402, 403f
examples, 400f, 401f
"I" dominance, 402
opening, 398–399
purposes, 398
credible, creditable, 535
Criticism, 313–315
Cross-cultural communication. See Intercultural communication
Cue-card method, 360–361, 361f
Cultsock: Communication, Culture, Media (www.cultsock.org), 10
Cultural differences. See also Intercultural communication
bad-news messages, 219
Canadians vs. Americans, 18
communication style, 20
context, 19–20, 19f

e-mail, 98
formality, 20
gestures, 14
individualism *vs.* collectivism, 20
time orientation, 20–21
Cultural synergy, 25
Customer complaint. *See* Complaint or claim message
Customer service representatives, 38

D

Daily newspapers, 264
Daimler AG, 169
Dangling modifier, 469
Dark matter, 263
Dash, 517–518
Dates, 501, 530
De-emphasizing ideas, 466
Decimals, 532
Decoding, 10, 16
Deepwater Horizon oil explosion, 60
Deference, 20
Deficient communication skills, 4
delicious, 103
Dell Computer, 108
Demographics, 23
Dependent clause, 61–62, 503–504
desert, dessert, 535
Desk rage, 306
Desktop computers, 87
device, devise, 535
Diagram Gallery (PowerPoint), 359
Diagrams, 280
Digg, 103
Digital dirt, 416–417
Digital portfolio, 407
Digital proofing, 75–76, 77f
Digsby, 98
Diligence and collegiality, 309f
"Dimensions of Occupational Changes in Canada's Knowledge Economy, 1971–1996" (Beckstead/Vinodrai), 5
Direct-mail sales letter, 168, 172, 173f. *See also* Sales and promotional messages
Direct opening, 59, 92
Direct pattern, 59–60
    advantages, 60
    audience, 59f, 225f
    collection letter, 192f
    feasibility report, 241
    justification/recommendation report, 238–239f
    negative message, 191f
    reports, 224, 225f, 272
    routine writing situations, 128
Direct quotation, 518
Direct-strategy collection letter, 192f
Direct-strategy negative message, 191f
Disability-biased language, 46
Disappointed customer, 203–204. *See* Complaint or claim message
disburse, disperse, 535
Discussion groups, 410
Disney, 109
"Distribute and print" environment, 8f
Diverse workforce, 23–25
Documenting your sources, 269–272, 455–464
    APA style, 238–239f, 456–458
    common knowledge, matters of, 270
    electronic sources. *See* Electronic references, citing
    endnotes, 455–456, 457f
    footnotes, 455
    how to document, 271
    MLA. *See* MLA style
    parenthetic method, 456

purpose of documentation, 270
References List, 458, 459f
source notes/content notes, 455
what has to be documented?, 270
Works Cited. *See* Works Cited
Doostang, 382
Dr. Guffey's Guide to Business Etiquette and Workplace Manners, 337
Drawing, 280
Dual appeal, 170

E

E-cruising, 318
E-mail, 90–98, 443–444
    all caps, 97
    Bcc, 443
    best practices, 93–96
    body, 92
    Cc, 443
    channel of choice, 38
    claim letter, 136, 137f
    closing, 93, 444
    components, 90–91
    composing offline, 96
    conciseness, 96
    correctness/accuracy, 96
    cover note with letter attachment, 226f
    cover note with memo attachment, 167f, 235f
    cover note with minutes attached, 329f
    cover note with résumé attached, 403f
    cultural differences, 98
    dangers, 94–96
    essential/critically important, 127
    example (effective e-mail), 444f
    formatting, 95f, 444
    graphic highlighting, 92
    humour/sarcasm, 97
    memos as e-mail attachments, 112, 167f, 235f
    netiquette, 97
    opening, 92
    personal use, 97, 125
    printing, 97
    professionalism, 17f
    promotional, 173–174, 175f
    reading and replying, 97
    reports, 228
    requesting information, 130f
    responding to customer complaint, 204f
    responding to customer request, 131f
    salutation, 91, 443
    sample, 94f
    sharing documents and information, 7, 128f
    skim value, 92
    spam, 97
    subject line, 91, 96, 443
    thank-you message, 145f, 146
    tips/pointers, 96, 97–98
    to line, 443
    tone, 48f, 87, 96
    top-of-screen test, 96
    transmittal (report), 281
    when used, 38f, 90
E-mail address, 17f, 96
E-portfolio, 407
effect, affect, 535
Electronic goodwill message, 147
Electronic mentoring, 409
Electronic messages, 89–90, 90–110
    blog, 90, 105–109
    e-mail. *See* E-mail
    IM. *See* Instant messaging (IM)

podcast, 89–90, 104–105
social media, 89, 101–103
text messaging (texting), 89, 98–101
wiki, 90, 109–110
Electronic presentations, 8f. *See also* Business presentations
Electronic references, citing, 271–272
    APA style, 458
    Works Cited, 462–463
Electronic report, 225
elicit, illicit, 535
Emily Post Institute, 147
Emotional appeal, 170
Empathy, 22, 41
Emphasis
    voice, 311
    writing, 465–466
Employability skills, 17
Employee bad news, 204–208
    announcing negative employee news, 207, 208f
    deliver the news personally, 205
    refusing workplace request, 206–207, 206f
    types of bad news, 204–205
    writing plan, 205
Employee communications, 39
Employee engagement, 39
Employee retention, 39
Employment advertisements, 310, 380, 383
Employment interview, 411–442
    actions to avoid, 422f
    answer questions confidently, 421–422
    asking your own questions, 427
    behavioural questions, 425–426
    challenging questions, 424
    "cheat sheet," 436
    concluding the interview, 427–428
    contact your references, 428–430
    "empty" words, 420
    follow-up after the interview, 430
    greeting the interviewer, 418–419
    hiring/placement interview, 412–414
    illegal and inappropriate questions, 426–427
    before the interview. *See* Pre-job interview activities
    kinds of interviews, 412–414
    nervousness/fear, 419
    nonverbal messages, 419–420
    post-interview activities, 428–430
    purposes, 412
    put yourself in employer's shoes, 420, 421f
    questions about experience/ accomplishments, 423
    questions about the future, 423–424
    questions to gauge your interest, 423
    questions to get acquainted, 422–423
    screening interview, 412
    situational questions, 424–425
    thank-you message to interviewer, 428, 429f
    virtual interview, 437, 438
Employment recommendation, 141–143
Employment-related blogs, 410
Employment search. *See* Job search
Employment web sites, 378, 380–382
"Empty" words, 420
Enbridge pipe rupture (Michigan), 60
Enclosure notation, 447
Encoding, 10
Endnote method, 282, 455–456, 457f
Endnotes, 540–546
Enelow, Wendy, 385

Enhanced job titles, 395
Enron, 308
ensure, assure, insure, 535
Enterprise Rent-A-Car, 101
envelop, envelope, 535
Envelope
    examples, 449f
    folding, 451
    mailing address, 449–450
    OCRs, 449
    Postal Service style, 449
    province/state abbreviations, 450f
    return address, 449
ePodcast Creator, 105
Essential clause, 504
Ethics, 307–308
    indirect pattern, 209
    plagiarism, 6, 7, 10, 267–269
    professionalism, 309f
    résumé, 395–396
    teams, 324, 324f
Ethnically biased language, 46
Ethnocentrism, 21
Evaluating Web sites, 255
every day, everyday, 535
Examples, 346
exceed, accede, 535
Excel, 279
except, accept, 535
Exclamation point, 517
Executive summary, 281, 286f
Experimentation, 57, 269
Explicit refusal, 197
Express Publishing, 186
Eye contact, 14, 16, 342f, 362
Eye messages, 22

F

Face-to-face communication, 38f, 310–316
Face-to-face group meeting, 38f. *See also* Business meetings
Facebook, 101, 102f, 174–176, 266, 382, 415
Facial expression, 14, 347
Faked attention, 12
Familiar words, 47
farther, further, 535
Favour
    refusing the request, 199–201
    requesting a favour, 162–164
    thank-you note, 145f, 146
Favourites, 267
Fax/fax cover sheet, 38f, 451–452, 452f
Feasibility report, 233, 238–240, 241f
Feedback
    communication process, 10
    diverse workplace, 24
    intercultural communication, 22
    learning to communicate, 3
    listening, 13
Feldman, Debra, 382
50 Cent, 186
Fight-or-flight response, 361f
Fillers, 66
"Finding the right words in awkward situations" (Harder), 304
Firefox, 265
First draft, 63–64
First-hand information, 57
First impression, 414–415
First-level heading, 275f
Flat, monotone voices, 311
Flattened management hierarchy, 5, 378
Flipchart, 348–349, 348f
Flow chart, 279, 279f
Footnotes, 282, 455
Forbes, Malcolm, 201

Formal proposal, 261–262
Formal report, 262–292. *See also* Report writing
appendixes, 283–284
background, 282, 287–288f
characteristics, 262
conclusions and recommendations, 282, 291f
defined, 262
definition of project, 263
documentation. *See* Documenting your sources
endnotes, 282
executive summary, 281, 286f
findings, 282, 288–291f
footnotes, 282
graphics. *See* Graphics
headings, 273–274, 275f
informal report, compared, 231f
introduction, 281–282, 287–288f
letter of transmittal, 281, 284f
list of figures, 281, 285f
organizational strategies, 272–273, 273f
outline, 273, 274f
plagiarism, 269–271
PowerPoint slides, 285
prefatory parts, 280–281
proposal, compared, 262
research, 264–269. *See also* Research
sample report, 283–292f
statement of purpose, 263
table of contents, 281, 285f
title page, 281, 283f
Works Cited, 282–283, 292f
Formality, 20
formally, formerly, 535
Forms of business writing, 86–302
bad news. *See* Negative writing situations
blog, 90, 105–109
e-mail. *See* E-mail
IM. *See* Instant messaging (IM)
letters. *See* Business letters
memo. *See* Memo
persuasive writing. *See* Persuasive writing situations
podcast, 89–90, 104–105
reports. *See* Report writing
routine writing situations. *See* Routine writing situations
social media. *See* Social media
text messaging (texting), 89, 98–101
wiki, 90, 109–110
Forum Nokia, 109
Four Seasons Hotels and Resorts, 230
Foursquare, 103
Fractions, 532
Fragments, 62–63
Free trial or sample, 171
Frequently misspelled words, 536–537
"Freshen up that online resume with original keywords" (Lee), 374
Frontloading, 60. *See also* Direct pattern
Functional headings, 232
Functional résumé, 384, 391f
further, farther, 535
Fused sentence, 63
Future perfect tense, 488
Future tense, 488

G

G/M Handbook. *See* Grammar/ mechanics handbook
Gabcast, 105
Galt, Virginia, 23
Gender-biased language, 46

Gender-neutral language, 46
General Electric, 107
General language, 70, 72
Generation Y, 44
Geographical or spatial arrangement, 272–273, 273f
George Brown College Library web site, 265
Gerund, 515
Gestures, 14
GigaSpaces, 176
Global competition, 5
Globe and Mail, 416
Goodwill message, 144–147
condolence note, 147
electronic channels, 147
five Ss, 144
replying to, 146, 147
sympathy message, 147
thank-you note, 144–146
Google, 266
Google Docs, 302
Google Drive, 302
Google Groups, 410
Google Images, 7, 359
Google Reader, 103
Google Scholar, 230
Google search engine, 6, 230, 265
Google Talk, 98
GoToMeeting, 9f
Grammar checkers, 7
Grammar/mechanics handbook, 474–537
capitalization. *See* Capitalization
confusing words, 535–536
diagnostic pretest, 474–478
frequently misspelled words, 536–537
parts of speech. *See* Parts of speech
profile, 478
punctuation. *See* Punctuation
Grandstanding, 12
Granovetter, Mark, 382
Graphics, 7, 274–280. *See also* Visual aids
bar chart, 276–277, 277f
diagrams, 280
drawing, 280
flow chart, 279, 279f
general principles, 274
illustrations, 280
line chart, 277–278, 278f
maps, 280
organizational chart, 279, 280f
overview, 276f
photographs, 280
pie chart, 278–279, 278f, 290f
slide presentation, 354, 354f, 359
software, 279–280
table, 275–276, 276f, 290f
Grasso, Davide, 174
grate, great, 535
Group interview, 413
Grouped bar chart, 277f
Groupthink, 24

H

Hall, Edward T., 15, 19
Handheld wireless devices, 8f
Handouts, 348f, 349, 363
Hard-copy letter. *See* Business letters
Hard proofreading, 75, 76f, 77f
Hard skills, 307
Hcareers, 382
Headings
clarity/conciseness, 232
consistency, 232
functional, 232
major, 273–274, 275f

quotation marks, 233
readability, 73
reports, 232–233, 273–274, 275f
second-level, 274, 275f
second-page, 448
talking, 232
third-level, 274, 275f
tips/pointers, 232–233
Helicopter parents, 438–439
Hewlett-Packard (HP), 176, 261, 262, 266, 412
Hidden job market, 409–410
Hidden keywords, 396
High-context cultures, 19–20, 19f
Hiring/placement interview, 412–414
hole, whole, 535
Horizontal bar chart, 277f
Hostile claim e-mail, 136, 137f
"How to Use a Company Twitter Account" (Bishop), 106
Hyundai Motors, 322

I

"I" view, 42
IBM, 18, 37, 101, 109, 262, 266
Idea generation, 57–58
Ideas in Action, 108
IdeaStorm, 108
Idioms, 22, 23, 27
illicit, elicit, 535
Illustrations, 280
IM. *See* Instant messaging (IM)
I'm happy, 43
IM spam (spim), 100
Imagery, 346
Imperative mood, 133, 488
Implied refusal, 197
imply, infer, 535
Importance (organizational pattern), 273f
Imprecise, dull wording, 49
Imprecise writing, 468
In-text citation, 271
APA style, 457–458
MLA style, 458–460
Indefinite pronoun, 487
Independent clause, 61, 503, 510–511
Index of Occupational Titles, 379
India, 18
Indicative mood, 133, 488
Indirect opening, 59, 92
Indirect pattern, 60–61
advantages, 61
audience, 59f, 225f
bad-news messages, 191–193, 209
ethics, 209
justification/recommendation report, 237–238
negative message, 191–193, 209
persuasive writing, 160–162
reports, 225, 225f, 272
Indirect persuasion strategy, 160–162
Indirect-strategy negative message, 191–193, 209
Individualism, 20
infer, imply, 535
Informal proposal, 258–261
attention-grabbing opening, 258
authorization, 261
background, 258
budget, 260–261
introduction, 258
plan, 258–259
sample proposal, 259–260f
staffing, 259–260
Informal report. *See also* Report writing
contractions, 231
feasibility report, 238–240, 241f
first-person pronouns, 231
formal report, compared, 231f

information report, 224, 233–234, 235f
justification/recommendation report, 237–238, 238–239f
letter report, 225, 226–227f
minutes of meetings, 245, 245f
overview, 231f
progress report, 234–237
summary report, 240–244
Informal research, 57–58
Information report, 224, 233–234, 235f
Information request, 129–130
Information response, 130–132
body, 132
closing, 132
e-mail response, 131f
opening, 132
subject line, 131
writing plan, 131
Information sources. *See* Research
Insert Command, 76, 84
Inside address, 445, 446f
Instagram, 89
Instant messaging (IM), 98–101
best practices, 100–101
importance, 38
McLuhan's "field," 10
online exchange, 37
presence functionality, 100
pros/cons, 100
sample, 99f
sharing documents and information, 7
SMS, 98, 100
texting speak, 70
when used, 38f
Instant Messenger, 98
Instruction message, 132–133, 134f
insure, assure, ensure, 535
Interactive advertising, 172
Intercultural communication. *See also* Cultural differences
ethnocentrism, 21
minimizing oral miscommunication, 22
minimizing written miscommunication, 22–23
stereotype, 21
tolerance, 21–22
Interjection, 479
Internal persuasive messages, 165–168
International networking sites, 382
Internet
browsers, 266
case sensitivity, 266
defined, 265
digital dirt, 416–417
evaluating Web sites, 255
online job search, 380–382
online networking, 409–410
search tips and techniques, 266–267
search tools, 266
slide presentation, 360
URL, 266
Internet access, 265
Internet Explorer, 265
Interoffice memos. *See* Memo
Interpersonal bad news, 204
Interview
finding career information, 379–380
finding information for reports, 268–269
job. *See* Employment interview
primary research, 268–269
Interview "cheat sheet," 436
Intimate zone, 15f
Intranet, 8f
Introductory clause, 504

iPhone, 8f, 99f, 265
iResponse App, 360
iRipoff.com, 203
Irregular verb, 488–489
Irving Oil, 159
is when, is where, 496–497
it's, 482
iTunes U, 104

J

Jargon, 23, 47, 68–69
Jing, 360
Job acceptance message, 432
Job ads, 310, 380, 383
Job interview. *See* Employment interview
"Job Interview Funny" (YouTube), 439
Job rejection message, 432
Job search, 373–442
    application form, 430–431
    application or résumé follow-up message, 431
    changing nature of jobs, 378
    cover letter, 398–403
    employment advertisements, 310
    finding career information, 378–380
    hidden job market, 409–410
    interests, 377
    job acceptance message, 432
    job interview. *See* Employment interview
    job rejection message, 432
    knowing what employers want, 308–310
    networking, 409–410
    online search, 380–382
    overview, 377f
    parental involvement, 438–439
    professionalism. *See* Professionalism/professional behaviour
    qualifications, 377–378
    read newspaper regularly, 416
    rejection follow-up message, 431–432
    resignation letter, 433
    résumé. *See* Résumé
    salary negotiation, 441–442
    traditional search techniques, 382–383
Jobs, Steve, 357
Journal of Business Communication, 265
Journalism pattern (organizational pattern), 273f
Judge, Barry, 107
Justification/recommendation report, 233, 237–238, 238–239f

K

Kelley, Robert, 360
Kent-Snowsell, Paul, 125
Key competencies, 17
Knowledge occupations, 5
Kruse, Carol, 174

L

Label the main idea, 466
Language, 44–49. *See also* Business writing; Word choice
Large Hadron Collider, 263
Lead-ins, 65
lean, lien, 535
Leaner medium, 37
Legal terminology, 43
Lendvai, Robert, 125
Letter. *See* Business letters

Letter of appreciation, 144–146
Letter of recommendation, 141–143
Letter of transmittal, 281, 284f
Letter proposal, 258–261
Letter report, 225, 226–227f
Letterhead, 445
LexisNexis, 464
liable, libel, 535
Library, 264, 265, 379
lien, lean, 535
Lilipad cities, 262
Line chart, 277–278, 278f
LinkedIn, 89, 382, 390–394, 410
Linking verb, 493
Lipset, Seymour Martin, 20
Listed items, 511
Listening, 313
    active, 13
    barriers, 12
    conflict, 315
    criticism, 314
    cross-cultural communication, 22
    diverse workforce, 24
Live chat, 38, 40f
Live Nation, 175f
LiveEnt, 308
Long lead-ins, 65
loose, lose, 535
Low-context cultures, 19, 19f
Lowe's Home Improvement, 412

M

Mailing lists, 410
Major heading, 273–274, 275f
Major publications, 519
Manuscript format, 228. *See also* Formal report
Maps, 280
Marriott Hotel, 20
McCain Foods, 107f, 266
McDonald's, 101
McLuhan, Marshall, 10
McLuhan's "field," 10
Media richness, 37
MediaWiki, 302
Meeting. *See* Business meetings
Meeting agenda, 325–326, 326f
Memo, 90. *See also* Memo report
    body, 112
    closing, 112
    e-mail attachment, as, 112, 167f, 235f
    formatting, 111f
    general principles, 451
    instruction message, 134f
    opening, 112
    persuasive message, 167f
    sample, 111f
    subject line, 112
    template, 110, 451
    transmittal (report), 281, 284f
    when used, 38f
Memo report, 226–227
    e-mail attachment, as, 112, 167f, 235f
    justification/recommendation report, 238–239f
    persuasive message, 167f
    tips/pointers, 239
    trip report, 235f
Merrill Lynch, 439
merx.com, 257
Metaphors, 346
MetLife, 101
Microblogging service (Twitter), 106
Microsoft, 109, 262, 410, 412
Microsoft Internet Explorer, 265
Microsoft LiveMeeting, 9f

Microsoft templates, 6f
miner, minor, 535–536
Mini browser, 265
Minutes of meetings, 233, 245, 245f, 329f
Minutes report, 245f
Misplaced modifier, 469
Mixed construction, 468–469
MLA Handbook for Writers of Research Papers, 458
MLA style, 458–464
    in-text citation, 458–460
    reference book (MLA Handbook), 458
    when used, 456
    Works Cited. *See* Works Cited
MMS (multimedia messaging service), 98
Mobile browser, 265
Modern Language Association (MLA). *See* MLA style
Modified block style letter, 446f, 448
Modifier
    compound, 493–494
    dangling, 469
    misplaced, 469
Molloy, John T., 307
Money-back guarantee, 171
Monitoring employee use of company equipment, 125
Monitoring employee use of Internet, etc., 125
Monster, 381, 381f, 438
Monster Career Advice, 437
Monster College, 381
Morita, Akio, 325
Morrisson, Joline, 348
Multifunctional printer, 8f
Multimedia messaging service (MMS), 98
Multiple line chart, 277, 278f
Mutual goals, 25

N

Names and titles, 312
National Occupation Classification (NOC), 379
National Post, 416
Needless adverbs, 66
Negative language, 45
Negative remarks, 313
Negative writing situations, 188–219
    apologizing, 194, 195
    claim refusal, 201–203
    closing, 198
    collection letter, 190–191, 192f
    company policy, 196
    compromise/alternative, 197
    cultural differences, 219
    cushion the bad news, 197
    direct writing strategy, 189–190
    disappointed customers, 203–204
    fairness, 197
    favour refusal, 199–201
    goals, 189
    good wishes, 198
    implied refusal, 197
    indirect writing strategy, 191–193, 209
    opening, 193–194
    passive voice, 197
    positive words, 196–197
    reader benefits, 196
    reasons, 195–197
    refusing requests and claims, 198–203
    resale or sales promotion, 198
    responding to customer complaints, 203–204, 204f

sharing bad news with employees, 204–208. *See also* Employee bad news
    special offers, 198
    timeliness of response, 189
Netflix, 102f
NetNewsWire, 103
Networking, 383, 409–410
New Community Rules: Marketing on the Social Web, The (Weinberg), 176
News aggregators, 103
Nike, 174
Noise, 10
Nokia, 109
Nominative-case pronoun, 481
Nonessential clause, 504
Nonverbal communication, 13–17
    appearance, 15–16
    employment interview, 419–420
    eye contact, 14
    facial expression, 14
    gestures, 14
    oral presentations, 347
    posture, 14
    space, 15
    territory, 15, 15f
    time, 15
    tips/hints, 16–17
Nonverbal distractions, 12
Note taking, 13
Notes (endnotes), 540–546
Noun, 72, 479–481
Noun-centred sentence, 71
Noun plurals, 479–480
Number style, 530–534
    addresses, 530–531
    ages, 532
    clock time, 530
    consecutive numbers, 531
    dates, 530
    decimals, 532
    fractions, 532
    general rules, 530
    money, 530
    percentages, 532
    periods of time, 531
    quick reference chart, 533
    related numbers, 531
    round numbers, 532
    telephone numbers, 531
    weights and measurements, 532
Numbered list, 73

O

Object of the preposition, 483
Objective-case pronoun, 481
Objectivity, 231–232
Observation, as source of information, 229, 269
"Obvious" words, 47
Occupational Outlook Handbook, 379
Office Depot, 439
Office of the Privacy Commissioner of Canada, 126
Office workspace, 8f
One-on-one interview, 413
O'Neill, Nick, 102
123people.com, 417, 435
Online advertising, 172–176
online communities, 108
Online interview, 413–414
Online job sites, 378, 380–382
Online networking, 409–410
Online report, 228
Online research databases, 265
Open mindedness, 13
Open office, 8f
Open punctuation, 446f

Opening
   adjustment message, 138–140
   cover letter, 398–399
   direct, 59, 92
   e-mail, 92
   indirect, 59, 92
   informal proposal, 258
   information response, 132
   memo, 112
   negative writing situations, 193–194
   persuasive writing situations, 161
   recommendation message, 141–142
Oral presentations. See Business presentations
Organizational bad news, 204–205
Organizational chart, 279, 280f
Organizational strategies (report), 272–273, 273f
Outdated expressions, 65–66
Outline
   formal report, 273, 274f
   oral presentations, 343f
   writing, 58, 58f, 59
Ownership words, 514

P

Panel interview, 413
Paragraph, 469
Paragraph coherence, 469–470
Paragraph length, 470
Parallelism, 68, 467–468
Paraphrasing, 270–271
Parentheses, 518
Parenthetical elements, 517
Parenthetical style (citing references), 456
"Parking lot" list, 327
Participatory management, 5
Parts of speech, 478–499
   adjective, 492–495
   adverb, 492–495
   conjunction, 496–497
   interjection, 479
   noun, 479–481
   overview, 479
   preposition, 495–496
   pronoun. See Pronoun
   verb. See Verb
Passive voice, 71, 197, 466–467, 487
Past participle, 489
Past perfect tense, 488
Past tense, 488
Past-tense verb, 489
Patience, 13
patience, patients, 536
"Patients Rewarded" (Fjetland), 5–6, 77, 78f, 228, 247, 397
PDF résumé, 397
PeekYou.com, 417, 435
Peer-reviewed academic journals, 264
Percentages, 532
Performance tests, polls, or awards, 171
Period, 517
Periodicals, 264–265
personal, personnel, 536
Personal anecdotes, 346
Personal use of company equipment, 97, 125
Personal zone, 15f
Personalized statistics, 346
Persuasive claims and complaints, 164–165, 166f
Persuasive favour request, 162–164
Persuasive writing situations, 160–187
   attention-grabbing opening, 161
   build interest, 161

complex claims and complaints, 164–165, 166f
   cover letter, 160, 398–403
   favour request, 162–164
   indirect strategy, 160–162
   internal persuasive messages, 165–168
   motivate action, 162
   persuading other employees, 165
   persuading your manager, 165–168
   reduce resistance, 161–162
   sales messages. See Sales and promotional messages
PETA, 186
Phishing, 100
Phone tag, 317
Photographs, 280
Pie chart, 278–279, 278f, 290f
Pinterest, 89
Pitch, 311
Plagiarism, 6, 7, 10, 269–271
Plain language, 47
plaintiff, plaintive, 536
Plural noun, 479
Podcast, 89–90
   ease of listening, 265
   how created, 105
   how used, 104–105
   promotional tool, 176
   RSS feeds, 105
Politeness Canada, 20
Pom Wonderful, 186
Pompous/pretentious language, 47
populace, populous, 536
Portable Document Format. See PDF
Positive degree (adjective/adverb), 492–493
Positive language, 44–45
Positive self-talk, 362
Positive tone, 41
Possessive-case pronoun, 481
Possessive pronoun, 482
Post-it fax transmittal form, 452
Posture, 14, 16
Powell, Julie, 102
PowerPoint, 8f, 356f, 369f. See also Slide presentation
Praise, 313
Pre-job interview activities, 414–419
   digital dirt, 416–417
   dress/attire, 418
   expect to explain problem areas in résumé, 418
   first impression, 414–415
   gather items to bring, 418
   greeting the interviewer, 418–419
   nervousness/fear, 419
   phone techniques, 414–415
   practise answers to possible questions, 416
   prepare and practise, 416
   research the target company, 415–416
   social media, 415
   success stories, 416
   travelling to/arriving at interview, 418–419
precede, proceed, 536
precedence, precedents, 536
Precise, vigorous words, 47–49
Precise verbs, 70–71
Preposition, 495–496
Presence functionality, 100
Presence technology, 9f
Present perfect tense, 488
Present tense, 488
Presentation enhancers, 348f
Presentation software, 5, 279. See also Business presentations
Presutto, Sara, 39

Prewriting, 35–36, 36–49. See also Business writing
Prezi, 8f, 127, 128, 357f. See also Slide presentation
Primary data, 264
Primary research, 57, 229
Prime Impressions, 16
principal, principle, 536
proceed, precede, 536
Professional associations, 380, 382, 383
Professional image, 17
Professional Letter template, 6
Professional-looking documents, 5–6
Professional networking sites, 382
Professional polish, 307, 308
Professional teams, 321–324
   collaboration, 324
   communication, 323–324
   conflict, 323
   ethical responsibilities, 324, 324f
   importance, 321
   oral presentations, 371
   positive/negative behaviour, 322, 322f
   procedures, 323
   purpose, 323
   shared leadership, 324
   small size, diverse makeup, 323
   TEAM, 323
   virtual team, 322
Professionalism/professional behaviour, 17
   appearance and appeal, 309f
   business and dining etiquette, 307, 337
   civility, 307
   courtesy and respect, 309f
   diligence and collegiality, 309f
   honesty and ethics, 307–308, 309f
   knowing what employers want, 308–310
   polish, 307
   professional/unprofessional conduct, 17f, 306–310
   reliability and responsibility, 309f
   social intelligence, 307
   soft skills, 307
   tolerance and tact, 309f
Profiling the audience, 39–41
Progress report, 233, 234–237
Project team, 5
Promotional e-mail, 173–174, 175f
Promotional message. See Sales and promotional messages
Pronoun, 481–486
   antecedent, and, 483–484
   appositive, 482
   case, 481
   coherence, 470
   common-gender, 483
   contractions, contrasted, 482
   indefinite, 487
   object of the preposition, 483
   possessive, 482
   statements of comparison, 482
   who/whom, whoever/whomever, 483
Pronoun-antecedent agreement, 483–484
Pronoun repetition, 470
Pronunciation, 311, 311f
Proofreading, 75–78
   hard, 75, 76f, 77f
   Internet search, 267
   PDF files, 77, 78f
   résumé, 397
   slide presentation, 355
   soft, 75–76, 77f
   Track Changes, 76, 84
   what to watch for, 75

Proofreading marks, 76f, 454
Propaganda, 105
Proper noun, 479, 523–524
Proposal, 258–262
   formal, 261–262
   informal. See Informal proposal
   professional association, 262
   report, compared, 262
   RFP, 257
   when used, 38f
Props, 348f
ProQuest, 464
Provinces, abbreviations, 450f
Public zone, 15f
Puffed-up accomplishments, 395
Puffery, 186
Pun, 22
Punctuation, 500–523
   apostrophe, 514–515
   brackets, 519
   colon, 511–512
   comma. See Comma
   dash, 517–518
   exclamation point, 517
   parentheses, 518
   period, 517
   question mark, 517
   quotation marks, 518–519
   semicolon, 510–511
PwC, 104

Q

Question-and-answer period (oral presentations), 363
Question mark, 517
Questionnaires/inventories (survey), 229, 268
Quotation
   colon, 511
   comma, 507
   within quotation, 518
Quotation marks, 518–519
   definitions, 519
   direct quotation, 518
   headings, 233
   Internet search, 267
   punctuation, 519
   quotation within quotation, 518
   short expressions, 518–519
   titles, 519

R

Racially biased language, 46
Rational appeal, 170
Readability, 71–75
   document design, 75–76, 75f
   headings, 73–74
   numbered/bulleted list, 73
   white space, 73
Reader benefits, 41
Really simple syndication (RSS)
   automatic updates, 9f
   how RSS works, 103
   promotional tool, 176
   sharing information from blogs, podcasts, etc., 105
Recommendation message, 141–143
   body, 142
   closing, 142
   examples, 143f
   opening, 141–142
   overview, 141
   tips/pointers, 143
Recommendation report, 237–238, 238–239f
reddit, 103
Redundancy, 67

Redundant words, 67
Reebok, 27
Reference initials, 447
References List, 458, 459f
Refusal situations, 198–203
  claim refusal, 201–203
  favour refusal, 199–201
  implied/explicit refusal, 197
  refusing workplace request,
    206–207, 206f
  writing plan, 199
Rejection follow-up message,
    431–432
Reliability and responsibility, 309f
Remote network clusters, 87
Repetition of key words/ideas,
    469–470
Repetitive words, 66–67
Replies and requests
  claim letter, 133–136, 137f
  favour request, 162–164
  information request, 129–130
  replying to complaints and
    complaints, 136–141. See
    also Adjustment message
  replying to goodwill message,
    146, 147
  replying to information or action
    request, 130–132
Report delivery, 228
Report formats, 225–228
Report title page, 281, 283f
Report writing, 223–302
  analytical report, 224
  clarity/conciseness, 231
  defined the project, 228–229
  delivery method, 228
  direct strategy, 224, 225f
  electronic format, 225
  feasibility report, 238–240, 241f
  formal report. See Formal report
  functions, 224
  headings, 232–233
  indirect strategy, 225, 225f
  informal/formal writing style,
    compared, 231f
  informal report. See Informal report
  information gathering, 229–230
  information report, 223–224
  justification/recommendation
    report, 237–238, 238–239f
  letter format, 225, 226–227f
  manuscript format, 228
  memo format, 226–227. See also
    Memo report
  memo report. See Memo report
  minutes of meetings, 245, 245f
  objectivity, 231–232
  PowerPoint format, 227
  progress report, 234–237
  proofreading, 231
  proposal. See Proposal
  purpose, 223
  summary report, 240–244
  template format, 228
  when report/proposal used, 38f
Report-writing styles, 231f
Request for proposal (RFP), 257
Research, 56–58, 263–269
  experimentation, 57, 269
  formal research methods, 57
  informal, 57–58
  interview, 268–269
  observation, 269
  primary, 57, 229, 268–269
  reports, 229–230
  secondary sources, 57, 230. See
    also Secondary research
  survey, 268
Research databases, 265

Research report. See Formal report
Resignation letter, 433
Résumé, 374–375, 383–397
  action verbs, 387
  awards, honours, activities, 388
  capabilities and skills, 388
  career objectives, 385
  caution (what to avoid), 396–397
  chronological, 383, 390f
  combination, 384, 392f
  consolidated headings, 396
  education, 386
  employment history, 386–387
  functional, 384, 391f
  honesty and ethics, 395–396
  length, 384
  LinkedIn, 390–394
  main heading, 385
  objective style, 397
  PDF, 397
  personal data, 388
  professionalism, 397
  proofreading, 397
  qualifications, 385–386
  readability, 396
  references, 389, 389f
  submitting, 397
  video, 394
  wordiness, 396
  work experience, 386–387
Resume Rescue, 378
Revising, 36, 64–78. See also
    Business writing
RFP (request for proposal), 257
Richer media, 37
Ringtone, 319f
Ritz-Carlton, Moscow, 230
Robert's Rules, 326
Rogers, 186, 266
Roots, 107
Rosan, Erick, 340, 342, 344, 360
Routine writing situations, 127–159
  adjustment message, 136–141
  complaint/claim letter, 133–136,
    137t
  direct method, 128
  goodwill message, 144–147
  instruction message, 132–133, 134f
  recommendation message,
    141–143
  replying to complaints and claims,
    136–141
  replying to information or action
    request, 130–132
  requesting information or action,
    129–130
  sharing information, 129
RSS feeds. See Really simple
    syndication (RSS)
Rudman, Gary, 102
Run-on sentence, 63

S

Safari, 265
Salary Calculator, 378
Salary negotiation, 441–442
Sales and promotional messages,
    168–176
  action, 171–172
  attention, 169–170
  blog, 176
  celebrity endorsements, 186
  desire, 171
  e-mail, 173–174
  enclosing unsolicited merchandise,
    186
  example sales letter, 172, 173f
  Facebook, 174–176
  interest, 170–171

misleading statements, 186
  online messages, 172–176
  primary goal, 168
  proving your claims, 186
  P.S. (postscript), 172
  puffery, 186
  RSS feed, 176
  Twitter, 176
  wiki, 176
  writing plan, 169
Salutation
  business letters, 446f, 447
  e-mail, 91, 443
  punctuation, 512
Samsung, 321
Samsung Galaxy, 99f
SAS, 109f
School career or counselling centre,
    378
Schultz, Howard, 269
Screening interview, 412
Sealed Air Corporation, 323
Search engines, 6, 265
Second-level headings, 274, 275f
Second Life, 412
Second-page heading, 448
Secondary data, 264
Secondary research, 57, 230,
    264–267
  blogs, 267
  books, 264
  Internet, 265–267
  online databases, 265
  periodicals, 264–265
  print resources, 264–265
  social media sites, 267
Seeking employment. See
    Job search
Segmented 100% bar chart, 277f
Segmented line chart, 277, 278f
Self-destructing, 96
Self-directed work, 5
Semicolon, 510–511
Sender-focused message, 43
Sentence
  comma splice, 63
  fragments, 62–63
  length, 62
  run-on, 63
  types, 61–62
  unity, 468–469
Sentence fragments, 62–63
Sentence interruptions, 518
Sentence length, 62
Sentence unity, 468–469
Sequential interview, 413
serial, cereal, 535
Series
  comma, 500
  semicolon, 511
Sexting, 100
SharePoint, 7
SharpReader, 103
Short message service (SMS), 98,
    100
Signature block, 446f, 447
Silence, 362
Simile, 346
Simple/complex (organizational
    pattern), 273f
Simple fractions, 532
Simple line chart, 277, 278f
Simple sentence, 61
Singular noun, 479
site, cite, sight, 535
Situational interview questions,
    424–425
6-x-6 rule, 351
Skype, 8f, 9f, 99
Slang, 23, 69

Slide presentation, 349–360
  6-x-6 rule, 351
  analyze the situation and purpose,
    350
  animation, 359
  audience, 350, 358, 360
  best practices, 356f, 357f
  bulleted lists, 352, 353, 353f
  colours, 351
  diagrams, 353–354, 353f
  familiarity with equipment, 357
  font, 359
  formatting, 354
  good/bad slides, 353f, 355f, 369f
  graphics, 354, 354f, 359
  hyperlinks, 359
  interact with audience, 360
  Internet options, 360
  is slide necessary?, 354
  organize the slides, 351
  practising and preparing, 358
  pros/cons, 348f
  putting it all together (step-by-step
    process), 358–360
  revise, proofread, evaluate, 355
  SmartArt graphics, 353f
  templates, 351, 352
  transition effects, 359
  visual clichés, 352
Smart Fortwo, 169
SmartArt graphics, 353f
Smartphone. See Cellphones and
    smartphones
Smile, 22, 317
SMS (short message service), 98, 100
Snitch.name, 417, 435
Social bookmarking, 103–104
Social enabled advertising, 172
Social intelligence, 307
Social media, 89, 101–103
  establish boundaries, 102
  Facebook, 101, 102f, 174–176,
    266, 382, 415
  how used, 101
  inappropriate photographs and
    "friends," 102–103
  job interview, 415
  LinkedIn, 89, 382, 390–394, 410
  Pinterest, 89
  potential risks, 101–102, 102–103
  promotional tool, 174–176
  secondary research, 267
  Twitter, 101, 106, 106f, 176, 266,
    382, 415
Social zone, 15f
Société Générale, 196
Sodexo, 412
Soft proofreading, 75–76, 77f
Soft skills, 17, 307
Source notes, 455
Southwest Airlines, 106
Space zones of social interaction, 15f
Spam
  e-mail, 97
  instant messaging, 100
Spatial arrangement, 272–273, 273f
Speaking skills. See Business
    presentations
Speech habits, 17f. See also Voice
Spell checkers, 7
Spelling, 7, 536–537
Spence, Chris, 396
Spim, 100
Spoke diagram, 353, 353f
Spreadsheet programs, 279
Sprint writing, 63
squidoo, 103
Stage fright, 361, 362f
STAR technique, 425
Starbucks, 103, 106, 108

State abbreviations, 450f
stationary, stationery, 536
StationM, 101
Stereotype, 21, 24
Stop words, 267
Straw, 103
Stress interview, 413
StumbleUpon, 103
Style in writing, 465–473
   active/passive voice, 466–467
   dangling and misplaced modifiers, 469
   emphasis, 465–466
   imprecise writing, 468
   mixed construction, 468–469
   paragraph coherence, 469–470
   paragraph length, 470
   parallelism, 467–468
   transitional expressions, 470
   unity, 468–469
Subject-verb agreement, 486–487
Subjunctive mood, 488
Subordinate clause, 197
Success stories (job interview), 416
Sumitomo Corporation of America, 261
Summarizing statement, 518
Summary report, 233, 240–244
Superlative degree (adjective/adverb), 493
Surface chart, 277, 278f
Survey, 229, 268
SurveyMonkey.com, 360
Sympathy message, 147
Synchronous communication, 10

T

Table, 275–276, 276f, 290f
Table of contents, 281, 285f
Tags, 102
Take Your Dog to Work Day, 308
Talking headings, 232
Taming the Beast (Bloch), 100
Tapscott, Dan, 37
Target, 103, 105
TEAM, 323
Team presentations, 371
Team writing, 7, 301–302
   collaboration software, 302
   collecting information, 301–302
   editing and evaluating, 302
   organizing, writing, and revising, 302
   planning, 301
   preparation, 301
Teamwork. *See* Professional teams
Tech-savvy youth, 4
Technical words, 43
Technological advancements
   collecting information
      electronically, 6
   correctness and precision, 7
   graphics, 7
   professional-looking documents, 5–6
   team writing, 7
   templates, 6
Technorati, 266
Teleconferencing, 9f, 38f
Telephone, 316–318
   job interview, 414–415
   mini-agenda, 316
   phone etiquette guidelines, 317–318
   phone tag, 317
   professionalism, 17f
   smile, 317
   three-point introduction, 317
   when used, 38f

Telephone "bridge," 9f
Telephony (VoIP), 8f
Template, 6
   fax, 452
   letters, 113
   memo, 110, 451
   reports, 228
   slide presentation, 351, 352
Terminal clause, 504
Territories, abbreviations, 450f
Testimonial, 171, 174
Text messaging (texting), 89, 98–101
"Texting lingo shows up at office" (Sankey), 2
Texting speak, 70
Thank-you message, 144–146
   employment interview, 428, 429f
   example, 145f
   favour, 145f, 146
   gift, 145
   hospitality, 146
The All Good Blog, 107f
"The Lodge," 107
their, they're, there, 494, 536
then, than, 497, 536
there's, 482
Thesaurus, 72
Third-level headings, 274, 275f
Third-person constructions, 43
Thought speed, 12
Three-point introduction, 317
3M Corporation, 325
Time orientation, 20–21
Title page, 281, 283f
Titles, 519
to, too, two, 536
Tolerance, 21–22
Tolerance and tact, 309f
Tone
   audience reaction, 41
   business writing, 43–44
   e-mail, 48f, 87, 96
   voice, 311
ToneCheck, 87
Top-of-screen test (e-mail), 96
Topical or criteria arrangement, 273, 273f
Track Changes, 76, 84
Transitional expressions, 470
Translator, 23
Travelocity, 103
Trillian Astra, 98
Trip report, 235f
True North Airlines, 106f
Twitter, 101, 106, 106f, 176, 266, 382, 415
two, to, too 536

U

Unbiased language, 45–46
Uniform resource locator (URL), 265
Union Pearson Express, 261
United Egg Producers, 186
Unity, 468–469
University of California at Berkeley, 255
Uptalk, 17f, 312
URL (uniform resource locator), 265

V

Value/size (organizational pattern), 273f
Vandebroek, Sophie V., 321
Verb, 70–71, 486–491
   action, 387
   irregular, 488–489

linking, 493
mood, 488
past participle, 489
past-tense, 489
subject, agreement with, 486–487
tense, 488
voice, 487–488
Verb-centred sentence, 71
Verb tense, 488
Verbal static (fillers), 362
Verbeek-Vingerhoed, Chantal, 413
Verizon, 412
Vertical bar chart, 277f
Video phone, 9f
Video résumé, 394
Videoconferencing, 9f, 38f
Vinodrai, Tara, 5
Virtual interview, 437, 438
Virtual private network (VPN), 87
Virtual team, 322
Visual aids, 347–349. *See also* Graphics
   flipchart/whiteboard, 348–349, 348f
   handouts/speaker's notes, 348f, 349, 363
   props, 348f
   slides, 348, 348f. *See also* Slide presentation
   video, 348f
Visual clichés, 352
Vivid adjectives, 72
Vivid words, 466
Vogel, Doug, 348
Voice, 310–312. *See also* Active voice; Passive voice
   emphasis, 311
   pitch, 311
   pronunciation, 311, 311f
   tone, 311
   volume and rate, 311–312
Voice conferencing, 9f
Voice mail, 319–321
   greeting, 320
   leaving messages, 320–321
   professionalism, 17f
   receiving messages, 320
   when used, 38f
Voice over Internet Protocol (VoIP), 8f
   providers, 98
Voice recognition, 8f
Volin, Kathryn J., 307
Volunteering, 379

W

Wahl, Andrew, 349
waiver, waver, 536
Walmart, 412
"Watch your (digital) mouth" (MacArthur), 87
"We" view, 42
Wealink, 382
Web 2.0, 9f, 32–33
Web-based feed readers, 103
Web conferencing, 9f
Web document builders, 5
Web site evaluation, 255
WebEx, 9f
Webinar, 9f
Webspy, 126
Weinberg, Tamar, 176
Weingarten, Rachel, 103
We're delighted, 43
WetFeet, 437
White space, 73
Whiteboard, 348–349, 348f

who, whom, 483
whoever, whomever, 483
whole, hole, 535
Whole Foods, 105
Wiki, 9f, 38f, 90
   database for knowledge management, 110
   defined, 109
   documentation, 110
   global reach, 109
   marketing tool, 176
   meetings, 110
   project management, 110
   sample, 109f
   tips/pointers, 110
Wiki knowledge base, 110
Wikipedia, 110, 176
Windows Live Messenger, 98
Windows Phone 7 ads, 34
Wipro, 18
Wireless-free quiet zones, 319f
Word choice, 68–72
   active/passive voice, 71
   cliché, 69–70
   concrete nouns, 72
   instant-message speak, 70
   jargon, 68–69
   precise verbs, 70–71
   slang, 69
   vivid adjectives, 72
Word processing programs, 5, 7
Word templates, 113
Wordy expressions, 64–65
Work environment, 5
Workforce diversity, 23–25
Workopolis, 378, 380, 381f
Workplace conflict, 315–316
Workplace criticism, 313–315
Works Cited, 282–283, 460–464
   book and web site titles, 460
   e-mail communication, 464
   electronic references, 462–463
   examples, 292f, 461f
   hanging indented style, 460
   italics and underscoring, 462
   journal articles, 461
   magazine titles, 461
   medium of publication, 460
   online posting, 464
   online research database, 464
   television/radio, 463, 464
Workspace, 8f
Worst- and best-case scenarios, 346
Writer's block, 63
Writing process, 35–36, 35f. *See also* Business writing

X

Xerox, 321
Xing, 382

Y

Yahoo! Groups, 410
Yahoo! Messenger, 98
Yahoo! Search, 265
"Yes, but" answers, 363
you should, you must, you have, 45
"You" statements, 201–202
"You" view, 42–43

Z

Zappos.com, 101, 413–414
Zones of privacy, 15, 15f